Youth Activism

Advisory Committee

MAMADOU DIOUF
University of Michigan
Ann Arbor, MI

JACQUELYNNE ECCLES
University of Michigan
Ann Arbor, MI

RICHARD M. LERNER
Tufts University
Medford, MA

DOROTHY STONEMAN
YouthBuild
Somerville, MA

JUDITH TORNEY-PURTA
University of Maryland
College Park, MD

SUDHIR VENKATESH
Columbia University
New York, NY

CLAIRE WALLACE
Institute for Advanced Studies
Vienna, Austria

RODERICK J. WATTS
Georgia State University
Atlanta, GA

WENDY WHEELER
Innovation Center for Community
   and Youth Development
Takoma Park, MD

Youth Activism

An International Encyclopedia

Volume 1: A–J

Lonnie R. Sherrod

Editor

Constance A. Flanagan and Ron Kassimir

Associate Editors

Amy K. Syvertsen

Assistant Editor

GREENWOOD PRESS

Westport, Connecticut • London

Library of Congress Cataloging-in-Publication Data

Youth activism : an international encyclopedia /
    Lonnie R. Sherrod, editor.
      p. cm.
    Includes bibliographical references and index.
    ISBN 0–313–32811–0 (set : alk. paper)—ISBN 0–313–32812–9
(v. 1 : alk. paper)—ISBN 0–313–32813–7 (v. 2 : alk. paper)
      1. Youth—Political activity—Encyclopedias.   2. Social action—Encyclopedias.
3. Political participation—Encyclopedias.   4. Social advocacy—Encyclopedias.
5. Student movements—Encyclopedias.   6. Youth development—
Encyclopedias.   I. Sherrod, Lonnie R.
HQ799.2.P6Y65   2006
320'.0835'03—dc22   2005019216

British Library Cataloguing in Publication Data is available.

Library of Congress Catalog Card Number: 2005019216
ISBN: 0–313–32811–0 (set)
        0–313–32812–9 (v.1)
        0–313–32813–7 (v.2)

First published in 2006

Greenwood Press, 88 Post Road West, Westport, CT 06881
An imprint of Greenwood Publishing Group, Inc.
www.greenwood.com

Printed in the United States of America

The paper used in this book complies with the
Permanent Paper Standard issued by the National
Information Standards Organization (Z39.48–1984).

10 9 8 7 6 5 4 3 2 1

We dedicate this encyclopedia to all those young people throughout history who have risked their own well-being, comfort, and safety to make the world a better place for their fellow men and women. They are our youth activists.

Contents

List of Entries

Guide to Related Topics

Adolescent and Youth Development

Acculturation
Adult Partners in Youth Activism
Adult Roles in Youth Activism
Child Labor
Civic Engagement in Diverse Youth
Civic Identity
Civic Virtue
Communication and Youth Socialization
Community Collaboration
Community Justice
Community Service
Developmental Assets
Emerging Adulthood
Empathy
Empowerment
Ethnic Identity
Flow: Youth Motivation and Engagement
Identity and Activism
Moral Development
Moral Exemplars

Peer Influences on Political Development
Personality and Youth Political Involvement
Positive Development
Prosocial Behaviors
Pubertal Timing
Rights of Participation of Children
  and Youth
Rights, Youth Perceptions of
School Engagement
School Influences and Civic Engagement
Service Learning
Service Learning and Citizenship Education
Social-Emotional Learning Programs
  for Youth
Social Justice
Social Responsibility
Social Trust
Spirituality
Voice
Volunteerism

Adult Involvement with Youth

Adult Partners in Youth Activism
Adult Roles in Youth Activism
Adultism
Athletic-Square Model of Youth Sport
Character Education
Civil Society and Positive Youth Development
Communication and Youth Socialization
Community Collaborations
Empowerment
Environmental Education (EE)
Ethnic Identity
4-H
Generational Conflict
Generational Replacement

Identity and Organizing in Older Youth
Intergenerational Programs and Practices
Juvenile Justice
Moral Exemplars
Parental Influences on Youth Activism
Political Participation and Youth Councils
Positive Youth Development, Programs
  Promoting
Racial Socialization
Urban Communities, Youth
  Programming in
Youth Commissions
Youth-Led Action Research, Evaluation,
  and Planning

Advocacy for Social Causes

Advocacy
Advocacy Day
American Indian Movement (AIM)
Animal Rights
Anti-Nazi Youth Resistance
Anti-Tobacco Youth Activism
Antiwar Activism
Campus Compact
Campus Crusade for Christ International
    (CCC)
Child Labor
Child Soldiers
Civic Environmentalism
Civil Rights Movement
Community Justice
Earth Force
Environmental Education (EE)
Feminism
Gay-Straight Alliances in Schools (GSAs)

Global Justice Activism
Grassroots Youth Movements
High-School Students' Rights Movement
    of the 1960s
Juvenile Justice
Labor Movement
Mental-Health Advocacy in Youth
Political Consumerism
Rights of Participation of Children
    and Youth
Social Justice
Social Movements
Student Action with Farmworkers (SAF)
Student Political Activism
Sustainability
Terrorism, Youth Activism
    Responses to
United Students Against Sweatshops
    (USAS)

Education

Acculturation
Adult Partners in Youth Activism
AmeriCorps
Athletic-Square Model of Youth Sport
Campus Compact
Campus Crusade for Christ International
    (CCC)
Catholic Education and the Ethic of Social
    Justice
Character Education
Citizenship Education Policies in the States
Deliberative Democracy
Democratic Education
Digital Divide
Diversity Education
Earth Force
Environmental Education (EE)
Gay-Straight Alliances in Schools (GSAs)
Global Citizenship Education (GCE) in the
    United States

High-School Students' Rights Movement
    of the 1960s
IEA Civic Education Study
Just Community High Schools and Youth
    Activism
Kids Voting USA (KVUSA)
National Alliance for Civic Education
    (NACE)
National and Community Service
Public Scholarship
School Engagement
School Influences and Civic Engagement
Service Learning
Service Learning and Citizenship Education
Social-Emotional Learning Programs
    for Youth
Student Political Activism
Student Voices Project
*Tinker v. Des Moines Independent School
    District* (1969)

Gender and Sexuality

AIDS Advocacy in South Africa
Chat Rooms, Girls' Empowerment and

Empowerment
Feminism

Gay-Straight Alliances in Schools (GSAs)
Gender Differences in the Political Attitudes
   of Youth
Hip-Hop Generation

MTV's Choose or Lose Campaign (1992–)
Punk Rock Youth Subculture
Queer, Sexuality, and Gender Activism
Riot Grrrl

Global and Transnational Issues

AIDS Advocacy in South Africa
Antiwar Activism
Arab Americans
Child Labor
Child Soldiers
Contested Childhoods
Demographic Trends Affecting the World's
   Youth
Environmental Education (EE)
European Identity and Citizenship
Global Citizenship Education (GCE) in the
   United States
Global Justice Activism

Global Youth Action Network (GYAN)
Immigrant Youth in Europe—Turks in
   Germany
Immigrant Youth in the United States
Political Consumerism
State and Youth, the
Sustainability
Terrorism, Youth Activism Responses to
Transnational Identity
Transnational Youth Activism
United Students Against Sweatshops (USAS)
Xenophobia
Youth Bulge

Historical Examples, Causes, and Movements

Advocacy Day
Animal Rights
Anti-Nazi Youth Resistance
Anti-Tobacco Youth Activism
Antiwar Activism
Child Labor
Child Soldiers
Civic Environmentalism
Civil Rights Movement
Civilian Conservation Corps (CCC)
Feminism
High-School Students' Rights Movement
   of the 1960s
Immigrant Youth in Europe—Turks in
   Germany
Immigrant Youth in the United States

Labor Movement
National and Community Service
Native American Youth
Palestinian *Intifada*
Public Art
Public Scholarship
Queer, Sexuality, and Gender Activism
Racial and Ethnic Inequality
Soweto Youth Activism (South Africa)
Student Political Activism
Terrorism, Youth Activism
   Responses to
Tiananmen Square Massacre (1989)
Xenophobia
Zapatista Rebellion (Mexico)
Zionist Youth Organizations

International Examples of Activism and Social Movements

AIDS Advocacy in South Africa
Anti-Nazi Youth Resistance
Australia, Youth Activism in
Contested Childhoods
Demographic Trends Affecting the
   World's Youth

Eastern Europe, Youth and Citizenship in
Europe, Comparing Youth Activism in
European Identity and Citizenship
Immigrant Youth in Europe—Turks in
   Germany
India, Youth Activism in

Indonesia, Youth Activism in
National Identity and Youth
Nigeria, Youth Activism in
Palestinian *Intifada*
Russia, Youth Activism in
Serbia, Youth Activism in (1990–2000)
Soweto Youth Activism (South Africa)

Statute of the Child and Adolescent
   (Brazil)
Tiananmen Square Massacre (1989)
Turkey, Youth Activism in
United Nations, Youth Activism and
Zapatista Rebellion (Mexico)
Zionist Youth Organizations

Law and Justice

Catholic Education and the Ethic of
   Social Justice
Community Justice
Democracy
Democratic Education
Gangs
Gangs and Politics
Homies Unidos
Juvenile Justice
Mental-Health Advocacy and Youth

Racial and Ethnic Inequality
Rights of Participation of Children
   and Youth
Rights, Youth Perceptions of
Social Justice
Social Responsibility
State and Youth, the
Statute of the Child and Adolescent (Brazil)
*Tinker v. Des Moines Independent
   School District* (1969)

Media and Internet Influences and Uses

Advocacy Day
Chat Rooms, Girls' Empowerment and
Communication and Youth Socialization
Digital Divide
Empowerment
Film/Video as Tool for Youth Activism
Global Justice Activism
Hip-Hop Generation

Mental-Health Advocacy in Youth
MTV's Choose or Lose Campaign (1992–)
New Media
Participatory Action Research (PAR) by Youth
Political Consumerism
Public Art
Punk Rock Youth Subculture
Terrorism, Youth Activism Responses to

Organizations and Programs

Advocacy Day
American Indian Movement (AIM)
AmeriCorps
Campus Compact
Campus Crusade for Christ International
   (CCC)
Civilian Conservation Corps (CCC)
Earth Force
4-H
Global Youth Action Network (GYAN)
Homies Unidos
Innovations in Civic Participation (ICP)
Intergenerational Programs and Practices
Jesuit Volunteer Corps (JVC)
KidSpeak

Kids Voting USA (KVUSA)
MTV's Choose or Lose Campaign (1992–)
National Alliance for Civic Education
   (NACE)
Participatory Action Research (PAR)
   by Youth
Student Action with Farmworkers (SAF)
Student Voices Project
United Nations, Youth Activism and
United Students Against Sweatshops
   (USAS)
Youth Commissions
Youth Leadership for Development
   Initiative (YLDI)
Zionist Youth Organizations

Political Context

Advocacy
Anti-Nazi Youth Resistance
Antiwar Activism
Arab Americans
Child Soldiers
Citizenship Education Policies in the States
Civic Environmentalism
Civil Rights Movement
Contested Childhoods
Deliberative Democracy
Democracy
Democratic Education
Demographic Trends Affecting the
    World's Youth
Diversity Education
Eastern Europe, Youth and Citizenship in
Europe, Comparing Youth Activism in
Gangs and Politics
Gender Differences in the Political
    Attitudes of Youth
Generational Conflict
Grassroots Youth Movements
High-School Students' Rights Movement
    of the 1960s
Indonesia, Youth Activism In
Labor Movement

Minority Youth Voter Turnout
MTV's Choose or Lose Campaign (1992–)
National and Community Service
National Identity and Youth
Nigeria, Youth Activism in
Political Consumerism
Political Participation and Youth Councils
Poverty, Welfare Reform, and Adolescents
Queer, Sexuality, and Gender Activism
Racial and Ethnic Inequality
Rights of Participation of Children
    and Youth
Rights, Youth Perceptions of
Russia, Youth Activism in
Serbia, Youth Activism in (1990–2000)
Social Movements
Social Networks
Social Trust
State and Youth, the
Student Political Activism
Sustainability
Terrorism, Youth Activism Responses to
Transnational Youth Activism
Turkey, Youth Activism in
Xenophobia
Youth Bulge

Positive Youth Development

Adult Partners in Youth Activism
Adult Roles in Youth Activism
Adultism
AmeriCorps
Athletic-Square Model of Youth Sport
Civic Engagement in Diverse Youth
Civic Identity
Civic Virtue
Civil Society and Positive Youth
    Development
Communication and Youth
    Socialization
Community Collaboration
Community Justice
Community Service
Developmental Assets
Diversity Education
Empathy
Empowerment

Flow: Youth Motivation and Engagement
4-H
Identity and Activism
Identity and Organizing in Older Youth
Innovations in Civic Participation (ICP)
Intergenerational Programs and Practices
Moral Cognition and Youth Activism
Moral Development
Moral Exemplars
National and Community Service
Parental Influences on Youth Activism
Peer Influences on Political Development
Positive Development
Positive Psychology
Positive Youth Development, Programs
    Promoting
Prosocial Behaviors
Rights of Participation of Children
    and Youth

Social Justice
Social Responsibility
Social Trust
Spirituality

Urban Communities, Youth Programming in
Volunteerism
Youth Leadership for Development
   Initiative (YLDI)

Religion

Campus Crusade for Christ International
   (CCC)
Catholic Education and the Ethic of
   Social Justice
Civic Virtue
Community Justice
Community Service
Empathy
Identity and Activism
Jesuit Volunteer Corps (JVC)

Moral Cognition and Youth Activism
Moral Development
Moral Exemplars
Prosocial Behaviors
Religiosity and American Youth
Religiosity and Civic Engagement in African
   American Youth
Social Justice
Spirituality
Zionist Youth Organizations

Social Background Factors

Acculturation
Arab Americans
Australia, Youth Activism in
Civic Engagement in Diverse Youth
Civil Rights Movement
Demographic Trends Affecting the
   World's Youth
Diversity Education
Emerging Adulthood
Ethnic Identity
Gender Differences in the Political
   Attitudes of Youth
Generational Replacement
Homies Unidos
Identity and Activism
Identity and Organizing in Older Youth
Immigrant Youth in the United States
Juvenile Justice

Minority Youth Voter Turnout
Native American Youth
Nigeria, Youth Activism in
Parental Influences on Youth Activism
Peer Influences on Political Development
Personality and Youth Political Involvement
Poverty, Welfare Reform, and Adolescents
Pubertal Timing
Queer, Sexuality, and Gender Activism
Racial and Ethnic Inequality
Racial Socialization
Religiosity and American Youth
Religiosity and Civic Engagement in
   African American Youth
Serbia, Youth Activism in (1990–2000)
Soweto Youth Activism (South Africa)
Spirituality
Transnational Identity

Social Relationships and Networks

Adult Partners in Youth Activism
Adult Roles in Youth Activism
Animal Rights
Anti-Nazi Youth Resistance
Anti-Tobacco Youth Activism
Antiwar Activism
Community Collaboration
Community Service

Developmental Assets
Gangs
Gangs and Politics
Gay-Straight Alliances in Schools (GSAs)
Global Youth Action Network (GYAN)
Grassroots Youth Movements
High-School Students' Rights Movement
   of the 1960s

Voices of Activism

Youth Culture

Preface

Why is youth activism so important? If democratic societies are to survive and flourish and if authoritarian governments are to become more democratic they need citizens who are informed and concerned and who take action when necessary to improve the status quo. How such citizens develop from childhood into concerned and active adults is a critical and relatively new topic for research, programs, and policy that impact youth. Both research and policy are increasingly recognizing the importance of activism. *Youth Activism: An International Encyclopedia* brings together this combined body of work.

Organization and Coverage of Topics

In this two-volume encyclopedia, the editors have assembled over 160 entries relevant to the topic of youth activism. The entries are arranged alphabetically by title and cover relevant research, programs, and organizations; current and historical examples of youth activism; and voices of activists. The encyclopedia addresses the phenomenon of activism conceptually by presenting research on activism and on youth civic engagement generally. It includes entries on aspects of youth development that are relevant to activism. It presents examples of youth activism historically and globally in the contemporary world. And it reviews programs and policies oriented toward promoting activism in youth and to giving them the competency and the opportunities they need to engage in activism. The entries were chosen to cover an array of issues germane to the topic but broader than the specific entry. The following topic categories are included:

- **Adolescent and Youth Development:** Young people are still growing into maturity and their developmental status may influence their tendency to engage in activism and the particular kinds of activism that appeal to them. Hence, it is essential to consider the developmental status of teens and youth. Topics such as the timing of pubertal development or their experience of "flow" as an example of serious engagement in activities relevant to activism are examples.
- **Adult Involvement with Youth:** Adults' involvement with youth makes an important contribution to their identity and their behavior. Hence, it is critical to examine how adults' involvement contributes to their activism.
- **Advocacy for Social Causes:** Activism is oriented toward promoting an issue or cause, for example, equal rights for the sexes or for gay and lesbian youth or environmentalism. Hence, one way of considering youth activism is by the causes for which youth advocate.
- **Education:** Of course, the education we offer youth is critical to whether they develop an activist orientation to citizenship. Education covers not just civic education but also

their engagement in school and other influences of school, such as its sense of community.

- **Gender and Sexuality:** Research has reliably found that there are gender differences in young people's political behavior. Sexual identity also may play a role. It is important to ask also how these factors contribute to the expression of activism in youth.

- **Global and Transnational Issues:** Young people are increasingly becoming engaged with global issues and often organizing transnationally to address them. Some of those issues are about the status of young people themselves in the world today. As an international encyclopedia it is important to examine how globalization and other transnational issues shape and inspire activism in youth.

- **Historical Examples, Causes, and Movements:** Any encyclopedia of youth activism must, of course, document examples that have occurred throughout history, such as the anti-Nazi youth resistance during World War II. While we have tried to be as comprehensive as possible, it is likely that we have not fully covered all possible examples, and for this we apologize and ask that readers let the press know of examples not covered.

- **International Examples of Activism and Social Movements:** As an international encyclopedia, we make a major effort to cover activism throughout the world. This means describing cases of youth activism in Nigeria or Russia and other countries. The third introductory essay discusses the issues involved in adopting a cross-national perspective. As with historical examples, we have made an attempt to be comprehensive, but such efforts inevitably fall short.

- **Law and Justice:** Certainly one factor contributing to activism in youth is their recognition of social injustices. Hence, law and justice issues are important to explore.

- **Media and Internet Influences and Uses:** In today's world the media and the Internet are ubiquitous parts of young people's lives and hence interrelate with their activism. Communication both influences activism by exposing youth to causes and offers vehicles such as chat rooms for engaging in activism. Young people also are using new forms of media for social activism.

- **Organizations and Programs:** We are particularly interested in societies' efforts to promote activism in youth throughout the world. Hence, one major category of entries is the organizations and programs that work with youth to promote activism. Originally, we envisioned that the whole second volume would be devoted to organizations and programs with the first devoted to research. However, we concluded that topics related to multiple categories, making any such division arbitrary; we then abandoned this plan and arranged all entries alphabetically. However, this original plan indicates how important we consider this topic. Although such programs are particularly widespread in the United States, we have tried to cover organizations and programs worldwide.

- **Political Context:** Of course, one important contributor to the expression of activism in youth is the political context in which they grow up. The international aspect of this encyclopedia makes that particularly important. Examples include democracy or civil society as well as child labor or community justice.

- **Positive Youth Development:** This encyclopedia explicitly adopts a positive outlook on youth development because we believe that activism exemplifies such an approach. This approach then directs both research and policy, and it follows decades of research and policy oriented toward fixing kids by preventing problems—as opposed to promoting positive development. This positive youth development approach is explained further in the first and second introductory essays. Several entries also contribute to articulating how this approach relates to particular topics, such as civil society or youth programs.

- **Religion:** Religion and spirituality play an important role in youth's political attitudes and behavior, and therefore also require coverage with respect to activism.

- **Social Background Influences:** Such factors as social class, race, or ethnicity, and culture are of paramount importance to any topic relevant to youth development, and activism is no exception. Hence, several entries attempt to explain how one or more of these factors influence development or activism.
- **Social Relationships and Networks:** Everyone lives in a social world, but social relationships are especially important to youth because they help to shape the course of their development. Hence, a number of entries address the social world of youth, for example, attending to adult roles or partnerships.
- **Voices of Activism:** In the same way that we cover examples of activism, we have also tried to cover the voices of individuals who identify as activists. In some cases, these folks are youth; in others, they are adults who reflect on the youthful origins of their activism.
- **Youth Culture:** Culture in the form of clothes, music, and lifestyle is especially important to young people and therefore requires attention. It relates in especially interesting ways to activism. Hence, a number of entries cover topics such as MTV or punk rock.

Many entries span several of these categories, but all touch upon at least one, and each of these topical categories is listed in the "Guide to Related Topics" with the entries we believe relate to each. Of course, any such categorization is intended to be a guide only and has an element of arbitrariness to it. So we urge readers to adopt whatever organization they think appropriate.

The three introductory essays that follow this preface, authored by the encyclopedia editors, cover the core general areas that underlie the two volumes; these essays deal, respectively, with civic engagement in youth, adolescence and youth as a life phase, and conceptions of activism, including the need for an international perspective. We hope that these three essays, longer than the typical entry, set the stage for the entries that follow and provide a full justification for the encyclopedia.

The entries range in length from 1,000 to 4,000 words, depending on the topic. Hence, the two-volume work is about 400,000 words and contains tables, graphs, charts, and a variety of black-and-white photos to illustrate some of the entries. Some photos or illustrations are specific to an entry; others just represent visual illustrations of activism. There is a general bibliography at the end of the work. Another appendix contains examples of important relevant organizations and Web sites. These appendices allow readers to pursue additional work in the area. Our ability to assemble a work of this magnitude on this topic offers further proof of the importance of youth activism in the modern world. Youth may not be offered much opportunity to take responsibility in today's world, but the material in this encyclopedia demonstrates that they take responsibility when they deem it to be necessary.

We offer one caveat on our overall coverage of this topic. While we attempted to include examples of youth activism from various ends of the political spectrum, our coverage ended up including substantially more entries connected to "progressive" organizations and concerns compared with conservative ones. We actually found it more difficult to recruit authors willing to write on examples of conservative or right-wing youth activism. But we do not see activism as a topic with political valence. Instead, youth are active in the causes they believe in, whether from the left or the right, and often in ways that make that distinction less sharp than we might think. We hope this encyclopedia offers some balance in this regard, if perhaps not as much as we would have liked.

Unique Contribution of This Encyclopedia

No definitive sourcebook exists to provide both an overview and a detailed understanding of issues on this important topic of youth activism. We often forget that our children are our future. If we do not do right by our children, society will suffer in the future when these children are participating adults. In no areas is this truer than for citizenship and activism. Hence, we hope that *Youth Activism* will be useful to many different readers and that they will use it for many different purposes. The two volumes of this encyclopedia should be a welcome addition to reference libraries at all levels. It should be useful to secondary-school teachers; to university students, professors, and college administrators; to youth program personnel; and to legislators concerned with youth. It should be of interest to youth themselves. Hence, the audience for this work should be individuals whose backgrounds and interests are varied—we expect that students, teachers, researchers, parents, program administrators, and others will be interested in this examination of youth activism. It is useful for multiple purposes from report writing to program design to folks who want to advocate for a cause. Different entries may be more or less relevant to different audiences and for different purposes, but the multidisciplinary coverage of research, programs, examples, and voices makes the coverage comprehensive and therefore maximally useful for almost any purpose.

The entries are written to the level of the general reader to maximize readability. Most entries at their end contain a short list of recommended readings for those who want more depth on a topic. Hence, the encyclopedia should be useful for the preparation of reports for school and for other such purposes. Youth activism is a topic of broad general interest because of its relevance to the lives of all citizens in all societies. Therefore, these two volumes should have tremendous appeal to scholars, students, policymakers, practitioners, and youth activists from many walks of life.

The encyclopedia has the following unique features:

- The positive focus on youth should increase the appeal to youth and all of those in society who work for the benefit of youth.
- The cross-disciplinary approach provides a comprehensive scope across a number of fields addressing an important topic.
- The international extent of its contents demonstrates the global relevance of the topic.
- The historical reach of its coverage, especially of examples of youth activism, increases its usefulness as a reference tool.
- It has considerable relevance to the development of programming and legislation regarding youth development.
- Entries are indexed and cross-referenced to tie the contents of the volume together in a coherent manner.
- The two-volume set includes material presented by leading scholars in the multiple fields that inform the subject and presents it in a highly readable fashion.
- The two-volume set also contains material by youth, by youth leaders, and by practitioners who work with youth in areas relevant to activism.

A Focus on Positive Youth Development

Youth today are often given a "bad rap." As a society we have concerned ourselves with the problems of youth: teen pregnancy, delinquency, substance use, school failure, and youth violence. As a result, the public typically holds negative and somewhat fearful views of youth (Gilliam and Bales 2001; Hein 2001). Although large majorities of young people are engaged in their communities, provide service to them, and get engaged in activism to improve public life, the media as well as many scholars focus on conventional political markers such as voting or reading newspapers and conclude that youth are politically disengaged. Debates continue about whether trends showing declines in these conventional political behaviors should be interpreted as declining political engagement among younger generations. In this volume, we have broadened the meaning of "political" and thus have focused on the breadth of new forms that youth activism is taking, as well as the new methods and means youth are using to achieve those goals.

Youth Activism presents youth in a positive perspective, illustrating how it is frequently youth who recognize when society needs a wake-up call, when we need to reject the status quo and make changes in laws, policies, and institutions. Of course, not all examples of activism would be regarded as positive, especially those that employ violence as part of their efforts. However, these non-positive examples are also covered. Overall, we do regard activism as a clear representation of the positive contribution youth can make to society. We believe this focus on positive youth development is one of the most important contributions of this encyclopedia. We hope that the numerous examples of activism, current and historical, will help to challenge the public's negative image of young people.

References

Gilliam, F., and Bales, S. (2001). "Strategic Frame Analysis: Reframing America's Youth." *Social Policy Reports*, 15 (3).
Hein, K. (2001). *Report of the President.* Annual Report of the William T. Grant Foundation.

Acknowledgments

Marie Larcada of Greenwood Publishing Group is responsible for inventing the idea of this encyclopedia and for approaching Lonnie Sherrod about doing it. He was, of course, thrilled at the idea that a press was interested in doing such a massive work on this topic. He immediately enlisted the help of colleagues Constance Flanagan and Ron Kassimir. We also enlisted the aid of Amy Syvertsen who has proven to be invaluable in completing such a massive undertaking. We prepared a proposal that was submitted to Greenwood Press and subsequently approved. That proposal contained suggestions for numerous entries, some of which we have kept and others abandoned. It was a long two-year process with contacts to numerous colleagues in numerous fields. To our delight, almost everyone we contacted recognized the importance of the topic and agreed to help. A few, of course, had to decline because of time constraints but always offered suggestions of other possible contacts. There were almost no topics that were abandoned because we could not find an author.

We were fortunate in enlisting the assistance of a number of nationally visible researchers and youth-development workers as an advisory board. Advisory committee members include equally prominent international scholars and practitioners: Mamadou Diouf, University of Michigan; Jacquelynne Eccles, University of Michigan; Richard Lerner, Tufts University; Dorothy Stoneman, YouthBuild; Judith Torney-Purta, University of Maryland; Sudhir Venkatesh, Columbia University; Claire Wallace, Institute for Advanced Studies, Vienna, Austria; Roderick Watts, Georgia State University; and Wendy Wheeler, Innovation Center for Community and Youth Development.

Advisory committee members were consulted at all phases of development of the encyclopedia, from compilation of the initial list of entries to final stages of development. They were an invaluable resource throughout preparation of the encyclopedia.

We also could never have completed this massive work without the extensive and valuable assistance of junior colleagues at our home institutions. At Fordham University Carlos Davila, Omar Quinones and Christopher Smith offered assistance to Lonnie Sherrod; of these three, Chris Smith's help was especially extensive and therefore helpful. At the SSRC, Sion Dayson has provided valuable support to a related project that Ron Kassimir is developing on youth activism and citizenship and contributed an entry to this encyclopedia as well. Amy Syvertsen from Pennsylvania State University was so involved in all phases from the beginning to the end of the project that it was only appropriate that she be made an editor. Finally, John Wagner at Greenwood Publishing Group offered far more help than is typical for any editor; we owe him a tremendous debt. Were it not for his assistance, this encyclopedia might never have come to fruition. Certainly, it would have appeared much later.

Introduction

The following three introductory chapters provide a general justification for this encyclopedia on youth activism. The chapters address the three components of the topic—activism and civic engagement, youth development and activism, and the political nature of activism including its international dimensions.

In the first chapter, Lonnie Sherrod considers activism and the development of civic engagement more generally. Some people would argue that activism is a form of civic engagement; others might say that they are very different things. Both, however, refer to people getting involved with the issues that concern their society and their world. In the second chapter, Constance Flanagan and Amy Syvertsen examine the nature of youth and discuss why, as an age-group, youth are especially likely to show activism. In the third chapter, Ron Kassimir examines the political nature of activism and why it is important to adopt an international perspective. Together these three chapters provide the background for readers of the encyclopedia to understand the collection of topics and to use the encyclopedia for developing a solid knowledge about those topics of concern to them.

Youth Activism and Civic Engagement

LONNIE R. SHERROD

In broadest terms, activism refers to action for social change. Activism thus addresses that tendency of youth to take action to change society when they view such action is necessary. Activism includes protest events and actions, advocacy for causes, and information dissemination to raise consciousness. Even writing a letter could however be considered to be activism. In general, it is behavior to promote causes. Examples of issues that have captured the activist attention of young people during the past decade are child labor, environmental protection, animal rights, sweat shops, and support for Palestine. Historical examples include Nazi resistance, civil rights, and the anti–Vietnam War movement of the 1970s, each an entry in this encyclopedia.

One interesting issue on which there is no agreement is whether behavior that challenges the status quo without being oriented to specific causes can be considered activism. RAP music, for example, often explores racism and challenges the status quo regarding race differences in our society. Some would therefore consider it to be activism. Others would argue that it is not sufficiently oriented to promoting change, that it just raises issues, whereas activism needs to promote a course of action. Furthermore, others might argue that it is destructive, whereas activism needs to be constructive. These are interesting and controversial questions. Hopefully the readers of this encyclopedia can use it to formulate their own definition of activism, but we do hope that the entries in this two-volume encyclopedia raise interesting issues about the boundaries of youth activism.

Scholarly interest in youth political activism waxes and wanes with the times and with the behaviors of youth. It increases when large numbers of youth are engaged in some form of political activism. It also increases (as it has today) when, by conventional indicators, large numbers of the younger generation appear to be disengaged from political issues. But it is clear that one unquestionable form of civic engagement is activism. Hence, we begin this encyclopedia on youth activism by describing the development of civic engagement in youth.

Whereas a commitment to the rule of law is an aspect of being a good citizen, a society that is "ruled by the people," as should be true of any democracy, also depends on citizens who make informed judgments, who at times object to policies and even disobey unjust laws, as they have in many movements for social justice. This is activism. Good behavior may be one aspect of citizenship, but so is activism or taking action to improve the nation-state, which is frequently not considered good behavior. Yet our conception of the good citizen and our societal ways of promoting the development of citizenship has to incorporate this activist component of citizenry if democracies are to thrive and remain healthy.

The exercise of good judgment as a component of citizenship involves assessing when behavior is needed to maintain the status quo and when it is necessary to take action to change it—to adopt an activist orientation. Throughout history, youth have been the segment of the population most likely to refuse to accept the status quo and to act to change society for the better. To some extent it is in the nature of youth and the developmental changes they experience in cognition to do so. The topic of youth activism is therefore a logical choice.

Furthermore, youth are frequently concerned with global or transnational issues, and many examples of youth activism occur outside the United States. As a result, activism, especially youth activism, is inherently a topic for which one must adopt an international perspective and attend to the direct impact of globalization. Aided by the Internet, new forms of networking and transnational coordination are occurring. Hence it is essential to adopt a global perspective when addressing the topic of youth activism.

The Development of Citizenship

Participating as a citizen in society is as important as working or forming a family, yet there has been much more attention to the development of schooling and work and on the formation of relationships and families than to the development of citizenship. This is a serious mistake. Societies throughout the globe have to understand how their youth develop into productive, capable adult citizens. Societies also need to provide opportunities for the development of citizenship through their social institutions.

Political scientist Robert Putnam (1996, 2000) has argued that civic engagement is at an all-time low in the United States, especially among young people. He cites indices such as voting, reading newspapers, and participating in civic clubs such as Kiwanis, all of which are lower today than a decade or two ago. He further argues that these indicators are much lower in youth, eighteen- to twenty-five-years-old, than in any other age-group. For example, youth vote less than any other age-group.

Putnam's argument is controversial. It has been challenged by other researchers, such as Youniss et al. (2002), who argue that civic engagement has not declined but has simply changed in nature. So, for example, youth may not read newspapers, but they get news from TV or the Internet. Participation in organizations may be low, but volunteerism, as in community service, is at an all-time high.

This controversy has, however, generated renewed interest in youth civic engagement so that both research and policy attention are increasing. This encyclopedia is one example of that increased attention. There have also been at least three special issues of academic journals focusing on this issue (Flanagan and Sherrod 1998; Niemi 1999; Sherrod, Flanagan, and Youniss 2002). Community service is now a national priority in the United States. There were several efforts in the United States during the 2004 presidential election to get youth to vote by organizations such as MTV, for example, Vote or Die. And there are a few magnet schools in the United States that are oriented toward civics education. Thus, attention to the development of citizenship is increasing.

Furthermore, there have always been international differences in attention to the development of citizenship. The French, for example, attend more to the promotion of citizenship in young people than do Americans. The social change in Eastern Europe during recent decades has also influenced youth's conceptions of citizenship.

The Socialization of Citizenship

There have been two major historical periods of research attention to the development of citizenship. The first in the 1950s reflected the developmental approach of that time and focused on early experience and socialization by the family. The second during the 1970s focused on social movements such as civil rights and the anti–Vietnam War protests. It therefore involved adolescents and youth but was not very developmental in orientation (Flanagan and Sherrod 1998). Now a new wave of research is emerging.

A variety of socialization influences during adolescence have been shown to relate to later civic behaviors such as voting, and we know a great deal about the socialization of political behaviors. Several forms of socialization have been shown to relate to later civic engagement as broadly defined: civic education (Jennings and Niemi 1974, Torney-Purta et al. 2001); school climate and teacher behavior (Battistich, Solomon et al. 1995, Flanagan and Tucker 1999); instructional style, such as encouragement of free dialog in school (Leming 1986, McDevitt and Chaffee 2000, Torney-Purta 2002, Torney-Purta et al. 2001); school extracurricular activities (Eccles and Barber 1999, Niemi and Junn 2000, Verba, Schlozman, and Brady 1995); family interest and involvement (Jennings and Niemi 1974); community service (Hart, Atkins, and Ford 1998, Walker 2002, Yates and Youniss 1996, Youniss and Yates 1997); participation in community programs (Larsen 2000); religiosity (Youniss and Yates 1997); aspirations for success and wealth (Kasser and Ryan 1993); the media (McLeod 2000); and demographic characteristics such as class and race (Flanagan and Faison 2001, Jankowski 1992, 2002, Spencer 1999).

Hence, a diverse number of factors in youth's experience have been shown to relate to later civic engagement. However, the relationships tend to be complex. For example, both the nature of civics education teens receive in school as well as factors such as school climate and teacher behavior have been shown to predict youth civic participation (Flanagan and Tucker 1999, Niemi 1999). Teachers who treat students fairly promote the development of just behavior in teens. Classes that promote open discussion of issues promote higher levels of understanding of civics materials. A large international study of the civic education of 14,000 fourteen-year-olds examined civic education and youngsters' understanding of citizenship and democracy in twenty-eight countries (Torney-Purta et al. 2001). There was little variability in civic knowledge, and overall it was not as high as we would want. Civics education should be of the same national priority as math and science; it is as important to functioning as an adult in society as are math and science (Sherrod 2003). Civic knowledge is also important because it is the single most important predictor of youth voting; students with more knowledge are more likely to vote in political elections (Torney-Purta 2002). Knowledge does not relate, however, to how young people vote—to their political attitudes. We do not know why some youth develop conservative views and others liberal ones, why some become Republicans and others Democrats.

Research is needed that addresses how differences in these socialization factors relate to different aspects of adult civic engagement. For example, one would not necessarily expect working on the yearbook to have the same impact as participating in student government. All youth for the most part get some civics education, so is it the student's performance in civics class or the nature of the class that has more influence? Very detailed and serious research is needed to specify the connections between youth socialization factors and aspects of adult citizen participation.

It is particularly important to understand the civic development of youth who may feel disenfranchised, such as poor or minority youth or sexual-minority youth (Sherrod, Flanagan, and Youniss 2002); these young people may be the most likely to be disengaged because they do not see the nation as offering them particularly good opportunities. But a democracy is based on the participation of all citizens so that it is just as important to understand the development of citizenship in these youth as in more affluent, mainstream teens and young people. Furthermore, the number of minority youth is increasing and will soon become the majority (Hernandez 1993). Diverse youth may develop allegiances to social institutions other than the nation-state, such as to their family, and it is essential to understand how these allegiances relate to the development of citizenship (Bogard and Sherrod 2005).

Community Service and Service Learning

Community service has also been recognized as a way to promote youth civic engagement since it serves to engage youth civically and youth community service correlates with other forms of civic engagement later in life. Some people, however, consider it to be a form of civic engagement, not just a precursor to it (Youniss et al. 2002). Others have considered that young people may do service as an alternative to other political participation, so that it may substitute for civic engagement (Walker 2002). For these reasons, there has been tremendous national policy and research attention to community service by youth.

There is a National Youth Service Act, a Corporation for National Service, AmeriCorps, and a variety of other government initiatives to promote service in youth. As frequently happens, these efforts have been launched without sufficient research. Youniss and Yates (1997) find that the nature of the service influences whether or not it has any impact on any aspect of youth development. Working in one's community (e.g., in a soup kitchen versus tutoring young children), doing service voluntarily as opposed to having it mandated, and having an opportunity to reflect on what you do in the service and how the people you serve are and are not like you are three factors that relate to impact. Not all service programs have these qualities. Research has also shown that youth serve for quite different reasons. Some young people serve because they want to help someone, others because their parents or religion expect it of them, and others for quite selfish reasons, such as the fact that it looks good on their records (Sherrod 2003). One would expect these different reasons for doing service to relate to different effects of service on the individual's development. Hence, the nature of youth's service, which can be quite heterogeneous, determines its impact. This may be one reason why the relationship between service and later civic engagement is so controversial.

Service learning is a form of community service that aims to connect doing service to academic benefits. According to the Corporation for National Service, service learning is defined as learning that involves students in community activities that complement their classroom studies (Corporation for National Service 2000). Thus, service learning is a form of applied education in which students doing community-based service relate their real-world experiences to their academic coursework. Sometimes courses may require students to do service in order to get some real-world experience. Students may also get additional credit for doing service.

Studies show that service-learning programs can have both academic and social benefits. More research has focused, however, on gains in civic development and social competencies. Students engaged in service learning do demonstrate prosocial benefits. Markus, Howard, and King (1993) found that undergraduate students in political science courses with a service-learning component exhibited greater levels of social responsibility, volunteerism, likeliness to donate to charity, appreciation of others, and civic-mindedness compared to their peers in similar classes without the service-learning component. Other studies found service-learning students demonstrated more initiative, greater responsibility, increased cultural awareness, social responsibility (Jenkins 1991), reduced global and individual alienation (Calabrese and Schumer 1986), increased global concern and decreased racial prejudice (Myers-Lipton 1994), and increased social-problem understanding and problem solving; they are also more likely to view themselves as agents of change (Yates and Youniss, 1996). Stukas, Clary, and Snyder (1999) reviewed findings in six areas: self-enhancement and self-esteem, understanding of self and world, expression of humanitarian and prosocial values, career development in regard to exploration of options, satisfaction of social expectations, and protection from problems. They reported some positive impact of service programs in all areas, based on systematic research, including experiments, but effects varied by server and by program characteristics.

There is less research focused on academic gains made by students in service-learning courses, and most research examining academic gains has focused on academically based programs. Cohen and Kinsey (1994) found, for example, academically based service-learning students to be more motivated to learn and more interested in their academic courses compared with their non-service-learning peers. Knowledge of relevant course content may increase as well (Hamilton and Zeldin 1987), and service students may interact more with faculty (Sax and Astin 1997). Some research has shown that grades may not differ as a result of service (Kendrick 1996); other studies have shown that youth do better academically and avoid risky behavior.

Research has also examined the characteristics of programs that relate to impact. For example, Stukas, Clary, and Snyder (1999) describe studies showing that students' level of autonomy and responsibility in their service work contribute to impact. Hence, service is a quite diverse experience for youth, and although it does relate to civic engagement, current research does not allow us to disentangle the specific relationships between youth's community service and later civic engagement.

Political Attitudes and Behaviors

Research has tended to focus on the political behaviors youth show, such as voting, or the knowledge that underlies such behaviors. However, political attitudes are a third aspect of civic engagement that merit equal attention. Attitudes may in fact mediate the relationship between knowledge and behavior (Sherrod 2003).

Research on attitudes asks youth about political issues that reflect a dimension relating to being politically conservative versus liberal or that relate to their understanding of political issues and explanation for current political realities. Youth may, for example, be asked why they think people are poor. Is it because they don't work hard enough, because they are not smart or are lazy—that is, is the individual responsible for being poor? Or are people poor because of structural constraints such as lack of opportunity? Interestingly, poor youth are more likely to attribute poverty to individual causes (Flanagan and Tucker 1999). At first these results seem surprising, but if you think about it, they make sense. If people are poor due to structural constraints, then they may be trapped. However, if the individual is responsible for being poor, then these youth can maintain the hope of escaping poverty through their hard work.

Attitudes are likely to shape young people's political behavior so that we need much more research on how youth come to form different types of attitudes about political issues such as poverty. Sherrod, Quinones, and Davila (2004) examined youth's reactions to September 11, 2001, in the United States. This dramatic event had as much impact on youth's political views as on their trauma or experienced fearfulness. Political knowledge did seem to protect youth from trauma; that is, those with more knowledge showed less fearfulness. Furthermore, their political views provided a lens through which they responded to the event. Youth concerned about issues reflecting a concern for others worried about impact on prejudice; those concerned about defense and other such "conservative" issues were concerned about continuing terrorism and the need to "get even" (Sherrod, Quinones, and Davila 2004).

There are also important sex differences in political attitudes. Overall girls tend to be more prosocial and boys more conservative. These differences are present by early adolescence. The school activities in which youth participate also relate to views; sports, for example, relate to more conservative views. More boys participate in sports, but it is not clear if sports contribute to the development of conservative views or boys become involved in sports because they are conservative (Sherrod and Baskir 2005). Still, political views are another aspect of youth's civic engagement about which we need more research.

Positive Youth Development

Citizenship and youth activism are certainly important ways that youth can make positive contributions to society. Too often youth are given a bad rap and are seen negatively by adults—as lazy, as troublemakers, as not making positive contributions. In fact, for many years our research and policy attention to youth carried an equally negative orientation.

In recent years, however, a new approach has arisen in the youth-development field. This approach moves beyond treatment and even beyond prevention to the promotion of development. This focus on the positive development of youth moves beyond fixing problems or eliminating defects. For several decades research and policy have been devoted to identifying and correcting problems of youth: high-risk sexual behavior, teenage pregnancy, school failure and dropout, substance use and abuse, violence, and crime. It was from this focus that the emphasis on risk factors became prominent. Because not all youth succumb equally to risks, the concept of resiliency emerged, and prevention efforts were developed. Although these efforts have enjoyed some success in reducing risks and health-compromising behaviors, their achievement is constrained by limited funding and by the limited evidence of sustained behavior change after programs have ended (Scales, Blyth, Berkas et al. 2000).

A focus on promoting the positive development of youth rather than on fixing problems leads to the development-promoting qualities of families and communities and to policies that make up for the shortfalls of the environments. If we provide the supports that youth need, all have the potential to beat the odds (Larsen 2000).

This approach is based on the contributions of several groups, such as the Search Institute, the International Youth Foundation, and the Youth Policy Forum (Scales, Blyth, Berkas et al. 2000). Both external and internal assets of youth have been identified and correlated with environmental and individual resiliency factors. Internal factors include commitment to learning, positive values, social competencies, and positive identity. Broad categories of external factors include family and community supports, empowerment, boundaries and expectations, and constructive use of time. The presence of risk behaviors is inversely correlated with assets. These assets, of course, interact in complex ways and vary substantially by community (Scales, Blyth, Berkas et al. 2000). However, this approach demonstrates how providing the means to meet youth's multiple developmental needs by ensuring protection, support, and opportunities across these important contexts is a preferred focus for intervention.

The interest in positive youth development is reflected throughout this encyclopedia. Several entries describe one or more aspects of this approach, and the topic of youth activism is viewed as one means of pursuing a positive approach to youth development. Activism is one of the most important ways youth can make a positive contribution to their societies. No one can continue to hold a negative view of today's youth after reading the examples of activism in this encyclopedia.

In Summary

The development of citizenship is increasing as an important topic for research and policy attention. This encyclopedia on youth activism is one example. However, more attention is needed on the early experiences that relate to later civic engagement, on community service as an important correlate, and on attitudes as potential mediators of knowledge and behaviors.

References

Battistich, V., Solomon, D., Kim, D., Watson, M., and Schaps, E. (1995). "Schools as Communities, Poverty Levels of Student Populations, Motives, and Performance: A Multilevel Analysis." *American Educational Research Journal*, 32: 627–658.

Bogard, K., and Sherrod, L. (2005). "Allegiances and Civic Engagement in Diverse Youth." Submitted to *Child Development.* Based on a paper presented at the International Society for Behavioral Development, July, Ghent, Belgium.

Calabrese, R., and Schumer, H. (1986). "The Effects of Service Activities on Adolescent Alienation." *Adolescence*, 21 (83): 675–687.

Corporation for National Service (2000). "About Us: Legislative History." Retrieved November 10, 2000, http://www.cns.gov.

Eccles, J., and Barber, B. (1999). "Student Council, Volunteering, Basketball, or Marching Band: What Kind of Extracurricular Involvement Matters?" *Journal of Adolescent Research*, 12: 287–315.

Flanagan, C., and Faison, N. (2001). "Youth Civic Development: Implications of Research for Social Policy and Programs." *Social Policy Reports*, 1.

Flanagan, C., and Sherrod, L. (1998). "Political Development: Youth Growing Up in a Global Community." *Journal of Social Issues*, 54 (3).

Flanagan, C., and Tucker, C. (1999). "Adolescents' Explanations for Political Issues: Concordance with Their Views of Self and Society." *Developmental Psychology*, 35: 1198–1209.

Hart, D., Atkins, R., and Ford, D. (1998). "Urban America as a Context for the Development of Moral Identity in Adolescence." *Journal of Social Issues*, 54: 513–530.

Hernandez, D. (1993). *America's Children: Resources from Family, Government, and the Economy*. New York, NY: Russell Sage Foundation.

Jankowski, M. (1992). "Ethnic Identity and Political Consciousness in Different Social Orders." *New Directions for Child Development*, 56: 79–93.

Jankowski, M. (2002). "Minority Youth and Civic Engagement: The Impact of Group Relations." *Applied Developmental Science*, 6 (4): 237–245.

Jenkins, T. (1991). "Student Affairs and Academic Affairs Collaborate through a Service-Learning Course Requirement." *Journal of College Student Development*, 32: 79–82.

Jennings, M., and Niemi, R. (1974). *The Political Character of Adolescence*. Princeton, NJ: Princeton University Press.

Kasser, T., and Ryan, R. (1993). "A Dark Side of the American Dream: Correlates of Financial Success as a Central Life Aspiration." *Journal of Personality and Social Psychology*, 65: 410–422.

Kendrick, R., Jr. (1996). "Outcomes of Service Learning in an Introduction to Sociology Course." *Michigan Journal of Community Service Learning*, 3: 72–81.

Larsen, R. (2000) "Toward a Psychology of Positive Youth Development." *American Psychologist*, 55: 170–183.

Leming, J. (1986). "Rethinking Social Studies Research and the Goals of Social Education." *Theory and Research in Social Education*, 14: 139–152.

Markus, G., Howard, J., and King, D. (1993). "Integrating Community Service and Classroom Instruction Enhances Learning: Results from an Experiment." *Educational Evaluation and Policy Analysis*, 15 (4): 410–419.

McDevitt, M., and Chaffee, S. (2000). "Closing Gaps in Political Communication and Knowledge." *Communication Research*, 27: 259–292.

McLeod, J. (2000). Media and Civic Socialization of Youth." *Journal of Adolescent Health*, 27: 45–51.

McPherson, P., and Zimmerman, D. (in press). (Eds) Simon, L., Kenny, M., Kiley-Brabeck, K., and Lerner, R. (in progress). *Learning to Serve: Promoting Civil Society through Service-Learning*. Boston: Kluwer Publishing.

Myers-Lipton, S. (1994). "The Effects of Service-Learning on College Students' Attitudes toward Civic Responsibility, International Understanding and Racial Prejudice." PhD diss: abstract and discussion of results. University of Colorado, Boulder, CO.

Niemi, R. (1999). "Editor's Introduction." *Political Psychology*, 20: 471–476.

Niemi, R., and Junn, J. (2000). *Civic Education: What Makes Students Learn*. New Haven, CT: Yale University Press.

Putnam, R. (1996). "The Strange Disappearance of Civic America." *The American Prospect*, 34–48.

Putnam, R. (2000). Bowling Alone: The Collapse and Revival of American Community. New York: Simon and Schuster.

Sax, L., and Astin, A. (1997). "The Benefits of Service: Evidence from Undergraduates." *Educational Record*, 78 (3–4): 25–32.

Scales, P., Blyth, D., Berkas, T., and Kielsmeier, J. (2000). "The Effects of Service Learning on Middle School Students' Social Responsibility and Academic Success." *Journal of Early Adolescence*, 20 (3): 332–358.

Sherrod, L. R. (2003). "Promoting the Development of Citizenship in Diverse Youth." *PS: Political Science and Politics*, April: 287–292.

Sherrod, L. R., and Baskir, L. (2005). "Gender Differences in the Political Interests of U.S. Teens." In *Journal of Research on Social Issues*, edited by Ittel et al. (in press).

Sherrod, L. R., Quinones, O., and Davila, C. (2004). "Youth's Political Views and Their Experience of September 11, 2001." *Applied Developmental Psychology*, 25: 149–170.

Sherrod, L. R., Flanagan, C., and Youniss, J. (2002). "Dimensions of Citizenship and Opportunities for Youth Development: The What, Why, When, Where and Who of Citizenship Development." *Applied Developmental Science*, 6 (4): 264–272.

Spencer, M. (1999). "Social and Cultural Influences on School Adjustment: The Application of an Identity-Focused Cultural Ecological Perspective." *Educational Psychology*, 34: 43–57.

Stukas, A., Clary E. G., and Snyder, M. (1999). "Service Learning: Who Benefits and Why." *Social Policy Report: Society for Research in Child Development*, 8 (4): 1–19.

Torney-Purta, J. (2002). The School's Role in Developing Civic Engagement: A Study of Adolescents in Twenty-Eight Countries." *Applied Developmental Science*, 6 (4): 202–211.

Torney-Purta, J., Lehmann, R., Oswald, H., and Schultz, W. (2001). *Citizenship and Education in Twenty-Eight Countries: Civic Knowledge and Engagement at Age Fourteen*. Amsterdam: IEA.

Verba, S., Schlozman, L., and Brady, H. (1995). *Voice and Equality: Civic Voluntarism in American Life*. Cambridge, MA: Harvard University Press.

Walker, T. (2002). "Service as a Pathway to Political Participation: What Research Tells Us." *Applied Developmental Science*, 6: 183–188.

Yates, M., and Youniss, J. (1996). "A Developmental Perspective on Community Service in Adolescence." *Social Development*, 1–26.

Youniss, J., Bales, S., Christmas-Best, V., Diversi, M., McLaughlin, M., and Silbereisen, R. (2002). "Youth Civic Engagement in the Twenty-First Century." *Journal of Research on Adolescence*, 12: 121–148.

Youniss, J., and Yates, M. (1997). "What We Know About Engendering Civic Identity." *American Behavioral Scientist*, 40: 620–631.

Youth as a Social Construct and Social Actor

CONSTANCE A. FLANAGAN AND AMY K. SYVERTSEN

Youth is an elastic category: where it begins and ends is subject to interpretation and is sensitive to social and historical context. Typically, this stage or time in the life cycle refers to persons in the adolescent and emerging adult years, people who are no longer children but "not quite" adults in the sense of assuming the independence and responsibilities typically associated with adulthood.

Depending on the socioeconomic and sociocultural traditions of a society, youth may be persons as young as thirteen and as old as forty. What has often been said about the period of adolescence applies even more so to the period of "youth." That is, the period of youth begins in biology and ends in culture. In other words, sexual maturity is a biological characteristic that marks the end of childhood with pubescence, a biological process that, in many parts of the world, occurs at earlier ages today than it did one hundred years ago. But sexual maturity is not a sufficient basis for being an adult. Assuming the responsibilities of adulthood requires emotional and social maturity as well.

Ultimately, attaining full adulthood also means that young people have to have opportunities available in their societies to exercise the rights and responsibilities of adulthood. It is difficult to be an adult and to assume the responsibilities it entails if, for example, there are few opportunities to be financially self-sufficient. Thus, high unemployment rates in South Africa, coupled with the fact that many South Africans remain in school into the third decade of life, were realities taken into account when the Constitution for the Democratic Republic of South Africa defined "youth" as persons between the ages of fourteen and thirty-five. In summary, youth is a social construction: its meaning varies according to the particular contexts in which people are making transitions from the dependencies of childhood to assume the responsibilities of adulthood.

In general, youth is the age range covered by the adolescent and early adult years. Adolescence itself is a sociocultural construction, recognized as a period of life in some societies but not in others. Adolescence, derived from the Latin word *adolescere*, is a period of growth and maturity (Muuss 1990). It was G. Stanley Hall, sometimes referred to as the father of adolescence, who initiated the scientific study of this distinctive developmental period. Hall (1904) referred to this time of life as one of *sturm und drang*—that is, storm and stress—rampant with psychological turmoil. Even today, it is a commonplace belief that raging hormones drive adolescent behavior and that one should expect adolescents to act in erratic and unpredictable ways.

An alternative—positive youth development—approach is now contesting the dominant paradigm of youth as problems that society must manage and control. Instead, the

PYD approach attends to youth as assets to their communities, focusing on the energy and vitality of youth, the fresh perspectives they bring to community issues, and the revitalizations that can happen to organizations and communities if youth are invited to a place at the table. Implicit in the PYD approach is the importance of the opportunities that a society and its institutions offer to a younger generation in order to allow them to practice the skills they will need as adults.

Historically, the changing needs of a society and the creation of institutions to fulfill those needs were factors associated with the construction of adolescence and youth as a separate stage of life between childhood and adulthood. Prior to the Industrial Revolution in Europe and the United States, the transition between childhood and adulthood was comparatively smooth. When there is relatively little change between generations in labor and lifestyles, the younger generation can learn the skills they will need as adults at the sides of their parents. There is no need for a separate period or place for training if all of the knowledge youth will need can be learned in daily practice alongside the older generation.

But the Industrial Revolution separated work from family life and changed the intergenerational equation. Increasingly, the generations were segregated in separate institutions, the older in industry and the younger in schools. The consequent age segregation, especially over time as schools assembled specific age-groups of students into different levels of education, ultimately led to the conceptualization of adolescence and youth as distinct phases of life. In Western societies the term "youth" became part of popular vernacular with the advent of universities as institutions where large numbers of youth congregated for the purposes of being educated and trained to take their place in the adult world.

In summary, the "storm and stress" of adolescence is not universal—it is less likely to occur in societies where the pace of change is relatively slow, where a younger generation can learn through practice alongside an older generation what they will likely be doing as adults. As periods of the life span, adolescence, and youth, while not universal, are more widespread than they once were. The length and meaning of these periods vary across cultures, times, and places. And, even within the same setting, the implications of this period of life vary, depending on whether one is male or female, rich or poor.

Moving from Adolescence to Adulthood

Although for years the end of the teen years was thought to signal the beginning of adulthood, in recent years the period of youth has become more protracted. Compared to their parents and grandparents, young people today are less able as they enter their twenties to take on the responsibilities, especially the financial responsibilities, of adulthood. In large measure this is due to the increasingly complex nature of adult life and the fact that jobs that allow people to support families demand higher levels of education.

Just as adolescence was coined as a term to refer to the unique stage of life between childhood and adulthood, terms such as emerging adulthood or the transition to adulthood are now being used. Such phrases draw attention to the mismatch between the capacities of individuals in their early twenties and the lack of institutional opportunities that would enable them to assume the roles of full adulthood (Settersten, Furstenberg, and Rumbaut 2005). This mismatch is a major reason why the term "youth" is so elastic with the age range changing according to the imperatives, challenges, constraints, and opportunities at particular historical moments.

Psychological Theories

According to psychologists, youth is a time in life for taking stock—of oneself and one's society. This is a time when people have to decide how they will earn a living, what they are good at, and what they care about. Erikson (1968) captured the developmental imperatives of youth when he described the key psychosocial tasks of these years as exploring and consolidating an identity. What he meant by identity was both an individual's conception of his/her uniqueness as well as a sense of authenticity between what s/he believed in and how s/he acted and finally, a sense of connection or solidarity with others who were similar in background or beliefs. In other words, youth need to figure out who they are, what other individuals and groups they fit with, what they believe in, how they make sense of the world, and who else believes in the same things that they do. Thus, compared to other age-groups, it is more common for youth to be exploring spiritual, religious, cultural, and political ideas and deciding which ones they believe in and can commit to.

As they explore what they care about and who they are, youth develop an ideology, a worldview, a system of ideas and beliefs that guide their choices in the present, as well as the decisions they make about the future. According to Erikson, developing an ideology was essential for youth because it helped them to organize, manage, and make sense of the vast array of choices the world presented to them. Furthermore, being true to oneself, acting in a way that is consistent with what you believe in, is important to youth. Erikson referred to this as fidelity to one's beliefs. He also discussed the human need for a sense of coherence or continuity of personal character. These references to authenticity in Erikson's work also are captured in the phrase popularized in contemporary youth culture, "keeping it real."

Compared to children, adolescents are better at assessing whether the way an individual acts reflects what s/he believes in, in part because adolescents are more capable of handling abstractions, like beliefs. Personal beliefs become a standard for prosocial action for adolescents, more than they were in childhood (Hart, Yates, Fogley, and Wilson 1995). By late adolescence, the significance of beliefs is apparent insofar as they are now a critical dimension of how youth think about themselves (Harter 1999).

In answering questions about who they are, what they believe in and stand for, youth inevitably will grapple with issues in their society and world. In other words, as they take stock of themselves, they also take stock of their social order. They grapple with the kinds of principles their society stands for and the direction its policies are taking. Erikson contended that continuity or consistency in a belief system was important for youth, and it appears that this consistency also applies to the political theories youth endorse. Flanagan and Tucker (1999) found that adolescents' political theories and explanations for social problems were significantly related to their beliefs and values. Democratic societies recognize that youth are capable of taking stock of their societies and of helping to determine the principles and policies of those societies. The exact age varies, but whether at sixteen, eighteen, or twenty-one, youth are accorded the right to vote in most democracies around the world.

As young people search for and develop meaning and purpose in their lives, they find others with similar world views. These may become soul mates. They may join cultural, religious, or political groups that reflect their ideologies and commitments. Youth may also develop an awareness that they are members of a generation with political issues that are unique to their generational group. For example, in South Africa the Black Consciousness and Young Lions generations united around the cause of fighting apartheid and realizing a democratic South Africa. Now that democracy has been achieved, HIV/AIDS is the challenge that today's younger generation must tackle in order to sustain democracy.

Political views evolve somewhat in adulthood, and political behaviors tend to mellow with age. But basic ideologies and values crystallize for most people during the period of youth. This is especially true for those who engage in political activism during their youth because they grapple intensely with issues, which raise contested values and beliefs about the just and fair way to organize a society.

Several longitudinal studies that followed into mid-life, activists in the American civil rights and antiwar movements as well as their nonactivist peers found that the activists remained committed in mid-life to the needs of minorities and disadvantaged groups and were active in politics in their local communities and in movements for women's rights, peace, and the environment (Marwell, Aiken, and Demerath 1987, McAdam 1989). At the same time, for many activists family values and practices also play a formative role, selecting young people into activism and reinforcing their commitments.

The political positions of student activists of the 1960s and their parents, especially mothers, were more liberal than those of their age-mates during the height of student activism as well as fifteen years later (Dunham and Bengston 1992). It is very likely that 1960s antiwar activists learned in their families that questioning authority and holding leaders accountable are responsible behaviors in a democracy. When Haan, Smith, and Block (1968) compared the families of antiwar protesters to those of non-protesters, they found that disagreement and debate about current events were more common among the families of protesters, suggesting not only that politics was a salient topic in those families but that an attitude of open-mindedness and a willingness to hear alternative views prevailed. Other longitudinal studies comparing the parenting behaviors of activists and nonactivists at mid-life found that certain core values were passed on to the younger generation. As parents, those who were youth activists were more likely to teach their children the importance of understanding others and of serving the common good (Franz and McClelland 1994).

Sociological Views

Youth is a group that sociologists and political scientists have studied because, ultimately, younger generations will replace their elders in the political process. Thus, focusing on the issues that matter to younger generations, the beliefs and world views they hold, and their relationships with older generations provides a glimpse of the future political landscape of a society. Political stability, continuity, and change in a society are matters that concern sociologists and political scientists, and thus, they are interested in the way that younger generations become part of the body politic. Relationships between generations figure prominently in two theories as explanations of political stability and political change.

The first, political socialization theory, focused on the integration of younger generations into the body politic and argued that they adopted the beliefs and behaviors of their parents and other socialization agents. This theory focused on the relatively smooth transition or continuity in political beliefs and behaviors across generations. According to this theory there is an intergenerational bargain implied in the process of social integration; that is a promise that the younger generation will enjoy the rights and reap the benefits of the social order if its members live by the rules and fulfill the responsibilities of membership in that social order. But socialization theory is less compelling in contexts of rapid social change when there is considerable discontinuity between those principles that organized society during the parents' formative years and the principles that dominate as their children come of age. For example, in Central and Eastern Europe in the early 1990s, the rapid pace of change from command to market economies and from single-party to multi-party rule meant that the practices followed by the parents' generation were less effective for the younger generation (Flanagan and Campbell 2003). However, even when there is little social change occurring in a society, no younger generation rubber stamps the beliefs of its parents. Rather, whatever continuity there is across generations occurs because the younger generation constructs in its own way a set of political beliefs and behaviors based on those it inherits.

Compared to political socialization theory, generational replacement theory was more interested in discontinuities in political beliefs and behaviors across generations. Proponents of this theory pointed out that, as increasing numbers of the younger generations replaced the declining numbers of their elders in society, it was inevitable that the political landscape would change. The size of the gap between the beliefs and values of the older and younger generations was thought to contribute to the degree of change in the political landscape. It is noteworthy, however, that studies of political activists in the 1960s found no generational gap in values. In fact, youth were acting on values that their parents had taught them.

According to this theory, adult socialization agents, including parents, were only one of the influences on a younger generation's political beliefs and behaviors. Peers, culture, media, and historical events were others. Indeed, the historical events occurring when a generation comes of age (i.e., in its youth), whether these be wars, economic recessions, civil rights, or suffrage movements, are defining issues with which the youth of that era grapple. One large retrospective study of American adults found that, regardless of age, the events those adults considered most important were the ones that had occurred during their youth (Schuman and Scott 1989). For similar reasons, age cohorts, that is, people born at the same time and who consequently go through their adolescence and youth at the same time, are often given generational labels that reflect the major historical events of their youth. And generational theorists note that early adulthood can be a politically defining time with lifelong consequences.

In his classic essay, "The Problem of Generations," Karl Mannheim (1952) argued that youth had a "fresh contact" with their social order, seeing it from new perspectives.

Because youth were not saddled with roles and responsibilities, Mannheim held that they were less firmly entrenched in social roles than they would be later in life. Indeed, although young adults face certain developmental imperatives, those who are unmarried and childless and not in permanent careers are less saddled with responsibilities or social roles than they will be a few years down the road. They are free to explore different ideas, values, lifestyles, religious and cultural traditions, and political views. And they are often in settings like college campuses where they are exposed to more alternative perspectives on social issues than they were in high school and also are less influenced by their parents' views.

According to generational theorists, college itself offered a particularly rich setting where young people had the chance to form new political reference groups. Away from the influence of their families of origin, youth could explore ideas with peers and with teachers, free from the ideological constraints of their families. An example is provided in Newcomb's longitudinal studies of undergraduate women who attended Bennington, a progressive women's college, in the 1930s. Exposure to the young faculty's perspectives on public issues—perspectives which departed from their parents' conservative convictions—was related to a shift in the women's positions toward greater identification with the policies of the New Deal (Newcomb et al. 1967). Thereafter, the realignment of their political views remained stable, even into the late adult years (Alwin, Cohen, and Newcomb, 1991). Similarly, Jennings (2002) compared high-school seniors who attended college in the late 1960s with their peers who did not attend college. He found that political attitudes were shaken up by the college experience but that, once crystallized, the attitudes of those who went to college were more stable thereafter.

Whether or not they attend college, youth tend to be free from the kind of informal social control that would constrain their thinking and behavior. Compared to children, they are less subject to older adults' authority and governance. And compared to those even a few years their senior, youth are less constrained by the social norms of co-workers or the conventions of social roles since they are less likely to be in permanent jobs or committed to particular social roles. This is one reason why youth are more likely than their elders to act on their political beliefs in unconventional ways, for example, through public demonstrations, acts of civil disobedience, or even more disruptive forms of political action. Historically, there have always been disproportionate numbers of youth in movements for social change. Since the 1830s in societies across the globe, youth have swelled the ranks of political protest movements and leveled demands for social change at the adults in charge (Braungart 1984).

One poignant account of the greater readiness of youth to take risks in the service of a political cause is provided in David Halberstam's book, *The Children*. In that work he chronicles the history of the Student Non-Violent Coordinating Committee (SNCC), whose nonviolent sit-ins at segregated lunch counters in the southern United States challenged the laws upholding segregation. Describing the group of young people who were preparing for the first sit-in, he observes:

> The four were all freshmen (students at the Agricultural and Technical College in Greensboro, NC)—freshmen which reflected something that was to be constant as the student movement grew throughout the South—the younger the potential volunteer, the

more willing he or she was to take risks (while the converse was generally true)—the older the students, the more they had a stake in terms of career and career expectations, and the less likely they were to join up (Halberstam, 1998, 92).

In general, youth are more tolerant than their elders of different lifestyles and of deviant behaviors. This tolerance of deviance, combined with the experimental nature of the period and the fact that deviant behavior peaks in the late adolescent years, all contribute to the popular and negative stereotype that youth have no self-control and could pose a danger to society. Historically, such stereotypes have been leveled against young political activists and used to dismiss the causes they espouse. The stereotype that the political activism of young people reflects their naïve and impetuous nature rather than an informed commitment to social justice has prompted some activists to shun words like "youth" or "young" when referring to their movements.

Compared to their elders, youth tend to feel invulnerable and are more inclined to take risks and act on their political convictions. In fact, taking risks and exploring alternative ideas are considered normative for youth. The "fresh contact" to which Mannheim alluded is another factor that may contribute to their activist tendencies. Compared to their elders whose views of justice may have more shades of gray, youth are more likely to see the world in right-and-wrong, just-and-unjust terms (Watts and Flanagan in press). And, compared to those whose sense of political efficacy may be moderated by age and experience, youth may be more inclined to act on the supposition that their cause is just and should prevail. Combined with their insistence on authenticity, it is not surprising that youth would be more inclined to act immediately and strongly on things they consider unjust.

Halberstam alludes to the divergence in political tactics advocated by different generations in the civil rights struggle. Whereas the older generation, aware of the dangers of nonviolent resistance to the activists' physical safety, urged caution, Halberstam says that the younger generation

> ... had come to sense in some intuitive way that the things they wanted to happen would happen only if they reached and crossed a certain danger point. An intuitive philosophy of the students in the Movement was born: The safer everything was, the less likely that anything important would take place. Changes would come only with risk: the greater the risk, the greater the change. The children were the first to understand that, Will Campbell thought, for they had not yet made the compromises which had been forced on their elders, and they were willing to resist those compromises, if need be, with their lives. They still lived in a world where the truth was absolute (Halberstam 1998, 276).

Mannheim pointed out that not all members of a generation will deal in the same way with the historical events occurring as they come of age. He used the term "generational units" to refer to these differences within a generation. Empirical support for this notion comes from longitudinal studies that show it is not the historical events as much as the way in which individual youth grapple with those events that predict their subsequent political positions (Jennings 2002). In any generation and with any historical event, youth can get actively engaged with the issues, can be interested bystanders, or can be disinterested and inactive altogether.

McAdam (1988) has argued that engaging in intense political activism during one's youth transforms identity in fundamental ways. He compared young adults who participated in the Mississippi Freedom Summer voter-registration drives in the southern United States with a group of their peers who volunteered to go but in the end did not participate. Although the period of time was short, the actions in which these volunteers were engaged were highly contested and their lives were on the line. According to McAdam, these facts, combined with the collective identity they experienced as part of a group powerfully committed to a cause, fundamentally transformed their identities and also disrupted subsequent life trajectories. It seems that the sustained commitment of young activists to social causes can eclipse other relationships. Several longitudinal studies have shown that intense activism in one's youth is related to a lower likelihood in adulthood of marrying or staying married and of having children (Franz and McClelland 1994, McAdam 1988).

Youthful risk taking is often considered a problem, but there are many contemporary and historical examples that show that youth's readiness to take risks invigorates organizations and political movements. When youth are in leadership roles in community organizations or commissions, their vitality and fresh perspectives reinvigorate the organization and its ties to the community and bring both the adults and the organization back to their core values (Zeldin, McDaniel, Topitzes, and Calvert 2000). During the decades of struggle against apartheid in South Africa, youth rejuvenated organizations such as the African National Congress and often advocated militant action (Ngomane and Flanagan 2003). Similarly, in the U.S. civil rights movement of the late 1950s and early 1960s, youth were instrumental in getting established organizations such as the NAACP to be more proactive and assertive (Oberschall 1989).

The fresh perspective and energy that youth can bring to an organization can benefit society as well. Keniston, for one, believes that there are moral and political benefits for individuals and for societies from the soul searching that goes on during youth:

> To be sure, those who have had a youth—who have seriously questioned their relationship to the community that exists, who have a self and a set of commitments independent of their social role—are never likely to be simple patriots, unquestioning conformists, or blind loyalists to the *status quo* (Keniston 1968, 272).

References

Alwin, D. F., Cohen, R. L., and Newcomb, T. M. (1991). *Political Attitudes over the Life Span: The Bennington Women after Fifty Years*. Madison: University of Wisconsin Press.

Braungart, R. G. (1984). "Historical and Generational Patterns of Youth Movements: A Global Perspective." In *Comparative Social Research*, vol. 1, edited by R. F. Tomasson. Greenwich, CT: JAI Press.

Dunham, C., and Bengston, V. (1992). "The Long-Term Effects of Political Activism on Intergenerational Relations." *Youth and Society*, 24: 31–51.

Erikson, E. (1968). *Youth: Identity and Crisis*. New York: W. W. Norton.

Flanagan, C. A., and Campbell, B., with L. Botcheva, J. Bowes, B. Csapo, P. Macek, and E. Sheblanova (2003). "Social Class and Adolescents' Beliefs about Justice in Different Social Orders." *Journal of Social Issues*, 59 (4): 711–732.

Flanagan, C. A., and Tucker, C. J. (1999). "Adolescents' Explanations for Political Issues: Concordance with Their Views of Self and Society." *Developmental Psychology*, 35 (5): 1198–1209.

Franz, C. E., and McClelland, D. C. (1994). "Lives of Women and Men Active in the Social Protests of the 1960s: A Longitudinal Study." *Journal of Personality and Social Psychology*, 66: 196–205.

Haan, N., Smith, M. B., and Block, J. H. (1968, November). "Moral Reasoning of Young Adults: Political-Social Behavior, Family Background, and Personality Correlates." *Journal of Personality and Social Psychology*, 10 (3): 183–201.

Halberstam, D. (1998). *The Children*. New York: Fawcett Books.

Hall, G. S. (1904). *Adolescence: Its Psychology and Its Relations to Physiology, Anthropology, Sociology, Sex, Crime, Religion, and Education*. New York: Appleton.

Hart, D., Yates, M., Fegley, S., and Wilson, G. (1995). "Moral Commitment in Inner-City Adolescents." In *Morality in Everyday Life: Developmental Perspectives*, edited by M. Killen and D. Hart. New York: Cambridge University Press.

Harter, S. (1999). *The Construction of the Self: A Developmental Perspective*. New York: Guilford.

Jennings, M. K. (2002, June). "Generation Units and the Student Protest Movement in the United States: An Intra- and Intergenerational Analysis." *Political Psychology*, 23(2): 303–324.

Keniston, K. (1968). *Young Radicals: Notes on Committed Youth*. New York: Harcourt, Brace, and World.

Mannheim, K. (1952). "The Problem of Generations." In *Essays on the Sociology of Knowledge*, edited by P. Kecshevich. London: Routledge and Kegan Paul (original work published 1928).

Marwell, G., Aiken, M. T., and Demerath, N. J., III. (1987). "The persistence of political attitudes among 1960s civil rights activists." *Public Opinion Quarterly*, 51: 359– 375.

McAdam, D. (1988). *Freedom Summer*. New York: Oxford University Press.

McAdam, D. (1989). "The Biographical Consequences of Activism." *American Sociological Review*, 54: 744–760.

Muuss, R. E. (1990). *Adolescent Behavior and Society: A Book of Readings*, 4th ed. New York: McGraw-Hill.

Newcomb, T. M., Koenig, K. E., Flacks, R., and Warwich, D. P. (1967). *Persistence and Change: Bennington College and Its Students after Twenty-five Years*. New York: John Wiley.

Ngomane, T., and Flanagan, C. (2003). "The Road to Democracy in South Africa." *Peace Review*, 15 (3): 267–271.

Oberschall, A. (1989). "The 1960 Sit-Ins: Protest Diffusion and Movement Take-Off." *Research in Social Movements, Conflict and Change*, 11: 31–53.

Schuman, H., and Scott, J. (1989). "Generations and Collective Memories." *American Sociological Review*, 54: 359–381.

Settersten, R. A., Jr., Furstenberg, F. F., Jr., and Rumbaut, R. G., eds. (2005). *On the Frontier of Adulthood: Theory, Research, and Public Policy*. Chicago: University of Chicago Press.

Watts, R. J., and Flanagan, C. A. (in press). "Pushing the Envelope on Youth Civic Engagement: A Developmental and Liberation Psychology Perspective." *Journal of Community Psychology*.

Zeldin, S., McDaniel, A. K., Topitzes, D., and Calvert, M. (2000). *Youth in Decision-Making: A Study on the Impacts of Youth on Adults and Organizations*. Chevy Chase, MD: National 4-H Council.

Youth Activism: International and Transnational

RON KASSIMIR

Few concerns are more ubiquitous across societies in different parts of the world than the worries about young people by their elders. Across continents, parents and politicians complain of young people as out of control, apathetic, or "living in their own world." Alternatively, they worry about youth as helpless or lacking a future given current social or control conditions. Whether young people are to blame for this supposed situation or are the innocent victims of what the journalist William Finnegan calls a "cold new world," the current state and future fate of young people are core to the hopes and fears of all societies.[1] At the same time, different societies have different definitions of who is a youth, what it means to be an adult, and what needs to happen for a young person to become a "proper" adult.[2] In other words, exactly what worries different people and nations about youth and how they worry depends on a range of factors—history, economics, culture, political systems, and so on.

When societies worry about young people as *political actors*, they worry about the kinds of citizens young people are right now in the present, the kinds of citizens they will become in the future, and the kinds of things that need to be done in the present to prepare young people to become "good" future citizens. Young people receive this kind of attention in part because they are presumed to be "incomplete" and not (yet) capable of fully responsible action and rational judgment. International concerns over the phenomenon of child soldiers, for example, stem both from a moral conviction that young people should be protected from participating in war and from a presumption that they are especially vulnerable and more impressionable and easily manipulated, including their being drawn into committing violent acts. Debates about where to set the voting age and other political rights are also tied to understanding the nature of youth from the perspective of their capacities and vulnerabilities.

Many young people around the world also think hard about themselves as political actors, now and in the future. Their worries often relate to the constraints put on their ability to influence the decisions and structures that shape their lives. In a sense, while many elders worry about the capacities of the young as political actors, many youth see limited capacity in their environments and of their elders to provide opportunities for the enactment of citizenship.

An International Perspective

It is because youth activism concerns both what young people are like as political actors in the present and what kinds of institutions and resources are available to enable (or limit) young people's politics that an international and comparative perspective on young people is so important. While worrying about young people may be universal, definitions of youth and of the transition to adulthood and citizenship vary across cultures. In addition, the knowledge and institutions that channel and shape (or exclude) youth, the legal and political frameworks that enable (or constrain) young people, and the resources available to them differ widely from one part of the world to another. Not least, what is understood as "activism" and its practical and normative importance to societies when young people engage in it varies. One of the intended contributions of this encyclopedia is to give a sense of the similarities and differences in youth activism in different parts of the world depending on resources, distribution of wealth and opportunity, political systems, and historical and cultural differences. At the same time, we must be attuned to how global change may, in some ways, be inducing similar experiences among young people, who themselves are connecting more and more across national and regional boundaries for the purposes of activism.

Depending on how activism is defined (see Sherrod's introductory essay and my discussion below), the research world may or may not lag behind the actual practices of young people around the world. There is a fair amount of research on young people as political actors with some work focused on the present, some on the future, and others on the relationship between the two.[3] In Western countries, principal attention has been paid to voting behavior, voluntarism, and the sources and effects of political socialization, especially civic education in schools. Much less is known about young people's participation in social movements or other efforts at changing the policies or behaviors of powerful institutions. Although the study of social movements took off at the height of young people's political mobilization in the 1960s (antiwar, civil rights, anticapitalist in the West; anti-colonial, nationalist, and anticapitalist in the developing world), research on political activism generally, and on young people's politics and civic engagement in particular, has tended to travel on parallel rather than intersecting tracks.

In the developing world interest in youth activism was connected in part to struggles against colonialism or empire. More recently, young people's politics in the postcolonial era has tended to focus on political violence and terrorism. While these are indeed forms of "activism," their extreme nature tends to gain far more attention than contemporary youth participation in nonviolent movements or other forms of public advocacy.[4] International media help to circulate global images of developing-world youth as "super-predators," just as national media in the United States have conveyed a similar image of male African American youth.

While not necessarily concentrated on activism, an increase in scholarly attention on young people has occurred in a world in which the activities and problems of young people have been a popular subject of social policy, public discourse, and media representations. From a demographic perspective, the weight of statistics in terms of the percentage of populations within specific age ranges is undeniable in terms of the youthfulness of populations, at least outside of industrialized countries. This has moved policymakers to put youth at the center of policy agendas in many parts of the developing world.[5] The United Nations' Youth Employment Network is one important recent example. In places where the age pyramid is reversed, such as Western Europe, concerns about young people are linked closely to debates over immigration given the relative youth of so many migrants looking for, and only occasionally finding, employment. In addition, certain iconic events have fueled interest in youth in different parts of the world—the Columbine killings in the United States, suicide bombers in Israel and Palestine, child soldiers in Sierra Leone, as well as the youthfulness of protesters opposing neo-liberal policies around the world. Certain issues—real and perceived—have also received attention and public discussion: youth disaffection from mainstream democratic politics as measured by low voter turnout in elections, youth unemployment and child labor abuses, youth gangs and criminality, drug use, crises in public education, child sexual abuse, access to "adult" content on the Internet, and so on. Many of these issues have become the object of activist causes, either by young people themselves, concerned adults, or cross-generational coalitions.

Research is still catching up with both the myths and realities of the contemporary lives of young people around the world and the broader consequences of their ideas and actions for their status as citizens. Part of the delayed reaction may be a certain fuzziness to the notion of "activism" both within societies and across cultures.

What Is Activism?

Activism is a difficult term to pin down as it is used in many different ways by a wide range of political actors as well as practitioners concerned with the civic engagement of others. In this encyclopedia, we define activism broadly to encompass both the different "actions" attributed to activism and the different kinds of knowledge, resources, and experiences that enable young people to engage in activism.

For scholars, policymakers, and advocates of youth programs, youth activism can range from voting in elections to participating in revolutions, from exposure to civic education to participation in debate clubs, voluntary work, and service provision, from working on behalf of political parties to gathering signatures to present a petition to political leaders. Activism is civic engagement, and the education and experience that prepare a young person for the roles, rights, and responsibilities of citizenship are all part of the process.

However, for young people (and others) who consider themselves activists, the *active* part of the word activism is paramount. Activism here is a more specific kind of participation in the following:

- Protest events and direct actions (nonviolent or violent)
- Ongoing advocacy campaigns to change the policies and behaviors of powerful institutions—governments, transnational corporations, international institutions
- Consumer boycotts and other uses of market power to effect change
- Information gathering and dissemination intended to influence media attention and the consciousness of the public regarding issues of concern

From the standpoint of an activist, *activism* is one form of civic engagement—and clearly not the most common type. The other phenomena related to youth politics and citizenship mentioned above may go together with or lead to activism but quite often do not. Activism implies *action* that expresses dissent, attempts to effect change, or works to place issues on the political agenda. It is usually (although not always) organized and occasionally linked to wider social movements, which may or may not play by the rules of mainstream politics and civic decorum. Todd Gitlin, former leader of SDS, recently wrote that "an activist is a different sort of *–ist*, for it's not your beliefs that make you one but your beliefs hooking up to your activities."[6] Oxfam's International Youth Parliament stated in their recent report that activism "can be broadly defined as efforts to create changes in the behavior of institutions or organizations through action strategies such as lobbying, advocacy, negotiation, protest, campaigning and raising awareness."[7]

This form of activism is not widespread among young people (or the rest of the population), at least most of the time. Even compared to voting—typically engaged in by smaller percentages of young people than other age-groups—activism in this sense is a relatively rare phenomenon. But its importance cannot be measured only by the numbers of young people participating. As witnessed in major protests and demonstration events such as those against the WTO in Seattle and elsewhere, activism has effects, even if the results are not always what the activists hoped for. Young people's activism may also affect their political engagement and citizenship practices later in life as adults.[8] In addition, activism may have peer effects. Even if it does not result in bringing in new recruits to a cause, activism may raise awareness of issues and expand imaginations of what is politically possible for a young person.

One other issue worth considering is whether activism is, by definition, a good thing for the individual and for society. It is virtually impossible to answer this question in the abstract—different people will inevitably have different views depending on how their political goals and ideologies match with the goal of the activist and the type of action. Most people who see themselves as activists are likely to consider activism a good thing. Conversely, if young people take action on behalf of a cause that self-proclaimed activists disagree with, the action might not merit the accolade of activism. Others, including most social scientists, are more likely to use activism as a term relating to actions that take on a range of moral, political, or ideological orientations. This would include young right-wing, anti-immigrant skinhead movements as well as antisweatshop campaigners, and the aims and practices of young, religiously inspired extremists as well as young members of mainstream religious organizations' social-change activities. Clearly, the term "activism" has largely been appropriated by those with "progressive" agendas in relation to human-rights and social-justice issues, including most kinds of transnational activism. But it is important to remember that much "non-progressive" activism may also come from young people who are marginalized, feel threatened, and seek to change the policies and behaviors of powerful institutions.

What counts as activism and how it is valued differs in different places. Under more closed political systems voting tends to be a sham exercise, and open dissent and public advocacy for change is simply impossible or suicidal. Political activism in such cases may be more hidden out of necessity, and consciousness raising and strategizing for action may take place surreptitiously or at formally nonpolitical gatherings like religious services. Alternatively, the youth wings of political parties may be openly "active" but sometimes in the sense of repressing the expression of opposing voices.

Whether or not it is allowed within the political system, youth activism is likely not to be seen as unambiguously good in most parts of the world, even apart from its political goals. All societies emphasize respect for older generations and, as mentioned, see young people as in some sense lacking in the wisdom of experience. In some places the public expression of dissent might be regarded as so severely disrespectful that self-censoring takes place among the young when it comes to social and political issues that concern them. The kinds of issues on which young people can "appropriately" address themselves may also vary—perhaps in one place pressing for access to education is seen as legitimate but not the content of the education. Also, in different degrees and in different ways, young women everywhere tend to have additional obstacles in their way regarding their engagement in activism given cultural expectations.

Lastly, the focus or targets of young people's activism are diverse. Activism may be on behalf of a very local cause—advocacy on behalf of more and better educational opportunities or, in places stricken with HIV/AIDS, programs to care for the afflicted and their dependents. At a national level, it could be protest against an authoritarian government or the promoting of policies to provide young people with jobs. While local and national objectives and audiences are still central to the work of youth activists, transnational activism has grown markedly in recent years, both in reality but also in the kinds of youth politics that attracts media attention.

A Transnational Perspective

Transnational activism (TA) refers to a range of internationally oriented and organized political engagements in which young people may be involved. While there is no detailed data, especially to compare over time, it is likely that TA, and especially young people's involvement in it, has grown dramatically in recent years.[9] There are several different shapes that transnational activism can take.

On one level, TA concerns issues or events either outside the native country of the activist (e.g., the human-rights situation in a specific country) or ones that are global in scope (e.g., the implementation or strengthening of internationally recognized child-labor laws). An example here might be an American student protesting against sweatshops in Asia or refusing to buy the products of companies using sweatshop labor.

A second kind of TA concerns engagement by local activists in addressing problems originating in or caused by (or perceived as originating in or caused by) forces outside his or her country. An example here might be a Latin American youth taking part in an organization promoting debt relief or fair trade or a Nigerian youth protesting against the environmental practices of a transnational oil company.

A third meaning of TA refers not to a specific issue but to the networks and alliances that form between activists based in different parts of the world. This may happen for certain issues, especially those seen as global in scope, but not necessarily for others. It implies a certain level of communication and even coordination across borders.[10]

Some TA issues are directly related to young people—that is, not only are young people active, but the goal of the activism is to change young people's lives. This could involve efforts to stop child soldiering or child labor (or, alternatively, to create employment for young people), extend political and other rights to young people, protect youth's legal status regarding juvenile justice and incarceration, reverse practices seen as discriminatory to young people based on gender or race, and provide wider access to education or health care.

Central to TA is the linkage of an issue to particular institutions seen as responsible for local or global problems or for not responding to solve them. Contrary to media images of what has been dubbed the "antiglobalization" movement that portray various groups and their alliances as incoherent at best or nihilist at worst, most have quite explicit targets or audiences whose practices they want to influence. These include transnational corporations; powerful countries and regions, especially the United States and members of the European Union; the International Financial Institutions (IMF, World Bank, WTO); the United Nations, NGOs and humanitarian agencies, and the media.

Underlying much of youth's involvement in TA is the question of the accountability of these institutions. Powerful institutions—many of which, in a local or national context, are considered as "external" or global—are seen as having great influence over people's lives and young people's futures. Yet, these institutions are not accountable to those whose lives they shape by the classic mechanisms of representative democratic government. Transnational corporations, formally accountable only to owners and shareholders, are seen as even more powerful in the current era in which the market and private sector is lionized and corporate identity is no longer bound up with nor their practices regulated by particular nation-states. As young people contemplate their futures (and those of others), it is not difficult to imagine concerns that such an accountability gap will grow. Indeed, most of these movements are not antiglobalization. Rather they appear to be directed toward an accountable globalization that sees the benefits (including economic ones) of an interconnected world but feels that they are unequally distributed and/or coming at too high a cost in environmental or other terms.

Clearly, not all youth are responding to this gap with activism or other kinds of civic engagement. Among those young people who are engaging, research on activist organizations, information technologies, and "political consumerism" has indicated a tendency to eschew formal political institutions, such as parties, for direct kinds of activism. In many cases a cynicism about formal institutions and politics shared by many youth is linked with an idealism related to directly addressing issues of social justice and accountability.

A Different Kind of Politics?

Beyond the issue of accountability there is one other key feature of transnational activism that prominently involves young people, although it is also apparent in other forms of youth activism. In some ways young people may be doing activism differently compared with previous generations—both older ones now and young ones in the past. The availability and the use of information technologies (IT) surely have something to do with this.[11]

Facilitated by IT, much youth activism, especially on transnational issues, operates more through networks and loose alliances than the more top-down structured political movements of the past. Many youth activists emphasize a participatory, consensus form of interaction and decision-making as a virtuous end in itself—although it is also presumed (correctly or not) that internal democracy makes the achievement of ultimate goals of social justice more likely and sustainable.

In some ways, there is nothing new about this for youth activism in the twenty-first century. A certain kind of idealism connecting with anti-authoritarianism has always been one variant of activism. Internal democracy is, in part, about setting a good example. As Gitlin wrote about 1960s student activists, "We were trying to build—or be—a better society."[12] IT does not create a focus on process and an organizational culture that attempts to marry decentralized structures with coordinated action, but it does enhance already existing tendencies. The Open Source movement, while addressing communication issues directly, may also serve as a model for sharing information and the tools to make it available. The creative and occasionally mischievous and illegal use of IT known as hacking may be refocused by "hacktivists" and others using IT in the service of political agendas.[13]

There is not enough hard information to declare that young people do activism and politics differently, but we can raise the right questions that would need to be answered in order to find out. We have noted the widespread sense around the world that young people are frustrated with and alienated from formal, hierarchical institutions. This includes not only those held as directly responsible for injustices but also those organizations involved in political mobilization—political parties and parts of civil society that are seen as overly bureaucratized and thus not themselves internally democratic. This is often seen connected to low voter turnouts among young people in many democracies. In such a context, do decentralized, looser, and heavily process-oriented forms of organization appeal to young people in their ambiguous status as not-yet-full citizens? Do they allow for types of participation, agency, and sense of self-efficacy not available through more formal institutions? Is "youthfulness" somehow connected to idealistic goals related to social justice, to sometimes uncompromising stances and penchant for risk-taking, to an insistence on room for shifting loyalties and easy entry into new groups and identities, and to a preference for informal structures?

Similarly, Juris has also pointed out that principles of self-management and autonomy are also core to transnational activism.[14] Are they also important for young people? With such a wide variety of causes and such a wide range of practices that can be considered "activist," young people may value being part of a broader movement without giving up their priorities or control of their agendas. At a time in their lives when they are establishing independence from parental authority, is this kind of autonomy and the peer-to-peer kinds of relationships that develop within it part of the establishment of a "political subculture" among youth?

In concluding, our understanding of contemporary youth activism—local and global, national and transnational—lags woefully behind the political practices of young people. While only a small percentage of young people are activists in the strong sense of the word, their numbers may be growing, the impact on their own futures as political actors is likely to be significant, and they may have effects on other young people—challenging them to engage in issues of accountability and democracy in new kinds of ways. Youth activists around the world are asserting their (global) citizenship in the present—*being* citizens while still in the process of *becoming* ones.

Notes

1. William Finnegan, *Cold New World: Growing Up in a Harder Country* (New York: The Modern Library, 1999).

2. See introductory essay by Flanagan and Bertelsen; also B. Bradford Brown, Reed W. Larson, and T. S. Saraswathi (eds.), *The World's Youth: Adolescence in Eight Regions of the Globe*

(Cambridge: Cambridge University Press, 2002); and Cynthia B. Lloyd (ed.), *Growing Up Global: The Changing Transitions to Adulthood in Developing Countries* (Washington, D.C.: National Academies Press, 2005).

3. For a good overview of some of these issues, see Lonnie R. Sherrod, Constance Flanagan, and James Youniss, "Dimensions of Citizenship and Opportunities for Youth Development: The What, Why, When, Where, and Who of Citizenship Development," *Applied Developmental Science*, 6 (4) (2002): 264–272.

4. For an exception, see Ann Mische, "Projecting Democracy: The Construction of Citizenship across Youth Networks in Brazil," in Charles Tilly (ed.), *Citizenship, Identity and Social History* (Cambridge: Cambridge University Press, 1996). On the involvement of South African youth in the anti-apartheid struggle, which fluctuates between violent and nonviolent strategies, see Monique Marks, *Young Warriors: Youth Politics, Identity and Violence in South Africa* (Johannesburg: Witwatersrand University Press, 2001). For an account of youth social protest in the former Yugoslavia, see Greenber's entry in this encyclopedia as well as Matthew Collin, *Guerilla Radio: Rock 'n' Roll Radio and Serbia's Underground Resistance* (New York: Thunder's Mouth Press, 2001).

5. For a rich analysis, see Elizabeth Fussell and Margaret E. Greene, "Demographic Trends Affecting Youth around the World," in B. Bradford Brown, Reed W. Larson, and T. S. Saraswathi (eds.), *The World's Youth: Adolescence in Eight Regions of the Globe* (Cambridge: Cambridge University Press, 2002).

6. Todd Gitlin, *Letters to a Young Activist* (New York: Basic Books, 2003), p. 4.

7. Carla Koffel, "Globalization of Youth Activism and Human Rights," in James Arvanitakis (ed.), Highly Affected, Rarely Considered: The International Youth Parliament Commission's Report on the Impacts of Globalization on Young People (Sydney: International Youth Parliament Oxfam Community Aid Abroad, 2003), p. 118. See http://www.iyp.oxfam.org/campaign/youth_commission_report.asp.

8. See Doug McAdam, *Freedom Summer* (New York and Oxford: Oxford University Press, 1988.)

9. The number of academic books, journalistic accounts, and participant treatises and memoirs regarding mobilization related to global issues has been voluminous over the past five years and shows no signs of stopping! One of the few accounts focusing on young people's involvement directly is Paul G. Aaron, *Youth Activism and Global Engagement*, OneWorld Special Report, Benton Foundation, http:/www.benton.org/OneWorldUS/Aron/aron1.html. Also see Mica Pollock, "Using and Disputing Privilege: U.S. Youth and Palestinians Wielding 'International Privilege' to End the Israel-Palestinian Conflict Nonviolently," in preparation. Youth activists in the United States have themselves recently published. Jee Kim et al., *Future 500: Youth Organizing and Activism in the United States* (New Orleans: Subway & Elevated Press, 2002).

10. See the influential book by Margaret E. Keck and Kathryn Sikkink, *Activists beyond Borders: Advocacy Networks in International Politics* (Ithaca: Cornell University Press, 1998).

11. See the contributions of Jeffrey Juris and others to this encyclopedia.

12. Gitlin, Letters to a Young Activist, p. 3.

13. See the entry on Political Consumerism by Michele Micheletti and Dietlind Stolle in this encyclopedia.

14. Jeffrey Juris, "Networked Social Movements: Global Movements for Global Justice," in Manuel Castells (ed.), *The Network Society: A Global Approach*, forthcoming.

References

Aaron, P. G. *Youth Activism and Global Engagement.* OneWorld Special Report, Benton Foundation. http:/www.benton.org/OneWorldUS/Aron/aron1.html.

Brown, B., Larson, R. W., and Saraswathi. T. S., eds. (2002). *The World's Youth: Adolescence in Eight Regions of the Globe.* Cambridge: Cambridge University Press.

Collin, M. (2001). *Guerilla Radio: Rock 'n' Roll Radio and Serbia's Underground Resistance*. New York: Thunder's Mouth Press.

Finnegan, W. (1999). *Cold New World: Growing Up in a Harder Country*. New York: The Modern Library.

Fussell, E., and Greene, M. E. (2002). "Demographic Trends Affecting Youth Around the World." In *The World's Youth: Adolescence in Eight Regions of the Globe*, edited by B. Brown, R. W. Larson, and T. S. Saraswathi. Cambridge: Cambridge University Press.

Gitlin, T. (2003). *Letters to a Young Activist*. New York: Basic Books.

Juris, J. "Networked Social Movements: Global Movements for Global Justice." In *The Network Society: A Global Approach*, edited by M. Castells (forthcoming).

Keck, M. E., and Sikkink, K. (1998). *Activists beyond Borders: Advocacy Networks in International Politics*. Ithaca: Cornell University Press.

Kim, J., de Dios, M., Caraballo, P., Arciniegas, M., and Taha, K. (2002). *Future 500: Youth Organizing and Activism in the United States*. New Orleans: Subway & Elevated Press.

Koffel, C. (2003). "Globalisation of Youth Activism and Human Rights." In *Highly Affected, Rarely Considered: The International Youth Parliament Commission's Report on the Impacts of Globalization on Young People*, edited by J. Arvanitakis. Sydney: International Youth Parliament Oxfam Community Aid Abroad. See http://www.iyp.oxfam.org/campaign/youth_commission_report.asp.

Lloyd, C. B., ed. (2005). *Growing Up Global: The Changing Transitions to Adulthood in Developing Countries*. Washington, D.C.: National Academies Press.

Marks, M. (2001). *Young Warriors: Youth Politics, Identity and Violence in South Africa*. Johannesburg: Witwatersrand University Press.

McAdam, D. (1988). *Freedom Summer*. New York: Oxford University Press.

Mische, A. (1996). "Projecting Democracy: The Construction of Citizenship across Youth Networks in Brazil." In *Citizenship, Identity, and Social History*, edited by C. Tilly. Cambridge: Cambridge University Press.

Pollock, M. (2005) Struggling for solidarity: The international solidarity movement as a snapshot of transnational youth activism. Youth activism: A web forum of the social science research council. http://ya.ssrc.org/transnational/Pollock/

Sherrod, L. R., Flanagan, C., and Youniss, J. (2002). "Dimensions of Citizenship and Opportunities for Youth Development: The What, Why, When, Where, and Who of Citizenship Development." *Applied Developmental Science*, 6 (4): 264–272.

Youth Activism

A

Acculturation. An individual who was raised in one culture and comes to live in another has to adjust to the new environment. This adjustment process is called acculturation: "Acculturation comprehends those phenomena which result when groups of individuals having different cultures come into continuous firsthand contact with subsequent changes in the original culture patterns of either or both groups." Traditionally such processes can be observed if individuals move from one culture to another (immigrants, guest-workers, exchange students, etc.). It is, however, also possible that a new culture actually enters an existing (cultural) system, thereby initiating change that can also be interpreted as acculturation. An example of this situation would be German unification, wherein the former communist system collapsed and was replaced by a Western system.

The term acculturation can be used in various ways—the easiest differentiation being that between process and outcome. Acculturative processes, that is, changes caused by ongoing cultural contact, can be seen in three different ways.

First, acculturative changes happen simply because of learning. The new environment offers another language, other behavioral norms and scripts. Immigrants need to acquire skills to continue their lives in the new context (shopping, public transportation, etc., may be organized in a different way). Acquiring skills through encounters with the new environment typically follows a learning curve, with a steep slope shortly after immigration, and relates to adjustment over time.

Second, acculturative changes are also the result of problems and difficulties an individual immigrant has to overcome, that is, immigration-related stressors, such as major life events (family disruptions through immigration) or everyday hassles (such as discrimination in school). These experiences can be very stressful in the beginning, but with time immigrants usually find ways to overcome such difficulties. Acquiring new skills according to this model relates to coping processes whereby immigrants gradually adapt to the requirements and challenges of the host society.

A third perspective argues that acculturative changes can be seen as group processes. Individuals define themselves as members of various social groups. If different social groups come together (immigrants versus nonimmigrants, majority youth versus minority youth, etc.), or if group affiliations change through the new societal status after immigration, behaviors, values, and opinions, as well as external appearance, may change according to the group identity. This enables ingroup association and outgroup differentiation.

The outcomes of acculturation may also be grouped in various ways, and a common distinction is made between psychological and sociocultural adaptation. Successful learning processes, which help to gain a better understanding of the new culture, predict fewer sociocultural problems. For example, navigating through the new society becomes easier, friendships can develop since the behavioral code is understood, and skills for shopping and daily life are gained. Psychological adaptation is related to issues like depressive symptoms, consumption of drugs and alcohol, or delinquency. Such outcomes are understood as markers of a failed coping process in the new environment. Adolescent immigrants may be especially overwhelmed by the normative challenges of youth that fall together with additional acculturation-related stressors.

Another way to describe acculturative outcomes relates to the degree of closeness immigrants maintain to their culture of origin and to the degree of adaptation toward the host culture. Two questions can be asked to measure the acculturative orientation of individuals: "Is it considered to be of value to maintain one's original culture and identity?" and "Is it considered to be of value to cultivate relationships with the larger society?" According to the answers (yes/no) to these two questions, four different acculturation orientations, that is, different patterns in the adjustment process are defined. If maintaining the original cultural background is deemed to be important, whereas contact to the host society is not, a separation strategy is employed. Where the opposite is true—strong association with the host society and no maintenance of one's own cultural traditions—an assimilative strategy is said to be used. The third strategy, integration, is defined by both positive relationships to the host society and maintenance of one's own cultural traditions. This acculturation orientation was found to be the preferred strategy of many immigrants. The fourth combination (no relations to hosts and no maintenance of elements of the own culture) can be interpreted in different ways. Either this shows a marginalization of individuals (loss of identity, loss of guiding cultural values) or it represents a high degree of individualization that includes loose ties to any social group. It may also show a transformation of the feelings of belonging and identity to a third social group, as in religious affiliation.

The question of which acculturative strategy is best for a successful adaptation to the new society has received much attention. Research from various countries shows that integration (in some studies also assimilation) predicts better outcomes in terms of adjustment. Immigrants with these acculturative strategies have been found to be healthier and happier than others. It has to be noted, however, that the success of a certain strategy also depends on attitudes of the host society. Attitudes shared in the host society about immigration in general and toward a specific group of immigrants in particular direct the way the majority and minority interact. An integration strategy by immigrants will be less useful when the host society refuses interaction and mutual relations and only accepts separation. If there is no match between the two perspectives, conflicts between immigrants and the host culture are likely to emerge.

Obviously, some immigrants blend into the host society without many difficulties, whereas others develop maladaptive behaviors and symptoms. Acculturative strategies and their interplay with attitudes of the host society foster or hinder a successful adaptation to the challenges of the new environment. Several moderators in the acculturation process that result in individual differences in the degree and the course of problems after immigration have been found. First, factors related to characteristics of the old or new context are considered responsible for this variation. Whether or not the country of origin was left willingly, having friends and family in the host (i.e., in the new) country, knowledge about and experiences with elements of the host culture or foreign cultures in general, the degree of multicultural experiences of the local population, or differences between culture of origin compared with the host culture are examples of contextual influences on the status of mental health after immigration. Second, factors related to the individual immigrant are known to be relevant to the severity of mental-health problems after immigration. For instance, optimism, flexibility, self-efficacy, and language competence are known to foster adaptation, whereas social anxiety increases difficulties in the acculturative process.

While the bulk of research on immigration and acculturation targets adults, the well-being of adolescent immigrants is very likely to be subject to similar influences, although there is only limited empirical evidence for this assumption. In the following, we want to summarize some additional factors that are known to direct and influence the quality of acculturative outcomes, especially among adolescent immigrants to another country.

During adolescence, identity development is a major developmental task that involves the acceptance of oneself as a person and provides an answer to the question of "who am I." The ethnic background of a person is known to be an important part of his or her identity. The process of identity development of minority adolescents involves identification with their social group (e.g., "I am Turkish"), a subjective feeling of belonging to this group, active identity exploration, and finally, the achievement of an ethnic identity. If an ethnic identity is successfully achieved, adolescents cope with experiences of discrimination more easily and report higher self-esteem, more optimism, and fewer depressive symptoms.

Language competencies represent another prominent source of better adjustment. Such skills relate to a better understanding of the host culture, fewer communication problems, less anxiety and loneliness, and less acculturation-related stress. Some research, however, shows a downside of language proficiency, whereby better language skills were found to be related to intensified substance use, such as cigarette smoking, and to anxiety problems. There are two reasons for this somewhat surprising effect: first, increasing abilities of the immigrants are not always mirrored by an increase of chances and options in the host society. Many immigrants remain in less fortunate socioeconomic positions with limited opportunities for social participation (e.g., getting a job,

taking part in social life, etc.). Such a mismatch between expectations and opportunities is likely to result in less favorable acculturative outcomes. Second, better language proficiency provides a greater understanding of subtle discrimination that may be reflected by poorer adjustment. Despite this downside, knowledge of the language can be assumed to be one of the most important assets that give adolescents the chance for social participation in the host society.

The factors mentioned so far (acculturation orientation, identity, and language) represent factors within a person, but the context also matters. For adolescents, the family, peers, and the school provide important sources of support. A warm, cohesive family climate helps adolescents to overcome the problems of acculturation more easily. Peer contacts (e.g., classmates and close friends) are equally important. Strong ties between host and immigrant peers can foster the adjustment process. For example, native peers can teach appropriate behavior and language use. However, the timing of such encounters is important. If contact is established too early after immigration, it can result in feelings of incompetence, the development of communication problems between members of both groups, and higher depressive symptoms. In the third context, at school, adolescents spend a substantial amount of their time, and immigrants are exposed to a large variety of majority and minority peers. On the one hand, adolescent immigrants experience discrimination more often at school than in any other context, which in turn relates to feelings of loneliness, higher levels of substance use, low self-esteem, acculturative stress, and problem behavior. On the other hand, the school context also provides many opportunities for learning, contacts to other (same or other group) adolescents, and social support. Friendships between members of social groups are more common if schools and classes provide opportunities for exchange.

Even though there has been a lot of research on single risk factors that may contribute to negative outcomes of acculturation, the interplay of different risk factors is not yet really clear. Moreover, the development of maladaptive behaviors in immigrant adolescents may also be fueled by more or less the same set of risks that are known to relate to problem behavior among nonimmigrant youth. It seems that a single risk (e.g., discrimination at school) is not sufficient to disrupt a successful acculturative process. New research shows that it takes a number of problems to initiate maladaptive behaviors, many of which are similar to factors known for nonimmigrant populations. The accumulation of unfavorable conditions and insufficient personal resources seems to erode adolescents' positive social bonds to normative values, leading into depression. Both of these factors (depression and eroded social bonds) are also related to elevated levels of delinquency in adolescence.

Even though some adolescent immigrants may be troubled by a number of risks and problems, this does not mean that a significant portion among them shows problematic behaviors of any kind. Most adolescent immigrants and minority adolescents do well, and the well-adjusted group exceeds the number of problematic adolescents in nearly all studies. Some groups even do better than the average. Asian Americans, for instance, often outperform other groups at school and have higher levels of educational attainment. The complex interplay of factors that direct positive outcomes after immigration is not yet fully understood and more research is needed to tailor intervention programs for immigrant youth at risk.

See also Civic Identity; Ethnic Identity; Identity and Activism; Identity and Organizing in Older Youth; Immigrant Youth in Europe—Turks in Germany; Immigrant Youth in the United States; National Identity and Youth; Racial and Ethnic Inequality; Racial Socialization; Transnational Identity; Xenophobia.

Recommended Reading

Berry, J. W. (1997). "Immigration, Acculturation, and Adaptation." *Applied Psychology: An International Review*, 46 (1): 5–34.
Chun, K. M., Organista, P. B., and Marin, G., eds. (2003). *Acculturation: Advances in Theory, Measurement, and Applied Research*. Washington, D.C.: APA.
McLoyd, V. C., and Steinberg, L., eds. (1998). *Studying Minority Adolescents*. London: Lawrence Earlbaum.
Schmitt-Rodermund, E., and Silbereisen, R. K. (1999). "Determinants of Differential Acculturation of Developmental Timetables among Adolescent Immigrants to Germany." *International Journal of Psychology*, 34: 219–233.
Ward, C., Bochner, S., and Furnham, A. (2001). *The Psychology of Culture Shock*. London: Routledge.

Peter F. Titzmann and Eva Schmitt-Rodermund

Activism. *See* Identity and Activism.

Adult Partners in Youth Activism. Adults can and should serve as partners with youth in activist efforts. Effective and sustained grassroots activism requires diversity of all types. Activism at its best brings together diverse groups for a common cause. It is critical, therefore, to create new roles for adults, rather than excluding them from youth activism. Partnership is one important role.

The health of any society depends upon the active participation of its citizens. Across the globe, citizens are embracing participatory democracy and progressive populism. These movements, which constitute "grassroots activism," call for citizens to push their leaders to enact policies that ensure the well-being of all citizens. Youth are emerging as integral players in grassroots activism. They are organizing, leading community change, solving community problems, and contributing to public policy. These efforts are based on the belief that youth can contribute in the here and now, rather than at some vague future time; can engage in real work, rather than simulations; and need to develop civic skills and capacities, rather than only classroom knowledge.

The engagement of youth is usually given a title: "youth in governance," "youth civic activism," "youth philanthropy," "youth as researchers," or "youth in public decision-making." These banners can be misleading. Rarely are youth going it alone. Gerison Lansdown (2001) provides a wealth of international examples of youth activism that makes this obvious, yet often forgotten, point. Youth activism demands, of course, that youth take a powerful leadership role in change efforts. In the most successful self-advocacy efforts by youth, Lansdown concludes that adults are serving as partners to young people in the roles of adviser, guide, administrator, and fund-raiser.

There are many reasons why community adults are being brought on as partners in youth activism. One reason is that adults have access to resources that many youth do not, such as networks of people, funds, or institutional power. A second reason is that adults may care about the same issues as youth. There are many adults who are committed to confronting racism and homophobia, cleaning up toxic chemicals from poor urban and rural localities, advocating for quality public education for all students, or advocating for youth rights and voice. Third, youth are often legally prohibited from forums of governance, such as school boards or boards of directors. Adult allies are necessary to change those laws. Finally, many youth are too busy to be full-time activists—they need to finish high school, work at jobs, and engage in the broad range of recreational and learning activities with friends and family that allow them to fully experience their adolescence.

A bottom-line lesson is this: effective and sustained grassroots activism requires diversity of all types. Activism, at its best, brings together diverse groups for a common cause. It is critical, therefore, to create new roles for adults, rather than excluding them from youth activism.

This lesson has a long legacy. Most modern grassroots activists trace their principles and approaches to the ideas of Paulo Freire. Freire (1983) taught that for people to change the oppressive conditions of their lives, they need critical literacy. In other words, they need to be able to accurately "read" the conditions of their lives, placing the events and difficulties of their lives into a broader context of community policies and social forces. Once a critical appraisal is done, action can then be taken. After a certain amount of action, reflection is undertaken to consider how the action has fit into the definition of the problem so far. Freire called this cycle of activism "praxis."

Critical to the praxis cycle are the processes of individual and group learning. When youth and adults are partners and allies in activism and engage in praxis they become co-learners, learning together and from one another. Such learning helps individual citizens gain control over their lives by raising their awareness and then imagining new alternatives and directions. This type of learning also helps groups and communities engage in activism because it permits people to collectively identify the underlying causes of community issues, not just the symptoms. This enables youth and adults to bring about long-lasting community change.

Grassroots activism involving youth is also based on theories of John Dewey. Dewey (1944) urged that public education be devoted to group learning and community building as much as to individual development. Dewey encouraged young people to be aware of their roles as citizens, including responsibility to raise their voices publicly, to make informed choices based on the common good, and to acquire the skills to make change happen. Like anything else, activism is a learned ability. For these reasons, Dewey urged schools to take civic education into the community, allowing students to learn from action-oriented experiences with peers and adults, and to start this learning process as early as possible.

When youth and adults are partners and co-learners in youth activism, there is high potential for success. However, because youth-adult partnership is a relatively new way of working, many cultures and countries, especially the United States, do not have well-established traditions for it. Thus, there are challenges to negotiate.

The key question is this: Who gets to define the problem that will be addressed by youth activism? The challenge to grassroots activism is to ensure that the voices of youth and adults are equally valued and heard. This means that activists working through youth-adult partnerships need to ensure that the adults relinquish sole definition of issues and problems and include the voices of diverse youth. The result is a richer and broader understanding that promotes community change.

For example, we have worked with one rural community in which many youth lobbied for a skateboard park. The youth were repeatedly dismissed by many adult residents as a "weird faction." The adults wanted to use the property for a family park. This prompted the young people to do a formal needs assessment. They conducted a survey of youth and adults about attitudes toward skateboarders and rollerbladers and gathered opinions about how the property should be used. The young people also led a community mapping exercise about public space. Their research found that there were many public spaces available for family recreation but none devoted exclusively to teens. Also found was a widespread desire of many youth for a skateboard park. After learning the findings, several adults agreed to partner with the youth in lobbying and together they succeeded in getting the property deeded for the skateboard park.

But that is not all. The young people observed an even more significant community problem during the research and mapping processes. The problem was that there were few youth involved in community-decision roles. The youth concluded that this was their priority issue, and over the past four years they have enlisted an increasing number of adults to help them address it. Now, there are youth involved in many roles of public decision-making,

and a community foundation has been established to promote youth service and youth philanthropy.

A bottom-line lesson is this: youth can define problems and teach adults about community issues in ways that propel successful community action. Also, the early and sustained involvement of youth and adults as partners in defining problems leads to positive "ripple effects." Over time youth and adults discover other, often more important, problems that they are able to address as allies.

The key question is this: what is the bottom-line motivation for engaging youth in grassroots activism? Effective grassroots activism depends on people agreeing about the purpose of change. During a decade of research, however, we have consistently found that community groups and local organizations struggle to reach consensus as to the bottom-line purpose for engaging youth in grassroots activism. For some, the purpose is social justice for youth, the rationale being that youth are entitled to be heard in all matters affecting them and to have their views taken seriously. Others are motivated to include youth because they believe that the skills and competencies of youth will lead to better community outcomes than if adults took the lead by themselves. Interestingly, however, most adults are motivated to include youth because they believe that the purpose of youth activism is to promote positive youth development. These adults believe that involving youth will help young people develop identity, social responsibility, leadership, and skills like public speaking.

The conflict is that while adults are motivated to support youth activism as a strategy for promoting youth development, almost all youth choose to engage in civic activism because of issues of social justice or community building. That is, adults are looking to help youth. In contrast, youth engage to promote a collective cause or to remedy a problematic community situation. Until these discrepancies in purpose are sorted out, it is difficult to embark on successful grassroots advocacy with youth and adults working in partnership.

An interesting case example brings home the point. The example tells the story of the establishment in the 1980s of a youth-run newspaper in New York City, one of the first of its kind. When the project was framed as exclusively "youth-run," adults were reluctant to interfere or give their advice, thinking that the major purpose was to have youth learn experientially how to put out a paper and run the operation. The paper had mixed success. Sometimes it operated well; at other times, it sputtered unsuccessfully. For this reason, the motivation and purpose was redefined as "to publish a newspaper that served the needs of New York teens." Toward that end, the most experienced youth and adults jointly made the key management decisions, while concurrently teaching the ropes and coaching the next generation of media activists so that they could hone their own leadership and publishing skills. Not only did the overall quality and sustainability of the paper increase, but youth development was also more effectively promoted.

A bottom-line lesson is this: when youth and adults clearly state their purposes and understand their own and one another's interests and motivations, there is a better chance for success. Once the purposes are out in the open, youth and adults can also learn that there may be benefits to having more than one purpose and to see how they can fit together into the big picture of grassroots advocacy.

The key question is this: who gets to make and carry out the key decisions? As discussed above, it is necessary for all to participate and consensus be reached regarding the problem definition and purposes of community activism. Equally important is that all find their own ways to contribute to implementation, be it as group facilitators and trainers, researchers, documenters and public communicators, organizers and planners, team members, and so on.

Youth and adults are wise not to overgeneralize about who may be right for which roles. It is easy to assume that adults know how to do things because of their ages and so they should be the teachers and youth the learners. This is not always true, of course. Community activism is, when all is said and done, about mobilizing groups of people to action. This is a strength that is not dependent on age. We, as have many others, observed many youth who are highly effective trainers, who are able to creatively engage and motivate others. We have seen these youth teach skills and processes to their adult partners. And who else but youth are better equipped to motivate their peers to action? Youth bring networks to community activism that could never be efficiently accessed by adults.

As Dewey reminds us, experience is the best teacher. Community activism requires both youth and adults who have experience and those who don't. The task is to involve the experienced activists, regardless of their age, as guides who are charged with bringing along those with less experience. Also, following Freire, it becomes clear that "inexperienced" persons have much to bring to the table. Activism is a collective construct. When people with different interests and levels of expertise come together as co-learners, teaching one another, success is promoted.

A bottom-line lesson is this: involving youth and adults as co-learners throughout community action ensures that many diverse persons will be involved in making and carrying out decisions. Additionally, both youth and adults should have the opportunity to choose their roles based on their interests and talents, thus ensuring that all persons have the motivation and skill to effectively participate.

A final lesson is this: negotiating power is always central to negotiating roles. Adults almost always come to a group with more institutional power than youth. The challenge is to find ways to share this power. As adults concede the power to control the process and outcomes in favor of a collaborative relationship with youth, new roles for youth and adults are created.

Youth and adults partnering in community activism is an exciting new avenue for practice and affords several interesting questions for future research. For example, since co-learning is a basic function of activism, what are the outcomes of this strategy? Do youth and adults learn the same sorts of things or in the same ways? How is activism advanced when organizations take the time to engage in co-learning? A second set of questions concerns roles and the nature of partnership between youth and adults. How can equitable youth-adult partnerships be best built for social justice and community change? A third set of questions concerns definition of issues and purpose and the connection of local action with larger movements. Local issues can often be traced to national, even global, trends and policies. How do the issues local youth and adults identify relate to larger trends and forces? A risk of activism work involving youth is that it be confined solely to the realm of "youth development." How can local partnerships of youth and adults connect to regional, national, and international coalitions and public-interest groups?

Across the globe grassroots activism is transcending boundaries between youth and adults. "Everyday people"—youth and adults—working together on issues that matter to the common good is the common theme. The movement encourages citizens to trust their own judgment, develop their own skills, and be motivated to share their experience and learn from others so that they can tackle complex issues. It is important to understand how youth and adults can accomplish these aims together and can be allies and partners in the work. Research, practice, and policy should all explore how youth and adults can best negotiate defining issues and problems, understanding of the larger purposes of their common work, and finding roles and power to achieve success.

See also Adult Roles in Youth Activism; Adultism; Emerging Adulthood; Gay-Straight Alliances in Schools; Generational Conflict; Generational Replacement; Grassroots Youth Movements; Intergenerational Programs and Practices; Moral Exemplars; Parental Influences on Youth Activism.

Recommended Reading

Camino, Linda (2000). "Putting Youth-Adult Partnerships to Work for Community Change: Lessons from Volunteers across the Country." *CYD (Community Youth Development) Journal*, 1 (4): 26–31. See http://www.cydjournal.org.
Camino, Linda (2000). "Youth-Adult Partnerships: Entering New Territory in Community Work and Research." *Applied Developmental Science*, 4: 11–20.
Dewey, John (1944). *Democracy and Education.* New York: Macmillan.
Freire, Paolo (1983). *Pedagogy of the Oppressed.* New York: Continuum.
Hefner, Keith (1988). "The Evolution of Youth Empowerment at a Youth Newspaper." *Social Policy* (Summer): 21–24.
Landsdown, Gerison (2001). *Promoting Children's Participation in Democratic Decision-Making.* Florence, Italy: UNICEF Innocenti Research Center. See http://www.unicef.icdc.org.
Skelton, Nan, Boyte, Harry C., and Leonard, Lynn Sordelet (2002). *Youth Civic Engagement: Reflections on an Emerging Public Idea.* Minneapolis, MN: Center for Democracy and Citizenship. See http://www.publicwork.org.
Zeldin, Shepherd, Camino, Linda, and Calvert, Mathew (2003). *Toward an Understanding of Youth in Community Governance: Policy Priorities and Research Directions.* Social Policy Report, Vol. 17 (3). Ann Arbor, MI: Society for Research in Child Development. See http://www.srcd.org.spr.html.
Zeldin, Shepherd, McDaniel, Annette, Topizes, Dimitri, and Calvert, Mathew (2000). *Youth in Decision-Making: A Study of the Impacts on Adults and Organizations.* Chevy Chase, MD: National 4-H Council. See http://www.atthetable.org.

Linda Camino and Shepherd Zeldin

Adult Roles in Youth Activism. Just outside of Boston, an experienced farmer imagined an intergenerational gathering of people working together to combat hunger and homelessness and developed the Food Project. He enlists adults and young people who use teamwork, creativity, and like-minded interests to create a sustainable metropolitan food system. In the process the group bridges communities traditionally divided by race, class, and physical distance and provides area food banks and homeless shelters with thousands of pounds of organic produce and dozens of volunteers each year.

In an effort to clean up their South Bronx neighborhood, the young people of Youth Force mobilized hundreds of local youth and adult residents to form tenant associations and demand needed repairs, created the Community Justice Center, and challenged the *New York Times* head-on for misrepresenting young people in the media. Through adult partnerships, the Community Justice Center offers young people legal aid and referrals to education, jobs, counseling, and other services, as well as individualized "court support" for young people going through the judicial system.

In Denver young people fought back against the school district's move to divide their high school into three academies, which resulted in both racial segregation and limited choices for students. Their organization, Students 4 Justice, holds the school accountable for its actions and partners with teachers and other administrators to create more equal learning opportunities and a better school climate. It also enjoys the support of adult partners who offer these young people a space to put their ideas in action and the opportunity to lead in the context of an adult-led organization, the Colorado Progressive Coalition.

In East Nashville a youth mobilization organization raised enough money to offer young people a unique opportunity to work directly in community organizations, evaluate their services, and report their findings back to the agencies that employ them during a summer-internship program. Thanks to dedicated staff and a receptive group of community partners, all vowing to support youth action, the "youth mobilizers" of the Youth Opportunities Network (an affiliate of the Community Impact! Net-

work) are helping these adult-led organizations and businesses realize their potential for building stronger ties to their community neighbors.

In Philadelphia a disenfranchised group of students came together to identify and address inequities in public education and soon began to make significant changes in their schools, such as getting up-to-date textbooks in classrooms, improving teacher quality, and winning state policy battles. With the support of adult allies such as teachers and district representatives, the Philadelphia Student Union is now a citywide, youth-led organization that serves as a powerful force in the community and a model for others around the nation.

These examples reveal a growing trend that has taken root in rural, urban, and suburban communities across the country. In each of these instances, young people play a role in changing communities for the better by addressing issues they care about in their schools, neighborhoods, and workplaces. All of these young people envision a community that has something to offer all of the people who live there, and they are using their talents to open up more possibilities for the next generation of youth.

Just as importantly, each of these examples also reveals adults playing significant roles in supporting and contributing to young people's work. While the roles they play are substantially different—ranging from leaders to allies, to cheerleaders and followers—their participation has significantly bolstered youth efforts.

But how do young people even begin to become such activists, and what happens when some youth are given the space to share their diverse opinions in a public forum and others are not? To answer these questions, we will explore adult roles in youth activism. While it's true that young people have a great capacity for creating change, when adults take responsibility for guiding that process, the possibilities are endless. Adults who cast aside preconceived ideas and come to the table with a real sense of partnership offer the needed

Youth Contributing to Communities

Young people and adults working together to create the necessary conditions for the successful development of themselves, their peers, families and communities

Communities Supporting Youth

Evidence that adult support matters

resources and encouragement that can allow a young person to make lasting social and community changes benefiting the entire community (as illustrated in figure titled "Evidence that support matters").

The stories described earlier are not simply exceptions to the rule. There are hundreds of examples that suggest young people are truly making important connections in their communities. Adult support helps fuel such efforts. While students sometimes take action alone, they seldom do so without the support of peers and adults. According to research by The Gallup Organization, young people are more than twice as likely to be involved in service if they are asked to do so. In the same survey young people indicated that support from significant adults was an important factor in helping them continue to serve (Hodgkinson, Weitzman, Crutchfield, et al. 1996). In numerous studies young people indicate that they are most likely to engage in service with others they respect and in communities of which they feel part (Peter D. Hart Research Associates 1998; Princeton Survey Research Associates 1998).

Outside support is as important for adolescents as for younger students, despite the common perception that teenagers are eager to do things on their own without the interference of parents, teachers, or other adults. Each of the surveys cited above focuses on young people in their teens—precisely those young people who are traditionally considered most likely to withdraw from adult support and guidance. Just as the survey data reveals the desire youth activists have for adult support, young people express the need directly as well. For example, in spite of the achievements of Students 4 Justice as a political force in their community, one member said, "Our teachers need to support us more. Right now they say, 'Why are you in Students 4 Justice? You're not going to get anywhere with it.' We need encouragement in the school, somebody to tell us, 'You can do it.'"

From a different perspective, a young person with the Food Project expressed her satisfaction with working side-by-side with adult volunteers and staff as a meaningful contributor to the organization's efforts. "I feel amazed, mature, and responsible," she said. When youth are supported by adults, they are more likely to report positive experiences. Research also suggests that young people with positive adult role models are significantly less likely to engage in such high-risk behaviors as violence, illicit drug use, and premarital sex (Bier et al. 1996).

Clearly, young people want the opportunity to partner with adults who are willing to work with them to create a better community. Adults themselves recognize the need for their participation and support in efforts that engage youth as activists. Many understand that the simple act of supporting such efforts can serve the community as a whole. This was the case in Lubec, Maine, where high-school students created a state-of-the-art aquaculture center to raise trout and salmon, reviving their community's declining fishing industry. While young people led this effort, adults quickly recognized how important their encouragement was for these youth activists and how much the struggling community needed their continued efforts. "Economic development starts by planting seeds—you never know what's going to come from it. Every student involved in the project is a seed we've planted," says Dianne Tilton, adult supporter. "All of these students may move away and never look back, but it seems more likely that they'll stay committed and stick around. You just don't know, but I think we need to take the chance."

The evidence suggests that adults can play important roles in supporting youth activism. The important question, then, is *how* adults do this—what roles they play, what actions they take, and what dispositions they take on when they support youth action. In some circumstances adult involvement in youth activism can in fact interfere with the process or lessen the experience. Much of this comes from the negative attitudes adults have toward young people.

In his publication *Adults as Allies*, University of Michigan researcher Barry Checkoway calls such behavior "adultism" and suggests that adults reflect on their attitudes, body language, and use of language that would seem disrespectful or condescending to a young person. For example, "You're so smart for your age!" and "When are you going to grow up?" and "What do you know? You haven't experienced anything!" are all phrases that suggest young people don't have the ability to be change agents.

Checkoway says, "The liberation of young people will require the active participation of adults. A good starting place is to consider and understand how we—today's adults—were mistreated and devalued when we were children and youth."

Consider, for example, the Hampton Coalition for Youth in Hampton, Virginia. This citywide initiative places more than 600 young people a year in leadership, policy, and decision-making positions. Now known across the country for its dynamic youth-adult partnerships, Hampton has a reputation as a classic example of youth activism. But the people behind this effort explain that these changes didn't happen overnight. One youth activist, Harmonie Mason, described her experience getting adults to look past her age and to take youth opinions seriously: "We don't want you to give us things because we're cute. We want you to

give us things because you understand the importance of what we're asking." To help build a sense of professionalism, young people attend meetings well organized and equipped with slick electronic presentations (see, e.g., Search Institute: 2001).

What, then, does adult support for youth activism look like in its most positive forms? Checkoway (1997) sets a productive course for answering this question. He suggests, "Adults play the key role in identifying, nurturing, educating, encouraging, counseling, advising, and inspiring young leaders." Both youth activism and adult roles in supporting it are remarkably diverse, yet a look at those efforts that successfully promote youth action reveals a common core of goals. To become activists, young people need to be aware of the issues around which they will act and be motivated to take action. They need to have the skills and capacities to act effectively, and they need concrete opportunities for action. Adults support this by doing the following:

1. *Fostering motivation.* Youth-centered efforts build young people's awareness of issues and root causes, deepening a sense of commitment and responsibility.
2. *Building capacity.* Youth-centered efforts help young people develop their leadership skills and deepen their understanding of community systems and strategies.
3. *Creating opportunities.* Youth-centered efforts provide young people with a range of opportunities to act on passions and use skills in ways that generate demonstrable outcomes or identify the skills necessary to evoke real change efforts.

The core role of adult allies is to help young people visualize their roles as activists in their communities and beyond. Adults can spark an interest in youth activism by showing young people local and national issues. Jessica, a student at Smith College, shares such an example. "I acquired a political consciousness as I grew up because my parents instilled it in me.... At the age of sixteen, meeting someone who had suffered brutal human-rights violations inspired me to action" (Muchhala 2000).

Adult supporters can influence the way the community looks at young people and the types of services and support youth need to develop. Keeping these ideas in mind will help adult supporters find allies in parents, teachers, business owners, community activists, and, most importantly, young people. Consider these following four assumptions, based on the evaluation of adult allies who effectively support youth activism in communities:

1. Adult allies have higher expectations for young people.

When the subject of children and teenagers comes up during conversation among adults, what words are used? Are they thought of as lazy, spoiled, disrespectful, or irresponsible? If you've heard adults sharing a similar opinion of young people, you're not alone. According to a study conducted by Public Agenda and the Ad Council, 57 percent of adults surveyed believed that today's children and teens will make America a worse place or will make little difference at all in the future. In a different study, 66 percent of adults believed that the percentage of teens who committed violent crimes had increased over recent years, when in reality it had declined. How does this viewpoint impact the way young people are treated in their roles as activists?

Many adults do envision a bright future for the young people in their families and neighborhoods. They expect these young people to pursue higher education and to eventually set a reasonable career path. It is doubtful, however, whether most adults have an image of young people as contributors and change makers. Nor do they realize the impact youth can have on people, places, institutions, policies, and ideas. The challenge for adult supporters is to create the public belief that young people are able and willing—and should be expected—to find ways to make sustained differences in the communities, organizations, and groups with which they are involved, while acting on issues they care about. Most importantly, this expectation must be reinforced in practice.

For example, one of the functions of the Food Project is to offer a weekly farmers' market, allowing residents to purchase much-needed produce at reasonable prices. This market fills a void in the community, places a level of responsibility on the young people who organize it, and has become a service on which residents depend. Greg Watson, an adult supporter affiliated with the Food Project and director of the Massachusetts Renewable Energy Trusts, describes the farmers' market as "a much-anticipated community ritual."

Expectations contribute to youth activism by creating the assumption among parents, peers, teachers, faith leaders, public officials, and business owners that all young people can and should make a difference. Without clear, broadly held expectations, opportunities for young people might never be created or realized.

2. Adult allies create an environment for action.

Based on what has been learned from researchers and practitioners in communities, we know a lot about environments that support learning and healthy development. These environments—which include such elements as safe, stable places; caring relationships; and opportunities for voice, choice, and contribution—are all relevant for youth activism contexts. The following illustrate such characteristics:

Safe, stable places. Young people need access to stable places where they feel safe and a sense of ownership. In addition to ensuring the physical safety of youth activists, adults can insist that young people have a predictable structure and a number of caring adults on whom they can rely.

Caring relationships. Positive, supportive relationships—among peers and particularly between youth and adults—are fundamental components of youth activism efforts. Adult allies provide guidance, show a genuine interest, and are supportive, attentive, and nonjudgmental.

Opportunities for voice, choice, and contribution. Youth activists need a range of formal and informal opportunities for age-appropriate participation and involvement in their families, schools, programs, and communities. Adult allies create a feeling of belonging and membership, increasing a young person's chances of achievement. At a minimum, adult supporters and leaders of community organizations can operate on the principle that young people should be given more choice and more roles in organizational activities in which they are involved, shifting from just receiving knowledge to creating knowledge and from being service recipients to being program planners and deliverers.

For example, adult allies in teachers' unions and the school districts supporting the Philadelphia Student Union help youth activists—young people who already have a visible and significant role in the community—have more bargaining power and a wider outreach. Former Philadelphia school superintendent David Hornbeck offered his sentiments for why such partnerships are important: "When we are successful [in changing schools] it will be, I am increasingly convinced, because 'the children shall lead us.' It will be their energy, their purity of purpose, their sense of justice and injustice that will sustain the effort in its most difficult moments."

3. Adult allies help youth link experiences into visible action pathways.

"Action pathway" is a term that describes the visions, directions, hopes, and dreams

young people can have for themselves and for their future. Once they begin to see themselves as activists, youth need ongoing options for meaningful participation in organizations and activities that they believe will make a difference to someone. Just as importantly, young people need to envision how they might build the skills that allow them to act on their interests and beliefs. Efforts to develop strong, young activists need to be intentional, and adult supporters can provide a sense of direction and a long-term vision.

Adult allies create action pathways for young people by ensuring that youth efforts are linked to real issues, that awareness building and analysis are a part of their experiences, and that youth have ongoing opportunities to put their skills and passions to work. Given some reason to believe they can and should make a difference, young people will often take the lead in creating their own pathways or in calling upon adults to help them get what they need.

It is also important to remember that young people can create action pathways and benefit greatly from involvement with organizations and programs that are not youth-centered, such as faith organizations, museums and theaters, businesses, and governmental planning bodies. Adult allies support youth in these environments by encouraging critical thinking, identifying resources that assist their work, and being available for help. Such experiences can be positive for the organization and the young person.

For example, when a candidate for city council in East Nashville wanted to connect with a young person who could convey youth interests and issues to policymakers, adult organizers of the Community Impact! Network immediately connected the candidate with Eric, a seasoned youth activist with strong organizational and communication skills. Eric recalls, "We live in the same neighborhood. I didn't know her before, and now we have a great friendship. Just imagine if every young person had someone in their neighborhood to call on like that. We need to build relationships with leaders in our city."

Youth are better prepared for the future when they are invited into real-time, real-impact activities, projects, and decision-making processes. These adult-led organizations not only have the capacity to prepare young people for making contributions and to support them in more general preparation, but they also have the capacity to engage youth with adults in real work, creating another pathway for mentoring opportunities and intergenerational-relationship building.

Action pathways are creating communities that actively engage all citizens and are helping build flourishing communities. Youth participation creates opportunities for young people to learn outside of the school walls, explore their individual talents, and develop networks and relationships with adult activists, business owners, and other community members. But it doesn't end there. When youth engage in ways that allow them to contribute something back to their communities, everyone wins. It is important that individual outcomes are balanced with community outcomes. Adults play an essential role in achieving this balance by pinpointing areas where young people need the most support and opening doors to more experiences that allow them to contribute their unique gifts and perspectives.

4. Adult allies encourage positive peer culture and connections.

Much of the focus of this discussion is on adults. Adults, however, are not the only ones who provide the necessary supports and conditions for youth activism. Young people look to peers as often as they do to adults for guidance and capacity. Eric at the Community Impact! Network says the key to the organization's success has been the relationships the youth have with each other and the desire they have to make a difference. "Many of the youth mobilizers have younger sisters and brothers that

they want to create a change for. They're thinking, 'I grew up in a situation, and I don't want the same to happen to them.' When you have young people saying they want to connect, it sparks energy. We go through the process of designing the project, and it's a lot of work, but even with all the work, they're committed to it."

A Diversity of Approaches

Many of the programs and organizations that support youth action have their roots in youth development. Some are rooted firmly in the traditions of civic activism, neighborhood development, or community organizing. Others focus squarely on the youth-action arena and act as hybrid organizations, blending individual youth-development efforts with community-change efforts. Just as these approaches to youth development are diverse, the approaches adult allies take toward supporting youth activists in these situations are equally diverse. Adult allies must keep in mind as they connect with youth-led, adult-led, and hybrid organizations that each offers a unique opportunity to support youth activism. Adult roles range from that of a supporter, offering networking opportunities and a bridge to the necessary professional resources; to a facilitator/coordinator, working daily with young people to develop their ideas in an adult-led effort; to a working partner, collaborating on an approach to create change.

Whom?

Traditionally, many youth-action organizations and programs are initiated by adults. Efforts such as the Community Impact! Network have received attention as successful youth-run initiatives sponsored and incubated by adult-run organizations. There are numerous other examples of adult-led efforts engaging youth as activists for local-, city-, and national-level change.

However, youth-led organizations are emerging, and increasingly, youth-led efforts such as Youth Force are receiving equal visibility as they demonstrate their power to inspire and engage young people as change agents in their schools, housing projects, and communities. Additionally, young people are meeting and acting "below the radar screen" in groups, clubs, and places unaffiliated with—and often unnoticed by—formal organizations.

These efforts are started and led by young people like Eric Braxton, a former youth activist who put off going to college to build Urban Retrievers, the organization that is now known as the Philadelphia Student Union. This organization is committed to helping young people find a voice and take action on issues that affect them with particular emphasis on access, quality, and equity in local public schools. Among such organizations, this drive to connect skills development to change efforts was particularly strong when youth were at the helm.

Where?

Youth-action opportunities are located in institutions throughout the community. Such opportunities are found in, and focused on, the full range of organizations and associations that make up the community's assets, such as the performing arts, education, human services, technology, civic activism, and spiritual outreach. The spheres in which young people can make a difference are the spheres of community life.

Guided by national volunteer rates, survey data show that young people age twelve to seventeen volunteer through organizations in which they participate the most heavily. Almost half (44 percent) the teens report they volunteer through religious organizations. One-third (36 percent) report they volunteer in or through youth-development organizations, and one-third (34 percent) volunteer in educational organizations (Hodgkinson, Weitzman, Crutchfield, and Heffron 1996). It is not surprising that the organizations that work most closely with youth become the bases for their volunteering. Such organizations are the logical hubs for efforts to increase the quantity, quality, and diversity of youth-action opportunities.

What?

Our national scan suggests that the kinds of programs engaging youth in purposeful action vary. The definitions of youth-action approaches are also different. Using the GOALS model, a set of definitions gathered from representatives of youth-action organizations (The Forum for Youth Investment and the Innovation Center for Community and Youth Development 1999), we can examine five action strategies—governance, organizing, advocacy, leadership development, and service—that help adults imagine their roles in youth action.

Governance. Youth activists assume decision-making and power-sharing roles and responsibilities that influence and determine an organization's strategic direction and how resources are allocated.

Organizing. Youth activists motivate other youth and adults to take action on a specific, common agenda that emerges from or resonates with their needs and concerns. Such efforts allow young people to build alliances across diverse populations.

Advocacy. Young people develop effective methods of articulating and presenting positions on issues that reflect the opinions of specific individuals, organizations, or groups. Advocacy is issue focused. It can be, but does not have to be, constituent based.

Leadership development. Young people develop basic and specialized skills needed to be effective leaders.

Service. Youth activists meet the needs of youth and adults through direct involvement, improving the conditions of their community, and effecting change.

Clearly, there are differences between various approaches to youth action. However, these approaches are linked to each other and offer young people opportunities to make a difference in the areas of governance, organizing, advocacy, service, leadership, voice, and entrepreneurship. Adult allies help financial contributors, policymakers,

Five Opportunities for Youth Action

Opportunities for Youth Action	Challenge(s)	One Approach
Governance	Youth are not always given decision-making power. They may be placed in roles they do not want or for which they are unprepared and in which adults are not always prepared to work with youth.	The Hampton Coalition for Youth engages a wide cross section of young people in civic and democratic life, particularly in shaping policy issues that directly affect Hampton, VA, youth. Young people partner with adults to identify issues in their community work as city planners and are appointed to serve on boards and commissions.
Organizing	A political agenda could outweigh meaningful youth engagement. This could potentially make it difficult to determine a clear goal, secure funding, and obtain buy-in from skeptical adult leaders.	Students 4 Justice is closely aligned with controversial issues, such as racial tracking and equity and access in Denver schools. However, adult organizers help youth balance activism with the desire to address important topics affecting school climate.
Advocacy	Youth can potentially address a range of issues. Some are not obviously relevant to the broader community, and adults wonder when and how they should direct or guide youth advocacy efforts.	Through Youth Force, young people reach out to adult residents as well as young people to create a strong following that allows them to place enough pressure on policy makers to see real results. Adult allies offer guidance that helps youth make ongoing progress.
Leadership Development	Leadership efforts are sometimes considered too vague, too future-oriented, elitist, and not directly connected to youth activism.	Since its inception, more than 500 students in the Philadelphia Student Union have addressed justice and democratic governance in schools and scored notable victories. These youth activists use leadership capabilities to partner with teachers, administrators, and district-level leaders, generating buy-in and creating opportunities.
Service	Service is often perceived as an opportunity for participation instead of activism. While it has the potential to spark youth-action efforts, service often doesn't live up to that potential in implementation.	The most tangible evidence of the Food Project's impact on the Boston area is the thousands of pounds of organic produce grown annually and distributed to the city's poor; the 2,500 hours volunteered at local soup kitchens and homeless shelters; and the compost and soil tests offered for free to resident gardeners. Youth and adults work collaboratively to offer a valuable service to their community and gain practical skills.

program planners, and nonprofit and for-profit organizations see the potential and benefits of supporting youth leadership and youth action.

Models for the Work: How Certain Approaches Can Fit Certain Communities

Efforts that have been successful in engaging youth as change agents were introduced throughout this entry and used as examples for the relevance of adult roles in youth action. By closely examining these efforts, adult allies can picture how youth activism fits into their own communities. The previous table illustrates five opportunities for youth action using the GOALS model described in the preceding section. Each examines the opportunities, the challenges facing many youth-focused efforts, and one real-life approach taken by youth activists and adults.

While every approach described is different, each offers young people opportunities to build skills, develop relationships, and engage in real community activism. Adult allies work with and for all of these efforts, contributing when youth activists need guidance in youth-led work and framing goals and making decisions that help young people see themselves as change agents. The approaches vary, but the end goal is the same: to give young people the space needed to become activists who care about their community and want to make a meaningful difference.

Around the world and across America, adults concerned with the well-being of youth and communities are supporting the trend that we call youth action by enriching and training young people who participate in efforts to improve their communities. However, adults can do even more to place the power of activism in the hands of youth. The simple but powerful vision is of young people working with adults in many fields to effect change in areas that are important to them. Adults who work with young people have to change, organizations have to change, and public attitudes have to change. Youth action is not just a program; it is an ongoing commitment to build capacity, harness motivation, and link youth to real opportunities within programs and organizations.

Fortunately, many of these programs are awakening to the potential of youth to join and enhance their efforts. The time is right for a surge forward in America's investment in youth action.

See also Adult Partners in Youth Activism; Adultism; Civil Society and Positive Youth Development; Community Justice; Community Service; Emerging Adulthood; Generational Conflict; Generational Replacement; Intergenerational Programs and Practices; Moral Exemplars; National and Community Service; Parental Influences on Youth Activism; Positive Development; Social Justice; Social Networks.

Recommended Reading

Beier, S., Beier, S. R., Rosenfeld, W. D., Spitalny, K. C., Zansky, S. M., and Bontempo, A. N. (1996). *The Potential Role of an Adult Mentor in Influencing High-Risk Behaviors in Adolescents.* Conducted by the Department of Pediatrics, Division of Adolescent Medicine, Albert Einstein College of Medicine at Yeshiva University, Bronx, NY; Montefiore Medical Center, Bronx, NY; the Adolescent/Young Adult Center for Health, Morristown Memorial Hospital, Morristown, NJ; and the Center for Community Health, New York State Department of Health, Albany, NY.

Checkoway, B. (1997). *Adults as Allies.* Battle Creek, MI: Kellogg Foundation.

Hodgkinson, V., and Weitzman, M., with E. Crutchfield, and A. Heffron. (1996). *Volunteering and Giving among Teenagers Twelve to Seventeen Years of Age: Findings from a National Survey.* Survey conducted by the Gallup Organization for Independent Sector. Washington, D.C.: Independent Sector.

Hawthorne, S. (2001). "Hampton Leads in Youth Engagement." *Assets: The Magazine of Ideas for Healthy Communities and Healthy Youth.* Minneapolis, MN: Search Institute.

Irby, M., Ferber, T., and Pittman, K., with J. Tolman and N. Yohalem (2001). *Youth Action: Youth Contributing to Communities, Communities Supporting Youth.* Community and Youth Development Series, Vol. 6. Washington, D.C.: The Forum for Youth Investment, Impact Strategies, Inc.

Muchhala, B. (2000). *Student Voices: One Year after Seattle.* Washington, D.C.: Institute for Policy Studies.

Peter D. Hart Research Associates (1998). *Leadership for a New Century: Key Findings from a Study on Youth, Leadership, and Community Service.* Conducted for Public Allies. Washington, D.C.: Public Allies.

Princeton Survey Research Associates (1998). *Young People's Community Involvement Survey: Report on the Findings.* Prepared for Do Something, Inc. New York: Do Something.

Tolman, J., and Pittman, K., with B. Cervone, K. Cushman, L. Rowley, S. Kinkade, J. Phillips, and S. Duque (2001). *Youth Acts, Community Impacts: Stories of Youth Engagement with Real Results.* Community and Youth Development Series, Vol. 7. Washington, D.C.: The Forum for Youth Investment, Impact Strategies, Inc.

Joel Tolman, Kalisha Davis, Karen Pittman,
and Merita Irby

Adultism. Adultism is a form of oppression and discrimination, comparable to that of racism or sexism in its underlying mechanisms. Adultism covers a range of behaviors, beliefs, and attitudes that are rooted in the unquestioned assumption that adults are inherently and necessarily better than young people. Adults are considered more moral, rational, considerate, civic-minded, responsible, intelligent, developed, mature, and able than young people. Thus, adults are deemed entitled to wield their power *upon* young people without securing their approval or cooperation. Adultist beliefs are most likely to be held and perpetuated by adults and by adult institutions (e.g., government, schools, and the media); however, even young people may internalize these beliefs, so that they come to believe that adults are fundamentally better than they are.

One need not agree with all aspects of the adultist perspective to appreciate what it has to contribute to our work with young people or as young people. Adultism is perpetuated not only through formal channels such as laws and policies but also through widespread institutions such as schools and informal channels such as family customs and cultural belief systems. Adultism may take on several forms—dismissal, stereotyping and prejudice, and disempowerment and repression.

Young people's opinions ("you don't know what you're talking about") and experiences ("it's just a stage") are frequently *dismissed* as irrelevant or as insensible simply because it is youth who hold those opinions or have those experiences. Why? Across the world youth are viewed as living through a stage of life that is transitional, a stage when they are learning to think and act like adults. In the meantime, they may be defined as "incomplete adults" regardless of how they might think or feel. This perception has some merit, in that youth is a time of life when bodies, minds, and identities undergo significant changes. However, we also walk a slippery slope if we view young people as little more than individuals who are undergoing a training period and who are living in an in-between phase of their lives. The danger is in not valuing—or even of actively dismissing—the abilities, insights, experiences, or contributions of young people. After all, if they are not "full" individuals, all they do or say is something that they will "grow out of"; this makes it easy to automatically dismiss their opinions as individuals. In fact, youth as a group can also be written off as if they had little to teach us about ourselves or about our society.

Youth organizations themselves may actively dismiss the opinions of their youth members or passively do so by failing to solicit or encourage their input into the organization's affairs. This is a common practice that, once examined, suggests that as adults we assume at times that young people have nothing to teach us that we do not already know. Around the world politicians also err by failing to speak to the interests and needs of young people, in part because many in this age-group are too young to vote.

As is the case with any group stereotype, adultist *stereotypes* of youth cast them in highly general terms that (a) assume that everyone fits the generality and (b) are typically not grounded in reality. Such stereotypes negatively inform our attitudes toward others, and prejudice is the result. Peer influence and pressure is one common example of a stereotype about youth. Generally, peer influence and pressure among young people is thought of in a negative light. Similarly, in many societies when large numbers of young people congregate together, it is typically viewed as a sign of trouble ("they couldn't possibly be up to any good"). In the United States, this stereotype is especially applied to youth of color.

Another form of adultist stereotyping can be seen in the negative portrayal of youth's lives and culture in scientific research, journalism, and social commentary. For example, disproportionate attention is given to such behaviors as juvenile delinquency, violence, drug and alcohol use, and academic failure, as if these were the norm among young people. In the United States, popular psychology books on adolescence that are marketed to parents and educators are filled with such stereotypes and one-sided depictions. Additionally, actions that are potentially positive or inspired are unfairly minimized as naïve or irresponsible. Such descriptions are applied, for example, to youth activism: social movements and protests are often dismissed on the basis that they primarily involve young people.

Adultism may also manifest itself through *disempowerment and repression*. Obvious forms of direct repression or violence include child physical and sexual abuse, rampant but underrated problems in numerous societies, and verbal violence, yelling and screaming at young people. Youth are also disempowered because they are denied rights that are afforded adults (e.g., the right to vote or participate in the political decision-making process) and because they are formally or informally excluded from positions of power and authority. For example, youth are barred from assuming positions of leadership in most organizations, including organizations such as schools, even though they form the largest stakeholder group.

Youth, finally, are subjected to *double standards* worldwide. For example, although

their teachers may scream at them, young students have no right to scream back. Young people are also denied rights because they are seen as lacking maturity and as being relatively weak—they require protection from themselves and from others. And yet they may be subjected to the same punitive standards and laws as adults. For example, in many countries youth under the age of eighteen can be charged as adults for their crimes even though they are otherwise deprived of adult rights. They may be tried in adult courts, held to the same standards of culpability, and sentenced to serve time in adult prisons even though they are not allowed to vote, drive, or run for political office. The notion of adultism has important implications for youth activism and youth work (see also Social Justice).

However, as with many considerations of justice, there is a tension between the problem of adultism and that of respect for cultural diversity. Practices that are seen as adultist are often derived from longstanding cultural traditions and, in essence, make up some of the cultural fabric. Respect for elders, for instance, is a principle of many "traditional" or non–Western cultures. And yet, it is also based on the notion of adultism, a practice that unduly and unfairly undermines youths' rights because it demands that they uncritically agree to everything that adults suggest or order of them. Those who endorse the concept of adultism are challenged to pursue a more just society without overly dismissing or disrespecting culture and culturally based practices, for doing so might prove ineffective and culturally biased.

See also Adult Partners in Youth Activism; Adult Roles in Youth Activism; Empowerment; Generational Conflict; Generational Replacement; Intergenerational Programs and Practices; Moral Exemplars; Parental Influences on Youth Activism; Social Justice.

Recommended Reading

Bell, J. (1995). *Understanding Adultism: A Key to Developing Positive Youth-Adult Relationships*. Somerville, MA: YouthBuild USA.

Cohen, R. (2004). "Adultism." *The School Mediator*, III (1).

Freechild Project: Promoting Young People + Social Change. See http://www.freechild.org/adultism.htm.

Swiderski, C., and Palma, P. (1999). Adultism *Is an "ism" Too.* See http://www.ctassets.org/fall1999/voice.cfm.

Omar Guessous

Advocacy. The Kidney Foundation of Canada Advocacy Handbook defines "advocacy" as follows: "Advocacy ... the act of supporting or arguing in favor of a cause, policy, or idea. It is undertaken to influence public opinion and societal attitudes or to bring about change in government, communities, or institutional policies."

Following this definition, successful advocacy can change people's behavior (e.g., by disseminating information on the importance of a "designated driver"), mobilize community groups (e.g., to clean up toxic industrial sites), alter government policies (e.g., having the federal government make illegal the redlining of poor neighborhoods), strengthen groups' internal and external communications (e.g., through providing up-to-date computer technology), alter public mind-sets (e.g., to see youth as resources, not as problems), and reorder marketplace activity (e.g., convince corporations to buy sustainably harvested timber). Needless to say, advocacy can be partisan, bipartisan, and nonpartisan. All sides of the political spectrum do it, from advocating for immigrant rights to changing how elections are financed. Sometimes the effort is a colossal failure (e.g., health-care reform under President Bill Clinton); sometimes it is a great success (e.g., repeal of estate taxes under President George Bush).

Well-known, recent examples of wider-community advocacy showcase the roles that can be played by individuals, working through nonprofit organizations that organize collective power to change public opinion, behavior, and laws. Anti-smoking advocacy has taken a long and successful road that included public awareness of health risks, sanctioning of the tobacco industry, and wide adoption of "no smoking in public places" laws. (Of course, the work isn't yet finished.) Advocacy focused on drunk driving (increased penalties and "designated driver" campaigns) is also very well known and documented. These successful advocacy movements began at the grassroots level, spearheaded by families of victims. As they built power and public awareness, broader campaigns involving both individuals and organizations came together to reshape overall public opinion and policy across the United States.

Do young people participate in advocacy defined in this way? Can and do youth play important roles in the complex processes of changing public opinion or shaping public policy? Are there ways that youth-directed advocacy itself changes public opinion or societal attitudes toward young people? And can such changes also lead to new policies that directly affect young people? What kind of youth-activist work is this, and where can it be found?

Youth are increasingly involved in advocacy. This entry provides a lens through which to understand youth advocacy. The lens brings two related ideas into focus with partial answers to the questions posed above about the intentions and results of youth-led social change:

That advocacy for a host of community and social changes is not the exclusive province of adult activists, politicians, or policy wonks but is the work of activist youth, too, and

That youth advocacy itself has the power to transform the public's very understanding of the needs and capacities of young people as able contributors to the betterment of communities and society.

What are some examples of youth advocacy? Though not (yet) as well known as the anti-smoking and drunk-driving campaigns mentioned above, youth-led advocacy drives are picking up heads of steam. Across the United States and around the globe, young people—alone or with adult allies—have begun to advocate for specific changes to policies and institutions that concretely improve their own chances for successful lives. In particular, youth are increasingly raising their collective voices to influence and improve the public systems with which they are most involved: education and juvenile justice. Public systems are the most likely targets for several reasons: youth live within them and therefore know them (schools and, unhappily, juvenile justice facilities), and, just as importantly, these systems garner the largest share of public monies and are thus ripe for public influence.

Young people also advocate for environmental protection, in response to globalization, and generally to increase the depth of opportunities available to themselves in their communities. Youth pursue their goals through organizing (see other encyclopedia entries), governance of community institutions (in nonprofits and by serving on civic committees), by producing media that express youth opinion and intention, and through service and other activities.

Support for youth civic engagement and advocacy is premised on a core tenet of positive youth development: that with the right infrastructure and opportunities, young people become strong community assets capable of full civic participation. Participation in advocating for change on a community problem can result in precise outcomes, as the examples below illustrate. By taking direct action, along with other community stakeholders, young people can consequentially improve the community institutions that support or fail them. In fact, recent advances in youth-development theory and research bolster the view that deep participation in nitty-gritty, youth-relevant community issues (e.g., education or justice reform, stewarding community institutions) is among the most effective means of promoting the healthy development of individual young people. An important benefit is the establishment of lifetime patterns of social interest and involvement.

Following are specific examples of youth advocacy, which are the results of direct-action organizing:

In Los Angeles, CA, at South Central Youth Empowered Through Action (SCYEA), young people have taken the reins and are working to directly improve educational opportunities for thousands of students in the community. SCYEA provides critical academic support and leadership development to high-school students in a notoriously underserved area of Los Angeles. As community advocates, high-school-aged youth in the program are highly engaged in planning and concretely pressing for reforms of South L.A.'s community institutions. Through organizing, youth have been able to reduce the number of tobacco and alcohol billboards near South L.A. schools and have created 120 of their own billboards conveying strong, positive prevention messages and advocating for improved, healthier behavior. More recently, after two years of research, building community awareness, and public education, students were able to directly influence the spending of a $2.4 billion statewide school-bond initiative, ensuring that $153 million was allocated for badly needed capital repairs for South L.A. schools. Once inserted, youth voices advocating for fairness and equity could not be denied.

In Philadelphia, students participating in an after-school organizing program focused on education reform, the Philadelphia Student Union, sought to inject youth planning and youth voice into public discussion as the district engaged a new superintendent of schools. The student union surveyed thousands of students on a range of topics and presented a fifteen-point platform for school reform to the superintendent and the press. The platform contained recommendations on school safety, improving instruction, deepening relationships between students and teachers, upgrading the physical school building plants, school nutrition, and so forth. This very public document energized students, and its recommendations encouraged the local press to see youth opinions as serious, substantive, and invested with first-hand knowledge.

The Youth Justice Coalition in California intensively develops youth through civic engagement and organizing training and then supports their efforts to improve a failing juvenile justice system. Prompted by stark disparities in public spending (in California, it costs $49,000 per year to incarcerate a youth versus $7,000 per year to educate one), an astounding 90 percent recidivism rate, and high-profile teen suicides as a result of conditions inside detention halls, youth have advocated for better conditions and services and more effective rehabilitation and prevention programs. They have been very successful. Effective advocacy efforts to date have included: (1) convincing city officials to halt plans to place youth in adult facilities where violence against and abuse of youth was rampant; (2) ensuring that prison officials enforced their own guideline that youth who are pepper-sprayed must receive medical attention within fifteen minutes of being sprayed (youth complained of waiting hours before seeing a nurse or being allowed to shower); and (3) establishing standing committees inside each detention hall made up of staff *and youth* who review all discipline and grievance procedures.

Youth service on community-institution boards allows peers and adults to see young people's capacities and interests firsthand. Formal research on the impacts of youth on board governance (on young people, adults, and organizations) shows great potential and strong effects. Professor Richard Zeldin of the University of Wisconsin has taken the lead on this now voluminous body of documentation and formal evaluation, which has been widely read, leading to many instances of youth being invited onto formerly "adults-only" boards. Dramatically, in the past year the national 4-H made its own policy determination to involve significant numbers of teenagers on every board within the 4-H system: from local clubs to regional divisions, to state offices, up through the national board of trustees of 4-H. Other large national youth-serving organizations are likely to follow with their own programs.

A second pathway to advocacy, working alongside direct-action organizing by individual groups, is pursued by intermediary organizations, which support and then unite *multiple* groups working toward the same advocacy goals. (Anti-tobacco and drunk-driving advocacy campaigns also harnessed this two-prong approach: direct action by individual groups, usually working locally; and collective advocacy, led by organizations skilled at uniting the work of multiple local groups, such as Mothers Against Drunk Driving.)

Intermediary groups are most frequently the formal advocates working to actualize the *collective* vision of young people, working to influence institutions and their fields through public education, research, communications, and documenting promising practices. Such "infrastructure groups" advocate on field or national levels for acceptance of young people as valid partners in consequential community decision-making processes (e.g., around financial resource allocation, public policy changes, improvements to a school district, proposed legislation, board memberships). The following are examples of this:

The Ella Baker Center for Human Rights, headquartered in San Francisco, has actively united multiple groups hoping to encourage reform of California's juvenile justice system. It has coordinated the efforts of over forty grassroots, youth-led groups that successfully challenged Alameda County's (Oakland, CA) plans to build a new facility doubling the number of residential beds for juvenile prisoners. The Ella Baker Center established a unified campaign called "Books Not Bars," which advocated for, and convinced county commissioners to back, *reduced* incarceration in the county, putting scarce resources into prevention and alternatives-to-incarceration programs. The question was asked loudly in the press: how can the county justify building more beds when juvenile crime in the county declined significantly and steadily for ten years? With this and other victories under its belt, the coalition finally pressured California lawmakers to agree to overhaul the entire California Youth Authority system, a process that will be completed by 2006. Young people advocated for approaches that placed priority on alternatives to incarceration, prevention rather than locking away youth. Youth voices advocating for these newer approaches, many of which are successful in other jurisdictions, are now firmly in the mix.

The Funders' Collaborative on Youth Organizing (FCYO) is an effective field-level advocacy organization. Through research and peer education, funding, and deliberate education of grant-makers, FCYO has helped to steadily increase the financial and capacity-building resources available to groups that use direct-action organizing, led by young people, to achieve a range of advocacy campaign goals. FCYO has been very successful in its advocacy efforts within the field of philanthropy: from 2000 to 2002 there was a 60 percent increase in funds available to youth organizing (from $14 million a year from fifty-nine foundations to $24 million a year from seventy-four foundations).

And here is the really big picture. Individual campaign efforts and consolidated ones pursued by intermediaries have an effect beyond their own specific campaign goals. They offer communities and the country at large a wider perspective on the positive power and new roles being played by young people. This is meta-advocacy: putting forward a new image of young people themselves as capable, full democratic participants in community life. If the work of youth on policy, public awareness, and behavior change becomes visible to a broad public, new roles for young people as partners in democratic enterprises will open up. And as these new roles are crafted, deeper public investment in youth will surely follow.

See also Advocacy Day; AIDS Advocacy in South Africa; Animal Rights; Anti-Nazi Youth Resistance; Anti-Tobacco Youth Activism; Antiwar Activism; Civil Rights Movement; Global Justice Activism; High-School Students' Rights Movement of the 1960s; Mental-Health Advocacy in Youth; National and Community Service; Social Movements; Social Responsibility.

Robert Sherman

Advocacy Day. Since 2000, delegations from neighborhoods and communities across New York state have converged once a year in Albany, the state's capitol, for an After-School Advocacy Day that calls for the continuation and expansion of local after-school programs. The day, which many observers and participants describe as filled with energy and enthusiasm, includes some one hundred meetings between local delegations and their state legislators or legislative staffers. Sitting alongside program providers and parents in those meetings are after-school students, who comprise the great majority of Advocacy Day participants. Including youth in Advocacy Day is both pivotal to its effectiveness and a valuable source of experiential learning. Lucy Friedman, president of The After-School Corporation (TASC), which co-sponsors the event, observes that it is increasingly clear that "positive outcomes for social and emotional development are a key benefit of after-school services" and that bringing youth together to support an institution they care about promotes those outcomes.

Advocacy Day, which brought approximately 1,200 people to Albany in February 2004 (with one hundred participating in a March "overflow" day), is a large and well-orchestrated event. Participants, who wear T-shirts with quotes and statements about the importance of after-school programs, spend the morning at a rally, which features speakers, performances by after-school groups, and role plays to prepare delegations for their sessions with legislators. Following a brief march to the capitol

More than 1200 students from across New York travel to the state capitol of Albany each year to participate in The After-School Corporation and Coalition for Afterschool Funding Afterschool Advocacy Day. *Courtesy of The After-School Corporation.*

building, delegations from the different localities meet with their legislators or legislators' staffers to make a case for maintaining or expanding after-school services.

In 2004, some 1,000 after-school students, ages eight to eighteen, with most between the ages of ten and thirteen, attended one of the two Advocacy Days. In some programs enrollees in a particular after-school activity participate as a group; in others, youth apply to attend individually. In part because resources and other constraints limit the number of youth a program can send to the event, staff use different criteria to decide who will attend. Many programs try to gauge students' level of interest in the day. For example, students in one program who took the time to

Students from the Hudson City School District traveled to Albany to be a part of After-School Advocacy Day and, after marching to the Legislative Office Building, were able to meet with staffers of State Senator Stephen Saland and share their goal of universal after-school programs for all children by 2010. *Courtesy of The After-School Corporation.*

write an essay on why they valued after-school services were more likely to be chosen.

Advocacy Day reflects the missions of its co-sponsors, TASC and the Coalition for After-school Funding (CASF). TASC was established in 1998 with a $125 million challenge grant from philanthropist George Soros, which is matched on a 3:1 basis. The organization's mission is to make quality after-school programs universally available and publicly funded in New York City, New York state, and across the nation.

To pursue its mission TASC examines and disseminates information on the operational experiences, best practices, and outcomes of a critical mass of programs, making grants to a wide variety of nonprofit groups, many of them community-based organizations, to manage school-based after-school programs throughout New York City and elsewhere in New York state. Today

the TASC network includes 187 New York City programs and 56 in other New York localities, collectively serving over 50,000 students in grades K through 12. Programs are led by full-time, year-round site coordinators, and they aim to provide educational enrichment, technological-skills development and homework help, combined with arts, sports, and community service.

CASF, founded in 2000 under the umbrella of the nonprofit Citizen Action of New York, is an after-school advocacy campaign consisting of over 350 member organizations. TASC was instrumental in creating CASF, and the organizations collaborate in promoting the availability of high quality after-school services in the state. Advocacy Day is an important ingredient of this work. While CASF takes the lead in organizing the event, TASC-sponsored programs account for a significant portion of the delegations, and TASC provides funds for buses, lunches, and T-shirts for all participants.

Adults who accompany students in TASC-sponsored programs to meetings with legislators and the lawmakers themselves describe the youth as engaged, confident, and well spoken. Assemblywoman Crystal Peoples recalls the young people in the Advocacy Day delegation as "very well prepared and able to articulate the importance of after-school services." "The youth take the lead," observes state CASF director Davia Gaddy-Collington. "Ultimately these meetings are between them and the legislator."

There is consensus that the key to a strong presence at the meetings is careful preparation. Programs typically brief students on topics such as the structure of the legislature, legislative perspectives, and the funding situation for after-school services. A number of programs also engage students in role plays, which are then reinforced with the ones staged at the Albany rally. CASF gives programs guidance as they prepare. Jenny Seaquist, a teacher-artist in a TASC-sponsored New York City program managed by the Educational Alliance, describes how using a role play of a legislative meeting developed by a CASF staff member, she and the staff member coached youth on how to respond to legislators.

Karen Scharff, executive director of Citizen Action of New York, CASF's parent organization, and Kate Pepe, CASF's organizer for western New York, offer two different but complementary perspectives on preparing students for the meetings. Scharff emphasizes the need to help students anticipate how sessions might unfold, describing training sessions in which youth are asked, "What do you want the legislator to do?" For example, she believes students should be told not to be satisfied when a legislator only praises them and promises, "I'll look into that," and that they should practice follow-up questions that press for specifics. At the

same time Pepe cautions against overly preparing youth to speak about their own experiences. She believes that they can make strong, unrehearsed statements about what after-school programs mean to them and that these are the messages that have the most power.

Students are told they may encounter a range of reactions from legislators. Most often, legislators engage well with youth. Seaquist recalls her class's meeting with a top aide of Senator Liz Krueger. Sequist said, "When they asked, 'Why doesn't the funding get through?' she told them, 'Some people want one thing, some another, and there's a need to compromise.' She was very respectful; it wasn't a dumbed-down answer." But Jennique Sanford, who is now seventeen and has attended two Advocacy Days, says some legislators have looked less interested than others. "You can see on their face—'whatever.' They're listening with closed ears." She adds that she has learned not to be overly frustrated by these kinds of reactions. "I would do it again, as long as I got a chance to speak."

Another facet of the preparation is ensuring that students understand that an Advocacy Day is more challenging than a recreational field trip. Pepe says that students should be told that the day will be long, that often they must be quiet, and that because of legislators' schedules and extended waits to go through security, they must also be patient.

For some youth, the most memorable part of Advocacy Day is the excitement of interacting with peers from across the state and of being part of a movement of thousands of people with a common purpose. Thus, a high point of the event for seventh-grader Dominique Scarfone, who is from a small upstate New York community, was "meeting other people," while for Sanford, who is from New York City, it was "seeing how many kids care about this and took the time to come." The rally, with chants, performances, and awards for individual advocates, reinforces this sense of cohesion.

Once Advocacy Day has ended, programs try to keep its issues and spirit alive. Many follow up with postcard campaigns and thank-you notes to the legislators they met. Scharff notes that legislators are presumed to respond most readily to "money or votes—and kids have neither." Nevertheless, she believes young people "change these dynamics. They are our most effective voice. If we were to be limited to taking only one constituency to Albany, it would be students." Legislators concur that the presence of young people matters, with several noting that youth "put a human face" on after-school services. "When children come to Albany themselves, it makes a difference," says Assemblywoman Peoples.

Pepe recalls a legislator challenging students by asking them, "Do you really go to the program everyday? What do you do when you're not there?" Pepe says, "And one girl spoke up immediately, 'We need this program because now all the kids do is hang out on the street corner.' And that shocked him. Of course, he knew this was happening, but it's different when someone is sitting in your office and describing the situation. After the kids spoke, he wrote a letter of support for the program to the Speaker." "These are not Gucci-clad professional lobbyists," says state Senator Sam Hoyt, a strong supporter of after-school programs, "but they can be a breath of fresh air. If they say to me, 'I need your help,' I will listen."

The visibility of large numbers of spirited youth on Advocacy Day signals that there is an organized movement for after-school services—and one that includes strong representation from the service users—increasing the likelihood that after-school interests will be factored into budgetary decisions. Another strategic value of youth participation, according to state Senator George Maziarz, also a vocal supporter of after-school programs, is that students connect to parents. Youth advocates can carry back a positive picture of a legislator to parents, and legislators, often parents themselves, are responsive to an issue raised by children.

Whatever influence students can exert on the legislative process, TASC and CASF would not invest energies in Advocacy Day without a belief that it offers youth important personal benefits. Listed below are three often intersecting pathways through which benefits reach youth:

Community service. TASC considers community service a critical ingredient of after-school programming, but compared with many other elements of the TASC program model—for example, sports and homework help—it tends to be more difficult to translate into programming. Advocacy Day and its preparation help staff meet this programming challenge by giving youth concrete opportunities to relate to the world outside their schools. "Youth who travel with adults to Albany to support a key neighborhood service ultimately feel more connected to their community," says Lucy Friedman. Moreover, according to Adelle Dix, who coordinates the TASC-sponsored Advantage after-school program, which is managed by the YWCA of Niagara Falls, NY, Advocacy Day enables youth to give back to that community. Rather than being only recipients of beneficial services in their neighborhoods, students contribute to efforts to keep the services alive.

Civic engagement. While students are taught they should engage in the democratic process, civic engagement can seem remote unless, as in Advocacy Day, young people have the chance to learn through experience. "Participating in the legislative process strengthens young people's knowledge of state government and lawmaking," says state Senate Majority Leader Joseph Bruno. "I believe exposure to the process in one's youth will greatly increase the chances that an individual will remain an informed and active participant in our democracy." Bruno and other legislators stress that Advocacy Day can teach skills of patience and compromise that are important to civic engagement but that do not always come naturally to young people.

Empowerment. While Advocacy Day helps students see that the democratic arena does not offer quick gratification for most demands, youth also learn that if they are organized and have a clear message, they can effect change. The TASC and CASF conceptualization of youth as central, not peripheral, to their delegations reinforces this sense of collective empowerment.

TASC also believes the taste of collective empowerment helps youth with the individual developmental task of acquiring a sense of self-efficacy—an achievement that is particularly important in a society that expects them to have the confidence to shape their futures. On Advocacy Day, Friedman says, youth "meet face-to-face with legislators and stakeholders, share their stories about what after-school programming has meant to them, and call for more funding. That is a powerful opportunity that helps youth think differently about their futures, what they are capable of, and their place in the world."

See also Advocacy; AIDS Advocacy in South Africa; Civic Engagement in Diverse Youth; Empowerment; Mental Health Advocacy in Youth; Social Responsibility.

Recommended Reading

National Research Council, Committee on Behavioral and Social Sciences (2002). *Community Programs to Promote Youth Development.* Washington, D.C.: National Academy Press.

Phia, S., and Miller, B. (2002). *We Can Do More: Improving the Quality and Impact of After-school Programs.* Wellesley, MA: National Institute on Out-of-School Time.

Reisner, E., White, R., Russell, C., and Birmingham, J. (2004). *Building Quality Scale and Effectiveness in After-school Programs.* Summary report of the TASC evaluation. Washington, D.C.: Policy Studies Associates, Inc.

Susan Blank for The After-School Corporation

African American Youth. *See* Hip-Hop Generation; Minority Youth Voter Turnout; Religiosity and Civic Engagement in African American Youth.

AIDS Advocacy in South Africa. The AIDS pandemic is the challenge for younger generations in a democratic South Africa that apartheid was for earlier generations. Post-apartheid South Africa has a very young population with 53 percent under the age of twenty-five. Within this population HIV infection rates are particularly high. It is estimated that 60 percent of all adults who acquire HIV become infected before they turn twenty-five. Within this context, youth have assumed the identity of the "urban warrior" invoked by earlier generations of youth in the struggle for liberation.

In apartheid (legitimized racial segregation which was abolished in the early 1990s), South Africa's youth were described in the popular media as "urban warriors" who led an activist social movement against legitimized inequality and oppression. That same image of activism is applied by today's youth as they take up the challenge of HIV/AIDS. The image also is used broadly in the media and public discourse about HIV/AIDS. And, just as in a pre-democratic South Africa when the state responded to the youth's insistence on a democratic agenda, the state is responding again today to the younger generation's demand to address HIV/AIDS as a human-rights challenge.

The current generation of youth has consciously linked the symbolic platforms (i.e., the historical events and achievements of the pre-democracy struggles) to elevate the HIV/AIDS struggle from a personal to a political level. Not only has the historical identity of the urban warrior been applied by the younger generation to HIV/AIDS activism but also to racism, increased rates of crime, violence, unemployment, and poverty. The activist campaign against HIV/AIDS has gone forward on many fronts. Youth have used the platforms of the pre-apartheid era to bring attention. They also have drawn from youth culture, the media, peer-to-peer campaigns, and a sense of generational solidarity via NGOs.

Historic Dates and Symbolic Heroes

Youth Day, celebrated on June 16, commemorates the youth social movement, which played an integral role in the abolition of apartheid laws. Today, the symbolic value of Youth Day is invoked to fight another social and political burden threatening the youth of South Africa. In June 1999, the National AIDS Program in the Department of Health and the National Youth Commission collaborated on an HIV/AIDS youth awareness initiative.

The collective memory concerning Youth Day goes back to June 16, 1976, when thirteen-year-old Hector Petersen died. Hector was the first urban warrior to publicly fall in the struggle for liberation. He was shot dead by the apartheid regime's security forces in the township of Soweto. The commemoration of his death was juxtaposed on Youth Day with the high rate of HIV infection in the younger population in South Africa. On this day the president of the National Association of People Living with HIV/AIDS, Mr. Nxesi, asserted that the history of Hector Petersen is the history of fighting for human rights, and HIV/AIDS is a human-rights issue. In this speech he emphasized that South Africa needs an activist approach in the fight against HIV/AIDS.

Roughly twenty-five years later, another young urban warrior became the symbol in the fight against HIV/AIDS. In 2001, twelve-year-old Nkosi Johnson became the youngest South African AIDS activist to fall. Johnson successfully fought and changed policies that kept HIV-infected children out of public schools. His openness about his infection exposed a government criticized for being slow to react to the disease and gave hope to South Africa's 4.7 million people with HIV. Thus, it is from Johnson's death and those of others like him that young activists in contemporary South Africa draw their courage and strength to fight and expose the realities of the HIV epidemic. Both Johnson and Petersen died while protesting unjust policies. The fact that Johnson was twelve and Petersen was thirteen puts a very young face on the struggles for human rights.

Media

The media is a second arena that youth have used in their fight for human rights. More than two decades ago, the media revealed the struggles of previous generations against apartheid in South Africa. In present-day South Africa the youth struggle against HIV is constantly portrayed in print and other media. For instance, one of the most popular dramas on television, known as *Yizo Yizo*, portrays how young people wrestle with contemporary issues including sexuality, violence, poverty, and HIV. Besides such dramatic presentations, the campaigns against HIV/AIDS are regularly covered—for example, high-profile leaders' speeches such as those of former South African President Nelson Mandela and Microsoft's Bill Gates in their appeals to younger generations. Other examples of campaign activities that are typically covered on the news include the work of AIDS activist organizations with a political agenda, like the Pan-African HIV/AIDS Treatment Access Movement. The leaders of this particular campaign draw from the tone and discourse of the Pan-Africanist liberation struggle. The slogan used in the earlier apartheid era—"We Are Angry. Our People Are Dying."—is again used in the contemporary struggle.

In general the portrayal of the younger generation in scholarly work and in the popular media is as an apolitical and extremely materialistic group. They have recently been labeled the "*Yizo Yizo*" generation after the popular SABC educational drama on television dealing with contemporary social issues in the country. Although, in general, the media portrays the younger generation in a stereotypically apolitical and passive light, the portrayal of youth activists against HIV/AIDS is quite positive. Indeed, both the media and government have adopted the youth activist image to encourage greater civic engagement among other members of the younger generation. Whether the apolitical image of the younger generation is accurate or not, the image of the young urban warrior and its connection to South African youth's history is invoked as an image to galvanize the younger generation.

In fact, in a 2002 survey by the Human Sciences Research Council (HSRC), 39 percent of young people aged eighteen to twenty-four indicated they were seriously concerned about the disease and felt it was the biggest threat to them. The survey also showed that, in contrast to the general population's resistance to condom use, the younger generation would more readily use condoms because they were concerned about AIDS. The public sector's strong attempt to instill an activist approach in the youth population with regards to HIV/AIDS issues is preceded by the social identity created by popular culture of present-day youth in South Africa.

Youth have also used the media as a direct mouthpiece to elevate their campaign. For example, the Associated Press reports that thousands of college students bearing AIDS–awareness posters marched through various South African cities calling for better programs to combat HIV. In the words of one of the student leaders, Kholiwe Botha, a member of the student council at the University of the Witwatersrand, "we need to spread the word about HIV/AIDS because the more that students know, the better able they are to make informed choices."

Youth Culture and Cultural Traditions

Popular youth culture is often used as a common medium aimed at addressing contemporary challenges facing young people in the country. For instance, in KwaZulu-Natal youth activist approaches are used to create awareness on HIV/AIDS. AIDS prevention messages are incorporated in song, dance, and street theaters. Similarly, Abo'm Rapper Against AIDS uses the popular music platform to spread its activist message that local hip-hop is waging war against HIV/AIDS.

Cultural relevance is an important aspect that youth take into account as they design projects. For example, the deputy president of the South African Youth Council reported that many young people ran projects in KwaZulu-Natal, where they play an

activist role in training members of the community to promote HIV/AIDS awareness within their specific sociocultural context. According to a study done by the Human Sciences Research Council, KwaZulu-Natal has the fourth highest rate of HIV infection in the country. Hence, it is no surprise that the AIDS movement in this province is more youth led as compared to other provinces in South Africa. One example is fifteen-year-old Andile Sithole who is educating fellow students in the province about HIV/AIDS. In a program run by Targeted AIDS Intervention. Sithole and his friends are challenging Zulu cultural taboos by talking about HIV/AIDS prevention. In Zulu tradition issues of sexuality are not commonly discussed, but young people within that tradition are questioning that practice. Insofar as sexual and behavioral practices are culturally based, education on HIV prevention has to take such contextual issues into account if it is going to be successful.

Peer-to-Peer Education and Nongovernmental Organizations

Peer-to-peer education refers to young people's efforts to speak directly to fellow members of their generation. This can be done at a personal level as well as via collective efforts through nongovernmental organizations. One such organization is ACTIVE YOUTH, a NGO that employs peer-to-peer activism to raise consciousness and educate youth on HIV/AIDS. Another peer-educator project in Soweto, Johannesburg, is the Township AIDS Project (TAP), a sexual education and HIV/AIDS prevention program. Peer-to-peer education often occurs through very informal and social networks. For this reason TAP has also established a number of clubs in the community that advocate and educate about HIV/AIDS issues in the township. According to YouthAIDS, another NGO, and in particular their Take Action initiative, youth who are in tertiary institutions need to be targeted because of high HIV prevalence rates which exceed 50 percent. Thus, YouthAIDS has encouraged the activist rhetoric, and many universities in South Africa have taken up the activist banner in the fight against the disease. For example, the University of the Western Cape in Cape Town has directed numerous initiatives in AIDS education and outreach to its student community. The University of KwaZulu-Natal's Treatment Action Campaign (TAC) advocates for students and staff to get tested. One of the TAC's principal objectives is to use lobbying, advocacy, and all forms of legitimate social mobilization to challenge any type of discrimination relating to treatment and care. The TAC challenges the university, the broader community, and even the government. In fact, the TAC was nominated for a Nobel Peace Prize in 2004 for bringing global attention to HIV/AIDS by taking the government to court to insist that treatment be made available to those infected with the disease.

YOUTHNET, another NGO, has established an out-of-school program that focuses on HIV prevention strategies and sex education. The organization targets street children and out-of-school youth to educate them about prevention strategies with regard to HIV infection. In summary, youth-led initiatives as summarized in the examples listed above have been the response of the current generation in a democratic South Africa to the challenge that their generation and their society face.

Several NGOs have targeted fifteen- to twenty-year-olds and made it their mission to reduce by half the number of HIV infections within a three- to five-year period. One of these, launched in September 1999, is "loveLife," a national AIDS collaboration, reported to be one of the most successful campaigns. It is a foundation-sponsored sex education and activism campaign that uses television, advertising, and the Internet to get youth talking about historically taboo topics. Tapping into contemporary youth culture, loveLife employs multiple strategies (ads in public transportation, dress codes, ads in the media) to send a consistent message of prevention. Perhaps for this reason, loveLife has the widest reach of any of the HIV prevention-education campaigns, reaching into urban and rural areas alike. loveLife attempts to achieve this through brand-driven, sustained, multidimensional national programs. It seeks to make condom use a natural element of youth culture and style. loveLife has a number of youth-friendly Y-centers across the country. According to Joel Makitla, a young person who manages a loveLife Y-center in Orange Farm, Johannesburg, and speaks to teenagers about gender and sexuality issues, loveLife reaches the youth through an active engagement with this population.

Similar to loveLife, the Youth4Life Foundation also has set a 50 percent reduction goal. According to their statement of policy, a unique aspect of the Youth4Life (Y4L) Foundation is the inculcating of an ethos of volunteerism among the youth of South Africa. Their goal is to recruit and train one million Y4L ambassadors by 2010 who will promote the Y4L habits for life strategy. In addition to their three- to five-year target of 50 percent reduction of new infections, Y4L has also set up a target of preventing any new HIV infections by the year 2020. Both Y4L and loveLife are youth led and are motivated by an implicit goal, that of instilling a sense of citizenship and social responsibility toward reducing HIV infections among the youth population.

A final initiative directed at getting the youth to actively engage in the fight against HIV/AIDS is the Nelson Mandela Foundation's 46664 AIDS Campaign, which was launched in Cape Town in November 2003 and is led by Mandela himself. The number 46664 was Nelson Mandela's prison number during his incarceration on Robben Island, denoting "Prisoner Number 466 during the Year 1964," which was used by prison wardens to refer to him instead of his name. Indeed, Mandela has now taken on the tough new role of leading the international fight against HIV/AIDS through his foundation as well as his children's fund with the same zeal and dedication he showed in leading the anti-apartheid campaign. It is interesting to note that the symbolic hero in both struggles is to a large extent embodied through the image of Mandela who, as a young adult in 1944, was one of the founding members of the African National Congress (ANC) Youth League, the political party that led the anti-apartheid struggle and won the first democratically held elections in South Africa after the fall of apartheid in 1994 and is still ruling the country even today. In a way the 46664 campaign represents the interconnectedness of the anti-apartheid struggle of the past and the current fight against the further spread of HIV/AIDS, especially by viewing HIV/AIDS as a human-rights issue and that HIV/AIDS has to be banished from the face of the earth in much the same way as apartheid was in 1994. In essence, the 46664 AIDS campaign is an international call to invoke global citizenship to curb the further spread of the disease, an effort that uses music, especially among the youth, as well as fundraising for the fight against HIV/AIDS via a Web site, http://www.46664.com. Many international and local musical icons, most of them youth themselves who took part in the first concert in 2003 that was held in Cape Town, were invited to Robben Island by the Nelson Mandela Foundation on the eve of the first 46664 concert in November 2003. In his speech to the musicians gathered, Mandela asserted that during his incarceration and that of the other freedom fighters on Robben Island, lobby campaigns for their release were launched internationally and that musicians in particular played an integral role in the campaign outside of South Africa to liberate the country. He concluded by stating that this time he was asking them to join forces to free our world from HIV/AIDS, especially among the youth. The first 46664 concert was extremely successful and raised millions of dollars to support the fight against HIV/AIDS both locally and internationally. The second 46664 concert is scheduled to be held in 2005 again in South Africa.

Conclusions

In South Africa during the era of apartheid youth had spearheaded a social movement that contributed significantly to eventually overthrowing legitimized segregation. In contemporary South Africa youth across the country, as individuals, as members of NGOs, and as students, are still engaged in mobilizing members of their generation to combat social problems such as HIV/AIDS. And it appears that their efforts are having an impact.

For example, compelling evidence exists that the incidence rate of HIV peaked during the late 1990s. Recent prenatal survey data shows that there has been a significant decrease in the rate of both HIV and syphilis infections among female teenagers between ages fifteen and nineteen. The reduction was primarily driven by changes in the behavior of youth in response to multiple interventions as described above. Clearly, the fight against HIV in South Africa will be won ultimately because of what happens in this important age-group, and therefore continued action including youth activism around the issue of HIV/AIDS is critical.

See also Advocacy; Advocacy Day; Mental Health Advocacy in Youth; New Media; Religiosity and Civic Engagement in African American Youth; Social Networks; Social Responsibility; Soweto Youth Activism (South Africa); Transnational Youth Activism; United Nations, Youth Activism and.

Recommended Reading

Department of Health (June 12, 1998). *Youth in South Africa Bears a Terrible Burden—HIV/AIDS.* Pretoria, South Africa: Department of Health. Retrieved April 21, 2004, http://www.doh.gov.za/docs/pr/1998/pr0612.html.

Department of Health (2004). "National HIV and Syphilis Antenatal Seroprevalence Survey in South Africa/2003." Pretoria, South Africa: Department of Health. Retrieved January 5, 2005, http://www.doh.gov.za/docsreports.

Everatt, D. (2002). "From Urban Warrior to Market Segment? Youth in SA 1990–2000." Development Update. *The Dead Decade? Youth in Post-apartheid South Africa. Quarterly Journal of South African National NGO Coalition and INTERFUND,* 3 (2): 1–39.

Parker, W. (2003). *Re-Appraising Youth Prevention in South Africa: The Case of loveLife*. Paper presented at the South African AIDS conference, Durban, South Africa.

Rehle, T., and Shisana, O. (2003). "Epidemiological and Demographic HIV/AIDS Projections: South Africa." *African Journal of AIDS Research*, 2 (1): 1–8.

Shisana, O., and Simbayi, L. (2002). *Nelson Mandela/HSRC Study of HIV/AIDS: South African National HIV Prevalence, Behavioral Risks, and Mass Media Household Survey 2002*. Cape Town, South Africa: Human Sciences Research Council Publishers.

Simbayi, L. C., Chauveau, J., and Shisana, O. (2004). "Behavioral Responses of South African Youth to the HIV/AIDS Epidemic: A Nation Wide Survey." *AIDS Care*, 16 (5): 606–619.

Allanise Cloete and Leickness Chisamu Simbayi

AIM. *See* American Indian Movement.

American Indian Movement (AIM). Native Americans have been united by a number of organizations focused on promoting their unique concerns. The National Congress of American Indians, the National Tribal Chairmen's Association, the National Indian Youth Council, and the American Indian Movement (AIM) collectively form the most modern Native American movement. In contrast to the other movements, AIM gained support in urban areas, nonreservation rural areas, and on reservations where tradition and ethnicity were not emphasized. Furthermore, it was considered to be a largely militant movement patterned after the Black Panther Party.

Formally founded in 1968 in Minneapolis, Minnesota, the American Indian Movement (AIM) was created with the purpose of protecting the rights of urban Native Americans facing poverty and police oppression. As AIM evolved into an organization, it began to emphasize the need for a national Native American identity and started to bring attention to a wide range of societal issues important to Native Americans including but not limited to the following: discrimination and police harassment, economic independence, control over natural resources, political autonomy of tribal reservations, revital-

ization of traditional culture and spirituality, and education of young Native American children.

The American Indian Movement was co-founded by Dennis Banks, Clyde Bellecourt, Herb Prowess, Eddie Benton-Banai, George Mitchell, and others. Later, Russell Means became one of AIM's main spokespersons. AIM's primary mission was to ensure the fulfillment of treaties that were made with the United States. During its existence, AIM has successfully brought lawsuits against the federal government for the protection of rights of native nations guaranteed in treaties. Demonstration, confrontation, and occupation were methods used to draw attention to the causes. Often these protests resulted in violence, arrests, federal prosecution, and the imprisonment of leaders of the American Indian Movement. In many cases, the militant methods used to draw attention to AIM's cause were considered dangerous forms of protest that alienated potential supporters of Native Americans. Some of the more notable protests organized by the American Indian Movement between the years of 1969 and 1973 include, but are not limited to, the following:

Occupation of Alcatraz Island. On November 11, 1969, fourteen Native American students briefly occupied Alcatraz, an abandoned federal prison in California, to bring attention to the educational needs of Native Americans that were exposed when the American Indian Center in San Francisco burned on November 1, 1969. On November 20, 1969, between eighty and one hundred Native Americans occupied the island. The occupation of Alcatraz served as a catalyst for gaining recognition for the American Indian Movement.

Trail of Broken Treaties. American Indian Movement leaders organized caravans beginning in Seattle, Washington, and San Francisco, California, in October 1972 that ended in Washington, D.C., during November 1972 with the week-long occupation of the Bureau of Indian Affairs (BIA) headquarters. The purpose of the event was to present a twenty-point manifesto providing ideas for the reorganization of the BIA and demanding the appointment of a committee to review treaty violations. At first the U.S. government agreed to the surrender terms but later denied the manifesto request for a committee to review treaty violations and prosecuted those involved with the occupation of the BIA headquarters. After this occupation government support was withdrawn from AIM survival schools in Minnesota, and AIM was classified by the Federal Bureau of Investigation (FBI) as an extremist organization.

Occupation of Wounded Knee, South Dakota. Local tribal groups on the Pine Ridge Reservation of the Ogallala Sioux contacted American Indian Movement leaders in a retaliatory move against the current tribal chairman who opposed the AIM movement. AIM activists were summoned to assist them in addressing corruption within the local tribal council and Bureau of Indian Affairs (BIA). Deplorable social conditions on the reservation added to the reservation's hostile political environment. A seventy-two-day occupation ensued, and later there was military engagement with federal officers. It is estimated that approximately 200 activists and 300 federal agents were involved in the siege. Activists ended the occupation after a negotiation based on the government's promise to discuss the Fort Laramie treaty of 1868 (a treaty viewed by many as granting sovereignty to the Sioux nation). However, there was never serious discussion of the 1868 treaty, and a backlash against the activists began on the reservation and across the nation. Eight months of criminal trials resulted from the occupation's events.

After these large protests, AIM lost its potency and support base largely because of dwindling human resources, financial support, and increasing disapproval of its selection of protest tactics. Although it lacked the membership of the original formal movement, the American Indian Movement members continued to draw attention to their cause during 1978 by organizing "The Longest Walk," a walk from San Francisco, California, to Washington, D.C., to protest anti–Native American legislation.

Scholars feel AIM's effectiveness may have dwindled because of a lack of efficient resource mobilization. In other words, the founders may have been more focused on the big picture than on the daily processes needed to maintain the organization's stability. In addition, the political climate of the United States during the 1960s may have been more conducive to the rise of this militant group than the political climate during other decades. For example, the 1960s are characterized as a dynamic decade of increased public protests and free speech. Whether protests were organized around social issues, the civil rights of minorities, opposition to wars, or the once-mandatory military draft, society's young adults began to openly question the status quo in the United States and the world. In other words, society began to look more favorably upon questioning the authority and decisions of leaders. A political climate favorable to inquiry about social issues prompted minority groups who had been silent for decades to raise their voices and draw attention to their situations either through the use of nonviolent or militant tactics. In many cases, minority groups chose to unite their voices by forming an organization to serve as a collective voice; such was the case with Native Americans and AIM.

At present, AIM exists as a network of independent regional chapters that are loosely affiliated nationally. Most recently, leaders of the American Indian Movement have been instrumental in organizing protests that oppose the use of native symbols, images, and names as mascots for collegiate and professional sports teams.

In general, the modern Native American movement can be credited with drawing attention to the need for education about cultural practices and instilling a sense of cultural identity and community in tribal youth. Tribal leaders do not want to perpetuate stereotypes of their people. Instead, tribal leaders want to increase understanding, acceptance, and appreciation of their culture. In fact, community and school-based cultural programs that include native language, history, and art are beginning to make their way into mainstream educational curricula and community programming. While learning to treasure their cultural traditions and understand the injustices of the past, young adults are encouraged to overcome adversity by becoming upstanding tribal leaders. Going on to higher education, giving back to their reservation communities, or taking ownership for decisions that affect their futures are three of the ways some Native American young adults are being taught to assist in the advancement of their tribal communities.

See also Native American Youth; Social Justice; Zapatista Rebellion (Mexico).

Recommended Reading

American Indian Movement (AIM). See http://www.aimovement.org.

Bonney, R. A. (1977). "The Role of AIM Leaders in Indian Nationalism." *American Indian Quarterly*, 3: 207–223.

Deloria, V. (1974). *Behind the Trail of Broken Treaties: A Declaration of Independence*. New York: Delacorte Press.

Dewing, R. (1985). *Wounded Knee: The Meaning and Significance of the Second Incident*. New York: Irvington Publishers.

Eisinger, P. K. (1973). "The Conditions of Protest Behavior in American Cities." *American Political Science Review*, 67: 11–28.

Howard, J., ed. (1970). *Awakening Minorities: American Indians, Mexican Americans, Puerto Ricans*. New Brunswick, NJ: Transaction Books.

Matthiessen, P. (1983). *In the Spirit of Crazy Horse*. New York: Viking Press.

McAdam, D. (1982). *Political Processes and the Development of Black Insurgency, 1930–1979*. Chicago: University of Chicago Press.

O'Brien, S. (1989). *American Indian Tribal Governments*. Norman: University of Oklahoma Press.

Orr, S. A. (2001). "Southerners." *Southern Living*, 36 (5): 44.

Ortiz, R. D. (1984). *Indians of the Americas: Human Rights and Self Determination*. New York: Praeger.

Stotik, J., Shriver, T. E., and Cable, S. (1994). "Social Control and Movement Outcome: The Case of AIM." *Sociological Focus*, 27 (1): 53–66.

Weyler, R. (1982). *Blood of the Land: The Government and Corporate War Against the American Indian Movement*. New York: Everest House.

Wilkins, D. E. (2002). *American Indian Politics and the American Political System*. Lanham, MD: Rowman & Littlefield.

Heather M. Jones

AmeriCorps. The Clinton administration created AmeriCorps in 1993 as a federal youth-service organization. Since then, AmeriCorps has become one of the most influential and effective mechanisms for involving American youth in community and national service. AmeriCorps "members," as volunteers are called, do everything from running literacy programs in elementary schools to environmental cleanup and designing urban renewal projects. AmeriCorps not only involves young people in the design and implementation of its projects; youth are one of the primary target groups for its various assistance programs.

Prior to AmeriCorps, the Commission on National and Community Service sponsored several models of youth service, including the Delta Service Corps (which sponsored programs in the Mississippi Delta region), and the time was ripe for the consideration of a national program.

The creation of AmeriCorps owes much to the personal support of Bill Clinton. Prior to his inauguration, focus groups had brought to his attention the increasing cost of tertiary education, thereby influencing Clinton to advocate a service program that would help pay for college.

President Clinton proposed the AmeriCorps program on March 1, 1993, the 32nd anniversary of the day John F. Kennedy announced his Peace Corps plan. AmeriCorps was intended to function as a domestic Peace Corps in that both agencies encourage service and reward for this service. AmeriCorps members work only on U.S. soil and serve for ten to twelve months, while Peace Corps members serve abroad for two years.

AmeriCorps is one of three components that are overseen by the Corporation for National and Community Service (CNCS),

Teenagers carry an AmeriCorps banner in a Martin Luther King Day Parade. *Courtesy of Skjold Photographs.*

the other two components being Senior Corps and Learn and Serve America. George W. Bush, in his January 29, 2002, State of the Union address, announced his "call to service" initiative. In tandem with this initiative, CNCS and its affiliated service programs, in addition to the Peace Corps and the Citizen Corps, are now part of the USA Freedom Corps.

The mission of AmeriCorps is to support and enhance local service programs, by using the following four guiding concepts:

1. *Getting things done*—Meeting communities' educational, public safety, and environmental needs.
2. *Strengthening communities*—Bringing people together from many diverse backgrounds in the community to solve local problems.
3. *Encouraging responsibility*—Using service and civic education to help local people take responsibility for meeting their own needs, rather than relying on others.

4. *Expanding opportunity*—Creating expanded opportunities for employment and education for AmeriCorps volunteers (members) through educational awards for services provided.

AmeriCorps programs, which begin in January, June, or September (CNCS 1 2003) are run by volunteers. Each year approximately 50,000 young people aged seventeen years or older volunteer for AmeriCorps. The members work twenty to forty hours each week. They cooperate with local, regional, or national organizations, such as Habitat for Humanity, Teach for America, and the American Red Cross to meet the needs of various communities. In return for their service, volunteers earn an annual living stipend, educational awards, and health benefits.

Three programs comprise the larger AmeriCorps structure: AmeriCorps* State and National, AmeriCorps* National Civilian Conservation Corps (NCCC), and AmeriCorps* VISTA. The focus areas of these groups are different, and each works with different types of local organizations.

AmeriCorps* State and National is the largest of the programs. Annually, 20,000 volunteers are placed in local service programs operated by about 21,000 nonprofits, state and local governments, and colleges and universities, as well as partnership programs between these groups. Volunteers do a great deal of work with literacy and education, such as teaching reading and writing to grade-school students and running after-school mentoring and tutoring programs.

AmeriCorps* National Civilian Conservation Corps (NCCC) is similar to the Civilian Conservation Corps started by Franklin Delano Roosevelt in the 1930s. This branch of AmeriCorps is a full-time residential program, which annually employs approximately 1,200 volunteers aged eighteen to twenty-four in team-based projects related to homeland security, the environment, and disaster relief. These teams are comprised of ten to fourteen members and are based on five college campuses in different parts of the United States. Training for NCCC members incorporates aspects of civilian, as well as military, service.

AmeriCorps* VISTA evolved out of the preexisting VISTA (Volunteers in Service to America) program, begun in the 1960s. VISTA has about 6,000 members and focuses on the eradication of poverty. Members of this AmeriCorps program work in low-income communities and their work addresses the issues of homelessness, education, health, and nutrition. VISTA members work in over 1,100 local programs, 15 percent of which are faith-based initiatives.

However diverse AmeriCorps programs may be, all programs focus on education, environment, public safety, human needs, and homeland security. These elements are deemed essential to ensure the well-being of the average American citizen.

Education has been one of the most popular areas of service for AmeriCorps members, who work in either rural or urban settings. AmeriCorps supervisors coordinate the types of service programs to be pursued with the host institutions and maintain contact with the members through weekly or daily contacts. Members are matched with schools depending on the skills needed by that school as well as the number of members required. AmeriCorps members assist in schools by tutoring and mentoring all ages. For example, some members coordinate adult education programs, while others conduct after-school and vacation activities.

Environmental programs have two main foci: maintenance projects and public education. In regards to the latter, members inform the local public about the need for such environmental programs, as well as the methods involved in their implementation. These projects often include health and safety seminars about environmental hazards. There is meticulous planning and monitoring involved in projects for the environment, and these programs usually deploy members in teams or crews under the direct supervision of AmeriCorps managers.

Members working with public-safety programs provide services to victims of domestic violence and their children. AmeriCorps members provide these services in the following three ways: 1) working in prosecutor offices as advocates for victims against their attackers in courtroom processes, 2) working at crisis centers to provide victims and their children with the available services or information about services, as well as counseling and referrals, and 3) working in civil courts to provide guidance for victims as they make decisions about the legal processes they wish to pursue. Public-safety programs also advocate drug-abuse prevention, improvement of relations between communities and their local police, provision of assistance for victims of violence and abuse, and the distribution of informational materials about safety measures to avoid victimization. Members also work to raise awareness for people at risk.

Human-needs projects are designed to alleviate the burdens of those who earn low incomes. Volunteers in human needs often work on a one-to-one basis with community members. AmeriCorps members provide three main spheres of service: (1) volunteers who work on independent-living projects for the elderly, disabled, and for low-income families, (2) volunteers who assist in the provision of preventative health services and the distribution of related informational materials to low-income families, and (3) volunteers who work as case managers for low-income families and the elderly on housing issues.

Homeland security is the newest of the focus areas for AmeriCorps service. Since 1995, AmeriCorps has worked with the Federal Emergency Management Agency (FEMA) to respond to dozens of emergencies. In the aftermath of September 11, 2001, President George W. Bush decided to increase the involvement of AmeriCorps members in homeland-security activities. Bush developed the Domestic Preparedness and Response Corps (DPRC) through which AmeriCorps members train and educate citizens in how to respond most effectively to an attack or other security-related emergency. Some of the DPRC's activities include organizing neighborhood patrols, providing emergency health information, and developing disaster response plans.

Two of the stated goals of AmeriCorps are to provide volunteers with the opportunity to attend college and to develop "an ethic of service and civic responsibility." Young people who volunteer for AmeriCorps service receive educational rewards of $4,725, which can be used to pay for college, vocational training, or to repay student loans for those who have already attended college. Eighty-five percent of AmeriCorps members surveyed stated that they would use (or had used) the educational awards AmeriCorps provides to enter university or pay off student loans. Many volunteers also received certification for skills they had mastered during

their terms of service, such as carpentry and child development.

Members hone invaluable skills through the implementation of their projects and gain confidence in their capabilities by noting the observable differences they make in the lives of their fellow community members. According to an independent evaluation of AmeriCorps conducted by Aguirre International, AmeriCorps members reported significant gains in several important skill areas: communications, interpersonal skills, analytical problem solving, knowledge of informational technology, and understanding of organizational structure and functioning.

Most AmeriCorps volunteers stated that it was important for them to serve at a job in which they could be of use to the community or could help solve social and economic problems.

One of the main benefits for groups that host AmeriCorps programs is an expansion in local service capacity. Data from over 500 AmeriCorps* State and National programs for the year 1997–1998 indicates that more than 17.6 million people benefited from the services AmeriCorps provided. About 2 million students received educational services and 250,000 children received care, instruction, or immunization. These are services that would not have been feasible had AmeriCorps not been involved—and these services have proved effective.

Another benefit for groups that have partnered with AmeriCorps is an increase in the quality of service. Jumpstart, a program that partners college work-study students with preschoolers in Head Start classrooms, expanded from eleven to thirty sites with the support of AmeriCorps. Also, about 58 percent of students tutored by AmeriCorps increased their reading level by a full year, and 39 percent were reading at their expected grade level, even though most were below their expected reading level when they started the tutoring with AmeriCorps members. Learn and Serve Higher Education observed major improvements in grade-school students' test scores, counseling and community service activities for juvenile offenders, and health planning for certain organizations, due to help from their AmeriCorps tutors, mentors, and volunteers.

The presence of AmeriCorps increases the likelihood of more volunteer service to nonprofit organizations than would normally be available. Small organizations have often been unable to spend the time, money, and energy to properly recruit new volunteers to their community development projects. Recently, AmeriCorps* Vista recruited approximately 283,000 volunteers, who worked for a total of 6.6 million hours at nonprofit organizations.

The formation of new partnerships and collaborations has also been beneficial to the growth of AmeriCorps projects. Interagency collaboration was one of the founding goals of AmeriCorps. Over the past ten years AmeriCorps has been able to bring together many organizations that had not previously worked together. AmeriCorps has linked homelessness organizations with many social-service providers and has created bridges between schools, service organizations, and businesses. The majority of organizations that have been involved with AmeriCorps members felt that working with AmeriCorps helped to strengthen community collaboration between itself and other agencies or institutions, and 70 percent stated that AmeriCorps had done "a good job" in creating innovations in provision of direct service to beneficiaries:

AmeriCorps has proven to be one of the few accessible means by which young people are able to get involved in national service activities in their communities in the United States. Volunteers are given the opportunity to be part of a positive and challenging social-change movement, contributing to serious work on important issues such as education, aid to the homeless, and environmental protection.

AmeriCorps began as the dynamic idea of an inspired presidential candidate who wanted to help young people with more affordable education, while also addressing local service needs around the United States. In the years since 1994 when its activities began, AmeriCorps has emerged as a comprehensive and successful national service program. It has trained and employed some 350,000 volunteers and created new or expanded social services in hundreds of agencies and small organizations. Volunteers have gained personal benefits in terms of education and skills, and communities have benefited through increased services, new partnerships, and a model for future success.

See also Jesuit Volunteer Corps (JVC); National and Community Service; Social Responsibility; Transnational Youth Activism; Volunteerism.

Recommended Reading

Aguirre International (1999). "An Evaluation of AmeriCorps: Summary." *Aguirre 1*. San Mateo: Aguirre International.

Aguirre International (1999). "AmeriCorps* State/National Direct Five-Year Evaluation Report." *Aguirre 2*. San Mateo: Aguirre International.

Commission on National and Community Service (1993). "What You Can Do for Your Country: Report of the Commission on National and Community Service." Washington, D.C.: Commission on National and Community Service.

Corporation for National and Community Service (CNCS) (2003). "AmeriCorps: Factsheet." *CNCS 1*. New York: USA Freedom Corps.

Corporation for National and Community Service (CNCS) (March 27, 2003). "AmeriCorps and Senior Corps Help AmeriCorps Stay Alert." *CNCS 2*. See http://www.nationalservice.org/news/pr/032703.htm.

Jastrzab, Joanne, Bernstein, Lawrence, Litin, Lisa, Brant-Campbell, Sytske, Stickney, Eric, and Giordano, Leanne (2001). "Serving Country and Community: A Study of Service in AmeriCorps." Washington, D.C.: Abt Associates.

Karasik, Judy (2003). "National and Community Service: Ten Years of National Service." Washington, D.C.: Innovations in Civic Participation.

Stroud, Susan (December 12, 2003). Interview.

Van Til, John (2000). "The Case of AmeriCorps: Conflict and Consensus in the Civil Society/Governance Relation." Speech, Rutgers University, Camden, NJ.

Waldman, Steven (1995). *The Bill: How the Adventure of Clinton's National Service Bill*

Reveal What Is Corrupt, Comic, and Cynical— and Noble—About Washington. New York: Viking.

Ariel Wyckoff, Kara-Kaye Colley, Brett Alessi, Grace Hollister, and Susan Stroud

Animal Rights. The modern animal rights movement is largely a product of the raised social and ethical consciousness of the mid- to late-twentieth century. Some proponents of animal rights were influenced by the civil rights or women's rights movements in the 1960s and 1970s. Long before these movements, however, religious leaders, philosophers, and children's advocates were thinking and writing about the treatment of animals. Henry Salt's *Animals' Rights* of 1892 was one such work. The American Society for the Prevention of Cruelty to Animals (ASPCA), initially founded in 1866 by Henry Bergh to protect children, was the first American organization to concern itself with the welfare of working animals. The ASPCA spurred the passage of the first effective animal-cruelty law in the state of New York. The Humane Society of the United States was first officially recognized as a group in 1954, working on issues such as companion animal overpopulation and slaughter reform.

Today's American animal rights movement began in earnest with small groups voicing their opposition to animal experimentation, the use of animals for fur, and the treatment of farmed animals. The first modern animal rights book to gain widespread attention was Australian philosopher Peter Singer's *Animal Liberation,* first printed in 1975, which helped to launch the animal rights movement as we know it today.

People for the Ethical Treatment of Animals (PETA), which is now the largest animal rights group in the world, was founded in 1980. PETA uncovered the abuse of animals in experiments in 1981 with the precedent-setting Silver Spring monkeys case. This resulted in the first arrest and conviction of an animal experimenter in the United States on charges of cruelty to animals, the first confiscation of abused laboratory animals, and the first U.S. Supreme Court victory for animals in laboratories.

People who support animal rights believe that animals are not ours to use for food, clothing, entertainment, experimentation, or any other exploitative purpose. They believe that people should consider the best interests of animals first and foremost and that this principle should be upheld regardless of whether the animal is a cute, useful to humans, or endangered.

There is a difference between supporters of the animal rights movement and those who work for animal welfare. Those who endorse the latter accept that animals have interests but allow those interests to be traded away if the benefits to humans outweigh the sacrifice. Supporters of the animal welfare movement believe that animals can be used as, for example, food, as long as "humane" guidelines are followed. Animal rights theories say that animals, like humans, have interests that cannot be sacrificed or traded away to benefit others. The animal rights movement operates under the belief that animals should have the right to equal consideration of their interests. For instance, a dog certainly has an interest in not having pain inflicted on him or her unnecessarily. We are, therefore, obliged to take that interest into consideration. However, animals don't always have the same rights as humans because their interests are not always the same as ours, and some rights, such as voting, would be irrelevant to animals.

Since its founding, PETA has taken these principles and widened the scope of its activism. With locations in North America, Europe, India, Asia, and the Pacific, PETA's campaign actions range from protests against the abuses of factory-farmed animals to promoting vegetarianism to protecting companion animals. PETA also tries to appeal to all age-groups. PETA2. com, a Web site and Internet community aimed at activists in their teens to mid-twenties, was launched in 2002 and gave young adults an outlet where their views could be made public.

Young animal rights activists march to promote the benefits of vegetarianism. *Courtesy of Skjold Photographs.*

The animal rights movement attempts to get people to look at their actions toward animals. They recommend that people consider actions that protect animals (e.g., maintain a vegan diet; purchase consumer goods that have been tested for safety *without* the use of animals; avoid animal-based clothing such as fur, wool, silk, and leather; avoid participating in forms of entertainment that rely on performances by animals constrained in unnatural settings who are forced to perform). Through protests, boycott, civil disobedience, and educational outreach programs, activist groups have made major strides toward animal liberation, particularly in the past fifty years. Some of the gains include the development of nonanimal laboratory testing methods; the proliferating of human-only circuses; stronger anti-cruelty laws, particularly on the state level; an increase in prosecutions of those who have abused animals; and growth of the vegetarian food industry.

See also Global Justice Activism; Social Movements; Social Networks; Social Responsibility.

Recommended Reading

Achor, A. B. (1996). *Animal Rights: A Beginner's Guide.* Yellow Springs, OH: WriteWare.
Singer, P. (1975). *Animal Liberation.* New York: HarperCollins.

Marci Hansen

Anti-Nazi Youth Resistance. The young dissenters who opposed the Nazi regime were remarkably resilient in the face of Nazi oppression and manipulation. Despite the threat of punishment and the pressure to conform, many young people found ways to resist Nazi tyranny. At times this resiliency arose from a youthful rejection of authority, but it was also motivated by a well-developed ethical awareness. Youth resistance in Nazi Germany was not a cohesive movement. It was manifested in a variety of forms that ranged from politically nondescript youth cliques to

Adolf Hitler is saluted by members of the Hitler Youth in Erfurt, Germany, in 1933. Anti-Nazi youth resistance was also prevalent, as this entry describes. *Library of Congress.*

well-structured groups with politicized world views.

Since the late-nineteenth century, youth had held a valued place in German culture. Germany was home to thousands of youth associations, clubs, and leagues. Although the vast majority of these youth groups were associated with particular political and religious organizations, many others developed independently of any supervisory organizations. These relatively unstructured groups eventually came to represent a youth movement commonly referred to as the *Wandervögel* (wandering birds). To a large extent the movement was a reaction to the moral rigidity of conservative Wilhelmian society. Young people sought escape by slipping away from their jobs, schools, and parents for hiking expeditions in the countryside. Characteristically, many of the youth groups rejected not only conservative bourgeois values but modern urban life as well. Typically, the *Wandervögel* romanticized traditional pre-industrial folk art and culture. The movement did not survive the carnage of World War I when

thousands of young men lost their lives. Following Germany's defeat, many young men, now disillusioned and militarized, found themselves reentering the ranks of German society. In the years of the Weimar Republic, many of these still young men increasingly found their place in the organized national youth leagues (*Bündische Jugend*). Others would join various political and religious youth leagues such as the Catholic Young Men's Association (*Katholischer Jungmännerverband*, KJVD), German Communist Youth Organization (*Kommunistischer Jugendverband Deutschlands*, KJVD), and the Socialist Workers' Youth (*Sozialistische Arbeiterjugend*, SAJ). Although the philosophical currents of the German youth movement remained influential in many of the national youth leagues, the *Wandervögel* group itself never fully regrouped after the war. A void remained where the independent youth movement once stood.

Various political organizations formed or renewed their youth groups after the war. Perhaps the most fateful was that of the National Socialist German Workers' Party (*Nationalsozialistische Deutsche Arbeiterpartei*, NSDAP). The NSDAP understood the potential force that youth represented in German society. In 1921 the Youth League of the National Socialist Party was formed; the organization was later renamed the Hitler Youth (*Hitler Jugend*, HJ). The HJ actually encompassed four major divisions. Males between the ages of ten and fourteen made up the *Jungvolk*; those between the ages of fourteen and eighteen were considered *Hitler Jugend*. Females were divided similarly; those between the ages of ten and fourteen were in the *Jungmädel*, and young women between the ages of fourteen and twenty-one were placed in the League of German Girls (*Bund Deutscher Mädchen*, BDM). Capitalizing on the frustrations of youth, the NSDAP began the HJ under a banner of rebellion. Young people were encouraged to defy their parents, teachers, and other authority figures when such individuals challenged Nazi views. Hitler Youth organized book burnings, challenged school teachers, and intimidated many of their adult neighbors. This new sense of power was a liberating experience for HJ members.

Having seduced young people through its rebellious rhetoric, the NSDAP turned its attention to solidifying its hold on their minds. The Nazi leadership focused on a critical area of youths' social development, their leisure time. The HJ bonded ideology to socialization through its many sponsored field trips, sporting events, and other extracurricular activities. During nighttime rallies, theatrical effects were used to give young people a sense of purpose. In this context youth stood not on the periphery of the Nazi movement but at its center. In addition to the political rallies, numerous film festivals drew youth in by the thousands. Accompanying this colonization of youth's leisure time was a massive propaganda effort. Wandering down a city street one was likely to encounter Nazi propaganda posters enticing boys and girls to join the movement. Images were used to imbue young people with a sense of agency.

The propaganda conveyed that youth stood at the forefront of a grand new movement in history. For many young people, joining the NSDAP's youth organization seemed like an opportunity to camp out forever.

Once the NSDAP consolidated its power in the Reichstag, all other youth organizations, with the exception of the Catholic youth leagues protected by Germany's concordat with the Vatican, were banned before the end of 1933. Employers and school officials pressured parents into enlisting their children in the HJ. Other youth organizations were offered the alternative of joining the HJ or disbanding. This process of consolidation resulted in an increase in the HJ's membership from 107,956 in 1932 to 3,577,565 in 1933 (Koch 1975). By March 1939, membership in the HJ was mandatory. National Socialist attempts to ideologically encode youth reflected Nazi indoctrination policies in general; however, the degree of attention paid to young people far exceeded that given to other segments of the population. Pressure to conform was also influenced by elements of terror. It is estimated that in the twelve years of Nazi rule over 3 million Germans were incarcerated. Thousands more were executed for the most trivial acts. Writing unfavorable remarks or speaking critically about the government could result in imprisonment, torture, or execution. Germans, regardless of their ideological views, were conscious of the state's police apparatus and the danger that nonconformity represented.

Despite the massive indoctrination effort by the NSDAP and the threat of punitive repercussions, many young people still rejected and confronted National Socialism. In the early years of the regime the vast majority of the young dissenters could be found in the disbanded political parties of the left. Although its membership stood at only 55,000, the members of the Communist Party's KJVD played a significant role in resisting Nazism (Zarusky 1997). The group held spontaneous demonstrations against the regime and actively dispensed anti-Nazi literature in cities like Berlin and Essen well into 1934. The young Social Democrats of the SAJ, although not as confrontational as the KJVD, also continued their political activities. After being disbanded by the Nazis, many members of the organization regrouped in leisure and hiking clubs like the Friends of Nature, where they maintained their political views and expressed their disaffection with the government (Zarusky 1997). In Bremen, for example, young Social Democrats in a Friends of Nature hiking club united with Communist youth to form a larger resistance network called the *Bremer Gruppe* (Bremen Group). The organization disbanded after its leaders were arrested in 1936 (Marßolek and Ott 1986). By the mid-thirties, increased police persecution led to the dissolution of most of these groups. Despite the liquidation of illegal youth organizations, youth dissent in Germany continued in a less structured milieu.

As early as 1937, youth began to seek each other out in unauthorized gatherings, clubs, and cliques. In Leipzig working-class youth joined groups like the Leipzig Hounds. Although spontaneous in its formation, the group appeared to be influenced by young Communists. The Hounds acknowledged one another with the Russian Youth Pioneers' greeting and listened to illegal broadcasts from Moscow (Zarusky 1997). The Hounds were precursors to a trend that developed in the later years of the Third Reich. Groups of working-class youth, most between the ages of sixteen and nineteen, began to consolidate in a variety of cliques and gangs. The majority of these groups identified themselves collectively as the Edelweiss Pirates. Increasing numbers of unauthorized youth cliques appeared throughout Germany in the late 1930s and early 1940s. They were known by such names as the Black Hand Group, Death Head Group, and Navajos. Typically, they congregated in parks, cafés, and other areas free from Nazi supervision. On weekends groups of these working-class boys and girls banded together and traveled about the countryside. The Pirates came to constitute a youth subculture with a shared identity that was expressed in their manner of dress, forms of cultural expression, and their celebration of freedom. The Pirates had a peculiar style that was antithetical to the Nazi image of youth. They typically wore checked shirts, dark short trousers, white stockings, and a variety of jewelry that usually included metal edelweiss flowers on their lapels (Peukert 1987).

The Edelweiss Pirates were not content to simply slip away from the control of adults and other authorities; instead, many chose to confront National Socialism. Pirates were infamous for attacking Hitler Youth patrols. These confrontations were often violent, and in some cases combatants were wounded or even killed (Becker 1946). Such incidents might lead some to believe that the Pirates' actions were merely examples of teenage hooliganism; however, when considered alongside their politicized rhetoric their motivations appear more complex. The Pirates demonstrated a politicized idealism that rejected Nazi authority, as the following lyrics demonstrate:

> Hark the hearty fellow sing!
> Strum the banjo, pluck that string!
> And the lasses all join in.
> We're going to get rid of Hitler,
> and he can't do a thing....
> Hitler's power may lay us low,
> and keep us locked in chains.
> But we will smash the chains one day.
> We'll be free again....
> We march by the banks of Ruhr and Rhine
> and smash the Hitler Youth in twain.
> Our song is freedom, love, and life,
> We're Pirates of the Edelweiss.

—Edelweiss Pirate Song (Peukert 1987)

Although lacking a structured political ideology, the Edelweiss demonstrated a political stance. Actions that in normal times might be attributed to simple juvenile delinquency had serious ideological connotations in the Third Reich. The fact that the Edelweiss Pirates rejected Nazi authority in the face of pressure and repercussions is a testament to their ethical awareness. This political disaffection toward the regime became more apparent at the end of the war when a number of Pirates were involved in raids on German military supply camps. On November 10, 1944, Barthel Schink, the sixteen-year-old leader of the Cologne Edelweiss Pirates, was hanged with thirteen compatriots for his involvement in raids. The types of resistance carried out by the Pirates ranged from common vandalism to overtly militant resistance. The fact that many of these youth chose a political tone for their actions indicates a conscious concern with the regime's despotic nature. Many of them could have carried out rebellious acts without political connotations. By choosing to denigrate National Socialism and Hitler, they placed themselves directly in the line of persecution.

Youth resistance to Nazism was not restricted to the actions of working-class youth. Middle-class youth also demonstrated resistance, albeit in a less politicized manner. The "swing movement" took shape in the German cabaret and nightclub scene in the late 1930s and managed to survive through World War II. Characteristically, swing youth enjoyed jazz music as well as American and British styles of dress. The swing youth represented all that was anathema to the Nazi ideal of youth. This is apparent if one contrasts a typical description of "swing kids" to that of the militant and masculine ideal of the Hitler Youth. The following appeared in a Hitler Youth report from 1942:

The predominant form of dress consisted of long, often checked English sports jackets, shoes with thick crepe soles, showy scarves, Anthony Eden hats, and an umbrella on the arm whatever the weather, and, as an insignia, a dress-shirt button worn in the buttonhole with a jeweled stone. The girls too favored a long overflowing hairstyle. Their eyebrows were penciled, they wore lipstick and the nails were lacquered. The bearing and behavior of the clique resembled their dress (Peukert 1987).

By the early 1940s the swing movement had a presence in most major German cities. Boys and girls drawn to this subculture challenged the conformist ideal of youth advocated by National Socialism. Militant haircuts and uniforms gave way to long hair and stylish clothing. More importantly, these young people were embracing a jazz subculture that was, according to Nazi officials, the product of racially inferior blacks and Jews. Authorities were further enraged that boys and girls were interacting beyond the gaze of adult supervision. Ignoring the warnings of authorities, swing youth chose to maintain their uninhibited jazz lifestyle, thus challenging Nazi indoctrination efforts. In this sense they represented a cultural-resistance movement. Breaking the swing movement became a pet project of SS leader Heinrich Himmler, and by the end of the war many of the swing kids found themselves in Nazi prisons and work camps.

In addition to the semi-political opposition of the Pirates and the cultural defiance of the swing kids, spontaneous anti-Nazi youth resistance also manifested itself in more clearly defined ideological forms. The White Rose group is a clear example of this type of resistance. The organization's core membership, Hans Scholl, Sophie Scholl, Willi Graf, Christoph Probst and Alexander Scmorrel, were medical students from Munich University. The initial group consisted mainly of students of Kurt Huber, a philosophy professor in the university. The origin of the group's name remains unclear, but it is rumored to have been taken from one of the members' favorite novels. Between June 1942 and February 1943 they carried out a large-scale anti-Nazi propaganda campaign. Although the core membership was located in Munich, students in other German universities also became involved in the leaflet campaign. The group's leader appears to have been Hans Scholl, a medical student. Hans, a former member of the Hitler Youth, became disenchanted with Nazi conformity and intolerance. Later, as a young recruit on the eastern front, he was further disillusioned by the atrocities he witnessed. Together with his sister Sophie and several classmates, Hans distributed a series of six leaflets that criticized the German War effort, drew attention to the plight of Jews, and called upon the German people to overthrow the Nazi regime. The very first leaflet addressed the issue of Nazi crimes as follows:

Nothing is so unworthy of a civilized nation as allowing itself to be "governed" without opposition by an irresponsible clique that has yielded to base instinct. It is certain that today every honest German is ashamed of his government. Who among us has any conception of the dimensions of shame that will befall us and our children when one day the veil has fallen from our eyes and the most horrible of crimes—crimes that infinitely outdistance every human measure—reach the light of day (Scholl 1970)?

The White Rose's campaign came to an end on February 18, 1943, when Hans and Sophie were arrested. A porter employed by the university spotted the two dumping a suitcase of leaflets onto a school courtyard. The arrests were highly publicized and the government was determined to make an example of the students. Roland Freisler, the grand inquisitor of the Reich, was flown in to perform the trial. After three days of court proceedings Hans, Sophie, and their friend Christoph were beheaded, a form of execution reserved for German citizens. Several months later, Professor Huber would meet a similar fate.

The White Rose students were not the only group of young Germans who would lose their lives attempting to rally fellow Germans against the regime. Helmuth Hubener and his friends Gehard Duwer, Karl-Heinz Schnibbe, and Rudi Wobbe also engaged in an anti-Nazi leaflet campaign two years earlier in Hamburg. The young people, with the exception of Rudi Wobbe, were members of the Church of Latter-Day Saints. The fact that most of the clique's members belonged to a religious minority in Germany may have influenced their actions, but the primary motivation behind their actions appears to have been Helmuth's obsession with the truth. Together with his friends, Helmuth transcribed illegal allied radio broadcasts and then disseminated the transcripts in local mailboxes, phone booths, and train stations. Helmuth also produced his own propaganda in addition to the transcripts. His leaflets shared much in common with those of the White Rose group; they called attention to the terrorist nature of National Socialism. One leaflet read:

German boys! Do you know the country without freedom, the country of terror and tyranny? Yes, you know it well but are afraid to talk about it. They have intimidated you to such an extent that you don't dare talk for fear of reprisals. Yes, you are right; it is Germany—Hitler Germany! Through their unscrupulous terror tactics against young and old, men and women, they have succeeded in making you spineless puppets to do their bidding (Holmes and Keele 1995).

Like the students of Munich University, seventeen-year-old Helmuth was decapitated on August 27, 1943. His young associates received prison sentences. The Edelweiss Pirates, swing youth, White Rose students, Helmuth Hubener group, and the many other young people who resisted the regime differed in the manner their resistance took; however, they each sought to maintain an independent identity outside of National Socialism. Resistance for the swing youth was primarily motivated by their desire to maintain a unique identity, but for the Pirates, White Rose students, and Helmuth Hubener group, resistance was fueled by ethical convictions. All these youth groups valued freedom over conformity.

What accounts for the sudden growth of youth cliques in the late 1930s and early 1940s? Disillusionment with the supposed revolutionary ideas of National Socialism is a primary factor. In the early days of National Socialism, the Hitler Youth group was presented as a revolutionary movement, an opportunity for youth to strike out against conventional authority. As the years progressed, the HJ became increasingly more demanding of young people's time and energy. The rebellious rhetoric and imagery of the organization lost its influence as

German society became increasingly conformist under the Third Reich. Having failed to maintain the interest of youth, the true nature of the regime became more visible. This development was no doubt compounded toward the end of the war, as the NSDAP's massive propaganda campaign became more transparent. Soldiers returning from the front lines of the war brought with them stories of defeat; such accounts conflicted with Nazi propaganda efforts. These factors contributed to a growing opposition against the regime by many of Germany's youth. The desire to escape the confines of the Hitler Youth and the party machine triggered more altruistic notions within young people. The majority of these young resisters had spent their formative years under the shadow of a massive propaganda machine that dominated their schooling and leisure time. Despite this intense programming, the Nazi regime was unable to completely control the consciences of all of Germany's youth. Many would resist the regime even at the cost of their lives. The youth resisters in Nazi Germany are not only significant because of their cultural, ethical, and political resiliency, they also impart an important lesson regarding the value of youth activism. Young people can play an important and positive role in society, this is evinced by the actions of those young people who chose to resist and confront Nazi tyranny while so many adults retreated into passivity.

See also Antiwar Activism; Eastern Europe, Youth and Citizenship in; Europe, Comparing Youth Activism in; European Identity and Citizenship; Immigrant Youth in Europe—Turks in Germany; State and Youth, The; Student Political Activism; Zionist Youth Organizations.

Recommended Reading

Becker, H. (1946). *German Youth: Bond or Free.* London: K. Paul, Trench, Trubner and Co.
Hoffman, P. (1977). *The History of the German Resistance, 1933–1945.* Trans. Richard Barry. Cambridge, MA: Harvard University Press.
Holmes, B., and Keele, A. (1995). *When Truth Was Treason: German Youth against Hitler.* Chicago: University of Illinois Press.
Horn, D. (1973). "Youth Resistance in the Third Reich." *Journal of Social History*, 7: 26–50.
Koch, H. W. (1975). *The Hitler Youth: Origins and Development, 1922–1945.* London: Macdonald and Jane's.
Marßolek, I., and Ott, R. (1986). *Bremen im Dritten Reich: Anpassung, Widerstand, Verfolgung.* Bremen: C. Schünemann.
Peukert, D. (1987). *Inside Nazi Germany: Conformity, Opposition, and Racism in Everyday Life.* Trans. Richard Deveson. New Haven and London: Yale University Press.
Scholl, I. (1970). *Students against Tyranny.* Trans. Arthur R. Schultz. Middletown, CT: Wesleyan Press.
Zarusky, J. (1997). "Youth Opposition." In *Encyclopedia of German Resistance to the Nazi Movement*, edited by W. Benz and W. Pehle. New York: Continuum.

Ron Van Cleef

Anti-Tobacco Youth Activism. Youth-led anti-tobacco activism is a movement to educate young people about the dangers of tobacco use and to empower them to take a stand against tobacco marketing campaigns that target teenagers. The Master Settlement Agreement—a landmark multi-state legal settlement against major tobacco companies to recover tobacco-related health care costs—spurred young people's creative energy to wage war against corporate tobacco and their products (i.e., bidis, cigarettes, cigars, kreteks, smokeless tobacco) by thinking outside of the box and sparking grassroots movements *by* teenagers *for* teenagers. In response to the tobacco companies' escalating investment in marketing to youth, young activists are striking back.

Findings from the Monitoring the Future survey reveal a steady decline in cigarette and smokeless tobacco use among eighth-, tenth-, and twelfth-grade students since its peak in 1996–1997; yet, a quarter of young people in the United States are still smoking when they graduate from high school. Furthermore, in the global context, one teen becomes addicted to tobacco every second.

The anti-tobacco youth movement can be subdivided into three principal domains: activism against corporate tobacco, participation in prevention efforts, and engagement in policy initiatives.

The growing popularity of smoking, especially among teenage girls, like the two sixteen-year-olds shown here, has helped spur youth anti-smoking activism. *Courtesy of Skjold Photographs.*

Activism against Corporate Tobacco

The success of corporate tobacco hinges upon addicting young people to tobacco products at an early age, thus increasing the odds of addicting young consumers for life. As a 1984 R. J. Reynolds memo states, "the renewal of the market stems almost entirely from eighteen-year-old smokers. No more than 5 percent of smokers start after age twenty-four" (Burrows 1984). Revealing and disturbing, this memo only came to light as a result of the Master Settlement Agreement.

The Master Settlement Agreement between corporate tobacco—Philip Morris, Brown & Williamson, Lorillard, R. J. Reynolds, Commonwealth Tobacco, and Liggett & Myers— and the attorneys general from forty-six states and U.S. territories: (1) restricts marketing and advertising tactics of corporate tobacco (e.g., brand-name sponsorship of activities, concerts, contests that have a youth audience); (2) establishes policies to restrict youth access to tobacco products; (3) requires that the industry provide funds for smoking cessation and prevention programs; and (4) requires a corporate commitment to compliance with the Agreement.

By making youth their target market, corporate tobacco secures an addicted customer base that will likely continue into adulthood. The motivation of youth activists stems from their response to the tobacco industry's attempt to dupe them and their peers into taking up the destructive habit of using tobacco products. Alluring advertisements in magazines with high levels of teen readership and well-placed cigarette smoking in PG-13 movies are just a few of the marketing strategies that corporate tobacco overtly and covertly employs to attract a young customer base. New generations of youth activists are not, however, willing to stand by idly as corporate tobacco targets youth culture. Instead, youth are organizing grassroots efforts to fight back. The truth® campaign is a prime example.

The truth campaign is the youth-engagement arm of the American Legacy Foundation, an independent public-health organization established by the Master Settlement Agreement that brings the effects of tobacco use into the limelight. Ultimately, truth strives to change social norms and reduce teen smoking by empowering young advocates with a forum to voice their contempt for tobacco products. Using innovative technology and marketing strategies, the campaign exposes corporate tobacco's deceptive marketing and manufacturing practices. Youth play an integral role in marketing development, production, and promotion of truth commercials and other social-marketing materials. The campaign's in-your-face, hard-hitting ads appeal to young adults' desires to voice their rights, demonstrate independence, and take a stand. In addition, the truth campaign has been acknowledged by the Monitoring the Future study as one of the reasons teen tobacco use has declined in the past four years. Similar state-level campaigns that foster attitudes that counter the industry's messages have also been shown to significantly decrease smoking initiation.

National media campaigns such as truth get young people interested in fighting for a tobacco-free generation. Once their interests are piqued, youth may research tobacco initiatives online. For example, the Campaign for Tobacco-Free Kids provides an interactive Web site where youth can exchange advocacy ideas and register to participate in the nationally recognized Kick Butts Day. Other anti-tobacco public awareness efforts include the World No Tobacco Day and the Great American Smoke-Out, sponsored by the World Health Organization and American Cancer Society, respectively. Each organization calls upon young people to take a stand against corporate tobacco by organizing public education and activism activities in their schools and communities.

In addition, youth-led organizations such as Fighting Against Corporate Tobacco (FACT) provide youth with a forum to become actively engaged. Through these organizations, youth unmask the facts about corporate tobacco by protesting and by spearheading letter-writing campaigns. Moreover, youth rebel against corporate tobacco by exposing corporate tobacco's less-than-reputable marketing practices.

Prevention Education

Tobacco-related diseases are the most preventable cause of death worldwide. Thus, prevention education can have an impact in minimizing the numbers of new tobacco users. Youth have found a place in these efforts. They increase awareness and educate peers about the dangers of using tobacco. Youth educators realize that the choice to use tobacco, ultimately, rests with the individual. As a way to debunk myths, provide education, and enhance self-esteem, young people have organized health campaigns on the national, state, and local levels to illustrate the dangers of choosing to use tobacco products.

In addition to national initiatives, state coalitions have formed to reinvent social norms regarding tobacco. For example, Teens Against Smoking in Kansas (TASK) promotes tobacco-free teens by bringing communities together with a unified voice against corporate tobacco. In Kansas thirty-five youth comprise the TASK Youth Advisory Council, which organizes Smoke-free Teens Are Rising (STAR) rallies and an annual youth leadership summit to educate young people on the dangers of tobacco use. A local TASK group, the Smoke-free Tigers Task Force, started with nine members and quickly grew to 400. They successfully lobbied the school board to prohibit smoking on school grounds, including at sporting events. TASK exemplifies the power of young people joining together to turn national initiatives into local action.

Young people can also participate in anti-tobacco educational activities through school-based clubs such as Teens Against Tobacco Use (TATU), which is co-sponsored by the American Lung Association, American Heart Association, and American Cancer Society. As TATU members, high-school students receive training to become peer educators, whereby, they teach middle-school students about the dangers of the tobacco industry's marketing strategies, the ingredients found in cigarettes (e.g., arsenic, ammonia, acetone) and smokeless tobacco, the local and national statistics regarding tobacco use, and the detrimental health consequences caused by tobacco products. This method of peer education is meant to provide young students with interactions among older peers as a form of positive role modeling against tobacco use. Often times the peer educators use innovative hands-on teaching strategies to engage younger students in the learning process. Moreover, peer educators help their younger peers to identify hobbies that can become their "anti-drug." For example, as a way to introduce themselves to a class of younger students, peer educators state their names and their anti-drug such as skiing, theater, music, and so on. Peer education has proven to be a successful pedagogy for tobacco-prevention efforts. Capitalizing on the power of positive peer pressure, teens serve as healthy role models for elementary- and middle-school students.

Policy Initiatives

Finally, youth are actively engaged in policy reform. Their initiatives include lobbying for increasing taxes on tobacco products, insuring that retailers are in compliance with laws prohibiting tobacco sales to minors and demanding that smoke-free public spaces exist. For example, members of the Youth Tobacco Prevention Corps in southern California challenged the city councils of Encinitas and Del Mar to ban smoking on public beaches. The idea came to corps members after completing a beach cleanup, where, in just one hour, they collected over 4,000 cigarette butts. City council members from both cities listened to corps members' concerns, but took no action. Young corps members, however, were relentless in their efforts to initiate policy change. So, they took the issue to the city council of nearby Solana Beach. After concluding that the smoking ban may prevent youth from smoking, the Solana Beach city council unanimously voted in favor of the public-policy change. One corps member summarized the experience by saying, "We made policy change, and we are only kids in high school. It's fun" (Goldberg 2003). Since then, other California cities have followed Solana Beach's lead on banning smoking on public beaches.

In conclusion, youth action drives the anti-tobacco movement. Young people have demonstrated leadership as they advocate against corporate tobacco, educate peers on the dangers of tobacco use, and take initiative in policy reform. The success of programs such as truth®, TASK, TATU, and the Youth Tobacco Prevention Corps are a testament to young people's abilities to push the anti-tobacco movement forward. Current trends in the movement suggest that young people's creative use of technology will allow them to take the movement global via Internet discussion boards, blogs, interactive Web sites for activists, and transnational public-awareness campaigns.

See also Civic Environmentalism; Grassroots Youth Movements; Political Consumerism; Social Responsibility; Student Political Activism; Transnational Youth Activism.

Recommended Reading

American Legacy Foundation (2003). truth® Fact Sheet. [Online]. Available at http://www.americanlegacy.org.

Burrows, D. (1984). "Strategic Research Report." [Online]. Available at http://tobacco-documents.org/youth/AmYoRJR19840229.Rm1.html.

Campaign for Tobacco-Free Kids. See http://www.tobaccofreekids.org.

Goldberg, K. (November 21, 2003). "California Town Bans Smoking on Beach." Speaker on National Public Radio. Available at http://www.npr.org/features/feature.php?wfId=1515903. Washington, D.C.: National Public Radio.

Johnston, L. D., O'Malley, P. M., Bachman, J. G., and Schulenberg, J. E. (2004). *Monitoring the Future National Results on Adolescent Drug Use: Overview of Key Findings, 2003.* Bethesda, MD: National Institute on Drug Abuse.

National Institute on Drug Abuse (January 2004). "High School and Youth Trends." [Online]. Available at http://www.drugabuse.gov.

Siegel, M., and Biener, L. (2000). "The Impact of an Anti-smoking Media Campaign on Progression to Established Smoking: Results of a Longitudinal Youth Study." *American Journal of Public Health*, 90 (3): 380–386.

Sly, D. F., Trapido, E., and Ray, S. (2002). "Evidence of the Dose Effects of an Anti-tobacco Counteradvertising Campaign." *Preventive Medicine*, 35 (5): 511–518.

Substance Abuse and Mental Health Services Administration (2003). *Results from the 2002 National Survey on Drug Use and Health: National Findings.* Office of Applied Studies, NHSDA Series H-22, DHHS Publication No. SMA 03–3836. Rockville, MD.

World Bank (1999). *Curbing the Epidemic: Governments and the Economics of Tobacco Control.* Washington, D.C.: World Bank.

Amy K. Syvertsen and Julie A. Scheve

Antiwar Activism. Antiwar and peace movements have a long history in the United States and around the world. Young people have often played a critical role in energizing and sustaining these movements. Here some important features of the antiwar movement as a whole, as well as a brief history of this movement in the United States, are provided. Particular attention is given to movements against the war in Vietnam and the more recent war in Iraq because of the very different roles young people played in these mobilizations.

Regarding antiwar movements in general, it is worth noting first that, for as long as there have been wars, individuals and groups have worked to challenge them. While there are many individuals and groups who have maintained their opposition to war for decades, this opposition has only been able to mobilize large numbers of people in certain periods. Political opportunities are critical for the successful mobilization of antiwar movements, as well as social movements in general. Despite the best efforts of committed organizers, broad antiwar mobilization is contingent on particular constellations of institutional politics and public policy that provoke and create space for mobilization. Such mobilizations, in turn, alter the political opportunities for the movements themselves as well as for their opponents.

Second, for antiwar movements to attract sufficient support to affect policy, they must grow beyond their traditional left and pacifist core and appeal to larger, more diverse constituencies. Some people and groups will always be sympathetic to the antiwar cause; however, in order to mobilize great numbers of people, the movement must appeal to more than just these core constituencies. This is done through "framing" efforts aimed at coalition building. Each of the successful mobilization surges during the last half century were built around a fairly simple and straightforward message that is delivered through what Snow and Benford call a "master frame": an interpretation of relevant events and conditions in ways that are intended to mobilize potential adherents and constituents, to garner the support of bystanders, and to demobilize antagonists. These master frames, such as "The World Says No to War," which was used in the recent anti–Iraq War mobilization, are able to appeal to a wide variety of different groups and individuals with divergent interests and concerns. As long as the difference between supporters and government policy is the most salient issue, both moderates and more extreme adherents within an antiwar coalition have incentive to cooperate with one another. Movement coalitions are, however, apt to dissolve when the government offers the prospect of influence, potentially transforming some movement demands into policy.

Finally, it is important to recognize that even when an antiwar movement disappears from the news and widespread mobilization ends, the infrastructure of a core remains in what Rupp and Taylor call an "abeyance" structure. Antiwar mobilizations are not isolated, sporadic events. Rather, they are tied together by networks of activists, organizational structures, and shared frames. The protest of 100,000 people at the height of the anti-Vietnam mobilization, for example, was just the visible tip of the iceberg of the antiwar movement. When the political context changes and widespread mobilization declines, the networks of individual activists and organizational structures remain, waiting for the next political opportunity to arise. This infrastructure proves critical during opportunities for remobilization.

There have been many significant antiwar mobilizations in American history.

Members of the University of Texas chapter of Students for a Democratic Society protest the Vietnam War in 1965. *Library of Congress.*

Every war conducted by the United States in the nineteenth century elicited organized protest and outright opposition: the War of 1812, the Mexican-American War of 1846, the Civil War, and the Spanish-American War of 1898. These antiwar movements challenged government policy, patriotic rhetoric, and the rationale for fighting. Early peace advocates before World War I have been characterized as mostly moral evangelists who elevated values derived from Christian and Enlightenment tradition into national standards. They were a prophetic minority in an age when war was almost universally considered an acceptable, perhaps inevitable, and even desirable way of settling international differences.

The introduction of the use of nuclear weapons by the United States at the end of World War II fundamentally transformed the antiwar movement. Nuclear weapons changed the perceived threat of war, raising public concern and giving activists a salient issue around which to organize. The National Committee for Sane Nuclear Policy (SANE), founded in 1957, and other groups issued appeals, staged international conferences, organized rallies, and ran newspaper and television advertisements calling for nuclear disarmament.

While opposition to nuclear weapons was the most consistent issue for the postwar antiwar movement, opposition to the Vietnam War was the most volatile. Universities across the United States were the first sites of organized antiwar opposition, and these protests quickly became highly visible to the news media. Students for a Democratic Society (SDS), an organization which would prove instrumental in the anti–Vietnam War movement, was founded in 1960 and had its roots in campus-based SANE chapters. SDS had a reputation for dynamic and dramatic student activism, although its recruits were mainly white and middle class.

After Lyndon Johnson began the bombing of North Vietnam in February 1965, SDS escalated their mobilization efforts.

Teach-ins against the war spread across U.S. campuses following the example set at the University of Michigan that March, when 2,500 students attended lectures and rallies devoted to the issue of the war in Vietnam. This was the first significant protest ever by American students against U.S. foreign policy. In April of 1965, SDS organized the first major protest against the war, the largest antiwar demonstration thus far in U.S. history. A march on the White House attracted over 20,000 people, mostly students. SDS's membership grew fourfold between December of 1964 and October of 1965, from 2,500 to 10,000, and the organization launched an anti-draft campaign in the fall of that year that swelled membership even further. By 1966 SDS was a loosely knit association of 151 chapters with 100,000 members, and in 1967–1968 organized student protests of the war in Vietnam were reported at 38 percent of universities in the United States.

The success of antiwar mobilization efforts and the increasingly violent protests produced a backlash against the movement in some sectors of the broader public. Nonetheless, by 1972 the U.S. Congress had effectively legislated the end of the war by withholding funds to continue the draft and provide supplies to continue fighting. McAdam and Su note that the antiwar movement can claim substantial credit for provoking opposition to the war, raising the costs of conducting it, and serving an agenda-setting role in which U.S. foreign policy received an unusual degree of scrutiny.

Why did young people, predominantly middle-class student populations, become so involved in the anti–Vietnam War protests? First, young people, particularly those in college, have more free time than other youth who work at paid employment, as well as older generations. At the time of the Vietnam War, there were not only more young people in general—35 million fifteen- to twenty-four-year-olds in 1970 as compared to 23 million in this age-group in 1960—there were also many more college students. The 8.6 million students in 1970, compared to 2.3 million in 1950, created a substantially larger pool of potential activists. Students also have the advantage of having high levels of sustained interaction and are consequently often more apt to organize. In addition, the military was increasingly relying on younger soldiers; the average age of a soldier in the Vietnam War was nineteen, whereas it had been twenty-six in World War II. This fact, as well as the issue of the draft, made the war personally salient for young people of the era.

After the Vietnam War protests, activists who were once engaged became increasingly involved in other movements, such as the women's movement, the environmental movement, and most notably the nuclear disarmament or "nuclear freeze" campaigns. Although there was a mobilization against the first Gulf War (1991), it quickly dissipated after the war began. The second war in Iraq, on the other hand, has been met with considerable and prolonged opposition. The movement against the war in Iraq is the largest antiwar movement that has ever taken place and is unique in its international reach and coordination of efforts. Demonstrations that occurred *before* the invasion of Iraq were larger than anti-Vietnam mobilizations that had taken years to organize.

The mobilization against the war in Iraq in the United States was coordinated by a number of social-movement coalitions, such as International ANSWER (Act Now to Stop War and End Racism), which was formed shortly after September 11, 2001, by the International Action Center. ANSWER skillfully mobilized demonstrations against the war in Afghanistan, and when the Bush administration began preparing for its attack on Iraq, the ANSWER coalition was first to mobilize. ANSWER was able to act quickly because it had experience with such work and the necessary organizing structure. Other coalitions such as United for Peace and Justice (UFPJ) were extremely broad and able to mobilize up to

200 organizations. The coalitions also took advantage of new technologies—ANSWER, United for Peace and Justice, Not in Our Name, and MoveOn used the Internet as a highly effective mobilizing tool. Alongside these national coalitions were a large number of local organizations that opposed the war. These coalitions included many organizations that were not traditionally concerned with antiwar activism, such as churches and other religious organizations, trade unions, and social-justice organizations of all kinds that turned at least some of their attention toward opposing the war.

There were many young people in the mobilization against the war in Iraq who brought verve and creativity to the demonstrations and took the lead in civil disobedience. However, the young people in this antiwar movement represented only a small minority of their generation and only a small proportion of the movement as a whole. This contrasted sharply with the movement against the war in Vietnam where the majority of activists were young and the movement was based on campuses. In comparison, U.S. campuses were relatively quiet during the mobilization against the Iraq War. At the time of the anti–Vietnam War protests, many older people who opposed the war had a difficult time finding a place in the movement. The recent antiwar movement against the war in Iraq was strengthened by the diversity of generations participating in it. However, young people play a particularly important and energizing role in social movements. Arguably, if there had been more of them in the recent antiwar effort, the movement and its capacity for influencing U.S. policy would have perhaps been strengthened.

There are many possible reasons why young people were less active in the anti–Iraq War protests. One reason for the relatively low level of involvement of young people in the recent antiwar mobilization is the absence of the draft. Today's college students also have less free time than college students of the 1960s and 1970s, with more of them working at paid employment while they attend school. Finally, today's young people grew up in the conservative culture of the last two decades which has promoted individual material success and in which collective action for a better world has often seemed unrealistic or futile.

Marullo and Meyer tell us that "peace activists usually lose—at least in terms of preventing their nation from going to war. But their actions often have significant consequences in terms of altering public opinion forcing policymakers to alter their goals, or undermining the institutional or political infrastructure that supports war-making." These activists are very important in changing the way that the public thinks about war, how nations decide to engage in war, and policies around which war will proceed. Antiwar activism is also important for the individual activists themselves, as it can be a bridge to participation in other movements and civic and political commitments later in life. In this way a young person's participation in the antiwar movement can be a first step in a lifetime of civic engagement.

See also Anti-Nazi Youth Resistance; Arab Americans; Child Soldiers; Civic Engagement in Diverse Youth; Global Justice Activism; Palestinian *Intifada*; Social Movements; State and Youth, The; Student Political Activism; Tiananmen Square Massacre (1989); United Nations, Youth Activism and.

Recommended Reading

Chatfield, Charles, with Kleidman, Robert (1992). *The American Peace Movement*. New York: Twayne Publishers.

Gilbert, Marc Jason (2001). *The Vietnam War on Campus: Other Voices, More Distant Drums*. Westport, CT: Praeger.

Klatch, Rebecca E. (1999). *A Generation Divided: The New Left, the New Right, and the 1960s*. Berkeley: University of California Press.

Marullo, Sam, and Meyer, David S. (2004) "Antiwar and Peace Movements." In *The Blackwell Companion to Social Movements*, edited by David A. Snow, Sarah S. Soule, and Hanspeter Kriesi. Malden, MA: Blackwell Publishing.

McAdam, Doug, and Su, Yang (2002). "The War at Home: Antiwar Protests and Congressional Voting, 1965 to 1973." *American Sociological Review*, 67 (5): 696–721.

Rupp, Leila, and Taylor, Verta (1987). *Survival in the Doldrums: The American Women's Rights Movement*. New York: Oxford University Press.

Snow, David A., and Benford, Robert (1992). "Master Frames and Cycles of Protest." In *Frontiers in Social Movement Theory*, edited by A. Morris and C. M. Mueller. New Haven, CT: Yale University Press, pp.133–156.

Catherine Corrigall-Brown

Arab Americans. The terrorist attacks of September 11, 2001, and the political, social, and military response to these events has put a spotlight on the Arab-origin population of the United States. Who are Arab Americans? They are immigrants and their descendants who came to the United States from Arabic-speaking countries of the Middle East. These countries include Algeria, Bahrain, Egypt, Iraq, Jordan, Kuwait, Lebanon, Libya, Mauritania, Morocco, Oman, Palestine, Qatar, Saudi Arabia, Sudan, Syria, Tunisia, United Arab Emirates, and Yemen. Iran is not included because Iranians speak Farsi or Persian, not Arabic.

How many Arab Americans are there? The 2000 census counted approximately 1.25 million people of Arab descent in the United States. Compared to other racial and ethnic minority groups, this population is not large. According to the 2000 census, there are more than 34 million African Americans, 35 million Hispanics, 10 million Asian Americans, and 2 million American Indians/Alaska natives. Among racial and ethnic minority groups counted in the census, only those of native Hawaiian and Pacific Island descent, who number less than 500,000, are a smaller group than Arab Americans.

The census, however, may have severely undercounted Arab Americans. Concerns about immigration status and prosecution by the government may lead people to avoid acknowledging Arab origin. Some analysts speculate that the United States may be home to more than twice as many Arab Americans as census figures suggest.

Immigration from the Arab world to the United States has a long history. The first wave of immigration began in the 1870s

A nineteen-year-old Arab American mother holds her baby at a September 11th memorial service. *Courtesy of Skjold Photographs.*

and lasted until World War II. These immigrants came primarily from the region of Syria and present-day Lebanon. They were overwhelmingly Christian. The second wave of immigration began after World War II and has lasted to the present day. Revolutions in Egypt and Iraq during the 1950s, displacement from Israel in 1967, and the fifteen-year civil war in Lebanon are among the events that prompted residents of those regions to migrate to the United States. The lifting of central immigration restrictions in 1965 opened the door, making immigration to the United States more feasible. The Arab immigrants who arrived since World War II differ from the earlier Arab immigrants in that they are more likely to be Muslims. Also, they are highly educated, and many seek employment as professionals.

So what was the composition of the Arab American population in the year 2000? The largest subgroup by far, about 36 per-

cent, had Lebanese ancestry. Syria and Egypt each contributed another 12 percent or so. Another 6 percent came from Palestine. Iraq, Jordan, and Morocco each contributed about 3 percent. About 24 percent of respondents who claimed Arab ancestry identified simply as "Arab" or did not select one of the countries listed above and were classified as "other Arab."

Arab Americans are an urban population, concentrated in certain states (especially California, New York, and Michigan) and in particular cities (Los Angeles, Detroit, New York, Chicago, and Washington, D.C.). They are well educated: less than one-fifth fails to hold a high-school degree, while more than one-third has a college degree. Family income among Arab Americans is higher than the national average. Of course, circumstances vary within this population. Despite Arab Americans' high average status, some Arab American groups are struggling just to get by.

Many people are surprised to learn that Arab Americans are much less likely to adhere to Islam than to Christianity. In fact, less than a quarter are Muslim. About two-thirds of Arab Americans are either Catholic or Orthodox Christian, another eighth being Protestant. There are, however, particular locales where the majority of the Arab Americans are Muslim.

Arab Americans have held uncertain status in the racial classification system of the United States. Although they are often judged to be "not quite white," they have not consistently received the legal protections granted to racial minorities. The case of *Saint Francis College v. Al-Khazraji* provides an example. An Iraqi-born man of the Muslim faith claimed racial discrimination when he was denied tenure at the college where he taught. It took a U.S. Supreme Court ruling, overturning judgments of lower courts, to give the professor a chance to prove he had been a victim of racial bias.

Only since the 1993 and 2001 terrorist attacks by Muslim extremists have Arab Americans been in the spotlight of public attention. Thus we have limited information about the attitudes toward this group held by other Americans. In fact, it is a fair guess that until recently, well-formed opinions about Arab Americans didn't exist in the minds of most U.S. residents. The best public opinion information we have comes from surveys conducted in 1992 and 1994 in the Detroit, Michigan, metropolitan area, where there is a substantial Arab American population. Reflecting the conception that Arab Americans are "not quite white," the surveys show that white Detroit residents view Arab Americans more negatively than they view other whites but not as negatively as they view blacks. Black residents view Arab Americans more negatively than whites do, perhaps because of tensions with Arab Americans running small businesses in black neighborhoods. White women are more likely than white men to hold negative views of Arab Americans, probably because they mistakenly equate Arab with Muslim and

object to the treatment of women in many Muslim societies.

In the wake of September 11, 2001, many Arab Americans and people mistaken for Arab Americans faced strained and hostile reactions—a few of them deadly—from other Americans expressing fear or seeking revenge. Also, the U.S. government undertook a number of efforts in the name of increasing security. For example, the FBI was given expanded power to search and monitor the communications of people who are suspected of criminal activity, even if no evidence of wrongdoing exists. Special registration was required of male U.S. residents who are citizens or nationals of certain Muslim countries, including those here on business or to attend school. The result was confusion, detentions, and the initiation of deportation proceedings against more than 13,000 men, most of whom were eventually shown merely to be waiting for permanent resident applications or to have minor visa problems.

In October 2001, the Congress passed the U.S.A. Patriot Act. The name stands for "Uniting and Strengthening America by Providing Appropriate Tools Required to Intercept and Obstruct Terrorism." This controversial act targets "nonresident aliens," those in the United States as international students, vacationers, business travelers, researchers, and so on, allowing surveillance, detention, and deportation without the standards of evidence usually required in U.S. justice institutions. Some 143 communities in twenty-seven states have adopted resolutions opposing the Patriot Act, and the American Civil Liberties Union has filed legal challenges to the act.

Detainment of Arab Americans began immediately after September 11, 2001, even before the Patriot Act was passed. Some were held on the basis of minor visa violations. Others were labeled "material witnesses" or "special-interest" detainees. Critics of such detentions claim they often amounted to preemptive incarceration based on a presumption of guilt. A number of Arab Americans were held for prolonged periods without receiving their Miranda rights, being allowed legal counsel, or having charges filed against them. For example, an Arab American physician was held for seven days without access to a lawyer or his family; no charges were ever filed against him. A dentist residing in California was arrested and transferred to a detention center in New York City, where he was held for several months, again with no charges ever filed.

Another measure taken shortly after September 11, 2001, was the development of an FBI "watch list" of people wanted for questioning about terrorist events. The list was widely distributed to public agencies and private companies, with requests to help find those named on the list. With time, many erroneous inclusions on the watch list have been identified, but the list was so widely distributed that it has been difficult or impossible for innocent people mistakenly listed to clear their names.

Several local, national, and international associations serve as vehicles for Arab American political, social, and cultural organizing. A number of these organizations were in existence prior to the terrorist attacks of September 11, 2001, but their activities changed in response to those events. Many now focus a great deal of their energy and resources on the political, legal, and social repercussions of September 11th. Several organizations provide legal counsel as well as information about civil rights laws and violations, federal rights and protections against discrimination, and issues such as religious freedom and traveling as an Arab American. Other important goals of these organizations include educating their communities and serving as resources for governmental agencies and political leaders who want to learn about Arab culture and the concerns of Arab Americans. Examples of organizations that provide such information are the Arab American Institute and the American Arab Anti-Discrimination Committee. These and other Arab American organizations work directly with policymakers on both local and national levels.

They also support political leaders who are of Arab descent or who take positions supportive of the Arab American community.

Two relatively new organizations serve important purposes. The Congress of Arab American Organizations is an umbrella organization that was launched in August of 2001 to enhance cooperation, communication, and coordination among the more than 120 local, regional, and national groups that serve Arab Americans. The Association of Patriotic Arab Americans in the Military was created in response to September 11, 2001, with the help and encouragement of the Arab American Institute. It is a nonpolitical association with the goal of highlighting the military service and sacrifice of Arab Americans. This is the first organization of its kind.

Arab student associations on college and university campuses are an important vehicle for youth organizing in the Arab American community. The Union of Arab Student Associations serves as an umbrella organization for eleven universities in the Washington, D.C., metropolitan area. In conjunction with the American Arab Anti-Discrimination Committee, they have sponsored conferences on Arab American student activism annually since 1999. Such programs complement those of national organizations that offer internship and scholarship opportunities to encourage Arab American students to prepare for future leadership positions.

See also Immigrant Youth in the United States; Terrorism, Youth Activism Responses to; Xenophobia; Zionist Youth Organizations.

Recommended Reading

American Civil Liberties Union. See http://www.aclu.org.
Arab American Institute Foundation (2002). *Religious Affiliation of Arab Americans*. See http://www.aaiusa.org/PDF/ancestry.pdf.
Human Rights Watch (2002). *Presumption of Guilt: Human Rights Abuses of Post-September 11 Detainees*. See http://www.hrw.org/reports/2002/us911/.
Saint Francis College v. Al-Khazraji, 483 U.S. 1011 (1987).
Samhan, H. H. (1999). "Not Quite White: Race Classification and the Arab-American Experience." In *Arabs in America: Building*

a New Future, edited by M. W. Suleiman. Philadelphia: Temple University Press, pp. 209–226.

Suleiman, M. W. (1999). "Introduction: The Arab Immigrant Experience." In Arabs in America, Building a New Future, edited by M. W. Suleiman. Philadelphia: Temple University Press, pp. 1–21.

"The Birth of an Arab-American Lobby" (October 14, 2000). The Economist, p. 41.

U.S. Census Bureau (1990). 1990 Census of Population and Housing, CP-3-2, Ancestry of the Population of the United States.

U.S. Census Bureau (2000). Summary File 3, Matrices P1, and PCT18.

Younis, A. L. (1995). The Coming of the Arabic-Speaking People to the United States. New York: Center for Migration Studies.

Suzanne E. Agha and Marylee C. Taylor

Athletic-Square Model of Youth Sport. Organized youth sports are perhaps the largest youth "organization" within the United States. On average 42 million children play sports each year. Youth sports have been recognized by researchers and laypersons alike as a vehicle to promote life skills and competencies. Sports give youth opportunities to increase their self-esteem, develop an appreciation of health and fitness, and even equip them with the skills necessary to become leaders within the community.

According to research, a win-at-all-costs atmosphere in a youth sports program can be harmful to a developing young person. Few children possess the talent to play competitive sports at the highest level; that is, most children will not grow up to be professional athletes. Therefore, the primary goals of youth sports should be to foster the development of general physical competence and to promote physical activity, fun, life skills, sportsmanship, and good health. Through sports youth can learn how to be self-reliant and how to seek the resources of others when needed, skills that will serve them well throughout life. Simply put, youth sport programs are meant to be community youth-development programs.

Athletic Triangle

In the past researchers identified the athletic-triangle model of youth sports—parents, coaches, and youth as each point of a triangle. Scholars theorized that the most important relationships involved in youth sports were among these three different categories of people. Although the athletic triangle addresses some very important participants within the youth sports arena, it overlooks another important participant—the community itself.

Bronfenbrenner's ecological theory (1979) provides an explanation of the importance of the interaction between individuals and the various levels of their environment. The ecological theory describes multiple interrelated, interdependent systems that interact with and influence individual behavior and development. The model places the individual (e.g., youth) within the middle of a circle with each system or level forming around the individual within concentric circles. The levels include the microsystem, mesosystem, exosystem, macrosystem, and the chronosystem. Two of these are especially relevant for youth sports: the microsystem and the macrosystem.

The microsystem includes people or places that involve day-to-day interaction. For youth elements of the microsystem include parents, teachers, peers, coaches, classrooms, and playing fields or courts. How this mini-society interacts with the youth can affect the youth's behavior and relationships. For example, participation in sports can increase peer acceptance and form social competence within this system. In fact, some scholars have argued that, with the exception of school, sports may be the most important social environment for many male youth.

The macrosystem is the culture in which the youth and the different systems function. The culture in which the youth participates is crucial for his or her development. A case in point is if the parents, coaches, sport organizations, or the community as a whole promote a "win-at-all-costs" environment, then the youth is more likely to cheat, possess unsportsmanlike attitude, engage in unsportsmanlike behaviors, or to have been turned off and even quit sports entirely.

Within these levels of the ecological model, youth sports participants explore their sports organization and community. Does the player feel that his or her relationship with his or her parents will be negatively affected by sports? Does the player feel that he or she must cheat to "win at all costs"? Does the community emphasize competition as the sole reason for sports? Do the media within the community help promote sportsmanship? Can the youth handle the pressure placed upon them by parents, coaches, players, and the community?

In thinking about these questions it is apparent we must educate the sports organizations as well as the community as a whole about positive youth development and the benefits of sports. The organizations have a responsibility to create an environment that is engaging and has the features that promote positive youth development, positive character, and sportsmanship.

In order for youth to receive the benefits of sports, the sport atmosphere must be positive and developmentally appropriate. Thus, the adults involved within the youth or sports organizations must understand youth development, achievement motivation, and interpersonal relationship skills. Youth participating in sports have the right to expect a developmental setting that promotes physical and psychological safety, clear and consistent rules or appropriate structure, supportive relationships, and opportunities for all the youth to feel as though they belong. Youth expectations could also include an environment that promotes positive social norms and that helps integrate family, school, and community. Finally, the youth should have opportunities to contribute to the system and to build their life skills.

Youth Sports and Community Youth Development

How can the needs of young players be met by parents, coaches, and the community? The first step is to recognize that we can no longer operate under the Athletic-Triangle Model. We need to update the model to meet today's issues. Youth sports are not only a family issue but also a community issue. Thus, the "athletic-square" model should replace the athletic triangle to draw attention to the fact that the youth, parents, coaches, and the *community* are all responsible in creating the positive youth sports environment needed to engender youth sports' benefits. The athletic square integrates the principles of community youth development (CYD). Community youth development involves creating opportunities for young people to connect to others, develop skills, and utilize those skills to contribute to their communities, which in turn increases their ability to succeed.

Young athletes also have some responsibility within the sports realm. They must be willing to listen and learn, communicate their needs, and play with good sportsmanship and character. In fact, according to the athletic-square model, youth have both the right and the responsibility to contribute to the community beyond the sports program. Therefore, sports programs and the adults who organize and volunteer in them must provide meaningful opportunities for youth to contribute both to the organization and community. Having several youth representatives on an organization's board and insuring that those youth have decision-making power equal to that of adult board members is one example of such a meaningful opportunity. Another example is having youth teams' members host an activity day at the sports arena for a group of younger children from the local school or day-care center. A more basic example would be requiring that a child and his or her parent(s) volunteer to sell snacks *or* be the announcer at games for youth of different ages. These examples build upon the key components of CYD: building skills, providing youth with a sense of belonging, and engaging youth as partners in building organizations and communities.

Because sports are a community youth development program, adults and youth have to *advocate* together for opportunities and structures that provide young people with sustained positive relationships with adults and opportunities to utilize newly acquired skills in the "real-world" experiences of their communities.

Youth sports that foster youth's personal competence are engaging them in the development of their abilities to do life planning, to be self-reliant, and to seek the resources of others when needed. The athletic-square model requires that parents, coaches, and community members recognize the power of youth sports as a teaching mechanism for character, good citizenship, and leadership.

See also Positive Youth Development, Programs Promoting; Urban Communities, Youth Programming in.

Recommended Reading

Bronfenbrenner, U. (1979). *Ecology of Human Development.* Cambridge, MA: Harvard University Press.

Daniels, A. M., and Perkins, D. F. (2003). *Putting Youth Back into Sports.* Brookings, SD: South Dakota State University.

Hodge, K., and Danish, S. (1998). "Promoting Life Skills for Adolescent Males through Sports." In *Handbook of Counseling Boys and Adolescent Males: A Practitioner's Guide,* edited by A. M. Horne and M. Kiselica. Thousand Oaks, CA: Sage Publications.

Perkins, D. F., and Borden, L. M. (2003). "Key Elements of Community Youth Development Programs." In *Community Youth Development: Practice, Policy, and Research,* edited by F. A. Villarruel, D. F. Perkins, L. M. Borden, and J. G. Keith. Thousand Oaks, CA: Sage, pp. 327–340.

Villarruel, F. A., Perkins, D. F., Borden, L. M., and Keith, J. G. (2003). *Community Youth Development: Practice, Policy, and Research.* Thousand Oaks, CA: Sage.

Walker, J., Marczak, M., Blyth, D. A., and Borden, L. M. (In Press). "Designing Developmentally Intentional Youth Programs: Toward a Theory of Optimal Developmental Success in Community-Based Learning Experiences for Youth." In *Organized Activities as Contexts of Development: Extracurricular Activities, After-school and Community Programs,* edited by J. L. Mahoney, R. W. Larson, and J. S. Eccles. Mahwah, NJ: Erlbaum.

Daniel F. Perkins and Ann Michelle Daniels

Australia, Youth Activism in. As with elsewhere in the world, youth have been at the forefront of activism and radical politics in Australia. More often than not, this has been associated with environmental causes, animal rights, anticapitalist protests, antiracism demonstrations, and antiwar marches. In other words, the mainstream of the "extreme" has tended to be oriented to left-wing or alternative progressive movements and ideologies. Young people are attracted to the hope and promise of building new futures, ones that are far removed from the wars, inequality, cruelties, and harshness of the present. The hallmarks of twenty-first-century activism appear to be a global focus and social networking, a strong antimaterialist ethic and orientation, little reliance upon traditional institutional supports and resources (such as the trade unions), and even less reliance on and respect for centralized leadership structures. Young people are active in ways that they can relate to and are comfortable with.

One of the ironies of youth activism is that when young Australians do get active, when they raise their voices and fists in remonstration against the powers that be, they are frequently subject to criticism. Youth are constantly told to "participate" in the lives of their societies, but there are strict "rules of the game" that dictate what is acceptable and what is not when doing so.

We begin by briefly reviewing the broad social context within which youth activism in Australia occurs. This is followed by discussion of the notion of youth agency, addressing the sorts of consciousness that accompany youth engagement in social-change movements and street politics. The final section explores the paradoxes of participation as these pertain to youth in Australia.

Activism and Social Context

Young people in Australia engage in civic life in many different ways. Many of the groups and institutions with which they are associated might not be seen as "political." Some are explicitly so.

Young Australians wave their national flag at a cricket match.

How and why young people become actively involved in this or that group or activity is shaped by the specific social context into which they are born. Activism, narrowly defined, tends to be a "middle-class thing." Traditional working-class neighborhoods and poorer suburbs are hardly hotbeds of political activism, although they are certainly focal points for other types of social engagement, such as youth cultures that include street dancers and graffiti artists, and teenage activities that include sports as well as drug use and drinking. Solidarity in this context is something that is molded at the neighborhood and community level. Supporting your friends and defending your own means dealing with everyday issues through existing social networks of family and friends. Work, money, babies, cars, entertainment—these needs, desires, responsibilities, and problems are at the center of a politics of everyday life. Activism in these circumstances is likely to be directed at authority figures such as the police and to involve confrontation in public spaces over the control and "ownership" of these spaces. Group defense of communal spaces and activities may mean, literally, taking over the streets, an assertion that "we live here and this is our place."

For many young people the politics of everyday life is shaped by direct experiences of racism, of discrimination, of homophobic violence, experiences that are often shared with others. In such instances there is greater likelihood of collective action that is focused, organized around concepts such as human rights and anti-discrimination, and linked across generations and across neighborhoods. The personal problem is represented as shaped by institutions and thus subject to concerted resistance and conscious reform. Disadvantage may be a great leveler, but repression and oppression can be generators of active dissent and propel people into action. Anti-Arab and anti-Muslim discrimination, for example, is having a major impact on young people around the country. Arab and Muslim youth feel that they are particularly at risk of harassment. According to a recent Human Rights and Equal Opportunity Commission report, this has led to feelings of frustration, alienation, loss of confidence in themselves, and loss of trust in authority. It has also been associated with a politicization of identity, where, for example, to be Lebanese, publicly and proudly, becomes a profound political statement. In the working-class, migrant suburbs of western Sydney, a new militancy is emerging.

Young people who are exposed to information and ideas about the wider world beyond their suburb, town, or region are also more likely to take an interest in global events and wider social trends. These events and trends may be reflected in what happens at the local level (as with music, videos, job opportunities), but they are best understood and dealt with in light of a broader vision of social structures. Education is thus an important component of the activist armory. It is also a stimulus to activism in the first place. No wonder that many private-school students join with their middle-class peers in government schools on issues of social justice and breaches of human rights. Those who "see" are those most likely to "act." Children of privilege are seemingly more likely to use that privilege as a stepping stone to righting the world of its wrongs. A material base free from want provides more possibilities for young middle-class people to campaign in support of their Third World cousins, animal companions, and forests and remote wilderness areas. Commitment to causes is made easier when food, shelter, entertainment, and school are rendered relatively unproblematic. Ironically, material wealth can beget the antimaterialist. Thus, movements toward some kinds of social change are enhanced.

A young person's immediate social context very much influences how and why they may engage in activism. What they do, and with whom they do it, is guided by the intersections of age, gender, ethnicity, and class. Where you grow up, the cultural universe you occupy, the position and status of your family and parents in the wider Australian social mosaic—all of these shape opportunity, socialization, and the formation of ideas and of social networks. Activism is both local and national, community-centered and global in orientation. It depends upon where you live.

Activism and Human Agency

Human agency is about knowingly and intentionally doing something in order to achieve certain ends. So how much agency is exercised by young people when they are attacking the bastions of capitalism or condemning the detention of asylum seekers? The short answer is that it varies. Young people join movements, groups, and demonstrations for a wide range of reasons, motivations, periods of engagement, and levels of intensity.

Thinking critically about agency is important for understanding notions such as "active citizenship," a form of agency which has received much contemporary attention in relation to young people and others, and which implies meaningful and significant engagement in and with key social institutions. An analysis of the relationship of young people to the mainstream institutions of society is a good starting point for understanding citizenship. To what extent are different groups of people able to participate fully in shaping civil society?

We can usefully distinguish between three dimensions of youth agency (see table titled "Dimensions of Agency"). In its most basic formulation, we might say that agency simply refers to conscious, goal-directed activity. It includes, for example, how young people "choose" their fashions, lifestyles, modes of speech and dress, and so on. It is concerned with individual or personal choices about things over which individuals have some measure of control. That is, the "choices" exercised tend to be based upon private goals linked to immediate social, economic, and

Dimensions of Agency

Private goals	Individual or personal choices (linked to immediate circumstances)
Public domain	Individual or collective project (linked to limited change/ maintenance of existing circumstances or institutions)
Social transformation	Collective project (linked to fundamental change in overall social order)

Source: White & Wyn 1998, p. 316.

political circumstances. Even where action takes place against mainstream institutions and fashions, this too tends to make reference to conventional (i.e., politically acceptable if not socially tolerated) patterns of behavior. The phenomenon of "fads," whether generated from the bottom-up (the street-level innovation of young people) or top-down by industry, represents a break with convention that strives in the end to *be convention* (witness the evolution, and some might say perversion, of hip-hop into a mass audience phenomenon).

Agency can also be defined in terms of collective or individual projects which have goals which are not simply personal but which are projected into the public domain. Here agency takes the form of (usually) organized attempts to modify, reform, or retain aspects of the existing social order. For example, the efforts of lobby groups, experts, youth, community workers, and others to change a particular law, to enhance a particular benefit, to protest against a particular government intervention, or to gain more resources are examples of this type of limited collective agency. Agency here is generally wrapped around the idea of tackling specific social problems, and action is conceived in terms of addressing specific, and immediate, public issues.

A third sense in which we can talk about agency is where there is a collective project which involves a conscious, self-reflective practice, one that is tied to wider political ideals and even utopianism. Direct and immediate social action is strategically linked to a larger social-change agenda.

This is perhaps best seen in some sections of the new social movements (such as the feminist, green, and gay and lesbian movements), as well as in reactionary social formations (such as neo-Nazi and white supremacy movements). Relatively few young people are directly engaged in social-transformation activity of this kind. It is also important to distinguish activities and groups according to specific ideological orientations, not all of which are emancipatory in nature. In other words, analysis of youth engagement in collective action for social change also demands analysis of the political goals and contexts of such action.

Young people in Australia are linked to social movements and specific events across these three dimensions of agency. Some young people throw themselves fully into activist work and lifestyles. "Ferals" are prominent defenders of Australian forests, living and protesting in remote bush areas as well as bringing their cause to city streets. The young socialists of the group Resistance often put all of their time and energy into political activity, and their dance and song is permeated by politics.

However, for many other youth activism is less about a vision of social transformation. Rather, it is contingent upon where they are at that particular moment in their lives. High-school antiracist marches include groups of friends, young people who do not like what is happening to their peers in the classroom, in the media, and in the formal political arena. Their "politics" is a politics of friendship, built in the here and now, and founded upon immediate circumstance (e.g., school-based relationships).

For many others, agency is less about a world vision than about specific issues or events. Rallies, protests, marches, and demonstrations can also be fun. They certainly get the adrenaline running, and they can be exciting places to be—as long as the issue is straightforward and "just."

Thus, activism reflects varying levels of commitment and different sorts of agency. For some young people it is something to "dip into" once and a while with their friends. For others it is a serious, and seriously taken, commitment. Many young people can't be bothered to participate at all. They have other things on their mind, or they face resistance from their peers and parents when expressing a wish to get more active.

Paradoxes of Youth Participation

One of the major stumbling blocks to youth activism has to do with the ways that young people's problems get defined, often displacing attention from the collective nature of their origins. The translation of *social* problems into *individual* ones is a process that tends to blame people for their own plight. Unemployment is due to lack of skills, education, or efforts to get a job. Detaining asylum seekers is necessary because they tried to enter Australia illegally. Indigenous people are poor because they get too many handouts. The message is clear: take responsibility for your own welfare because nobody else is going to. The social processes of individuation delegitimate and undermine a collective sensibility.

This is compounded by a general lack of political education in Australian society. Schools do little to encourage knowledge about, or participation in, conventional politics. Most young people (and older people) are disillusioned with the mainstream political parties and parliamentary systems. In their minds governments fail to deliver the goods; politicians lie and gain even bigger electoral wins; war is justified on the basis of phantom evidence. Nobody listens because all they do is talk.

Young people do become active; they do participate in the political world around them. But this places young people at the fulcrum of a series of paradoxes related to the nature of their activism.

Young people are accused constantly of being apathetic. The Generation X hype of the 1990s, among other things, reinforced the idea that young people only care about themselves. Alternatively, participation and activism is seen to be reserved only for the truly committed, the truly active, the truly agitated. Activism is thus presented as an "either-or" proposition: totally apathetic versus totally active. Analysis of how young people actually live their lives, however, tells us that young people can be both at the same time. It depends upon the day, their relationships, their resources, and their interests. There are few people at either end of the activism continuum.

Activism is presented as one-dimensional in other ways. Some forms of activism are seen as legitimate, others not. Some forms of activity are seen as activism; some are not. Is the production of Zines, by and for young women, an activist activity? Is watching the Gay and Lesbian Mardi Gras with friends an activist activity? Is it only direct participation in street demonstrations that counts, or are there other means of being and becoming an activist? Activism is usually associated with transgressive actions, those that challenge and seek to transcend existing ways of doing things. But what if a youth attends the illegal rave party in the public park, not because of progressive politics and its agenda of democratization of public spaces— but because it is fun? Where do the lines between activism and adrenaline cross?

The complaint of youth apathy is frequently contradicted in the actions of the young. In Australia high-school kids have organized and participated in great numbers in events such as antiracism marches, antiwar marches, and reconciliation marches (related to indigenous people and the colonialism legacy). Youth have been prominent in demonstrations against capitalist business, the World Bank, and the International

Monetary Fund (IMF). They have been active on refugee issues, bringing their passion to defend asylum seekers against enforced detention. They are central players in the fight over environments and protection of animals from cruelty and extinction. Certain types of events tend to be particularly well attended by young people.

The following significant mass-action events demonstrate this participation:

High school marches against *racism*. These were organized by and for young people in 1998 in protest against the policies and propaganda of the One Nation Party (a right-wing, racist, populist party) and its fellow travelers in the mainstream political parties.

Mass demonstrations against *capitalism*. This was especially the case in Melbourne on September 11, 2000, when thousands of people converged around Crown Casino, site of the World Economic Forum, to protest against the WTO, the World Bank, the IMF, and other institutions and institutional supporters of capitalism.

Persistent agitation against *environmental degradation*. This has largely featured anti-logging protests, often in remote parts of the bush, but has also included mass demonstrations in cities, and particularly targeted the practice of clear-cutting of old growth forests.

Not surprisingly, the active presence of young people at such events, as activists, has in turn been accompanied by conservative critiques. Activism outside conventional political channels (such as youth parliaments, political parties, and the ballot box) often meets with disapproval. Moreover, if young people do engage in these alternative types of activism, then they "don't really know their own mind." That is, they have been duped by adult activists, by members of far-left socialist organizations, by the idealistic Greenies. Activism that even remotely smacks of the collective form of agency gets redefined as not really the activism of youth.

Ironically, youth activism inside of so-called "approved" forums is also often dismissed as not being "real" activism. Young people, it seems, are damned if they do and damned if they don't. In this instance the criticism often originates from outside commentators—usually youth-studies academics who identify with some sections of the Left. The criticism has much the same substance as the previous one. That is, young people who enter into local government youth groups or school councils or youth parliaments are seen to be under the guidance (read: control) of adults and are forced to follow protocols appropriate to the organization in question. Following rules and receiving some kind of training are equated with the young people "not knowing their own minds" and simply slotting into someone else's agenda.

The reality, however, is a bit more complicated. Activism is always learned behavior. One does not become a fully fledged activist overnight. It requires learning from those around you—the language, the techniques, the chants, the organizational structures, the key ideas, who your friends are, who the enemy is. Whether it be in a new social movement or your local council, there is a period of adjustment and training as one moves further into the activist sphere.

In addition, socialization into activism and participatory practices does not mean that we leave our brains behind. Young people have demonstrated that they use public forums of all kinds to express what they feel and think. In some cases, it may well be that young people are heavily influenced by others around them, but this is not unusual for a person of any age. On the other hand, structured or organized youth forums can allow for types of youth participation that actually do have bite, that will indeed impact upon policymaking and wider political decisions. Acknowledging the limitations of conventional and more institutionalized avenues of youth participation ought not to be the same as saying that such opportunities will not have any effect. For example, the involvement of young people in local government forums (equivalent to municipal councils) can change the wider political climate. This is especially so in regard to "law-and-order" environments in which youth, when provided with a chance to voice their opposition to moral panics and anti-youth legislation, have occasionally been able to implement youth-friendly policies and practices.

It is important to be skeptical about formal mechanisms, but the cynicism of the armchair critic misses the potential and potency of organized channels of youth participation. Observation of federal and state youth forums shows that very often governments and political parties do selectively choose participants and that the agenda and processes (such as roundtables and consultations) preclude the possibility of unfettered participation and the setting of alternative goals and values. It is well known that managing young people's participation and channeling it into mainstream outlets is attractive politically for governments faced with potentially difficult social issues and active social movements. Nevertheless, *local* government is often constituted as quite a different kind of arena. Here, young people do have more scope to shape policy and to engage in civic participation that, in many cases, mirrors the concerns of the new social movements. Activism that takes conventional form is still activism if it challenges the broader rules of the game and the values that those rules are seen to uphold.

Conclusion

Youth activism in Australia is complex, contradictory, and ambiguous. There are many ways in which young people can be active and many criticisms of them regardless of how, or even whether, they are. Young people engage in "politics" for myriad different reasons with differing motivations, levels of political consciousness, and degrees of commitment.

Most activism is associated with progressive causes and social-justice agendas in the Australian context. Some young people, a small handful, engage in the politics of fear and dabble with the far-right politics of the neo-Nazis. Many thousands more, however, subscribe to environmental movements and support human-rights organizations. And in the middle are the vast numbers of young people who "do their own thing"—until life and circumstances force them to "become active."

See also Demographic Trends Affecting the World's Youth; Eastern Europe, Youth and Citizenship in; Europe, Comparing Youth Activism in; European Identity and Citizenship; Immigrant Youth in Europe—Turks in Germany; Immigrant Youth in the United States; India, Youth Activism in; Indonesia, Youth Activism in; Nigeria, Youth Activism in; Palestinian *Intifada*; Serbia, Youth Activism in (1990–2000); Soweto Youth Activism (South Africa); State and Youth, The; Statute of the Child and Adolescent (Brazil); Tiananmen Square Massacre (1989); Transnational Identity; Transnational Youth Activism; Turkey, Youth Activism in; United Nations, Youth Activism and; Xenophobia; Zapatista Rebellion (Mexico); Zionist Youth Organizations.

Recommended Reading

Glenorchy City Council (2003). *Face the Challenge, Take the Risk, Enjoy the Ride: A Local Government Guide to Youth Participation*. Hobart, Australia: Tasmania Department of Education, Tasmania Office of Youth Affairs, Glenorchy City.

Healy, S. (1999). "Generation X? Young People and Politics." In *Australian Youth Subcultures: On the Margins and in the Mainstream*, edited by R. White. Hobart, Australia: Australian Clearinghouse for Youth Studies, pp. 200–208.

Human Rights and Equal Opportunity Commission (2004). *Ismae—Listen: National Consultations on Eliminating Prejudice against Arab and Muslim Australians*. Sydney, Australia: Human Rights and Equal Opportunity Commission.

McDonald, K. (1999). *Struggles for Subjectivity: Identity, Action, and Youth Experience*. Cambridge: Cambridge University Press.

Poynting, S., Noble, G., Tabar, P., and Collins, J. (2004). *Bin Laden in the Suburbs: Criminalizing the Arab Other*. Sydney, Australia: Sydney Institute of Criminology.

Vromen, A. (2003). "'People Try to Put Us Down ...': Participatory Citizenship of 'Generation X'." *Australian Journal of Political Science*, 38 (1): 79–99.

White, R., and Wyn, J. (1998). "Youth Agency and Social Context." *Journal of Sociology*, 34 (3): 314–327.

White, R., and Wyn, J. (2004). *Youth and Society: Exploring the Social Dynamics of Youth Experience*. Melbourne, Australia: Oxford University Press.

Wierenga, A. (1999). "Imagined Trajectories: Local Culture and Social Identity." In *Australian Youth Subcultures: On the Margins and in the Mainstream*, edited by R. White. Hobart, Australia: Australian Clearinghouse for Youth Studies, pp. 189–199.

Rob White

B

Brazil. *See* Statute of the Child and Adolescent (Brazil).

Bulges of Youth. *See* Youth Bulges.

C

Campus Compact. Campus Compact advances the public purposes of colleges and universities by deepening their ability to improve community life and educate students for civic and social responsibility. Founded in 1985, Campus Compact has deliberately assisted presidents, faculty, staff, and students in strengthening higher education's commitment to community development and student civic engagement. In 2002 Campus Compact launched an intentional effort to support the voice and power of college students in public life. This initiative seeks to establish students as vital stakeholders on campus and to mobilize them to be agents of community and institutional change.

Campus Compact is a national coalition of more than 950 college and university presidents—representing some 5 million students—who are committed to fulfilling the civic purposes of higher education. As the only national higher-education association dedicated solely to campus-based civic engagement, Campus Compact promotes public and community service that develops students' citizenship skills, helps campuses forge effective community partnerships, and provides resources and training for faculty seeking to integrate civic and community-based learning into the curriculum.

Campus Compact's membership includes public and private, two- and four-year institutions across the spectrum of higher education. These institutions put into practice the ideal of civic engagement by sharing knowledge and resources with their communities, creating local development initiatives, and supporting service and service-learning efforts in areas such as K–12 education, health care, the environment, hunger and homelessness, literacy, and senior services. To support this membership the Campus Compact network includes one national office and thirty state offices.

In 2001 in response to increasing public debate around student involvement in communities and decreasing interest in politics, Campus Compact set out to gain a better understanding of how members of the current generation understood their own civic engagement and education. A gathering of thirty-four college students from across the country resulted in the publication of the student-written book, *The New Student Politics: The Wingspread Statement on Student Civic Engagement.* The students took deep exception to the idea that they were not engaged but rather indicated that they needed to deal with problems directly, as part of the process of getting involved in public policy or politics. The students also made it clear that they believed that doing the work of diversity was doing the work of democracy and that, in their service work, many were engaging in communities very different from the ones in which they grew up. They acknowledged that this was difficult and took a level of understanding that they did not readily find in their coursework.

Soon after this gathering, Campus Compact launched a large student mobilization effort, Raise Your Voice–Student Action for Change, designed to increase community and political involvement on hundreds of campuses. The idea of the campaign is to provide motivation, tools, and space for students to take action on issues of their choosing, whether direct service, policy, advocacy, electoral politics, dialog on public issues, or community organizing. At the same time Campus Compact hosted a gathering of national student organizations to build connections between groups, issues, and strategies in order to broaden the overall experiences and effectiveness of students.

Raise Your Voice mobilized student organizers in seventeen states to work with students on campuses in those states while deliberately co-creating opportunities for student leaders to guide the initiative. Campus Compact's work with students through Raise Your Voice focuses on three areas:

Linking student public and community service to democratic action and the many strategies needed to affect social change by connecting students to the conventional political system and elected officials;

Providing students with the opportunities to discuss and learn about how higher education works and what needs to be done to build commitment to student civic engagement and create engaged campuses; and

Building state and national networks of students connected to other campuses and communities involved in similar efforts who have the skills, like community-mapping and public dialog, to build and mobilize their community.

Days at the statehouse, dialogs with elected officials, and training on how to be effective advocates for public policy are examples of opportunities created by and for students involved with Raise Your Voice at Campus Compact. As a result students have met with local, state, and national elected officials addressing issues that they care about, from the global economy to the cost of tuition, and the importance of higher education's civic engagement. Started in 2003, many of these efforts occur during Raise Your Voice–A Month of Action, during which over 250 campuses and 100,000 students across the country coordinate activities to speak collectively about the importance of civic engagement in higher education.

Networks of students created by Campus Compact have a distinct impact on student voice in efforts on campus to increase civic engagement and have often given more passion and sense of immediacy to these efforts as they move forward. These students have acted as a bridge between service and advocacy groups, as well as creating opportunities for student voice in campus decision-making. As a result, students have lobbied for increased service-learning opportunities on campus, created ongoing spaces for students to discuss public issues, and have played critical roles in building campus-community partnerships. Co-written by students, *Students as Colleagues: Expanding the Circle of Service-Learning Leadership* documents the ways that students are leading course-based service-learning programs on campuses across the country.

In 2004 Raise Your Voice student leaders from across the country gathered to discuss their experiences mobilizing other students and advocating for increased commitment to civic engagement on campus and to document lessons learned from student civic engagement. The central theme of this conversation was the critical role that a college or university plays in modeling civic engagement for students. National Raise Your Voice student fellows are issuing a call for colleges and universities to realize their role as critical institutions in communities.

Early assessment of Raise Your Voice has indicated that service learning is positively associated with every kind of student engagement from volunteering to voting. Additionally, training, mentoring, and supporting students in their community engagement using many tested, effective interventions (i.e., peer-to-peer recruitment, hubs for civic engagement on campus, collaboration between civic engagement approaches) have led to deep levels of involvement that go beyond simplistic notions of volunteerism and enable students to become engaged and effective community members.

Campus Compact's award programs recognize students every year on the state and national level for their ongoing commitment to strengthening communities and finding innovative solutions to real-world problems. Through Campus Compact, students have the opportunity to speak out and take on leadership roles on the national level. Campus Compact's unique structure connects students to presidents, faculty, legislators, and others in order to advance community and civic engagement as well as public policy that supports campus-community partnerships and engaged campuses.

Student voices are critical not only to increasing the breadth and depth of young people and students involved in their communities and public life but also to creating an expectation that going to college should provide many opportunities to learn about and participate in public life. To this end Campus Compact is working with the Princeton Review to publish *Colleges with a Conscience*, a guide for prospective college students on the culture of activism and civic engagement on campuses across the country.

Campus Compact challenges all of higher education to make civic and community engagement an institutional priority and supports student action toward this goal. For more information on Campus Compact and Raise Your Voice go to http://www.compact.org.

See also Campus Crusade for Christ International (CCC); Civic Virtue; Community Service; Emerging Adulthood; Empowerment; Social Justice; Social Responsibility; Student Political Activism; Volunteerism.

Recommended Reading

Germond, T., Love, E., Moran, L., Moses, S., and Raill, S. (In Press). *Raise Your Voice: Lessons Learned*. Providence, RI: Campus Compact.

Long, S. (2002). *The New Student Politics: The Wingspread Statement on Student Civic Engagement*. Providence, RI: Campus Compact.

Williams J., Longo, N., and Zlotkowsk, E. (In Press). *Students as Colleagues: Expanding the Circle of Service-Learning Leadership*. Providence, RI: Campus Compact.

Abby Kiesa

Campus Crusade for Christ International (CCC). With a budget that exceeds $350 million and over 24,000 full-time employees, Campus Crusade for Christ (CCC) serves as the organizational basis for social engagement and activism based on an evangelical mission for students at 1,029 college campus in 152 countries. The size of CCC makes it one of the largest evangelical organizations in the United States. The location of CCC at college campuses, environments that are often hotbeds of activism, combined with the membership of an age-group likely to be involved in activism (see also Emerging Adulthood), makes CCC an important source of resources and organization for a great deal of youth activism.

Founded in 1951 by William "Bill" Bright (1921–2001) at the University of California at Los Angeles, the mission of the interdenominational CCC is to "take the gospel of Jesus Christ to all nations." Bright created an efficient and standardized approach to evangelism by narrowing Christianity's message to the following four spiritual laws:

1. God loves you and offers a wonderful plan for your life.
2. Man is sinful and separated from God, thus cannot know and experience God's love and plan.
3. Jesus Christ is God's only provision for man's sin.
4. We must individually receive Jesus as Savior and Lord.

The four spiritual laws have been published in a booklet, which Crusaders use to achieve the first of three imperatives that define the Crusade mandate: win, build, and send. Once a person is "won" to Christ, the crusader helps the individual develop an understanding of the Christian faith through a systemized study of the "basic principles." To augment the building stage, CCC has published ten booklets, which contain the "transferable concepts" (TCs). TCs are ideas or truths that can be transferred or communicated from one person to another without distorting or diluting their original meaning. The booklets include topics like "How You Can Experience God's Love and Forgiveness" and "How You Can Be a Fruitful Witness." After the building stage individuals are supposed to then evangelize to others.

Although evangelism may not be typically what is thought of when considering the word "activism," religious activism often involves the same mechanisms and motivations that inspire social or political activism. Additionally, evangelical religion tends to be a very "public faith" and often leads to social and political engagement based on religious values. Like social and political activism, religious activism works toward changing society through engagement based on a religious value system as opposed to political, social, or other bases of action. As its training materials state, CCC sees itself as a movement that "will transform their campuses and make an impact around the world."

In the 1970s and 1980s, CCC used massive rallies and blunt proselytizing to attract potential converts. Today, the group relies on more subtle and innovative techniques. In one campus-wide campaign, fliers are posted across campus asking, "Do you agree with Joe?" After the flyers have created a buzz, the campus newspaper publishes an ad stating what Joe believes, which tends to be one of the four spiritual laws. On a designated day following the advertisement, several hundred CCC adherents appear on campus wearing brightly colored T-shirts that say, "I Agree with Joe." CCC then holds a discussion session at which a student (the person's name corresponds to the name of the individual in the ad campaign) describes his or her beliefs.

One of the less novel proselytizing techniques used by CCC is to distribute Christian materials widely. Over 1.5 billion copies of the booklet containing the four spiritual laws have been published in over one hundred languages and distributed across the world. On college campuses CCC gives students thousands of Christian books, CDs, and videos. In the fall of 2000, CCC gave, for example, 200,000 freshman "survival kits," which contained Christian materials along with a questionnaire asking students if they would like to "know God personally." The campus ministries of CCC have been flexible and innovative in creating specialized packages for their message. They have developed specific materials and resources for students in athletics, fraternities, sororities, ethnic minorities, international students, and those training to be in the military.

One of the large-scale distribution projects that have become a signature of CCC is the Jesus film. The film was produced in the late 1970s by John Heyman, who had co-financed major movies such as *The Rocky Horror Show* and *Marathon Man*. In 1979 Warner Brothers released the two-hour film *Jesus* which presented the life of Jesus based on Luke's gospel. Although the film received a lukewarm reception, CCC quickly began to distribute it widely. As of April 2001, 1.5 billion people had seen the film, making it the most-translated movie ever. According to Campus Crusade's calculations, "tens of millions" have "responded" to the message.

As an evangelical movement, the main purpose of CCC is to convert individuals to Christianity. To succeed in this goal, CCC's method of choice has been described as "aggressive evangelism." This method, in contrast to those of similar groups like Inter-Varsity Christian Fellowship, has been critiqued by some as too "in your face" and even insensitive to the beliefs of others. Some religious leaders have, for example, called efforts to produce mass mailings of the Jesus film close-minded, conveying the message that alternative religious expressions are not valid. Others have called the group's campaigns deceptive, because Campus Crusade does not always identify itself up front as the sponsor. To the students who belong to CCC, the issue is not about sensitivity but the importance of their mission and their opinion that their beliefs are ultimately the "right" ones.

Although the group's primary focus is proselytism, CCC has been involved in politics. Because Bill Bright, the group's founder, has always supported Republican and conservative causes, the CCC has become associated with religious and political conservatives. Additionally, CCC relies on donations to support their efforts, and the donors tend to be individuals or groups on the political right. In one of their more visible campaigns, CCC attempted to act as a religious and political countermovement to the radical student activity from the political left that occurred on many college campuses during the 1960s. Demonstrating their flexibility in presentation but not in message, Bright and CCC held campus rallies that often adopted the language of the student counterculture movement such as "Revolution Now!" but redefined the terms to suit their mission of evangelism. Hence, "revolution" was redefined to mean a "spiritual revolution," and Jesus was portrayed as the revolutionary leader.

More recently the group has been involved in controversial campaigns about sexual abstinence, heterosexuality, and race relations. During one National Coming Out Week, for example, CCC placed advertisements in university newspapers that contained testimonies from former homosexuals. While twenty-five school newspapers ran the ads, some refused and others published them next to editorials stating that the paper disagreed with the advertisement's content. In another incident, CCC unsuccessfully tried to run an advertisement in East Tennessee State University's student newspaper honoring Martin Luther King Jr.'s birthday and black history month. The ad contained the headline, "And now a racist remark from God," followed by the words of John 3:16, and then the quote, "I love them all." It also contained text that read, "People forgiven by God have changed hearts, the kind nec-

essary to end racism." The paper had previously run one of CCC's ads proscribing homosexuality. As a result of the negative response, the paper was particularly cautious about including CCC's advertisements. After showing the black history month ad to African American students and staff, the paper rejected it, stating that it was "misleading, needlessly sensationalistic, and racially insensitive." The paper gave CCC an opportunity to submit another ad, which they did.

Campus Crusade for Christ has also drawn criticism from groups who feel like the organization is competing with actual churches. As a nondenominational group, CCC states clearly that it is not a substitute for membership and participation in a local church. Some Christians who do not welcome their aggressive evangelism have argued that CCC's message and methods frame all of Christianity in a negative way. Other religious organizations on campuses and elsewhere complain that CCC makes religious dialog difficult if not impossible. Similarly, some Christian leaders have criticized CCC's standardized approach to Christianity as overly simplistic and superficial.

Despite these criticisms, Campus Crusade for Christ International holds a strong presence among organizations that support and encourage activism among youth. It provides a wealth of resources and an extensive international network of individuals and organizations to support youth activism on a macro scale. At the same time CCC provides many programs aimed at smallscale local activism on campuses and in communities.

See also Campus Compact; Catholic Education and the Ethic of Social Justice; Religiosity and American Youth; Religiosity and Civic Engagement in African American Youth; Spirituality; Student Political Activism; Zionist Youth Organizations.

Recommended Reading

Flake, C. (1984). *Redemptorama: Culture, Politics, and the New Evangelicalism.* Garden City, NY: Anchor Press.

Krapohl, H. R. (1999). *The Evangelicals: A Historical, Thematic, and Biographical Guide.* Westport, CT: Greenwood Press.

Lee, S. (August 10, 1998). "Jesus Draws." *Forbes,* 162 (3): 58–59.

McMurtrie, B. (May 18, 2001). "Crusading for Christ, amid Keg Parties and Secularism." *The Chronicle of Higher Education,* 47 (36): A42.

Quebedeaux, R. (1979). *I Found It! The Story of Bill Bright and Campus Crusade.* San Francisco: Harper and Row.

Reina, Laura. (February 17, 1996). "Campus Paper Rejects Religious Ad." *Editor and Publisher,* 129 (7): 26–27.

Sharn, L. (March 7, 1996). "Campus Crusader: Decades of Work, a Prestigious Award." *USA Today,* 09A.

Zoba, W. M. (July 14, 1997). "Bill Bright's Wonderful Plan for the World." *Christianity Today,* 41 (8): 14–27.

Christopher Scheitle and Amy Adamczyk

Catholic Education and the Ethic of Social Justice. Insofar as there is an identifiable Protestant ethic that prizes the individual, in contrast to the group, and the value of the mundane everyday world, there is, by comparison, a Catholic ethic which gives priority to the common good over the individual and using one's talents to better the lives of others, especially those in need. Of course, both ethics are abstractions that are not necessarily descriptive of the way people function. Further, in a pluralistic nation such as the United States, there is overlap between ethics so that sharp boundaries are countered by shared outlooks that are due to mutual adaptation. Nevertheless, the generalized Catholic ethic can be found clearly in select places, in particular those that are sponsored by the Catholic Church for the purpose of promoting its outlook on life, society, and morality. Catholic schools are one such place, as their role is to socialize young people to sustain and enrich this ethical orientation.

Catholic schools in the United States have a rich history. One factor in their establishment was an effort on the part of Irish, German, Polish, and other ethnic groups to maintain their culture and identity in differentiation from one another. Another impetus was the desire to retain Catholic identity in light the dominant Protestant culture. These two forces combined to lay the groundwork for Catholic schools whose growth continued unimpeded from roughly 1880 through 1965. The former date coincides with the second large wave of immigration that brought many and diverse Catholic groups to this country. The latter date corresponds to the end of the Second Vatican Council, which opened the church to the modern world, and the coming of age of the American Catholic population, symbolized by the election of John F. Kennedy as president.

It is difficult to estimate the proportion of Catholic children that attended Catholic schools, but in industrial cities such as Chicago, it may have been as high as 50 percent in the post–World War II era. More recent estimates put the proportion much lower. Nevertheless, current enrollment is about 2.5 million students in grades K through 12. At least that many more children are estimated to attend classes of religious instruction once per week. Whatever the number at any moment in history, it is clear that over the past 125 years, millions of Catholic children have grown up with formal exposure to religious doctrine and principles of right behavior within the framework of the Catholic ethic.

Communication of the Catholic ethic to children and youth can be understood best by the fact that for most of the past 125 years, religious and moral instruction was led by adults who had made a formal commitment to the religious life. These avowed adults viewed teaching as part of their commitment, with each religious order (e.g., School Sisters of Notre Dame, Sisters of Charity, Christian Brothers) bringing a unique history and offering a particular emphasis regarding the ethic. The following example is presented from an institution that is owned and run by the Jesuits:

The distinctiveness of a[n] ... education stems from our Jesuit heritage, which calls for students to find their unique gifts and talents and become leaders in service to others. It is based on a 450-year-old Jesuit tradition which is shared by

[Jesuit] institutions around the world.... We seek to develop skills that will help our graduates take leadership in building a better world.... Students are encouraged to act on their commitments and values through service to others.

There is hardly a Catholic school that would not be able to articulate its place within a similar tradition. Thus, it is not surprising that our recent survey of a random sample of 189 Catholic secondary schools (estimated at 10 percent of the total), produced the following results. Seventy-seven percent of the schools said that community service was required of all their students. This figure compares with 51 percent of religious, but non-Catholic secondary schools (N = 112).

Given choices on a five-point scale (1 = not very much, 5 = very much), schools responded as follows to a question about the rationale for service:

"Service is a religious duty." The mean response was 4.98.
"Service implements principles of social justice." The mean response was 4.88.
"Service integrates scriptural precepts into life." The mean score was 4.77.
"Service is an adjunct to the teaching of doctrine." The mean score was 4.10.

For the purpose of comparison, mean scores were lower at non-Catholic religious schools for the four items, although scores followed a similar pattern. The largest differences occurred on the items assessing social justice. The Catholic school mean was 4.88 with the other religious schools having a mean of 3.79.

What do the students do in their service? In order from most to least often, they partake in food and clothing drives, tutor or coach younger children, tutor or coach disadvantaged youngsters, visit and assist the elderly, take peer-leadership roles, work in short-term projects such as summer camps, and do functionary work for nonprofit organizations. Finally, when asked about religious and civic justifications for service, the Catholic schools responded by agreeing to both principles weighting social justice at a mean of 5.00 and civic responsibility at 4.48. The corresponding scores for the other religious schools were 4.38 and 4.64, respectively. These four mean scores clearly indicate that religious schools view religious and civic missions as compatible and, most likely, complementary.

It is a well-established fact that churches in the United States are a major source of service opportunities. On the one hand, many churches operate social-service sites (soup kitchens, health care, counseling, etc.), and on the other hand, churches supply volunteers for various service sites beyond their own. It is also known that churches are a resource that provides members with civic skills and civic interest. Putting these data together, one can see that the service emphasis that starts during the school years is carried on by churches for older members throughout the life cycle. In summary, the Catholic ethic of service is put into practice in schools and sustained outside of schools for the purpose of enacting social justice and making society better for everyone, thus perpetuating the Catholic ethic in principle and in practice.

See also Campus Crusade for Christ International (CCC); Religiosity and American Youth; Religiosity and Civic Engagement in African American Youth; Spirituality.

Recommended Reading

Allahyari, R. A. (2000). *Visions of Charity: Volunteer Workers and Moral Community.* Berkeley: University of California Press.

Greeley, A. (2000). *The Catholic Imagination.* Berkeley: University of California Press.

Hallinan, M. T. (2000). "Conclusion: Catholic Education at the Crossroads." In *Catholic Schools at the Crossroads*, edited by J. Youniss and J. J. Convey. New York: Teachers College Press, pp. 201–220.

Kerestes, M., and Youniss, J. (2003). "Rediscovering the Importance of Religion in Adolescent Development." In *Handbook of Applied Development Science: Applying Developmental Science for Youth and Families*, Vol. I, edited by R. M. Lerner, F. Jacobs, and D. Wertlieb. Thousand Oaks, CA: Sage, pp. 165–184.

Meagher, T. (2000). "Ethnic, Catholic, White: Changes in the Identity of European American Catholics." In *The Catholic Character of Catholic Schools*, edited by J. Youniss, J. J. Convey, and J. A. McLellan. Notre Dame, IN: University of Notre Dame Press, pp. 190–218.

Morris, C. (1997). *American Catholics: The Saints and Sinners Who Built America's Most Powerful Church*. New York: Times Books.

Tropman, J. E. (1995). *The Catholic Ethic in American Society: An Exploration of Values*. San Francisco: Jossey-Bass.

Verba, S., Schlozman, K. L., and Brady, H. E. (1995). *Voice and Equality: Civic Volunteerism in American Politics*. Cambridge, MA: Harvard University Press.

Walch, T. "The Past Before Us: Three Traditions and the Recent History of Catholic Education." In *The Catholic Character of Catholic Schools*, edited by J. Youniss, J. J. Convey, and J. A. McLellan. Notre Dame, IN: University of Notre Dame Press, pp. 176–189.

James Youniss

CCC. *See* Campus Crusade for Christ International (CCC); Civilian Conservation Corps (CCC).

Character Education. Character education is a role that schools fulfill in helping to foster the development of prosocial, moral capacities and tendencies of students. While some consider this a controversial role, it has been a central part of schooling—in fact, often *the* central part of schooling—throughout human history. Certainly the classic Greeks (e.g., Socrates, Plato, and Aristotle) understood this clearly. So did the founding fathers of the great experiment in American democracy. Thomas Jefferson argued that democracy depends upon "public-spiritedness" which must be taught. Benjamin Franklin argued that "only a virtuous people are capable of freedom." It is clear that schools not only can but also are obligated to focus on educating for character.

Furthermore, it has been argued that educators cannot avoid character education even if they wanted to. Aristotle noted that "all adults involved with children either help or thwart children's growth and development, whether we like it, intend it or not." Educators frequently concur, recognizing that teachers inevitably impact the development of their students, including their character, whether they want to, intend to, or not. The goal of character education is to systematically, intentionally, and positively foster the development of students' character.

But how can they do that? This has been a matter of great debate as long as people have thought about good and evil. What impacts character? What makes a person inclined and able to promote the welfare of self and others? What can schools do to make this optimally possible? That is precisely the mission of character education.

To do this, one first has to clearly define character. Various definitions exist. The Character Education Partnership, the national character-education professional organization, defines character as "understanding, caring about, and acting upon core ethical values" (sometimes referred to as the *head*, *heart*, and *hand* of character). This recognizes that character is multifaceted, including cognitive (understanding/head), affective (caring about/heart), and behavioral (acting upon/hand) components. Others have even more complex definitions, but the bottom line is that character is (a) psychological, (b) multidimensional, (c) developmental, and (d) ethical. Character is the set of psychological characteristics (e.g., emotions, thinking, conscience, values, social skills, motives, etc.) that leads one to be able to do the right thing.

The next step is to understand how character develops. This is actually a very complex issue, largely due to the complexity of character itself. We know that character begins to develop as early as eighteen months of life and continues throughout one's life span. We know that family is the primary influence on the development of character, largely through parenting and the modeling of family members. Across families, schools, and other influences, the primary means of impacting character development are how people treat the child, how people treat each other in the child's presence, and what significant others espouse. Of course, the clarity and consistency both within and across these influences also affect their impact.

Most importantly, character is affected by caring deeply for children, setting high but possible (and supported) expectations for children, modeling desirable character traits, authentically empowering children (i.e., giving them a "voice" in their families, schools, etc.), and helping them understand how their behavior affects others (and how important that is to you). These are all things that parents, teachers, and other adults who interact with children can do to foster the development of character. All of these, furthermore, are based in extensive psychological research.

Ideally, character education is a comprehensive school-reform project. Many schools try to compartmentalize character education as a discrete set of lessons, part of student government or counseling, a monthly assembly or set of posters or announcements, a reward or recognition program. But effective character education is accomplished when it pervades the entire life of the school, that is, when it is in the curriculum, discipline code, mission statement, extracurricular activities, professional development, leadership style, classroom management philosophy, and student government, to name a few.

School leadership is critical. It is difficult to shift the culture of an entire school if the school's administration does not understand character development and character education or is not fully committed to promoting it as a top educational priority. Effective school-reform leaders also need to know how to shepherd the development of a caring, professional learning community among the adults who work in the school. Only when the vast majority of the staff "get it" can it be institutionalized for the students' developmental benefit.

Effective character education programs tend to (a) be multifaceted (i.e., they use multiple, typically six to eight, strategies); (b) use peer interactive strategies like class meetings and cooperative learning; (c) invest heavily in professional development;

(d) integrate character education into the academic curriculum; (e) directly teach social and emotional competencies like conflict resolution and anger management; (f) encourage or even require student service to others (e.g., community service, classroom helping roles, service learning); (g) promote the discussion of ethical issues; (h) model good character (e.g., staff modeling, other adult modeling, peer mentors); (i) involve parents and other community members in meaningful ways; and (j) empower student voices (e.g., authentic student government, democratic classroom management, student-led parent conferences).

Many educators are daunted by what they perceive as a set of new duties added to their already "full plate." However, character education is not something to add to the "plate," rather character education "is the plate." In other words, character education is not an addition but a different way of running classrooms and schools. Furthermore, an investment of time, energy, and professional development in character education pays off in the long run by recapturing school time that would have been wasted on motivating students, managing student misbehavior, and classroom disruption. Some of the most common benefits of character education documented in research are accelerated development of social-thinking skills, increased prosocial behavior and attitudes, better problem-solving skills, reduced drug use, reduced violence and aggression, improved general school behavior, more knowledge about and healthier attitudes toward risk behaviors, greater emotional competency, improved academic achievement, and increased emotional attachment to school. This list demonstrates the robust effects of successful comprehensive character education on students' development. It impacts students' ways of thinking, their feelings, and their behaviors. It increases positive development and reduces negative development. And it not only fosters character development but also improves learning and academic achievement.

It should be no surprise that when students are respected and challenged with high expectations, when they are taught the social and emotional skills necessary for an effective life, and when they regularly interact with adults who model democratic behaviors, then these students develop positive character, bond to their schools, and learn more. On the other hand, when schools are demeaning to students (e.g., treat them as immature, incompetent, and dangerous) and saddle them with boring curricula, and when adults are inconsistent and model undesirable characteristics, then those settings tend to produce students of poor character.

There is a growing science of character education that is built upon solid research evidence and knowledge of the psychological development of children. If schools pay attention to this body of knowledge and commit to the dual purpose of schools (i.e., intellectual and character development), then our schools, our children, and our society will all benefit.

See also Civic Virtue; Democratic Education; Diversity Education; Environmental Education (EE); IEA Civic Education Study; Just Community High Schools and Youth Activism; National Alliance for Civic Education (NACE); Prosocial Behaviors; School Engagement; School Influences and Civic Engagement.

Recommended Reading

Beland, K. *Eleven Principles Sourcebook*. Washington, D.C.: Character Education Partnership.

Berkowitz, M. W., and Bier, M. C. (2004). "Research-Based Character Education." *Annals of the American Academy of Political and Social Science*, 591: 72–85.

Bier, M. C. (In Press). *What Works in Character Education*. Washington, D.C.: Character Education Partnership.

Lickona, T. (1991). *Educating for Character*. New York: Bantam.

Marvin Berkowitz

Chat Rooms, Girls' Empowerment and. While many parts of the world and social groups are still disadvantaged in accessing the Internet, in Western societies girls and

Especially for girls in Western countries who have Internet access, online chat rooms are becoming an increasingly powerful source of ideas and information.

boys have gained more or less equal access. There is increasing awareness of the importance of access to and use of the Internet for equal opportunity regarding life chances. The Internet not only functions as an information medium but also as a communication medium. There are strong reasons to believe that girls benefit from communicating on the Internet. The specific conditions of chat-room communication provide opportunities to act in alternative ways to the gender-specific and often subconscious conduct in real life. Girls gain self-confidence, learn about gender-specific expectations and attributions, and learn how to contest them. Girls as well as boys experience new ways of acting in chat rooms that may also be transformative in real life.

Since the mid-1990s, the Internet has become more and more part of everyday work and leisure time in Western societies. But the Internet is still not a democratic medium to which all men and women have equal access. Despite its increasing availability, a "digital divide" exists between industrialized and developing countries as well as between social classes within industrialized countries.

Many researchers argue that access to the Internet depends on level of education. Higher education especially tends to lead to higher incomes, which increases the possibilities for Internet access. Social inequality produces a digital divide, and at the same time the digital divide increases existing inequalities or produces new ones.

In contrast to social inequality based on age, class, and ethnicity, gender differences decrease with the further distribution of the Web. Once disproportionately used by males, the Internet is now accessed by men and women almost equally. In Austria, 45 percent of Internet users are female. In the United States, there are even more women than men using the Internet. Globally, however, gender differences still remain. Overall, women use the Web less frequently and less intensively than men.

Young people are most likely to use the Internet. In Austria, 91 percent of the age-group fourteen to nineteen are Internet users. The proportion of girls and boys is well-balanced, but they differ in how they use the Web. Whereas girls are likely to have to use a modem and a telephone connection, boys are more likely to be able to use a fixed connection. As a result, boys spend more time online than girls on average. Boys and girls also differ in what they use the Web for. Girls like to communicate and to search for concrete information, whereas boys surf around, play, and also use more technically complicated applications (downloads of programs and MP3s)—a distinction related to different Internet connections.

Chatting is the favorite activity of young people on the Internet. In Austria, 80 percent of girls and boys younger than fifteen use chat rooms; 40 percent of the population younger than fifteen use them frequently. For young people below nineteen, 5 percent are frequent chat-room users. The numbers for American girls and boys are similar. An American study shows that girls and boys spend the same amount of time in chat rooms, whereas Austrian boys chat a little less than girls. In Austria, migrant youth use chat rooms slightly more than the average.

On a technical level there are different kinds of chat rooms. The first provider of such synchronous communication was IRC (Internet Relay Chat), but today Web Chats are most commonly used. Visual chats also exist where the chat participants can display themselves using avatars (e.g., comic figures). Chat communication can also be supported by Web cams or acoustic transmission. Related to chat rooms are instant-messenger systems (e.g., ICQ). The user saves his or her friends ("buddies") in the computer, and when one of them goes online, the program recognizes them und informs the user.

Chat providers usually offer not only one but many different rooms, and the participants choose one room or more in which to chat. The separate rooms tend to have certain target groups, for example a certain age-group coming from a particular place. Chat rooms deal with a range of topics. Most chat rooms that young people use are "flirt chats," meaning that the young chatters want to get to know new people and communicate with them. For young people chat rooms are experimental. New and sometimes otherwise forbidden behavior can be tried. For example, a boy with low self-confidence may dare to address a girl. Or a girl may insult a boy in a way that she would not do in real life. Research shows that long-term contacts between chatters do not develop very often, not to mention friendships and relationships. Usually teenage chat partners do not meet each other in real life, although they tend to act as if the main goal of chatting is to set up a date in real life. They often exchange phone numbers, too, but actually, the exchange seems to be more important than possible phone calls.

Unlike face-to-face communication, chat allows one to take part in several conversations simultaneously. Experienced users chat with up to ten people in separate conversations at the same time. Conversations can be either held in a common room where other people also have their own conversations, or two (or more) chat partners use a separate, "private" room.

An important feature of the communication is its nonbinding character. Chatting involves neither duties nor responsibilities. Usually users can decide for themselves if and when to quit a conversation. They do not have to fear any consequences in real life resulting from their actions. In the worst case they get banned from a certain chat room, but even then all they have to do is to find a new nickname and they can participate again. Certain codes of behavior exist that operators may enforce. For example, operators may discourage "flooding" (too many chunks by one person) or rude name-calling.

In contrast with face-to-face communication, facial expression and gesture are not possible in chat rooms. Users substitute the missing physicality with emoticons and acronyms. Emoticons are represented by a large variety of "smileys" (smile faces), and acronyms are abbreviations that are used to express certain feelings or behaviors (e.g., "lol" for "laughing out loud"). Users can thus exercise control over their own display and personae—unwanted appearances through posture, facial expression, and sounds are not visible. This may increase the feeling of security and help to overcome one's inhibition to get in contact with others. Furthermore, people do not appear contextualized in chat rooms. This means that people can communicate with others with whom they would not talk if they knew how they looked. Physical attractiveness and social-class status are less important in chat rooms than in real life. However, virtual

interactions still involve imagining the bodies of others.

The absence of physicality in virtual communication has lead to the assumption that, while on the Internet, people display an identity other than the one they hold in real life, including gender identity. Recent research shows that changing one's gender identity is most common in Multi-User Dungeons (or MUDs, virtual role plays), where people represent themselves through a self-made figure. In chat rooms, there is no deconstruction or reconstruction of the body, but the participants interact with the use of their imaginations. Because we assume that the gender identity of our partners is their "real" one, credibility plays an important role—if a person says that she or he is female or male, the chat partner develops certain perceptions and expectations concerning the gender-specific online behavior of the other person. If these expectations are not fulfilled, it will not be long until the chat partner will conclude "that there is something wrong." This means that even in chat rooms it is not easy for anyone, male or female, to change his or her gender identity and remain credible. Studies show that only 5 percent of chat-room users change their gender identity. Young people are especially preoccupied with developing their gender identity. It is new and interesting to them to present themselves or to be perceived as adolescent girls or boys. There is no need for the teenagers to try a new gender identity; experiments with their own identity are exciting enough.

Some observers regard the process of gender swapping as defensive conduct, that is, women use it as a mask to make themselves invisible in order to avoid sexual harassment on the Internet. Other authors describe a more progressive and subversive motive for gender swapping by helping to reduce gender hierarchies. Men, for example, use the anonymity of chat rooms to present themselves more emotionally, while women act more aggressively than in real life.

Research carried out in Vienna and Los Angeles shows that teenage girls and boys do not "swap gender." On the contrary, it is important for them to let the chat partners know about their "real" gender identity. They often represent their gender identity immediately by choosing certain nicknames. Girls make their gender membership explicit in order to be recognized as girls. Thus, they use girls' first names or add "-girl" to the name. If a nickname is gender neutral, everyone regards the person as male. Young people also represent their gender membership with a stereotypical use of nicknames. The girls present themselves as sexually attractive (e.g., "sexygirl"), the boys as active in public life (e.g., "subculture"). After this initial display of gender, various forms of representation of the "real" gender identity can be found in the chat communication of the girls and boys. For example, the boys expect the girls to behave in a more passive way in the conversations, and they are surprised when the girls ask many questions instead of just replying to the boys' questions. The boys want to know what the girls look like, while the girls are more interested in the boys' activities than in their looks. For girls, the main intention of chatting is having a nice or thrilling conversation, whereas the goal of the boys is to get the girl's phone number and arrange a date in real life. Accordingly, young people show gender stereotypical behavior in many aspects, emphasizing their real-life gender identity. But regarding the specific conditions of chat rooms, there are also possibilities for atypical behavior.

Under some circumstances, girls can benefit from chat-room interactions compared to interactions in real life. While in cross-gender communication men tend to decide which themes are to be discussed, in chat communication girls have as much control of the topics as their male chat partners. The fact that the boys cannot interrupt their contributions allows girls to both introduce the themes that interest them and also contribute as much as the

boys. They insist on their interests and are usually successful in spite of occasional opposition. Often they achieve their goal—having a nice or thrilling conversation and not exchanging telephone numbers. If they do not approve of the development of the conversation, they can exercise the option of quitting without explanation and consequences. They fight against stereotypical gender attributions and seem to enjoy arguments with their partners. In the context of flirting, girls present themselves as independent from possible boyfriends, and they fight against the pet names the boys use for them. They also offer compliments to their partners and do not wait until the boys start to flirt with them. Because they cannot be judged by their physical appearance, it is easier for them to act with more self-confidence than in real life.

It is instructive to look at the interactions of girls and boys outside chat rooms and how they relate to virtual interactions. At the youth centers where one study was conducted, the girls invented a game in which they hold a higher, more powerful position than the boys they are chatting with: They do not start to chat with a stranger as usual, but they begin a conversation with a boy who is also currently chatting in the youth center. The boy of course does not know who he is chatting with and the girls make fun of him. They play with gender stereotypes; for example, they describe themselves as very sexually attractive and ask for a date, which girls usually never do. This shows that they are very much aware of gender-specific expectations. They do not simply follow the expectations but play with them and use them to kid the boys.

In face-to-face interactions people cannot control their posture, facial expression, and sounds that follow gender-specific attributions and the expectations that we tend to perform subconsciously. Being "invisible" therefore means two things for the girls: First, divorced from face-to-face contact, they gain awareness of gendered expectations. Second, girls are especially used to being judged by their physical appearance. Because of their invisibility, they experience a new freedom. On the one hand, it helps them to gain self-confidence, enabling them to express their own desires and needs and also to fight for them. On the other hand, it also provides the possibility of behaving against gender-specific expectations or to play with them. These two consequences— growing self-confidence and behaving against expectations—go hand in hand. Without more self-confidence the awareness of gendered attributions and expectations would not lead into actual alternative ways of acting.

Our society is more and more determined by media. Young people grow up in a digitalized world and spend a growing amount of time using new media which increases its relevance and impact on values and behavior. New media support individualization processes and flexible structures of relationships and everyday life. They provide a chance for opening up traditional or rigid values that determine gender-specific behavior. Girls are clearly experimenting— their behavior in chat rooms is not only different from their behavior in real life, but they also start to transfer alternative ways of acting into real life. The experiences that the girls and boys have in chat rooms should not be regarded as exceptional but rather as central to their lives. We do not yet know if, how, and how fast gender roles and attributions will change through the impact of new media. However, we can assume that the experiences had in virtual reality will not remain irrelevant for real life.

See also Digital Divide; Empowerment; Gender Differences in the Political Attitudes of Youth; New Media; Riot Grrrl.

Recommended Reading

Beißwenger, M., ed. (2001). *Chat-Kommunikation. Sprache, Interaktion, Sozialitaet and Identitaet in synchroner computervermittelter Kommunikation. Perspektiven auf ein neues Forschungsfeld.* Stuttgart: Ibidem-Verlag.
Cooper, J., and Weaver, K. D. (2003). *Gender and Computers: Understanding the Digital Divide.* Mahwah, NJ, and London: Lawrence Erlbaum Associates.
Doering, N. (2000). "Geschlechterkonstruktionen und Netzkommunikation." In *Soziales im Netz. Sprache, Beziehungen und Kommunikationskulturen im Internet,* edited by C. Thimm. Opladen: Westdeutscher Verlag.
Norris, P. (2001). *Digital Divide: Civic Engagement, Information Poverty, and the Internet Worldwide.* New York: Cambridge University Press.
Turkle, S. (1995). *Life on the Screen: Identity in the Age of the Internet.* New York: Simon and Schuster.
Waechter, N. (2004). *Doing Gender and Doing Ethnicity. Eine Untersuchung der Interaktionen von jugendlichen MigrantInnen in Chat rooms.* Dissertation. Universitaet Wien.

Natalia Waechter

Child Labor. Child labor has reemerged as a major issue in the last two decades of the twentieth century. This reemergence comes with two key differences: the issue is now global in scope, and it involves children and young people as activists in the debate over child labor. Earlier anti–child labor campaigns were hardly concerned with the exploitation of the hundreds of millions of children working in colonial plantations, village industries, and peasant farms. But today's anti–child labor campaigning is firmly connected with conditions in the developing world. Similarly, until recently concerned adults spoke and acted in the name of children, rarely if ever allowing them to express their views or take leadership roles. Today, working children are actively organizing themselves to engage in actions to advance their own interests.

The background for recent concerns about child labor and how to address them lie in the crisis sweeping over much of developing world that began in the 1970s. Governments of developing countries received loans from financial institutions such as the International Monetary Fund (IMF) and the World Bank in exchange for introducing far-reaching economic and social reforms (Structural Adjustment Programs or SAPS) that deeply affected living standards. Children's food and health

Spindle boys working in a Georgia cotton mill c. 1912. *Copyright Bettmann/Corbis.*

programs were stopped; the cost of education became prohibitive for many; prices of basic commodities, rents, and services exploded; and countless workers in government service were laid off. In many cases an adult wage was not sufficient to buy the family's basic food requirements. Excluded from schools that they could no longer afford, millions of children were faced with the necessity of working for their family's livelihood.

As a response to the entering of large numbers of children into work, two contending camps emerged: *abolitionism* and *protagonism*. Abolitionists organize in support of a ban of child labor, demanding that education be made affordable, accessible, and compulsory. Protagonists demand the right to work in dignity and the protection of children's jobs. For the latter, the problem is not the fact that children work but that they are exploited. Education should be an option open to children that can be combined with work but not a compulsion and certainly not a way of abolishing child labor.

Abolitionists get most of their support from adult—mostly Western—organized labor. They believe that developing societies are doomed to remain poor and underdeveloped if they fail to educate their children and have them work from a tender age in backbreaking, unskilled jobs. Children are seen as in demand not for their special qualities as workers but because they are docile and cheap. If sufficient political and moral pressure is built up, adults could replace child laborers. Failing to act against child labor would have a deleterious effect on adult employment in both developing and developed societies. Adult jobs and wages must be protected against what they see as unfair competition from children.

For protagonists, abolitionists are insensitive to the urgent survival needs of those in extreme poverty—including children—in the developing world. Abolitionists, in their view, underestimate working children's ability to shoulder responsibilities toward their families and see them narrowly as victims of poverty. Instead, protagonists see children as active agents involved in the remaking of their own societies who value what they learn at work and demand the right to organize to defend their interests. Protagonists claim to represent voices of children working in agriculture and in the unorganized, informal sectors of the urban economy. These children form the vast majority of working children whom the debate on child labor all too often forgets.

The tensions between protagonists and abolitionists are reflected in the terms they use: while abolitionists consistently use the term "child labor" to stress that they are talking about an unacceptable form of labor, protagonists prefer the term "working children" to emphasize that the majority of the world's children work for a living and at the same time that this it does not make them any less children than their nonworking peers in wealthier classes or countries.

Protagonists have triggered debates on the political and economic role of children in society and helped draft labor laws that recognize that children in the developing world normally work from an early age. They have mobilized and drawn strength from a range of international meetings and declarations meant to unite working children behind a program of action. A historical landmark was reached in 1996 in the south Indian town of Kundapur, where an international meeting of working children produced the "Kundapur Ten Points." The movement is supported by a number of nongovernmental organizations (NGOs) and international organizations. Representatives of the movement have been welcomed at the UNICEF summit, A World Fit for Children (2002), in New York and at the World Bank. However, the movement's global impact has been less extensive than that of the abolitionist lobby who mobilized the major Global March against Child Labor and who have effectively used the media to promote young heroes of the anti–child labor movement.

In the 1990s, threats of U.S. boycotts against countries accused of making use of child labor in their exports hung over the preparatory discussions for the World Trade Organization (WTO). Threats were based on U.S. Senator Tom Harkin's draft bill, the Child Labor Deterrence Act (1992), that prohibited the importation of goods produced by child labor into the United States. A freshly created Senate Child Labor Committee produced a thick report with the telling title *By the Sweat and Toil of Children* substantiating the large-scale involvement of children in the production of imported goods. Exporters, consumer associations, and trade unions lobbied intensely to induce the North American and European governments to support a "social clause" as a condition for WTO membership. The social clause would bar membership to countries found wanting in respect of their core labor standards, including the prohibition of child labor. To increase pressure, the anti–child labor lobby threatened in 1994 to boycott Bangladesh's garment industry. Accused of making extensive use of child labor, the industry exported about 150 million shirts a year to the United States. The threat induced Bangladeshi exporters to fire, virtually overnight, about 50,000 children, mostly girls. Thousands of children reacted furiously, picketing the factory gates and attempting to obtain indemnity for the loss of their income. They lost the battle.

Months later many of them were found in risky and badly paid jobs in the informal service sector. The number of those back in school was negligible, although this was the ostensible goal of the anti–child labor lobby. After millions of dollars had been spent to set up special schools, register the children, and provide them with stipends, the results remained disappointing. On further inquiry, it became clear that the working children had already taken on adult responsibilities and were now more worried about how to pay the rent and buy food for their younger siblings than schooling.

The first WTO meeting rejected the idea of including a social clause as a condition for membership and referred the issue to International Labor Organisation (ILO) in Geneva. In 1973 the ILO had adopted a convention that prohibited the employment of children under age fifteen (*ILO Convention 138*). Claiming that the convention was unsuitable to their situation of underdevelopment, South Asian governments declined ratification. The ILO prepared a new convention on the worst forms of child labor (*ILO Convention 182*) to which South Asian governments could not object since it specifically dealt with crimes against children such as sexual exploitation, the use of children in drug trafficking, and war. That convention was adopted in 1999.

Countrywide consultations to draft Convention 182 started in the course of 1996. In the Netherlands it was suggested that since the 1989 UN Convention on Children's Rights (CRC) granted children a right to participation, working children should be consulted. The Dutch ministry received the idea positively and decided to fund an international consultation of working children. A number of NGOs from the developing world with a record in child participation were requested to send delegates to what was soon to be known as the "Kundapur meeting."

Kundapur is a small town in Karnataka, South India, where *Bhima Sangha*, an organization of working children, hosted this first international meeting of representatives of working children. About thirty working children, representing as many countries, were brought together and discussed for two weeks their common concerns. This resulted in the "Kundapur Ten Points," listed below:

1. We want recognition of our problems, our initiatives, proposals, and our process of organization.

2. We are against the boycott of products made by children.
3. We want respect and security for ourselves and the work we do.
4. We want an education system whose methodology and content are adapted to our reality.
5. We want professional training adapted to our reality and capabilities.
6. We want access to good health care for working children.
7. We want to be consulted in all decisions concerning us at the local, national, or international level.
8. We want the root causes of our situation, primarily poverty, to be addressed and tackled.
9. We want more activities in rural areas and decentralization in decision-making, so that children will no longer be forced to migrate.
10. We are against exploitation at work, but we are for work with dignity with hours adapted so that we have time for education and leisure.

The delegates agreed on three points: first, that as workers they have a right to exist; second, that this right must be protected from those who want to abolish child labor; and third, that acknowledging this right does not redeem adults from taking responsibility for children's well-being. Though demanding respect for their work and taking a firm stand against boycotts, working children do not want to compete with adults for jobs. They recognize the latter's duties toward children and propose to be their allies in a common struggle for the dignity of all workers. Their wish to organize separately is born out of the dreaded effects of anti–child labor campaigning and their exclusion from trade unions, not from a sense that their interests are separate from those of adult workers. It is worth considering further three of the key organizations from the developing world that had important roles to play at Kundapur.

1. *Bhima Sangha.* In the early 1980s, trade-union activists in South India discovered

that many children attended the meetings they held for workers in the informal sector. Child labor being prohibited, none of the regulations applicable to adult workers were applicable in the event that the worker was a child (no minimum wage, no job protection, no security, etc.). Children were also barred by law from union membership. The situation was likely to worsen, as the ILO was putting pressure on the Indian government to ratify Convention 138. Activists of a NGO named the Concerned for the Working Children (CWC) undertook to draft a child-labor law that instead of prohibiting all types of employment would seek to protect working children from exploitation. The bill made a distinction between unacceptable, exploitative work in particularly dangerous sectors—for example, glass manufacturing, carpet weaving, szari-embroidery, and brass work—and work that was not dangerous. In 1986 the Indian government passed the Child Labor Prohibition and Regulation Act in which some of the CWC-propositions were accepted.

Realizing that most of the working children in Bangalore were migrants from rural areas, CWC activists started projects in surrounding villages to provide education and occupational training to working children. In 1989 they launched a newspaper for and by young workers. The newspaper encouraged the formation of small groups, eventually leading to the founding of *Bhima Sangha*, a working children's union that now has a membership of 16,000 (see http://www.workingchild.org). *Bhima Sangha* organizes elections of *Makkala Panchayats* (children's village councils), runs a training center for working children (*Namma Bhoomi,* Our Land), and keeps close links with a union for youths older than eighteen.

The organization's position on child labor is that while governments must strive to eradicate poverty, children should have the right to work in safe and dignified occupations that leave room for education, leisure, and personal development. Education is not seen as an alternative to work but as a universal right. For children who have to work, education and occupational training should be provided in appropriate, accessible ways, deliver recognized diplomas, and prepare young workers to become agents of change. Coupled with such education, children's work can help break the cycle of poverty and oppression.

2. *African Movement of Working Children and Youth (AMWCY).* Also in the early 1980s, activists involved in the Africa-based organization Environmental Development Action in the Third World (ENDA) were confronted with increasing numbers of children migrating to West African cities in search of a livelihood. With twenty-one other branches in southern countries, ENDA is a large NGO promoting an activist, empowerment approach to development. A first meeting of street and working children was held in Grand Bassam, Ivory Coast, in 1985. Convinced of their ability to identify and sustain actions on their behalf, participants requested from ENDA the creation of a section for children and youth. The Youth and Child Workers program (YCW) was created in 1985 to train young people in self-organization (see http://www.enda.sn/english). Youth from twenty-five African countries became involved in the training. On May 1, 1992, a group of young maids in Dakar, Senegal, decided to participate in the celebrations of Workers' Day. Other working children in Dakar as well as in other Senegalese cities soon joined in. Trade unions welcomed the initiative. In 1994 delegates of the movement of working children and youth in Senegal met in Bouaké, Ivory Coast, with activists from Burkina Faso, Ivory Coast, and Mali. They drafted a list of twelve rights that would inspire the Kundapur Ten Points. The meeting marks the beginning of the Mouvement Africain des Enfants et Jeunes Travailleurs (African Movement of Working Children and Youth, AMWCY). Local groups include porters, shoe shiners, rag pickers, and maids. Maids are particularly active and well organized. Members of AMWCY also contributed to

the official UN document A World Fit for Children (2002) and take pride in their efforts to put working children's rights on the front burner.

3. *MANTHOC* (Peru). In 1976 when the Peruvian state was under a military dictatorship, massive layoffs swelled the ranks of children and youth working in the streets in the informal sector. These children and youths faced horrific working conditions. Charitable responses from churches and the voluntary sector rescued a few children but failed to equip them to survive independently. Drug trafficking worsened the situation, turning poor children into targets of police repression. Young militants of the leftist Catholic Young Christian Workers started organizing children to "strengthen their power as social actors." The idea was to prepare them for active union membership as adults. In the summer of 1979, the children decided to name their organization MANTHOC (Movement of Working Children and Adolescents from Christian Working-Class Families). MANTHOC did not propose to eradicate child labor but to defend the rights of children as workers. It sought to foster not just an individual but also a collective social and political identity for these children. Children must become actors engaged in social change.

Participatory democracy plays a central role: the movement is both a critique of "adultism" and of western conceptions of childhood which would make children socially invisible and exclude them from public life. It rejects the abolitionist stance that reduces working children to mere victims of poverty: work is a key ingredient of the identity of those the movement calls "NATs" (*Niños y Adolescentes Travajadores*/Working Children and Youth). From a young age NATs have to deal with the cruel reality of exploitation. Even though society fails to recognize them as economic and social actors, they are in practice the "protagonists" of their own lives. MANTHOC's achievements are wide-ranging—persuading local authori-

ties to repair bridges and roads used by children, developing and piloting curricula for NATs, tackling abusive employers, and negotiating better working conditions. In 1996 the Peruvian Ministry of Education started special programs for NATs in nine of Lima's primary schools. In 1998 MANTHOC signed an agreement with city authorities stating that it would create 600 jobs for NATs over the next two years. MANTHOC is a member of the National Movement of Peruvian Young Workers (MNNATSOP), a federation set up in 1996 representing nearly 10,000 children between ages seven and fourteen.

Thus, the working children's movements that played a major role in Kundapur not only had a well-developed agenda of action but had also networked internationally and could count on growing support both from governments and from the nongovernmental sector. Supporters of working children were flown to Kundapur from all over the world as observers. They were impressed that the children took pride in their work and that they did not want to be patronized. Rather, they claimed the right to be taken seriously as workers.

However, in May 1998 when thousands of working children and NGO activists from all corners of the world were marching through the streets of Geneva to lobby the upcoming ILO meeting on draft Convention 182, Kundapur delegates were to meet with great disappointment. The marchers did not want children to be recognized as workers. They demanded immediate action to "stop child labor now."

When the WTO rejected the social clause, the International Confederation of Free Trade Unions (ICFTU) started mobilizing governments, employers, workers, and public opinion in favor of a new ILO convention that could be used to the same effect. There would be a big difference, however; the WTO has a system of sanctions that the ILO lacks. The main weapon of the ILO is public pressure. All energy was therefore concentrated on raising public awareness worldwide against child labor. It was hoped that the Global March against Child Labor would achieve that effect (see http://www.globalmarch.org).

Hosted by the South Asian Coalition Against Child Servitude (SACCS) in New Delhi, the Global March drew inspiration from a variety of Indian experiences. Attempting to stop the privatization of state-owned companies, Indian trade unionists found allies in U.S. trade unions trying to protect jobs against the effects of business outsourcing jobs to low-wage countries. Both felt that child labor in South Asia stood as a symbol for what organized labor would increasingly face in the future if it failed to act. SACCS had some success with rescue operations of children pledged by their parents to an employer against a loan (bonded-labor children). The use of *sathyagraha* (literally "insist on truth"), Gandhi's famous method of nonviolent protest, had also granted SACCS a reputation as an effective organization in mustering public support.

Backed by sizeable funding from international donors and chiefly European and North American governments and trade unions, the Global March soon grew into a formidable media-machine. According to the march organizers, a thousand organizations in 107 countries mobilized a million children, collected 7 million signatures, and covered a total of 80,000 kilometers. As highlighted in the plan of action, the goals of the Global March were not to organize children as workers but to restore them to childhood with an emphasis on education as an alternative to work. To refute accusations of neglecting children's right to participation, once in Geneva the organizers put a Swiss youth organization in charge of holding a workshop in which the child participants would be discussing their work and their actions. They were not to make a public statement, although the spokesperson of the youth organization did offer to summarize publicly the conclusions of the workshops and openly conveyed the children's criticism of adults' control of the march's agenda.

The Global March was nevertheless the culmination of years of activism in which children, although never allowed to take the lead, had played an active role. During the Amsterdam conference (1997) in preparation for the ILO meeting of 1998, the Dutch minister for welfare was, for instance, presented by Dutch school children with a petition carrying tens of thousands of signatures to stop child labor. In many other countries children took a host of initiatives to back the campaign in favor of the new convention. Two child personalities were particularly influential: the Pakistani Iqbal Masih of the Bonded Labor Liberation Front (BLLF) and the Canadian Craig Kilburger, founder of Free the Children.

Iqbal Masih was reportedly only four years old when his father bonded him to a carpet manufacturer against a loan. He worked the loom for fourteen hours a day, rarely allowed to leave the premises of the factory. When about ten he attended a meeting of the Bonded Labor Liberation Front. He was successfully freed from his employer and became an activist in the organization. His frail looks and passionate engagement with the cause of exploited children combined to guarantee his growing media success. When he was awarded the Reebok Youth in Action Award (1994) for his work and traveled to Sweden and the United States, his success as a symbol of public mobilization against child labor was at its height. His career was dramatically put to an end when, in April 1995, Iqbal was murdered in his home village. He was only twelve. Though it is unclear whether the murder had any political connotations, the killers were never caught. During his funeral, a girl, also a former bonded laborer, declared: "The day that Iqbal died, a thousand new Iqbals were born."

The next day the story of Iqbal's murder appeared in the *Toronto Star,* deeply impressing twelve-year-old Craig Kilburger. He and his school friends soon decided to set up Free the Children (FTC). As new children joined, FTC started spreading information about child labor in schools. Craig also addressed a trade-union meeting in Toronto where FTC was promised substantial funds for its work. Craig decided to make a trip to Asia where he met with organizations fighting child labor including Child Workers in Asia (CWA) in Bangkok, BLFF in Pakistan, and SACCS in Delhi and Calcutta. He was awarded the Roosevelt Freedom Medal and the State of the World Forum Award. In 1998 he was named a Global Leader of Tomorrow at the World Economic Forum in Davos.

The organization's aim is to fight child labor so that working children can enjoy a childhood in school with sufficient time to play. FTC's slogan "Children can free the children" articulates the activists' belief that children are the legitimate spokespersons of other children. FTC takes issue with the consumerist "Western" child who is treated as a vulnerable being incapable of taking responsibility. Children in the West are brainwashed to be consumers and define themselves according to what they *have* and not to what they can *do*. FTC activists are aware of the privilege of living in a supportive environment. But even then, they also know that when it comes to important decisions and official matters, children are usually refused a say. FTC's first objective is "to free children from poverty, exploitation, and abuse" in the developing world. In addition to advocacy, the organization fundraises for rehabilitation centers for bonded-labor children, school buildings, medical services, and income-generating activities for working children's parents.

The most striking difference with working children's movements is that FTC is an organization for, not by, working children. It is more concerned with supporting the international campaign against child labor than engaging with the dignifying aspects of work. Craig, a middle-class kid from the suburbs propelled to the world stage of international human rights, stands for what responsible citizens, even children, can do to mobilize public opinion for the plight of hundreds of millions of downtrodden children in the developing world. He typically ignores the reality of child labor in the wealthy part of the world. His engagement seems to draw more inspiration from a belief in the power of good intentions than from an analysis of the hard reality of child exploitation. However noble, freeing child laborers is not enough. Once free, how will they live? This is the core of the protagonist critique of abolitionism.

In spite of declarations of good intentions, anti–child labor campaigning has been driven by the concerns of well-organized, relatively privileged adult workers in North America and Europe. To lend support to their concerns about the consequences of a global free market, they have made exploited children in the developing world into icons of the dangers confronting labor in the absence of firm action. Reactions have been of two kinds: international business has refused to include labor standards in international trade regulations and referred the issue to the toothless ILO, and children's movements have profited from the situation to rise to world attention. Youth activists remain, however, divided on whether their actions should privilege the worker or the child. Those who want all children to have a carefree childhood tend to occupy positions of privilege that they want to extend to children believed to be lacking in or denied the essential experiences of childhood. They unwittingly assume an attitude that working children take as patronizing. The latter derive pride and self-respect from the role they play in society. A critical debate is now underway on the nature of both childhood and work from which working children can no longer be excluded.

See also Adultism; Child Soldiers; Labor Movement; State and Youth, The; Statute of the Child and Adolescent (Brazil).

Recommended Reading

Hobbs, S., McKechnie, J., and Lavallette, M. (1999). *Child Labour: A World History Companion.* Oxford: ABC-CLIO.
Invernizzi, A., and Milne, B. (2002). "Are Children Entitled to Contribute to International

Policy Making? A Critical View of Children's Participation in the International Campaign for the Elimination of Child Labor." *Journal of Children's Rights*, 10 (4): 403–431.

Kielburger, Craig, with Kevin Major. (1998). *Free the Children: A Young Man Fights Against Child Labor and Proves That Children Can Change the World.* New York: Harper Perennial.

Kuklin, S. (1998). *Iqbal Masih and the Crusade Against Child Slavery.* New York: Holt.

Levine, S. (1999). "Bittersweet Harvest, Children, Work, and the Global March against Child Labor in the Post-apartheid State." *Critique of Anthropology*, 19 (2): 139–155.

Liebel M. B. (2004). *A Will of Their Own, Cross-Cultural Perspectives on Working Children.* London and New York: ZED.

Myers, W. E. (2001). "The Right Rights? Child Labor in a Globalizing World." *Annals of the American Academy of Political and Social Science*, 575 (1): 38–55.

Nieuwenhuys, O. (1994). *Children's Lifeworlds: Labor, Gender, and Welfare in the Developing World.* London and New York: Routledge.

Stasiulus, D. (2002). "The Active Child Citizen." *Citizenship Studies*, 6 (4): 507–538.

Olga Nieuwenhuys

A young member of a pro-government militia group poses with his gun during the Liberian civil war in 1993. *Copyright Patrick Robert/Sygma/Corbis.*

Child Soldiers. Although children have often been depicted as passive and innocent, they are increasingly actors in political struggles and armed conflicts. Worldwide, an estimated 300,000 children, defined under international law as people under eighteen years of age, are soldiers in organized military groups such as government armies, armed opposition groups, and paramilitaries. Most child soldiers are boys, but, depending on the conflict, significant numbers may also be girls. Although the ages of child soldiers vary across conflicts, some of which feature child soldiers as young as six or seven years old, most child soldiers are teens between the ages of fourteen and seventeen. The largest numbers of child soldiers are in Asia and Africa, though significant numbers also exist in Latin American countries such as Colombia. Research on child soldiers is relatively new, however, and it is inherently difficult to collect accurate numbers due to the fog of war and the desire of armies to hide their exploitation of children.

Children's participation in war is not new, but it has increased owing to the recent changes in the nature of armed conflict. Most wars are now fought not between countries but between rival groups within particular countries. The dominant weapons used are low-tech and include widely available lightweight weapons such as AK-47 assault rifles. Using such small, light weapons, which in sub–Saharan Africa cost about as much as a chicken, children can be effective combatants. In addition, most wars are fought in and around communities, resulting in large numbers of civilian casualties, mass displacements, and extensive destruction of homes and infrastructure. As discussed below, many children join armed groups because their parents have been killed or they have no other means of meeting basic needs.

The term "child soldiers" is best viewed in critical perspective. The term "soldiers" elicits images of fighters; yet many child soldiers are not combatants but serve roles such as porters, cooks, spies, sex slaves, and general laborers. Moreover, many children are recruited forcibly, making it problematic to imply that they had joined voluntarily. For these reasons some analysts prefer terms such as "children associated with armed groups" or "abducted children." Regardless which term is used, it is vital to recognize the significant diversity that exists among children in armed groups. Furthermore, definitions of "childhood" and "youth" are culturally constructed and vary widely across cultures. In much of sub–Saharan Africa, childhood ends when a person has completed the culturally appropriate ritual of manhood or womanhood, typically around the age of fourteen years. Since calling sixteen- or seventeen-year-olds "children" can be inappropriate, some local people and analysts prefer to talk of "minor soldiers." "Youth soldiers" is also a frequently used term, though the category "youth," too, varies across cultures. Whereas in Western societies teenagers are thought of as youth or adolescents, in Sierra Leone a 40-year-old man may be considered a youth. It is impossible to resolve these issues here. According to the UN Convention on the Rights of the Child and its Optional Protocol on Children and Armed Conflict, eighteen is the minimum age for participation in armed conflict. Therefore, in this entry child soldiers will be considered persons under eighteen.

Entry into Armed Groups

Governments such as those of the United States and the United Kingdom regularly recruit people under eighteen, although this requires parental consent and cannot entail participation in hostilities. Worldwide, some of the largest child recruiters are governments, as the army of Myanmar (Burma) alone includes over 50,000 children. At field level, commanders often recruit children because they are readily available, are relatively controllable and obedient, and, lacking a sense of their own mortality, are willing to take exceptional risks. Sadly, some commanders view chil-

dren as expendable or as people whom they can convert through terror tactics into brutal killers. Broadly, recruitment occurs through a mixture of coercion and "voluntary" means. As shown below, however, voluntary recruitment occurs in a context of such deprivation and difficulty that it strains the ordinary meaning of the term.

Forced or coercive recruitment occurs in many ways. In northern Uganda, the so-called Lord's Resistance Army (LRA) has abducted over 10,000 children since 2001 and has abducted even more over two decades of armed conflict against the Ugandan army. Children's entry into the LRA involves extreme terror as LRA soldiers abduct children at gunpoint, often from schools, and take them into the bush or across the border into Sudan for military training. Children who attempt to escape are killed or severely beaten, as are those who fail to carry their heavy loads. Girls are typically assigned to a particular soldier as his "wife," although sex slavery is the more appropriate term since the failure to provide sexual service is punishable by death. Most children manage to escape from the LRA after a short time, whereas others stay with the LRA for years. Still others are born into the LRA, for example, in military camps in Sudan, and spend nearly all their formative years with the LRA.

Although northern Uganda is an extreme case, forced recruitment occurs also in many other countries. During the Taliban era in northern Afghanistan, Taliban commanders established a quota system that required villages to provide a particular number of youths to serve as soldiers, typically for a period of several months. Wealthy families protected their children by paying poor families to offer their sons instead or by sending their sons to neighboring Pakistan. As this example suggests, children from poor families are at increased risk of child soldiering. A similar quota system was used by the National Union for the Total Independence of Angola (UNITA), the opposition group that fought government forces in Angola's decades-long war. In Angola UNITA commanders threatened to destroy villages unless their leaders presented a particular number of youth for military service. In countries such as Colombia, forced recruitment has occurred through roundups wherein soldiers round up all the young people in a public area such as a market and load them onto a truck, which carries them to military camps where training occurs.

In many situations, children choose to become soldiers for family-related reasons. In Sierra Leone, some youth joined an armed group to be with a family member who had joined recently or to protect families that the government had not protected. Children may also join to escape negative family situations. In Sri Lanka, for example, a girl soldier reported that she joined the rebel group to escape mistreatment and the prospect of forced marriage. In situations of extreme poverty, it is not uncommon for parents to encourage their children to join the army as a means of earning an income that can be used to help support the family.

Prestige, power, excitement, and the desire for new competencies also serve as powerful motives that lead some youth to join an armed group. In Angola some children joined the military out of desire for the prestige of wearing a uniform and the power felt by wielding a gun, potent incentives for children who grow up feeling powerless. Children are attracted also by the excitement of soldiering. Child soldiers from both Sierra Leone and Liberia, for example, have told the author that they relished the thrill of battle, putting one's life on the line, and experiencing the special bonds and solidarity that develop with one's comrades under combat conditions. Others, who themselves had become commanders before they had reached age sixteen, said they enjoyed assuming leadership positions, exercising skill in combat, and being respected by their troops. In Sierra Leone, many youth joined the Revolutionary United Front (RUF) rebel group because

it provided opportunities for training and education that the government had not made available.

For many teenagers, social injustice and ideology provide powerful push-pull mechanisms that encourage soldiering. In South Africa, for example, many black youth who grew up during the apartheid era had become profoundly frustrated and angry over their mistreatment and the extreme social inequalities that existed. Seeing few other opportunities for creating social justice, they increasingly regarded violence as an acceptable instrument for achieving equality, adopted the ideology of the liberation struggle, and willingly sacrificed themselves and others for their political cause. Similarly, in Palestine many youth espouse the ideology of the liberation struggle and find meaning in the violence they engage in. A useful working hypothesis is that youth, being idealistic, are particularly drawn to ideologies of liberation struggle since they are defining their identity and searching for meaning. Particularly in a context saturated with injustice, humiliation, and lack of opportunity, it is not surprising that many youth become highly politicized, define their identity and make meaning in liberation struggles that depict violence as an appropriate instrument for achieving social change.

In many situations, desperation blurs the boundaries between forced and voluntary recruitment. Children who cannot feed themselves, protect themselves from attack, or obtain access to health care, for example, may join an armed group to meet these basic needs. Orphans and children who have been separated from their caretakers often face such difficult circumstances and are at high risk of recruitment, as are poor and minority children. In such situations, choice occurs but few options exist, and choices are made amid such extreme hardship and depravity that it begs the question of what is voluntary.

As this brief overview indicates, children join for many different reasons and in a wide variety of circumstances. This diversity cautions against monolithic images of child soldiers and also against simplistic images of children either as willing, eager warriors or as passive victims who had done what was necessary to survive.

Roles, Experiences, and Impacts

Children perform a wide variety of roles in armed groups. Since the roles vary by context, it is difficult to make broad generalizations that apply to most child soldiers. Although many children are combatants, many are in noncombat roles such as porters, cooks, laborers, or bodyguards. Quite often, young children are used as spies since they are small and can pass themselves off as civilians more easily. Typically, children serve multiple roles by serving, for example, as laborers around camp and as combatants in the field. Older children, typically those between fourteen and seventeen years old, may serve as commanders.

Recent research indicates that child soldiers' roles vary according to gender and context. In conflicts such as those in northern Uganda and Sierra Leone, girls are often sex slaves who are forced to service their captors or are assigned "husbands." Failure to comply with the demands for sex can lead to severe punishment, including death. In Angola, which emerged recently from forty years of war, girls who had been abducted by the rebel group UNITA were forced to dance all night to entertain the male troops, and they also provided sexual services for men. In other conflicts, such as those in Sri Lanka and the Philippines, armed opposition groups such as the Liberation Tigers of Tamil Elan (LTTE) in Sri Lanka had strong rules that prohibited sex with female soldiers. In addition, females have been potent fighters in numerous conflicts. In conflicts such as that in Sierra Leone, some women have become commanders. Overall, this evidence counters stereotypical images of women in armed groups as sex objects. Gender is also complicated in regard to boys. Although girls are the most common targets of sexual abuse, boys may be tar-

geted as well. In Afghanistan, for example, it was not uncommon for older male troops or a commander to sexually exploit smaller, younger male recruits. Much remains to be learned about the interplay between gender and children's roles in armed conflict.

Children's roles in armed conflict vary not only by situation, gender, and context but also according to children's choices. Although the range of choices is very limited and confined in most cases to roles that violate children's rights, it is nonetheless important to remember that children actively make choices even in a regime of terror. For example, some children in armed groups try actively to cultivate noncombat roles. In Sierra Leone, one enterprising young woman took care of the younger children, and once her expertise in this role had become apparent, she was permitted to spend much more time looking after young children than fighting, spying, or related activities. In northern Uganda, some children who had been abducted asked to perform assignments that they believed offered the greatest opportunities of escape. Even the role of sex slave can involve a conscious choice to perform that role rather than be killed. The young person's recognition that this was a choice compelled by survival needs is important in making meaning out of a very difficult situation. The realization that one had to submit sexually as a means of survival is a powerful mechanism of avoiding or decreasing self-blame, a powerful tendency among many survivors of sexual exploitation. A child soldier who views his or her experience as "what I had to do in order to survive" may have a very different ability to heal and to move on than someone who blames himself or herself for what happened.

Although child soldiers often make decisions based on survival concerns, their motives exhibit considerable variety, complexity, and evolution. Some youth report that they enjoy and even crave the excitement of fighting and the strong bonds that develop between fighters who have faced life and death situations together. Shaped by a system in which rewards such as access to health care and additional protection are given to those who exhibit the greatest bravery, zest for fighting, or willingness to take on the most dangerous assignments, some children take on roles such as assassins and torturers. In countries such as Sierra Leone and Liberia, where child soldiers were pumped up on drugs, boy soldiers often performed roles such as terrorizing and mutilating civilians and burning villages. Not uncommonly, in those situations the boy soldiers adopted nicknames such as "Rambo" and "Cock and Fire" that showed their machismo and fearlessness. Ideology, too, influences children's roles in armed groups. Among the LTTE, for example, some young girls have become suicide bombers not only through coercion but through socialization in a social system that portrays the LTTE fight as a valiant struggle for liberation and teaches that martyrdom is the greatest honor attainable. More prosaic motives also shape the roles of child soldiers.

Regardless of how children enter particular roles, the nature of the roles has a powerful influence on the children's experiences. A child combatant, for example, has in many cases been a perpetrator who has killed someone, whereas someone whose main role was as a sex slave may not have experienced hurting anyone directly. In addition, combat and noncombat roles vary greatly in regard to exposure to death. A child whose main role is as a spy, for example, may fear death himself or herself but may not have actually engaged in killing or seen people dying or being killed. In contrast, a child who has risen through the ranks and become a commander or a lead combatant may have frequently killed people, seen people dying, and witnessed horrendous events and scenes. These different experiences can lead to very different patterns of injury, risk, and outcome for child soldiers. A child who is a frontline combatant, for example, has much greater risk than a noncombatant of injury due to landmines, shooting, and other forms of attack.

In turn, the nature and the frequency of children's life-threatening experiences influence how children are affected by their war experiences. In general, a child who is abducted and who stays with an armed group for a relatively short time has a greater chance of full recovery than does someone who has been a soldier for a long time. One useful way to think about this is in terms of risk accumulation. The longer one is in the field as a soldier, the greater is the likelihood that one will be caught in an attack, experience severe hunger or malnutrition, contract a disease that is treated poorly or not at all, or be exposed to sexually-transmitted infections, including HIV/AIDS. Over time, one is exposed to multiple risks, which accumulate. Research indicates that risk accumulation often causes harm to children.

Although attention often focuses on physical injury and disabilities, child soldiers themselves often report that some of the worst wounds of war are emotional, social, and spiritual. For example, a former boy soldier in Angola reported that his biggest problem was that at night the spirit of the man he had killed came to him and asked, "Why did you do this to me?" In the local belief system, the boy was haunted or polluted spiritually by the unavenged spirit of the man he had killed. This was understood not as an individual problem but as a communal problem since the resulting spiritual discord could lead to family or communal misfortune such as bad health, crop failure, or more fighting. Although Western-trained psychologists often speak of trauma and mental illness in the aftermath of children's war experiences, this example shows the importance of understanding youth's perspectives on how they have been affected. Often, young people's interpretations are colored by wider social beliefs, many of which are at odds with Western beliefs and world views.

Reintegration and Civic Reengagement

Some media portrayals of former child soldiers have depicted them as damaged goods or a "lost generation" who have little hope for positive lives as civilians. Experience in many war zones, however, counter these stereotypes. Following soldiering, children take diverse paths, most of which lead back into civilian life. In some cases former child soldiers return home spontaneously, without special assistance. Often, however, UNICEF and other agencies arrange a process of disarmament, demobilization, and reintegration of former child soldiers. Through disarmament, child soldiers lay down their weapons, and through demobilization, they officially leave armed groups. Demobilization often entails a stay of several weeks or months in an interim care center that meets basic needs for security, health care, and food; offers psychological support for children affected by war; and enables the process of tracing, that is, of finding the child's parents or extended family members.

The reintegration process takes a longer period of time and faces numerous challenges. Local villages may fear former child soldiers, stigmatize them as troublemakers, or want to attack them for having attacked local people. Viewing the child soldiers as perpetrators, communities often do not recognize that the child soldiers had suffered and need support. Lacking education and means of earning a living, former child soldiers frequently doubt their ability to fit back into civilian life and to create a sustainable, meaningful role. Girls who had become pregnant may be stigmatized for having had babies out of wedlock and may have difficulties getting married.

Although reintegration processes vary by context, they typically include five key elements, the first of which is community preparation. This includes dialogs with local officials and leaders to raise awareness about the importance of young people returning home, about the need to support them and to avoid stigmatizing them, and about the ways in which the children have suffered. It also includes discussions with parents, teachers, and others in the community about the problems that may arise

as former child soldiers return home and ways of supporting them. For example, many people may not recognize that problems of aggressiveness may be effects of the children's war experiences rather than a sign of bad character. Parents and teachers need to anticipate such problems and have skills and strategies for addressing them.

Second is the process of reuniting children with their families. Often this entails physical accompaniment of the children home since there may be risks of re-recruitment. Third, there is often need of spiritual support to rid the children of perceived spiritual impurities that threaten them and the community. In Angola, for example, local healers may conduct special purification rituals for child soldiers such as the boy referred to earlier.

Fourth, returning child soldiers need support in developing life skills that give them a means of earning a living and taking on a positive role in the community. Whether learned through mentoring or more structured classes, these skills may include literacy, communication, business, and vocational skills such as carpentry, tailoring, or collective agriculture. Fifth, former child soldiers need to have the opportunity to earn a living and to achieve a positive social role. Small loans with regular payback provide the opportunity for former child soldiers to earn a living. Their adjustment to civilian life is aided as community people see them employed and assuming constructive roles as workers and parents. Throughout all aspects of the reintegration process, there is a need for trained social workers to provide follow-up support to the returning soldiers and their families, employers, and teachers.

Field experience has shown consistently that in supporting former child soldiers, it is vital to support all youth since all youth in war zones have been affected and since selective assistance to former child soldiers creates jealousies and social divisions at a moment when social unity is needed. Field experience has also shown that former child soldiers should be active leaders and participants in the process of reintegration. Having enormous creativity, youth are constructive problem-solvers who can be engaged as agents of their own protection and rehabilitation. Here again, one sees that former child soldiers are not passive victims or beneficiaries of programs but active agents who can help construct a positive future.

See also Antiwar Activism; Child Labor; Contested Childhoods; Palestinian Intifada; Serbia, Youth Activism in (1990–2000); United Nations, Youth Activism and.

Recommended Reading

Apfel, R., and Simon, B., eds. (1996). *Minefields in Their Hearts: The Mental Health of Children in War and Communal Violence.* New Haven, CT: Yale University Press.

Brett, R., and McCallin, M. (1996). *Children: The Invisible Soldiers.* Vaxjo: Rädda Barnen.

Coalition to Stop the Use of Child Soldiers (2004). *Child Soldiers Global Report 2004.* London: Coalition to Stop the Use of Child Soldiers.

Cohn, I., and Goodwin-Gill, G. (1994). *Child Soldiers.* Oxford: Clarendon Press.

Honwana, A. (1999). "Non-Western Concepts of Mental Health." In *The Refugee Experience*, Vol. 1, edited by M. Loughry and A. Ager. Oxford: Refugee Studies Programme, pp. 103–119.

McKay, S., and Mazurana, D. (2004). *Where Are the Girls? Girls in Fighting Forces in Northern Uganda, Sierra Leone, and Mozambique: Their Lives During and After War.* Montreal: International Centre for Human Rights and Democratic Development.

Wessells, M. (2002). "Recruitment of Children as Soldiers in Sub-Saharan Africa: An Ecological Analysis." In *The Comparative Study of Conscription in the Armed Forces* (Comparative Social Research, Vol. 20), edited by L. Mjoset and S. Van Holde. Amsterdam: Elsevier, pp. 237–254.

Wessells, M. G., and Monteiro, C. (2004). "Culture, Healing, and Post-conflict Reconstruction: A Community-based Approach to Assisting War-affected Children." In *Handbook of Culture, Therapy, and Healing*, edited by U. P. Gielen, J. Fish, and J. G. Draguns. Upper Saddle River, NJ: Erlbaum.

Michael Wessells

Children's Rights. *See* Political Participation and Youth Councils; Rights of Participation of Children and Youth; Rights,

Youth Perceptions of; Statute of the Child and Adolescent (Brazil).

Choose or Lose Campaign. *See* MTV's Choose or Lose Campaign (1992–).

Citizenship Education Policies in the States. The education commission of the states' National Center for Learning and Citizenship (NCLC) conducted a comprehensive scan of state policies that support citizenship education. The complete scan, which includes all fifty states and the District of Columbia, is available on the NCLC website at http://www.ecs.org/nclc. This entry discusses some indicators of effective citizenship education policies based on the preliminary scan and provides examples of innovative approaches to citizenship education taken in a number of states.

A recent national report, *The Civic Mission of Schools*, argues that civics education should help young people acquire and learn to use the *skills*, *knowledge*, and *attitudes* that will prepare them to be competent and responsible citizens who are informed and thoughtful, participate in their communities, act politically, and have moral and civic virtues. According to *Every Student a Citizen* (2000), a report of the National Study Group on Citizenship in K–12 Schools, education for citizenship requires that students acquire a "democratic self." This democratic self involves two components: first, the ability to identify one's personal stake in public deliberation and decision-making and second, recognition of one's membership in a community and one's role in establishing and maintaining the common good. Being an effective citizen also requires a number of civic skills, such as the capacity for critical judgment and reflection, the capacity for critical inquiry, and the ability to participate in public deliberations impartially and objectively. While an ability to influence public policy clearly requires knowledge of public institutions, the emphasis of the Study Group is on citizenship as a "craft" whereby the citizen constantly refashions the institutions and processes among which he or she lives, rather than simply accepting them as "givens." Citizenship implies ownership of the community and a stake in its success.

Clearly, a conceptualization of citizenship as ownership requires knowledge of the institutions of government. Thirty years ago high-school students completed an average of three civics courses before graduating. Today the average has dropped to one course, generally taken during the senior year. U.S. history courses thus provide students with much of what they learn about government and their rights and duties as citizens. Yet, knowledge of the historical and political development of the United States and the structures of government without attention to the development in students of the democratic self does not necessarily lead to active engagement in civic affairs. If our goal is to produce an active citizenry, we must provide students with opportunities to gain an array of skills, knowledge, and attitudes that enable them to participate fully in the political and civic life of their communities. Citizenship education must foster in students an orientation toward action and the skills and confidence to act effectively. Classroom instruction aimed at expanding content knowledge is necessary but not enough; students must be provided with opportunities to learn and practice civic skills by addressing real issues with real consequences.

Many schools and classrooms already provide opportunities for students to learn and practice civic skills. These include service-learning programs, simulations of public decision-making, discussion of current events and issues, extracurricular and cocurricular programs, internships, and others. But these efforts are rarely institutionalized through state or district policy. This failure to institutionalize opportunities for students to practice civic skills, combined with the American tradition of local control of education, means that citi-

zenship education in American public schools is somewhat idiosyncratic. High-quality citizenship education is often dependent upon the efforts of a few dedicated educators and community members. If these individuals leave or change jobs, there is no assurance that the quality of the citizenship education program will be maintained.

Wide variation exists in the extent to which state policies address citizenship education. Forty-one states have statutes specifically providing for the teaching of government, civics, and/or citizenship. While forty-one states and the District of Columbia have a course or credit requirement in government or civics for high-school graduation, only five of those states currently require students to pass an exit exam to graduate (Alabama, Georgia, Louisiana, New Mexico, and New York). West Virginia will require four social-studies credits, including one credit of civics, for high-school graduation for students entering ninth grade in 2005. Alabama, Maryland, Ohio, Texas, and Virginia are in the process of phasing in exit or end-of-course exams as a requirement for high-school graduation.

Assessment and accountability systems remain a primary focus of state education-reform efforts, but less than half of state systems address civics. Twenty-two states' assessment systems include knowledge of government or civics, while fourteen states include performance on civics/government or social-studies assessments within their accountability systems.

For students to meet the standards, schools must provide appropriate opportunities to learn. Under the federal No Child Left Behind Act (NCLB), states are required to develop school "report cards" based on students' performance on state reading, math, and science assessments. But as NCLB forces states to hold schools increasingly accountable for students' reading, science, and math scores, social studies may receive less emphasis. Currently only ten states include civics or social studies in their school accountability program. If the state and federal funding on which schools depend continues to be determined by students' performance on reading, math, and science tests, this number is not likely to increase.

Many advocates of citizenship education support the use of community service or service learning. Every state is eligible to receive federal funding to support service learning, and twenty-six states and the District of Columbia have some kind of policy on service or service learning—although the nature of these policies varies widely. The Corporation for National and Community Service, the federal agency that provides funding to support service learning, recently began requiring that states receiving funds through its Learn and Serve America program ensure that students' service-learning experiences enhance their understanding of civic responsibility and help them connect their service to broader civic participation and to the history of democracy in America.

Although state educational policy usually focuses on schools, citizenship education can take place both in schools and the community. According to a recent publication by the National Association of Secretaries of State (NASS), for example, 89 percent of secretary-of-state offices currently partner with schools, and 78 percent work with community organizations to promote voting among young people. Under the federal Help America Vote Act of 2002 (HAVA), states will receive funding earmarked for student-voter education and outreach efforts. NASS reports that 69 percent of secretary-of-state offices plan to introduce new voter education programs for teens and young adults as a result of HAVA funding. NASS also reports that 75 percent of states currently have laws allowing minors to serve as election workers, and nine secretaries of state and three state elections boards have developed or are developing training programs for student poll workers.

Thirty-nine states currently have policies designed to support the development of patriotism in students through recitation of the Pledge of Allegiance. Although the educational value of such requirements is debatable, thirty-four states currently require schools to provide the opportunity for students to recite the pledge. Two of the thirty-four state requirements have been challenged in court. An injunction is currently in place against Colorado's new pledge requirement, while Pennsylvania's has been ruled unconstitutional. In most states pledge requirements apply only to elementary schools or students, and most states also allow students to opt out on religious or other grounds.

State standards and curriculum frameworks or guidelines are most often used to influence civic education in the classroom. Following is a state-by-state list of some examples of state standards and frameworks that encourage active civic engagement through the teaching of civics:

Alabama—The state's social-studies course of study includes content standards for civic responsibility, which include language about "civic problem-solving" including (a) identifying a problem, gathering information, generating possible solutions, developing and implementing an action plan; and (b) evaluating the responsibilities of citizens, including civic responsibilities such as obeying the law, paying taxes, being informed, participating in the political process through such activities as voting, working in a campaign, holding office, attending rallies, writing letters, and petitioning.

Arkansas—The social-studies frameworks include a "power, authority, and governance" strand. One content standard states that "students will demonstrate an understanding of the ideals, rights, and responsibilities of participating in a democratic society." One of the student learning expectations for grades five through eight is for students to "develop a project to serve the school, community, state, or nation." The document's description of the subject of civics and government includes a statement that "the formal curriculum should be augmented by related learning experiences, in both school and community, that enable students to learn how to participate in their own governance."

Hawaii—The social-studies content standards include a political science/civics strand, which addresses governance/power/authority; democracy; global cooperation, conflict and interdependence; citizenship/participation; and political analysis. The citizenship/participation standard for grades nine through twelve includes students taking "action to gain larger community involvement on the issues, e.g., a service-learning project."

Maryland—The introduction to the state social-studies standards states that "it is the responsibility of social studies to prepare young people to identify, understand, and work to resolve problems that confront them, their communities, the nation, and the international community." The rationale for the political-systems standard includes a statement that "students should be provided with opportunities to develop the skills and attitudes necessary to become active citizens."

Nebraska—Although the state standards focus more on enhancing students' understanding of history and the institutions of government than on civic engagement, the social-studies framework encourages "increased opportunities for students to get involved in civic activities in the school and community" through activities such as having students plan and implement a community-improvement project, interview community leaders, provide voluntary service for community agencies, and make maps of the community.

North Carolina—The North Carolina standard course of study includes grade-level competencies, such as "competency four" for the tenth-grade citizenship course: "The learner will explore active roles as a citizen at the local, state, and national levels of government." Objective 4.04 is "demonstrate active methods of promoting and inhibiting change through political action." Objective 4.08 is "participate in civic life, politics, and/or the government."

Oregon—Oregon's civics standard is "understand participatory responsibilities of citizens in the community (voluntarism) and in the political process (becoming informed about public issues and candidates, joining political parties/interest groups/associations, communicating with public officials, voting, influencing lawmaking through such processes as petitions/initiatives)." Another standard emphasizes the influence on government of individual and group support or dissent.

Vermont—Vermont's "framework of standards and learning opportunities" recommends schools provide learning experiences with personal, community, or global relevance; opportunities to participate in democratic processes in the school and community; and ways for students to apply knowledge to "real needs."

West Virginia—The instructional goals and objectives for social studies include content standards for citizenship and civics/government across grades, with grade-level objectives under each standard. Citizenship objectives include community service, student participation in school and community governance, community problem-solving, citizen influence on public policy, and taking and defending positions.

Wisconsin—The "model academic standards for the social studies" include five content standards, including "political science and citizenship: power, authority, governance, and responsibility." Within this standard are performance standards for grades four, eight, and twelve that include participating in debate on public-policy issues, mobilizing public opinion, various forms of civic action, and finding and using information to understand an issue and take a position.

In addition to state standards and curriculum frameworks, many states have experimented with other unique ways of augmenting classroom instruction in citizenship education, including the following:

Connecticut—The state's Challenge to Educational Citizenship Award program, sponsored by the state Student Advisory

Council on Education and the governor's office, recognizes student-organized service projects.

Hawaii—Hawaii's Politics and the School program allows political candidates to make speeches to students; allows non-candidate political representatives to be invited to schools to discuss their party and its policies and platforms; and encourages youth political clubs. In addition, Hawaii's Board of Education maintains a controversial issues policy which states that "student discussion of issues which generate opposing points of view shall be considered a normal part of the learning process."

Michigan—The Michigan Civics Institute produces lesson plans; maintains a speakers bureau for schools that includes lawmakers, lobbyists, and executive-branch staff; provides legislative updates designed specifically for students; and sponsors the House Civics Commission and the Michigan Youth Caucus. The commission is a bipartisan, ad hoc committee of lawmakers that holds public hearings across the state to listen to bill ideas from students. The caucus, created and staffed by high-school and college students around the state, provides students with online tools and offline meetings and conventions to facilitate the creation of the Michigan Youth Caucus platform.

In what may be an indicator of concern among state lawmakers about a persistent decline in civic participation among young people, several state legislatures have established legislative committees or commissions to monitor civic education and make recommendations for action to the legislature and other state leaders. They include the following:

Alabama—In 1994 the legislature established the Alabama Compact for Leadership and Citizenship Education to increase the availability of youth leadership and citizenship programs, extend community and other leadership programs to rural and underserved areas, and serve as a resource for community and youth leadership programs. Alabama also established the Citizenship Trust, a public-education corporation of the state and its American Village civic-education classroom, which provides resources and programs to enable and encourage students "to serve and lead their communities, state, and nation as active, responsible, informed, and law-abiding citizens." The legislative Joint Committee on Civic Education provides oversight and recommendations with respect to the compact and the trust and reports annually to the legislature on the state of civic education.

Rhode Island—The Commission on Civic Education was established by the legislature recently to appoint committees to study areas of concern and report their findings to the legislative leadership and the commissioner of education four times per year.

Maine—The Commission to Study the Scope and Quality of Citizenship Education was established by the state legislature this year to examine (a) the extent to which citizenship education, including service learning, is currently included in the visions, missions, values, and practices of Maine school administrative districts and institutions of higher education; (b) the extent to which existing pre-service and in-service professional development programs for educators address citizenship education; (c) national models with the potential for preparing Maine students to be active and engaged citizens; and (d) models for involving students and giving them a voice in governance and providing opportunities for student engagement and leadership. The commission submitted a report with recommended legislation to the legislature by December 3, 2003.

Other states, including the following, have recently enacted policies to support citizenship education in some unique and innovative ways that include student-voter registration, simulated elections, elected student councils, and even the involvement of students in the development of state policy:

Connecticut—Public Act No. 03-54, enacted June 3, 2003, established an official statewide student-voter registration drive and encourages students to learn about civics and participate in the democratic process. Public Act No. 03-108, enacted the same day, allows students aged sixteen or seventeen to work at polling places as checkers, translators, and voting-machine tenders.

Illinois—House Bill 0030, signed by the governor July 22, 2003, requires the state Board of Elections and state Board of Education to jointly develop a simulated election program for K–12 students to be conducted at actual polling places with volunteers and private funding in conjunction with the general election. The law requires both boards to develop and offer an educational component of the program and rules.

Maine—House Paper 557, enacted in June 2003, requires the state education commissioner, secretary of state, and director of the Office of Substance Abuse to develop recommendations to establish a permanent youth-advisory committee in the executive branch to serve as a resource for any state agency charged with developing, implementing, or enforcing policies that relate specifically to youth.

North Carolina—Senate Bill 795, an Act to Enhance and Further Implement the Provisions of the Student Citizen Act of 2001, encourages elected student councils in high schools and middle schools to provide opportunities for students to have input into policies and decisions that affect them. The purpose, according to the act, is "to build civic skills and attitudes such as participation in elections, discussion and debate of issues, and collaborative decision-making." The act also encourages discussion of current events, especially in social studies and language-arts classes. Local school boards are encouraged to teach the responsibilities of service and good citizenship. The act also instructs the state Board of Education to consider incorporating into the School-Based Management and Accountability program a character and civic-education component, which may include a requirement for student councils. The act was included in the budget bill signed by the governor on June 30, 2003.

Whether in response to concerns about declining civic engagement or as an effort to promote patriotism, this brief overview illustrates the variety of ways in which states are attempting to educate students for citizenship both inside and outside the classroom. The NCLC's fifty-state policy scan (available at http://www.ecs.org/nclc) provides a more complete look at state education policies aimed at fostering citizenship, including state graduation requirements, standards, assessment, accountability, statute, recent or pending legislation, administrative code, and statements by state superintendents or state Boards of Education in support of citizenship education.

The scan provides a barometer of state policies concerning citizenship. The kinds of civic competencies (knowledge, skills, and dispositions) that students of various ages need are also discussed in a paper by Torney-Purta and Vermeer. The importance of schools as institutions where these competencies are developed cannot be overestimated. The resources outlined in this article provide a foundation for a set of policy options and technical assistance available to state policymakers and educational leaders seeking to improve the way their states educate young people for citizenship.

See also Character Education; Civic Engagement in Diverse Youth; Civic Virtue; Civil Society and Positive Youth Development; Democratic Education; Diversity Education; Environmental Education (EE); Global Citizenship Education (GCE) in the United States; IEA Civic Education Study; Just Community High Schools and Youth Activism; National Alliance for Civic Education (NACE); Prosocial Behaviors; School Engagement; School Influences and Civic Engagement; State and Youth, The.

Recommended Reading

Carnegie Corporation of New York and CIRCLE: Center for Information & Research on Civic Learning & Engagement (2003). *The Civic Mission of School.* New York: Carnegie Corporation of New York.

Corporation for National and Community Service (2003). *Learn and Serve America School-Based Formula Programs 2003 Application Guidelines.* Washington, D.C.: Corporation for National and Community Service.

Education Commission of the States (July 2000). *Every Student a Citizen: Creating the Democratic Self.* Denver, CO: Education Commission of the States.

National Association of Secretaries of State and Youth Vote Coalition (July 2003). "New Millennium Best Practices Survey." Washington, D.C.: National Association of Secretaries of State and Youth Vote Coalition.

Torney-Purta, J., and Vermeer, S. (April 2004). *Developing Citizenship Competencies from Kindergarten through Grade 12: A Background Paper for Policymakers and Educators.* Denver, CO: Education Commission of the States.

Terry Pickeral and Jeffery J. Miller

Civic Education. *See* IEA Civic Education Study.

Civic Engagement in Diverse Youth. Civic engagement can be expressed through knowledge, behaviors, and attitudes. These three domains of engagement are measured and sometimes become operational differently for youth and adults. First, youth civic knowledge is typically measured by the National Assessment of Education Progress (NAEP) Civics Report Card for the Nation, which is given to approximately 22,000 fourth-, eighth-, and twelfth-grade students every few years. Second, since youth under eighteen years old are not old enough to vote, developmental researchers have expanded the more traditional definition of civic behaviors—voting and obeying laws—to include having a sense of belonging to and contributing to a group larger than the self. Youth, even those under eighteen, can practice civic engagement by obeying laws, participating in community service, demonstrating an allegiance to a religious institution, and through involvement in extracurricular activities at school like student government or team sports. Third, youth civic attitudes are particularly important since they may set the stage for adult political participation and civic behavior. High-school students have well-formed attitudes about issues that are directly relevant to their lives.

Youth have opportunities to express their civic engagement across a number of

A fourteen-year-old mentor helps a six-year-old child learn to read as part of an after-school reading program. *Courtesy of Skjold Photographs.*

different contexts. Contexts of civic engagement that have been examined include school, family, community, religion, working, and voting. Civic engagement can also be expressed by holding certain attitudes about what it means to be a citizen. The level of participation across these contexts sometimes varies as a function of individual and familial factors like gender, immigrant status, socioeconomic status, race, and ethnicity. For example, the percentage of females participating in community service is consistently higher than males.

The opportunity to engage in civic activities is also facilitated or constrained by neighborhood resources. For example, youth living in neighborhoods with fewer adults to structure activities and supervise youth will be less likely to participate in community service than youth living in high-resource communities. Cultural and environmental contexts shape youth attitudes about the role of government in people's lives and youth's own role as future citizens. Therefore, it is important to understand various environmental and cultural forces from the familial level to the macro level of policy and general attitudes in a society that contribute to youth's understanding of their role as future citizens and hence, their engagement in society.

The first domain of youth civic engagement involves civic knowledge and is typically assessed by the NAEP Civics Report Card. The last civics assessment was in 1998, and the next scheduled assessment is for 2006. According to the 1998 results, 28 percent of white youth and 26 percent of Asian/Pacific Islander youth in the eighth grade achieved proficiency in civics knowledge. The percentages for black, Hispanic, and American Indian youth were 7, 8, and 11 percent, respectively. The percentage of twelfth graders achieving proficiency increased by 2 to 5 percent for all subgroups except American Indians, who decreased by two percentage points. These results mirror science-, reading-, and math-proficiency scores and may reflect both the higher risk status of black

and Hispanic children for educational lags as well as the increased likelihood that they attend lower quality schools. Therefore, when comparing groups on civic knowledge, it is important to examine the types of schools youth attend since they are one pathway through which youth gain important civic information.

The second domain of civic engagement is assessed by civic behaviors. Civic behaviors include community service, service learning, extracurricular activities, working, and voting. Each one of these civic behaviors will be discussed in turn.

Four significant factors predict community service activities among students in the sixth through twelfth grades: (1) gender, with female students more likely to participate than male students; (2) language, with those speaking English at home as opposed to another language more likely to participate; (3) race, with white students more likely to participate than black or Hispanic students and black students more likely than Hispanic students to report service participation; and (4) family level of education, with students whose parents had a higher level of education more likely to take part in community service than students with less-educated parents.

It may be that some students who are preparing to go on to college participate in community-service activities for self-interested reasons like building their résumé for college entry. Youth participate in community service for various reasons, which are related to their political views. For example, youth with an interest in political issues related to having a concern for others reported engaging in community service to help others. On the other hand, youth most interested in political issues related to self-interest reported doing service for reasons related to self-promotion like "it looks good on my record."

Service learning connects volunteerism or community service to academic learning. The number of schools promoting service-learning activities has significantly increased from 1996 to 1999. Fifty-two percent of students reported participating in community service in 1999. Fifty-seven percent of those students reported a service-learning component. In 1999 Hispanic students were more likely to attend schools that arranged and required community service than white students (28 percent and 16 percent, respectively). Twenty-two percent of black students reported attending such schools. Therefore, the extent of service learning within a school environment as well as what youth need to do to prepare for their future are two important elements that contribute to the extent that youth participate in community service.

School extracurricular activities like participating in clubs and groups are important youth activities that may be good practice for adult civic engagement. Females and students from higher socioeconomic strata are more likely to participate in school activities than males and students from lower socioeconomic backgrounds. There is also a connection between doing well in school and participation in school-based, extracurricular activities. The ability of low-income youth to participate in activities may be constrained by other activities that are important in their context of living. For example, family duties like doing chores and taking care of siblings may be necessary activities for youth whose families have fewer resources than their peers from higher-income families. So while duties that contribute to family well-being may displace time that could be spent in community service or school activities they may also be a precursor to adult civic engagement.

Immigrant status and ethnicity are linked to family allegiance and time spent on household duties. First-generation immigrant high-school students report higher rates of spending time on familial duties than nonimmigrant families. Asian and Latin American students in particular report higher rates of family connectedness than students from European American backgrounds. This trend for immigrant youth to report higher family allegiance

was also found for college students. College youth from immigrant families report more of a commitment to their families than students with parents born in the United States. This commitment translates into time spent on familial duties, in that immigrant youth spend more time on familial duties than youth born in the United States and with parents born in the United States. This is especially true if immigrant parents do not speak English. The behaviors of immigrant youth reflect their attitudes toward family commitment in that youth from immigrant families are more likely to report that they *should* support and assist their families than youth from nonimmigrant families. Time spent on familial duties among this population displaces time available for academic involvement as well as other youth civic activities.

African American youth are more likely to spend time with their parents than white youth. The time they report spending with their families does not change with age, as in other populations of youth. Typically, as European American suburban youth enter the adolescent years, they spend less time with their families, but this trend is not commonly found among youth of color. These differences in time spent with families are probably reflections of differences in norms and family values between African American and European American families.

Teenagers from families experiencing an economic crisis have been found to contribute to the household financially and participate in household chores more than teens whose families do not experience an economic crisis. Youth transitioning from high school into young adulthood are also more likely to assist their families if they are of lower socioeconomic status. These findings are consistent with a nationally representative sample of twelve- to seventeen-year-olds who reported whether or not they felt close to their parents. Youth from the lowest income bracket (< $10,000) reported feeling closest to their parents, and those with the highest family income (> $100,000) reported feeling the least close to their parents (78 versus 64 percent for mothers; 66 versus 53 percent for fathers).

These findings, which indicate an increased family allegiance among first-generation youth versus third-generation youth, among low-income versus higher-income youth, and among youth whose families experience an economic crisis versus those families who do not experience an economic crisis, suggest that youth participate in family activities because their assistance is needed more in these families. The racial and ethnic subgroup differences may also indicate cultural differences between nonimmigrant European American families and immigrant families and families of color living in the United States.

Religious institutions provide a context for civic engagement through their community-service activities. It has been suggested that civic engagement among immigrant youth may be more likely to take place through their place of worship than other contexts like school. Religious participation varies by individual characteristics among youth. In 2002 females in the eighth, tenth, and twelfth grades were more likely than males to report weekly religious attendance (48 versus 41 percent; 44 versus 39 percent; and 37 versus 32 percent, respectively). Subgroup differences were also found by race. Across the years from 1991 through 2002, black youth reported consistently higher rates of weekly religious attendance and were almost twice as likely as white youth to say that religion was an important part of their lives.

While the percentage of youth from various subgroups significantly differs in participation in certain traditional civic activities like working, there is more similarity across groups in other activities like voting. Working is considered a civic activity, even among youth who are not yet considered adults. In 2002 there were differences in rates of working by gender, age, and race/ethnicity. Females sixteen to nineteen years old were consistently more

likely to report working than their male counterparts, and the percentage of youth working increased during the adolescent years. The percentage of youth working also differs by race/ethnicity. While over 80 percent of eighteen-year-old black, non-Hispanic youth reported being employed, they were less likely to report being employed than Hispanic and white, non-Hispanic youth (81.1, 88.3, and 93.9 percent, respectively). Macro-societal factors like lack of jobs in resource-poor, inner-city neighborhoods and racial discrimination in the job market are thought to contribute to racial disparities in employment rates. There are fewer differences between black and white youth in another traditional civic activity—voting.

Whereas black youth eighteen to twenty-five years old were just as likely to vote in a presidential election as white youth (34 and 33 percent, respectively), Hispanic youth were significantly less likely to vote (15 percent). Studies using datasets that indicate immigrant status show that although they vote less than white Americans, immigrants show high rates of voter registration. While immigrant adults try to keep a "low profile" overall, some groups do participate in other political activities extensively. Immigrant youth Americanize relatively quickly yet still retain their ethnic identities and engage in civic activities when issues arise that are relevant to their groups.

Evidence that immigrant youth Americanize quickly is found in immigrant youth's preference for English and their adoption of American dress and food. While integrating into American society, immigrant youth maintain their cultural identities, as evidenced by their self-identification labels. They retain some part of their national identity and define themselves as ethnic Americans. Civic attitudes among immigrant youth have been found to differ from native-born youth or youth whose parents were born in the United States.

Civic attitudes are the third domain of youth civic engagement. There are two general types of civic attitudes among diverse youth: proactive and traditional. Proactive attitudes include things like "defending the rights of minorities" and "helping the needy." Traditional attitudes include "respecting the flag" and "being patriotic." Overall, teenage girls report significantly higher levels of proactive attitudes, and teenage boys are higher on traditional attitudes. Youth with parents born in another country are more likely to endorse traditional civic attitudes than youth whose parents were born in the United States. There do not seem to be significant differences in proactive attitudes by immigrant status among adolescents. Understanding the political context in countries where immigrant families come from could provide insight into why immigrant youth are more likely to endorse traditional attitudes than nonimmigrants. Additionally, the reasons why they immigrated to the United States could provide further information on these differences. It is likely that immigrants who stay in the United States for longer periods of time and have experienced discrimination will hold more proactive views than youth that never experience discrimination. Evidence supporting the view that groups who experience discrimination hold more proactive civic attitudes can be found by comparing the future civic goals of black and white youth.

In most years between 1996 and 2002, black twelfth graders were twice as likely as white twelfth graders to report the following future civic goals as extremely important (the following percentages are averages across twelve data points): (1) "being a leader in my community" (23 versus 12 percent); (2) "working to correct social and economic inequalities" (19.5 versus 9.4 percent); and (3) "having lots of money" (44.3 versus 21.9 percent). Black youth were also consistently more likely than white youth to indicate that "making a contribution to society" is extremely important (26.3 versus 21.2 percent). Black and white twelfth graders were equally

likely to rate that "having a good marriage and family life" was extremely important with over 70 percent for both groups throughout the years from 1976 to 2002.

For black youth having proactive future civic goals and wanting to be financially successful reflects contextual differences in the lived experiences of black and white individuals in the United States today. Black individuals consistently experience higher rates of racial discrimination than any other group in the United States and are more likely to live in poverty. Therefore, it is not surprising that more than twice the number of black youth rated correcting social and economic inequalities and making lots of money as extremely important.

Family racial socialization is a process whereby parents prepare their children of color for racial discrimination by conveying messages about what it means to be black in a white-dominated society. "Preparation-for-bias" messages are associated with positive outcomes for children of color. A preliminary investigation of the impact of perceived parent racial socialization messages on high-school students' perception of what it takes to succeed in America found that positive socialization messages that aim to prepare youth for discrimination are associated with students reporting that it is important to work harder than the next person to get ahead in society. Similarly, economically disadvantaged students were both more likely to aspire to materialistic goals and to report that their families emphasized being economically self-reliant. Therefore, racial discrimination and parent socialization experiences among youth of color and economically disadvantaged youth shape youth civic attitudes and future civic goals.

How diverse youth view American society and how American society facilitates their integration will contribute to the development of a civic identity, which serves as a foundation for civic-related behavior as adults. It is important to consider the different contexts experienced by diverse subgroups of youth during their formative years when considering the development of civic identity. Considering the coinciding steady decrease in white, non-Hispanic children and the increase in Hispanic and Asian/Pacific Islander children as a percentage of the child and adolescent population and how youth from diverse groups engage in American society will predict the future of civil society in the United States.

See also Civic Identity; Civic Virtue; Civil Society and Positive Youth Development; Diversity Education; Global-Justice Activism; Religiosity and Civic Engagement in African American Youth.

Recommended Reading

Elder, G. (1974). *Children of the Great Depression: Social Change in Life Experience.* Chicago: University of Chicago Press.

Elder, G., and Conger, R. D. (2000). *Children of the Land: Adversity and Success in Rural America.* Chicago: University of Chicago Press.

Fuligni, A. J., and Pedersen, S. (2002). "Family Obligation and the Transition to Young Adulthood." *Developmental Psychology*, 38 (5): 856–868.

Fuligni, A. J., Tseng, V., and Lam, M. (1999). "Attitudes toward Family Obligations among American Adolescents from Asian, Latin American, and European Backgrounds." *Child Development*, 70: 1030–1044.

Hart, D., and Atkins, R. (2002). "Civic Competence in Urban Youth." *Applied Developmental Science*, 6 (4): 246–257.

Hughes, D., and Chen, L. (1997). "When and What Parents Tell Children about Race: An Examination of Race-Related Socialization among African American Families." *Applied Developmental Science*, 1 (4): 200–214.

Hughes, D., and Dodge, M. A. (1997). "African American Women in the Workplace: Relationships between Job Conditions, Racial Bias at Work, and Perceived Job Quality." *American Journal of Community Psychology*, 25 (5): 581–599.

Larson, R. W., Richards, M. H., Sims, B., and Dworkin, J. (2001). "How Urban African American Young Adolescents Spend Their Time: Time Budgets for Locations, Activities, and Companionship." *American Journal of Community Psychology*, 29 (4): 565–597.

Sherrod, L., Flanagan, C., and Youniss, J. (2002). "Dimensions of Citizenship and Opportunities for Youth Development: The What, Why, When, Where, and Who of Citizenship Development." *Applied Developmental Science*, 6 (4): 264–272.

Stepick, A., and Stepick, C. D. (2002). "Becoming American, Constructing Ethnicity: Immigrant Youth and Civic Engagement." *Applied Developmental Science*, 6 (4): 246–257.

Tseng, V. (2004). "Family Interdependence and Academic Adjustment in College: Youth from Immigrant and U.S.–Born Families." *Child Development*, 75 (3): 966–983.

U.S. Department of Education, National Center for Education Statistics (1999). *National Assessment of Educational Progress, 1999. Trends in Academic Progress: Three Decades of Student Performance.* Washington, D.C.: U.S. Department of Education. See http://nces.ed.gov/nationsreprtcard/civics/newresults.asp.

U.S. Department of Health and Human Services (2003). *Trends in the Well-Being of America's Children and Youth.* Washington, D.C.: U.S. Department of Health and Human Services.

Wilson, W. J. (1995). "Jobless Ghettos and the Social Outcome of Youngsters." In *Examining Lives in Context: Perspectives on the Ecology of Human Development*, edited by P. Moen and G. H. Elder. Washington, D.C.: American Psychological Association, pp. 527–543.

Kimber Bogard

Civic Environmentalism. Most of the eye-catching headlines on the environment in the United States today are about some government regulation that has just been passed or repealed or some protest against the siting of a hazardous waste or other facility that might increase harm to residents nearby. What often gets much less notice is the constructive action of citizens themselves to protect and restore the ecosystems around them, often in collaboration with a broad range of community groups and even with some of the adversaries they may have previously seen only on the opposite side of a courtroom or picket line. In recent years many citizen groups have come to realize that protest, lawsuits, and regulation—while essential tools for activists—have real limits for improving and restoring ecosystems over the long run and even for protecting the health of people most at risk from multiple environmental hazards. Increasingly citizens and government regulators have turned to a variety of other methods that

A group of seventeen-year-old high-school students plants a tree on Arbor Day. *Courtesy of Skjold Photographs.*

can be grouped under the term "civic environmentalism." And young people have played essential roles in many of the civic innovations of recent years.

Civic environmentalism emerged as a distinct paradigm within the environmental field in the 1990s, although similar innovations were underway at least a decade earlier. Civic environmentalists generally support federal regulation and recognize the substantial gains achieved since the 1960s in controlling point-source pollution (i.e., pollution from identifiable points such as a smokestack). But they argue that command-and-control regulation, pollutant by pollutant, is often inadequate in the face of the multiple sources of nonpoint pollution and threats to entire ecosystems. Here the problems are simply too complex for a one-size-fits-all regulation to work effectively. Regulation needs to become more creative and more catalytic of collaborative, place-based problem solving that engages a broad range of citizens, institutions, and organized stakeholders, including traditional adversaries, in a process of continuous, mutual learning and adaptive management. The holistic and integrated science of ecosystems requires far richer civic approaches than those typically found in polarized interest-group competition that too often results in policy stalemates.

Protecting and restoring a watershed, for instance, may involve a wide array of groups. A boating association might educate its members about not dumping waste into a river or bay and might provide a way for its members to report suspicious behavior by other boaters. An environmental group may help them with educational materials and its "baykeeper" boat might help monitor the health of the bay. Young people from local schools or colleges might train on the "baykeeper" and learn to collect and analyze data as part of their science classes. Their YMCA and 4-H clubs might help raise baby oysters and plant them in the bay to help restore natural filtration, and oyster fishermen might collaborate with them or provide some funds for their projects. An aerial photography class at a community college might collaborate with a local scuba-diving club to develop a state-of-the art database on invasive species, and homeowners' associations and churches might enlist members week after week to help remove them with their own hands. The local Grange (a cooperative organization representing farmers' collective interests) fifty miles away might host a barbeque where farmers come to hear about the latest sustainable-agriculture practices and hear from fishermen how their pesticides eventually migrate downstream to harm their catch. Farmers and ranchers who have been battling environmentalists for years may come to recognize that they need to develop a common strategy to prevent further ecosystem destruction and subdivision of the land for vacation homes by people who rarely live in the area and who may have little stake in a sustainable landscape.

In addition, officials from the state and federal environmental agencies or fish and wildlife services might help facilitate information sharing and collaboration so that local stakeholders can develop effective strategies that suit their specific ecosystems and make them capable of continuous learning and improvement. Most of these groups may come to recognize that battling in court for years, even when they eventually win a legal victory, will not do nearly as much to protect the watershed as finding ways to pool their knowledge and collaborate in the everyday work of restoring nature. And this work can be done in a way that does not violate the intent of environmental laws and does not remove the capacity for conflictual mobilization if some partners fail to act in good faith.

There are now tens of thousands of such civic environmental projects across the United States. They take many different forms and have even developed into distinct grassroots movements: the watershed movement, community-forestry movement, sustainable-communities movement, restoration movement, grassroots ecosystem-management movement, and land-trust movement. In the last several years the environmental-justice movement, which has been notable for its militant protest and legal tactics, has also begun to place special emphasis on the collaborative problem-solving model in its work in inner-city and other poor and minority areas.

The movement among environmental educators frequently links to these other movements, as teachers and students find creative ways to work in partnership with local civic associations and public agencies. For instance, Earth Force—a premier environmental education network—develops such partnerships through its Community Action and Problem Solving Program in various cities, as well as through its Global Rivers Environmental Education Network, which has affiliated middle- and high-school groups and educators in every state and several other countries (see also separate entry on Earth Force). The Student Conservation Association develops conservation-leadership and community-building skills among a national network of teams of high-school and college students, whom it places for extended periods of time with some 350 federal, state, and local agencies and environmental groups. The National Association of Service and Conservation Corps which includes 116 corps in thirty-one states and the District of Columbia also develops work and civic-leadership skills among low-income young people through conservation and other service projects.

Increasingly, public agencies have made civic environmentalism an important component of their work and the National Academy of Public Administration has recommended to Congress that it become central to reinventing environmental protection for the information age. At the U.S. Environmental Protection Agency there are a number of programs that support initiatives to build the civic capacities of young people. Its Chesapeake Bay program, for instance, provides grants and staff support to help establish local civic partnerships across a 64,000-square-mile drainage area. Through this program, schools and youth groups can get trained as "citizen monitors." The Office of Environmental Justice helps disadvantaged communities develop capacities for collaborative planning for pollution prevention and risk reduction, such as lead poisoning. The National Park Service has worked with the River Network to survey several thousand watershed associations, adopt-a-stream groups, and river and lake stewardship groups in order to help build a more robust watershed movement. State agencies in Massachusetts, California, Oregon, Washington, and elsewhere have redesigned their water protection programs to work in collaboration with watershed associations and other local conservation groups.

While civic environmentalism did not emerge as a youth movement, young people have quickly stepped in to make vital contributions. And for the coming years they are well positioned to do even more. Schools and colleges have enormous opportunities to link classroom education to hands-on work monitoring and restoring ecosystems (see also entry for Environmental Education). Such work develops academic competence while utilizing knowledge in a practical way that motivates young people and inspires adults with whom they work. Their volunteer monitoring can provide essential data that government agencies often cannot afford to collect on their own. Youth doing hands-on work can help groups locked in combat see beyond animosities and begin to collaborate on projects that are meaningful, productive, and fun. Youth groups (e.g., YMCA, 4-H, Boys and Girls Clubs, religious youth ministries) are capable of contributing millions of hours annually of work that no agency could ever imagine doing. They can help communities regain real ownership of their environmental problems. And they can do all this while working in sustained partnership with civic associations, businesses, and regulatory agencies.

See also Earth Force; Environmental Education (EE); 4-H; Sustainability.

Recommended Reading

Baker, M., and Kusel, J. (2004). *Community Forestry in the United States: Learning from the Past, Creating the Future.* Washington, D.C.: Island Press.

Barlett, P., and Chase, G., eds. (2004). *Sustainability on Campus: Stories and Strategies for Change.* Cambridge, MA: MIT Press.

Earth Force (1999). *Earth Force Community Action and Problem Solving: Teacher Manual.* Alexandria, VA: Earth Force.

Gobster, P. H., and Hall, R. B., eds. (2000). *Restoring Nature: Perspectives from the Social Sciences and Humanities.* Washington, D.C.: Island Press.

House, F. (1999). *Totem Salmon: Life Lessons from Another Species.* Boston: Beacon.

Kemmis, D. (2001). *This Sovereign Land: A New Vision for Governing the West.* Washington, D.C.: Island Press.

Shutkin, W. (2000). *The Land That Could Be: Environmentalism and Democracy in the Twenty-first Century.* Cambridge, MA: MIT Press.

Sirianni, C., and Friedland, L. (2001). *Civic Innovation in America: Community Empowerment, Public Policy, and the Movement for Civic Renewal.* Berkeley: University of California Press.

Stevens, W. (1995). *Miracle Under the Oaks: The Revival of Nature in America.* New York: Pocket Books.

Weber, E. P. (2003). "Bringing Society Back." In *Grassroots Ecosystem Management, Accountability, and Sustainable Communities.* Cambridge, MA: MIT Press.

Carmen Sirianni

Civic Identity. Identity is the crux of adolescent development. During adolescence, the crossroads of childhood and adulthood, youth transition from being defined primarily by their parents to defining themselves. The quest for self-definition forces teenagers to confront questions of who they are and who they want to become. But the questions do not end there. People often speak of identity as if it ends with the self; however, this approach fails to acknowledge the logical extension of adolescents' search: defining who they are as members of their communities.

Civic identity is the result of a developmental process whereby one constructs his or her role as a citizen. In other words, civic identity is the way a person conceives of his or her relationship to and connection with the community and larger society. We might also call this political identity. In common parlance there is a false distinction between the words "political" and "civic." In people's minds "political" often refers to the business of government: voting, serving on the city council, and participating in partisan politics. The word "civic," by contrast, is conceived as nongovernmental activities such as volunteering to lead a Girl Scout troop or spearheading a community beautification project. However, as Walzer explains, the two words have similar roots: the word "citizen" is derived "from the Latin word *civis*; the Greek equivalent is *polites*, a member of the polis, from which comes our political" (Walzer 1989, 211). Hence, "civic identity" and "political identity" can be used interchangeably to describe the process whereby a person comes to understand his or her rights and obligations as an engaged member of society.

Adolescence and early adulthood provide a unique opportunity for youth to understand and appreciate their role as citizens. Mannheim (1952) argued that adolescence is a period when youth have a "fresh contact" with society. That is, as youth engage with the polity with less parental monitoring than they had as children, they become increasingly aware of society's impact on their day-to-day actions. Simultaneously, they become cognizant of their ability to influence society and its institutions. It is often in very basic ways that young people learn about their rights and responsibilities within the polity. To illustrate this point, consider when we get our driver's licenses. By passing the government's operator test, we earned the *right* to drive an automobile, but with every right comes responsibility. Licensed drivers must drive safely, obey traffic laws, adhere to emissions standards, and share the road with other drivers. As drivers, we are *responsible* not only for our safety, but also for the safety of pedestrians, other drivers, and the environment.

Adolescents' civic identities evolve over time and depend on the accumulated experiences they have in their families, schools, and other community institutions. Suppose two teenage friends, Matt and Jared, are leaving the arcade when a person begging for spare change approaches. Matt, commenting under his breath that the person's too lazy to get a job, dismisses the beggar. Rather than following suit, Jared stops and gives the guy a couple of dollars. Why did these friends react so differently? Most likely, their different reactions reflect distinct civic attitudes and identities which the two youth have developed through different sets of life experiences. For example, Jared may belong to a church group that volunteers two hours a week at the local soup kitchen. His experiences working with people in the soup kitchen have likely resulted in greater empathy for the hardships that people face (e.g., low wages, high cost of living and of housing). He is also likely to be more aware that the roots of homelessness have many structural and systemic causes and cannot be reduced simply to blaming individuals for the problem. Jared, therefore, sees the beggar not as a *homeless* person, but as a *person* without a home. By contrast, Matt may have had fewer opportunities to interact with people experiencing these types of hardships, thus making it difficult for him to empathize. Matt equates being homeless with being unmotivated. This example illustrates how social experiences form the basis for our civic attitudes (i.e., what we consider the basis of the social problem). It also illustrates how actions reflect our civic identities (i.e., Jared feels a personal obligation to help a person in need). He doesn't have to think much about it because such behavior is just so consistent with who he is—in other words, with his civic identity.

It is important to remember that one's civic identity does not develop overnight, nor does it occur in isolation. Rather, civic identity forms over time through varied experiences and contexts. Young people consolidate their civic identities by making sense of the social experiences that occur in the context of their families, schools, and communities. Activities and relationships in each of these institutions are the means by which youth understand and define what it means to be a citizen.

Families significantly influence civic-identity development by teaching values. In the past, researchers have argued that children form their civic identities by talking to their parents about political ideas such as party choice and voting preference. However, it may be difficult for youth to relate to political parties when they are too young to cast ballots. Nevertheless, youth are old enough to learn family values, which in turn shape their civic identities.

For example, families who take the initiative to recycle teach their children to respect the environment, and as a result, these youth are more apt to develop a sense of responsibility for preserving local parks, forests, and streams. Similarly, parents who volunteer in community organizations model civic participation for their children. Participating in community organizations is one of the activities through which youth explore their civic identities. In such organizations young people develop an understanding of themselves as part of a larger public. They develop a sense of obligation to the group. Participation in such organizations in one's youth is a powerful predictor of civic engagement in adulthood.

Like families, schools play a pivotal role in shaping civic identity. Historically, society has charged schools with the tasks of educating and motivating young citizens. In part, schools achieve this goal by teaching courses such as history, civics, and government. But, content knowledge alone is not enough; schools must also develop the younger generation's civic skills and interests. Today, civic education fosters civic identity "not by teaching about democracy but by providing hands-on training for future participation" (Verba, Schlozman, and Brady 1995, 425). Student government and many other school organizations, with the exception of sports, cultivate civic commitments in adolescents. Inclusive school climates promote the development of civic values by insisting on tolerance, facilitating open debate, and encouraging perspective-taking.

Another trend in education is the adoption of experiential, intercurricular service-learning projects. The premise of service learning is that students' learning comes alive when they discover how concepts learned in school can be applied to community issues. Similar to community service, youth who are engaged in service learning volunteer their time to benefit others and the community-at-large, but service learning also incorporates a reflective component. Think of a tenth-grade horticulture class that designs a butterfly garden for the town square. Students spend the semester growing plants, perfecting the layout, and working with community collaborators to secure funding and equipment. Throughout the service-learning process, students collectively reflect on their roles, the skills they have learned, the public spaces they share with others, and the impact they have had on their community. Participation in service-learning activities not only allows students to develop their individual civic identities but also promotes a sense of group solidarity. Working side by side to complete the project provides students with a unique opportunity to come together and realize their collective ability to make positive changes in their community. Thus, service learning has the unique potential to bring the students, the class, the curriculum, and the community together for the common good. This experience of solidarity with the community, what we might call a "sense of place," is integral to the students' civic identities.

A sense of belonging and commitment to the community is essential to adolescent civic-identity development. Participation in community organizations (e.g., 4-H, theater groups) and institutions (e.g., school, church) evokes a sense of community ownership in youth. By participating in such organizations, adolescents begin to feel responsible for the common good that includes the well-being of others as well as the preservation of public spaces and goods. These informal organizations, or "schools of democracy" as Tocqueville called them (1848/1966), provide adolescents with a prosocial reference group and a set of core civic values with which to identify. Adolescents who actively engage in the community feel they have a voice and a stake in public affairs. Conversely, youth who do not feel like they count in the community become disaffected. Disaffected youth have no close emotional ties to the community and feel apathetic toward participating in the community. More often

than not, these youth come from communities that lack the community cooperation and financial backing to support youth-development programming, such as after-school and Big Brothers/Big Sisters programs. Failure to provide extracurricular activities (e.g., recreational, civic, artistic, religious, academic, and service clubs) can confirm disaffected adolescents' belief that they do not count. In contrast, communities that engage youth and invest in their futures lay the groundwork for a participatory democracy.

Adolescents' family, school, and community experiences shape how they define themselves as citizens well into adulthood. Studies routinely confirm that participation in youth organizations such as Boys and Girls Clubs, school council, and Young Pioneers has long-lasting influences on civic participation into adulthood. Youth involved in organizations during adolescence are more likely to participate in organizations as adults. This trend continues in volunteerism. The long-term effects of civic participation are not, however, reserved wholly for organizational involvement. The same effects hold true for short, intense stints of political activism; albeit, they are less common. In 1964 more than 1,000 young adults, most of whom were white, well-educated northerners, volunteered to participate in the Mississippi Freedom Summer civil rights voter-registration campaign. The project lasted three quick but intense months. Volunteers submerged themselves in black communities to register voters and provide the basic literacy skills required for voting. Participation in Freedom Summer significantly shaped the volunteers' relationship to society. Many of these volunteers continued grassroots work in their communities into mid-life. Regardless of form—long-term and common or short-term and intense—civic participation binds citizens to the polity and shapes their sense of themselves as civic actors.

Political participation manifests itself in countless ways. Whether people donate blood, serve on a youth governance board, join scout troops, or write opinion letters to the editor, they are developing their civic identities. The transitional nature of adolescence (i.e., a time for exploring options for one's identity while moving from childhood to adulthood) makes it the optimal time for youth to try new experiences that in turn reinforce the values that define their civic commitments. In short, civic identity is how one defines and fulfills one's rights and responsibilities as a citizen.

See also Acculturation; Ethnic Identity; Identity and Activism; Identity and Organizing in Older Youth; National Identity and Youth; Racial and Ethnic Inequality; Racial Socialization; Transnational Identity.

Recommended Reading

Colby, A., and Damon, W. (1992). *Some Do Care: Contemporary Lives of Moral Commitment.* New York: The Free Press.
Erikson, E.H. (1968). *Identity: Youth and Crisis.* New York: Norton.
Flanagan, C. A. (2004). "Volunteerism, Leadership, Political Socialization, and Civic Engagement." In R. M. Lerner, and L. Steinberg, eds. *Handbook of Adolescent Psychology.* 2nd ed. Hoboken, NJ: Wiley, pp. 721–745.
Flanagan, C. A., and Tucker, C. J. (1999). "Adolescents' Explanations for Political Issues: Concordance with Their Views of Self and Society." *Developmental Psychology,* 35 (5): 1198–1209.
Hart, D., and Fegley, S. (1995). "Prosocial Behavior and Caring in Adolescence: Relations to Self-Understanding and Social Judgment." *Child Development,* 66: 1346–1359.
Mannheim, K. (1952). "The Problem of Generations." In *Essays on the Sociology of Knowledge.* London: Routledge and Kegan Paul, pp. 276–322. (Original work published 1928).
Verba, S., Scholzman, K. L, and Brady, H. E. (1995). *Voice and Equality: Civic Voluntarism in American Cities.* Cambridge, MA: Harvard University Press.
Walzer, M. (1989). "Citizenship." In *Political Innovation and Conceptual Change,* edited by T. Ball, J. Farr, and R. L. Hanson. New York: Cambridge University Press, pp. 211–219.
Yates, M., and Youniss, J., eds. (1998). Roots of Civic Identity: International Perspectives on Community Service and Activism in Youth. Cambridge, MA: Cambridge University Press.

Amy K. Syvertsen

Civic Virtue. Civic virtue can be defined as the combination of knowledge, commitments, and actions of individuals that serve to promote the flourishing of democratic civil society. If we understand civic virtue then we are able to respond to questions such as: Why do some youth become engaged in activism related to social issues? What characteristics or principled commitments lead some to feel compelled to act on behalf of others? Why are some youth motivated to speak out or engage in resistance when they witness injustice? The exploration of such questions is essential to understanding civic engagement and activism among youth. Furthermore, those concerned with the civic education of youth need to consider the values and attitudes that are most likely to support active citizenship among youth.

Civic education is vitally important in a pluralistic, liberal democracy. By contrast, authoritarian orders have little need for citizens who consult their conscience on social issues. One of the best-known proposals for an authoritarian style of government is Thomas Hobbes' *Leviathan.* Hobbes described a commonwealth in which a sovereign ruler is all-powerful and the liberty of a subject "lieth ... only in those things which, in regulating their actions, the sovereign hath praetermitted (such as the liberty to buy and sell, and otherwise contract with another; to choose their own abode, their own diet, their own trade of life, and institute of their children as they themselves see fit; and the like)" (Hobbes 1994, 138). In other words, a person in such a society is allowed to make choices in some private matters, so long as the sovereign (i.e., the ruler) has permitted him or her to do so. Hobbes argued that such a form of government is advantageous in that it prevents the war of all against all and the "solitary, poor, nasty, brutish, and short" life that otherwise would exist. Modern liberal democracy is based on a foundation that rejects Hobbesian totalitarianism, and thus much more is expected and demanded of citizens of a liberal democracy.

There have been arguments recently that suggest that citizens of the United States are not living up to the expectations of democratic citizenship. Our civic discourse seems distorted by twenty-four-hour cable news shows in which *talking heads* have become *shouting heads* and "gotcha" tactics prevail over reasoned and civil deliberation. Citizens appear more and more divided politically, isolated socially, and entrenched economically. Whether or not one accepts a crisis mentality, it is clear that civic education for democratic citizenship is important and multifaceted. In addition to knowledge and skills related to democratic theories, structures, and processes, youth in democratic societies must develop civic virtue.

The concept of civic virtue has been explored by a wide variety of philosophers and educators concerned with democratic citizenship. Perhaps the first person to record his ideas on the subject was Aristotle. In the *Nicomachean Ethics,* Aristotle remarked:

For even if the good is the same for an individual as for a city, that of a city is obviously a greater and more complete thing to obtain and preserve. For while the good of an individual is a desirable thing, what is good for a people or for cities is a nobler and more godlike thing (Aristotle 1094b).

Aristotle argued that this commitment to the common good arises in people through action and habituation: "We become just by doing just actions, temperate by temperate actions, and courageous by courageous actions" (Aristotle 1103b).

Several philosophers since Aristotle, such as John Locke, Immanuel Kant, and John Stuart Mill, have reflected upon the virtues necessary for liberty, moral character, and civil society. Much of this thinking has centered on the problem of reconciling individual liberty with the broader needs of the community. Many of the ideological differences related to social and economic policy issues in a democratic society tend to revolve around this problem. The tension between individual liberty and the common good poses a complex challenge for education in a pluralistic democracy, yet recent scholars have attempted to resolve this dilemma by seeking to identify ideals and practices that move beyond this apparent dichotomy.

Amy Gutmann has suggested that the dichotomy between individual freedom and civic virtue is a "morally false choice." She argues:

We stand at a philosophical and political impasse unless we can defend an alternative to communitarian solidarity—which insists that children be educated to accept the singularly correct and comprehensive conception of the good life—and liberal neutrality—which insists that education not predispose children toward *any* [emphasis in original] conception of the good life (Gutmann 1993, 3).

Gutmann proposes that democratic education embrace the ideal of "conscious social reproduction" that is based upon the principles of nonrepression, nondiscrimination, and democratic deliberation. The principle of nonrepression guides educators to "cultivate the kind of character and the kind of intellect that enables people to choose rationally (one might say autonomously) among different ways of life." The conscious social reproduction of democratic society requires nonrepressive education that will "teach those civic virtues—such as veracity, nonviolence, toleration, and mutual respect—that serve as foundations for rational deliberation of differing ways of life." Gutmann explains that this nonrepressive form of education must be for everyone and thus, nondiscriminatory. Education that is nonrepressive and nondiscriminatory is vital to the health of a democracy since "the effect of educational discrimination is often to repress, at least temporarily, the capacity and sometimes even the desire of disfavored groups to participate in politics or to assert their own preferences in life" (Gutmann 1993, 4). Finally, Gutmann asserts that democratic education must cultivate students' capacity for democratic deliberation, decision-making, and self-governance while instilling social responsibility. Such an education requires teaching virtues of democratic character such as "veracity, self-discipline, nonviolence, toleration, mutual respect for reasonable differences of opinion, the ability to deliberate, to think critically about one's life and one's society, and therefore to participate in conscious social reproduction" (Gutmann 1993, 8).

The outcome of Gutmann's proposal—citizen participation in the effort to reproduce democratic society—is significant for those concerned with youth activism. A primary goal for democratic educators is fostering a tendency among youth to act and participate in accordance with civic virtue. As Robert Audi explains:

Virtue is not a mere capacity for good deeds, but a settled tendency to do them for an appropriate reason. Civic virtue, in particular, is constituted—at least as conceived as appropriate to citizenship in a liberal democracy—above all in relation to protection and promotion of the flourishing of civil society. This implies a disposition on the part of citizens to participate in sociopolitical decisions and a determination to do so with respect for the freedom and autonomy of other citizens (Audi 1998, 170).

Audi theorizes that there are six important dimensions to virtue: situational, conceptual, cognitive, motivational, behavioral, and teleological. Let us explore these dimensions by imagining a scenario in which two youth named Colin and Isabel have a disagreement over environmental protection. If Colin and Isabel have developed a commitment to civic virtue we would expect them to act in a particular way when confronted with an opportunity for democratic deliberation that requires mutual respect for differences of opinion. The situational dimension, described by Audi, would require that both Colin and Isabel recognize that this disagreement has placed them in a *situation* that calls for the application of particular civic virtues. The conceptual dimension requires that both youth are able to recognize that the *concepts* of respect, nonviolence, veracity, self-discipline, and comprehensible and reasoned deliberation apply to this situation.

Within the cognitive dimension, we would expect that both Colin and Isabel have developed *knowledge and skills* related to the relevant concepts. In this case, both Colin and Isabel should possess the understanding and skills needed to show respect for another with whom one disagrees and to engage in deliberation that is truthful, nonviolent, and comprehensible. The motivational dimension would call for both Colin and Isabel to possess the *desire* to engage in democratic deliberation. Both youth would possess the motivation to engage in deliberation for the purpose of understanding another's viewpoint and thoughtfully consider these alternative views, rather than desire to humiliate, defeat, coerce, or otherwise "show him or her."

The behavioral dimension encompasses the actions that Colin and Isabel take in this situation. If civic virtue has been effectively fostered within Colin and Isabel, both youth should *act* based upon their cognitive understanding of the virtues called for in this situation and their desire to live in accordance with these principles. Their actions might take a variety of forms from conversation to participation in political organizations that support their respective causes. Finally, within the teleological dimension both Colin and Isabel could reflect upon their actions—spontaneously and after time has passed—to consider how their actions are serving or have served desirable *ends*. If we adopt Gutmann's conception of the democratic ideal, then the realization of these ends should serve to promote the conscious social reproduction of a nonrepressive, nondiscriminatory, deliberative democracy.

Both Gutmann's conception of conscious social reproduction of democracy and Audi's explanation of six dimensions of virtue are helpful for educators seeking to cultivate civic virtue and a commitment to positive social action within youth. It seems apt to consider democracy as something to which each generation must give birth. This reproduction does not equate to replication. To extend the reproductive metaphor, we do not wish to *clone* our democracy with each subsequent generation, rather we seek to *give birth* to new forms of social order that maintain some of the characteristic "genes" that are essential to civil society. We do this consciously and deliberately while honoring the principles of freedom of thought and justice for all persons. Similarly, Audi's dimensions of virtue do not constitute a linear and fixed approach to virtue but offer some insight into the tasks for educators of youth. Fostering civic virtue in youth requires educational attention to civic knowledge, civic skill and abilities, and civic action. If we return to the questions posed at the beginning of this essay, our response could reasonably be that youth who become engaged in activism related social issues, who feel compelled to act on behalf of others, and who are motivated to respond to injustice possess civic virtue.

See also Civic Identity; Democracy; Democratic Education; Empathy; Innovations in Civic Participation (ICP); Moral Development; Moral Exemplars; National and Community Service; School Influences and Civic Engagement; State and Youth, The; Student Political Activism; Volunteerism.

Recommended Reading

Aristotle (2000). *Nicomachean Ethics*, edited and translated by R. Crisp. Cambridge: Cambridge University Press. (Original work completed approximately 330 BCE.)

Audi, R. (1998). "A Liberal Theory of Civic Virtue." *Social Philosophy and Policy*, 15 (1): 149–170.

Farrell, J. P. (2001). "On Learning Civic Virtue: Can Schooling Really Play a Role?" *Curriculum Inquiry*, 3 (2): 125–135.

Gutmann, A. (1993). "Democracy and Democratic Education." *Studies in Philosophy and Education*, 12 (1): 1–9.

Hobbes, T. (1994). *Leviathan*, edited by E. Curley. Indianapolis, IN: Hackett. (Original work published 1668.)

Leming, J. S. (1996). "Civic Virtue: Common Ground for Character Education and Law-Related Education Professionals." *Update on Law-Related Education*, 20 (1): 29.

Milson, A. J. (2001). "Fostering Civic Virtue in a High-Tech World." *International Journal of Social Education*, 16 (1), 87–93.

Null, J. W., and Milson, A. J. (2003). "Beyond Marquee Morality: Virtue in the Social Studies." *The Social Studies*, 94 (3): 119–123.

Oakes, J., Hunter-Quartz, K., Ryan, S., and Lipton, M. (2000). "Becoming Good American Schools: The Struggle for Civic Virtue in Education Reform." *Phi Delta Kappan*, 81 (8): 568–576.

Putnam, R. (2000). *Bowling Alone: The Collapse and Revival of American Community*. New York: Simon and Schuster.

Andrew J. Milson

Civil Rights Movement. The civil rights movement (1950s–1960s) marked a pivotal change in the treatment and status of African Americans, particularly in the Deep South. Fueled primarily by young activists and leaders, the civil rights movement mobilized people across the United States, especially African Americans in the South, to challenge the legal system of Jim Crow segregation. Utilizing protests, boycotts, sit-ins, and other nonviolent tactics, young activists shaped the movement and led the nation to a new understanding of rights, equality, and democracy. The civil rights movement made visible the intellectual, physical, and spiritual motivations of a new generation of activists. These young leaders and activists would demand that their country confront the troubling issues of segregated and unequal education, systemic violence against black Americans, discrimination in the use of public accommodations, and a basic denial of the right of blacks to vote throughout most of the South—known more generally as the system of Jim Crow segregation.

While many people date the formal start of the civil rights movement at 1955 with the beginning of the Montgomery bus boycott, it is important that we remember the numerous individuals, groups, and organizations that have struggled throughout the history of this country to secure the equal rights of African Americans. These individuals, organizations, and groups would help set the stage for the massive mobilization throughout the South that would come

An Atlanta police officer drags an African American high-school student to the paddy wagon during a 1964 demonstration against restaurant segregation. *Library of Congress.*

to be designated the civil rights movement. For example, long before the Montgomery bus boycott, the National Association for the Advancement of Colored People (NAACP) led a litigation strategy that sought to legally nullify many of the laws that guaranteed the secondary treatment of African Americans. Prior to the formal beginning of the civil rights movement the NAACP won court cases that led to the overturning of a number of laws meant to restrict black voting, such as the grandfather clause and the all-white primary. These efforts, while successful at times, were hard to come by and underscored the limits of a purely legal strategy to win the equal rights of black Americans. It was apparent that a legal strategy would need to be paired with on-the-ground mobilization.

Some of the necessary mobilization resulted from the killing of Emmett Till. Many argue that it was the murder of Emmett Till that truly galvanized the country and directed, in particular, the white public's attention to struggles for civil rights. Till, a fourteen-year-old from Chicago who was sent to Money, Mississippi, to visit relatives, was murdered in August 1955. Two white men took Emmett Till from his uncle's house in the middle of the night, accusing him of speaking inappropriately to a white woman. His body would later be found in the Tallahatchie River, having been brutalized nearly beyond recognition. His mother, Mamie Bradley, made the courageous decision to have an open casket during the funeral so the entire world could see the violence that daily threatened the lives of African Americans in the South. She also allowed *Jet* magazine to publish pictures of young Emmett's tortured body so that a larger group of people could witness this atrocity. In this case, it was the torture and death of a fourteen-year-old boy who refused to conform to irrational norms of white supremacy that helped set the stage for the civil rights movement.

Interestingly, actions taking place on a different continent, as Indian people struggled for independence from Britain, would also shape and contribute to the future civil rights movement. Specifically, the actions and ideas of Mohandas "Mahatma" Gandhi (1869–1948) would provide young activists and leaders in the civil rights movement, like Martin Luther King Jr., with new strategies and tactics for pursuing their rights. Gandhi helped lead the movement that resulted in the liberation of India from British imperialism. This movement was based on a philosophy of nonviolent protests, galvanizing an entire nation to take a peaceful stand against the oppressive colonizers. Dedicated to restoring India's independence, Gandhi employed nonviolent tactics to achieve advantageous social and political objectives. Imprisonment, numerous beatings, and death threats were not enough to dissuade him from his cause. His ability to affect change through peaceful mass mobilization and protest garnered widespread support, both regionally and internationally. The result was India's liberation from British rule in 1947.

The nonviolent protests of Mahatma Gandhi in India provided young African American organizers and activists in the South with a new model for realizing their objectives. Young leaders of the emerging civil rights movement, such as King, would have a chance to put these new tactics into practice during the Montgomery bus boycott of 1955. The moment to take action surfaced when a defiant Rosa Parks refused to give up her seat on a bus to a white man in Montgomery, Alabama, on December 1, 1955. Far from being a spontaneous reaction, Rosa Parks was not the first African American in the south to refuse to give up her seat. In fact, earlier in 1955, fifteen-year-old Claudette Colvin was arrested in Montgomery for refusing to give up her seat to a white person. Black city leaders considered mobilizing around her case but made a decision not to when they discovered that young Colvin was pregnant. Thus, even in the earliest stages of the movement, young activists were prepared to sacrifice and to lead.

Once word spread that Rosa Parks, a longtime NAACP activist, had been arrested for refusing to give up her seat to a white man, members of the NAACP and the Women's Political Caucus decided to plan a one-day boycott in response to her arrest. Led by Jo Ann Robinson of the Women's Political Caucus plans were put in place and information circulated asking African Americans not to ride the buses. King, the new, young minister at Dexter Avenue Baptist Church, was elected president of the Montgomery Improvement Association (MIA), a new organization started to lead the boycott effort. King was only twenty-six-years-old when he took on this leadership position. However, independent of his age, he demonstrated a mature and engaging leadership style that allowed him, in conjunction with other city leaders, to launch a nonviolent attack against the institutionalized system of racism. By creating their own transportation system and picketing the Montgomery bus line for over a year, the MIA led efforts that eventually resulted in the desegregation of the bus line. The Montgomery bus boycott displayed the power of intellectually and spiritually charged youth leaders and activists in the grueling battle against racism. Through the work of groups such as the MIA, the NAACP, and the Women's Political Caucus, the Montgomery bus boycott became a catalyst, motivating other young protesters to stand up and contest the oppressive racial practices and laws that degraded African Americans across the nation.

Young, often formally educated, African Americans emerged as the leaders of a new organized opposition to white supremacy and specifically Jim Crow segregation in the South. And while King and other young, religious southern leaders would go on to develop the Southern Christian Leadership Conference (SCLC) in 1957 as a means to coordinate continued organizing against Jim Crow throughout the South, other sources of youth activism and leadership also emerged. One such example is the Student Nonviolent Coordinating Committee (SNCC). SNCC and its leaders present one of the most complete pictures of the preponderance of youth activists involved in shaping the civil rights movement. SNCC not only brought together a group of youth organizers that would go on to shape politics in the United States for the next forty years—individuals such as John Lewis (now a member of the U.S. Congress), Marion Barry (former mayor of Washington, D.C.), and Julian Bond (current NAACP chairman)—it also brought to the fore a new style of leadership, more democratic and radical than was evident in organizations like the SCLC. Formally begun in April 1960, SNCC set out on a path to allow student and youth leadership to dictate a new direction of struggle in the civil rights movement. SNCC leaders and members would use the talents, resources, courage, and insight of young people to make a difference in the struggle for rights and equality for black people through nonviolent protests.

On February 1, 1960, four first-year students at North Carolina Agricultural and Technical College decided to stage a sit-in at the lunch counter of a Woolworth's store in Greensboro, North Carolina, to protest its policy of maintaining segregated lunch counters. While the four young men involved in the protest eventually left the store as it was being closed without having been served, the next day nearly thirty students returned to continue the sit-in protest. Over the next few months the number of young people participating in sit-ins

would continue to grow. It is reported that by 1961 nearly 70,000 students had joined in this effort. And while much of the sit-in activity was confined to the South, there were also students and youth activists in the North who picketed the northern branches of southern stores who refused to serve black Americans.

The sit-ins were designed to visibly protest the segregated lunch counters and call into question the basis for such practices. The sit-ins were, thus, a two-front attack; protesters physically opposed the segregated lunch counters by attempting to dine at the stores, and they also brought the national spotlight to another dimension of the system of racial inequality pervasive throughout the South. With the increased national attention came unwanted publicity from those whites committed to a system of racial stratification in which blacks received less and were treated as second-class citizens. And while sit-ins like those in Nashville put the young, idyllic protesters in harm's way, jeopardizing their safety, the Nashville students and other young people throughout the South were unwavering in the face of violent assaults. The sit-in tactics garnered support from both local black communities as well as from empathetic liberal whites, putting more pressure on the South to desegregate and abolish Jim Crow.

In the wake of the success of the early sit-in mobilization there was increasing talk about how to formally organize the students and young people involved in these protests. Organizations like the SCLC and the NAACP hoped to convince these young activists to align with their organizations. Ironically, Ella Baker of the SCLC, a strong opponent of traditional models of charismatic male leadership, helped organize a meeting of sit-in activists at Shaw University in April 1960. At that meeting Baker forcefully encouraged students to start a new independent organization that would not be under the leadership of any of the established civil rights organizations. The students present agreed with

Baker and decided to form the Student Nonviolent Coordinating Committee (SNCC).

As the sit-in movement progressed, the SNCC received assistance from more eager youth committed to affecting change, whatever the cost. Suffering from beatings, racial epithets, possible expulsions from school, and imprisonment, the students fervently moved on toward change. In Nashville, officials resorted to jailing the students for extended periods, but the success of the sit-in movement generated a legion of student demonstrators to replace their recently removed compatriots. The police would remove row upon row of student activists only to have the seats immediately filled by more supporters. Building on the accomplishments of the Nashville demonstrations, the sit-in movement took hold nationwide with youth from across America challenging and confronting segregation through peaceful means. Even imprisonment, which would tarnish their records and make it difficult for future employment, did not discourage young activists from building a national movement.

The SNCC continued to play an instrumental role in organizing and leading the civil rights movement in new directions. After the widespread success of the sit-ins, the SNCC began organizing and sending newly trained leaders to other parts of the country to conduct more demonstrations. In Albany, Georgia, SNCC field secretaries in concert with NAACP youth councils began organizing area high-school and college students for a sit-in at a white bus terminal (December 1961). The area was deprived of college students because only one university was located in the immediate region. As a result, high-school students played a large role in the movement. As the sit-in transpired, the Albany officials arrested more people than at any other sit-in action throughout the movement. This time, high-school students largely filled the jails. This also occurred in a Birmingham, Alabama, protest organized by James Bevel in 1963. Over 6,000 students between the

ages of six and sixteen were assaulted and then detained by Birmingham police officers. This practice evolved into a new direct-action strategy—filling the jails.

Prior sit-in strategies anticipated that participants would spend some limited time in jail and then post bond shortly thereafter. The new strategy called for filling the jails and having people, often young people, remain in jail until they had served their time. Regardless of rank or influence, the collective movement deemed it necessary to crowd the jails to argue for change. Given the sheer numbers of demonstrators, the jails quickly filled beyond capacity, leaving city officials with few options for resolving the situation. Imprisoning the protesters was no longer a sufficient solution and reiterated the need to construct new methods for handling the protesters. The direct-action strategy created more difficulties for city officials than they could handle, forcing them to make concessions to the movement. While prominent figures such as Martin Luther King Jr. spent a significant amount of time in jail, unknown activists committed to the struggle for equal rights spent most of the time in jail. Often these activists were young people who defied the instructions of their parents not to be involved in what they perceived as dangerous protests. These young people, however, knew that freedom and equality would only be won by taking a stand—and so they did.

In 1961 young protesters would again demonstrate their courage and commitment when they boarded buses destined for the South on what were called "freedom rides." Organized by the Congress of Racial Equality (CORE), the freedom rides, similar to other previous protest strategies created by the young organizers, took the issue of civil rights and equality straight to their white oppressors. Young demonstrators from CORE, SNCC, NAACP youth councils, SCLC, and white liberal supporters from northern states decided to charter and integrate buses and travel through some of the most volatile southern strongholds in an attempt to challenge Jim Crow segregation in transportation as practiced throughout the south. The "Freedom Riders" understood the dangers of their journeys, yet they pushed forward with unabated passion. They were unrelenting in their confrontation with injustice, even though the states through which they traveled offered no protection. Not surprisingly, freedom riders did not encounter the full force of white resistance until they entered Alabama where they were brutally beaten. Mobs of white southerners attacked the Freedom Riders and firebombed the bus with police visibly absent. Despite this treatment the young activists were committed to the freedom rides and vowed to continue. This time, however, the resistance came from the bus company who refused to continue.

As in other student- and youth-led mobilizations, when officials attempt to stop one group of activists by beating or arresting them, another group emerges to take their place and carry on the fight for justice. The freedom rides are another example of this tradition. When activists in Nashville learned that the original freedom riders would not be able to continue, students in the area led by Diane Nash went to Birmingham, Alabama, to continue the freedom rides. Eventually, the Nashville students would be allowed to restart the freedom rides. However, they, too, would be met with violence when they arrived in Montgomery, Alabama. Again, however they vowed to continue, and not even King's urging to stop would deter them. They departed for Mississippi. In Mississippi they were not greeted by the traditional mob violence of white southerners. This time Mississippi officials arrested the Freedom Riders. The group was sentenced to sixty days in the state penitentiary. Again, others came to continue their ride of protest, and many of these young activists were also arrested and beaten. In the end, their protests would help to secure true desegregation of interstate bus travel.

The freedom rides once again exhibited the complexities of the dilemma that troubled the nation. The nonviolent activists routinely suffered from violent offenses, often resulting in bodily harm, permanent emotional scarring, and extended time in jail. The young activists and the civil rights movement in general, looked to alleviate and remedy the chronic inequality and racism that plagued the nation. The resilience of the Freedom Riders served as a testament to the commitment and empowerment that the young activists offered to the civil rights movement while facing a reticent nation. Through the young activists' ardor for equality and exhausting efforts, the conceptualization of race and race relations in American society would never be the same. The Freedom Riders perseverance, along with that of their supporters, began to embolden the nation to correct the injustices faced by so many African Americans and other people of color in the United States.

Another powerful and notable moment in the civil rights movement, which demonstrates the importance and independence of youth activism, was the August 28, 1963, March on Washington. Increasingly, it was recognized that the systemic racial inequality that was the focus of the civil rights movement was no longer, or never was, just an issue for the Deep South but one for the entire nation to consider, and the March on Washington provided a national stage for addressing the problem. President John F. Kennedy, having introduced a new civil rights bill in 1963 that had yet to be passed by Congress, called upon the established leadership of the civil rights movement to demonstrate public support for the measure. After mass-mobilization efforts in major southern cities, many of the established civil rights organizations joined forces to organize the largest collective effort demonstration for civil rights. On August 28, 1963, over a quarter of a million people took part in this historic event staged in front of the Lincoln Memorial.

The march would feature the most recognized symbol of the movement, Martin Luther King Jr., as the primary speaker, with members of the participating organizations contributing speakers as well. As the day went on a division occurred between the more militant leaders of the SNCC and other more mainstream organizers. The speech that was to be given by John Lewis of the SNCC was thought to be too radical and critical of the federal government for the conciliatory tone of the march. After numerous revisions his speech found approval, and he was allowed to speak at the march. The tension over the speech, however, signified the increasing ideological independence of many young activists, tiring of the nonviolent strategy and rhetoric that they believed won, at best, incremental victories. The passions of the young organizers and their experiences in the Deep South, where on a daily basis black people faced deadly violence, caused tension and rifts between younger and older, more mainstream civil rights leaders both in terms of tactics and ideological beliefs. As the civil rights movement began to move to the North, a new philosophy of "Black Power" would contend with the ideas of nonviolence and integration for the hearts and minds of youth activists.

However, during the March on Washington the civil rights movement's objective appeared in a relatively coherent form with King presenting the illustrious words that concretized his legacy and defined the tone of the movement—"I have a dream." In the speech King detailed the vision for a new, brighter America in the days and years to come, one that was no longer riddled with injustice and inequality but filled with egalitarianism and tolerance for the multitude of different races and ethnicities that constituted the American population. King's eloquence, fervor, and profound statements captivated his national audience and left a lasting imprint on America's collective consciousness.

King's dream of a better America where equality is real to each and all is still being realized today, much to the credit of young activists. The civil rights movement serves as the pinnacle of youth activism. The movement displayed the raw power and impact of youth activism. The young demonstrators provided the momentum for affecting change in a society desperately in need of reconstruction. The activists employed their intelligence, passion, courage, physical numbers, and commitment to challenge both the country and the more traditional leadership of the civil rights movement. Through the extra-systemic participation of youth in the civil rights movement, a new conception of equality, rights, and democracy emerged in America.

The disparate approaches of the youth activists and that of the older generations, by working in concert, significantly advanced the work of reconstructing American institutions and practices to ensure equality and justice for all. The civil rights movement, through the leadership, guidance, and work of young people and their organizations helped to effectively begin the process of desegregating schools (enforcement of *Brown v. Board of Education*) and other public facilities. Furthermore, their combined efforts, along with the work of supportive whites, ended legal racial discrimination in the workplace and military, successfully secured the Civil Rights Act (1964) and Voting Rights Act (1965), and solidified the citizenship of African Americans. The longevity of the civil rights movement and the subsequent accomplishments are a tribute to the essential work of young activists.

See also Antiwar Activism; Democracy; Diversity Education; Ethnic Identity; Minority Youth Voter Turnout; Racial and Ethnic Inequality; Racial Socialization; Religiosity and Civic Engagement in African American Youth; Social Justice; Soweto Youth Activism (South Africa); Student Political Activism.

Recommended Reading

Blackside, Inc. (1986). *Eyes on the Prize: America's Civil Rights Years.* Alexandria, VA: P.B.S. Video/WGBH Boston.
Carson, C. (1981). *In Struggle: SNCC and the Black Awakening of the 1960s.* Cambridge, MA: Harvard University Press.

Halberstam, D. (1998). *The Children.* New York: Random House.

Marable, M. (1991). *Race, Reform, and Rebellion: The Second Reconstruction in Black America, 1945–1990.* Jackson: University of Mississippi Press.

McAdam, D. (1985). *Political Processes and the Development of Black Insurgency, 1930–1970.* Chicago: University of Chicago Press.

Morris, A. D. (1984). *The Origins of the Civil Rights Movement: Black Communities Organizing for Change.* New York: The Free Press.

Payne, C. M. (1996). *I've Got the Light of Freedom: The Organizing Tradition and the Mississippi Freedom Struggle.* Berkeley: University of California Press.

Ransby, B. (2003). *Ella Baker and the Black Freedom Movement: A Radical Democratic Vision.* Chapel Hill: University of North Carolina Press.

Williams, J. (1987). *Eyes on the Prize: America's Civil Rights Years, 1954–1965.* New York: Viking Penguin.

Kyle Hodges and Cathy J. Cohen

Civil Society and Positive Youth Development. Civil society—"the nexus of families, groups, neighborhoods, and associations" (Wilson 1993, 246)—is composed of the social mores, customs, values, and ideals of a people that ensure democracy. These social constructions or social institutions are not the components of government. In fact, government is only a means created "by the consent of the governed" to make systematic the availability to citizens of social justice and democratic opportunities. Civil society is, then, the "space" between individuals and government that assures that social justice and democracy are features of the social order and not a "gift" of government (see O'Connell 1999).

Certainly, after the attacks on America of September 11, 2001, ideas surrounding the concept of civil society have attracted more attention from both scholars and the general public, in part because of the difference between the ideology of the perpetrators of the attacks and the concepts of democracy and freedom providing the foundation of the idea of America (Lerner in press) and the question of how to maintain American institutions and freedoms while mounting an effective domestic and international response to the attacks. Framed by this growing interest in the institutions of society that keep a nation democratic and free, scholars studying positive youth development (PYD) have proposed that when youth show exemplary PYD, that is, when they thrive, they manifest an integration of their moral and civic identities that serves to maintain and enhance civil society.

One model of this relation between thriving youth and civil society focuses on the role of mutually beneficial, bidirectional relations between youth and society—relations termed "adaptive developmental regulations." We argue that such developmental regulations account for the linkage between positive, indeed exemplary, individual development (i.e., thriving) and the presence of institutions guaranteeing individual freedom and opportunity (e.g., as indexed by institutions, policies, and social programs reflecting social justice and equity).

Exemplary positive youth development or thriving involves a young person who—within the context of his or her individual set of physical and psychological characteristics and abilities—takes actions that serve his or her own well-being and, at the same time, the well-being of parent, peers, community, and society. A thriving young person is on a life path that eventuates in his or her becoming a contributing adult member of a civil society.

Thriving is enabled by a civil society that supports the rights of the individual to develop his or her abilities as best he or she can and in ways he or she values. Such a society can only exist when the people act to support, protect, and extend the societal institutions affording such liberty for all of its citizens. When individuals act in this manner because of their belief that such actions constitute the "right thing to do" and that these actions define the morally correct path, then there is a mutual, or reciprocal, relationship between individual thriving and civil society, which may be represented as "thriving individual ← → civil society."

This relationship involves the development in a person's life of a sense of self (a self-definition or an "identity") wherein civic engagement and moral thought and action are synthesized. This integrated civic and moral identity has its roots in humanity's evolutionary heritage and in the translation of this history into human development across the life span (Lerner in press). In human life integrated moral and civic identity may emerge prototypically in adolescence when the person's self-definition is undergoing significant and singular changes.

When humans across their life spans become more willing and more able to contribute to the maintenance and perpetuation of a social context that supports the health and prosperity of individual development, a civil society is constructed. Lerner terms this "individual ← → civil society" relationship *liberty*. In other words, when there are mutually beneficial exchanges (healthy developmental regulations) between individuals and civil society, then optimal development—*thriving*—is occurring. As well, when there is both maintenance and perpetuation of the institutions of civil society that enable individuals to contribute in healthy ways to self and to their social worlds, there is a "thriving individual ← → civil society" relationship. Lerner has argued that a society within which liberty exists is the epitome of a social order enabling relations between people and contexts to develop in a manner consistent with the evolutionary strategy requisite for the survival and the optimal functioning of the human species and of individuals within it (Lerner in press).

If it is in fact the case that integrated moral and civic identities may emerge prototypically in adolescence, when the person's self-definition is undergoing significant and singular changes, then the "thriving individual ← → civil society" relationship is actualized through the attainment of a synthesis between moral and civic identity, and young people attain

several key characteristics of positive development. We suggest, as have others (e.g., Eccles and Gootman 2002; Lerner in press; Lerner, Fisher, and Weinberg 2000; Roth and Brooks-Gunn 2003), that "five Cs" may be used to represent the key features of positive youth development: competence, character, confidence, social connections, and compassion. Together, these five characteristics enable an adolescent to make an optimal, or idealized, transition to the adult world. When these five characteristics place the young person on a life path toward a hopeful future, the youth is manifesting exemplary positive development: he or she is thriving. Such a youth will become a generative adult, a person making simultaneously productive contributions to himself or herself, to family and community, and to civic life. The individual will develop, then, a "sixth C," that is, contribution.

A moral and civic commitment to maintaining and to perpetuating a civil society marked by liberty means that one is thinking and behaving in ways that make contributions beyond those accruing to the self. Productive contributions to civil society involve acting to enhance people and institutions that extend in time and place beyond one's self. Such actions exemplify transcendence—feelings about and commitments to things that are beyond one's own existence. Transcendence is the essence of a sense of spirituality. We believe that spirituality, conceived of as transcendence, is a potent emotional force energizing individuals to invest their selves in other people, including future generations; in their communities and larger society; and in ideas and values of their culture, for example, a religious faith or the idea of America.

There are five sets of interrelated ideas found in the present conception of civil society and positive youth development: First, there is a universal structure for adaptive developmental regulations between people and their contexts. This structure involves mutually beneficial relations between people and their social worlds, and may be represented as "individual ← → social context." Second, these mutually beneficial, "individual ← → social context" relations have their historical roots in humans' integrated biological and cultural evolutionary heritage. Third, when instantiated in ideal ways, adaptive developmental regulations involve reciprocally supportive relations between thriving individuals and social institutions supporting the freedom of individuals. Fourth, thriving youth have noble purposes; they have an integrated moral and civic sense of self that impels them to transcend their own interests and contribute to others and to society in ways that extend beyond them in time and place (Damon, Menon, and Bronk 2003). Fifth, this idealized relation between individuals and society may be realized within diverse cultural systems.

When mutually beneficial person-context relations involve the support of individual freedom and the maintenance and perpetuation of a civil society, then liberty is most likely to exist. Youth are maximally likely to thrive, and reciprocally, a democratic and just society is most likely to flourish.

See also Civic Virtue; Positive Development; Positive Youth Development, Programs Promoting.

Recommended Reading

Eccles, J., and Gootman, J. A., eds. (2002). *Community Programs to Promote Youth Development*. Washington, D.C.: National Academy Press.

Damon, W., Menon, J., and Bronk, K. C. (2003). "The Development of Purpose during Adolescence." *Applied Developmental Science*, 7: 119–128.

Dowling, E., Gestsdottir, S., Anderson, P., von Eye, A., and Lerner, R. M. (2003). "Spirituality, Religiosity, and Thriving among Adolescents: Identification and Confirmation of Factor Structures." *Applied Developmental Science*, 7 (4): 253–260.

Lerner, R. M. (In press). *Liberty: Thriving and Civic Engagement among America's Youth*. Thousand Oaks, CA: Sage Publications.

Lerner, R. M., Dowling, E. M., and Anderson, P. M. (2003). "Positive Youth Development: Thriving as a Basis of Personhood and Civil

Society." In *Applied Developmental Science* [Special Issue], edited by L. Wagener and J. Furrow, 7: 172–180.

O'Connell, B. (1999). *Civil Society: The Underpinnings of American Democracy*. Hanover, NH: University Press of New England.

Roth, J. L., and Brooks-Gunn, J. (2003). "What Is a Youth Development Program? Identification and Defining Principles." In *Enhancing the Life Chances of Youth and Families: Public Service Systems and Public Policy Perspectives*, Vol. 2 of *Handbook of Applied Developmental Science: Promoting Positive Child, Adolescent, and Family Development through Research, Policies, and Programs*, edited by F. Jacobs, D. Wertlieb, and R. M. Lerner. Thousand Oaks, CA: Sage Publications, pp. 197–223.

Wilson, J. Q. (1993). *The Moral Sense*. New York: Free Press.

Richard M. Lerner, Sarah M. Hertzog, and Sophie Naudeau

Civilian Conservation Corps (CCC). The Civilian Conservation Corps (CCC) was the most popular of President Franklin D. Roosevelt's programs to combat the Great Depression; it was also America's first and largest civilian national service program. Between 1933 and its termination in 1942, the CCC put over 3 million unemployed young men (and older veterans) from families who needed economic help to work on a wide range of environmental conservation projects, planting trees, clearing trails, preventing soil erosion, building dams, fighting fires, and more. Individual enrollees worked in the CCC for an average of nine months in exchange for room and board in forest camps, other necessities, and $30 per month (of which approximately $25 was sent home to help support their families). Administratively, the federal government took the lead: the Department of Labor oversaw enrollee selection, the Departments of the Interior and Agriculture planned and supervised the work projects, and the Department of War ran the camps.

The Great Depression had hit young adults particularly hard. In 1933 over one-third of the nation's nearly 15 million unemployed were under age twenty-five.

In August 1933, President Franklin Roosevelt has lunch at a Civilian Conservation Corps camp in Big Meadows, Virginia. *Library Congress.*

The specter of a "generation lost" loomed large. Further, the state of the environment was perilous. Decades of industrialization had taken its toll, and poor logging and farming practices had led to deforestation and soil erosion—creating the infamous "Dust Bowl." Prior to the 1930s the United States lacked any official conservation policy. The CCC addressed the problems of youth unemployment and environmental degradation in tandem—in the words of one official, by sending the "threatened resources of America's youth ... to the rescue of the devastated and endangered resources of the forest, waters, and soils." Central to the CCC were two key principles: reciprocity and collaboration. The program operated on the understanding that both the participants and the nation were to benefit and that together the government and the citizenry—including the CCC's young, disadvantaged enrollees—could accomplish important public purposes.

The CCC enrollees and others—their families, local communities, and the country as a whole—benefited in a variety of ways. Enrollees were provided with a standard of living, including food, lodging, clothing, and health care, that many of them had never had, or had had and lost. In the process the nation benefited from "manhood saved," a good in and of itself but one that became particularly important with the coming of World War II. Enrollees also benefited from the CCC's education program. By 1939 approximately 75,000 illiterate enrollees had learned to read and write, and another 700,000 enrollees had added to their education by taking elementary- or high-school-level classes. Job training was also stressed. Through both on-the-job training and classes, enrollees learned specific job skills, as well as how to do "an honest day's work" and do it well. The nation benefited from a better educated, more highly skilled workforce. The nation and enrollees also benefited from the fact that the camps brought together young men from various backgrounds. As former enrollee Al Hammer explained, "I hadn't gotten out much, and this gave me a chance to meet and work with people different than me from all over the country—farm boys, city boys, mountain boys all worked together." This contributed to what the CCC director called "the up-building of a national culture."

There was more. Enrollees' families benefited from the wages that were sent home. For many it meant the difference between being able to make ends meet and not. But enrollees also benefited from being able to help. Most of them had never had the opportunity to make a substantial contribution to the family income; to do so gave them a sense of pride. Further, communities near the CCC camps benefited from CCC and enrollee spending, the hiring of local woodsmen as supervisors, and of course, from the CCC's environmental work.

The amount of work completed by the CCC was staggering. In 1937 alone, enrollees planted 365,233,500 trees, contributed 1,047,227 man-days of firefighting, built 1,081,931 check dams, and laid more than 9,960 miles of telephone lines, and these were just four of the 150 total major types of work. In just its first two years of operation CCC enrollees had furthered state and national forest and park development by ten to twenty years. While this was clearly of benefit to the public and posterity, it also mattered very much to the enrollees, to those who were responsible for its accomplishment. One observer noted, "There has come to the boys of the corps a dawning understanding of the inspiring and satisfying fact that they are taking an integral and indispensable part in a great program vitally essential to the welfare, or possibly even to the ultimate existence, of this country."

And there were the views of the enrollees themselves, summed up simply and powerfully by enrollee Harry Dallas: "There was pride in the work. We built something, and I knew I helped and saw the result. It was something you could take pride in, and there wasn't a lot of pride available in those days."

Youth activism in the CCC was principally, and importantly, channeled into enrollees' conservation work. Further, all camps had enrollee leaders and assistant leaders, many had "safety sentinels," recreation committees, and discussion groups, and some had camp governance advisory councils. However, in most camps work supervisors from the Departments of Agriculture and the Interior determined project priorities and work assignments; hence, enrollees' had little input into the nature and organization of their work. In addition, enrollees' ability to influence camp administration and CCC policies, or to engage in discussion or take action on public issues of the day, was sharply limited by army commanders, many of whom were afraid of potential "agitators," and by the president's opposition to an organization that would represent current and former enrollees. Nonetheless, through their participation—and most importantly their work—in the CCC, enrollees were taking action on two of the most serious challenges facing the country, its endangered environment and the economic crisis. As expressed by enrollee Allen Cook, the CCC "was not only a chance to help support my family but to do something bigger—to help on to success this part of the president's daring new plan to down 'Old Man Depression.'"

The CCC was terminated shortly after World War II began, when the depression lifted and young men's labor was needed on farms, in industry, and in the military. Despite its short history, its legacy is extensive. Americans benefit to this day from the CCC's environmental contributions. While many of these go unnoticed, plaques commemorating the CCC's work can be found in state and national parks around the country. Furthermore, millions of its enrollees went on to contribute to their country and communities through their military service, their other work, and their community involvement, becoming part of what has come to be called "America's greatest generation."

Finally, the CCC has inspired youth programs across the decades. At the federal level the Job Corps and the Youth Conservation Corps, both founded in the 1960s, were variations on the CCC theme, and the Young Adult Conservation Corps of the 1970s was patterned even more closely on its principles. Between the mid-1970s and mid-1980s, state governments began creating their own youth conservation programs and expanded them into urban areas, adding a new dimension to the old CCC idea. These initiatives received increased funding and attention in the early 1990s, with the creation of new federal national and community-service grant programs, particularly AmeriCorps. In addition, AmeriCorps created a special program—the National Community Conservation Corps (NCCC)— that is directly modeled on the CCC. Today thousands of young people are benefiting from and creating benefits for the public through programs that are connected across the generations to the Civilian Conservation Corps.

See also AmeriCorps; State and Youth, The; United Nations, Youth Activism and.

Recommended Reading

Boyte, H. C., and Kari, N. N. (1996). *Building America: The Democratic Promise of Public Work*. Philadelphia: Temple University Press.

Butler, O. (1935). *Youth Rebuilds*. Washington, D.C.: The American Forestry Association.

Cole, O. (1999). *The African American Experience in the Civilian Conservation Corps*. Gainesville: University of Florida Press.

Hill, F. E. (1935). *The School in the Camps: The Educational Program of the Civilian Conservation Corps*. New York: American Association for Adult Education.

Jackson, D. D. (December 1994). "To the CCC: Thanks for the Memories and Monuments." *Smithsonian*, 25 (9): 66–78.

Oliver, A. C., and Dudley, H. M., eds. (1937). *This New America: The Story of the C.C.C.* New York: Longmans, Green and Co.

Melissa Bass

Communication and Youth Socialization. Television use became a prime suspect when scholars began searching for causes of the four-decade decline in civic participation. Some thought that the rising levels of television watching displaced time that people would have spent in civic activity (Putnam 2000). Others have argued, however, that this apparent decline is actually a change in the form rather than the amount of participation (Ladd 1996). We can at least agree that the rates of engagement in public life have not kept up with the increase in education levels over the past fifty years. Critical for youth development is evidence showing that the gap in civic engagement between young and older adults has widened in recent years. For example, the gap in voter turnout between the younger, eighteen to twenty-four age-group and older adults grew from 17 percent in 1972 to 1980 presidential elections to 21 percent in the 1988 to 1996 period. Youth in the most recent cohorts are also less knowledgeable and pay less attention to the news than their parents did at their age. Furthermore, they are less trusting of their fellow citizens, and even when they do vote, their action is not as likely to be accompanied by other civic actions as was the case in previous generations.

Heavy television viewing is associated with lower civic activity among both adolescents and younger adults. This finding should be interpreted cautiously, however, for several reasons. First, this finding only holds for formal political activity and discussion, but not for less formal civic activities and learning. Second, displacement may not be the key mechanism. A focus on time spent with television may mask important differences in the effects of various forms of television *content*. Watching of situation comedies is a clear deterrent to civic action, while social dramas appear to have a modest positive effect. News viewing tends to show positive effects.

The popular interest in television also diverts attention away from the much stronger role played by the print media. Although a majority of citizens say they get most of their political information from television news, research has consistently shown they learn more from reading newspapers and newsmagazines. This distinction, unfortunately, is overlooked by many in the academic community who focus their critiques on television while ignoring the positive effects of the print media. Indeed, the decades-long decline in civic participation is more likely a direct result of the erosion of newspaper readership rather than the rise of television. The growing use of the Internet, particularly among the young, is a new source of print-news content and influence on socialization that in time may overtake the influence of both television and the newspaper.

The Dominant Socialization Model

The origins of communication approaches to socialization were partially a reaction against the dominant political-science functionalist model of the 1960s. The dominant model asserted that it was necessary for citizens to learn a basic set of "facts," beliefs, and behaviors reflecting a "unified political system." The agencies entrusted with socialization—first the family, then the schools, and later the news media—would act as conduits in transmitting to the neophyte citizens what mature citizens knew and practiced. The young would move steadily and irreversibly toward positive political maturity. Measurement of knowledge and other criteria were thought to be nonproblematic and objective. This top-down transmission model did not fit very well then or now. Changes in contemporary society have made it even less appropriate. Parental modeling and parental affective and punishment practices showed little influence

on adolescent civic socialization in the early socialization research.

Communication Approaches to Socialization

Forty years of communication research has radically altered the traditional model of political socialization. In common with other social-science fields, there has been a revision of the conception of the developing youth as a passive recipient of influence to that of a more active participant in seeking and using information to make sense out her or his external world. Of course, this is not to say that individuals are always systematic and rational in processing information. Rather, the new approach asserts that under certain circumstances they are active and capable of making connections and going beyond narrow self-interest to work for the common good. Their civic potential is by no means fixed in childhood and changes can and do take place well into adulthood.

The stability bias of the earlier model, reflected in portraying societies as unified wholes, has given way to focusing on communities as arenas where many forces with differing interests are contending. Earlier criteria of successful socialization, particularly affiliation with a political party and trust in government, seem more problematic today. The early focus on political *outcomes* came at the expense of ignoring *processes* that are vital to democracy. The processes of deliberation—the thoughtful processing of information from mediated and interpersonal sources, listening to diverse points of view, turn-taking in discussion, and working out compromises—are no less important than adopting attitudes supportive of the political system.

The idea of an active audience has important implications for learning how youth use media. As mentioned earlier, time-spent media measures are insensitive to *exposure* and *attention* to specific types of content that have differing effects. Television viewers often combine watching with other activities. Today's youth typically spend seven hours a day using media, most of which involve using two or more media simultaneously. It is thereby important to obtain self-reported information about the person's typical level of *attention* as well as their *exposure* to particular forms of media content. For television news especially, this produces much stronger effects on learning than does exposure alone.

To more fully understand media effects, communication research has gone beyond the *what* and *how much* of media use to examine the questions of *why* and *how* content is used. The why question is addressed by examining the *gratifications* sought from content. For example, seeking information increases attention to hard news and facilitates learning, whereas seeking escape or diversion lessens attention and learning from news. Recent research indicates that strategies individuals use to process information from the news media are crucial to understanding civic engagement. *Reflective thinking* about issues encountered in the news or in conversations with others greatly facilitates forming the connections needed for civic learning and participation while the tendency to *skim* or *scan* the news for familiar topics is a deterrent to engagement.

The socializing influences of mass media on youth are often complemented and reinforced by communication with parents and peers. How parents communicate with their adolescent children has been found to be more important to civic socialization than is how politicized parents are. The failure of adolescents to model the political savvy of their parents may reflect the tendency of many well-educated parents to see citizenship as "natural," or as the exclusive responsibility of schools. To the extent that conversations inside the home or outside of it with friends include discussion of social and community issues, they may play a key role in the development of civic identity.

Communication and Adolescent Development

To assess the impact of media use and interpersonal communication on the devel-opment of adolescent civic identity, we must consider two factors: the *level* of use or occurrence and strength of *effect*. This is analogous to the distinction between dosage and effectiveness in the evaluation of prescription drugs. For example, it may be that newsmagazines have very few young readers, but they can be highly effective sources of information among those who do read them.

Levels of communication and civic engagement. Adolescent use of news content from traditional print and broadcast media sources is dwarfed by their consumption of entertainment content in these media, videos, computer games, CDs, and the like. Nonetheless, there is a significant gain in news consumption from early to late adolescence that parallels a slightly greater gain in various indicators of civic engagement: political interest, knowledge, efficacy, and participation. Discussion of issues with friends also becomes more common, but the gain is less than that for either news use or civic engagement. Family communication patterns also change during the adolescent years. Parents are somewhat more likely to encourage encountering controversial social issues and speaking out and to lessen their demands for avoiding conflict and conformity. These changes contribute to adolescent civic learning and activity.

The growth in news consumption as part of adolescent development is encouraging, but the long-term prospects for traditional news media are somewhat ominous. Newspaper circulation has been in decline for three decades, and network news viewing has fallen sharply in recent years. For the first time, a majority of younger parents are no longer daily consumers of news, and this may reduce the likelihood that their children will become active citizens. Some even claim that young people now learn most about public affairs through the monologues of late-night talk shows hosts such as Jay Leno or John Stewart.

Use of the Internet by the most recent cohorts may partly offset the loss in consumption of traditional news media. Adolescent access to computers and the Internet in schools has grown rapidly in the past decade, but at this time we don't know how *access* translates into a pattern of information-seeking that would persist into adulthood. How computer use is taught in the classroom is doubtless the key to the future contribution of the Internet, and there are some problems here as well. Overall, teachers of computer skills are themselves not well trained, and those who are tend to be in schools in affluent neighborhoods (Packard Foundation report 2001). As a result, low-income youth tend to be taught only simple skills of word processing while affluent students are guided into learning the more cognitively complex skills of information searches that facilitate processes important to civic activism.

Communication Effectiveness. Reading of hard-news content in the newspaper has the strongest media effects, after demographic and other controls, in conveying knowledge, stimulating discussion, and shaping attitudes among adolescents. The strength of its effects remains as strong in recent years as they were thirty years ago. Attentive television news viewing has positive though weaker impact, while, as mentioned earlier, television entertainment viewing has modest negative effects in certain cases. No research has thus far examined the claim that most of what some youth know about politics they get from watching late-night talk shows such as *The Tonight Show* or *The Daily Show*. Reflection, recalling, and trying to make sense about issues seen in the news has a strong effect on civic engagement well beyond that of attentive exposure to the news.

Issue discussion with parents and peers, although much less frequent than talk about other topics, continues to encourage attentive news-media use and reflection and to stimulate civic engagement. Finally, communication influences increase in strength from early to late adolescence indicating that development is a function of both the level and potency of positive communication behaviors.

The lack of systematic evidence prevents any conclusion about the overall net effect of adolescent Internet use. Computer access and frequent use do not guarantee positive effects on civic activism. Results from simplistic "time spent online" measures have been used to assert erosion of psychological well-being, social trust, real-world ties, and community involvement. Other research that finds positive effects for young adults suggests more optimistic outcomes for adolescents. The balance of positive and negative Internet effects clearly depends on how the new technology is taught and used. The attractiveness of the Internet and other new media at least presents an opportunity for classroom and school-based programs to foster adolescent civic development.

Communication and Young-Adult Development

While the research presented earlier has documented the low levels of civic engagement among younger adults and particularly in the most recent age cohorts, it has been less successful in explaining *why* today's youth appear to be uniquely disengaged as citizens. Many of the same demographic characteristics that for decades have been known to influence participation continued to do so for contemporary youth. These traditional demographic sources of influence merely *locate* the differences. A better understanding of the current situation requires deeper evidence of the *processes* by which young adults connect their life situations to the expectations of civil society. Unfortunately, surveys specifically focusing on young adults are rare, except for studies of college students, and national surveys of adults generally provide too few young-adult cases (100–150). Fortunately, some recent studies that have both communication and civic engagement measures are sufficiently large to allow detailed analyses.

We should avoid assuming continuity and an upward trajectory of either communication or civic patterns from adolescence to early adulthood. Early adulthood is a period of rapid change and differentiation. The young adult is likely to have moved away from his family and its influence into a very different milieu of a new community or neighborhood and lifestyle. Much of the earlier social support for civic engagement from parents, peers, school, and church is removed, and new civic allegiances and identities must be formed. Young adults are likely to lack characteristics and ties that strengthen civic engagement. Compared to older adults, they tend to be new to the neighborhoods in which they live and anticipate moving away in the next five years. Politically heterogeneous and involved neighborhoods may act as contextual influences on activism beyond the young adult's individual characteristics. They are also more likely to be ethnic minorities, unmarried, and without religious membership. Not surprisingly, social interactions with friends and work associates are frequent among young adults, and they play a critical role in all aspects of their lives including the development of their civic identity.

Levels of Communication and Civic Engagement. The large Social Capital Community Benchmark Survey (2000) allows us to compare two groups, each comprised of more than 2,000 young adults (age eighteen to twenty-two and twenty-three to twenty-seven) with older adults (McLeod, Shah, and Yoon 2002). Although younger adults are generally less active than older adults, the extent of difference varies across indices of civic engagement. Differences are largest for voting, political/public-affairs interest, and knowledge. More moderate differences are shown for trust in people and efficacy. Volunteering and other forms of civic participation are more similar for younger and older adults. Newspaper reading, measured as days per week, reveals a pattern of very low readership from age eighteen to the mid-thirties, fol-

lowed by a sharp increase from age forty onward (McLeod, Scheufele, and Moy 2002). Newspaper use in the 2000 presidential campaign was similar; only 25 percent of those under thirty read campaign stories compared to more than 50 percent among those over age forty-five (Sotirovic and McLeod 2004). Television news is similar to newspaper reading with extremely low news viewing in the eighteen to twenty-two age-group; however, growth begins earlier among those age twenty-three to twenty-seven and approaches older adult levels by the mid-thirties. Campaigns and world events appear to reach young adults mainly through television. In noncampaign periods they watch television news only slightly more often than they read newspapers; during presidential campaign periods, for example, more than three-fourths of all age-groups report watching a campaign story on television news with less than a 10 percent gap between young adults and older adults. Internet use, measured in hours, reveals a pattern that is the mirror image of that of newspaper reading, declining linearly from its peak in the eighteen to twenty-two age category. The heavy Internet use by young adults implies a potential for stimulating activism. Closer examination of how and why young adults use the Internet generates a more complex picture. While learning is an important goal of Internet use among young adults, they infrequently read news and are more likely to use it for leisure (e.g., video games) and consumer purposes. This may change somewhat during elections and crises. More than 40 percent of young adults read a political story from the Internet in the 2000 election campaign—almost double the proportion for those fifty and older.

Communication Effectiveness. Communication effects rarely have been evaluated for specific age-groups. Newspaper reading, which has the strongest impact on learning and participation for adults generally, is among the strongest positive influences on civic engagement among young adults in the Benchmark (2000) survey (McLeod, Shah, and Yoon 2002). Newspaper reading stimulated political interest, civic knowledge, citizen efficacy, volunteering, and civic participation. Furthermore, the strength of effects among young adults was at least as strong as among those over thirty-five. This is supported in analyses of media effects on political knowledge during the 2000 election campaign (Sotirovic and McLeod 2004). The effects of reading newspaper stories about the campaign were equally strong among the young as among older adults, and the youngest age (eighteen to twenty-three) produced the most potent effects of any age-group. The problem involved in using newspaper reading as a way of spurring young-adult activism seems to be one of low use and not an inability of youth to learn from print media.

We know less about the effects of television on young adults because adequate measures are lacking. Time spent with television has modest negative effects, slightly higher than those for older adults in the Benchmark study. Watching television stories about the campaign generated positive effects on political knowledge but weaker than those for reading newspaper stories. Television campaign-news effects are strongest among the eighteen to twenty-three group, eligible to vote for the first time, and weakest in the twenty-four to thirty age category. Overall, they are equal in strength to those of older adults. Effectiveness is a particularly crucial question for Internet use because of its very heavy use among younger adults. Internet use, measured in the Benchmark survey by hours spent online, has significant positive influence on age eighteen to twenty-two adults' knowledge, interest, volunteering, and civic participation. Internet effects for the youngest adults tend be stronger than for adults over thirty-five years old. More appropriate use measures from the DDB Lifestyle survey revealed that Internet use for search and exchange of information was related to both trust in people and

in civic participation among the youngest adult cohorts. Again, these Internet effects were stronger than for older adults. The campaign context provides further evidence of stronger Internet effects among young adults than among older citizens. The effect in the eighteen to twenty-three age-group was twice as strong as in any other age category. The potential of the Internet to enhance youth activism is thus documented in both its high level of use and potency of impact among today's youth cohort.

Communication for Activism and Equality

If various forms of mediated and interpersonal communication contribute to the civic engagement of adolescents and young adults, the question becomes: how could these communication processes be better used to further stimulate youth activism?

Promoting Activism. One approach would be to devise strategies to increase use of news and other content beneficial to civic engagement. Another approach is to focus on teaching youth how to better seek and process information from the content they use that would facilitate their civic activism. This form of media literacy involves learning cues for focusing attention on certain content, using critical and reflective thinking, and making connections with past information and between isolated facts and issues. In addition, opportunities for discussion and deliberation, potentially about public affairs or documentary content, may also be potent. The traditional news media, newspapers and television news, present somewhat different challenges in promoting activism. The problem for using newspapers for activation is largely a matter of how to increase youthful exposure in the face of a decline in readership that is especially noticeable in the youngest cohorts. To the extent that young audiences do read newspapers, their beneficial effects on civic engagement are equal to those for older adults. Television news viewing is more common than newspaper reading among younger audiences, but here the problem is the weakness of its effect on civic engagement. The problem of television news resides in the deficiencies of its content, and thus efforts to teach youth how to use it more effectively are not likely to stimulate learning and action.

We should not assume that strengthening the impact of communication on civic engagement is solely a matter of changing how youth consume news content. Historical changes in news content toward crime and sensational "infotainment" content in both newspapers and television news may be partly responsible. While it is difficult to see how those interested in promoting youth activism could affect changes in media content, there are some hopeful signs that news content may be moving in directions more favorable to activism. Concern with declining circulation has lead many publishers to see "creating a sense of community" as a goal for their newspapers. Many local television stations have joined with newspapers in projects of civic/public journalism that may include youth in the community. Media professionals claim they are shifting this focus to stories that deal with broader issues and the search for solutions while cutting back on routine coverage of meetings. If these efforts and claims constitute an enduring change in news content, they may greatly aid youth activism.

The Internet offers great potential for promoting youth activism. It is widely used among both adolescents and young adults. Along with other new-media technology, Internet use has become a part of youth culture providing an area of autonomy and competence beyond that of their parents in many cases. When used for information search and exchange purposes, the Internet has positive effects on civic engagement far stronger than those for older adults. The problem with using the Internet for expansion of youth activism is how to stimulate its use for informational acquisition and public expression purposes in the face of other purposes that are at best irrelevant for activation. While most school assignments do involve information search, the lack of adequate training for teachers remains a problem.

Achieving Equality. The major justification for promoting youth activism is that it could increase the current low level of citizen participation in democracy. Given the evidence that communication and civic engagement patterns developed in youth carry over to later adulthood, increases in youth activism today would benefit democracy for many years to come.

No less important as a justification for youth-activism efforts is that they could lead to a greater voice for young people whose interests are underrepresented in the political arena. The age gap in participation is by no means the largest or most important to consider. Education, income, gender, and minority-group status all have strong influences on communication as well as on civic engagement and political power. Thus, any change induced through communication should be evaluated for its consequences for closing or widening existing gaps in civic engagement.

Education and the Internet provide striking examples of gaps in equality. Education of parents of adolescents, along with income, is a strong determinant of where adolescents go to school and whether there is access to the Internet in the home. Adolescents with more educated parents are thus more likely to use the Internet for searching and exchanging information that facilitates activism. Those whose parents have less education are less likely to be taught information skills for the computer in school and to practice them at home. The result is a widening educational gap in civic engagement.

School-based programs using communication strategies should be evaluated for their effects on existing gaps. A Kids Voting program that used strategies that fostered the interdependence of media, families, and discussion networks produced increases in adolescents' knowledge, self-efficacy, and trust and a reduction in cynicism. It also produced some unexpected "trickle-up" adolescent-to-parent effects. The program strongly stimulated attentive and reflective media use and interpersonal discussion with family and friends, which led to civic engagement. The Kids Voting program was at least as effective for those from lower-status homes as from higher-status homes. It reversed the common gender gap by being more effective for girls than for boys in stimulating attention to campaign news and in conveying knowledge. The program was roughly equivalent in its effect on minority and nonminority youth.

Status gaps in civic engagement have seldom been examined in the developmental context. The effects of college attendance were starkly revealed in a reanalysis of the Benchmark (2000) study. Those who had graduated from college exhibited a positive growth trend beginning with the age-group of twenty to twenty-seven through ages thirty-six to sixty-five in volunteering and participation, while the levels for those who did not go on to college were essentially flat. Gaps increased roughly 50 percent, grown through the adult life course. Communication may have contributed to this growing gap. The increase in newspaper reading with age is twice as great among those attending college. In addition, interpersonal networks grow more diverse with age in the college group but remain homogeneous for those with less education. Newspaper reading and network diversity both contribute to civic engagement.

Programs and strategies for fostering youth activism would benefit from attention to both mediated and interpersonal communication. The popularity of the Internet and other new media among youth and the centrality of interpersonal relationships at this stage of the life cycle suggest the importance and utility of incorporating communication into strategies for change.

See also Intergenerational Programs and Practices; Kids Voting USA (KVUSA); New Media; Participatory Action Research (PAR) by Youth; Positive Youth Develop- ment, Programs Promoting; Social Networks; Student Voices Project.

Recommended Reading

Chaffee, S. H., McLeod, J. M., and Wackman, D. B. (1973). "Family Communication Patterns and Adolescent Political Socialization." In *Socialization to Politics*, edited by J. Dennis. New York: Wiley, pp. 349–363.
Eveland, W. P., McLeod, J. M., and Horowitz, E. M. (1999). "Communication and Age in Childhood Political Socialization." *Journalism and Mass Communication Quarterly*, 75 (4): 699–718.
Huckfeldt, R., and Spraugue, J. (1995). *Citizens, Politics, and Social Communication*. Cambridge: Cambridge University Press.
Kraut, R., Patterson, M., Lundmark, V., Iiesler, S., Mukopadhyay, T., and Scherlis, W. (1998). "Internet Paradox: A Social Technology That Reduces Social Involvement and Psychological Well-Being?" *American Psychologist*, 53: 1017–1031.
McLeod, J. M., Scheufele, D. A., and Moy, P. (1999). "Community, Communication, and Participation: The Role of Mass Media and Interpersonal Discussion in Local Political Participation." *Political Communication*, 16 (3): 315–336.
McLeod, J. M., Shah, D. V., & Yoon, S-N. (2002). "Informing, Entertaining, and Connecting: The Roles of Mass Communication for Youth Civic Socialization." Paper presented at the meeting of the Society for Research on Adolescence, April, New Orleans, LA.
Putnam, R. D. (2000). *Bowling Alone: The Collapse and Revival of American Community*. New York: Simon and Schuster.
Roberts, D. F. (2000). "Media and Youth: Access, Exposure and Privatization." *Journal of Adolescent Health*, 27S: 8–14.
Shah, D. V., Kwak, N., and Holbert, R. L. (2001). "'Connecting' and 'Disconnecting' with Civic Life: Patterns of Internet Use and the Production of Social Capital." *Political Communication*, 18: 141–162.
Sotirovic, M. and McLeod, J. M. (2004) "Knowledge as Understanding: The Information Processing Approach to Political Learning." In *Handbook of Political Communication Research*, edited by L. Kaid. Mahwah, NJ: Lawrence Erlbaum Associates, pp. 357–394.

So-Hyang Yoon, Jack M. McLeod, and Dhavan V. Shah

Community Collaboration. Since its birth in 1862, the tripartite mission of the American land-grant university has been teaching, research, and service (see Bonnen 1998; Enerson 1989). Today, these three missions are embraced by all universities, public and private. However, in the last decade, service has been reconceptualized by many academic leaders as outreach to or, when a more integrated, systemic model is adopted, engagement with communities (see Kellogg Commission 1999; Lerner and Simon 1998). In part, these revised views of service have been based on the belief that a fundamental purpose of universities is to improve the lives of children, families, and communities and that such a contribution may frame the knowledge-generation, transmission, preservation, and application functions of universities.

Universities have addressed the challenge of linking faculty scholarship and student education and improving the lives of children, families, and communities by attempting to integrate the traditional three parts of the mission of higher education. By building and enacting models through which this integration may occur, universities and communities can collaborate to facilitate the translation of university-developed knowledge into policies and programs of meaning and value to the community.

A key issue that arises in the enactment of this integrative, collaborative agenda is the specification of models that may be used by universities to pursue all components of their mission in manners that are valued by both campus and community. Over the last ten years, a model of community collaboration and learning has evolved in a manner that integrates the missions of the university and that engages scholars and students in service to and collaborations with their communities.

While this community-collaborative model may be seen as an instance of service learning, we suggest it is in fact distinct. We believe, as do Kenny, Simon, Brabeck, and Lerner (2002), that the community-collaborative model rests on a different "knowledge base for establishing 'engaged' universities that promote civil society and successfully integrate outreach scholarship into the core fabric of the institutional agenda" (12) and that, as such,

"this vision requires, then, either a broader, more inclusive definition of the civic engagement or service learning concept or, in turn, a differentiation of the expectancies that are currently subsumed under the label of service learning" (7).

The community-collaborative model provides a human-development knowledge base as a means "though which universities seek to involve students in the life of the community" (Kenny, Simon, Brabeck, and Lerner 2002, 9). This model stresses that human development derives from dynamic relations between the developing individual and the multiple levels of his or her ecology. These levels range from biology through culture and history. The embeddedness of history means that there is always a temporal, and hence a change, component to human development, and as such, patterns of human behavior seen at one time and place may vary across historical periods and contextual (e.g., community) settings. Accordingly, there is always some potential plasticity in human development, that is, there is always some chance that changes in the relations between individuals and their contexts can promote systematic alterations of the human life course.

Plasticity in these individual-community relations represents a strength in all people, that is, the opportunity for change, for improving the course of human development, for making it more positive. Within the human-development literature, the recognition of the potential for positive development has created a focus on youth that, at least in part, is due to the historically unprecedented challenges of health and behavior affecting the likelihood of their positive development (e.g., Lerner 1995; Perkins and Borden 2003). In addition, the focus on positive youth development (PYD) has emerged as a means to counter the "deficit" model of youth development that has characterized the literature on adolescence for one hundred years (e.g., Hall 1904).

The literature pertinent to PYD provides evidence that the several characteristics of such functioning (e.g., the "five Cs" of competence, confidence, character, positive social connections, and caring; Lerner, Fisher, and Weinberg 2000) are facilitated by assets that exist in the communities within which young people live. These "nutrients" for healthy development may be associated with mentorship by a caring adult, safe settings within which youth can use their time constructively, and opportunities to interact in settings where youth participation and leadership is valued. These developmental assets have been identified as typically present in community-based organizations serving youth, and there is growing evidence that when young people are involved in such organizations not only is the probability of the development of the "five Cs" enhanced but, as well, there is evidence for the emergence of a "sixth C," contribution to community. In other words, a commitment to civic engagement is created.

Based on the literature pertinent to human development, generally, and to PYD more specifically, the community-collaborative model provides at least two levels of rationale for the broad, campus-wide integration of the tripartite mission of the university. First, the positive development of the young people studying at universities is enhanced through activities that contribute to community life; simply, college student civic engagement is identified as a vehicle for the promotion of PYD among community members (who, in turn, as PYD proceeds, become themselves more civically engaged). Second, community engagement provides college students with a broad sampling of the ways in which variation in the levels of organization extant within the physical and designed ecology of human life moderate the natural and social facets of our world. With this conceptual frame, community collaboration becomes a method through which professors from a broad array of disciplines can engage their students in "real-world laboratories" affording a richer understanding of the basic and applied dimensions of the physical and social sciences and the humanities.

Moreover, community needs are defined by the community members themselves, and this role of community partners provides a greater likelihood of more balanced collaboration, relevant projects, more consistent university-community partnerships, and more comprehensive, sustainable, and far-reaching outcomes. This set of potential outcomes of community collaboration may inspire more community enthusiasm in collaboration with university efforts.

However, the community-collaborative model is not free of challenges and limitations. The model requires a more integrative approach across the several disciplines that are needed to understand and enhance the array of individual and contextual variables that may influence the course of positive youth-community relations and thus of the outcomes of greater civic engagement and community contribution.

Accordingly, adequate implementation of the model may require new institutional structures and reward systems, which are a challenge to implement and finance. Such comprehensive efforts require a fundamental commitment from the top-down (from the highest levels of the administration) and from the bottom-up (from lecturers and junior faculty members) to succeed.

Moreover, the community collaborative model linking PYD and civic engagement needs to be rigorously evaluated. Key issues to be addressed include whether this approach usefully promotes an integration of the cultures of the university and the community, serves the goals and needs of both settings, and is effective, scalable, and sustainable.

The need for university-community collaboration has never been greater. Communities represent a potentially rich instance of critical contexts for human development. Describing and explaining the course and outcomes of individual-community relations constitutes, therefore, a fundamental focus of cutting-edge scholarship about the human-development system.

It is crucial, for both the advancement of developmental science and for the advancement of value-added contributions between higher education and communities, to determine the most mutually successful environment for service and outreach scholarship. We believe that the community-collaborative model we have described may prove to be a productive and perhaps optimal means to serve the three pillars of private and public universities—teaching, research, and service/outreach. However, at this writing, this belief awaits systematic empirical documentation.

See also Community Justice; Community Service; Empowerment; Just Community High Schools and Youth Activism; National and Community Service; Social Networks; Urban Communities, Youth Programming in.

Recommended Reading

Benson, P. (1997). *All Kids Are Our Kids: What Communities Must Do to Raise Caring and Responsible Children and Adolescents.* San Francisco: Jossey-Bass.
Bronfenbrenner, U. (2001). "Human Development, Bioecological Theory of." In *International Encyclopedia of the Social and Behavioral Sciences*, edited by N. J. Smelse and P. B. Baltes. Oxford: Elsevier, pp. 6963–6970.
Eccles, J., and Gootman, J. P. (2002). *Community Programs to Promoted Youth Development.* Washington, D.C.: National Academy Press.
Enerson, H. L. (1989). *Revitalizing the Landgrant Mission.* Blacksburg, VA: Virginia Polytechnic Institute and State University.
Hall, G. (1904). *Adolescence.* New York: Appleton.
Kenny, M., Simon, L. A. K., Brabeck, K., and Lerner, R. M., eds. (2002). *Learning to Serve: Promoting Civil Society through Service Learning.* Norwell, MA: Kluwer Academic Publishers.
Lerner, R. M. (2002). *Concepts and Theories of Human Development.* 3rd ed. Mahwah, NJ: Lawrence Erlbaum Associates.
Lerner, R. M. (2004). *Liberty: Thriving and Civic Engagement among America's Youth.* Thousand Oaks, CA: Sage Publications.
Lerner, R. M., Fisher, C. B., and Weinberg, R. A. (2000). "Toward a Science for and of the People: Promoting Civil Society through the Application of Developmental Science." *Child Development*, 71: 11–20.

Sarah M. Hertzog, Matan Chorev, Jason Steinman,
and Richard M. Lerner

Community Justice. Community justice is a new way of thinking about and responding to crime. It implements a holistic continuum of care and restoration, providing for prevention, intervention, diversion, commitment, probation, reentry, and aftercare services. This approach tries to balance the needs of the victim with the consequences for the offender and the community. It also tries to involve all of these parties (victim, offender, families, and community members) in the process of restoring justice and repairing harm. The guiding principles of community justice include repairing harm caused by crime, reducing risk to the public, and empowering the community.

Juvenile justice systems across the country have become complacent in addressing the needs of victims, offenders, and communities. Most operate with a certain degree of passivity and disconnection from the offender, the victim, and the community. There is a lack of sensitivity to the victim in the response to the crime or occurrence as well as a lack of accountability of the offender for the harm caused to the victim. The community is almost never involved in the decision-making process. Sanctioning is based on the offense and does not utilize the offender's strengths. And the current system does little to develop the competencies of the offender such that he or she would be less likely to offend again. States are not satisfied with the present situation, and a modern-day movement is transforming the future of the juvenile justice system. Community justice is part of that movement.

Community justice is a new framework for juvenile justice reform that seeks to engage citizens and community groups both as clients of juvenile justice services and as resources in a more effective response to prevent crime and prompt restorative activities when a crime occurs. Its mission attempts to ensure that juvenile justice intervention is focused on basic community needs and expectations. Communities expect justice systems to improve public safety, respond to juvenile crime, and habilitate and reintegrate offenders. True balance is achieved when juvenile justice professionals consider all three of these needs and goals in each case and when a juvenile justice system allocates its resources equally to meeting each need.

Basic community needs, including those of the victim, offender, and the community-at-large, are understood and addressed as follows:

Accountability. Traditionally, accountability has been viewed as compliance with program rules or as "taking one's punishment." However, crime is sanctioned most effectively when offenders take responsibility for their crimes and for the harm caused to victims, when offenders make amends by restoring losses, and when communities and victims take active roles in the sanctioning process.

Competency. Most rehabilitative efforts in juvenile justice today are still centered on fairly isolated treatment programs that are not well accepted by the public. A balanced and restorative justice approach to offender reintegration suggests that rehabilitation is best accomplished when offenders build competencies, leave the system more capable to live responsibly and productively, and strengthen relationships with law-abiding adults. Furthermore, competency development will increase their ability to become contributing members of their communities.

Public Safety. Although locked facilities must be part of any public-safety strategy, safe communities require more than incapacitation. Because public safety is best ensured when communities become more capable of preventing crime and monitoring offenders and at-risk youth, a balanced strategy cultivates new relationships between juvenile justice professionals and schools, employers, and other community groups. A problem-oriented focus ensures that offenders' time under supervision in the community is structured around work, education, and service. It also establishes a new role for juvenile justice professionals as resources in prevention and positive youth development.

Restorative Practices

Many states (e.g., Arizona, Illinois, and Florida) are developing programs at the community level. Different program models are available to implement principles and community-based practices, including victims' services, community service, arbitration, community probation, community supervision, community conferencing, and mentoring.

Victims Services. The victim is brought to a central role when an offense occurs and an offender is identified. The crime victims are encouraged to participate in the determination of reasoned restorative responsibilities that must be fulfilled by the offender. Identifying the victim as a primary customer of the justice system also causes the realignment of resources to ensure that victims have access to information about their rights, trauma counseling, help with determining value of their loss, and assistance with complete restitution recovery.

Community Service. Restorative community work service projects are very effective in supporting the following three community-justice principles:

1. Public Safety—When properly managed, community service increases face-to-face supervision, removes the offender from the community during high-crime hours, monitors substance abuse, and provides project and community bonding and opportunities for positive reinforcement, a sense of accomplishment along with positive role modeling and peer culture.

2. Accountability—The ability to earn money in order to pay restitution to the victim and complete the community-service requirements to the victim and the community are inherent in community-service programs.

3. Competency Development—Involving offenders in restorative work experiences can increase their opportunities for obtaining work skills and vocational exposure and offer real-life application.

Community-service projects that are restorative in nature most often originate as a result of collaboration between community members, business owners, neighborhood residents, and government staff. This collaboration is solicited and welcomed in the community-justice system.

Community Decision-Making Models

Community decision-making models, otherwise known as community-conferencing models, involve a range of options for juvenile justice systems. These models provide for a response to youth crime that balances the needs of the victim, the community, and consequences for the offender and that each are involved in the process to the greatest extent possible. The community-conferencing models implemented nationally include: victim-offender mediation, reparative boards, family-group conferencing, and circle sentencing. While these practices have traditionally been utilized in the justice system, they have been adapted by schools to deal with disputes, disruptive behavior, and, in some cases, as alternatives to arrest for misdemeanor offenses.

Circle sentencing is a version of traditional practices used by aboriginal tribes in Canada and American Indians in the United States. The "circle" members (e.g., victim, offender, families, justice and social-service staff, community residents, and law enforcement) all participate in a consensual discussion for the sentencing plan. Their strategy is to address their concerns in repairing the harm caused by the criminal-act process within a holistic, reintegrative context.

Family Group Conferencing, based on Maori tribal dispute-resolution tradition in New Zealand, involves those persons most affected by crime (e.g., the victim, the offender, family, friends, and key supporters). A trained facilitator guides discussion on how the affected parties have been harmed by the offense and how the harm may be repaired. Participants are involved in the resolution of the delinquent act.

School staff have increasingly utilized conferencing for truancy and suspension intervention.

Victim-offender mediation is the most common of these practices in the United States. Victim-offender mediation programs are increasingly being referred to as victim-offender reconciliation programs and victim-offender dispute programs. These programs are most commonly used in less serious juvenile crimes. The process, however, is increasingly being used for serious and violent juvenile and adult crimes. A trained mediator brings the victim and the offender and a family member together in a safe, structured setting where they discuss the impact that the crime has had on them. A final settlement is reached at the end of the mediation process. Peer mediations are a popular means to resolve disputes in school settings.

Reparative boards are a community sanctioning response to crime, known by such terms as *community panels, neighborhood accountability boards*, or *community diversion boards*. Most reparative boards primarily handle nonviolent, minor offenses. Boards may be comprised of students, teachers, school resource officers, school staff, and community members. Members of these boards conduct face-to-face meetings with offenders who have been diverted from the formal juvenile justice process. The board develops assignments and case plans for the offender, monitors compliance, and reports on case completion to the court. Justice system stakeholders (i.e., judges and prosecutors) are increasingly utilizing these restorative practices as diversion and alternative sanction methods to the formal juvenile-court process.

Conclusion

Community justice has emerged as a social movement for justice reform. Braithwaite suggests that community justice has become "the slogan of a global social movement" and that it will become a "profoundly influential social movement throughout the world" in the twenty-first century. Community justice has captured the interest of a growing number of practitioners, academics, and policymakers for its promise to "do justice" differently and better, as well as its model for systemic, rather than simply programmatic, juvenile justice reform.

Advocates believe that it is possible to envision a more empowering, holistic, community-justice agenda for the future of the justice system. Moving a juvenile justice system to prevent crime, transform the response to crime to one based on restorative activities, and adopt appropriate policies and practices requires leadership, vision, and communication among system partners, victims, offenders, and community. In its challenge to society, the journey of restorative justice also requires a deep commitment to long-term systemic change that is grounded in a spirit of collaboration, renewal, and hope.

See also Community Collaboration; Community Service; Empowerment; Juvenile Justice; National and Community Service; Social Justice; Social Networks.

Recommended Reading

Bazemore, G. (1999). "After Shaming, Wither Reintegration: Restorative Justice and Relational Rehabilitation." In *Restorative Juvenile Justice: Repairing the Harm of Youth Crime,* edited by G. Bazemore and L. Walgrave. Monsey, NY: Criminal Justice Press, pp. 155–194.

Bazemore, G., and Day, S. (1998). "Beyond the Punitive Lenient Duality: Restorative Justice and Authoritative Sanctioning for Juvenile Corrections." *Corrections Management Quarterly,* 2 (1): 1–15.

Bazemore, G., and Umbreit, M. (1999). *Conferences, Circles, Boards, and Mediations: Restorative Justice and Citizen Involvement in the Response to Youth Crime.* Ft. Lauderdale: Florida Atlantic University, Balanced and Restorative Justice Project.

Bazemore, G., and Umbreit, M. (February 2001). "A Comparison of Four Restorative Conferencing Models." *Juvenile Justice Bulletin.* Washington, D.C.: U.S. Department of Justice, Office of Juvenile Justice and Delinquency Prevention.

Braithwaite, J. (1994). "Thinking Harder About Democratizing Social Control." In *Family Conferencing and Juvenile Justice,* edited

by C. Alder and J. Wundersitz. Canberra: Australian Institute of Criminology, pp. 199–216.

Daly, K., and Immarigeon, R. (1998). "The Past, Present, and Future of Restorative Justice: Some Critical Reflections." *Contemporary Justice Review,* 1 (1): 21–45.

Karp, D., and Walther, L. (2001). "Community Reparative Boards: Theory and Practice." In *Restorative Community Justice: Cultivating Common Ground for Victims, Communities, and Offenders,*, edited by G. Bazemore and M. Schiff. Cincinnati, OH: Anderson Publishing.

O'Brien, S. (2000). *Restorative Juvenile Justice Policy Development and Implementation Assessment: A National Survey of States.* Ft. Lauderdale: Florida Atlantic University, Balanced and Restorative Justice Project.

O'Brien, S. (2003). "A Small Place Making a Big Impact: Deschutes County, Oregon, and Restorative Justice." *Juvenile and Family Justice Today.* Reno, NV: National Council of Juvenile and Family Court Judges.

O'Brien, S., and Hansen, J. (Summer/Fall 2003). "Community Partnerships: A Case of Restorative Justice in Schools." *The Resourcer.* Osprey, FL: National Association of School Resource Officers.

O'Brien, S., Maloney, D., Landry, D., and Costello, D. (Summer 2003). "Bringing Justice Back to the Community." *National Council of Juvenile and Family Court Judges Journal,* 54 (3): 35–46.

Pranis, K. (1998). "Promising Practices in Community Justice: Restorative Justice." *Community Justice: Concepts and Strategies.* Lexington, KY: American Probation and Parole Association.

Stuart, B. (1996). "Circle Sentencing—Turning Swords Into Ploughshares." In *Restorative Justice International Perspectives,* edited by B. Galaway and J. Hudson. Monsey, NY: Kugler Publications, pp. 193–206.

Umbreit, M. (1997). "Humanistic Mediation: A Transformation Journey of Peacemaking." *Mediation Quarterly,* 14 (3).

Umbreit, M., and Carey, M. (1995). "Restorative Justice: Implications for Organizational Change." *Federal Probation,* 59 (1): 47–54.

Van Ness, D., and Strong, K. H. (1997). *Restoring Justice.* Cincinnati, OH: Anderson Publishing Company.

Sandra O'Brien and Gordon Bazemore

Community Service. The notion that community involvement positively impacts the well-being of society is embraced by many, including the U.S. federal government (e.g., the National and Community Service Act of 1990; the National and Community

Teens pick up leaves during a community cleanup in St. Paul, Minnesota. *Courtesy of Skjold Photographs.*

Service Trust Act of 1993) as well as influential international bodies (e.g., the United Nations General Assembly—2001 Year of Volunteers). *Community service* is a critical component of involvement, and youth are important players in community-service efforts. In fact, volunteering among high-school students in the United States recently reached its highest level in fifty years. Two-thirds of adult volunteers began volunteering when they were young, and those who begin volunteering as youth are twice as likely to volunteer as adults. Successful efforts to increase volunteerism and community service among youth, therefore, have the potential to positively affect individuals and communities as a whole both now and well into the future.

Involvement in, or service to, a community is generally conceived of as prosocial behavior, or actions that are intended to help others or to have beneficial social impact. It includes a number of different activities that are geared toward enhancing the common good such as serving on community boards and committees, voting, and working (both paid and unpaid) with nonprofit and community organizations (e.g., hospitals, shelters, schools). Most often this involvement is in local and geographically-defined communities, like a city, but it can also take place in relational or interest-based communities in which members are geographically dispersed and may or may not know one another personally (e.g., work on environmental protection or on behalf of people living in poverty in other locations). A specific form of community service, *volunteerism*, can be defined as willingly giving time working for the good or welfare of others without expectations of compensation or reward. Volunteering can be informal, as when neighbors help one another, or it can be formally institutionalized in organizations and agency-based programs.

Social scientists, policymakers, educators, and parents are interested in the question of *why* people become and stay involved in community service and volunteerism. By and large, the explanations have tended to focus on explanations that relate to either sociological or psychological predictors of volunteerism.

The sociological factors that have been related to community service and volunteering tend to emphasize people's personal and financial resources. For example, greater wealth and education are related to higher rates of volunteerism among adults, and people who live in small towns tend to engage in community service and volunteerism more than people who live in large cities. Volunteering in organizations is also most often performed by European Americans, women, and individuals with higher incomes. These and other demographic variables have been related to volunteerism among youth. In one representative study, younger volunteers were more likely to be female; in addition, religiosity, membership in school organizations, and academic achievement (specifically, higher grade-point averages) were all positively related to inclinations to volunteer. Previous community service and volunteerism also predict later similar involvement, although it is unclear if this prior work actually causes people to engage in service activities later on. For example, it may be that certain people are simply more prone to volunteer than others. Their parents or other adult role models may have encouraged service work, or they might be part of a generation for whom volunteering and public service are common and reinforced activities. These individuals may start volunteering relatively early on and consistently engage in volunteer activities over the course of their lives. Finally, research suggests that people who have many social connections and are embedded in relatively dense social networks (i.e., they attend church, belong to clubs, participate in community meetings, etc.) are more likely to volunteer than people with fewer social connections.

One model of civic volunteerism incorporates these sociological factors in explaining why youth engage in community service. Specifically, this model identifies three different factors that lead to volunteerism. The first set of factors revolves around the availability of resources such as time, money, skills, and education. The second is engagement, which encompasses individual dispositions such as feelings of efficacy and concern for the common good. The third is recruitment, which is simply being asked to participate. Recruitment can occur either as an invitation for voluntary participation or in the form of a requirement to engage in community service. Each of these factors increases the likelihood of any individual volunteering, with volunteering especially likely among individuals with more resources, greater engagement, and those who are asked or compelled to volunteer.

A number of psychological factors also predict volunteerism. The research on this topic has mainly focused on the role of personal needs or motivations. One useful distinction from psychological research on motivation describes differences between extrinsic versus intrinsic motivation. Extrinsically motivated behavior is enacted because of external demands or rewards, such as coercion, pressure, or requirement. Intrinsically motivated behavior, on the other hand, consists of actions that are rooted in an individual's own free will and expressions of self. People engage in these behaviors because they enjoy them and find them inherently rewarding.

The implications of this distinction for community service and volunteering among youth are made clearer in the context of *service-learning programs*. Service learning is generally considered to be a course-based, educational experience in which students are required to participate in organized community service and often to then reflect on the service activity. The goal of these activities is to enhance students' academic outcomes, sense of civic responsibility, and intentions to engage in community service in the future, if not to provide them with "real-world" experiences that are relevant to current coursework or career goals. Some schools and school districts require a certain number of service hours or activities as a condition for students to graduate. Thus, service learning reflects a situation in which youth engage in volunteer work but, at least initially, for extrinsic reasons (e.g., to meet course requirements). Because prior volunteerism is a strong predictor of later volunteering, one way to think about service-learning programs is as attempts to extrinsically motivate students to engage in community-service work with the hope that these actions will be transformed into intrinsically motivated and continuing behaviors.

Another approach to motivation that has been usefully explored in understanding volunteerism is a functional approach that emphasizes individual needs and goals. Specifically, this approach suggests that individuals choose situations and experiences in order to meet personal needs and goals and that different people may engage in the same behavior but for different reasons. From this perspective, then, to understand why people engage in and continue volunteering, one must look at the needs and goals that are likely to be served by different volunteer activities. To the extent that psychological needs and motivations are able to be met by volunteerism, people should be likely to sign up to serve and also to continue to devote time and energy to community-service activities. When volunteer activities and motivations are mismatched, volunteerism and continuing service are reduced.

Several broad categories of personal needs and motivations for volunteerism have been identified in research. Some can be considered relatively altruistic or other-focused in nature such as the desire to express personal religious or humanitarian *values* or to act on *community concern.* Other motivations are relatively egoistic or self-focused in nature and include desire to gain new knowledge or *understanding*, to meet *social* or *personal development* goals, to enhance *career* preparation or contacts, or even for purposes of *self-enhancement,* such as to increase feelings of self-worth. Research utilizing a functional approach to volunteering, which is consistent with an emphasis on intrinsic motivation, has shown great promise in helping to answer questions about why people volunteer. The simple answer is that different people volunteer for different reasons. Future research is needed to better understand these motivations and their determinants. In addition, there is psychological theory and evidence that suggests that the importance of different motivations is likely to vary with a person's age.

There is no doubt that community-service impacts the recipients of service, as when an illiterate child learns to read or a political candidate is elected. However, there are other consequences of community-service work, and these varied consequences can emerge at both an individual level and at a community level.

Individual-level consequences of community service include the changes that people experience as a result of their service involvements. One individual-level outcome that has received considerable attention from researchers, and especially in service-learning contexts, is change in personal identity. Research suggests that youth who participate in community-service activities are likely to develop civic identities that include a sense of responsibility to the community. Compared to nonparticipants, youth who participate in community-service projects also have been found to have greater intentions for future community service as well as enhanced feelings that they can help to change society. They also are more likely to vote and to belong to community organizations, even years later.

Service-learning programs can also enhance academic development, improve learning, and lead to better leadership and interpersonal skills. The findings of one longitudinal study of high-school students involved in prosocial volunteer activities showed that these students performed better academically, were more likely to be enrolled in college at age twenty-one, and were less likely to engage in risky behaviors such as drinking alcohol and skipping classes. Volunteering has also been related to the development of greater educational aspirations and intrinsic work values. Community service by youth also seems to lead to the internalization of prosocial values and attitudes and to a greater appreciation of diversity and more complex understanding of social problems.

Volunteering over the life course is also related to better physical health and reduced mortality. Some researchers suggest that people who are involved in their communities experience fewer colds, heart attacks, strokes, and cancer than people who are not involved. Better mental health, as indicated by higher self-esteem, personal happiness, life satisfaction, and decreased depression, has also been related to community service and volunteerism. Thus, helping others through community-service work has important and reliable positive consequences for the individuals who engage in it. At this point, the mechanisms responsible for these individual-level effects are not entirely clear. Future research is needed that will systematically examine and test some of the different hypothesized pathways of these effects.

One critical issue in achieving positive consequences, and one that has yet to receive much research attention, is the role that motivations and perceptions of motivations play. For example, research findings indicate that different types of motivations can impact volunteers' reactions to and perceptions of community service as well as whether or not they continue their active engagement in service work. Requiring youth to engage in community service (to meet graduation requirements, etc.) may actually have an undesirable effect. As external pressure is applied and as youth perceive a loss of control over their own decision-making they may resent the service work they have to perform and be less likely to engage in similar activities in the future. Thus, psychological research needs to consider if and how extrinsically motivated service work can be transformed into behaviors that are performed for intrinsic reasons. To the extent the individuals are able to have their own needs and goals met through service work or develop personal identities of themselves as volunteers, they report greater satisfaction with their work and stay involved longer.

Finally, communities benefit from active involvement of their members. Citizen involvement, as for example though community-service work, is thought to be a marker of and to produce social capital. That is, social connections and networks have value. Social interaction with neighbors, membership in associations, and involvement in political, religious, and service institutions is believed to heighten norms of reciprocity and trust, which in turn provide broad foundations from which citizens can work together to ameliorate social problems.

Active engagement of community members also contributes to a heightened psychological sense of community, or the feeling that one is part of a meaningful collective. It includes the perception of interdependence with other members of the community. This feeling is likely to produce greater willingness to share one's own resources with others. Psychological sense of community also has been linked to being likely to be registered to vote, being active in neighborhoods, participating in community organizations, espousing support for specific public good policies (e.g., public school taxes), and general political participation.

In short, community involvement and volunteerism seem to lead individuals to feel more positively about and more strongly connected to the people around them and their communities. In reciprocal fashion, these feelings are linked to greater willingness to engage in community affairs and to work for the reduction of social problems. Thus, communities can be transformed and societies changed through the service work of their members.

As suggested throughout, research findings support the notion that numerous positive consequences, both at individual and the community levels, are related to participation in community service and volunteerism. Although these activities take time and energy and may require individuals to forego other important activities, they positively impact their recipients. They also change and benefit the individuals who engage in them as well as the broader community. Furthermore, research has generated considerable knowledge about why, and under what conditions, people engage in community service. However, an important next step is to determine if certain types or categories of motivation lead to more positive outcomes. It will also be critical to rigorously test the hypothesized causal relationships between motivations, community-service activities, and individual- and community-level consequences. Information that would be gleaned from this research would permit researchers and practitioners to more clearly link the determinants of community service to actual service work and on to its consequences. Based on this knowledge, individuals who work in volunteer organizations and service-learning programs would be able to design youth programs and interventions so as to ensure successful outcomes and maximize benefits for the recipients of service activities, for the youth who provide them, and for the community-at-large.

See also Community Justice; Developmental Assets; Moral Exemplars; National and Community Service; Volunteerism.

Recommended Reading

Clary, E. G., and Snyder, M. (1999). "The Motivations to Volunteer: Theoretical and Practical Considerations." *Current Directions in Psychological Science*, 8: 156–159.

Eccles, J. S., and Barber, B. L. (1999). "Student Council, Volunteering, Basketball, or Marching Band: What Kind of Extracurricular Involvement Matters?" *Journal of Adolescent Research*, 14: 10–43.

Johnson, M. K., Beebe, T., Mortimer, J. T., and Snyder, M. (1998). "Volunteerism in Adolescence: A Process Perspective." *Journal of Research on Adolescence*, 8: 309–332.

Omoto, A. M., Snyder, M., and Martino, S. C. (2000). "Volunteerism and the Life Course: Investigating Age-Related Agendas for Action." *Basic and Applied Social Psychology*, 22: 181–198.

Stukas, A. A., Snyder, M., and Clary, E. G. (1999). "The Effects of 'Mandatory Volunteerism' on Intentions to Volunteer." *Psychological Science*, 10: 59–64.

Wilson, J. (2000). "Volunteering." *Annual Review of Sociology*, 26: 215–240.

Yates, M., and Youniss, J. (1996). "A Developmental Perspective on Community Service in Adolescence." *Social Development*, 5: 85–111.

Allen M. Omoto and Anna M. Malsch

Contested Childhoods. Youth are often agents of transformation or catalysts of change. Sometimes they contribute to profound alterations in the way people live. How young people think about changing their world or how they attempt to do so in practice is not well documented. We acknowledge that there are contested child-

hoods and that youth struggle to change difficult situations. Yet, official records seldom detail the nature and effects of their revolt. Young people's involvement in the stand against oppression that leads some into conflict, even war, is a form of activism especially misunderstood.

Communities that have been caught up in war view children's involvement in violence in ways that are contingent on the nature, length, and ferocity of the conflict; the choice or lack of choice the young had in participating; the actions they carried out; and the consequences for members of their families. Clearly, attitudes toward the young who fight against oppression and for liberation differ profoundly from attitudes toward the young who kill and maim as members of warring groups. Conflict is too ancient in its rules of honor, training, justification, and goals and too widespread and changeable now to allow for easy summaries. The first step in understanding may be to analyze current descriptions of and attitudes toward war. Dominant ones seem out of touch with present conflagrations.

I have seen a variety of reactions to children's involvement in war: inconsolable loss when one has died or been hurt beyond recovery; absolute sadness for the damage trauma has inflicted; a harsh turning away; a quick reincorporation into the family fold; a tolerance of madness; patience with extreme behavior, yet impatience with young adults who fail to overcome their suffering and resume full responsibilities; quiet revenge; open compensation for loss caused; and some attempts to reassert control over the young and some letting go. I have seldom seen at the community level anything that matches the generalization, caricature, and categorical dismissal of young fighters that permeates current public and policy discourse, especially in the media and on the Internet, and even in NGO reports.

The young contribute to society as producers, reproducers, and social actors. In themselves, they hold the values for adults of continuity, meaning, pleasure (involving all of the five senses), and status. Apart from the inherent value of children (*never all children nor every person's children nor* those deemed to be unqualified by physical, mental, emotional, or behavioral stipulations, for example, the shade of skin color), children work in and on the frame, structure, norms, directions, and rituals of society, and the interaction is two way. A migrant worker in Cape Town who had been forced by apartheid laws to live apart from his wife and children for all of his working life once told me that, apart from the pain of not having been able to live with them, he had been denied the right to have his children make him grow.

Documenting Young People's Activism

The nature of war is complex in its scale, motive, conduct, and spread. Some of the analytical tools we bring to bear on the topic are outdated, especially in regard to the description of the effects and involvement of the young. Children are always caught up in conflicts whether as targets, fighters, messengers, servants, bush-wives, onlookers, or entrepreneurs. Children's behavior and reactions vary. We know little of the effects of war, national debt, unemployment, famine, and institutional devastation in breaking the lives of the young. The lines of accountability are seldom traced. Too often the young are discarded and, like plastic bags, they are seen to litter the landscape and pollute the environment. Too seldom are their manufacturers asked to take responsibility for their products.

Uncertain events or occurrences may influence present action: the outbreak of war, arms sales that flood a region with the weapons of war, the imposition of free-market trade rules that are unequal in their effects, international institutional machinations or attempts at social engineering, or the devastation of famine. It is always possible that opportunities can be seized in the face of change, releasing creative responses and reaffirming efforts to entrench human rights.

There is often little room left for individuation, for the description of the full range of children's connections, for the open-minded examination of trauma and recovery, for the acknowledgment of cowardice and heroism, or for the consciousness of possible harm or protection in reactions to any given situation. Any aspect of the way we live when it is ironed flat in the communication of our understandings is a potential lie, whether it comes in the guise of a myth, symbol, ritual, label, policy, or photograph.

Writings about youth activism tend to generalize patterns found in specific contexts and to simplify young people's motives, strategies, and solidarity with peers. In consequence, young people's own analysis, initiative, innovation, leadership, and labor are obscured, and the pain and loss they endure is not addressed. Not that youth is innocent: there is little room for sentimentality or romance in documenting the responses of the young to brutal force or oppression. Nor, however, is there reason to ignore serious intent and ethical behavior on their part. One young man who had been a leader in the struggle against apartheid in South Africa in a rural town said that he was most proud of one action he had taken during a decade of resistance: to have stood before a crowd of angry youths bent on burning a young man to death and insist that they allow the man to speak in his own defense against the accusation that he was an informer. The man spoke and was released unharmed.

It is difficult to document youth activism partly because people move through the age categorized as youth quickly, relative to the time span allotted to adulthood. They move from positions of little power in the public arena to positions of command (for some, usually men) in society and, it seems, easily distance themselves from earlier experiences. Age is an important ingredient in social awareness and the seniority it affirms can allow adults to assert their interests over those of the young.

Some of the literature on children's labor demonstrates that, through their contribution to production and reproduction, youth affect the environment and the nature of social relations. It is less easy to see what the young who become embroiled in war and resistance contribute. I have worked with children in Zimbabwe and South Africa following the conflict that engulfed each country during the fight for liberation, and it is with regard to these particular conditions that I make the following observations. I found that many of the young made conscious decisions to become fighters, against great odds, for carefully thought out reasons; that many reentered the fray again and again even after being very badly hurt and/or tortured and even when other options existed; that many held strong moral positions; and that many grew into persons of extraordinary stature and political astuteness. To substantiate these claims would require more space than can be claimed here. The likelihood is that if children and youth are not granted status as contributors to and sculptors of society, they will be more readily treated as objects of charity, missionary zeal, pawns in economic and political games, or their interests will be ignored.

It is easier to expound on the aspect that describes and disparages the destructive side of some of the young. Apart from hearts, there are at least four sorts of things that sizeable groups of young people seem intent on breaking: norms, conventions, rules; limbs, lives, themselves (self-destruction such as suicide, inordinate risk taking—including sexually-related risk); ties and relationships; and oppression. To some degree they must break current strictures in preparation for the new, for the young receive from their elders very little that they do not reinvent themselves. The young quiz the character of society and in so doing shake it and shape it. They probably seldom, if ever, break social order so profoundly as to unalterably change it except under adults' direction and with their compliance. Yet, they can frighten, distress,

and upset order quite dramatically. The Zezuru healers with whom I worked in 1992 and 1993 in Zimbabwe recognize the limits of young people's responsibility, and when things go awry for them or their worlds fall apart, then the healers hold adults accountable, and they are called to look to themselves for the reasons. The reasons are likely to be found in the spiritual, political, communal, familial, or moral spheres.

But the young can help to break oppression. In South Africa the young fought their oppressors under the apartheid regime for over thirty years and did so in great numbers after the Sharpeville massacre of 1976. At least 24,000 people under the age of eighteen were detained and the majority of the over 21,000 testimonies taken by the Truth and Reconciliation Committee were about the consequences for the young of gross human-rights violations, including death and torture. The young took their stand against their oppressors with deliberation; in doing so, they assumed the mantle from their elders. No war or conflict is clean, kind, or gentle-mannered. The part of the youth in ending a tyrannous regime was major; yet there has been precious little recompense.

How Young People Think about Changing Their World

The conditions that lead youth to revolt and turn against existing structures in society include their experiences of armed conflict, oppression, slavery and bondage, and severe economic deprivation. Let us consider the role of youth in armed conflict. They may be forced or coerced into participation either directly or by the nature of circumstances. J. M. Coetzee (1999) suggests that " ... wars are waged by children on children at the instigation of grown-ups." Or they may elect to participate for a variety or reasons. Faced with violence, many will eschew a passive role in their own interests or in the interests of others, especially their kin. They are agents in their own life trajectories that, in turn, affect the experiences of those close to them. Besides, their political engagement has force and this is taken into account in the strategy of leaders in some arenas. Their labor, both as combatants and in an array of other tasks, is valued, and a variety of means, including coercion, will be used to draw them into wars. I do not mean to underestimate the forces of control that are exerted over the young, nor the power of obligations and duties that are carved into patterns of family relations, social negotiations, and political orders that hold the young and inform their decision-making. Nevertheless, it is hard to keep the young from exploring, sharing moral positions, formulating sets of moral tenets, and acting in accord with them—whether others see their arguments as right, logically coherent, or in the best interests of individuals or groups.

During the 1990s I worked closely with twenty-four men (and less closely with many others) who in the 1980s had been young political activists and leaders, and they described their inductions and participation differently. The main impetus for their involvement came from the value they placed on relationships with kin, neighbors, or friends. They took action, at least in part, on behalf of others to end their poverty, humiliation, and oppression. They did not act only out of excitement, boredom, or the spirit of adventure, or as clients. In their views, they joined in the conflict as politically conscious actors and in full awareness of the danger to self and with the painful knowledge that, in entering the fray, they were likely to place their loved ones in danger and to cause them pain. It seems to me that many of the young make decisive and conscious choices about entering into situations of conflict. This view does not deny the influence of propaganda and political passions.

I have taken a description of how young people in a rural town in South Africa became active in the struggle against the oppression of the apartheid state from interviews with a man, whom I shall call Sipho, who joined when he was a schoolboy, aged fifteen. The young, Sipho said,

"were no longer prepared to accept second- or third- or fourth-class citizenship in the country of our birth." They drew on their seniors' experiences to stoke their adolescent rebelliousness and shake off restrictions including the authority of elders and the constraints of poverty. They sought the means to redefine themselves, and their models were "the Mandelas on Robben Island." Besides, they had few outlets for their energies, and politics offered a means for expressing their frustrations. He added, "Ours was a grassroots outburst that found resonance with national political grievances.... Most of us were high-school students or higher-primary students. It was easy to link these school struggles with community struggles because we realized that we were fighting one enemy."

Sipho offered a range of reasons why the young committed themselves to the fight. They include the following: the desire to leave childhood behind, move away from parental discipline, and take charge of their lives; to grow intellectually; to gain respect, even reverence, from others; for some, the attraction of instilling fear in others; and to seek adventure. Some, he added, were stimulated by stories of heroes and others by ideas of self-sacrifice for a vital cause, or in anticipation of reward under a new government, or because they feared being singled out as collaborators if they refused to join student protests. Sipho often included a wide arc of possible motivations and actions (some of which did not apply to him), and he was always careful to point out that some comrades abused any power they acquired by, for example, settling personal scores. A few behaved like little tyrants. He observed that when the euphoria of defeating the apartheid regime had dissipated under the weight of challenges of transformation, the inflated egos of a few leading activists collapsed. "They lost," he said, "their grip on the community because politics suddenly was nationally determined."

For Sipho, participation in political action in which demands for change were being made on a powerful, authoritarian state required of the individual that a constant effort be made to achieve a level of consciousness—one requiring vigilant self-monitoring. In reflecting on his own and his colleagues' contribution to the struggle for freedom, he mixed a serious evaluation of their purpose and achievement with a wry acknowledgment of motives and commitment tainted by personal flaws, desires, and ambitions. He was aware that few avoided falling into traps laid by ambition or passion. Many of them, at one time or another, sought self-enhancement or yielded to self-indulgence or misused authority (especially over kin or young women) or paraded self-righteousness or sought to slake their hunger for admiration. Sipho granted the value of political education, yet he was wary of the uses to which rhetoric and propaganda could be put. He acknowledged that the predicament in which young women activists landed was an extremely difficult one and that too often men "violated our fellow women comrades in the struggle. We disrespected them. Yes, we abused them. Yes, we ... lied and cheated. We used our status to have access to ... them. It was not uncommon." His generic use of "we" obscures his actions and ethical positions: he was speaking, once again, with serious intent and mockery. I don't know the extent to which he was making fun of himself in only giving a man's view of the women's position. One of his most valued and highly revered colleagues was a young woman—she was an executive member of the command group in the area.

How the Youth Fought

Whatever draws the young into making a stand against governing structures in society, the work entailed is hard. In the town that we are using as our example in seeking to understand some forms of activism among youth, there was a marked difference between leaders and the crowd. For leaders, harsh reality had to be faced: ideology and illusion could lead one into error.

Revolt required pragmatism. An activist may begin with curiosity, with avid listening to people's stories of mistreatment, and with careful observation of the conditions under which the underprivileged were forced to live, especially the conditions under which they labored. He or she may respond with a flaring of anger against easy targets plus an explosion of patience and a search for action. Meanwhile, elders were likely to comment on one's naïveté. Sober learning and meticulous examination were necessary steps before responsible leadership could be assumed.

In Sipho's view, one became obsessed with the control of self as any activist must. Reflection brought an appreciation of the need to understand how to contain and direct energy in organizations. Sipho's attitudes were influenced by the political attitudes he heard expressed at home, especially by those of his mother whom he characterized as an early feminist in terms of her strength and independent thinking. He was influenced, too, by two teachers, one of whom had been a hot-headed militant who had suffered physically while protesting the policies of a territorial governor who was a puppet of the apartheid system. Sipho was inducted into political action by scholars senior to him at school. He was an activist for more than a decade and suffered torture, imprisonment, and exile. He now holds a senior position in the town's local council and continues to participate in national political structures.

Youth's engagement in political action is often seen in isolation from the context in which transformation occurs, or it is characterized in terms of antagonism across generations. However, young people's activism can spring from a long gestation of political discussion and practice that includes careful induction of the young by their elders. Involvement in conflict that results from demands for change can incorporate the young for a brief time or for many years. In South Africa, youth fought the security forces of the apartheid state for over twenty years and many of their leaders spent ten to fifteen years of their lives in the struggle. Few of them were left unscathed: thousands were imprisoned and tortured—not once, but again and again. Some died. All of them lived with danger and fear. As Sipho suggested, not all activists lived up to the pure ideals and ethics of the contest and some betrayed the cause and their comrades, but they often did so under physical and psychological pressure from their enemies. However, many were heroic in their drive for freedom and in their integrity, courage, and endurance. While the constraints they faced were formidable, the possibilities were exciting, particularly the opportunity to participate in securing democracy.

Conclusion

It is difficult to observe, record, and document the particularity of youth's involvement in major political conflagrations, partly because of the nature of conflict that surrounds demands for change in governing structures or the rejection of oppression—it is clandestine and dangerous so that observation at the time of action is often impossible. With the end of conflict, individual contributions tend to be molded into a general story that suits a new dispensation whether it be toward the realization of ideals or nationalist ambitions. The retrieval of details about young people's contributions demands that close attention be paid to specific life trajectories and an accounting of sacrifice that may conflict with interpretations favored by others, especially powerful groups intent on molding a tale of history that bolsters specific interests, which often exclude the role of the young, just as they do the role of women. Ethnographic studies can add to the accumulated data on what the young think about and do in relation to revolt and may, therefore, help to correct the bias in the accounting of history.

The Child Soldiers Global Report 2004's Africa regional overview claims that there are 100,000 children in war and conflict in Africa alone. Much of the writing about children in war and efforts to assist them when conflict ends focuses on their victimhood. Few are regarded as having been fighters in their own right, and few are formally demobilized with pensions or other benefits. As long as there are wars, some young people will participate in order to protect their families, their communities, their land, their resources, and themselves, or to stand against oppression. If we are to understand the nature of war and its effects, we need to acknowledge and document the parts played by the young and costs entailed.

See also Antiwar Activism; Child Soldiers; Palestinian *Intifada*; Soweto Youth Activism (South Africa); United Nations, Youth Activism and.

Recommended Reading

Boyden, Jo, and De Berry, Joanna, eds. (2004). *Children and Youth on the Frontline: Ethnography, Armed Conflict and Displacement*. Oxford: Berghan Books, 2004.

Coalition to Stop the Use of Child Soldiers (2004). *Child Soldiers Global Report 2004*. London: Coalition to Stop the Use of Child Soldiers. See http://www.child-soldiers.org/resources/global-reports.html?root_id=159andcategory_id=165.

Ross, Fiona (2002). *Women and the Truth and Reconciliation Commission in South Africa*. London: Pluto Press.

Pamela Reynolds

CRC. *See* Rights of Participation of Children and Youth; Rights, Youth Perceptions of; United Nations, Youth Activism and.

D

Deliberative Democracy. Deliberative democracy is citizen-to-citizen politics; the objective is collective problem solving through collective action. People aren't likely to act together if they don't first decide together what actions to take. Deliberation is a means for making collective decisions, hence the name "deliberative democracy." Deliberative democracy emphasizes public interactions and opportunities to act and think together. It also presumes that the purpose of political life is not to satisfy individual ambition but to create a good life for all.

Young people voice many of the same criticisms of politics other Americans do, but there are important differences. While adults show anger and frustration, young people battle feelings of pessimism and alienation. Despite charges that the younger generation is totally preoccupied with their own self-interests, they are no more uncaring than the older generation is apathetic. The good news is that young people care a great deal. The bad news is that they can be quite cynical about the way the political system operates and pessimistic about their ability to change the situation for the better.

Young people who care about issues are often at a loss as to how to act on their concerns in an effective way. Many don't think the political system effectively addresses the problems they care about. In addition, they are turned off by the tone of politics. There are those who believe the political system is "a system I'd never want to be a part of" or that "politics has nothing to do with my life." This attitude is reflected in young people's poor voting record.

Young people can also fall into the trap of focusing more on their rights, more on what government should do for them, than they do on their own responsibilities as citizens. They see citizenship, at best, as a deferred responsibility. But it would be a mistake to conclude that young people can't be engaged. Their attitudes aren't yet solidified—they are open to imagining a different kind of politics. While they may not normally spend much time thinking about politics, when pressed on the subject they say things such as "there needs to be a better way." What they see happening in politics is different from what they would like to see. Given an opportunity, young people eagerly seize the chance to imagine what politics could be.

The question of what *should* happen in politics is difficult for young people to answer because they frequently lack a common language to explain what is on their minds. Conversations often center on the most basic element of politics, political debates, which often appall them. Politics appears to be a never-ending series of contests, not about solving problems but about who wins.

Young people know what is missing in the political discussions they criticize—a diversity of perspectives, listening, and the careful weighing of tradeoffs. They can even identify what they would need in order to practice a different kind of politics—the ability to keep an open mind, to stand in another person's shoes, to change, and to make decisions with others. What young people are looking for in politics is very close to what deliberative democracy values.

Young people who deliberate today are tapping into one of America's oldest and most distinctive political practices. It can even be argued that public deliberation was a major force in creating the United States. Deliberative forums, called town meetings, came well before the American Revolution and Constitution, paving the way for both.

Public deliberation is one name for the way people go about deciding how to act on public matters. Participants in public deliberations share opinions, concerns, and their own experiences with an issue and then weigh the costs and benefits of various approaches for action against the things they hold most dear. They struggle with the difficult choices that every issue entails, considering the pros and cons of each option. Often called "choice work," public deliberation does not usually end in consensus or total agreement but rather in a range of possible responses to a problem. Deliberation helps clarify purposes and sets a direction for action. The problem often gets redefined during the process, which can open the door to new and more diverse political actors. Public deliberation creates a "public voice," which is the articulation of how citizens think when confronted with a difficult decision.

Public deliberation is neither a partisan argument nor a casual conversation conducted with polite civility. Public deliberation is a means by which citizens make tough choices about difficult issues and directions for their communities and their country. It is a way of reasoning and talking together.

One way for young people to experience public deliberation is through forums, such as the National Issues Forums. Issue books on the topic they have chosen present issues in a nonbiased, nonpartisan manner and are framed in terms of three or four options for dealing with an issue—never just two polar positions. Young people participate in these forums for a variety of reasons, including personal growth and changing the political system.

Not everyone finds deliberation useful. Some young people leave forums frustrated because their expectations aren't realized as soon as they thought they would be. Most, however, believe the effects are cumulative and are convinced a public dialog can have a lasting influence. And they do want something that will endure because they don't just want to make improvements—they want a different kind of politics.

Young people encounter deliberative democracy in a number of places. Some get involved at their high schools through deliberative forums in classrooms. Others attend forums on their college campuses.

Still other young people deliberate in youth organizations. One of the issues has been how to combat the forces that put some youngsters at serious risk from drugs, crime, poverty, and parental neglect. Young people are at risk in many American cities. Expelled from school, these young Americans roam the streets with nothing to do but get into trouble. In Birmingham, Alabama, citizens have done more than worry about the problem. Each year, a number of eleven- to fifteen-year-olds are expelled for being involved in assaults or incidents involving a gun, knife, or other weapon. The best these kids have to look forward to is returning to school the next fall already labeled as troublemakers, knowing they have to repeat a grade. "What are you going to do with that person?" asked Peggy Sparks, director of the Birmingham public schools' Community Education Department.

To address that question, Sparks convened deliberative forums all over the city. City officials and staff from youth organizations served as moderators and recorders—roles that allowed them to participate but kept the meetings from being the usual public hearings. The moderators encouraged participants of all ages to weigh carefully a variety of approaches for dealing with the problem, not just one or two specific solutions. The goal was to create some common ground for action, some sense of direction, and an appreciation for the interdependence of different purposes so people could act together.

One of the directions participants settled on led to a program called CARES, or Comprehensive At-Risk Educational Services, run by young people at eight high schools. According to Sparks, 350 young people now serve on advisory councils and conduct weekly meetings. Other programs that grew out of the forums include a teen employment program and Camp Birmingham, a youth-run camp for low-income youngsters.

CARES' greatest success is that it gives young people a chance to learn how to make difficult choices together. And listening to the forums has given Sparks a much greater understanding of what young people think the problems are, and that helps her know how her department can engage them in solving their own problems.

Many universities are concerned about problems in the collegiate culture and about what kind of civic skills their students will have. In Oxford, Ohio, Miami University is using student deliberations to devise strategies for combating alcohol on its campus. Purdue University has also had forums on the same issue and reports a significant reduction in alcohol-related problems as a result.

At Wake Forest University, Professors Katy Harriger and Jill McMillan are leading a democracy-fellows project. They would like to find out if experience in public deliberations, coupled with classroom instruction, will reduce college students' cynicism about their ability to make a difference in politics and lead to more political engagement.

These are just a few examples of how young people participate in deliberative democracy. Public deliberation is one element of a politics that results in a variety of collective actions. Before choices can be made, problems must be named in public terms that resonate with the things that people hold dear. Then they must be framed in a way that allows people to consider all of their options for action. And after deliberation, people and organizations have to commit themselves to do the things that have been called for in the deliberation. In the end, these same folks have to decide, again deliberatively, if what they accomplished was what they intended—or whether their intentions need to be reconsidered. But even though the choice work people do is just one of the tasks that make up the work of citizens, it is central. It is a doorway into a politics where citizens—even the youngest—can make a real difference. Just knowing *that* is the most powerful knowledge a young American can have.

See also Democracy; Democratic Education; Public Scholarship; the State and Youth.

Recommended Reading

Creighton, J. A., and Harwood, R. C. (1993). *College Students Talk Politics.* Dayton, OH: Report to the Kettering Foundation.

Harriger, K. J., and McMillan, J. J. (2004). "Public Scholarship and Faculty Role Conflict." *Higher Education Exchange*: 17–23.

Mathews, D. (2002). *For Communities to Work.* Dayton, OH: Kettering Foundation.

Mathews, D., and McAfee, N. (2003). *Making Choices Together: The Power of Public Deliberation.* Dayton, OH: Kettering Foundation.

Melinda D. Gilmore and David Mathews

Democracy. Democracy is widely regarded as an essentially contested concept, an idea whose meaning is continually evolving and fundamentally unresolved. Changing concepts of democracy over time often reflect deeply held political convictions. An acute understanding of democracy requires examining its historical evolution from classical Greek democracy through early republicanism to constitutional governments and then modern democratic politics. Some of the greatest challenges facing democratic societies today were also faced by earlier democracies. These include problems of political participation, democratic communication, and the relationship between cultural diversity and global politics.

The word democracy is derived from the Greek word *demokratia* which means rule (*kratos*) by the people (*demos*). However, this translation gives rise to the quixotic notion that *classical Greek democracy* was egalitarian. In the Athenian city-state only a male citizen over the age of eighteen could participate in democratic politics. Under the reforms of Pericles in 450 BCE an individual had to be born of two Athenian citizens in order to obtain citizenship. Women were effectively excluded, as was a substantial portion of the Athenian population, including those who were either slaves or resident aliens. Nevertheless, the degree of direct participation in governance by the Athenian population is impressive.

The primary organ of democratic governance in Athens was the Assembly (*Ekklesia*). In the Assembly male citizens would gather to deliberate and vote on matters that affected every facet of Athenian life, both public and private. Such matters might include anything from finance to religion, from public festivals to war, from treaties with foreign powers to regulations governing ferryboats. The agenda of the Assembly was often set by the Council, a body of 500 citizens elected to serve as the full-time government of Athens. However, the Council had no power in direct decision-making as such right was reserved to the assembled people. All male citizens who attended the Assembly were granted the privilege to speak. In this regard, Athens was very much a direct democracy, since all matters of political importance were discussed and voted on by the people. Upon cessation of discussion, issues were usually brought to a vote by a show of hands, although occasionally a secret ballot was held.

In *Politics*, Aristotle notes that to participate in popular governance individuals must be at leisure, that is, freed from their financial obligations so as to have time to reflect upon pertinent political issues as well as to participate in deliberation and legislation regarding them. A democratic system cannot work and may even be detrimental to the well-being of the city-state if citizens do not have time to formulate a coherent and well-informed perspective on relevant political issues. To ensure that political participation did not become a luxury of the wealthy, Athenian citizens were paid by the city-state to attend Assembly. The extent to which some citizens could directly participate in formal political discussion and procedures, and in a manner that was both meaningful and significant, established a standard of democratic governance that has not yet been matched on so large a scale.

Some of the foremost Greek thinkers expressed ambivalence, even hostility, to this level of democratic governance. In his *Republic*, Plato claims, those best suited to rule are philosophers since they have most fully developed their faculty of knowledge and are more capable of formulating decisions that are not subject to base desires and petty ambitions. Plato moderates this position in the *Statesman*, arguing that rule by the many is inferior to rule by one or rule by the few when the state is constructed around a sound legal code. When no such code exists rule by the many is preferred so that no one individual can rule perniciously, unchecked by either law or citizen. Although less derogatory than Plato, Aristotle ranks democracy best among the bad regimes. Democratic citizens, who enjoy political equality, may seek equality in all respects, form factions against those they perceive to be somehow advantaged, and create instability in the city-state. However, Aristotle ultimately does not regard the masses as unfit to rule. Indeed, rule by the collective can overcome individual shortcomings, creating a whole which is better than the sum of its parts.

Aristotle also states that all forms of rule by one, few, or many, have the potential to be pernicious if the rulers desire only to increase their personal gain. His observation that all forms of government are potentially perverse served as the motivation for *early republicanism*. While democracy emphasizes rule by the many and venerates the virtue of political equality, republicanism advocates a government that incorporates the interests not only of the masses but also of the elites and of a single ruler. Republican thinkers argue that when one segment of society—whether the many, the few, or the one—possesses a monopoly over political power, the state becomes unstable. As the Roman statesman Marcus Tulius Cicero notes, even the most benevolent monarch may on a whim become a tyrant, the most excellent few may be tempted to conspire against the many, and the many are too often transformed into a mob or are divided by faction. Classical republicanism posits that a government must have a *mixed constitution* to be legitimate and stable.

From approximately 500 BCE to 23 BCE, the Roman Republic exemplified this ideal. It consisted of three branches: an executive branch comprising magistrates elected by a popular vote of propertied citizens; a Senate of 300 elites chosen from a pool of former magistrates; and the popular assembly, directly elected by all Roman citizens. While the Roman Republic did not employ the measures of direct democracy practiced in ancient Athens, it did implement methods of popular control over government policies vis-à-vis the popular assembly. However, the influence of the masses was mitigated by the executive branch and the Senate creating a system where the masses and the elites held power but where neither held it exclusively. The enduring success of the Roman Republic made it a political model that had a profound influence on the formulation of government in future states including the city-states of Renaissance Italy and the United States.

The end of the Roman Republic marked the beginning of an era of democratic desolation. With few exceptions, democratic governance became a rarity, and the western world in particular came to be dominated by monarchy and feudalism. In the seventeenth century, democracy once again began to emerge. In *The Second Treatise of Government*, a defense of the Glorious Revolution of 1688 and *constitutional government*, John Locke asserts that individuals form a society for the purpose of protecting their lives, liberty, and estates. To ensure that these rights are not violated, Locke argues that laws may only be formulated with the consent of society and by a legislature selected by the public. Although Locke restricted full rights of citizenship to property owners, his argument for government by consent was of great influence to partisans of democracy. His influence can be seen in the American Declaration of Independence in which Thomas Jefferson echoes Locke by proclaiming that all individuals have a right to life, liberty, and the pursuit of happiness.

Unlike Locke, Jean-Jacques Rousseau, patron saint of the French Revolution, did not believe that popular government should exist to protect private interests. Rousseau believed that the right to property espoused by Locke was not a natural right that all are entitled to but rather existed only as a construct of a materialist and inequitable society. For Rousseau the quintessential question for society concerns how individuals may come together and form a society for the purpose of promoting their greater preservation without sacrificing the freedom they possessed before society. Rousseau claims this can only be done through a *social contract* in which individuals give up all of their rights to the community as a whole. Since each individual forfeits liberties to the entire community, no one individual has undue privilege or influence. Through their equal position each person is sovereign while at the same time no person is sovereign. According to Rousseau, the sovereign is the multitude united in one body and since it consists of the individuals within the body, it cannot have any interest opposed to them. The desire of the social body of individuals united through their common condition of equality is termed the *general will*. It guides all social action and prevents civil undertakings from being abusive or tyrannical. Rousseau's political thought had extraordinary influence on the leaders of the French Revolution and continues to be influential for contemporary theorists.

The emergence of *democracy in the United States* illustrated that modern democratic states would be afflicted by many of the same controversies as the ancient democracies. Like Cicero in Rome, James Madison feared the potentially deleterious effects of mass politics in America. Notable among these was the fear of *faction*. In *Federalist #10*, Madison notes that differences of opinion are inevitable in society as long as individuals, who are fallible, retain their liberty. He regards individual freedom as inalienable but thinks that the factions produced by individuals pursuing their different goals must be controlled. Madison particularly fears majority factions because they have the power to undermine the public good and violate the rights of other citizens. For Madison and other Federalists, the dilemma of faction could only be resolved through the establishment of a strong centralized government in which representatives make political decisions. Like Madison, Alexis de Tocqueville feared the oppression of the few at the hands of the many. Yet, while Madison believed this quandary to be best remedied by the creation of a strong central government, Tocqueville advocated the formation of strong *civic associations* where individuals could preclude tyranny by unifying behind a common cause. As we see below, Tocqueville's assertion that a vigorous democracy requires a high degree of civil participation among the masses remains significant in democratic political thought to this day.

Since the time of the ancient Greeks it has been apparent that democracy was plagued by many internal complexities and contradictions. However, with the proliferation of *modern democracy* this fact became ever more apparent. How should democratic decisions be made? Who should make them? Are there any topics that should be immune to democratic decision-making? What should be done about groups that are systematically disadvantaged in democratic systems or who adhere to a set of moral values that conflict with certain democratic norms? Attempts to address these questions as well as many others have led contemporary theorists to formulate several different ways of thinking about democratic processes.

Three distinct, although related, approaches to democracy shape contemporary discussions. Each builds on and cuts across earlier themes. In the first, democracy is understood in terms of political processes that aggregate the choices and interests of citizens. Citizens express their preferences by choosing political officials and, less directly, public policies through a process of competitive elections. *Aggregative democracy* emphasizes rational or strategic action on the part of candidates, constituents, interest groups, lobbyists, parties, and political officials. It is a politics of logrolling and pork barrels, trade-offs and compromises. Public officials are "brokers" or "entrepreneurs," and citizens are the clients they represent and the consumers they satisfy. When electoral and legislative processes are fair and just, political decisions and public policies reflect the most intense and/or common preferences of the citizenry. However, like earlier attempts to represent individual interests, those processes neither presume nor promote a public good which is more than the sum total of private interests.

A second concept moves democracy beyond a politics of casting votes to discussing issues, beyond aggregating preferences to achieving understanding. *Deliberative democracy* focuses on cooperative interactions between citizens that enlarge their perspectives, potentially transforming private interests into public judgments. Echoing earlier attempts at direct democracy, political decisions result from discussions that ideally include everyone and on equal terms. Those terms include a commitment to rational discourse, a willingness to give reasons for political positions, and to seek—if not reach—mutual understanding and consensual decisions. Recently, deliberative theorists have proposed expanding concepts of political discourse beyond rational argument to include, for example, greeting, rhetoric, and storytelling. Recognizing that public debates are often initiated by political protests of social movements, they also stress the intersections between claims for democratic justice and struggles for cultural recognition. However, like aggregative democrats, deliberative democrats prioritize the pursuit of justice within established legal and institutional frameworks. With this they make a major concession to the increased scale of modern economic and political systems.

A third approach examines democratic processes beyond the boundaries of the traditional political activities, interests, and institutions. *Agonistic democrats* address the ways in which new identities are formed and how they then transform politics as usual. Agonistic democracy places political *agon* (struggle) at the center of democratic life. Here political differences involve more than competing candidates and contending arguments. Agonistic democrats invoke a visceral politics and stress affective, embodied, and extralinguistic features of public discourse. Cultural politics—dance, film, music, theater—mobilizes citizens whose discursive styles, frames of reference, and articulated needs challenge the limits of political institutions. New social movements, they argue, shift back and forth, up and down, between an established legal-institutional framework and this transformative politics, using the resources of both registers to sustain a vital civil society. However, a visceral politics can be used to manipulate a mass citizenry as well as empower it, to revitalize democratic processes or to undermine them. Recognizing this danger, agonistic democrats would limit political rhetoric to so-called noncoercive forms, to media and messages that connect particular with general interests.

The common themes which run throughout these discussions of democracy suggest continuing challenges facing democratic politics. First, there is the question of *participation* by all citizens at all levels of democratic politics. Voter turnout, party membership, union membership, and church attendance are declining in advanced industrialized democracies. In OECD (Organization for Economic Cooperation and Development) nations, overall voter turnout has dropped from roughly 80 percent in the 1950s to 70 percent in the 1990s. It continues to decline despite rising levels of education, once an important predictor of political participation. Robert Putnam discusses this decreased participation as a problem of civic disengagement which he traces to a decline of social capital. Most simply, his theory of social capital stresses the significance of social networks in democratic nations. Among the effects of modernization is a loss of community ties and the increasing privatization of public life. According to Putnam, citizens are becoming spectators of democratic politics rather than its participants. In modern democracies opportunities for citizens to engage in political discussions and debates have decreased. Professional politicians increasingly supplant the solidarity of social movements, and the connections between citizens are attenuated, limited to private networks, and often based on leisure and sports activities. Modern democratic citizens are, in Putnam's most famous phrase, increasingly "bowling alone."

A second overlapping problem concerns the forms of political communication available to democratic citizens. As Benjamin Ginsberg notes, the "voice of the people" expressed in elections is limited in its scope (e.g., selection from the available candidates), frequency (e.g., choices occur every two, four, or six years) and intensity (e.g., each citizen receives only one vote). Turnout remains higher among better educated and more affluent citizens, an indication that social capital, like other forms of capital, is unequally distributed. In this context, it is important to recognize that social capital is not necessarily democratic and can even work to undermine democratic processes. More inclusive forms of participation—debates, hearings, protests—potentially allow marginalized citizens to express their as yet unrecognized needs. However, members of oppressed groups must still attain political power if they are to successfully address longstanding injustices.

These alternative discourses of oppressed groups reflect the growing diversity of citizens within democratic nations, as well as the increasing *globalization* of contemporary politics. The rise of multinational and transnational corporations and the accompanying erosion of state sovereignty pose additional challenges to democracy. Regional and international institutions are needed to address issues—environmental, monetary, security—beyond the control of nation-states and to protect the civil, economic, and political rights of citizens across national borders. Among political theorists, David Held and Fred Dallmayr have proposed *cosmopolitan democracy,* a combination of regional and global as well as national institutions to govern our changing world. Collective institutions like the European Union and the United Nations, as well as political movements ranging from Amnesty International to Greenpeace, support the possibility of such transnational democracy. Longstanding questions about the limits of democratic citizenship and political participation reemerge here and are joined by new ones about human rights and global community. They illustrate that democracy remains an essentially contested concept, today on an ever-increasing scale.

See also Deliberative Democracy; Democratic Education; the State and Youth; Student Political Activism.

Recommended Reading

Arblaster, A. (1987). *Democracy.* Minneapolis: University of Minnesota Press.
Connolly, W. (1999). *Why I Am Not a Secularist.* Minneapolis: University of Minnesota Press.
Dallmayr, F. (2001). *Achieving Our World: Toward a Global and Plural Democracy.* New York: Rowman and Littlefield.
Dryzek, J. (2000). *Deliberative Democracy and Beyond: Liberals, Critics, Contestations.* New York: Oxford University Press.
Ginsberg, B. (1982). *The Consequences of Consent: Elections, Citizen Control, and Popular Acquiescence.* New York: Addison-Wesley.
Putnam, R. (2002). *Democracies in Flux: The Evolution of Social Capital in Contemporary Society.* New York: Oxford University Press.
Young, I. (2000). *Inclusion and Democracy.* New York: Oxford University Press.

Joshua L. Vermette and Nancy S. Love

Democratic Education. In a recent study, political scientists John Hibbing and Elizabeth Theiss-Morse found that the vast majority of Americans purposely avoid political participation, recoiling from what they see as a conflict-ridden system driven by narrow self-interest. To combat this problem, Hibbing and Theiss-Morse advocate loading the civic-education curriculum with hotly debated political issues to teach young people that controversy is not an unfortunate byproduct of democracy but one of its core and vital elements. In this article we describe and evaluate two of the most promising approaches to teaching about controversial public issues: classroom deliberation and youth-activism projects.

Deliberation refers to a form of discussion different from debate in that the goal is not to convince others of the superiority of one's own views but rather to learn as much as one can about the issue being discussed. In some cases deliberation results in consensus—on one of the original positions advanced, on a compromise position, or on an entirely new position that becomes evident only during the course of the discussion. In other cases the participants leave the discussion still in disagreement but with a more nuanced understanding of the issue and greater clarity on the precise points of contention.

As a pedagogical tool, deliberation most typically takes place among students in a classroom setting. By contrast, in a youth-activism project students participate directly in political life outside the classroom, often through designing and implementing an action plan in response to an identified social problem. While classroom deliberation engages students in the study of political issues, activism projects offer them opportunities to act on their beliefs and to effect change at the local, state, national, or even international levels.

These two approaches to engaging students in the study of controversial issues hold an advantage over other prevalent methods in that they teach civic skills that students are likely to use in their own lives. For example, in methods such as moot courts and Model United Nations, students get to mimic how adults make decisions in some of the world's most important institutions, but rarely will they get a chance someday to participate in these institutions themselves. By contrast, all students will have opportunities outside of school to deliberate with others on controversial public issues and to engage in civic activism.

In the remainder of this entry, we review the academic literature on the deliberation and youth activism approaches to teaching about controversial public issues, and we examine the most prominent curricular examples of each approach. We find that deliberation and activism have tended historically to be used in isolation from each other. For example, the Public Issues curriculum, developed by Donald Oliver and James Shaver, focuses almost exclusively on deliberation and thus falls short of teaching students how to effect social change in a world where rational discussion often fails to alter the opinions and actions of people in positions of power. Conversely, Project Citizen, perhaps the most widely used curriculum based on the youth-activism model, tends to skirt deliberation of the most significant political controversies associated with the activism projects the students undertake. What results is a largely unreflective form of civic engagement. We conclude the article by proposing a set of design principles for a democratic-education curriculum that capitalizes on the merits of both deliberation and action.

The idea that deliberation of controversial issues should be a central feature in a democratic-education program is not new. An influential report on the social studies issued in 1916 encouraged schools to create "Problems of Democracy" courses that emphasized contemporary political issues. Enthusiasm for this approach continues today, as evidenced by the recently released *The Civic Mission of the Schools* report, which recommends that schools "incorporate discussion of current local, national, and international issues and events into the classroom, particularly those that young people view as important to their lives" (Carnegie Corporation and CIRCLE 2003, 6).

At least four reasons have been offered in support of the deliberation approach, perhaps the most obvious being the unique civic space that many schools provide. As Amy Gutmann writes, "Schools have a much greater capacity than most parents and voluntary associations for teaching children to reason out loud about disagreements that arise in democratic politics" (1999, 58). This is because the student population in many schools is more ideologically diverse than one would expect in a family, club, or religious organization. This diversity of views makes classrooms ideal places to promote what Gutmann deems the most important component of democratic education: "rational deliberations of competing conceptions of the good life and the good society" (1999, 44).

A second argument in support of this approach concerns the knowledge, skills, and dispositions that students gain from discussing controversial public issues. As it turns out, recent empirical research confirms much of what the 1916 education report hypothesized. For example, Patricia Avery finds a positive correlation between discussion of complex policy issues (especially civil liberties controversies) and the development of tolerant attitudes and an understanding of why tolerance is important in democratic societies. Walter Parker uses the term "democratic enlightenment" to refer to the numerous benefits that he believes result from such discussions: "literacy, knowledge of the ideals of democratic living, knowing which government officials to contact about different issues, the commitment to freedom and justice, [and] the disposition to be tolerant of religious and other cultural differences" (2003, 34).

Third, classroom deliberation appears to foster increased political engagement outside the classroom. A study involving 90,000 students in twenty-eight countries by the International Association for the Evaluation of Educational Achievement (IEA) finds that when students report to have "experience[d] their classrooms as places to investigate issues and explore their opinions and those of their peers," they are also more likely to exhibit higher levels not only of civic knowledge and support for democratic values but also of participation in political discussion and political engagement. Molly Andolina and her colleagues find that students who report that they discussed political and social issues in class with other students holding differing opinions are more likely to say that they also participated in civic activities such as signing a written petition, taking part in a boycott, and following political news most of the time.

Finally, many have argued that deliberation is democratic action in its own right: engaging with others in political discussions both inside and outside the classroom has the potential to make people politically smarter and to strengthen their sense of connectedness to the body politic. This is why many democratic theorists and educators believe that deliberation is both a cause and an effect of democracy itself. When the masses (as opposed to just the political elite) engage in deliberations of controversial issues, it is a sign of political equality—that all citizens are presumed capable of making decisions about matters of public concern.

One of the earliest and most widely used examples of the deliberation approach is the Public Issues model, developed as part of the Harvard Social Studies Project in the 1970s. The model involves selecting for discussion public policy issues that bring to the fore tensions between core democratic principles, such as liberty versus property. For example, students might deliberate on whether the state should legalize physician-assisted suicide or whether the U.S. Congress should prohibit Internet sites from publishing materials that threaten public safety. Diana Hess and Julie Posselt, who have examined classrooms utilizing this model, report that as the semester progressed, most students became more effective participants in deliberations and that their affinity for such discussions increased.

Some, however, have criticized curricular models that focus solely or primarily on deliberation. Fred Newmann has argued that in many cases "educational practice neglects the most crucial component in democratic theory: the right of each citizen to *exert influence in* (in contrast to 'thinking critically about' or 'taking an active interest in') public affairs" (1975, 4). Newmann's critique came before research was available that suggested a correlation between deliberation in school and participation in civic life. Nevertheless, it stands to reason that if the educational objective is civic participation, students should be provided with hands-on experiences working on real community problems.

While rationally discussing social problems with those who disagree is surely a key component of civic life, other activities are no less important, such as boycotting and "buycotting," grassroots organizing, collective bargaining, fundraising, civil disobedience, lobbying policymakers, and campaigning for political candidates. Particularly for groups who lack access to power and who face an entrenched opposition, is it not enough to learn in school only how to talk civilly about public issues. Disempowered groups also need training in how to gain political leverage and effect change even when others refuse to listen to what they say. Focusing democratic education solely on deliberation, then, may serve to sustain current social hierarchies.

To address these concerns about programs based on discussion of controversial issues, a number of educators have followed Newmann's advice and engaged youth directly in civic action outside the classroom. In the vast majority of cases this approach has taken the form of voluntary or mandatory community service, although some examples do exist of programs that engage students in what might be called *activism*, as opposed to service.

There is evidence that students learn a great deal from high-quality service-learning projects. Not only do their academic skills improve, but well-crafted programs can also help develop students' sense of civic responsibility. At the same time, such programs tend to rely on a narrow view of what it means to be an involved citizen. As Joel Westheimer and Joe Kahne argue, most community service programs implicitly or explicitly define citizenship as acting "responsibly" in the community, for example, "picking up litter, giving blood, recycling, volunteering, and staying out of debt" (2004, 242). Westheimer and Kahne note at least three problems with this conception of citizenship as personal responsibility: "first, the emphasis placed on character and behavior can obscure the need for collective and often public sector initiatives; second, this emphasis can distract attention from analysis of the causes of social problems; and third, volunteerism and kindness are put forward as ways of avoiding politics and policy" (2004, 243). In this way, community service projects tend to avoid political controversy altogether, promoting a largely unreflective form of civic action.

Activism projects can be distinguished from community service in that the former regard civic engagement as inherently political. They aim for students not simply to volunteer their time but rather to understand that any means of addressing a community problem is likely to please some members while angering others. Westheimer and Kahne identify a definition of citizenship advanced by many of these programs that contrasts with the "personally responsible citizen" of the community-service programs. This second type of good citizen—the "participatory citizen"—has intimate knowledge of how social institutions and government bodies operate and knows what sorts of tactics will be necessary to advance a given political objective. To give students the knowledge and skills necessary to influence public policy, activism projects based on the participatory ideal have students go through the various steps in the process of fomenting change: locating which organization or government body has the authority to address the issue, assessing the relative power of the competing interest groups involved, and designing and implementing a plan of action.

The participatory model addresses many of the shortcomings of community service, but its definition of citizenship has limitations of its own. The programs Westheimer and Kahne identify as subscribing to this model tend to be so concerned with teaching students the political savvy needed to advance a given cause that they skirt the larger question of which causes are worth fighting for in the first place. Unlike the community-service programs, students engage in a political analysis of the issue(s) being addressed, but this analysis goes only so far. It focuses on such questions as where different interest groups stand on the issue and what specific steps might be involved in a given plan of action. It does not, however, ask students to consider whether the issue under investigation is merely a symptom of a much larger, systemic problem.

Westheimer and Kahne locate a small number of programs that deal with these larger questions. These "justice-oriented" programs, as they call them, define good citizenship as having a broad understanding of the root causes of social problems and of the relationship between local phenomena and societal institutions. In these programs students engage in political action, such as community organizing and protesting, that fall outside the mainstream and that aim to alter the distribution of power in society. To clarify, while the personally responsible citizen might volunteer at a food drive, the participatory citizen would understand how to organize the drive. Meanwhile, the justice-oriented citizen would be asking why people are going hungry in the first place and looking for ways to eradicate poverty altogether.

One way of describing the shortcomings of both the community-service and the participatory approaches is to say that students learn how to become involved—either as responsible individuals or as politically motivated citizens—but do not end up discussing the wider implications of whatever actions they engage in. In short, both of these approaches could benefit from the addition of a deliberation component in which students would discuss these larger questions. With the justice-oriented approach, however, Westheimer and Kahne find that students end up knowing a great deal about the systemic causes of social problems and the kinds of solutions that might uphold standards of justice but not as much about how to "work the system" to see their ideas come to fruition. In other words, the justice-oriented model is vulnerable to a critique similar to that leveled against deliberation-based programs: students develop informed opinions on what sorts of political actions are needed but never learn how to effect concrete social change.

There is nothing to say that a single program could not both engage students in discussions about social justice and yet also teach them how to effect piecemeal change—as the cliché goes, "think globally, act locally." Few programs have succeeded in doing so, however. We believe that this fact may stem both from the public pressure placed on teachers to refrain from involving their students in radical political activity, as well as from the organizational difficulties of administering a program that has multiple and far-reaching goals.

To illustrate some of these challenges we have chosen to examine one particular youth-activism program in depth. The program, called Project Citizen, is for middle-school students and is sponsored by the Center for Civic Education. While not the only such program, its widespread use across the United States, its liberal funding by the federal government, and its promotion in numerous other countries make it worth focusing on at some length.

The principle component of Project Citizen is an "action plan" that a class or youth group develops together in response to a community problem they identify. The class rarely actually implements the plan, but they do often present it to community leaders as part of a statewide exhibition. The development of the action plan consists of five main components:

Identify a problem to study. The curriculum guide offers students some suggestions, such as gang violence, inadequate resources for childcare, low voter turnout, and environmental degradation.

Gather information. During this phase, students interview community members and examine print and electronic sources to identify the most salient features of the problem, as well as its most viable solutions. Little emphasis, however, is placed on gathering information about the root causes of the problem the students have selected.

Examine solutions. Students research competing views on how to address the problem.

Develop your own public policy. During this phase, the class comes to consensus on a public policy that best addresses the problem identified.

Develop an action plan. In the final phase students decide how they can best influence the appropriate government body to implement their plan of action.

By having students interview government, business, and community leaders to determine their views on the chosen problem and their preferred means of addressing it, Project Citizen teaches students the skills needed to become actively involved in civic affairs. As such, the program most closely subscribes to the idea of the "participatory citizen." It focuses on political action rather than service, but it stops short of engaging students in discussion of the most politically contentious issues involved, such as the root causes of the problem identified and the broader social and economic implications of the "solution" the class has devised. Thus, although the curriculum prompts much classroom deliberation—for example, on what problem to tackle, how to address it, what community resources to utilize, and how to balance the competing interests of different community groups—discussion stops short of the crucial questions asked by the "justice-oriented citizen."

What we find most troubling about Project Citizen's approach, however, is that it requires the entire class to settle on one community problem and one way of addressing it. Perhaps as a result of trying to reach consensus, many classes participating in the program end up choosing issues that spark little or no disagreement, such as erecting a new stop sign at a local intersection. They thus lose the opportunity to deliberate about the more contentious issues, along with the numerous educational advantages associated with such deliberation. Alternatively, if the class selects an issue that is in fact highly controversial, the class might ultimately settle on an action plan whose goals or methods a sizable minority of students flatly disagree with. These students thus might learn the unfortunate lesson that political engagement is not about empowerment—acting on one's beliefs—but about coercion—following the dictates of the group. We find this problematic because while citizens may have responsibilities to abide by laws they may not agree with, they are under no obligation to actively promote the establishment of such laws, nor to advance causes they do not support. For these

reasons, Project Citizen may promote a form of political engagement inauthentic to the way actual citizens behave.

At the same time, there may be sound educational reasons for this sacrifice of authenticity. A program that focuses the attention of the entire class on one problem and has them select one public policy solution allows the class to delve deeply into a common topic and teaches crucial consensus-building skills. Moreover, a single class project is clearly easier for teachers to manage than if groups of students within a single class were working simultaneously on several different problems, or even advocating competing policy solutions to a shared problem. This sort of tension is common in democratic education. The more authentic a curricular approach is to actual participation in the world outside of school, the more difficult it often is to administer.

This trade-off becomes especially acute when the inclusion of politically controversial content is at issue. Returning to the point made by Hibbing and Theiss-Morse, that Americans' low levels of political engagement stems from their aversion to conflict, it is reasonable to assume that such aversion also applies to teachers and school administrators. Despite the educational advantages of including controversial issues in the curriculum, school faculty and staff have many reasons to avoid doing so, from placating potentially angry parents, to avoiding racial, ethnic, or religious conflict in the classroom, to disrupting their own reassuring vision of America as a land of unity and consensus. It is therefore understandable that while programs such as Project Citizen do allow for deliberation of controversial issues, they in no way ensure that such discussion will take place. Other action-oriented programs, such as community service, seem specifically designed to teach young people about civic engagement without the risks thought to accompany the inclusion of controversial issues. At the same time, it is hard to see how young people could learn to maneuver comfortably and effectively in a world riddled with conflict if they are taught in school a sugarcoated version of civic life.

The two approaches to civic education examined in this entry—deliberation and youth-activism projects—have the potential to help young people develop into thoughtful and engaged citizens. Each by itself, however, has significant limitations. Programs such as the Public Issues curriculum, which customarily lacks an activism component, tend to put too much emphasis on the liberal ideal that social and economic problems could be solved if only people would sit down together and discuss their differences of opinion. Such a paradigm ignores the stark reality of a stratified society in which some groups can advance their agendas no matter what the opposition says in protest. Meanwhile, participatory approaches such as Project Citizen succeed in getting students to understand the tactics necessary to accomplish a political goal but tend to skirt classroom deliberation of the most contentious issues involved. In effect, students fail to learn that becoming involved in public affairs always entails making choices about how to position themselves in relation to the myriad groups competing for power and resources. Thus, as in the case of deliberation-based approaches, youth-activism projects run the risk of giving students a skewed picture of civic life that downplays social hierarchies and political battles.

In light of these concerns, we propose three design principles to consider when developing a civic-education curriculum. First, we believe that programs should include both deliberation and activism components. By discussing, for example, competing perspectives on the problem of poverty, students can come to understand which policy options are most likely to produce which kinds of results. They can come to see that each choice involves trade-offs that have political implications (e.g., increases in taxation, transformation of racial or gender hierarchies, or realign-

ment of party coalitions). At the same time, involving students in community projects designed to test the theories discussed in class, can teach them the sorts of tactics that can be used to further a political agenda. In this way, students can become both more thoughtful and more empowered citizens.

This brings us to our second point, that even a well-structured, comprehensive program will not necessarily focus students' attention on the most hotly debated and significant political issues of the day. Rather, it will take a concerted effort on the part of curriculum writers and teachers to expose students to competing perspectives in all phases of the project, from choosing which social problems to address (indeed, in deciding what counts as a "problem" to begin with), to assessing possible responses, to devising an action plan. Students by and large will not discover on their own those perspectives that fall outside what is available in the mainstream media, nor will they necessarily see the wider political implications of the various choices they make. Thus, teachers and curriculum designers might assemble resources and devise classroom activities that direct students' attention to the diversity of perspectives on the issues examined and to the larger social and economic processes to which these issues relate.

Finally, although we recommend that students be taught to consider ideas that they may not initially agree with, we feel it is inauthentic—and highly undemocratic— to compel them to participate in political projects that they do not support. In the case of Project Citizen, the whole class still could together select a problem, deliberate on its various causes, and investigate different policy options, but when it comes to deciding which option to pursue, we would advocate letting each student make this decision individually. Thus, returning to the example of poverty, one group of students might choose to volunteer at a soup kitchen, while another group worked with legislators to develop a welfare-to-work program, and a third group lobbied the city council to establish a living-wage law. While infusing controversial public issues into the democratic-education curriculum is clearly not an easy task, it can make for a more authentic civic-education curriculum—one that prepares students to participate in a democratic society where conflict appears to be the norm.

See also Character Education; Citizenship Education Policies in the States; Civic Virtue; Deliberative Democracy; Democracy; Diversity Education; Environmental Education (EE); IEA Civic Education Study; Just Community High Schools and Youth Activism; National Alliance for Civic Education (NACE); Prosocial Behaviors; School Engagement; School Influences and Civic Engagement.

Recommended Reading

Andolina, M. W., Jenkins, K., Keeter, S., and Zukin, C. (2002). "Searching for the Meaning of Youth Civic Engagement: Notes from the Field." *Applied Developmental Science*, 6 (4): 189–195.

Avery, P. G. (2002). "Political Tolerance, Democracy and Adolescents." In *Education for Democracy: Contexts, Curricula, Assessments*, edited by W. C. Parker. Greenwich, CT: Information Age Publishing, pp. 113–130.

Carnegie Corporation of New York and CIRCLE: Center for Information and Research on Civic Learning and Engagement (2003). *The Civic Mission of Schools*. New York: Carnegie Corporation of New York.

Center for Civic Education (2004). *We the People—Project Citizen*. See http://www.civiced.org/project_citizen.php.

Gutmann, A. (1999). *Democratic Education*. Rev. ed. Princeton, NJ: Princeton University Press.

Hess, D., and Posselt, J. (2002). "How High School Students Experience and Learn From the Discussion of Controversial Public Issues." *Journal of Curriculum and Supervision*, 17 (4): 283–314.

Hibbing, J. R., and Theiss-Morse, E. (2002). *Stealth Democracy: Americans' Beliefs about How Government Should Work*. Cambridge and New York: Cambridge University Press.

Newmann, F. M. (1975). *Education for Citizen Action: Challenge for Secondary Curriculum*. Berkeley, CA: McCutchan.

Oliver, D. W., and Shaver, J. P. (1974). *Teaching Public Issues in the High School*. Logan: Utah State University Press.

Parker, W. (2003). *Teaching Democracy: Unity and Diversity in Public Life*. New York: Teacher's College Press.

Torney-Purta, J., Lehmann, R., Oswald, H., and Schultz, W. (2001). *Citizenship and Education in Twenty-eight Countries: Civic Knowledge and Engagement at Age Fourteen*. Amsterdam: International Association for the Evaluation of Educational Achievement.

Westheimer, J., and Kahne, J. (2004). "Educating the 'Good' Citizen: Political Choices and Pedagogical Goals." *PS*, 37 (2): 241–248.

Diana Hess and Eric Freedman

Demographic Trends Affecting the World's Youth. The world's population reached 6 billion in 1999, with children under the age of fifteen making up one-third of the population in developing countries and nearly half in sub–Saharan Africa. While the number of children and youth is large relative to previous generations in many countries, their share of national populations varies considerably.

Age Structure and Youth

A population's recent history of fertility, mortality, and migration determines the proportion of people at any given age. Fertility decline reduces the proportion of children, and mortality decline increases the proportion of the surviving elderly, both of which cause the population to age. Europe, North America, and other countries where the demographic transition from high to low fertility and mortality is largely over are characterized by low growth rates and aging populations. In most of Latin America, East Asia, and some of the Middle East and South Asia, the decline of mortality and fertility began more recently, and fertility still supports moderate population growth. In sub–Saharan Africa, the rest of the Middle East and South Asia, and several countries in Latin America, mortality is not as low as it is in places where it declined earlier. Here, fertility remains relatively high and in combination with higher mortality results in youthful populations and relatively rapid population growth.

These regional groups of countries have sharply varying age distributions. People under age fifteen make up almost half of the population in countries that have not started or are at the beginning of the demographic transition (with a median age of seventeen), a third of the population of countries that are mid-way through the demographic transition (with a median age of twenty-three), and less than a quarter of the population in the countries where the demographic transition is nearly completed (with a median age of thirty-four) (United Nations 1993; United Nations 1990). In the coming years these large groups of young people will become adults, but in the meantime the relative burden their numbers place on working adults in their societies will have important implications for how they fare later on. When half of the population is under age seventeen, the demands on schools and other social institutions are enormous. Each of these different age structures poses challenges for governments trying to provide for their populations. When the numbers of young people and their demand for age-specific goods and services like education and health care fluctuate rapidly, these changes are more likely to be experienced as social problems.

A summary measure of changes in age structure is the dependency ratio, which compares the relative size of the youngest and oldest segments of the population (aged zero to fourteen and over sixty) with the population most likely to be economically productive (aged fifteen to fifty-nine). A large youth-dependency ratio emerges when children are surviving infancy in greater numbers but fertility has not yet declined. After fertility declines, particularly if it falls sharply, a smaller youth-dependency ratio becomes inevitable, emerging about twenty years later when the large youth generation enters the labor market. Finally, when fertility and mortality are both low, the large numbers born before the fertility decline age into economic dependency, relying on a working-age population made smaller by fertility decline. During the interval in which the overall dependency ratio is small, demographic forces can contribute to economic growth and development if nations are prepared to take advantage of the situation.

The East Asian "miracle" provides the most impressive example of the positive role that age structure can play in economic growth. The huge birth cohort resulting from the East Asian mortality decline in the 1940s and 1950s reached the labor market about twenty years later. The large youth-dependency ratio had suppressed per capita income growth, but after 1970 the greater proportion of workers and the government's investments in education and job creation facilitated per capita income growth. By 2010 this low dependency ratio will have vanished as the many workers of the economic miracle retire and are supported by the smaller working-age cohorts that followed them. East Asia made the most of this transient opportunity, investing heavily in education and health services, and they have reaped the rewards of having done so (Leete and Alam 1999).

Dependency ratios and the periods of demographic opportunity vary significantly between regions. North America, Oceania, and Europe are nearing the end of a period of low dependency resulting from intense childbearing after World War II and have begun to face the problems associated with growing elderly populations. On average, elderly dependency now exceeds the youth-dependency ratio in Europe, North America, and Oceania, an unprecedented demographic situation that demands careful allocation of resources across the population age structure. Although immigration to these countries may slow population aging by adding to the youthful population, it is hardly sufficient to reverse the trend. Asia and Latin America and the Caribbean are currently experiencing low elderly dependency ratios and declining youth-dependency ratios. Both regions have prepared for it by investing in children and youth, but Latin America's economic crises have diminished economic opportunities for youth. Africa can invest in the huge youth population that will soon become workers by investing in youth with education, health care, and improved living conditions. Unless governments prepare well for this "demographic opportunity" by creating opportunities for young people, disaster may result as large cohorts of inadequately prepared youth enter adulthood.

When youth have relatively few opportunities for work and schooling, they often make decisions that affect both local age structures and economic growth. One way in which young adults attempt to access better education, employment, housing, and in other ways improve their life chances is through rural to urban and international migration. However, this generally youthful migration flow also leads to urban underemployment and unemployment as urban population growth exceeds labor demand, and the dislocation can carry substantial costs in loss of community and culture for the migrants. In industrialized countries in Western Europe and North America, one solution to the shrinking of the population has been to incorporate international migrants, particularly from the developing world. This international movement creates social networks that channel money, trained labor, and new ideas back into developing countries.

In sum, births, deaths, and migration are some of the few predictable factors shaping a country's future. Youth in developed countries are in relatively small cohorts in aging populations. Youth in developing countries are in large cohorts likely to be followed by similarly large cohorts but smaller dependency ratios if they have fewer children of their own. This demographic change can provide new opportunities for youth if governments invest in young people in a timely manner.

Investments in Youth

Parents and communities invest in children and youth by providing for their health, education, and preparation—physical, vocational, and cultural—for productive adulthood. When young people come of age in a context of low dependency ratios they potentially contribute to economic growth and development by translating those investments into economic productivity. However, the demographic and economic context in which youth cohorts come of age shapes how much parents and society are able to invest in young people.

The experiences of Europe and North America and the industrialized countries of East Asia suggest that large birth cohorts benefit in times of economic expansion because parents and governments are able to invest generously in youth. Furthermore, markets in healthy economies expand to accommodate large cohorts, creating economies of scale. In response to a large generation of young people, for example, schools grow in size and number, health and recreation services expand, and entrepreneurs compete for growing markets. In times of economic stagnation, large youth cohorts may be shortchanged with regard to social investments, as occurred in Latin America. There, the growth potential offered by low dependency ratios was weakened by a lack of social investment in youth, as we can see from regional trends in educational participation.

Developed countries in the 1990s were characterized by nearly universal primary and secondary education among school-age youth, while nearly half of postsecondary-age youth participated in higher education. Rather than trying to increase school participation, educators are developing curricula appropriate for contemporary labor markets. In eastern Asia and Oceania, where the demographic window of opportunity is closing, primary education is all but universal and secondary education is widespread. In recent decades there, participation in secondary education has increased by 40 percent and in tertiary education by 160 percent, as governments and families continue to take advantage of the mutually reinforcing effects of economic growth and low dependency ratios.

Latin America and the Caribbean countries have not been able to take advantage of low dependency ratios, since in the 1980s and 1990s, also known as "the lost decades," recession and overwhelming foreign debt have commanded governments' financial resources. Although primary- and secondary-education levels are similar to those of eastern Asia and Oceania, there has been relatively little growth in education at the secondary and tertiary levels.

In southern Asia, the Arab States, and sub–Saharan Africa between 78 and 95 percent of primary-school-age youth are enrolled, although low attendance and failure to progress to upper grades are critical threats to raising education levels. In these regions primary-school participation has increased relatively little, while participation rates in secondary and tertiary education have increased more, reflecting growing disparities by class, ethnicity, and sex in investments in youth. Indeed, throughout the developing regions, public spending per student on higher education is between seven and forty-four times greater than spending per student in primary school, in contrast with a ratio of 2.5:1 in the OECD (Organization for Economic Co-operation and Development) countries. Since the rates of return to investments in primary and secondary education are greater than investments in tertiary education in developing countries, this represents significant inequity in public spending.

Spending on health has a disproportionately positive impact on young people in developing countries where life expectancy at birth is low. However, investments in early health have been impeded by low levels of economic growth in many developing regions. The work still to be done in achieving health for all is shown by the gap of over thirteen years in life expectancy at birth between industrialized countries and developing countries, a gap that has decreased by only 3.6 years since 1970. While youth may not face as many direct health risks as children and the elderly, by this age they have learned the health practices that will carry them through the rest

of their lives. Thus practices ranging from hygiene and diet to use of medical services and healthful sexual practices are important for further increasing life expectancy in developing countries.

The major causes of death for youth are accidents, homicide, and suicide. These causes of death are largely preventable with appropriate education and mental-health care. In sub–Saharan Africa and other places where prevention efforts are weak, however, HIV/AIDS has become an increasingly important cause of death. The epidemic is fueled by official denial of the disease, reluctance to provide young people with information about sexual health, and low capacity to test and treat those who are infected.

Adolescents everywhere need resources and incentives to learn healthy sexual practices and delay early childbearing. The sexual activity, contraceptive use, and fertility of adolescent girls and, to a lesser extent, boys are areas of adolescent health that have received international research attention due to concern about early childbearing and its contribution to population growth. Adolescent girls are frequently sexually active but have little knowledge of reproduction or contraception and even less access to reproductive-health services. As girls' schooling becomes more widespread and marriage is delayed, premarital, unplanned, and unwanted pregnancies and births increase. Western European countries are among the only ones that consistently provide young people with the skills and information to negotiate their sexual relationships safely and responsibly.

The more parents and societies invest in young people, the greater their productive potential in young adulthood. The timing of their entry into the workforce, marriage, and parenthood reflects these levels of investment. In most developing countries with low levels of compulsory education, young men become economically active in their teens when they leave school. In contrast, adolescent girls in these countries are unlikely to enter the labor force after finishing school, often because female employment is discouraged and marriage and childbearing are encouraged at young ages. In developed countries where young men and women may often stay in school into their early twenties, they begin working in their twenties unless school is combined with part-time employment or apprenticeships. By staying in school longer, young people have more to offer employers when they begin work.

The earlier marriage and parenthood occur, the fewer resources young men and women are likely to have to offer to their children, as the transitions often mark the end of investment in one generation and the beginning of investment in the next. From Lesotho to Luxembourg, over 90 percent of men aged fifteen to nineteen remain single. The proportions of women aged fifteen to nineteen remaining single vary far more across regions and countries. The majority of women typically marry in their late teens in sub–Saharan African countries, the Middle East, and western and southern Asia. In contrast, more than 80 percent of East and Southeast Asian women remain single throughout their teens. More than 90 percent of women in the Caribbean nations remain single at this age, while only 70 to 89 percent of women in Central and South America do so.

The associations between women's early entry into family roles, lower autonomy, social status, and education and higher fertility and poor child outcomes make young women's early marriage and childbearing a cause for concern. Adolescent fertility rates are highest among women in sub–Saharan Africa, ranging from fifty to over 150 births per 1,000 women aged fifteen to nineteen. In other developing regions young women also begin to have children at young ages, although the rates are not as high and are declining in many places. The lowest teen birth rates (zero to twenty-four per 1,000 women aged fifteen to nineteen) occur in Western Europe, East Asia, Canada, and Australia. In these more advanced indus-

trialized countries young women generally attend school or begin working in their teens, and it is unusual to begin having children so young. Among industrialized countries, the United States' exceptionally high teen birth rate is attributed not to greater sexual activity but to young people's limited access to information, sex education, and contraception.

While time spent in school may delay marriage and parenthood by maintaining youth as "children" in their parents' households, it also changes young people's ideas and expectations. Literacy and access to information exposes young adults to a broader range of ideas. Globalization and its implications for markets, trade and the spread of ideas and values powerfully transmits the notion that in youth one should be free of adult responsibilities and develop individual talents and interests. Rapid urbanization in many developing countries erodes traditions that encourage early entry into adult roles and more communal values. In rural societies economic and cultural incentives like dowry or "bridewealth" have typically encouraged parents to arrange children's marriages relatively early, for example, but these incentives are often diminished in urban contexts.

As youth are drawn into urban and global economies, they are better able to adapt and thrive if fortified with good health and education. However, these investments in youth vary within countries as well as between countries. Without substantial economic growth and government programs to redistribute resources to children with fewer parental resources, poverty and inequality in the parents' generation will be transmitted to their children. Inequality in income or consumption is an important indicator of the social inequities that shape the transition to adulthood. The greatest inequalities occur in sub–Saharan Africa, Latin America, and the Caribbean. The most equitable societies are in Europe, particularly Eastern Europe and Scandinavia, where income redistribution policies have reduced inequality.

The characteristics of households themselves and their focus on and capacity for rearing their children also contribute to inequality. Divorce, separation, widowhood, and nonmarital childbearing all increase the chances that children may live with nonbiological parents or in single-parent homes. These varied family structures are sometimes associated with poor health, education, and adjustment outcomes for children, especially in families where workers are distributing support among more people.

Children in households headed by women on their own are more likely to be living in poverty. Reducing adult household earners and caregivers from two to one significantly reduces the income of the household and the children in it and also reduces the time the parent—most often the mother—can devote to caring for children. Around the world, men's roles as husbands and as parents are increasingly separate, and fathers are often absent from their children's households. Female-headed households with dependent children are common in sub–Saharan Africa, Latin America, the United States, and Western European countries.

Another threat to household income is the HIV/AIDS epidemic, which by 2001 had orphaned 13.4 million children under age fifteen globally, 11 million in sub–Saharan Africa. In almost every sub–Saharan African country, over 10 percent of all children are orphans and many other children live with one or more HIV-positive parent. General measures of child health and well-being are eroded by the loss of a child's mother or by fostering. Although extended families have traditionally taken in orphans, the numbers of orphans produced by the HIV/AIDS epidemic are overwhelming the working adults available to support them. As a result, children are increasingly being abandoned or compelled to care for younger siblings and dying parents, losing their chances for schooling and adult nurturing.

The poverty of parental households often drives young people and their parents to great lengths to earn money. In many developing countries youth move from rural to urban areas to earn money to send back to their parents. Migrant children who work as domestic servants are vulnerable to domestic violence and abuse because they are frequently indebted to their employers for the costs of transportation, room and board, and because labor laws rarely protect domestic workers. False promises of jobs and money may lead parents to sell or give away their children, and trafficking is most widespread in Asia. Every year over 2 million children, mostly girls, although the number of boys is increasing, are trafficked and sold for sexual purposes. Trafficking exploits youth in every way, destroying their prospects for education, health, and their present and future well-being.

Inequality as a Brake on Investments in Youth

Providing health care, education, and opportunities to work is critical to promoting the well-being of all youth and fostering their hope for the future. Making this investment in young people is especially difficult for countries with large international debts (e.g., many Latin American countries) and economies in transition (e.g., Eastern Europe and the Commonwealth of Independent States). When the population is growing but the economy is growing very little, as in sub–Saharan Africa and South Asia, the challenges are even greater.

Income *inequality* further reduces the prospects of many youth, but it has increased even in the countries best positioned to reduce it through income redistribution programs. Persistent inequality is one of the dangers for youth of the over-reliance on markets to distribute the public goods of health, education, and opportunities for employment. Recent analyses of the relationship between inequality and development affirm that "gross inequities between people not only are unjust but represent a squandering of human resources and a potential brake on socioeconomic development" (United Nations 1997).

Over the past thirty years, however, the gap between the rich and the poor has widened, both between and within countries. From 1960 to 1993, the gap between average per capita incomes in industrialized and developing countries tripled, and the richest one-fifth of the world's population went from taking 70 percent to taking 85 percent of global income. The gap between the poorest developing countries and other developing nations has disturbingly widened further.

Young people face exceptional conditions today as a result of their absolute and relative numbers. There is little predictable about the future, but one thing we do know is the number of young people coming of age in the next few decades. Their numbers are a direct indication of future demand for schools, health care, and employment training. Their share of the population points to the competition youth will face for public resources. A country's ability to prepare for these youth cohorts depends on its place in the global economy, the attention it gives to planning for the future of its young people, and international assistance.

See also AIDS Advocacy in South Africa; Australia, Youth Activism in; Europe, Comparing Youth Activism in; European Identity and Citizenship; Immigrant Youth in Europe—Turks in Germany; Immigrant Youth in the United States; India, Youth Activism in; Indonesia, Youth Activism in; Nigeria, Youth Activism in; Palestinian *Intifada*; Serbia, Youth Activism in (1990–2000); Soweto Youth Activism (South Africa); State and Youth, The; Statute of the Child and Adolescent (Brazil); Tiananmen Square Massacre (1989); Transnational Identity; Transnational Youth Activism; Turkey, Youth Activism in; United Nations, Youth Activism and; Xenophobia; Zapatista Rebellion (Mexico); Zionist Youth Organizations.

Recommended Reading

Alan Guttmacher Institute (1998). *Into a New World: Young Women's Sexual and Reproductive Lives*. New York: Alan Guttmacher Institute.

Bloom, D. E., and Canning, D. (April 14, 1999). *The Demographic Transition and Economic Growth in the Middle East and North Africa*. Paper presented at the Fourth Annual Conference of the Middle East Institute and the World Bank.

Fussell, E. (2002). "Youth in aging societies." In *The Future of Adolescence: Societal Trends and the Transition to Adulthood in the Twenty-first Century*, edited by J. Mortimer and R. Larson. New York: Cambridge University Press.

Fussell, E., and Greene, M. E. (2002). "Demographic Trends Affecting Youth around the World." In *The World's Youth: Adolescence in Eight Regions of the Globe*, edited by B. B. Brown, R.W. Larson, and T.S. Saraswathi. New York: Cambridge University Press, pp. 21–60.

Jejeebhoy, S. J. (1995). *Women's Education, Autonomy, and Reproductive Behaviour: Experience from Developing Countries*. Oxford: Clarendon Press.

Leete, R. and Alam, I (1999) "Asia's Demographic Miracle: 50 Years of Unprecedented Change," *Asia-Pacific Population Journal*, 14 (4): 9–20.

Lloyd, C. B., and Desai, S. (1992). "Children's Living Arrangements in Developing Countries." *Population Research and Policy Review*, 11: 193–216.

Massey, D. S., Arango, J., Hugo, G., Kouacouci, A., Pellegrino, A., and Taylor, J. E. (1999). *Worlds in Motion: Understanding International Migration at the End of the Millennium*. Oxford: Clarendon Press.

McLanahan, S., and Sandefur, G. (1994). *Growing Up in a Single Parent Home: What Hurts, What Helps*. Boston: Harvard University Press.

Mensch, B. S., Bruce, J., and Greene, M. E. (1998). *The Uncharted Passage: Girls' Adolescence in the Developing World*. New York: The Population Council.

UNAIDS, UNICEF, and USAID (2002). *Children on the Brink 2002: A Joint Report on Orphan Estimates and Program Strategies*. Washington, D.C.: The Synergy Project.

United Nations (1993). "Age Structure Changes in 1950–1990." *Demographic Yearbook Special Issue: Population Aging and the Situation of Elderly Persons*. New York: United Nations.

United Nations Development Program (1999). *Human Development Report*. New York: Oxford University Press.

United Nations Education, Scientific, and Cultural Organization (UNESCO) (1998). *Statistical Yearbook*. New York: United Nations.

Elizabeth Fussell and Margaret E. Greene

Developmental Assets. Over ten years ago Lerner and Miller (1993) predicted that the

1990s would be a decade in which community coalitions would surface and make important contributions to our understanding of community contexts as they influence child and adolescent development. Whitlock and Hamilton (2003) use the term "community youth development" to define the growing number of community-wide, youth-focused initiatives driven by coalitions and alliances that have a rich environmental presence that is independent of youth development programs and organizations. They also identified Search Institute (SI) and its developmental asset framework as a prime model influencing and shaping community youth-development efforts.

There is reason to suspect this interest in collective community action on behalf of the developmental well-being of young people stems in part from disappointment within the helping professions, and among the general public, over the value of more conventional intervention designed to change problematic trends and prevent or reduce the presence of risk factors among children and adolescents. These approaches tend to utilize interventions targeted exclusively at individuals or, at best, discrete collections of individuals within a particular developmental setting such as families or schools. Most fail to take the social determinants of development into account.

Significant changes are occurring in response to many of these concerns. For one thing, within the policy, research, and practice arenas it has become increasingly evident that more strength-based and comprehensive approaches to promoting the healthy development of young people require a deeper understanding community and neighborhood influences. Benson and Pittman (2001) argue that the shift away from deficit-based perceptions of youth problems and related conceptions of youth remediation toward a more strength-based approach to youth development constitutes a paradigm shift that may be seen as a social movement.

Moreover, federal funding has gradually shifted greater service-delivery responsibility to state and local units of government and actively promoted community-level interventions. Finally, numerous foundations have also made community a favored context for improving the well-being of young people.

Over the past decade, SI has synthesized research on the factors leading to healthy development for children and youth. The literature scan and synthesis led to the creation of the "Forty Developmental Assets," which identify "building blocks" of healthy development that help young people grow up healthy, caring, and responsible. The developmental asset framework adopts an ecological perspective as it takes into account and emphasizes all of the primary socialization contexts and processes for youth across the middle- and high-school years. It identifies the multiple community settings from which supports and opportunities for the acquisition of developmental strengths can emerge. Individuals, families, schools, neighborhoods, youth-serving organizations, and religion are all viewed as the prime settings and sources contributing to development. The framework also pays particular attention to interactive and reinforcing developmental processes across community settings. In doing so it articulates the kinds of relationships, social experiences and habitats, and patterns of interaction, norms, and competencies over which a community of people, through its socializing systems, has considerable influence and control.

The developmental asset perspective also embraces the maxim of collective social responsibility for fostering human development. This notion of "everyone's responsibility" is a theme that was reinforced from SI's national investigation of asset-based community initiatives. There is an implied understanding that all members of the community "are in this together" and no one person, sector, or organization can or should try and do it alone. Communities making use of the developmental asset framework to promote community-based human development seek to energize a critical mass of community members and stakeholders, who comprehend that advancing human development is a fundamental investment in youth and their community that can make a real difference in the lives of young people and enhance the common good.

Extensive research conducted by SI for well over a decade has confirmed the significance of developmental assets for young people. Analyses of Search Institute's 1999–2000 aggregate dataset of 217,277 young people in grades six through twelve across the United States demonstrate the relationship between developmental assets and a wide range of developmental milestones.

The most striking and consistent finding of SI's research is that too few youth experience enough of the developmental assets in their daily lives. Young people report having, on average, only nineteen of the forty assets. While there are slight variations across communities and different subgroups of youth, the variation does not detract from the overall lack of young people's exposure to these developmental nutrients. Across hundreds of communities surveyed throughout America, 15 percent of young people report having zero to ten of the forty developmental assets. Another 41 percent indicate that they experience eleven to twenty assets, and 35 percent indicate that they experience twenty-one to thirty of the assets. Only 9 percent experience thirty-one to forty of the developmental assets, a level that we consider to be "asset rich." Overall, the vast majority of young people in the United States surveyed by Search Institute do not experience an adequate level of developmental assets, and a sizeable proportion face the particular challenge of experiencing ten or fewer of these assets.

These findings take on even more importance when it becomes clear that low levels of developmental assets appear to serve as a slightly better predictor of engagement in high-risk behaviors than demographic factors, such as living in poverty and/or being from a single-parent family, which the public and policymakers typically view as putting young people at risk.

The absence of developmental assets among America's youth and an accompanying fragile community foundation and infrastructure for human development constitutes an enormous social challenge and serves as a call for activism around the theme of securing youth health and well-being. And, once communities awaken and decide to take action, the assets define developmental targets worthy of pursuit.

Numerous adults in these asset-based community youth development initiatives see themselves as part of a social movement in which central agenda items entail promoting youth development and youth activism. They assume the mantle of human development activists, who also understand youth have important roles to play in the expression of collective social action. By virtue of their actions these adult champions help young people see and appreciate their own unique qualities and special gifts, rouse young people to identify and fully explore their interests and aspirations, encourage young people to be inquisitive in order to learn and develop, open doors for young people to experience unique opportunities and grow, create relationships with young people that lead to deep impressions and long-lasting impact, and assist young people in building bonds to their communities.

A recent research project conducted by SI with a group of adult activists in Kansas and their counterparts across the country led to adult identification of mentoring, youth leadership development, policy formulation, and the organizational advancement of youth-serving agencies as the ways they see themselves making a difference for young people and helping youth become activists. The following quote illustrates how one adult activist spoke of enhancing youth through the policy arena: "I guided a group of teenagers to become leaders instead of lawbreakers by encouraging them to help change a skateboarding law that they were repeatedly violating. They presented their case to lawmakers and convinced them to change the law. They learned a good lesson on democracy and that older folks do at times listen to teenagers."

Adult activists also credit youth leadership development with making a difference for young people. On that particular issue an activist stated, "I helped and supported a group of youth to start their own after-school homework help program, Feed Your Brain. It is still youth led and is helping over 25 percent of the youth in local middle schools."

As quoted below, other adult activists described similar experiences and efforts to strengthen youth leadership skills:

"As a trainer, mentor, and coach to college students, I develop them into more confident leaders."

"I am currently a director of a community initiative. I have responsibility of six communities with students as the leaders."

"Our organization operates through a lens of youth-adult partnership and collaboration, beginning with youth and adult members of our board of directors; all members of our staff are trained to promote youth-adult teams to participate in our community initiatives; and youth are put in leadership roles."

"I work side by side with young people to model youth-adult partnership practices, treating them as respected colleagues and resources."

These examples show how youth are engaged in active problem solving, and assume leadership responsibilities in constructive activities. The adults did not *do* it for youth. Instead, they facilitated and fostered youth activism. In both cases adults held to the general understanding that youth have to be given opportunities to take charge and make decisions. And, even more importantly, youth must have experiences to actually *practice* leadership and engage in decision-making.

Other data from the SI research project suggested that adult activists believe they impacted and promoted young people's human development by enhancing their self-worth and self-esteem; through improving adult engagement with young people; by diffusing the asset/positive youth development message through publications, presentations, and media; and by strengthening youth programming.

Various expressions of less adult-facilitated—and more independent—youth activism are also evident in these asset-based community youth development initiatives. Youth serve as decision-makers, advocates, planners, councils, funders, evaluators, and administrators. Young people from an asset-oriented community youth development coalition in Traverse City, Michigan, serve on youth advisory councils across a five-county region. These youth make decisions about activities, events, and new strategies. The Healthy Community Initiative of Greater Orlando's Youth Philanthropy program highlights youth serving as funders. In this effort youth were trained in the general grant-making process. They then assessed grant applications and awarded funds to youth-based initiatives. The appeal and benefit of this youth civic engagement activity is that it provides an opportunity for youth to work together and to connect and compliment the knowledge and skills sets each of them brings to recommending and carrying out thoughtful ideas and actions.

Local youth in Lawton, Oklahoma, participate in leadership training where they become teen trainers who go on to teach their peers about social pressures, such as early sexual involvement. When asked why they participated in the leadership training and other activities and what was meant by their comment of "making a difference" in their community, one female youth focus-group participant shared the following:

Making a difference in my community, to me, would be ... by doing what I'm doing to help bring down teenage pregnancy ... because I remember ... when I was in seventh grade there were four girls [who got] pregnant.... They were supposed to graduate with me in two years. So, by doing this, hopefully I can get that rate down, in and making ... a more positive environment for them to grow up in. Or for ... when my thirteen-year-old sister gets in high school, she will know not to do this. She will follow after me or follow after Brooke or follow after Jennifer. And they will see us as a positive role model and want to be more like us, instead of seeing the people that are in the corner having sex or in the corner doing dope, you know, doing whatever. So, basically, trying to make my community a better place for the young people that are growing up in it now ... because of the negative influences that are in my community now, if there weren't people like me ... like all the people who care, then we're just all going to go to heck before too long.

Youth activism also entails advocating for themselves and youth in general. They are aware of the judgmental behavior and stereotypes adults hold toward them, and they are motivated to challenge the public's deficit-based and negative perceptions of youth. One youth illustrated this perception when she noted, "I mean, they [adults] see the word 'teenager,' and they think, 'Oh, my goodness. Nothing but a bunch of rambunctious, rude, obnoxious people.' They don't give us a chance to be ourselves. They don't really realize that there's more to us than loud music and lots of laughter, you know?" Consistent with this youth's view, an Orlando youth-initiative participant shared the following personal experience:

Seniors usually view youth in a very bad eye. In one particular instance, I was driving down the road, and there was an old guy walking down our street. I looked at him and smiled, and he looked at me and he gave me this look like, "What are you doing? You're smiling at me? What is that for?" ... it was very weird to see that perception from that. And then ... that's when it hit me, that these seniors really do view us [youth] as not such good things.

Because youth are typically viewed negatively and as problems, communities often appear less likely to welcome them into their civic forums. Some youth have used the media as a way to combat stereotypes and judgments held against them. A group of youth from a community-based youth development initiative in Portland, Oregon, advocated for more balanced and positive media coverage of youth and stories about youth. The effort by this group of young people led to a partnership with a regional newspaper and the development and contribution to "The Zone." This column focused on positive youth stories, particularly ways in which youth are positively contributing to their communities. This is a compelling example of how young people have countered adults' negative perceptions of youth and how youth have a desire to strengthen their communities. As one youth put it, "I think a lot of people in the community have a false idea of like teenagers and like what we do. So like being on the board and us representing teenagers and youth can just help us get a better image I guess."

Youth participants in a SI research project about these asset-based community youth development initiatives consistently spoke to the need for leadership roles and opportunities in which they were offered and given the opportunity to be in positions of leadership. Youth went on to describe other activist situations, captured under the theme of *youth efficacy*. This entails youth describing the value of feeling active or involved in decision-making about their lives and in their communities. They spoke positively about participating in and having influence over decisions concerning themselves and their communities.

As youth become activists in the civic realm and manifest leadership, they have the opportunity to learn about their obligations and positive contributions they can make to the betterment of their immediate communities and the larger society. The ultimate appeal and benefit of youth activism is that it provides an opportunity for youth to work together and to connect and compliment the knowledge and skills sets each of them brings to recommending and carrying out thoughtful actions and ideas.

Cumulatively these efforts all serve as a testament to the importance of developing the leadership capacity of youth around civic engagement. Then, youth activists are not only manifesting successful development but also becoming part of a social movement dedicated to bringing about social change.

See also Civil Society and Positive Youth Development; Moral Development; National and Community Service; Positive Youth Development, Programs Promoting.

Recommended Reading

Benson, P. L. (1997). *All Kids Are Our Kids: What Communities Must Do to Raise Caring and Responsible Children and Adolescents.* San Francisco: Jossey-Bass.

Brooks-Gunn, J., Duncan, G. J., and Aber, J. L., eds. (1997). *Neighborhood Poverty: Context and Consequences for Children*, Vol. 1. New York: Russell Sage Foundation.

Burt, M. R., Resnick, G., and Novick, E. R., eds. (1998). *Building Supportive Communities for At-Risk Adolescents: It Takes More Than Services.* Washington, D.C.: American Psychological Association.

Finnegan, W. (1999). *Cold New World: Growing Up in a Harder Country.* New York: Modern Library.

Gold, S., and Ellwood, D. (1994). *Spending and Revenue for Children's Programs.* Washington, D.C.: The Finance Report.

National Research Council and Institute of Medicine (2000). *From Neurons to Neighborhoods: The Science of Early Child Development.* Washington, D.C.: National Academy Press.

National Research Council and Institute of Medicine (2001). *Community Programs to Promote Youth Development.* Washington, D.C.: National Academy Press.

Scales, P. C., and Leffert, N. (1999). *Developmental Assets: A Synthesis of the Scientific Research on Adolescent Development.* Minneapolis, MN: Search Institute.

Marc Mannes and Shenita Lewis

Digital Divide. The "digital divide" is the foremost equity issue of the digital age. This divide may be defined as the gap between those persons or groups of people who have the opportunity for regular access to the Internet and people who have irregular or no opportunity to access the Internet. In fact there are numerous observable divides. When talking about the Internet,

there are two primary types of divides: (a) the divide between those who have access to the Internet (i.e., infrastructure, hardware, and software) and those who do not; and (b) the divide between those who have the relevant skills to use the Internet effectively and those who do not. Each kind of digital divide, whether it is based upon age, class, disability, gender, geography, or race, is impacted in different ways by these two types of divides.

The former type of divide is more recognized in the United States and international policy circles, especially in the field of education. For example, most of the focus upon the "digital divide" in U.S. education policy has been the creation of the federal "e-rate plan," a system of regulations that provides schools and other public institutions with access to the Internet at a cost less than what the marketplace demands. The majority of attention has been placed on access to the Internet without assuring that different groups of people have the skills necessary to access the Internet. Within each type of divide there are numerous distinct kinds.

Social equity is central to the digital divide. There is always the question of how fair it is that some people do not have access to or can not access the Internet because they lack the necessary skills. There are a variety of individual and social dimensions to the digital divide. How many times have you been in class or work situations where the teacher or employer took it for granted that everyone in the class had similar access to the Internet, software applications, or the knowledge of how to use the Internet? Many individuals in fact do not have the knowledge or access necessary to take advantage of the full resources available on the Internet, thus precluding them from full participation in our digital age. On this deeply personal level, many people struggle to take advantage of the full benefits of the digital age.

Besides this personal level, the digital divide also has a social dimension. Many leaders in the United States and abroad claim that computers and the Internet are necessary for the development of the economy and society. The different kinds of access and skills that various groups of people have concerning the Internet means that not all groups in society are ready or able to take advantage of the digital age. Increasingly, government and business resources and services are *only* available on the Internet. Furthermore, many cultural activities are only present through the use of digital technology. If distinct groups of people lack the skills and resources to access the Internet, then they are excluded from that which is becoming the norm of democratic social participation in the digital age. Since the policies of the United States and other countries do not guarantee universal service or education about the Internet, this medium of communication is viewed by many as exclusive.

Various groups of people that do not have access to the Internet or the relevant skills to exploit the Internet represent the distinct kinds of divides. These include the divides based on age, class, disability, gender, geography, and race. When talking about age, it seems at times that the Internet is primarily geared toward the young or those who grew up developing their computer skills. The elderly, who grew up and lived their lives in a distinct technological age, represent a group of individuals who have trouble finding the resources or skills to access the Internet. Even many baby-boomers, whose generation was highlighted by the advent of the computer, seem lost or find it difficult to gain the computer skills necessary to access the Internet. Furthermore, these older age-groups are no longer enrolled in the formal education system, which is the normal way in which people gain computer skills. This divide based on age calls out for informal education remedies that ensure lifelong learning of essential skills.

Besides the digital divide based on age, there is another set of skills and access issues based on one's socioeconomic background. The access issue is relatively easy to see. On both the national and international levels, the poorer classes generally do not have the resources to buy computers or acquire dial-up or broadband access to the Internet. Yet the skills issue seems against common sense. The main way in which people learn about the Internet is either on the job or in schools. In schools at least there should be equal access since all social classes attend schools where computers are used. However, children from more privileged families typically have access to computers at home *and* at school. They also may have had access as preschoolers. And their parents may be more familiar with computers and the academic advantages they offer.

A third group in need of Internet-related skills and resources are the disabled. Over the past decade, there have been tremendous leaps in adaptive and assistive technology that allows persons with disabilities to better manage their disabilities and gain a better life. Increasingly this computer technology is enabled or enhanced through access to the Internet. Yet these advances all come at a tremendous personal and social price. The cost of this technology is prohibitive for many people whose resources often barely cover daily care and medical treatment. This is unfortunate since the technology itself can be enabling. Besides assistive technology, access to the Internet offers networking capacity that allows disabled individuals to achieve a sense of community while struggling with conditions that often isolate them. This networking capacity is more than a social tool. Disabled individuals are using the Internet to enhance their careers and carve a position for themselves in society. This capacity further aids in the movement for self-advocacy and political activism for the disabled to fight for their rights, including the right of access to advanced technology and full participation in society.

Gender also plays a role in the digital divide, particularly in terms of use of technology. The typical first-wave computer user—the so-called "techie"—is a young male who has gained his knowledge through habitual use of the computer. Many girls have either not been trained or exposed to the benefits of digital technology in their lives. Although, notably, this divide has diminished over the past few years. One way to ensure that this divide closes is to make sure that the actual information available on the Internet keeps the female audience in mind. This may help increase their interest and exposure to the Internet, defying typical stereotypes about whether males or females are more capable of exploring and exploiting this medium.

The digital divide can be a matter of geography, that is, where an individual lives can impact his or her access. Compared with other regions such as cities and suburbs, rural areas of the developed world and the entire developing world stand to benefit the most from the networking capacity of the Internet. For these underdeveloped regions to build their local economies, it is necessary for them to achieve access to the wider world as well as to network with other small communities in their region. But there are infrastructural costs associated with introducing this technology. It would be very expensive to connect everyone in the United States to the Internet using traditional dial-up means. Access using traditional dial-up for the most distant potential users to the communications backbone in the United States would cost approximately $5,000 per user—a total cost of several billion dollars.

Nonetheless, there are far less costly alternatives for connecting people in distant areas. As computer and digital technology evolve, people in underdeveloped regions have the possibility to leapfrog generations of technology and achieve access through either broadband connections or satellite technology. Furthermore, many rural areas are crossed by the communication backbone infrastructure leading to more populated destinations. If there was a way to aggregate the demands of these small communities, which entails that all communications networks

are joined together, this increased demand would promote the whole region's access. Thus, more private users would have access to Internet resources. Informal avenues of education are increasingly sponsored by community activism that aggregates the resources of the community in order to spread access to the various technologies.

There is also another way to harness community resources so as to increase access to the Internet. Through the creation of "community-access centers" (CACs) that provide instruction in and access to computers and the Internet, the community has the dynamic opportunity to provide equal access to all educational consumers. CACs in particular provide an important resource for students after the normal school hours. CACs can be situated in a school after hours, a public library, a government office, another public institution, or even on a commercial basis in cyber-cafés. CACs are a short-term solution that grants the opportunity for the aggregation of community resources to achieve equal access to the different educational technologies.

Finally, race is a category that has important implications for the digital divide. For example, according to the National Telecommunications Infrastructure Agency's *Falling through the Net* report (2002), rural black households have the lowest level of access of any group. The digital divide stretches to the inner city, where large populations of minorities live. Even though the residents of inner cities are surrounded by communication infrastructure, many people are still struggling to afford a computer, let alone an Internet connection. One method that has proven successful in many regions to remedy this situation, especially in minority areas, is the development of community-access centers. These centers not only present the opportunity to gather users in one place and organize the social resources to provide access, they offer a place where users can gain the necessary skills to use the Internet.

What direction are we heading in a digital society that is not inclusive? One hundred years ago, numerous people did not have the means or the wherewithal to access the telephone network. Many people were simply scared of the "talking machine." Following the government commitment to universal service, people began to realize that telephones are necessary for modern life. This perceived necessity is the reason why our society pays for universal telephone service—it is a social as well as an economic good. Increasingly, computers are achieving the same status, yet many government officials and business leaders are reluctant to invest, or provide the regulations, for the establishment of universal Internet service. Furthermore, this way of communication needs methods of universal education to reach out to all segments of society. These struggles for universal service and education are the only means through which socially conscious individuals may ensure that the digital divide does not continue over the long term. The social space that is created by the digital media should promote as much democratic participation as the norms of the actual society that created it.

See also Diversity Education; Generational Conflict; New Media; Poverty, Welfare Reform, and Adolescents; Racial and Ethnic Inequality; School Engagement; School Influences and Civic Engagement; Social Justice.

Recommended Reading

Ansell, S., and Park, J. (2003). "Technology Counts 2003: Tracking Tech Trends." *Education Week*, 22 (36): 43–44.

Gillet, S. E. (2000). "Universal Service: Defining the Policy Goal in the Age of the Internet." *The Information Society*, 16: 13–21.

Grimes, S. (2000). "Rural Areas in the Information Society: Diminishing Distance or Increasing Learning Capacity?" *Journal of Rural Studies*, 16: 13–21.

Haddad W., and Draxler, A. (2002). "ICT for Education: Potential and Potency." In *Technologies for Education*, edited by W. Haddad and A. Draxler. Paris: UNESCO, pp. 28–41.

Inglis, A., Joosten, V., and Ling, P. (2002). *Delivering Digitally: Managing the Transition to the Knowledge Media*. London: Kogan Page.

Kenny, C. (2001). "Prioritizing Countries for Assistance to Overcome the 'Digital Divide.'" *Communication and Strategies*, 41: 17–36.

Organization of Economic Cooperation and Development (2001). *Information and Communication Technologies and Development: Territorial Economy*. Paris: Organization of Economic Cooperation and Development.

U.S. Department of Commerce (November 1999). *Falling through the Net: Defining the Digital Divide*. Available at http://www.ntia.doc.gov/ntiahome/fttn99/FTTN.pdf.

U.S. Department of Commerce (October 2000). *Falling through the Net: Defining the Digital Divide*. Available at http://search.ntia.doc.gov/pdf/fttn00.pdf.

Robin L. Clausen

Diversity Education. The global market in which American corporations do business has become highly competitive. The demographic makeup of the U.S. population is changing dramatically. More and more individuals are choosing to celebrate their differences instead of compromising their uniqueness to "fit into" the mainstream culture. These are three important reasons why the topic of diversity education has become the center of much attention in the political, educational, and business arenas of our nation.

Since the 1980s, Fortune 500 corporations, government agencies at all levels, and large and small nonprofit organizations have all been doing "diversity work." Today, units on diversity are being added to elementary and secondary school curricula, and courses that focus on diversity are being offered—and required—on many college campuses.

Today's youth are more likely to face the challenges of interacting and working with people different from themselves than did their parents and grandparents. The ability to relate well to all types of people in the workplace is a leadership skill that is becoming increasingly important. Understanding, accepting, and valuing diverse backgrounds can help young

Like this group of high-school friends posing in front of their lockers, the American student population is becoming increasingly diverse. *Courtesy of Skjold Photographs.*

people thrive in an increasingly global environment.

Simply stated, diversity means differences. Human diversity means differences among people. It is all of us in our rich and infinite variety. One author defines diversity as "the mosaic of people who bring a variety of backgrounds, styles, perspectives, values, and beliefs as assets to the groups and organizations with which they interact" and suggests that "valuing diversity is a celebration of our humanity, of our individual uniqueness, as well as our group commonality" (Rasmussen 1996). People differ from one another in many ways. These differences can be referred to as dimensions of diversity. The major dimensions can be categorized as primary and secondary. The primary dimensions are unalterable and have extremely powerful effects on our lives. Most scholars agree

that age, race, ethnicity, gender, physical and mental ability, and sexual orientation are primary dimensions of diversity. The secondary dimensions are important in shaping us, but we have some measure of control over them. Secondary dimensions include, among others, education, income, work background, geographic location, religious beliefs, marital status, parental status, and military experience. Although differences come to mind when we think about diversity, an equally important aspect of diversity education is a focus on commonalities among people. While people differ from one another in many aspects, they are also like others in many ways. Diversity education encourages people to appreciate both similarities and differences between people.

The research related to youth attitudes toward diversity is fairly limited. A number of studies, however, have found that many high-school students hold negative images of racial and ethnic minorities, and many have sexist attitudes. In addition, members of most ethnic and racial groups hold at least some prejudicial attitudes and beliefs about the members of other groups. Even students who consider themselves free of prejudice frequently recognize their hidden biases and animosities when issues of sexual orientation arise. Studies have found that youth, aged twenty-one or younger, are the most common perpetrators of violence against gays and lesbians, responsible for 50 percent of all reported incidents.

Young people are often also the victims of prejudice and hate crimes related to sexual orientation. In a national survey of fifteen- to twenty-four-year-old lesbian, gay, and bisexual youth, 80 percent had been victims of verbal insults; 44 percent had received threats of attack; 30 percent had been chased or followed; 17 percent were victims of physical attack; and 10 percent had been assaulted with a weapon.

Race is another dimension of diversity that can impact the type of interactions that youth may or may not have with others.

The U.S. Census Bureau predicts that between the years of 1995 and 2025, the population of the United States will increase by 72 million. By the end of this thirty year period, the Asian population is expected to have doubled. The African American population is expected to comprise 16.5 percent of the new growth; the Hispanic/Latino population is expected to comprise 44 percent of the new growth, and the white population is expected to decline by 9 percent.

Children begin to notice differences in race around the age of three. Our attitudes and opinions about race are formed, shaped, and, many times, distorted consciously and unconsciously by our families, friends, communities, and the images that we see and do not see during our growing years. While many social scientists believe that racial tensions and conflict have worsened over the past several years, others argue that race relations have improved dramatically. Public figures such as Colin Powell, Oprah Winfrey, and Tiger Woods are idolized by all.

Yet a look at trends in the racial segregation of communities and schools suggests that the opportunity for youth to interact with peers from different racial and ethnic backgrounds is becoming more challenging. Almost fifty years after the U.S. Supreme Court outlawed segregation in schools, minority students are more likely to attend classes in racial isolation. This is due, in large part, to the fact that housing is increasingly segregated by how expensive it is. Since ethnic minority families are typically less able to afford middle- or upper-income housing, they are more likely to be concentrated in poorer neighborhoods. And the schools that draw from those neighborhoods have a student body composed largely of ethnic minorities. Additionally, some middle-class neighborhoods become segregated when people of color move in and whites move out of the neighborhood. This pattern has been termed "white flight."

Nationwide, nearly 70 percent of African American students and 75 percent of Latino students attend predominantly minority schools, according to data collected in 1997 for the Civil Rights Project at Harvard University. A high percentage of African American and Latino students are in schools where 90 percent or more of their classmates are minorities, while the typical white student is enrolled in a school where more than 80 percent of his or her classmates also are white. The need for diversity education is even greater when youth have fewer opportunities to meet others who are different from them.

Income is a secondary dimension of diversity that affects the opportunities of young people. Today, there is a growing gap between the rich and the poor in this country. The middle class is shrinking. More than 38 million Americans live below the poverty line. Of these poor, the largest groups are women and their children. Being poor can be particularly difficult for youth in a society where what you have, to a large degree, defines who you are. Youth are bombarded with messages that suggest that higher-income people are "normal" Americans, while those with lesser incomes have less value. Such messages come from the media, from the expectations of teachers and other influential adults, and from peers in school and social groups.

Too often those with more privileged status assume the myth that most poor people have brought this situation onto themselves. It is assumed they are poor because they haven't worked hard enough. The truth is that many poor people are hardworking men and women. They are the chambermaids in hotels; the adults who cook in fast-food restaurants; the cafeteria workers in school lunchrooms; and the nurse's aides who make sure patients have clean rooms and clean bodies. For those people, poverty is not a result of a lack of motivation or an unwillingness to work hard. It is a result of the low wages many working people are paid.

Without the money to purchase the symbols of status that others enjoy, youth from poor families find themselves in situations where they may be joked about, put down, ridiculed, or ignored by more privileged peers. Poorer youth may go to great lengths and sacrifices to acquire the "in" brand of running shoes or jeans in order to feel a positive identity and sense of belonging.

The effects of classism (i.e., the belief that people with higher incomes or social status are better than those with lower incomes) can have long-term impacts on both the poor and the more privileged. Youth from low-income families may hear and internalize messages that they are inferior and that may translate into hostility toward the more privileged. Feelings of inadequacy and resentment may persist into adulthood. Middle- and higher-income youth may develop a false sense of superiority.

One of the biggest reasons for the increase in diversity in the United States is immigration. While the United States–born population grew by nearly 33 million in the 1990s, the foreign-born population increased by 11 million during that same period. Between 1991 and 2000, an average of 900,000 foreigners were admitted as legal immigrants to this country each year. American classrooms are experiencing a large influx of immigrant students. In addition to diversity in race and cultural backgrounds and customs, many immigrants who enter the country speak a language other than English as their first language. A survey of youth attitudes toward diversity found that while most youth believed that the ability to speak another language is a valuable skill, about one-third of responders said they get irritated when around people who do not speak English.

Family structure is an additional dimension of diversity affecting youth. Today, the families in which many youth grow up are anything but traditional. The traditional family with father as breadwinner and mother as full-time homemaker and child-care provider is becoming increasingly unrepresentative of families in this country. Today, youth are reared in dual-earner families, single-parent families (both single mothers and single fathers), stepfamilies,

blended families, adoptive families (both two-parent and single), lesbian and gay families (two moms or two dads), biracial and multiracial families, and in families where grandparents have assumed the role of parents. While attitudes toward family structures vary, with some considered "appropriate" and others considered "deviant," it is important to remember that a family, whatever the makeup, is about love and caring for its members.

Gender is an important dimension of diversity. The woman's liberation movement of the 1960s and 1970s and legislation such as Title IX of the 1972 Education Amendments of the Elementary and Secondary Education Act of 1965 and the Women's Educational Equality Act of 1994 had a positive impact on the opportunities for women in the school setting. However, the types of courses and careers boys and girls are encouraged to consider and the opportunities for participation in sports are still influenced by sex-role stereotyping. And once young men and women enter the workplace, sexual harassment, discrimination, and the "glass ceiling" continue to be challenges related to gender.

Many other diversity-related issues confront youth. As the median age of Americans continues to get older, youth will need to relate effectively with a growing senior population. As the religious diversity of this country continues to grow, there will be a need for greater religious tolerance As the inclusive-education movement continues, a greater number of students with physical and mental disabilities and challenges will be placed in the regular education classroom and educated alongside their peers without disabilities. Acceptance of differences will become increasingly important.

In response to the growing diversity in our country, there is a push by advocates of social justice for multicultural education. One author defines multicultural education as "an approach to teaching and learning that is based upon democratic values and beliefs and that affirms cultural pluralism within culturally diverse societies in an interdependent world.... Multicultural education argues that the primary goal of public education is to foster the intellectual, social, and personal development of *all* students to their highest potential" (Bennett 2003, 14). While the definitions of multicultural education vary somewhat, most include the following dimensions: use of equitable pedagogy, the rethinking of the curriculum from multiple perspectives, increasing one's cultural awareness and competence to effectively function in cross-cultural interactions, and the commitment to combat prejudice and discrimination in all its forms.

American institutions have recognized the need for diversity-education programs that promote greater understanding among our diverse cultures in a variety of settings. Courses in elementary and secondary schools are being revised to consider subject matter from multiple perspectives. Not only, for example, is history of the westward movement by early American pioneers being considered from the viewpoint of the pioneers, it is also being considered from the viewpoint of Native Americans who were also impacted by this movement. A growing number of Web sites are designed to assist educators with curricula, activities, and suggestions for infusing diversity into the educational program.

Students at both the secondary and college levels have opportunities to participate in study-abroad and exchange programs that provide students a chance to experience a different culture. At the college and university level, an increasing number of diversity-related courses and programs are being offered. Majors are available in women's studies, African and African American studies, Latino studies, East Asian studies, and Jewish studies, for example. Many colleges and universities support multicultural/diversity centers and commissions that offer workshops, seminars, guest presentations, and multicultural activities that encourage students to explore diverse cultures, groups, and ways of thinking.

Businesses, corporations, and nonprofit organizations consider the cost of diversity training a wise investment of their resources. Workshops and training programs focus on various diversity-focused topics such as recruiting and hiring diverse employees, sexual harassment, laws related to access and disability issues, religion in the workplace, issues related to sexual orientation, ageism, and conflict resolution.

Diversity education does not have to depend on a formal program. Create your own independent-study project. Opportunities abound. Volunteer to work at a soup kitchen, visit a church of a religion different than your own, volunteer your time at a nursing home, shop in a community where the dominant language spoken is not your language, invite someone you know from a different culture to your home for dinner and ask them to talk about their culture. Take advantage of opportunities to increase your diversity education.

See also Character Education; Citizenship Education Policies in the States; Civic Engagement in Diverse Youth; Civic Virtue; Democratic Education; Environmental Education (EE); IEA Civic Education Study; Just Community High Schools and Youth Activism; National Alliance for Civic Education (NACE); Prosocial Behaviors; School Engagement; School Influences and Civic Engagement.

Recommended Reading

Banks, J., and Banks, C. A. M., eds. (2001). *Handbook of Research on Multicultural Education*. San Francisco: Jossey-Bass.

Bennett, C. I. (2003). *Comprehensive Multicultural Education: Theory and Practice*. 5th ed. Boston: Pearson Education.

Berril, K. T. (1990). "Anti-Gay Violence and Victimization in the United States: An Overview." *Journal of Interpersonal Violence*, 5 (3): 274–294.

Colvin, R. L. (June 12, 1999). "Racial Segregation Growing in Public Schools, Study Finds." *San Francisco Chronicle*, p. A-3.

Crawley-Long, K. (1995). "Resources for Teaching White Students about Issues of Race." *The Clearing House*, 68 (3): 134–137.

Erickson, J. B., Hasbrouck, S., and Hogan, D. (1995). "Indiana Youth Poll: Youth Views of Racism, Sexism, and Poverty." ERIC Document Reproduction Service No. ED 386612.

Gardenswartz, L., and Rowe, A. (1993). *Managing Diversity: A Complete Desk Reference and Planning Guide.* New York: Irwin Professional Publishing.

Hershberger, S. L., and D'Augelli, A. R. (1995). "The Impact on the Mental Health and Suicidality of Lesbian, Gay, and Bisexual Youths." *Developmental Psychology*, 31: 65–74.

Ingram, P. (1997). "Attitudes of Pennsylvania Governor's School Scholars toward Diversity." *NACTA Journal*, 41 (4): 11–17.

Orfield, G. (2001). *Schools More Separate: Consequences of a Decade of Resegregation.* Cambridge, MA: The Civil Rights Project, Harvard University.

Polakow-Suranky, S., and Ulaby, N. (1990). "Students Take Action to Combat Racism." *Phi Delta Kappan* 71 (8): 601–606.

Rasmussen, T. (1996). *The ASTD Trainer's Sourcebook: Diversity.* New York: McGraw-Hill.

Patreese Ingram

E

Earth Force. Earth Force develops middle-school resources that are equal parts service learning, environmental education, and civic education. Earth Force projects are designed to deliberately promote civic engagement, community involvement, lasting change, and youth voice. Earth Force projects blend these elements into a form of service learning that prepares middle-school students to successfully participate in the civic life of their communities. Below are three examples of how the Earth Force community problem-solving process guided school group advocacy projects.

Tired of seeing blight every day, a sixth-grade class in inner-city Charleston, South Carolina, decided to do something about the run-down houses and abandoned lots around their school. The students were not content to temporarily clean up the area and ended up assuming a leadership role in the city's long-term effort to revitalize its neighborhoods. They helped transform their neighborhood by sharing data and working with the city council, the mayor, and other city officials. Eventually, they were tapped to be liaisons between the city and neighborhood residents, a role that included hosting a community forum to examine different revitalization plans. Students have not only seen tangible improvements in the neighborhood, they have gained the confidence and skills needed to tackle future problems that confront them.

Middle-school science students in Rochester Hills, Michigan, were alarmed to find high levels of sediment in the Clinton River after testing the river's water quality. Their teacher encouraged them to observe local land uses and to discover what was causing the sediment problem. The group discovered that a builder had cleared a lot without using the proper silt fencing. They researched state and local laws and found that the builder was violating the law without facing any consequences. After an unsatisfactory meeting with the builder, the students secured a stop-work order covering the entire site until the proper silt fencing was erected.

Seventh-grade students in Denver, Colorado, knew their tap water had an unpleasant taste. As their teacher helped them test the tap water in the school and in their homes, the group discovered alarmingly high lead levels in many homes near the school. They worried less about the water's taste once they learned about the effects of lead in drinking water. The students thought at first that Denver Water must be responsible for the high lead levels, but they found the culprit to be older pipes, which are the responsibility of the homeowners. Rather than try to change or enforce a policy, the Denver students decided to educate local residents about the lead problem and about low-cost filters that would remove most of the lead.

The core community problem-solving process at the heart of all Earth Force programs consists of six steps. Earth Force students begin a project by conducting an inventory of the environmental conditions in their community. They define boundaries, look for problems, and identify assets. They then work with their teacher to develop criteria for selecting a problem to address, apply those criteria, and choose a problem. Next, they conduct thorough research on the policies, practices, and

A student from West Ashley High School talks to a local TV station about student efforts to protect natural diversity through an Earth Force project. Lowcountry Earth Force worked with teachers to coordinate a policy and practice research symposium, which would give students in different classes the opportunity to come together and meet with community partners to share project ideas with one another. The P.O.N.D. (Protecting Our Natural Diversity) Symposium brought together more than 130 students and nine community experts to discuss plans for Earth Force projects. *Courtesy of Earth Force.*

leaders that affect their problem. The goal of this step is to steer projects toward effecting a long-term change in people's behavior, either through educating the public or advocating policy outcomes. Students then examine options for changing policies or practices and select a strategy based on criteria they help develop. They make this choice only after hearing the vast array of views in the community about how best to solve the problem. Then students take civic action to try to change policies or practices. At a minimum, this usually requires them to identify audiences, customize messages, build alliances, and engage other citizens. Finally, students look back and ahead, reflecting on their successes and challenges and determining how citizen involvement can continue to affect their issue.

The Earth Force process is built on the 1978 Basic Citizenship Competencies Project, written by Richard Remy of Ohio State University and Mary Jane Turner of the Social Science Education Consortium. Remy's and Turner's seven essential citizenship skills are listed below along with a description of what Earth Force students do to practice those skills.

Acquiring and using information. Students gather, organize, and evaluate information from numerous conflicting sources.

Assessing involvement. Students discuss the consequences of personal and group activity (and apathy) in the public sphere.

Making decisions. Students analyze values, goals, and consequences for various alternatives, such as deciding the geographic limits of their community.

Making judgments. Students develop, apply, and assess criteria underlying personal and group choices, such as which problem to select.

Communicating. Students develop, present, and support views on public issues.

Earth Force Logo. *Courtesy of Earth Force.*

Cooperating. Students interact with others using democratic principles.

Promoting interests. Students advocate specific changes in policies or practices.

These skills are best learned through real-world practice, which also provides Earth Force students with a lesson in how democracy works. They may learn that real power resides outside the formal political structure. They may identify which offices and levels of government are open and accessible. They may also find out that being well-informed earns them respect from officeholders, which enables them to advocate for policy change rather than to be props in a pro forma photo op. Finally, they may begin to identify where self-interest and public interest intersect, that is, they can see that protecting natural resources or the health of the public is in their own self-interest.

The quality of an Earth Force project depends on skilled teachers as much as on the curriculum. Youth voice permeates the Earth Force process, so teachers are trained to let students direct the process free of pressure to pursue an adult's agenda. Teachers are also trained to explicitly incorporate civic skills such as gathering information, group problem solving, or public speaking into Earth Force projects; students do not gain civic skills merely as a result of doing projects. Finally, teacher reflection is encouraged through regular Earth Force teacher meetings led by Earth Force staff mem-

bers in the communities where Earth Force operates.

Core Elements of Civic Service Learning

Service learning is an increasingly common practice in schools and research continues to show that it is an effective teaching method. Yet research also suggests that student gains are temporary unless service-learning projects have some duration and feature extensive student voice. Short or episodic projects and those that address adult-defined needs seem to have little lasting effect on student growth. At the core of the Earth Force process are three elements that are critical in engaging youth in authentic experiential education.

Projects must transcend short-term efforts, such as park cleanups, and engage youth to be active leaders in creating lasting community change by addressing the policies and practices at the core of a problem.

The sixth-grade students of Morey Middle School in Troutdale, Oregon, are a great example of how to clean a park in a lasting way through civic action. They were able to restore a run-down park while addressing the issue of animal habitat loss. They helped create a new landscape design and planted 700 new plants around the park's pond to encourage wildlife to return to the area. More importantly, the students made presentations to other schools, the school board, and city council, encouraging them to invest money and time in keeping the park clean.

Action plans must be based on balanced research that the students conduct early in the process. Understanding an issue from a variety of perspectives gives youth credibility and helps them become agents of effective and lasting change.

In Charleston, South Carolina, a group of young people from Springfield Elementary School wanted to do something about the declining swordfish population. Polite chuckles could be heard when the "cute kids" started to present their case at a public hearing held by the National Marine Fisheries Service (NMFS). When the students made an effective presentation based on balanced and thorough research, however, the audience began to see the young people as civic contributors, not just "cute kids." The students had talked to local and national environmental organizations as well as to the people who fish and process swordfish. They made the case that the current regulations allowing fishing practices such as long-lining are not sustainable in the long run. These same students went on to identify elementary schools near other NMFS hearings across the country and wrote to the schools to explain the importance of changing swordfish policies. They also participated in a local press conference about the issue and were invited to Washington, D.C., to participate in a press conference and to speak to their congressional delegation. One year later, the students celebrated progress toward their main goal as the coast from the border of the Carolinas to the Florida Keys was closed to all long-lining.

The process must be truly youth-led with youth choosing the issue and creating a plan of action. The goal is to teach them how to make policy judgments for themselves, not to follow anyone else's agenda.

In Denver, students at Place Middle School wanted to assess the health of the stream that runs next to their school. Their focus changed when the students discovered that several of their classmates in wheelchairs could not reach the riverbank. The students successfully worked with local officials to make the riverbank accessible to people with physical disabilities. Ramps have now been installed to provide access to a paved riverside trail for wheelchair users.

Results

The Center for Youth and Communities (CYC) at Brandeis University has conducted the Earth Force evaluation since 1997. There are two overall purposes for the evaluation: to improve organizational operations and to determine the impact of the program on educators and students. Student and educator surveys indicate that taking part in Earth Force enhances students' civic skills, attitudes, and knowledge. They learn to identify local environmental issues, collaborate, conduct research, and express their views. They also develop increased confidence, efficacy, belief in the value of long-term solutions to environmental problems, and understanding of diverse viewpoints.

Understanding how educators respond to the program is crucial to Earth Force. Although 58 percent of surveyed teachers say that leading projects increases their workload, 97 percent say they would strongly recommend the program to colleagues. Nearly 94 percent call the support they receive from Earth Force staff members good or excellent.

The educator surveys measure the program's impact on educators as well as on their students. Participating in Earth Force increases teachers' levels of environmental knowledge, their commitment to improving the environment, and their emphasis on environmental issues in their teaching. It also makes educators more aware of resources in the community that can be used to improve their teaching and increases their use of student-led projects in the classroom. Finally, educators say Earth Force increases their satisfaction with teaching, their professional confidence, and their belief in the ability of young people to make a difference in the community. The entire evaluation report can be found at www.earthforce.org.

Conclusion

As the institution in which students spend significant time, schools should help young people become active community problem-solvers. Experiences that carefully combine environmental education and service learning can develop students' civic competencies and convince them that core course content can be put to good use. Equally important, students learn that their efforts can improve community conditions, and that apathy has consequences as well.

To Get Involved

Earth Force reaches 39,000 young people each year in seventeen states and is always looking to expand into new areas. Materials and educator support are delivered through field offices and partner organizations, which are listed at http://www.earthforce.org. Groups interested in joining the network of partners should contact Earth Force at earthforce@earthforce.org.

See also Advocacy; Civic Environmentalism; Environmental Education (EE); Positive Youth Development, Programs Promoting; School Influences and Civic Engagement; Sustainability; Youth-Led Action Research, Evaluation, and Planning.

Recommended Reading

Bransford, J., Brown, A. L., and Cocking, R. R. (2000). "How People Learn: Brain, Mind, Experience, and School." Expanded ed. Washington, D.C.: National Academies Press.
Center for Information and Research on Civic Learning and Engagement (CIRCLE). See Web site at http://www.civicyouth.org.
Education Commission of the States. See Web site at http://www.ecs.org/clearinghouse.
National Service-Learning Clearinghouse. See Web site at http://www.servicelearning.org.

Additional Web Sites

Three organizations that offer programs similar to Earth Force are Public Achievement, the Constitutional Rights Foundation, and Kids Consortium. Some provide free lessons and newsletters on their Web sites, which are provided below:
Public Achievement: http://publicachievement.org
Constitutional Rights Foundation: http://www.crf-usa.org
Kids Consortium: http://www.kidsconsortium.org

Scott Richardson

Eastern Europe, Youth and Citizenship in.

In postcommunist Eastern Europe, the citizenship status of young people has been transformed. The space for activism and other forms of civic participation has increased drastically. At the same time, youth livelihoods in the present and future are less secure under current economic and political conditions.

The roots of citizenship in Eastern Europe can be traced to the liberation movements against the great empires in the region in the nineteenth century: Turkish, Russian, and Austro-Hungarian. Unlike the western part of the continent, Eastern Europe experienced the simultaneous formation of independent nation-states and of state welfare systems in the late nineteenth and early twentieth century. Hence, the notion of citizenship was both strongly linked to the responsibilities of defending the state and its borders and to an active understanding of citizens' participation in one's country's development, rather than as a juridical status under state sovereignty and a passive endowment of rights.

Under the Communist regimes in the region in the second half of the twentieth century, youth were officially proclaimed to be the builders of the "bright Communist future." But rather than citizenship and rights, the official ideology stressed that youth's most significant mission was in the construction of Communism. A strong emphasis was placed on obligatory military service for men for a set period of time (two or three years in different countries) and on defending the Socialist camp (i.e., the Soviet bloc) against imperialist invasion (perceived as coming mostly from NATO). During one-party rule, youth activism lacked any autonomy. Indeed, it was possible only through the channels of the official youth organizations named *Komsomol* (Communist Youth League) in most countries.

In this period, youth activism took three major forms: (1) strategic participation on the part of youth leaders; (2) forced participation by the majority of young people; and (3) voluntary escapism in informal youth subcultures. The first route led to a career in the party and state structures and consequently to an incorporation in the so-called "nomenclature"—the thin layer of privileged political cadres. For the majority of youth the *Komsomol* and its clubs provided free access to sports and arts and leisure in return for not questioning the status quo. The third form—autonomous youth self-expression—was labeled "anti-state" and "pro-imperialist" and met with oppressive measures, which rendered political meaning to an essentially nonpolitical cultural youth activity.

Youth studies at the time deepened our understanding of citizenship by elaborating the idea of "juventization." The Romanian sociologist Mahler argued that young people fulfilled their role of citizens by producing new values and changing society accordingly. The goal of youth activism should not simply be the social integration of each new coming generation into the existing institutions, norms, and practices. It had to be nothing less than the "rejuvenation" of society. His theory had a powerful critical dimension in arguing for the opening of society to youth's innovative potential rather than their current dependence, submissiveness, and alienation.

The 1989 revolutions in Eastern Europe were, in part, authentic youth revolts against the repressive governments. Independent youth movements joined the mobilization of other groups, which eventually toppled the Communist regimes one after the other. Youth activism took a multiplicity of forms: peaceful and violent demonstrations, singing during marches, ecological and peace protests, hunger strikes and road blocks, and happenings and performances.

The breakdown of the authoritarian regimes created new conditions for youth citizenship in the countries in the region. Youth were freed not only from the paternalistic control of the omnipotent party-state but also from its previously generous welfare support. The transition from a centrally planned economy to a market one established many opportunities for entrepreneurship for the young, as well as giving rise to youth unemployment that often surpassed 25 percent. Many new educational institutions came into being, both state and private, formal and informal, but the wider access to postsecondary and higher education was accompanied by an increasing number of early school leavers without any qualifications. With the quick dissolution of the official youth organiza-

tion, young people lost even their formal representation in the new political institutions as the newly formed youth associations and clubs had a very thin membership and lacked influence in the multiparty politics. Many groups, including young members, had their citizenship rights threatened by regional wars and ethnic tensions and consequent displacement and emigration.

Under postcommunism the concept of citizenship assumed new meanings together with societal changes in the direction of liberalization of the economy and politics. Many youth researchers in the region turned to the classical concept of T. H. Marshall, defining citizenship as a set of universal rights attached to one's membership in the nation-state. They stressed a wider range of rights and duties, such as the right to information, housing, health, and meaningful leisure. Others embraced a more proactive understanding, linking citizenship to youth civic participation. This participatory approach to citizenship explored youth initiatives from a problem-solving perspective, taking a well-defined problem (e.g., unjust conditions in need of change), mobilizing resources for participation (individuals, group structures, influential allies), and affecting outcomes (effects on individuals, organizations, communities, and societies).

Youth activism in postcommunist Eastern Europe has followed three basic patterns: (1) participation in institutional politics (e.g., voting, support for and membership in political parties); (2) protest activities (e.g., demonstrations, marches, new social movements); and (3) civic engagement (e.g., activity in youth associations, community involvement, volunteer work).

Beyond membership in the youth sections of major political parties, distinct channels for young people's participation under postcommunism are the youth political parties of which the Federation of Young Democrats (*Fidezs*) in Hungary and the Youth Party of Slovenia (SMS) are good examples. *Fidezs* developed from a protest movement in the late 1980s and established itself as an alliance of young people (the upper age limit being thirty-five) that challenged the gerontocratic elite of the Communist Party. In the mid-1990s it transformed into the Hungarian Civic Party winning the parliamentary election in 1998 and forming a coalition government headed by thirty-five-year-old Prime Minister Victor Orban. SMS was founded in Slovenia in 2000 not as an association of people of a certain age but as a party acting in defense of young people's interests and encouraging their participation as citizens. That same year SMS won seats in the national parliament and has since performed as a constructive opposition, offering a new approach to politics and a fresh vision for the country's future.

Participation in elections in the region has started to decline as elsewhere in modern societies. However, when young people feel that the democratic developments in their countries are threatened, they turn to the ballot boxes in impressive numbers, as in Bulgaria in 1997 and Slovakia in 1998. Specific, concrete issues quickly mobilize youth, who then often claim the public space in their cities to protest governmental decisions, voice environmental concerns, or defend minority rights.

Youth participation experiments have spread to new spheres and found new forms. Young people are building communities online or in youth cultural scenes. Research has documented a widespread dislike of formal structures and a growing inclination to search for individual solutions. New, more flexible, and often individualized ways of practicing citizenship are staging consumer boycotts, recycling, and reducing water consumption.

Immigration from countries left outside the European Union after the recent 2004 accession wave, such as Bulgaria, Romania, Moldova, and Ukraine, is not necessarily a negation of citizenship driven by a desire to participate in Western markets and welfare systems. It is also a striving for individual integration and a criticism of the slow and ineffective efforts of their countries' integration into the European Community.

In conclusion, the development of youth citizenship in Eastern Europe has led to its expansion in at least three respects: (1) including active citizen participation in social change as well as the passive acquisition of rights in the life course, such as the right to vote, to drive a car, to own property, to receive a guaranteed income, and others; (2) embodying not only formal membership in a political community, in its institutions and organizations, but also informal practices of identity creation such as spontaneous youth activism, lifestyle initiatives, cultural creativity, and sports; and (3) to push the borders of citizenship beyond the nation-state to a wider community—a regional one such as Eastern Europe, the Balkans, and the Baltics; a supranational one such as Europe; or a transcultural one, such as those represented by global youth cultures.

Emphasizing the active dimensions of citizenship does not mean that it is only young people who bear the duties of being active citizens in their postcommunist societies and exempting governments from reciprocal responsibilities to the young generation. The new political elite in the region is still expected to develop democratic and participatory youth policies appropriate to the new conditions of young people. Active citizenship is a reciprocal process between the authorities and young people, an arena where rights and responsibilities are defined, claimed, and defended. Youth in Eastern Europe struggle for their rights to participate in and shape the course of the social transformation in their societies.

See also Australia, Youth Activism in; Demographic Trends Affecting the World's Youth; Europe, Comparing Youth Activism in; European Identity and Citizenship; Immigrant Youth in Europe—Turks in Germany; Immigrant Youth in the United States; India, Youth Activism in; Indonesia, Youth Activism in; Nigeria, Youth Activism in; Palestinian *Intifada*; Russia, Youth Activism in; Serbia, Youth Activism in (1990–2000); Soweto Youth Activism (South Africa); State and Youth, The; Statute of the Child and Adolescent (Brazil); Tiananmen Square Massacre (1989); Transnational Identity; Transnational Youth Activism; Turkey, Youth Activism in; United Nations, Youth Activism and; Xenophobia; Zapatista Rebellion (Mexico); Zionist Youth Organizations.

Recommended Reading

Apostolov, A. (2001). "A Culture on the Periphery? Bulgarian Youth in Discourses of Space." In *Transitions of Youth Citizenship in Europe: Culture, Subculture and Identity*, edited by A. Furlong and I. Guidikova. Strasbourg: Council of Europe.

Chisholm, L., and Kovacheva, S. (2002). *Exploring the European Youth Mosaic: The Social Situation of Young People in Europe*. Strasbourg: Council of Europe.

Chuprov, V., and Zubok, J. (2000). "Integration versus Exclusion: Youth and the Labor Market in Russia." *International Social Science Journal*, 164: 171–182.

Kovacheva, S. (2000). *Keys to Youth Participation in Eastern Europe*. Strasbourg: Council of Europe.

Machacek, L. (2001). "Youth and Creation of Civil Society." In *Youth, Citizenship and Empowerment*, edited by H. Helve and C. Wallace. Aldershot: Ashgate.

Mahler, F. (1983). *Introducere in Juventologie*. Bucaresti (English Summary in *IBYR-Newsletter* 1/1984).

Marshall, T. H. (1952). *Citizenship and Social Class*. Cambridge: Cambridge University Press.

Tivadar, B., and Mrvar, P., eds. (2002). *Flying over or Falling through the Cracks? Young People in the Risk Society*. Ljubljana: Office for Youth of the Republic of Slovenia.

Wallace, C., and Kovatcheva, S. (1998). *Youth in Society: The Construction and Deconstruction of Youth in East and West Europe*. London: Macmillan.

Siyka Kovacheva

EE. *See* Environmental Education.

Emerging Adulthood. Youth activism occurs especially during the years from age eighteen to twenty-five, the period that many scholars now call "emerging adulthood." Emerging adulthood is the period of the life course that is in between adolescence, when most people are dependent on their parents and live in their parents' households, and young adulthood, when most people have "settled down" into adult roles of marriage, parenthood, and steady employment. During emerging adulthood, most people in industrialized societies are more independent of their parents than they were as adolescents, but they have not yet entered the obligations that structure adult life for most people.

There are features that distinguish emerging adulthood as a period of the life course (Arnett 2004):

• It is the age of *identity explorations,* of trying out various possibilities in the areas of love, work, and ideology.
• It is the age of *instability*, when many changes of direction take place in love, education, and work.
• It is the most *self-focused* age of life because it is a time when most people do not have daily obligations either to their parents or to a spouse and children.
• It is the age of *feeling in-between*, in transition, neither adolescent nor adult.
• It is the age of *possibilities*, when hopes flourish, when people have an unparalleled opportunity to transform their lives.

Each of these five features helps explain why emerging adulthood is a time when activism is at a high point. Emerging adulthood is the age of identity explorations and part of this involves ideological explorations—that is, emerging adults are in the process of deciding what they believe about political, social, and religious issues. As they explore these issues, they may reach conclusions that inspire them to make a commitment to activism. For example, an emerging adult who concludes that the world's wealth is unfairly distributed may decide to join the antiglobalization movement or an organization that assists people in developing countries. Or, an emerging adult who has decided to embrace a particular religious faith may decide to express that faith through participation in a religious service organization.

Emerging adulthood is a time of instability, that is, a time when people make frequent changes in their lives, for example, in their educational directions, jobs, romantic partners, and places of residence. This instability enhances the possibility of activism. Because emerging adults tend to lack enduring commitments, they risk less if they participate in activism. They may not worry as much if by participating in activism they risk losing their jobs; their jobs tend not to last long anyway, so they are used to ending one job and finding another. They usually do not have to worry about who will pay the mortgage if they leave for weeks, months, or even years for the sake of an activist commitment—few of them own houses, and they frequently move from one residence to another. This instability and the way it limits the depth of their roots in any one place makes activism more likely for them than for adults who have commitments that would present obstacles. For example, they could spend a year or more in an activist organization such as AmeriCorps or the Peace Corps, which would be much more difficult for adults who have long-term commitments.

Emerging adulthood is a self-focused age in the sense that people in this age period tend to be concentrating on their own self-development and their preparations for adult life, and they are less constrained by ties to others than people in other age periods. Children and adolescents are constrained by their parents, who set the rules of the household and decide where the family will live. Most adults are constrained by commitments—to a spouse or romantic partner, to children, to a long-term job. These constraints can make activism problematic. Adolescents usually cannot take part in activism without their parents' consent. Because they are dependent on their parents, they cannot leave home to pursue an activist cause. Adults may be reluctant to take part in activism without their partner's support and may have commitments to family and work that make it difficult to find time for activism.

The self-focused nature of emerging adulthood makes activism more likely.

Many of them leave home to live independently and do not need their parents' consent to engage in activism. Even if they continue to live at home, typically they have much more independence than adolescents do, which would include more freedom to take part in activism if they wish. Because they are not typically committed yet to a spouse or children, they would not be prevented by those ties from pursuing activism.

Similarly, the experience in emerging adulthood of feeling in between adolescence and adulthood also supports the likelihood of engaging in activism. Emerging adults do not feel like they are simply living an extended adolescence—they feel different from adolescents, more mature. They feel different from what they expect to feel in adulthood, too—less settled, less committed. They are aware that they are in a special time of life, when they have more freedom than they had as adolescents or will have as adults; activism may be one of the things they choose to do with that freedom. They realize that once they are in adulthood their freedom will be curtailed by adult responsibilities, so they may see their emerging adult years as the time to engage in activism, before the responsibilities of adult life descend upon them.

Finally, emerging adulthood is the age of possibilities, when people tend to have high hopes for their lives, high expectations that adult life will work out very well for them. They expect, almost universally, to end up with a good job and to find a desirable marriage partner (Arnett 2000). For some, this personal idealism transfers over into the public arena as well. They believe the world could be better than it is, and they take part in activism as a way of contributing to making the world more like they believe it should be. For example, in Eastern Europe in the 1980s, the "Velvet Revolution" that overthrew the Communist governments in that region was created in large part by young people (mainly college students) who were fed up with the corruption and oppression of their governments and were willing to take risks in order to improve their societies (Macek and Rabusic 1994).

Although all five of the features that distinguish emerging adulthood as a developmental period can be said to contribute potentially to activism, only a minority of emerging adults actually take part in it. In fact, emerging adulthood is for many people a period of disengagement from political and social issues. For example, emerging adulthood is a low point for participation in conventional politics (Van Hoorn, Komlosi, Suchar, et al. 2000). In most industrialized countries, emerging adults are less likely to vote or join organized political parties than older adults are. Similarly, emerging adults engage in volunteer work less than adolescents and less than adults past emerging adulthood. They are less likely to do volunteer work such as helping with a food drive or visiting a nursing home.

Nevertheless, there is a segment of emerging adults who participate in activism, and this segment is large enough to make emerging adulthood the period of life when activism is most likely to take place. There have been many examples in the past century of activist movements led and/or staffed principally by emerging adults: in China, the Cultural Revolution of the 1960s and the Tiananmen Square democracy movement of the 1980s; in Eastern Europe, the Velvet Revolution of the 1980s that led to the overthrow of communist dictatorships; in the United States, the antiwar movement of the 1960s and early 1970s; and in many countries, the current antiglobalization movement.

Similarly, activist volunteer work that involves an extended, full-time commitment of a year or more tends to be done mainly by emerging adults. Three examples in the United States are the Peace Corps, AmeriCorps, and Teach for America. Over half the volunteers in the Peace Corps are aged eighteen to twenty-five, and in AmeriCorps and Teach for America nearly all the participants are eighteen to twenty-

five-year-olds. These programs pay very little money and often require volunteers to move to where they are needed. Consequently, they are most likely to find their volunteers among emerging adults, who usually do not have to provide for anyone but themselves and who are most likely to be able to be unfettered enough to be able to move to a new location relatively easily.

Thus, emerging adulthood is a polarized period in terms of activism, with the majority focusing on their own lives and having little interest in either activism or conventional political involvement and in contrast, a significant minority committed to activism and making substantial contributions to activist movements and volunteer programs. Emerging adults are both *less* likely to engage in conventional politics and *more* likely to engage in activism. In one national survey in the United States, only 28 percent of college freshmen said they were interested in politics, but 81 percent had done volunteer work, and 45 percent had participated in a political demonstration (Kellogg 2001).

Historically, in diverse countries, many of the activists in protests involving emerging adults have been college students. There are several reasons why emerging adults who are college students might be especially likely to be involved in activism. First, college students are by definition among the most educated emerging adults in their societies because in most societies only a minority of emerging adults attend college. Greater education makes college students more aware of social issues that might inspire them to become activists. Second, sometimes college students have professors who inspire activism by what they teach and who may even serve as activist leaders. Finally, the college environment brings emerging adults together into a common setting. This common setting provides opportunities for emerging adults to find others who share their activist passion and allows them to exchange information about opportunities for activism.

See also Adult Partners in Youth Activism; Adult Roles in Youth Activism; Adultism; AmeriCorps; Generational Conflict; Generational Replacement; Identity and Organizing in Older Youth; Intergenerational Programs and Practices.

Recommended Reading

Arnett, J. J. (2000). "High Hopes in a Grim World: Emerging Adults' Views of Their Futures and of 'Generation X.'" *Youth and Society*, 31: 267–286.

Arnett, J. J. (2004). *Emerging Adulthood: The Winding Road from the Late Teens through the Twenties.* New York: Oxford University Press.

Kellogg, A. (January 2001). "Looking Inward, Freshmen Care Less About Politics and More About Money." *Chronicle of Higher Education*, A47–A49.

Macek, P., and Rabusic, L. (1994). Czechoslovakia. In *International Handbook of Adolescence*, edited by K. Hurrelmann. Westport, CT: Greenwood Press, pp. 117–130.

Van Hoorn, J. L., Komlosi, A., Suchar, E., and Samuelson, D. A. (2000). *Adolescent Development and Rapid Social Change: Perspectives from Eastern Europe.* New York: State University of New York Press.

Yates, M., and Youniss, J. (1999). *Roots of Civic Identity: International Perspectives on Community Service and Activism in Youth.* New York: Cambridge University Press.

Jeffrey Jensen Arnett

Empathy. Empathy, in the most general sense, refers to the reactions of one individual to the observed experiences of another and has long been viewed as a fundamental social skill which allows the individual to anticipate, understand, and experience the point of view of other people. Empathy is an emotional reaction to another's emotional state or condition that is similar to what the other person is feeling or would be expected to feel. This is different from sympathy, which is an emotional response based on another's emotional state or condition that consists of feeling of sorrow or concern for the other. Empathy and concern for others appear to be universal, involuntary responses—if one attends to the relevant cues, one responds empathically—that may have had survival value in human evolution. The capacity for empathy serves as the foundation for relationships and also provides a basis for coping with stress and resolving conflict while adding to the quality of life and the richness of human social interactions. Empathy also seems to play a key role in the development of social understanding and positive social behaviors.

Some theorists have considered empathy to consist of *either* cognitive reactions or emotional responses. In recent years it has been argued that empathy may best be considered a set of related constructs including both emotional and cognitive components. The cognitive components of empathy consist of perspective-taking skills. Perspective taking is an individual's ability to imagine what someone else is thinking or feeling by taking account of one's own and other's perspectives. Such abilities help adolescents to choose responses that are most likely to achieve desired results and maintain positive interpersonal relationships. Emotions sometimes complement cognitive processes in perspective taking. The emotional facets of empathy are characterized by feelings of warmth, compassion, and concern for another person. It is a growing belief among psychologists that our understanding of empathy can improve only with the recognition that there are both emotional and cognitive components to a person's empathic responses. One advantage of this multidimensional approach to empathy is that by clearly defining the different types of reactions to others that can be called empathic, we may explore the systematic similarities and differences between these types of empathy and their implications for other behaviors.

Once an individual reaches the adolescent years, both perspective taking and emotional empathy increase. Self-reflective perspective taking and other-oriented judgments tend to emerge in late childhood and increase through adolescence. During late childhood and early adolescence, as children develop the ability to think about others and situations in more abstract terms (perspective taking), they also gain the ability to react emotionally with the distress of others who are strangers or with groups of people. Adolescents are therefore not just able to empathize with familiar individuals but also with unfamiliar groups of people such as stigmatized populations (e.g., people with HIV/AIDS, the homeless, racial or ethnic minorities). As adolescents move into high school they are able to gain a more sophisticated understanding of other peoples' plights. They are able to draw on a rich knowledge base derived from numerous social experiences and so they become ever more skillful at drawing inferences about people's psychological characteristics, intentions, and needs. By late adolescence an individual has gained the ability to consider multiple perspectives and incorporate them when analyzing and acting upon situations.

While empathy generally increases with age, gender differences in empathy have been found. Girls consistently score higher than boys on measures of empathy between nine years old and sixteen years old. It can be speculated that girls are more empathic than boys because of differences in the socialization of emotion in boys and girls. From an evolutionary point of view, empathy might have had survival value in women by strengthening the mother-child attachment.

In the past ten years there has been an increasing interest in the topic of empathy. This interest is probably due to the association of empathy with altruistic behavior and social competence. If empathy plays a role in the development of valued social behaviors, they are of obvious theoretical and applied significance. However, there is relatively little research that has been conducted on the development of empathy during adolescence. Much of the research concerning adolescence focuses on their involvement in or risk for engaging in negative behaviors. Most research on empathy during adolescence has an emphasis on juvenile offenders and their lack of empathy. Few studies have focused on positive youth development and how to promote empathy during the adolescent years.

Empathic responding has been the cornerstone of several theories of altruistic behavior. Altruism is any purposive action on behalf of someone else with the ultimate goal of increasing another's welfare. Research indicates that feeling empathy for a person in need is an important mediator in helping. Empathy is associated with the desire to reduce another person's distress or need and, therefore, is likely to lead to altruistic behavior. The developmental mechanism that is typically used to explain age-related changes in altruism is the increasing ability of the individual to take the point of view of the other person. In order for an individual to act altruistically, one must have the ability to understand another's needs and view the situation from another's perspective. As an individual gains the skills of considering multiple perspectives, he or she is better able to consider the various points of view of groups of people and therefore has the potential to act more altruistically. Therefore, when considering altruism, perspective-taking skills are critical.

Although most developmental psychologists would agree that the development of perspective-taking capacity is central to the development of altruistic behavior, most would also agree that perspective taking alone is not sufficient to promote altruistic action. Emotional empathy and its relationship to altruism also need to be understood. This sense of empathy to the abstract person is an important concept when considering altruism. This ability allows adolescents to see others as individuals who have unique personal identities.

Research on adolescent empathy suggests that changes during adolescence increase the likelihood for individuals to participate in altruistic behaviors. Adolescent altruism is rarely studied, but altruism increases with age, and characteristics related to adolescence may promote this increase in altruistic behavior. During adolescence, individuals become more mature and an increase in moral reasoning enables individuals to carry out actions that they once could not do. Also, adolescents become involved in more intimate relationships with peers, which may foster and promote altruism.

Nancy Eisenberg, a psychologist at Arizona State University, has been conducting a longitudinal study on the development of empathy and altruism. Her research found that during adolescence higher rates of emotional empathy and perspective taking are related to higher rates of helping behavior and altruism. Interestingly though, her research also found that self-centered behavior, which dropped off sharply from early childhood to eleven to twelve years old, increased somewhat at fifteen to sixteen years old. From fifteen to twenty years of age, self-centered behavior continued to increase slightly. Most of the nineteen and twenty year olds did not verbalize principles such as responsibility to the self. Rather, they simply seemed to have weighed long-term and important costs to the self versus the needs of the other more carefully and realistically than when in high school. In other words, in late adolescence individuals' concern with achieving success and independence is heightened, and therefore they focus on their own needs before helping others with their needs. This does not represent a decrease in empathy but rather an increase in the cognitive capacity to understand and evaluate one's own needs more logically.

Despite much uniformity of opinion regarding the significance of empathy, there is much controversy as to the mechanisms by which the capacity for empathy develops and whether empathy can be taught. There are studies which have attempted to teach empathy through a variety of means. Since empathy has a cognitive component there is great capacity for improving empathy if interventions target these cognitive processes. Programs should encourage adolescents to look at commonalties across cultures and different groups to minimize in-group empathic bias. There

are several existing programs that focus on empathy and emotional understanding that have shown successful results. However, it is not yet clear whether these changes persist in real-life situations. Increased development and implementation of these programs will likely be productive in enhancing altruistic behavior and decreasing antisocial behavior in children and adolescents.

See also AIDS Advocacy in South Africa; Civic Virtue; Moral Exemplars; Prosocial Behaviors; Religiosity and American Youth; Religiosity and Civic Engagement in African American Youth; Spirituality.

Recommended Reading

Davis, M. H. (1983). "The Effects of Dispositional Empathy on Emotional Reactions and Helping: A Multidimensional Approach." *Journal of Personality*, 51: 167–184.
Eisenberg, N. (1990). "Prosocial Development in Early and Mid Adolescence." In *From Childhood to Adolescence: A Transitional Period? Advances in Adolescence*, Vol. 2, edited by R. Montemayor, G. R. Adams, and T. P. Gullotta. Newbury Park, CA: Sage, pp. 240–269.
Eisenberg, N., Carlo, G., Murphy, B., and Van Court, P. (1995). "Prosocial Development in Late Adolescence: A Longitudinal Study." *Child Development*, 66: 1179–1197.
Eisenberg, N., Miller, P. A., Shell, R., McNally, S., and Shea, C. (1991). "Prosocial Development in Adolescence: A Longitudinal Study." *Developmental Psychology*, 27: 849–857.
Hoffman, M. L. (2000). *Empathy and Moral Development: Implications for Caring and Justice*. Cambridge: Cambridge University Press.
Moore, B. S. (1990). "The Origins and Development of Empathy." *Motivation and Emotion*, 14: 75–80.

Jason J. Barr

Empowerment. Empowerment is a buzzword in the field of youth programs and is believed to be a necessary precursor for youth activism. However, there has been little theoretical or empirical analysis of the meaning of empowerment as it applies to the lives of young people. Discussions of empowerment have been located in diverse fields, including health, human services, and organizational behavior. Most previous studies of empowerment focus on adult processes, and as such, the overall discussion of empowerment is constructed according to adult frames of reference and experiences. How does empowerment develop, and what are its implications for young people and their communities?

The concept of empowerment was introduced in the field of community psychology in the early 1980s as an alternative approach for social and policy change. This shift was an attempt to move away from prevention-based approaches, in which professional experts act as leaders, to a collaborative model, where community members become engaged in solutions to community problems. The leading definition of empowerment, which is grounded in this perspective, states that "empowerment is the goal of enhancing the possibilities for people to control their own lives." This concept of empowerment has both a value orientation of working in the community to promote goals, aims, and strategies for social change and a theoretical component that acknowledges the existence of many social problems because of larger structural inequalities.

Recent discussions of empowerment describe it taking place at three levels: psychological, organizational, and community. Most studies of empowerment focus on psychological empowerment. Psychological empowerment has been defined as "the connection between a sense of personal competence, a desire for, and a willingness to take action in the public domain." The concept includes intrapersonal, interpersonal, and behavioral components. The intrapersonal component refers to how people think about their capacity to influence social and political systems. The interpersonal component refers to the transactions between individuals and environments that enable one to successfully master social or political systems (including knowledge of resources and causation, critical awareness, and development of problem-solving skills). Finally, the behavioral component refers to the specific actions an individual takes to

influence the social and political environment via participation in community organizations and activities.

Much of the theoretical and empirical research on psychological empowerment examines participation, which is a manifestation of the links between the intrapersonal, interpersonal, and behavioral. Studies of adults have shown that participation in community organizations has a direct and positive effect on an individual's psychological empowerment. Further, individuals who report high levels of empowerment participate in more community activities than their counterparts. Individuals with a critical awareness about how to exert power to create change in their community environment (another indication of psychological empowerment) report greater levels of both participation in formal organizations and sense of community.

Less attention has been given to empowerment at the organization and community levels. According to Zimmerman (2000), at the organizational level are empowered and empowering organizations. An empowering organization may not necessarily impact policy but provides members with opportunities to develop skills and feelings of control in settings where people with similar interests share information and experiences and develop a sense of identity with others. Finally, community empowerment is reflected by a structure that incorporates interconnected coalitions promoting involvement and resources for its members and attention to community issues.

Many of the critiques of theories of empowerment speak to the limitations of current conceptualizations when applied to empowerment of young people. One of the primary critiques of empowerment theory is that psychological empowerment needs to be linked with actual manifestations of power; clearly this is relevant when applying the concept to young people, whose actual power to act may be structurally limited. More specifically, it is argued that thinking about empowerment typically has focused on the individual level, while power is fundamentally a social phenomenon. In focusing on psychological empowerment, feelings of empowerment are measured rather than any empirical power, influence, or ability to act with consequence. Empowerment becomes a dichotomous condition that applies to an individual (e.g., a youth is either empowered or unempowered) with little attention to the structural dimensions that inhibit or support the manifestations of empowerment.

More generally, critics of empowerment studies point out the dominant cultural assumptions underlying concepts of empowerment. Prevailing notions of empowerment fail to address how social power produces and sustains inequality via systems of oppression. Specifically, in addition to a focus on individualism, others have pointed to the grounding of empowerment models in traditionally masculine concepts of mastery, power, and control with relative ignorance of traditionally feminine concepts of communion and cooperation. While empowerment is understood as being context and community specific, most research fails to recognize that the existing models and definitions of empowerment are adult-specific. Recognizing this limitation, several recent studies have proposed models for understanding the development of youth empowerment.

There are unique implications for the concept of psychological empowerment when applied to young people. At the intrapersonal and interpersonal levels, many social institutions and cultures do not acknowledge or allow the capacity of young people to influence social and political systems. As a result, at the behavioral level examples of specific individual action by young people in communal activities are exceptional. At the same time, contexts that promote youth participation in meaningful community activities for positive social change provide important examples of youth engagement and empowerment, and emerging research on community/youth development parallels the research on empowerment among adults. Empowerment at the community level for youth would mean intentionally including youth voice in community-level decision-making.

At the organizational level, empowering organizations are shown to be ones that not only provide a supportive context but also are based on commitment to youth-adult partnerships. Such strategies result in empowerment at the organizational and psychological levels. Organizations that try to equalize power differentials between youth and adults, while at the same time making adult power transparent, have been more successful at carrying out collaborative action plans. Cargo, Grams, Ottoson, Ward, and Green (2003) describe youth empowerment as occurring as a transactional process between a welcoming social climate created by adults and an engagement of youth. Specifically, when youth control the organizational process with the assistance and facilitation of adults—that is, power is transferred to youth, and they become responsible for voicing, decision-making, and action—there are positive changes in youth development and in the social integration of young people into the community. Youth-adult partnerships may also result in an "empowered" organization, with youth and adults bringing different strengths to the table.

Results of this recent work are encouraging, but transcending cultural ideas about the ways that youth and adults relate to one another is a constant challenge for empowerment among young people. Specifically, the idea that well-intentioned adults can "empower" powerless young people has been critiqued. Youth empowerment comes about through self-activity; the adult role is to help create and structure experiences in ways that can facilitate youth empowering themselves—a role that is inconsistent with most notions of adult responsibility for supervision and expert guidance of youth. Others challenge the assumption that power can be transferred from one group to another and argue that attempts to empower youth actually serve to socialize youth into the status quo rather than providing them with the tools to challenge their disempowerment. Ironically, there are no known studies that directly consider the ways that young people describe their own definitions and understandings of what "empowerment" means to them.

Youth empowerment programs can build self-esteem and life skills while meeting real community needs, thus creating opportunities for youth to guide decisions that affect their lives. However, the objectives of youth empowerment programs differ depending on whether the emphasis is youth development or social justice. For those with a youth development emphasis, the goal is to enhance the life options of youth involved; those with an emphasis on social change or social-justice champion youth empowerment as a strategy for social change.

Chinman and Linney (1998) offer a youth development model of empowerment for adolescents that merges theoretical perspectives from appropriate developmental theory, identity development, bonding and social control, and rolelessness. According to this model, the adolescent empowerment cycle is one in which youth engage in a process to develop a stable, positive identity by experimenting with roles and incorporating the feedback of others. Participation in positive, meaningful activities, learning useful and relevant skills, and being recognized are central characteristics of the initiation of the empowerment cycle. As a result of this bonding development process (action-skill development-reinforcement), this model predicts that adolescents will feel more confident and will have critical awareness and self-efficacy.

Ginwright and James (2002) propose a social-justice youth development framework to understand youth political engagement. The main questions addressed by this framework are: What role can youth play in forging a democratic society and creating more equitable institutions? How can adults support sociopolitical development among youth? And what can be learned from youth organizing and its impact on the development of young people? These authors focus on marginalized youth to examine the social issues they confront and explore how they creatively respond through organizing, political education, and identity development. The principles of this framework include analyzing power in social relationships, making identity central, promoting systemic social change, encouraging collective action, and embracing youth culture. The social-justice youth development approach makes the serious social problems and conditions that young people face more explicit than traditional youth development approaches. Furthermore, this approach supports youth development by not only seeing youth as assets but also as agents capable of transforming their environments.

See also Adult Roles in Youth Activism; Community Collaboration; Parental Influences on Youth Activism.

Recommended Reading

Cargo, M., Grams, G. D., Ottoson, J. M., Ward, P., and Green, L. W. (2003). "Empowerment as Fostering Positive Youth Development and Citizenship." *American Journal of Health Behavior*, 27 (Supplement 1): S66–S79.

Chinman, M. J., and Linney, J. A. (1998). "Toward a Model of Adolescent Empowerment: Theoretical and Empirical Evidence." *The Journal of Primary Prevention*, 18 (4): 393–413.

Crenshaw, P., Mitchell, W., Bonton, R., and Green, E. (2000). "Youth Empowerment and Youth Research: Expertise, Subjection, and Control." *Youth and Policy*, 69: 1–16.

Ginwright, S., and James, T. (2002). "From Assets to Agents of Change: Social Justice, Organizing, and Youth Development." In *Youth Participation: Improving Institutions and Communities*, Vol. 96, edited by B. Kirshner, J. L. O'Donoghue, and M. McLaughlin. San Francisco: Jossey-Bass, pp. 27–46.

Zimmerman, M. A., and Rappaport, J. (1988). "Citizen Participation, Perceived Control, and Psychological Empowerment." *American Journal of Community Psychology*, 16 (5): 725–750.

Anna Muraco, Stephen T. Russell, and Aarti Subramaniam

Environmental Education (EE). Environmental education (EE) was first defined by William Stapp of the University of Michigan in 1969. He described it as education aimed at producing citizens who were knowledgeable about the environment and problems associated with it, aware of how to help solve these problems, and motivated to work toward solutions. Thus, from its beginning EE has encompassed not just knowledge and awareness of content matter but action skills designed to enhance citizenship. Environmental education had its beginnings in the fields of nature study, environmental science, and outdoor and conservation education. Since that time it has grown to encompass parts of these fields while preserving its own individuality.

In 1970 the U.S. Congress passed the Environmental Education Act which highlighted education as an instrument to improve and protect the environment. The act also saw education as the means for addressing the public's increasing concerns about environmental quality and sustainability. In 1975, prompted by the perception that the field needed clarification concerning its direction, the international community drafted a commonly accepted definition at the United Nations Educational, Scientific and Cultural Organization (UNESCO) meeting in Belgrade, Yugoslavia. Three years later at the world's first Intergovernmental Conference on Environmental Education in Tbilisi they refined the definition of EE further and composed a declaration that is widely used today: "Environmental education is a learning process that increases people's knowledge and awareness about the environment and associated challenges, develops the necessary skills and expertise to address the challenges, and fosters attitudes, motivations, and commitments to make informed decisions and take responsible action."

This declaration also stated the components and objectives of EE as follows:

Awareness and sensitivity to the environment and environmental challenges;

Knowledge and understanding of the environment and environmental challenges;

Attitudes of concern for the environment and motivation to improve or maintain environmental quality;

Skills to identify and help resolve environmental challenges; and

Participation in activities that lead to the resolution of environmental challenges.

This then became a working definition for the field with the understanding that the field and its meaning would evolve with educational research findings and as more stakeholders were consulted. It is widely accepted today that environmental education is an educational process that fosters knowledge, values, attitudes, and an understanding of humans' relationship with the environment with the goal of responsible environmental behavior. Decisions about what responsible environmental behavior means are not preordained but are decisions made by people at particular times and in particular contexts. Indeed, this is a critical part of the definition of EE because the field itself does not advocate a particular action or viewpoint. Rather it aims to provide individuals with the ability to weigh the various sides of an environmental issue, to formulate their own informed opinions, and to take action to resolve specific issues, should they deem that actions are necessary. Thus, skills of critical thinking and problem solving are fundamental to the definition and practice of EE.

Today, debate continues about what exactly a program has to be to fit the term "environmental education." Although in practice, the majority of EE takes place in informal settings such as nature centers and parks, many theorists of EE would argue that these programs cannot truly be considered EE because they do not address all of the goals of an EE program. There is general agreement that EE should be rooted in outdoor education and nature education—where the field began—but it is also generally agreed that EE is more than knowledge about and appreciation of nature and the outdoors.

Currently, the trend in North America is for EE programs to aim to instill "environmental literacy" in participants. This term can be defined as a person's ability to analyze and understand the quality of fitness of the environment and the capability of taking appropriate action to maintain or improve the status of the environment. It is a process that begins with awareness and ends with civic action. To achieve this ultimate aim, environmental education must be a series of ongoing lessons that enforce the goals of the discipline throughout life.

Environmental education can be thought of in many ways. It its broadest sense, it incorporates formal and informal education that focuses on raising awareness, forming values and attitudes, and building knowledge and skills in people, which leads to responsible environmental behavior. While EE often incorporates field trips and stand-alone lessons in science class, it is the coupling of knowledge about science, nature, and the environment with other civic skills that is a key defining feature of an environmental-education program.

Nature and outdoor education continue to be essential foundations for EE. To learn about animal habitats and natural resources, there is no substitute for the real thing. This learning is not only factual in terms of environmental knowledge but also personal in terms of an individual's values and attitudes. The motivation to preserve the natural environment can be based on a personal moral stance or on a desire to preserve the natural environment for recreational use. So whether going on field trips helps students learn to respect the rights of animals and plants to exist or whether going on such trips simply means students want to preserve nature for the future recreational use of themselves and other human beings, from an EE point of view, the success of the field trip is in motivating students to preserve the environment.

Ultimately, the goal of environmental literacy is not accomplished by field trips or nature study alone. Neither can EE be relegated to science class. EE is not a stand-alone discipline but an interdisciplinary program that incorporates the natural sciences, language arts, and social studies among other disciplines. For example, to appreciate how the ecology of an area has changed over time as humans have inhabited a particular geographical area, students would have to learn about the geography of the region and natural ecological interactions, as well as the social, cultural, and economic history of humans interacting with the natural environment and using natural resources.

Environmental change is not an easy concept for young people to understand and only by delving into the natural and human history of an area can they come to see the implications of human actions for that environment. Because an understanding of environmental impairments and solutions is not based solely on the natural sciences but also depends on knowledge about human culture, economics, and politics, the study of environmental education has to encompass these fields as well. Furthermore, if students detect a problem and want to take action, they will need skills in writing and public speaking, to name two, which they are likely to learn in language-arts classes.

Another applied example of EE is the holistic education students would need in order to monitor water quality. To monitor water quality there is a set of scientific skills that students can learn by applying observational, chemical, and biological principles to a stream ecosystem. It would be important for students to learn a basic scientific understanding of the concept of a watershed and the ecological concepts and interactions naturally occurring in the stream. By testing the chemical parameters, surveying the types of biological life found in the stream, and observing the smell, color, and other physical conditions of the stream and bank, they would gain an idea of the health of the waterway.

But skills in monitoring water quality are not enough. If students detect a problem such as high levels of phosphates and no organisms sensitive to pollution in the water, they have to appreciate scientifically what this means about the health of the stream. In addition, they would have to be able to research and analyze where the pollution was coming from. The latter requires a set of skills in observing and researching land use in the area and scientifically analyzing what human and environmental causes could be behind the impairments to the water.

Furthermore, students would have to gain the civic skills necessary to engage stakeholders in the area who might play a role in affecting water quality. Stakeholders could include organizations, companies, groups, or individuals whose actions might affect the water quality, such as homeowners polluting the water with chemical fertilizers or organizations working to monitor and protect it. In this part of their environmental education experience, students might engage experts who could help verify the problems the students identified or who could inform the students about local policies and practices that might affect water quality. And, if the students want to take action, they have to know how to decide on an action project that they can implement, how to present their case, and how to hold the powers-that-be accountable to preserving the safety and quality of the public's water.

The entire EE process would take place in a number of different settings and would engage educators and environmental practitioners in various ways. It may begin in a science class as students learn ecological concepts associated with waterways, continue on a field trip to a nature study area where students could actually monitor the water, and culminate with a classroom teacher and experts from a nonprofit watershed council working together to help students implement an action plan. In this way students benefit from working with experts in education who know how to teach them concepts and skills in an impartial manner, as well as environmental experts who can provide insights into politics and community practices that play a role in the health of natural ecosystems.

There is still debate among practitioners about the precise meaning and definition of environmental education. But there is no question that the field is gaining recognition nationally and throughout the world. Although currently there are no EE certification programs in formal education, there are national organizations working on certification programs and working to integrate EE into all aspects of education by incorporating it in teacher education programs. Increasingly, universities are offering courses in the discipline. Many state departments of education now recognize it as a legitimate subject for formal education and are adding EE programming into requirements for classroom education.

See also Character Education; Citizenship Education Policies in the States; Civic Environmentalism; Civic Virtue; Democratic Education; Diversity Education; Earth Force; IEA Civic Education Study; Just Community High Schools and Youth Activism; National Alliance for Civic Education; Prosocial Behaviors; School Engagement; School Influences and Civic Engagement.

Recommended Reading

Heimlich, J. E., and Daudi, S. S. (April 1997). "Environmental Education: As Defined by the Practitioners." *Advancing Education and Environmental Literacy*, 15. EETAP Resource Library.

Heimlich, J. E., and Daudi, S. S. (May 1997). "Evolution of Environmental Education: Historical Development." *Advancing Education and Environmental Literacy*, 16. EETAP Resource Library.

Stapp, W. B., et al. (1969). "The Concept of Environmental Education." *Journal of Environmental Education*, 1 (1).

United Nations Educational, Scientific and Cultural Organization (UNESCO) (October 14–26, 1977). "Final Report--Tbilisi." Paper presented at the Intergovernmental Conference on Environmental Education, Tbilisi, Republic of Georgia.

U.S. Public Law 91-516. The Environmental Quality Education Act. Enacted October 30, 1970.

Weber, B., Lesure, B., Sivek, D., Heimlich, J. E., and Daudi, S. S. (November 2000). "Impact of Environmental Education Activities on Environmental Literacy of Learners." *Advancing Education and Environmental Literacy*, 93. EETAP Resource Library.

Erin Gallay

***Estatuto da Criança e Adolescente* (ECA).** *See* Statute of the Child and Adolescent (Brazil).

Ethnic Identity. Ethnic identity is a dynamic, multidimensional construct that refers to one's identity, or sense of self, as a member of an ethnic group. Ethnic identity is not a fixed categorization but rather a fluid and dynamic understanding of self and group that changes with age, time, and context. An ethnic identity is constructed and modified as people become aware of other groups and of the ethnic differences among groups and attempt to understand the meaning of their ethnicity within the larger setting. It is a central defining characteristic of many individuals, particularly those who are members of minority or lower-status groups and is of particular importance during adolescence. While the term "ethnic identity" is sometimes used to refer only to the label or group name with which individuals choose to describe themselves, the concept is much broader, encompassing the feelings, attitudes, and cognitions associated with one's group membership.

An understanding of the role of ethnic identity in human interactions is essential in a world in which the populations of most countries consist of people from different ethnic or cultural groups. Ethnic identity has become increasingly important as a result of population changes and movement across national borders. Although ethnic identity is of relatively little salience for ethnically homogeneous populations or among members of dominant majority groups, there are few people today who can remain unaware of, or unexposed to, cultural differences in behaviors, attitudes, and practices. Exposure to others who are different from oneself raises fundamental questions about who one is culturally, what group one belongs to or identifies with, and how one feels about one's group membership. These are the central issues of ethnic identity formation. The ways in which these issues are resolved have important implications for how individuals feel about themselves, how they view society, and how they interact with individuals who are culturally different from themselves.

The foundation for the formation of an ethnic identity is established through early experiences with ethnicity. The family provides the initial basis for feelings about what is normal and comfortable, and these feelings are generally supported in the immediate community. In homogeneous settings, familiar practices are not recognized as ethnic. When children encounter others who are different in appearance, language, or behaviors, they begin to categorize and label themselves and others. Children learn their ethnic self-label between the ages of four and seven years, although the age varies with the group and the amount of contact with other groups. By eight or ten years of age, children with exposure to other groups develop an understanding of ethnic constancy (the fact that their ethnicity does not change over time or with superficial changes such as clothing).

As children's thinking abilities develop, their understanding of ethnicity becomes more complex. Young children understand ethnicity in literal and concrete terms, defined by food, customs, and language. With increasing cognitive competence in middle childhood, children develop a group consciousness and begin to understand ethnicity in terms of norms, values, and inter-group attitudes.

Socialization plays an important role in the content and meaning children attach to ethnicity. Children's feelings about their ethnicity are influenced from an early age by their families and communities. When families provide positive images of their ethnic group, children's early feelings about their group are likely to be positive. A strong and vital ethnic community supplies a context in which children can form a positive sense of their group. As long as they remain within a supportive ethnic community, individuals may give little thought to the meaning or implications of their ethnicity.

However, children are influenced as well by messages from other groups and the larger society. When an ethnic group is disparaged by others, held in lower esteem, or subjected to stereotypes, negative messages about one's group may become internalized. In that case, children are likely to hold conflicting or negative feelings about their ethnicity and may express the desire to belong to another group. Models of ethnic and racial-identity formation have described a type of identity in which adolescents prefer dominant culture over their own and try to imitate it. For example, an ethnic minority youth may adopt the styles of dress and behavior of the majority group.

Ethnic identity is of particular significance during adolescence and young adulthood, at the time when young people are exploring and establishing their sense of identity. The process of identity formation involves developing a sense of self in important areas of one's life. With the onset of adolescence, a number of changes typically make issues of identity and ethnicity more salient. In modern, industrialized societies, adolescents face choices regarding future careers, religious and political values, personal relationships, gender, and lifestyle. These choices initiate a period of exploration and consideration of alternatives in order to make decisions in key areas that can serve as a guide for the future.

The exploration of one's ethnicity is part of this process, especially for ethnic minority youth. During adolescence, young people typically move from more homogeneous neighborhoods and primary schools to more diverse settings, such as secondary schools, jobs, and leisure activities. Young people become increasingly aware of cultural differences among groups, as well as of discrimination and unequal opportunities. The chance to socialize with or date peers from other groups raises questions about youth's willingness to form close relationships with peers from outside their own group and about parents' receptivity to such relationships. These experiences typically lead to questions about the meaning of their ethnicity and its role in their lives.

This search for a meaningful ethnic identity involves learning about the history, customs, accomplishments, and current status of one's group. The process can lead to a wide range of reactions, both positive and negative. Minority youth may become aware of social problems within their ethnic communities. If they have supportive families or mentors, these youth may begin to think about ways to help their neighborhoods. They may be motivated to aim for educational and career goals that would allow them to contribute to improving their communities. The idealistic motivations of young people at this age provide an opportunity for interventions that promote involvement in communities.

On the other hand, as they see problems in their ethnic groups and learn about inequality and discrimination, minority adolescents may become angry and disillusioned. They may feel that change is not possible and that there is little they can do with their lives. When legitimate means of identity development and ethnic affirmation are perceived as unavailable, hopelessness can result, sometimes leading to antisocial actions. Some youth decide it is not worth trying to find a constructive identity; rather, they develop a negative or oppositional identity that leads to a rejection of mainstream society and possibly behavior that is destructive to themselves and others. Interethnic violence often results from feelings of threat to one's ethnic identity, including the inability to be accepted for who one is.

The optimal outcome of the ethnic identity formation process is the achievement of a secure and confident sense of one's ethnicity. Erik Erikson points out that true identity depends on the support which young people receive from the collective sense of identity characterizing the social groups significant to them: their class, nation, or culture. An achieved ethnic identity results from an understanding of the culture, history, and accomplishments of one's group, as well as the difficulties that it has faced. This mature sense of self as an ethnic group member includes positive feelings about one's group and is a source of personal strength and positive self-evaluation. Feeling secure about one's own ethnic identity is also associated with more positive attitudes toward other groups. An achieved ethnic identity is related to the ability to understand the perspective of other groups, to adopt a multicultural perspective, and to see the place of one's own group in a larger perspective. Multicultural education programs that expose children and adolescents to diverse cultures and allow for the expression of a range of ethnic traditions and customs can both promote development of ethnic identity and make a positive contribution to intergroup relations.

Ethnic identity has been widely studied using questionnaires that assess the strength of commitment to one's ethnic group, together with the extent to which one has developed a clear understanding of the meaning and implications of one's ethnicity. The strength of ethnic commitment varies across ethnic groups depending on the past history and current status of the group. Ethnic identity is generally stronger among minority group members who have experienced negative stereotyping and discrimination. A secure ethnic identity may serve to buffer individuals from such experiences, through an affirmation of their ethnicity in the face of negative messages and experiences. In the United States, African Americans, who have suffered the greatest amount of discrimination, consistently show a stronger ethnic identity than other groups. Substantially lower levels of ethnic identity are found among members of the dominant majority, for example European Americans in the United States.

As minority group members develop a sense of their own group membership, they also face issues regarding their national identity (i.e., their sense of belonging to the larger society). The way in which these two identities interact is an important factor in the well-being of ethnic group members. Ethnic minority young people differ in the extent to which they think of themselves as belonging to the larger society. Some youth—particularly those who are racially distinct from the dominant majority—may not think of themselves as having a national identity. For example, in the United States some nonwhite youth may not think of themselves as American because of a perception that being American means being white. These young people may remain separated from the mainstream and be unable to find productive roles and identities in society. Other youth perceive the country as being made up of people from many different cultural and ethnic backgrounds and feel that they are part of the diverse society. Individuals who both identify with the larger society and maintain a strong ethnic identity can be described as having a bicultural identity.

Research suggests that the most adaptive outcomes for individuals in multicultural societies result from being bicultural and having bicultural competence, that is, being able to get along comfortably in two (or more) cultural settings. Most ethnic minority adolescents report having a bicultural identity, although they differ in how they handle involvement with two cultures. Some maintain generally separate identities and alternate between them; for example, Mexican American youth may feel Mexican at home and American at school. Others combine the two cultures to form a single blended identity as Mexican American. Both types include a strong ethnic identity, and both seem to provide a satisfactory way of being bicultural.

Adolescents of mixed ethnic or racial backgrounds, that is, youth who have parents from two different groups, face special challenges in forming an ethnic identity. Multiracial or multiethnic children are typically aware at an early age of being different from each of their parents, and they learn that they do not fully belong to any of the obvious ethnic groups in their environment. As adolescents, they are likely to face a more difficult task of achieving a group identity. Identification with the group of only one of their parents implies rejection of the other parent. An environment in which there are other biracial people with whom they can explore their experience can help multiethnic or multiracial adolescents achieve a secure identity as biracial.

Developmental processes underlie the formation of ethnic identity in childhood and adolescence, but ethnic identity may be renegotiated throughout life in response to individual, contextual, and historical changes. Ethnic identity varies in the short term over differing contexts with strong ethnic feelings emerging in settings where ethnicity is highly salient, such as traditional ethnic celebrations, and receding in settings which de-emphasize ethnicity. Many bicultural individuals experience variation in the strength of their group identities as they move between ethnic and nonethnic contexts and change their language and behaviors to suit the context. Ethnic groups themselves change over time, and our understanding of ethnic identity must be continually revised and updated. Nevertheless, the strong feelings associated with ethnic group membership suggest that ethnic identity will remain a powerful force in society for the foreseeable future.

See also Civil Rights Movement; Nigeria, Youth Activism in; Racial and Ethnic Inequality; Racial Socialization; Religiosity and Civic Engagement in African American Youth; Serbia, Youth Activism in (1990–2000); Transnational Identity; Transnational Youth Activism.

Recommended Reading

Bernal, M., and Knight, G., eds. (1993). *Ethnic Identity: Formation and Transmission among Hispanics and Other Minorities.* Albany: State University of New York Press.

Phinney, J. (1990). "Ethnic Identity in Adolescents and Adults: A Review of Research." *Psychological Bulletin*, 108: 499–514.

Phinney, J. (1992). "The Multigroup Ethnic Identity Measure: A New Scale for Use with Diverse Groups." *Journal of Adolescent Research*, 7: 156–176.

Phinney, J. (1993). "A Three-Stage Model of Ethnic Identity Development." In *Ethnic Identity: Formation and Transmission Among Hispanics and Other Minorities*, edited by M. Bernal and G. Knight. Albany: State University of New York Press, pp. 61–79.

Phinney, J., and Devich-Navarro, M. (1997). "Variations in Bicultural Identification among African American and Mexican American Adolescents." *Journal of Research on Adolescence*, 7: 3–32.

Quintana, S. (1998). "Children's Developmental Understanding of Ethnicity and Race." *Applied and Preventive Psychology*, 7: 27–45.

Rockquemore, K., and Brunsma, D. (2002). *Beyond Black: Biracial Identity in America.* Thousand Oaks, CA: Sage.

Wijeyesinghe, C., and Jackson, B., eds. (2001). *New Perspectives on Racial Identity Development: A Theoretical and Practical Anthology.* New York: New York University Press.

Jean S. Phinney

Europe, Comparing Youth Activism in. A widespread image of young people in the media and among some scholars is that they are inactive in political life, that they are alienated from politics, and that they are not even interested in voting. There are fears that young people are becoming more and more cynical about conventional politics that do not address their needs and interests. In aging European societies, young people are a smaller and smaller proportion of the electorate, which may be one reason why politicians are prepared to overlook their interests, especially when it is older persons who are benefiting the most from the welfare system. Some people have described this as a generational conflict of interests.

The former Communist countries of Central and Eastern Europe have only allowed free elections for some fifteen years and

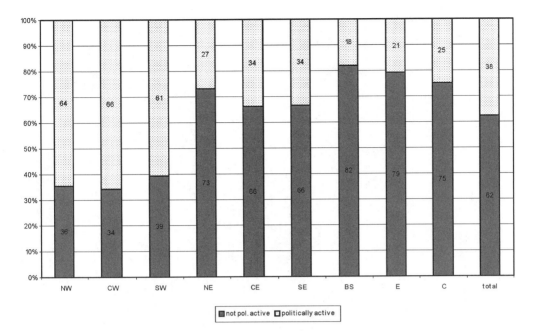

Political activism by region (see abbreviations on this page)

even now not all of them are fully democratic. Are young people there more enthusiastic about participating in politics?

Data from the World Values Survey carried out from 1995 to 1998 in many countries can help in understanding young people's engagement in politics in different regions. The total sample size was 7,740, and young people were counted as those between ages sixteen and twenty-five. The countries were grouped into geographical regions to make the sample more representative, as shown below:

NW: The Northwest (N=518) includes Norway (164), Sweden (163), and Finland (191).

NE: The Northeast (N=527) is the Baltic region including Lithuania (168), Latvia (217), and Estonia (142).

CW: The Central West (N=296) is represented by West Germany (133) and Switzerland (163).

CE: The Central East (N=854) includes Hungary (116), the Czech Republic (137), the Slovak Republic (148), Poland (149), East Germany (112), and Slovenia (192).

SW: The Southwest is represented by Spain (N=1,596).

SE: The Southeast (N=990) includes Albania (201), Croatia (221), Macedonia (165), Montenegro (37), Bosnia Herzegovina (180), and Serbia (186).

BS: Bulgaria (179), Romania (218), and Moldova (157) belong to the Black Sea region (N=554).

E: The East (N=926) includes Tambov (part of Russia) (67), Belarus (315), the Ukraine (316), and Russia (228).

C: The Caucasus region (N=1,479) includes Georgia (445), Armenia (541), and Azerbaijan (493).

Although only one-third of young people are interested in politics, 56 percent do occasionally discuss politics. Three-quarters of young people stated that they did not think that politics was important for their lives, so this seems to confirm the stereotype that most young people are not engaged in politics.

Next, we turned to the kinds of political actions that young people had actually carried out. Here we also found that only a minority of young people were actually engaged in politics: 28 percent had signed a petition; 22 percent had attended a demonstration; 9 percent had joined in boycotts,

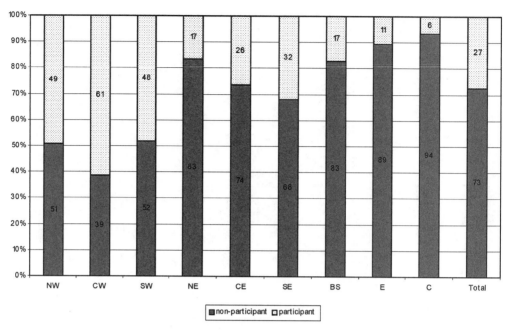

Civic participation by region (see abbreviations on page 241)

7 percent in strikes, and 2 percent in occupations. We should note that the demonstrations against engagement in the war in Iraq, for example, mobilized large numbers of young people, but these were still only a minority. However, a very large number had voted or were prepared to vote—about 90 percent. Hence, there is less evidence that young people in Europe do not want to vote, and in focus groups and interviews they claimed that they saw voting as something that all citizens should be obliged to do. We should be aware that in some parts of Europe voting is required by law. If we put all these kinds of political activism together and look at the regional differences, we find that there is much more political activism in Western Europe than in Eastern Europe (see figure titled "Political activism by region"). Hence, more mature democracies encouraged more political activism.

But political engagement can take many forms. For example, are young people active in civil society or as members in political organizations? Civic organizations include church and religious organizations, sports organizations (most common

among young people), arts and music organizations, charity organizations, and others. We found that two-thirds of young people did not belong to any organization; 20 percent participated in one civic organization and only 8 percent in two or more. There were important regional differences, and once more young people in Western Europe were much more active than those in Eastern and Central Europe (see figure titled "Civic participation by region").

Far fewer young people belonged to political organizations, by which we mean political parties, trade unions, environmental organizations, and professional associations. Only 6 percent of young people belonged to any of these organizations, and only 1 percent belonged to two or more. We should note though that in some parts of Europe trade-union membership is compulsory in many workplaces, so this might have pushed up the engagement. Political participation was slightly higher in Western than in Eastern Europe, but differences were small because it was generally very low everywhere.

So does this mean that many observers were correct in assuming that young people are apathetic, cynical, and disengaged from politics? To answer this question we would need to look beyond conventional forms of political activism like those we have described so far. There are a number of other ways in which young people can be active, and perhaps they are more interested in other kinds of issues.

For example, young people are far more active in a range of different kinds of involvement in ecological issues. Forty-one percent of young people said that they had chosen to buy household products that they thought were more environmentally friendly, and nearly half (45 percent) had reused or recycled something rather than throwing it away. Altogether 42 percent had tried to reduce water consumption for environmental reasons, and 13 percent had signed petitions aimed at protecting the environment, while 9 percent (almost one in ten young people in Europe) had made a donation to an environmental organization. Furthermore, more than half of young people (54 percent) were prepared to pay higher prices to protect the environment. Altogether, 20 percent had carried out several of these activities, 46 percent only some of these activities, and only one-third had never done any of the above activities. Although young people in Western Europe were more actively engaged in these types of activities, environmental issues were something that engaged large numbers of young people in both Eastern and Western Europe. Most interestingly, young women were most concerned about the environment, while young men were most often engaged in conventional politics.

Hence, it is certainly the case that only a minority of young people are actively engaged in conventional politics, and these are found more in Western than in Eastern Europe, and more of them are young men rather than young women. However, we can also detect another trend in young people's political activism: environmental activism. This was widespread across Eastern and Western Europe (although more common in Western Europe), and rather than representing a conventional kind of political engagement (e.g., joining an organization), it took the form of *lifestyle politics*. The way young people did their shopping and their propensity to recycle or to change their lifestyles in an environmentally friendly way can be considered a new kind of political activism. Therefore, we should take a broad definition of "political activism" when assessing young people's orientations and activities.

See also Australia, Youth Activism in; Demographic Trends Affecting the World's Youth; Eastern Europe, Youth and Citizenship in; European Identity and Citizenship; Immigrant Youth in Europe—Turks in Germany; Immigrant Youth in the United States; India, Youth Activism in; Indonesia, Youth Activism in; Nigeria, Youth Activism in; Palestinian *Intifada*; Russia, Youth Activism in; Serbia, Youth Activism in (1990–2000); Soweto Youth Activism (South Africa); State and Youth, The; Statute of the Child and Adolescent (Brazil); Tiananmen Square Massacre (1989); Transnational Identity; Transnational Youth Activism; Turkey, Youth Activism in; United Nations, Youth Activism and; Xenophobia; Zapatista Rebellion (Mexico); Zionist Youth Organizations.

Recommended Reading

Wilkinson, H., and Mulgan, G. (1995). Freedom's Children: Work, Relationships and Politics for Eighteen to Thirty-four-Year-Olds in Britain Today. London: Demos.

Claire Wallace

European Identity and Citizenship. The development of the European Union (EU) has created a new relationship between people in different European countries: they are now fellow citizens entitled to live and work in anywhere in the EU. While many view the EU as bringing positive change, there is also the potential for developments to be perceived negatively, for instance, as a threat to national employment through an increase in nonnational migrants or through feeling a loss of control of national laws and practices. Issues related to European integration may have particularly strong impact on young people. How the next generation views these issues and how they feel about being part of Europe are thus critical to the future of the EU. Generally, young people experience both frustrations and enthusiasm about being part of Europe and being European citizens. However, there is much variation across youth from different European countries. While young people are often described by the media as politically apathetic, research has found that they are, in fact, interested in political issues but are often alienated from party politics, finding more relevance in activities beyond traditional political structures.

The concept of citizenship itself is complex. It has many different meanings, changes over time, and is used in different ways by different groups. For some it is simply a formal legal category that conveys entitlement to claim basic rights by being a citizen of a country. Others use the concept with a focus on actions for the benefit of a wider community rather than solely for the benefit of the individual. Thus citizenship actions may be caring for others, taking part in community organizations, or participating in protests and demonstrations.

For young people citizenship is especially related to their employment status and autonomy. Recent social change has had a massive impact on the lives of young people, which gives them a very different experience than that of their parents and grandparents. With the decline of heavy manufacturing industries and the rise of economic uncertainty in many sectors across Europe, many young people are unemployed or forced into jobs for which they are overqualified, understimulated, have insecure contracts, are poorly paid, and work in poor conditions. The prospect of finding a job for life, which might have been guaranteed in previous generations, has today become a rare commodity. With the loss of industrial jobs and greater insecurity in employment has come the need to be more educated and skilled to compete

in the workforce. This has meant that many more young people stay in education longer. Without a job with a living wage it becomes harder for young people to start up independent households of their own. The transition from being a youth to being an adult has thus lengthened with dependence on parents and/or the state for longer periods. In Britain, as in other countries, the transition out of the parental home is not a one-way ticket anymore with young people sometimes having to return to the parental home if their employment ends.

Thus, many young people do not enjoy a full complement of citizenship rights until increasingly older ages. In fact, in Britain the state itself has made this situation worse by withdrawing state benefits to young people until they are older. This affects their ability to position themselves in society and can contribute to young people's social exclusion at a time when they need the most support. Constraints on becoming financially independent diminish the ability to practice citizenship or engage in community life by such actions as attending group meetings or affording membership fees. The insecurity caused by social upheaval and the lengthening of childhood before formal citizenship is obtained may help explain the lack of certain sorts of citizenship actions that are often the subject of media complaints about apparently apolitical or apathetic young people.

There has been concern recently that while people may receive rights through being a citizen, few are active in the fulfillment of these rights, and even fewer are active within their communities. Examples of attempts to increase "active" citizenship include introducing citizenship as a formal aspect of the school curriculum in England and Wales and the development of a comprehensive training book on citizenship, youth, and Europe by the Council of Europe (2003). The development of a European parliamentary focus on young people has also emphasized citizenship.

It is up to the public authorities to bridge the gap between young people's eagerness to express their opinions and the methods and structures which society offers. Failure to do so might fuel the "citizenship deficit," or even encourage protest (European Commission 2001, 10).

In Europe the EU has added another level of formal citizenship to that of the nation. All citizens of countries within the European Union are formally European citizens, who have the following rights and entitlements:

- The right to move freely and to reside in the territory of member states;
- The right to vote and to stand as candidates in local and European Parliament elections in the member state of residence;
- Entitlement to protection in a non-EU country in which a citizen's own member state is not represented, by the diplomatic or consular authorities of any other member state; and
- The right to petition the European Parliament and to apply to the European ombudsman. *See* http://europa.eu.int/comm/archives/abc/cit3_en.htm.

The EU officially came into being in 1993 following the signing of the Maastricht Treaty in 1992. Enthusiasts of the EU see it as an opportunity to develop a "people's Europe" in which people feel a strong sense of being European. Attempts to develop such a sense of European identity have been made by the EU through the creation of symbols of commonality such as a European Union flag, anthem, and the euro currency.

While the EU has brought positive economic change, especially to poorer nations in Europe, there is also the potential for developments to be perceived negatively, for instance, as a threat to national employment through an increase in nonnational migrants, or through feeling a loss of control of one's own country through the intrusion of European laws which alter common national practices. Thus, in some countries there is still debate about whether it is wise to be a part of the EU, and issues such as the introduction of the euro currency are hotly contested with some countries, such as Denmark, finding their citizens voting "no" in a national referendum on its use.

A large study titled "Orientations of Young Men and Women to Citizenship and European Identity," conducted between 2001 and 2004, funded by the European Commission looked at youth, citizenship, and European identity (see http://www.sociology.ed.ac.uk/youth/). This research was carried out with young people aged eighteen to twenty-four at ten sites across Europe: the city of Vienna and the Bregenz area of Vorarlberg in Austria, the cities Chemnitz and Bielefeld in former East and West Germany, Madrid and Bilbao in Spain, Manchester and Edinburgh in Great Britain, and the capital cities of Prague in the Czech Republic and Bratislava in the Slovak Republic, formerly part of Czechoslovakia. The sites were chosen as contrasting pairs with different relationships to the nation (or former nation in the case of the former Czechoslovakian cities). For instance, Madrid is the capital of Spain and has a strong identification with the nation, while Bilbao is situated in the Basque country and has a strong regional identity and less of an affiliation to the rest of Spain.

Young people have different experiences of citizenship depending upon which country they come from, whether they are employed, whether they receive financial support, whether that support comes from the state or their parents, and whether they are themselves parents and full-time caregivers, usually mothers, of their children. Thus, citizenship can be shaped by the nation in which one resides and varies across different national histories, cultures, and institutional practices. In addition, a young person's age, socioeconomic circumstances, and gender will likely affect her or his citizenship orientations and behavior. Youth in various parts of Europe experience different lives despite commonalities of age and a certain level of shared culture (such as new forms of communication and global trends in youth culture) and experiences (such as high youth unemployment in comparison to other age-groups). For example, in Spain and in other parts of the Mediterranean, young people tend not to leave their parents' houses until they are in their late twenties, by which time they may have succeeded in finding work or have married. In the northern countries in Europe, particularly in Scandinavia, young people tend to leave home at the age of eighteen or nineteen, often to go to university, training, or work. There is more state support in the northern European countries, which is absent in Spain and other Mediterranean countries. This support makes it more feasible for youth, even those who do not study or work, to leave home.

Some European countries are marked by distinct social histories that still have ramifications for the current activism of youth. Former Communist societies in Europe do not have a tradition of political action because social movements did not operate under Communism, although volunteering was expected and became a normalized activity. This is evident in the higher rates of volunteering undertaken in some former Communist countries. In Bulgaria in 1990 and 1991 young people took part in the protests that eventually led to change in the government and even helped to establish new forms of parliamentary democracy following the political change. However, since the radical start of the new democracy, some young people who had high hopes following the collapse of Communism soon found themselves feeling pessimistic as the transformations they envisaged failed to materialize as quickly as they had imagined. Since the fall of Communism, young people are more educated in citizenship and democracy, and there has been a growth in the numbers attending youth groups.

Many national variations can be identified in terms of citizenship behaviors, but there are limited gender differences. For example, in the "Orientations of Young Men and Women to Citizenship and European Identity" study, young people from Edinburgh and Manchester showed

the least enthusiasm for voting in European elections. There was more readiness to vote for members of the European Parliament in Bratislava and Prague despite the fact that the right to vote in a European election had not yet even been obtained, as the Czech and Slovak Republics were still in the process of joining the EU. Young people in Austria were the most committed to voting. Spannring, Wallace, and Datler (2004) suggest that this comes from young people in Austria having a better understanding of the EU, stronger second-language skills, and greater experience with other countries and that these factors flow into an interest in the European political process.

However, while young people in Edinburgh and Manchester were alienated from the formal political processes, they were still engaged in social and political issues. The alienation of many from party politics was expressed in their saying that no political party represented their views. They thus refused to vote. However, the same young people expressed interest in and willingness to discuss a range of topics related to politics and citizenship.

This combination of concern with politics with an avoidance of formal, political institutions is generally the case across Europe and may bode well for citizenship, so long as it is "activated." Historical differences do matter, however. For example, markedly fewer young people in the Czech and Slovak Republics were engaged with citizenship, perhaps explained by the lack of campaigning organizations dealing with such issues, a legacy from former Communist days.

Only minorities of young people were involved in organizations, clubs, or societies, but again with significant differences. Only 10 percent of young people in Manchester and in Bratislava were members of clubs compared with 45 percent in Bregenz in Vorarlberg, Austria. With the exception of Madrid in Spain and Bratislava in the Slovak Republic, men tended to be members of clubs much more frequently than women. Sports clubs were the organizations where most of these memberships were held.

The worry for politicians in Europe is that if people are alienated from formal political structures but protest activities have become the norm, then the future holds great difficulties for the smooth running of democracies. Not surprisingly, politicians and advocates of current democratic structures are keen to encourage young people into more formal political structures. For instance, in Britain and elsewhere in Europe, youth councils and parliaments have developed for young people to have their say in the running of issues, usually local ones. The Eurobarometer (2001) survey of young people suggests that a large number of young people believe that active participation would be most encouraged by asking young people's viewpoints (46 percent) as well as providing youth-specific information campaigns (45 percent). The European Youth Parliament brings together young people from various parts of Europe to discuss current issues in relation to youth. These forums support young people's interest in broader politics and provide the opportunity to be involved and to learn how they can work to see their input making a difference.

Another crucial issue receiving attention from researchers and policymakers is how young people feel about their locality—their region, their nation, and Europe—and to see which was the most important to them. The "Orientations of Young Men and Women to Citizenship and European Identity" study suggests that more young people express attachment either to their nation or to their region than to Europe. The proportion of respondents expressing attachment to Europe was particularly low among residents of Edinburgh, Scotland. This was surprising, given that Scottish people are sometimes cited as potentially having a strong feeling of being European. The claim is sometimes made that Scots turn away from Britain and toward Europe in reaction to their perceived situation as a nation which does not have the power to run itself independently but is subsumed into Great Britain.

When young people were asked about whether they considered themselves European citizens, respondents in Germany and to a lesser extent Spain tended to think of themselves much more frequently as European citizens than those in Great Britain and the Czech and Slovak Republics. Interestingly, when asked how frequently they thought of themselves as global citizens, more Spanish youth reported feeling this way than those who felt European. Once again, only a very few people in the British and Czech and Slovak sites thought of themselves in this way with any frequency. This suggests that young people in Spain (and also Germany) may frequently focus beyond the EU borders, while young people in England and Scotland are very inward-looking, not focusing beyond the boundaries of their respective nations.

One apparently positive factor is impact of language skills and visits to other European countries. A sense of being European can be developed by encouraging the learning of foreign European languages and making personal contacts across Europe beyond national borders. These findings suggest that schemes set up by the EU to promote the experience of young people in different nations have the potential to raise the sense among participants of being European.

In concluding, young people's access to the full rights of citizenship is not automatically acquired at eighteen because their transition from the family to independent adult lives is often thwarted by unemployment, the need to train or to be educated for longer, lack of finances to move out of their parents' homes, and lack of resources to take part in organizations. However, this does not mean that they are unwilling to be active citizens.

Current research suggests that young people are concerned about many social and political issues, but such expressions are left inactivated or are activated through political conduits outside formal political structures. Many young people feel frustrated with party and parliamentary politics and believe that their opinions will not be heard or make a difference. While there is the possibility for many more young people to develop a European identity, few currently have a strong sense of one. However, a sense of being European is stronger in some countries than others, reflecting historical differences and opportunities to travel across European boundaries, to learn languages and take part in exchanges with peers from other European countries. Overall, the idea of a "people's Europe" seems very distant at present.

See also Australia, Youth Activism in; Demographic Trends Affecting the World's Youth; Eastern Europe, Youth and Citizenship in; Europe, Comparing Youth Activism in; Immigrant Youth in Europe—Turks in Germany; Immigrant Youth in the United States; India, Youth Activism in; Indonesia, Youth Activism in; Nigeria, Youth Activism in; Palestinian *Intifada*; Russia, Youth Activism in; Serbia, Youth Activism in (1990–2000); Soweto Youth Activism (South Africa); State and Youth, The; Statute of the Child and Adolescent (Brazil); Tiananmen Square Massacre (1989); Transnational Identity; Transnational Youth Activism; Turkey, Youth Activism in; United Nations, Youth Activism and; Xenophobia; Zapatista Rebellion (Mexico); Zionist Youth Organizations.

Recommended Reading

Council of Europe (2003). *Under Construction: Citizenship, Youth and Europe.* Strasbourg: Council of Europe Publishing. Available at http://www.jugendfuereuropa.de/static/common/download.php/132/tkit7.pdf.

Eurobarometer (2001). "Young Europeans in 2001: Results of a European Opinion Poll." Brussels: European Commission. Available at http://banners.noticiasdot.com/termometro/boletines/docs/paises/europa/ue/2001/ue_young_summary_en-2001.pdf.

Eurodesk, providing information about young people and Europe. See http://www.eurodesk.org/new/.

The European Union. See http://europa.eu.int/.

The European Youth Parliament, an international, nonpartisan organization that aims to raise young people's awareness of European issues. See http://www.eyp.org/intro.htm.

European Commission (2001). *White Paper: A New Impetus for European Youth.* Brussels: European Commission. Available at http://europa.eu.int/comm/youth/whitepaper/download/whitepaper_en.pdf.

Flanagan, C., Jonsson, B., Botcheva, L., Csapo, B., Bowes, J. M., Macek, P., Averina, I., and Sheblanova, E. (1999). "Adolescents and the 'Social Contract': Developmental Roots of Citizenship in Seven Countries." In *Roots of Civic Identity: International Perspectives on Community Service and Activism in Youth,* edited by M. Yates and J. Youniss. Cambridge: Cambridge University Press, pp. 135–155.

Fuss, D., Garcia Albacete, G., and Rodriguez Monter, M. (2004). "The Role of Language Skills and Foreign Country Experiences in the Development of a European Identity." *Sociológia,* 36 (3): 273–292.

Grundy, S. (2003). "Views and Actions of Citizenship amongst Young Adults in Europe: Looking at Gender and National Differences." Paper presented at the 2003 European Sociological Association Conference, Murcia, Spain. Available at http://www.sociology.ed.ac.uk/youth/docs/SG_murcia_paper.pdf.

Grundy, S., and Jamieson, L. (2003). "Are We All Europeans Now? Local, National and Supranational Identities of Young Adults." Paper given at the British Sociological Association Conference, York. Available at http://www.sociology.ed.ac.uk/youth/docs/UK_BSA_paper.pdf.

Grundy, S., and Jamieson, L. (2004). "Action, Reaction, Inaction? Young Adults' Citizenship in Britain." *Sociológia,* 36 (3): 237–252.

Iacovou, M., and Berthoud, R. (2001). *Young People's Lives: A Map of Europe.* Colchester: Working Papers of the Institute for Social and Economic Research, University of Essex. Available at http://iserwww.essex.ac.uk/pubs/iserreps/002.pdf.

Jamieson, L., et al. (2003). Working paper 1F: Report of international, national and regional variation in surveys of European Identity (All Partners) September 2003. Available at http://www.sociology.ed.ac.uk/youth/Research_docs.html.

Jamieson, L., et al. (2005). Orientations of Young Men and Women to Citizenship and European Identity." Available at http://www.sociology.ed.ac.uk/youth/.

Roker, D., Player, K., and Coleman, J. (1999). "Young People's Voluntary and Campaigning Activities as Sources of Political Education." *Oxford Review of Education* 25 (1 and 2): 185–198.

Spannring, R., Wallace, C., and Datler, G. (2004). "'If You Have a Grandpa Send Him to Europe': Attitudes of Young Austrians towards the EU Elections." *Sociológia,* 36 (3): 253–272.

Sue Grundy

F

Feminism. Feminism is the belief in the social, political, and economic equality of the sexes. It exists as a movement grounded in grassroots activism as well as a theory developed and studied in academia. Feminism considers the collective interests of women in economic, social, and religious contexts and explores questions of gender, power, and culture. In addition, feminism acknowledges the experiences of individual women and their choices about their bodies, education, careers, religion, and family life.

Mary Wollstonecraft's *A Vindication of the Rights of Woman,* published in 1792, is often cited as one of the first works of explicitly feminist writing. Prior to that however, the words and actions of women ranging from the Greek poet Sappho to the writer and mystic Hildegard to Egyptian queen Cleopatra to the British monarch Elizabeth I exhibited what can be described as aspects of feminist thought. These include a critique of the systemic ways in which women have been at a disadvantage to men in patriarchal societies, that is, those run by men. This includes the inability to hold property, vote, or divorce; it also includes the restricted options for women's participation in educational, work, and religious settings.

While most historical women cited today as feminists would not have been known as such during their own time, their lives are important markers in the evolution of feminism. Furthermore, feminist activism is closely linked to other movements, such as abolition, civil rights, and antiwar movements. It is essential to note feminism's changing and multifaceted nature and its fluctuating boundaries. However, feminism in the United States can be considered as a series of waves. As such, feminism's more formal roots are said to lie in the nineteenth-century emergence of the idea that women were at a disadvantage in a patriarchal society. This is often referred to as the first wave of feminism. The first women's rights convention at Seneca Falls, New York, in 1848 marked the first real organization of women in pursuit of expanded rights. Led by abolitionists Elizabeth Cady Stanton and Lucretia Mott, the convention put forth a listing of discrimination against women, the "Declaration of Sentiments." This became an influential document in the feminist movement. Other activists like Susan B. Anthony, Charlotte Perkins Gilman, Victoria Woodhull, and Virginia Woolf, through their writings and actions, further helped to articulate arguments for women's interests and rights. These included the right to vote as well as increased creative and career opportunities. It was not until 1920, however, that the nineteenth amendment gave women the right to vote, and women continued to struggle to have the time and chance to pursue the arts, education, and fulfilling careers.

The second wave of feminism, often marked from the early 1960s through the 1970s, saw even greater social and political action for and by women. In 1963 Betty Friedan published *The Feminist Mystique,* a book that articulated the dissatisfaction many women felt and argued that women would not find fulfillment only from marriage and motherhood. This book was a catalyst for the establishment of more formal networks of activism by women; for instance, Friedan founded the National Organization for Women in 1967. She was also a leader in the struggle for the Equal Rights Amendment, which was passed by Congress in 1972 but has yet to be ratified by the necessary number of states.

Throughout the 1960s, 1970s, and 1980s feminists organized around a number of other issues. Women formed consciousness-raising groups where they gathered to discuss their lives, held marches, and conducted teach-ins to educate themselves and men about inequalities. They promoted reproductive rights, including abortion and contraception, and saw the 1973 *Roe v. Wade* Supreme Court decision that legalized abortion. They fought for economic parity, working to bring more women into male-dominated professions, and to make salaries equitable. They also drew attention to the objectification of women in the media and inequalities in athletics. The passage of Title IX in 1972 required schools to provide equal opportunities for male and female athletes and has dramatically increased the number of women who participate in sports. Women also brought their gender to the forefront in the arts, making women's issues and perspectives more prominent.

As feminism expanded its reach it also opened itself up to dissension. Betty Friedan and NOW were accused of not welcoming lesbians, and women including Gloria Steinem, who started *Ms.* magazine in 1972 and founded the National Women's Political Caucus and Women's Action Alliance, were faulted for focusing primarily on the concerns of white, middle- and upper-class women. One notable critic is the writer Alice Walker, who used the word "womanism" to describe a fuller kind of feminism that included the experiences of black women. Other writers, like Audre Lorde and Adrienne Rich demanded that individual feminists and feminist organizations broaden their agendas. Feminism also faced critics who questioned its very existence.

This second wave coincided with much other social upheaval in the United States, and many women took on leadership roles in the antiwar and civil rights movements. It came to be understood that while feminism provides an umbrella for the advocacy of women's rights and concerns, it does not pertain to one way of thinking or acting. In addition to conflict among feminists who identify as straight and as lesbians and those who are white and women of color, there are differences among those concerned with the Western and non-Western world and those who do not include men with those who do. There is also discord between feminists who are grassroots activists and those who work in the academic world. Within academia, feminism has entered into disciplines including sociology, linguistics, literature, history, and psychology. Feminist scholars promote the inclusion of women and argument from women's perspective in these various disciplines. For example, a history class with a feminist perspective might include the diaries and letters of women as important texts for understanding a particular historical period. The ideas of female philosophers and writers such as Simone de Beauvoir, bell hooks, Hélène Cixous, and Luce Irigaray have also contributed to feminist thought. In addition, by the 1990s women's studies classes and departments, with their interdisciplinary approaches to considering issues of gender, gained prominence on many college campuses.

The beliefs of feminism have become so commonplace that many women no longer identify them as such, nor do they call themselves feminists. However, groups like NOW and the Feminist Majority hold the view that women's rights and interests are still in jeopardy. They continue to focus on the lack of women in politics; the objectification of women in the media, including advertising; and pornography. Feminists also work for women's health issues, including access to emergency contraception and health care. In the workplace, feminists focus on the continued pay disparity;

the "glass ceiling," which indicates the low numbers of women in executive roles; and family leave, which helps working men and women take time off to care for children or parents. International issues like female mutilation and educational opportunities for girls are also important feminist issues. In addition, sexual harassment and violence are active areas of feminist work, particularly on college campuses.

In fact, it is younger women who are considered to be the third wave of feminism. Newer organized groups like the Third Wave Foundation promote their interests with financial support, and more established women's organizations like NARAL, ProChoice, the Feminist Majority, and NOW court this younger generation. Having grown up with the benefits that second-wave feminists fought for, younger women often bypass organized feminism for a more individual kind. Some older feminists believe this could be detrimental to the gains they made and worry that their causes are not being advanced. Many young feminists, however, are less interested in specifically women-centered activism in the United States and often turn to women's issues in other countries. They are also often more concerned with social issues like hunger, the environment, and gay rights. Many third-wave feminists put forth an increased emphasis on the claiming of language like "bitch" and "slut" as well as their own sexuality. They express their feminism through individual action: how they speak, dress, and act. Still, some young activists are organizing by starting and running high-school and college women's centers and by participating in campus events like "Take Back the Night," a national event to protest sexual assault. They also push for more female professors, particularly in traditionally male fields, and for courses about women. Young feminists have also showed their unique brand of activism through the formation of activist groups like the Radical Cheerleaders, who cheer at rallies, often for other social issues.

While feminism's face, theories, and activism have changed over time, the basic belief in the social, political, and economic equality of the sexes remains constant.

See also Chat Rooms, Girls' Empowerment and; Gender Differences in the Political Attitudes of Youth; Riot Grrrl.

Recommended Reading

Friedan, B. (2001). *The Feminist Mystique*. New York: W. W. Norton.
Labaton, V., and Lundy Martin, D., eds. (2004). *The Fire This Time*. New York: Anchor Books.
Walker, A. (2003). *In Search of Our Mothers' Gardens: Womanist Prose*. New York: Harcourt Brace.

Kate Dube

Film/Video as a Tool for Youth Activism. Film has been used as a tool for social activism and historical documentation since the early 1900s. Producers have addressed and captured issues such as racism, politics, human rights, intolerance, and social reformation. *The Birth of a Nation* by D. W. Griffith depicts in chilling clarity the racial assumptions and tension of the late 1800s. John Ford portrays the images and challenges of poverty following the depression in his early 1940s film *The Grapes of Wrath*. Rory Kennedy also documents the issues of poverty in her 1990s film *American Hollow*. In the twenty-first century, Michael Moore of *Roger and Me*, *Bowling for Columbine*, and *Fahrenheit 9/11* challenges myths about capitalism and terrorism and our sanguine views of acceptance of violence in America. Along with the Hollywood blockbusters are the independent films created to challenge and document historical issues. Video has also begun to take its place in the visual arts as the less expensive and more accessible counterpart to film.

Recently, a younger generation of producers has taken up this method of creative activism. Adolescents and young adults have adopted video as a medium for challenging popular culture and perspectives, creating dialogue among peers about issues that concern them, and expressing their personal views. This relatively new form of expression is also a means whereby young people can challenge the way they are represented in the media. Finally, as the young Anne Frank was able to use her writing to provide a descriptive historical account of her experiences with the Holocaust, youth are now using film as a means to document current issues and social change.

A tool for civic engagement and activism, video offers youth the rare opportunity of framing, separating, and analyzing the reality surrounding them. With video, youth analyze issues that concern them, such as violence, depression, inequality, suicide, stereotypes, and poverty. Often, these are issues that have bothered young people, ones they have wanted to analyze and address but were without means to raise them. As a consequence, they had learned to ignore and/or accept these issues passively. However, when youth bring a camera into their local community, these issues surface through dialog and events and are captured by the camera as evidence that the problems exist. When the youth later review their captured footage, a distance is created between the issue of concern and the young producers, allowing for discourse, analysis, and speculation on future change. The ability to fast-forward, rewind, and pause allows for repeated examination at whatever pace the youth need to establish and examine individual perspectives. In a sense, they are given the opportunity to manipulate reality into a pace that allows them to consider what is actually occurring, instead of the quick pace of real-life experience, which rarely allows for reflection and analysis.

Over the past decade, a large variety of social programs have been organized to encourage and assist in this new form of youth activism. The Human Rights Watch (HRW), a national organization promoting the protection of human rights, has created an annual international film festival in which it encourages youth producers to exhibit their material. To offer further support to the youth film movement, the Human Rights Watch started a program that offers training and materials to teachers and after-school programs to conduct film workshops and media education for students. It is HRW's goal to "inspire youth to actively critique mainstream media and to produce videos that reflect their own unique perspectives on human rights issues."

Samples of the issues that youth have addressed through this program include sexuality, urban development, militarism, and poverty. An example of a piece created by students receiving support from HRW is the film *Some Place to Call Home*. This piece, created in 1996, was produced by a group of students living in foster homes. The film depicts challenges of living in transitory housing through the eyes of the youth in the foster-care system. In 2003 a new group of high-school students decided to build upon the original work by tracking each of the students filmed in the original piece. This second piece is titled *Not Me, Not Mine: Adult Survivors of Foster Care*. *Not Me, Not Mine* further elaborates on the lives of the original producers as they have grown up and out of the foster-care system. This film is currently in the HRW 2003–2004 film-festival library and is available as an educational resource for schools and other institutions.

Educational Video Center (EVC) is another program which offers youth the opportunity to use film as a means of activism. This center serves groups of teens from poverty-stricken areas in New York City by offering a semester-long, credit-bearing program. EVC encourages students to examine their surroundings and address the issues that are present in their environment. One young girl created a film which confronted the poor living conditions of her tenement complex. After speaking with neighbors, gathering signatures for a petition requesting attention to the poor conditions, and documenting a number of infractions against her landlord, the resulting footage landed her an interview on the

Today show. Shortly after the program aired, her landlord sold the building, and the necessary changes were made.

Other students in the EVC program have created films that have challenged unequal educational opportunities, drug use among peers, racial tension between Jews and African Americans, and the juvenile criminal-justice system. In speaking of the motivation behind the creation of these films, one student said the following: "I like telling stories that matter. Not idiotic stories about asteroids hitting the earth [or] a woman running away from a serial killer. I like telling stories that you can watch and you can learn something from—like, 'I can't believe that's going on, I should do something about it.' [They're] really social change media, things that you watch that make you want to act." EVC provides an opportunity for youth to use film as a mode to critically and actively examine their social conditions, peer influences, and cultural perspectives.

Using film has also led a large number of adolescent youth to reexamine how they themselves are represented in mainstream media. An awareness of the generally negative representation of youth in modern culture has led many youth media groups to produce films challenging and redefining who youth are. Reel Grrls is an after-school media program offered exclusively to female adolescents. Beyond teaching media literacy skills, this program offers young women the opportunity to critically examine women's portrayal in mainstream media and analyze the effects this imagery has on their own self-image and perspectives. One of the first films produced through this program, *Reel Grrls* is a composite of public-service announcements (PSAs) consisting of animation, self-reflection, music, and humor to challenge the representation of adolescent women in the media and the effect this representation has upon their lives. This film has been voted one of the top ten videos of the year for young people by the American Library Association.

In Minnesota there is another group of young adults taking mainstream images into their own hands and providing broader perspectives. A statewide video project, titled Community Video, sponsored by the Orton Foundation, is providing rural youth the opportunity to examine concerns within their own communities. One group in particular has decided to directly challenge the stereotypes they feel are held within their immediate community. This particular community is relatively diverse due to a local reservation of Native Americans. The racial tension and clichés formed within the high-school setting have concerned a small group of local teens. As a topic for their film, they decided to have their community and peers define "what is normal." When completed, this film will be shown to the community-at-large in a local public space. It is the hope of this young group of producers that their peers and fellow community members will realize that there is not one standard for normalcy and thus help to defuse some of the current tension.

Literally hundreds of media literacy programs are forming to provide young adults with opportunities to have voices within their communities and society. Because the images captured on film are based on the decisions of young people, these films provide an archive, a historical documentation of current experience and culture through the eyes of adolescents and young adults. These productions are being shown both nationally and internationally, creating dialog and recognition of local and global concerns. As Steven Goodman, the founder of EVC, states, "Video documentary enables students to bear witness to their social conditions and look for solutions.... We tend to go through life almost being lulled into accepting our conditions, but there's something about video that captures life, reframes it, positions it." This creative form of activism allows youth to reveal visually and realistically issues that concern them and not only ask that change occur but suggest directions change should take and ways to make it happen.

See also Digital Divide; MTV's Choose or Lose Campaign (1992–); New Media; Participatory Action Research (PAR) by Youth; Positive Youth Development, Programs Promoting.

Recommended Reading

Davies, S., Pinkett, R. D., Servon, L., and Wiley–Schwartz, A. (2003). "Community Technology Centers as Catalysts for Community Change: A Report to the Ford Foundation." Plainfield, NJ: BCT Partners.
Educational Video Center: http://www.evc.org/.
Feuerstein, M. (1999). "Media Literacy in Support of Critical Thinking." *Journal of Educational Media*, 24 (1).
The Freechild Project: Young People and Social Change: http://www.freechild.org/index.htm.
Goodman, S. (2003). *Teaching Youth Media: A Critical Guide to Literacy, Video Production, and Social Change*. New York: Teachers College Press.
Johnson, L. L. (2001). *Media, Education and Change*. New York: Peter Lang Publishing.
Kinkade, S., and Macy, C. (2003). *What Works in Youth Media: Case Studies from Around the World*. Takoma Park, MD: Forum for Youth Investment, International Youth Foundation.
Tolman, J., and Pittman, K., with Cervone, B., Cushman, K., Rowley, L., Kinkade, S., Phillips, J., and Duque, S. (2001). *Youth Acts, Community Impacts: Stories of Youth Engagement with Real Results*. Community and Youth Development Series, Vol. 7. Takoma Park, MD: Forum for Youth Investment, International Youth Foundation.
Video Machete: http://www.videomachete.org/about.html.

Carmen M. Hamilton

First Amendment. *See Tinker v. Des Moines Independent School District* (1969).

Flow: Youth Motivation and Engagement.
Youth clearly need to be motivated to show activism and they need to show some engagement in the activity. There is a long history of research in psychology on motivation and engagement. Sometimes people, including youth, report a subjective experience that they enjoyed so much that they were willing to go to great lengths to experience it again. This we have called the flow experience; flow is an extreme form, in a positive sense, of motivation or engagement. The defining feature of flow is intense experiential involvement in moment-to-moment activity. This entry describes the development of this idea of flow in the context of psychological research on motivation.

Psychological accounts of motivation often start with the assumption that human beings have "needs" or "drives" for a few wired-in goals, such as self-preservation and reproduction, and that all other motivations are if not reducible, then at least based on such needs. For example, Maslow's hierarchy of needs assumes that survival takes precedence over all other considerations, and no other need becomes active until survival is reasonably assured. On closer examination, however, this simple causality seems much less convincing. A species needs to take care of many other priorities besides survival and reproduction to survive. At the human stage of evolution, where adaptation and survival depend increasingly on flexible responses mediated by conscious thought, members of the species had to be motivated by curiosity, by the willingness to take risks, to explore, and to try new things in order to master and control a hostile and changing environment.

It makes sense to assume that natural selection favored those individuals and their descendants who enjoyed acts of mastery and control, just as survival was enhanced when other acts necessary for survival, such as eating and sex, became experienced as pleasurable. The idea that the ability to operate effectively in the environment fulfills a primary need is not new in psychology. In Germany Karl Groos (1901) and Karl Bühler (1930) elaborated the concept of *funktionlust* or "activity pleasure," which Jean Piaget included in the earliest stages of sensori-motor development as the "pleasure of being a cause" that drove infants to experiment (e.g., Piaget 1951). In more recent psychological thought, Hebb (1965) and Berlyne (1960) focused on the nervous system's need for optimal levels of stimulation to explain exploratory behavior and the seeking of novelty, while White (1959) and DeCharms (1968) focused on people's need to feel in control, to be the causal agents of their actions. Later Deci and Ryan elaborated on this line of argument by claiming that both a need for competence and a need for autonomy were innate psychological needs that must be satisfied for psychological growth and well-being. But the theories that provide explanations for why people are motivated to master and control tend to be distal. In other words, they provide sensible explanations, typically based on an evolutionary framework, for why such behaviors should have become established over many generations, in order to support the reproductive success of individuals. However, for an activity pattern to become established in a species' repertoire, it has to be experienced as enjoyable by the individual. To explain how this happens, a proximal theory of motivation is needed.

A "phenomenological account" of motivation is examined in the present article. It tries to look very closely at what people actually experience when they are involved in activities that involve mastery, creativity, and autonomous behavior, without prejudging the reasons why such experiences exist. This line of explanation assumes that the human organism is a system in its own right, not reducible to lower levels of complexity such as stimulus-response pathways, unconscious processes, or neurological structures. Such an explanation is not incompatible with motivational accounts based on simpler needs. Quite often the two perspectives support each other, driving the organism in the same direction. But it is also often the case that genetically programmed instructions may come in conflict with the learned ones or that the unconscious forces press in a direction contrary to what the phenomenological reality suggests.

The phenomenological account focuses on events occurring in consciousness. It is what has come to be called the flow experience. This concept emerged over a quarter century ago as a result of a series of studies of what were initially called autotelic activities, that is, things people did for the sheer sake of doing, without expectation of any subsequent reward or outcome.

The initial question was: why do people perform time-consuming, difficult, and often dangerous activities for which they receive no discernible extrinsic rewards? This was the question that originally prompted a program of research that involved extensive interviews with hundreds of rock climbers, chess players, athletes, and artists. The basic conclusion was that in all the various groups studied, the respondents reported a very similar subjective experience that they enjoyed so much that they were willing to go to great lengths to experience it again. This we eventually called the flow experience because in describing how it felt when the activity was going well, several respondents used the metaphor of a current that carried them along effortlessly.

In other words, flow is a subjective state that people report when they are completely involved in something to the point of forgetting time, fatigue, and everything else but the activity itself. It is what we feel when we read a well-crafted novel or play a good game of squash or take part in a stimulating conversation. The defining feature of flow is intense experiential involvement in moment-to-moment activity. Attention is fully invested in the task at hand, and the person functions at his or her fullest capacity. It is a state often reported by athletes and artists but also by people involved in everyday activities. For instance, Mark Strand, former poet laureate of the United States, in one of our interviews described this state while writing as follows: "You're right in the work, you lose your sense of time, you're completely enraptured, you're completely caught up in what you are doing.... When you are working on something and you are working well, you have the feeling that there's no other way of saying what you're saying." (Csikszentmihalyi 1996, 121).

The intense experiential involvement of flow results in three additional subjective characteristics commonly reported: the merging of action and awareness, a sense of control, and an altered sense of time. Action and awareness sometimes merge. We typically devote a good deal of mental energy to thoughts that are irrelevant to what we are doing at the present moment. We think of past accomplishments, future possibilities, pending obligations. During flow, however, attentional resources are fully invested in the task at hand, so that objects beyond the immediate interaction generally fail to enter awareness.

One such object is the self. Respondents frequently describe a loss of self-consciousness during flow. In the terms that George Herbert Mead introduced, the "me" disappears during flow, and the "I" takes over.

One advantage of such a compelling focus of attention is that most of the irrelevant distractions excluded from consciousness tend to be stressful or depressing. The default option of consciousness is a chaotic review of things that one fears or desires, resulting in a phenomenological state I have elsewhere labeled "psychic entropy"(Csikszentmihalyi 1988, 1993). In flow, attention becomes ordered around the pursuit of a clear goal, resulting in the exclusion of thoughts and feelings that we experience as negative.

During flow, we typically experience a sense of control—or, more precisely, a lack of anxiety about losing control that is typical of many situations in normal life. This sense of control is also reported in activities that involve serious risks such as hang gliding, rock climbing, and race-car driving, activities that to an outsider would seem to be much more potentially dangerous than the affairs of everyday life. Worrying about whether we can succeed at what we are doing—on the job, in relationships, even in crossing a busy street—is one of the major sources of psychic entropy in everyday life, and its reduction during flow is one of the reasons such an experience becomes enjoyable and thus rewarding.

William James noted in 1890 that duration seems to increase when "we grow attentive to the passage of time itself." During flow, attention is so fully invested in the task at hand that there is little or none left over to devote toward the mental processes that contribute to the experience of duration. As a result, persons in flow typically report time passing quickly.

Flow experiences are relatively rare in everyday life, but almost everything—work, study, or religious ritual—is able to produce them provided certain conditions are met. Past research suggests three conditions of key importance. First, flow tends to occur when the activity one engages in contains a clear set of goals. These goals serve to add direction and purpose to behavior. Their value lies in their capacity to structure experience by channeling attention, rather than being ends in themselves.

A second prerequisite for flow is immediate feedback. The actor needs to negotiate the continually changing environmental demands that are part of all experientially involved activity. Immediate feedback serves this purpose—it informs the participant how well he or she is progressing in the activity and dictates whether to adjust or maintain the present course of action. It leaves the participant with little doubt about what to do next, thereby promoting the sense of control that so often accompanies flow.

Of course, positive feedback is preferable, as this improves the sense of competence. However, because flow takes place at a high level of challenges, occasional failure is inevitable. From a phenomenological viewpoint failure is not necessarily aversive, as long as the person knows why it occurred. No climber wishes to fall off the rock face, but the possibility of falling is what keeps the mind and the body concentrated on the task. Without an occasional fall the activity would soon become meaningless.

Finally, entering flow depends on establishing a balance between perceived challenges and perceived skills. This condition is reminiscent of the concept of "optimal arousal" but differs from it in highlighting the fact that what counts at the phenomenological level is the perception of the demands and abilities, not necessarily their objective presence.

When perceived challenges and skills are well-matched, as in a close game of tennis or a satisfying musical performance, attention is completely absorbed. This balance, however, is intrinsically fragile. If challenges begin to exceed skills, one typically becomes anxious; if skills begin to exceed challenges, one relaxes and then becomes bored. These subjective states provide feedback about the shifting relationship to the environment and press the individual to adjust behavior in order to escape the more aversive subjective state and reenter flow. The following figure shows a simple diagram summarizing the way the ratio of challenges and skills usually impacts subjective experience.

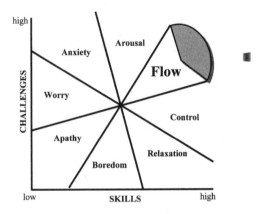

Thus at the phenomenological level it is the dynamic balance between challenges and skills that provides optimal experience, and thus the maintenance of this balance becomes intrinsically rewarding. In terms of more distal explanations, the balance between these two dimensions of experience allows for the gradual development of ever higher skills and thus leads to the enhancement of competence.

In their review of what the most revered thinkers of the past have written about education, the editors of the synopticon to the *Great Books of the Western World* (Adler 1987, 271) had this to say:

One opinion from which there is hardly a dissenting voice in the great books is that education should aim to make men [*sic*] good as men and citizens. "If you ask what is the good of education?" Plato writes "'[T]he answer is easy' that education makes good men, and that good men act nobly ..." Thus it would seem to be a common opinion in all ages that education should seek to develop the characteristic excellences of which men are capable and that its ultimate ends are human happiness and the welfare of society.

If this were truly the "common opinion in all ages," one would think that by now educators would have found a way to turn children into happy individuals and useful citizens. This, however, is hardly the case. Teachers are not expected to help children to be happy and to support what is good for society. Instead, each year more than the previous one, they are expected to help them get high scores on standardized tests measuring the latest version of abstract mental skills. There is little agreement about what constitutes optimal development in adolescence and what we can do to help it along.

If we assume that the human species has been around for 2 million years and that the average life span during this period was thirty years, then by this very conservative estimate about 70,000 human generations have followed one another on this planet. This continuous chain of lives includes 70,000 weak links, the times when the knowledge painfully accumulated up to that time had to be passed on to the next generation so that it would not vanish from the face of the earth. For better or for worse, the chain has held so far. But in the past four generations or so, the transmission of vital knowledge has changed dramatically. Universal mandatory schooling has taken over this task, an educational practice modeled on the production processes that were so successful in the factories of the Industrial Revolution of the eighteenth century and before that in the few schools attended by members of the future clergy. Some of the most dubious assumptions underlying this form of education are: (1) that children learn best by listening passively; (2) to abstract material; (3) while physically confined; (4) deprived of any meaningful choice; (5) responsible only for their own individual learning; and (6) while feeling either bored or anxious.

The list could go on and on. Suffice to say that this is not how young people learned during the first 69,996 generations of human existence. It is doubtful that we will be as successful as they were if we continue to follow the educational principles on which schooling has been based in the last four generations By contrast with the above scenario, it is useful to consider the developmental implications of the flow model. As individuals master challenges in an activity, they develop greater levels of skill, and the activity ceases to be as involving as before. To continue experiencing flow, they must identify increasingly greater challenges. Experiential goals thus introduce a principle of selection into psychological functioning that fosters growth and stretches a person's existing capacities.

This positive relationship between flow and positive youth development has been demonstrated in a number of studies that have used the experience sampling method (Csikszentmihalyi and Larson 1984) to examine the phenomenological experience of students within school settings. In longitudinal research with talented adolescents, students still committed to pursuing their talent area at age seventeen were compared to peers who had already disengaged. Four years earlier, those who were still committed had experienced more flow and less anxiety than their peers while engaged in school-related activities; they were also more likely to have identified their talent area as a source of flow. In a longitudinal study of students talented in mathematics, Heine (1996) showed that those who experienced flow in the first part of the course performed better in the second half, controlling for their initial abilities and GPA. Also controlling for initial abilities, Wong and Csikszentmihalyi (1991) found that immediate, experience-based motivation was a better predictor of the difficulty level of classes students subsequently chose than their motivation to achieve long-term academic goals.

In addition to enhancing positive outcomes, longitudinal research on resilience suggests that a subjectively optimal matching of challenge and skill in daily life may protect against negative outcomes. In a national sample of American adolescents, teenagers who had experienced high adversity at home and/or at school but had access to extracurricular and other challenging activities, who were involved in these activities and felt success when engaged in them, were much less likely to have problems years later. The ability to get involved in flow activities appears to mediate many developmental obstacles, and allow young people to become fruitfully engaged in productive, growth-producing activities. The ability to enjoy challenges and then master them is a fundamental meta-skill essential to individual development. Yet many obstacles prevent individuals from experiencing flow. These range from inherited genetic malfunctions to forms of social oppression that reduce personal freedom and prevent the acquisition of skills.

But even in the most benign situations flow may be difficult to attain. For instance, in our society at present, most parents are determined to provide the best conditions for their children's future happiness. They work hard so they can buy a nice home in the suburbs, get all the consumer goods they can afford, and send the children to the best schools possible. Unfortunately none of this guarantees that the children will get what they need to learn to enjoy life. In fact, a growing number of studies suggest that excessive concern for safety, comfort, and material well-being is detrimental to optimal development. The sterile surroundings of our living arrangements, the absence of working parents and other adults who could initiate young people into the joys of living, the addictive nature of passive entertainment, the reliance on material rewards, and the excessive concern of schools with testing and with disembodied knowledge, all militate against learning to enjoy mastering the challenges that life inevitably presents.

Thus understanding how flow works is essential for social scientists interested in improving the quality of life. Transforming this knowledge into effective action is not easy. But the challenges this task presents promise almost infinite opportunities for enjoyment for those who develop the skills necessary to master them.

See also Civic Engagement in Diverse Youth; Religiosity and Civic Engagement in African American Youth; School Influences and Civic Engagement.

Recommended Reading

Adler, M. J., ed. (1987). *Great Books of the Western World*, Vol.1. Chicago: Encyclopedia Britannica.

Berlyne, D. (1960). *Conflict, Arousal, and Curiosity*. New York: McGraw-Hill.

Conti, R. (2001). "Time Flies: Investigating the Connection between Intrinsic Motivation and the Experience of Time." *Journal of Personality*, 69 (1): 1–26.

Csikszentmihalyi, M., and Csikszentmihalyi, I., eds. (1988). *Optimal Experience: Psychological Studies of Flow in Consciousness*. New York: Cambridge University Press.

Csikszentmihalyi, M., and Larson, R. (1984). *Being Adolescent*. New York: Basic Books.

Csikszentmihalyi, M., and Schmidt, J. A. (1998). "Stress and Resilience in Adolescence: An Evolutionary Perspective." In *The Adolescent Years: Social Influences and Educational Challenges*, edited by K. Borman and B. Schneider. Chicago: University of Chicago Press.

Csikszentmihalyi, M., and Schneider, B. (2000). *Becoming Adult: How Teenagers Prepare for the World of Work*. New York: Basic Books.

Csikszentmihalyi, M., Rathunde, K., and Whalen, S. (1993). *Talented Teenagers: The Roots of Success and Failure*. New York: Cambridge University Press.

Deci, E. L., and Ryan, R. M. (1985). *Intrinsic Motivation and Self-Determination in Human Behavior*. New York: Plenum.

Shernoff, D. J., Csikszentmihalyi, M., Schneider, B., and Shernoff, E. S. (2003). "Student Engagement in High School Classrooms from the Perspective of Flow Theory." *School Psychology Quarterly*, 18 (2): 158–176.

Mihaly Csikszentmihalyi

4-H. The Cooperative Extension system was established by an act of Congress in 1914 through the Smith-Lever Act. A partnership among federal, state, and local governments, the Cooperative Extension's mission is to enable people to improve their lives and communities through learning partnerships that put knowledge to work. Nationally, there are over 3,000 county extension offices with Cooperative Extension educators who are the conduits for disseminating research-based information from land-grant universities to the people in their communities. The youth development program of the Cooperative Extension is the 4-H. Research-based information is disseminated to rural, suburban, and urban youth through several types of 4-H programs and clubs. Youth learn by doing as 4-H members in community clubs, project clubs, and after-school clubs, or through school enrichment experiences and as individual members with adult helpers.

Through 4-H programs, youth can enroll in projects and programs in a variety of curriculum areas such as citizenship and civic education, science and technology, environmental education, leadership and personal development, communications and expressive arts, animal and plant sciences, and nutrition and health. In the process, youth learn and practice important life skills, apply leadership skills, acquire a positive self-image, and learn to respect and get along with others.

More than 7 million youth, ages five to nineteen, participate in 4-H Youth Development experiences in all fifty U.S. states, its territories, and at U.S. Army installations worldwide.

4-H Youth Development is the only youth program that ties both public and private resources to the sole purpose of supporting the positive and successful development of youth. 4-H is also an international youth program. There are 4-H and related programs in over eighty countries around the world. These programs operate independently, as there is no international

Kids aged three to seven work on a 4-H clay project. *Courtesy of Skjold Photographs.*

4-H organization. However, through international exchanges, global education programs, and communications, youth are connected through 4-H. State 4-H programs support international exchanges of 4-H alumni and other young adults who live with host families in foreign countries to increase global awareness, develop independent study interests, and improve language skills.

4-H began over one hundred years ago. Early 4-H programs focused on providing practical, hands-on learning to rural youth. Researchers at experiment stations of land-grant colleges found that adults would not readily accept new agricultural discoveries, but youth would try these new farming practices and share their successes with adults. Thus, rural youth programs became a vehicle for the introduction of new agricultural technology to adults. 4-H programs grew and became available to urban youth in the 1950s. The focus of 4-H then became the personal growth and life-skills development of the 4-H member. Life-skills development (i.e., decision-making, communication, problem solving, leadership) was included in all 4-H projects, activities and events so that youth would become contributing, productive, self-directed members of the community.

The 4-H Pledge, learned by all 4-H members, highlights the commitment of youth to learning and service: "I pledge ... My head to clearer thinking, my heart to greater loyalty, my hands to larger service and my health to better living, for my club, my community, my country, and my world."

4-H members pledge their hands to greater service, and many 4-H clubs interpret this as a call to give back to their communities through volunteer work, service learning, and community activism. In 2001 over half a million 4-H youth were involved in citizenship and civic education programs. Many youth are involved in county 4-H councils, youth advocacy committees or on local youth councils as 4-H representatives. These councils and committees become excellent learning laboratories for youth to demonstrate their advocacy capabilities and become involved citizens. Youth participation on committees and in youth organizations such as 4-H is a predictor of future membership and leadership positions in community-based organizations.

4-H club members are involved in a wide variety of service-learning or community-action programs with varying levels of youth activism. Some examples include 4-H clubs and youth serving as peer facilitators for prevention programs, organizing collection efforts for food and necessities for needy families or service men and women, adopting a road to keep it free of litter, taking on a project that addresses food insecurity and hunger in local communities, engaging in community mapping to identify gaps in youth recreational areas, joining planning and planting efforts in community gardens, volunteering to answer phones for a community referral line, and becoming involved in intergenerational programs.

Some national 4-H efforts are underway that support youth activism at the community level. In 2002, the National 4-H Council (the private, nonprofit partner with the National 4-H headquarters and CSREES, USDA) received funding from the U.S. Department of Agriculture (USDA) to implement the Engaging Youth, Serving Community project. One of the project objectives is to improve the abilities of youth and adults in rural communities to work in partnership to address community needs. Pilot projects are taking place in forty-nine states and Guam through their respective land-grant institutions, including numerous historically African American colleges and Native American institutions. Youth are encouraged to work with diverse partners toward common goals and to increase the number of youth in rural communities who become engaged in community problem solving via governance and partnership with adults in community organizations and agencies.

Environmental stewardship is another national 4-H community-action initiative supporting youth activism. Using the community development process, the environmental stewardship program seeks to involve youth as full partners with adults to address environmental challenges. Youth and adults are encouraged to develop their leadership skills and to find creative community-based solutions to challenging environmental problems.

The National 4-H Cooperative Curriculum System offers a curriculum, Public Adventures, for 4-H and other youth to teach them how to contribute to the world around them while developing a lifelong commitment to active citizenship. Youth are provided with experientially based learning opportunities to help engage them to act confidently, competently, and with integrity in the public world. The handbook that accompanies the curriculum teaches citizenship in the content on active public engagement.

The Innovation Center for Community and Youth Development has partnered with the 4-H organization to create two resources featuring strategies for promoting youth-adult partnerships as a means of strengthening youth and communities involved in social change and youth development. "Creating Youth-Adult Partnerships" and "Youth-Adult Partnerships: A Training Manual" are two curricula available from the Community Innovation Center and being used in 4-H programs nationwide. Both resources are included in the National 4-H juried curriculum collection.

See also Earth Force; Empowerment; Global Youth Action Network (GYAN); Innovations in Civic Participation (ICP); National and Community Service; Positive Youth Development, Programs Promoting; Student Action with Farmworkers (SAF); Urban Communities, Youth Programming in.

Recommended Reading

4-H Cooperative Curriculum System (2005). Available at http://n4hccs.org.
Innovation Center for Community and Youth Development. (1996). *Creating Youth-Adult Partnerships*. Available at http://www.theinnovationcenter.org.

Innovation Center for Community and Youth Development (1996). *Youth-Adult Partnerships: A Training Manual.* Available at http://www.theinnovationcenter.org.

National 4-H (2005). Official Web site available at http://www.4husa.org/.

National 4-H Cooperative Curriculum System (2003). *Public Adventures.* Available at http://www.n4hccs.org.

National 4-H Council (2005). Available at http://www.fourhcouncil.edu/.

National 4-H Council (2005). *Engaging Youth, Serving Communities Projects.* Available at http://www.fourhcouncil.edu/rydYIG.aspx.

National 4-H Headquarters (2005). Available at http://www.national4-hheadquarters.gov/index.htm.

Claudia Mincemoyer

G

Gangs. The word "gang" has many different meanings and usages. For example, the *American Heritage Dictionary* defines a gang, at least when speaking of human beings, as follows: "1. A group of criminals or hoodlums who band together for mutual protection and profit. 2. A group of adolescents who band together, especially a group of delinquents. 3. *Informal.* A group of people who associate regularly on a social basis. 4. A group of laborers organized together on one job or under one foreperson: a railroad gang." The *Oxford Dictionary* offers the following definition: "10. a. Any band or company of persons who go about together or act in concert (chiefly in a bad or depreciatory sense, or associated with criminal societies). *transf.* A social set. *Colloq.*"

These definitions demonstrate the manifold meanings related to many words in the English language. Whereas the most commonly used modern meaning(s) and concept(s) of gangs relate to negative behaviors and activities associated with criminality, it has been proven that "gangs" can and often do participate in positive activities. History reveals that the ranks of notable and sometimes distinguished individuals are filled with people who were once participants in "gang" and "hoodlum" behavior and/or activities. However, the gangs being discussed here can be defined as groups of individuals recognized as collectives that represent themselves by use of a specific name, wearing of certain identifying clothing, colors, markings, and so forth and generally closely associated with specific territories, although this may be loosely based as many

modern "gangs" have territories throughout the entire globe.

Research demonstrates that circumstance and situation oftentimes dictate and motivate behavior and activity. As individuals and/or groups change their circumstance and/or situation, they may often change their activities and/or behaviors. The motivation for criminal and/or socially unacceptable behavior is frequently dictated and driven by circumstance and situation. Whereas gangs, as defined above for this entry, are widely known for their participation in criminal and violent activities, it is noted here that this is not always or necessarily the sole purpose for their existence.

Understanding the reasons that young people are drawn to "gangs" is not difficult when one considers the fact that groups, clubs, and other organizations are the very fabric of society. The child or young person who associates with or joins a gang is typically functioning in the same manner as any other member of society by associating with other individuals that share the same interests and concerns that he or she does. In communities where threats were once or are still prevalent and when no apparent and readily available protection exists, gangs have historically evolved and thrived. The primary motivation for most gangs has historically been control of their territory or environment. Whether the threat has been perceived as members of rival gangs, other ethnic groups, or others, the origins of most gangs are found in the need for a collective to protect what they view as their territory, their friends and families, and themselves.

The criminal enterprise aspect of gang activity has typically been the result of the need to acquire assets to ensure the proliferation and continuation of the gang (organization). As revealed in research conducted in Detroit, Michigan, over a twenty-year period, gangs may be developed for or evolve to a point of existing strictly for the purpose of generating profits. This type of gang, known as the *corporate gang*, distinguishes itself from two lower levels of gangs known as *territorial gangs* and *scavenger gangs*.

While gangs can represent a problem for communities, they can also represent a tremendous asset if they are convinced to participate in efforts to solve problems within their communities. Incidents involving Chicago gangs in recent years demonstrate how gangs can be assets within a community. When a young girl was raped in their community, a directive from the gang leader who was incarcerated arranged the identification, location, and arrest of the rapist, which led to his successful prosecution. A second situation involved the successful signing up of over 10,000 voters for a Chicago election when the same gang leader instructed gang members to mobilize and ensure voting efforts in their community.

Historically, young men in particular, but also young women that are active in "gangs," have been motivated to participate in community activism and efforts to improve conditions where they live. As evidenced in the two Chicago examples, the potential exists to have gangs become community assets rather than liabilities. To achieve success in transitioning gangs from liabilities to assets it is imperative that dialog be established with gang members and perhaps more importantly, gang leadership. Understanding the motivating factors specific to a gang is important, but respecting gang members is of even greater critical importance.

The dynamics associated with interaction between gang members and other members of a community are often strained initially, but given effort (particularly by those outside of the gang), significant progress can be made with tremendous results being achieved.

See also Gangs and Politics; Urban Communities, Youth Programming in.

Carl S. Taylor, Virgil A. Taylor, and Pamela R. Smith

Gangs and Politics. Youth gangs around the world have had a complex and shifting relationship to politics and social movements. While gang activity is often a product of youthful alienation and lack of conventional opportunities, gangs have at times been drawn into grassroots, nationalist, religious, and revolutionary mass activity. Gangs have also played both political and paramilitary roles in support of powerful elites, and have organized politically in defense of the underground economy. Past experience with political activism demonstrates that when social movements do not address the concerns of the most socially excluded and marginalized, gangs will institutionalize and take destructive forms. On the other hand, political movements that include the interests of the socially excluded can gain the gangs' support and have a better chance of reducing local violence and advancing their aims.

There have been three distinct periods of youth gang political activity. The earliest gangs were "primitive rebels," mafioso in Italy and triads in China who had their origins in resistance to foreign rule—the Spanish Habsburgs and the Q'ing Dynasty. These Sicilian, Italian, and Chinese groups were not pure social movements but combined nationalist appeals with the pedaling of protection and control of gambling, prostitution, and drugs.

In London groups of "hooligans" were a sixteenth-century byproduct of urbanization. During the nineteenth-century Chartist rebellion, it was claimed that hooligans of all sorts pitched in on the side of working-class organizations. But it was the United States that developed the paradigmatic use of the gang in local political affairs. Immigrants from Ireland, Poland, Italy, and other countries in the 1800s came to U.S. cities and sparked periods of intense ethnic and class conflict. The building of urban machines relied on ethnic politics, and clashes between immigrant groups were the norm in Boston, New York, and many cities. In New York City the dominant Yankees were challenged by the Irish who mobilized "voting gangs" to intimidate rivals. Corner kids who gathered in loosely organized groups were recruited by politicians to bully Tammany Hall's electoral opponents. These second-generation children were attracted to gangs both as an act of rebellion against their more traditional parents but also as ethnic solidarity.

Racism against African Americans and Mexicans has also been an undercurrent in U.S. white ethnic gang life. In New York City, Irish gangs led the assaults on African Americans during the Civil War "draft riots," and Klan activity helped keep Los Angeles' Mexicans politically quiescent in the early twentieth century as well as terrorize southern blacks. The nadir of racist gang activity was to occur in Chicago in the period after World War I.

Youth gang politics in Chicago, as in New York City and elsewhere, mainly consisted of gang members acting like thugs on Election Day on behalf of the Democratic Party. But unlike in other cities, ethnic gangs in Chicago were also part of an ongoing violent enforcement of a segregated, racial order. Chicago's white "social athletic clubs," or gangs tied to the Democratic Party, were responsible for the intensity and duration of the 1919 race riot that killed thirty-eight people.

In Asia gangs were political actors in several countries, tightly linked to the heroin trade. For example, the Green Circle, a Chinese triad, led the slaughter of Communists for Chiang Kai-shek in 1927 and was a major ally of the ruling Kuomintang. In the 1940s, the Binh Xuyen gang in Saigon became politicized while members served time in prison with Nationalists and Communists—an indication of things to come. Corsican gangs played a major role in Southeast Asian heroin trafficking and worked with French military and intelligence organizations.

Gang involvement with politics, however, would change abruptly with the worldwide upsurge of the 1960s. Oppressed peoples around the world mobilized as part of national liberation and revolutionary struggles. In South Africa youth gangs in Soweto and other cities joined with the African National Congress (ANC) and Pan Africanist Congress (PAC) in mass demonstrations and in opposition to the apartheid regime. Nelson Mandela explicitly called on the ANC to win over the gangs to the cause of liberation. As political alternatives appeared more promising, the alienation of poor youth was channeled into political parties, as in Northern Ireland and New Zealand. Gangs, as organizations of the street, typically stayed active in the underground economy. Bank robbery, extortion, and other gang tactics were adopted by revolutionary movements from Uruguay's Tupamaros to the Irish Republican Army.

This dual character of youth gangs can be most clearly seen in the United States. In Chicago the Conservative Vice Lords, the Blackstone Rangers, and the Black Gangster Disciples began to organize multineighborhood branches at the end of the 1950s. White ethnics had resisted black residential mobility, and white and black gangs fought continually in schools and on corners. Black gangs were involved in petty hustling but were also drawn to the emerging civil rights movement.

By the late 1960s, all Chicago's major black gangs had become involved in running social programs, starting businesses, and dabbling in local politics. When Martin Luther King Jr. came to Chicago in 1966, he moved into an apartment in Lawndale, home of the Vice Lords, met with them, and encouraged their involvement in his housing campaign. The three major black gangs formed a coalition called LSD, which stood for lords, stones, disciples, and took part in the struggle for jobs in the construction of buildings of the

University of Illinois-Chicago. The three gangs met regularly with Fred Hampton, leader of the Illinois Black Panther Party, and discussed how to mobilize the most disadvantaged sectors of the black community.

Puerto Rican and Mexican gangs also were pulled into politics. The Young Lords were a Chicago Puerto Rican street gang that became politicized during the same time. They also allied with the Black Panther Party and encouraged Young Lords chapters to be formed across the U.S., most notably in New York City. Chicano and Mexican American gang members also took part in the Brown Berets and other left-wing political movements. In Los Angeles, Crips and Bloods also engaged in radical politics as did the Savage Nomads, the Ghetto Brothers, and other New York City gangs.

There were constant tensions between the gangs and revolutionary organizations. The Black Panthers were recruiting from the same youthful, mainly male, populations as the gangs. The U.S. government, through programs such as the now infamous COINTELPRO, provoked conflict between the gangs and revolutionaries, in some cases resulting in gun battles.

The involvement of gangs in politics in the 1960s was curtailed by repression that forcibly transferred the gangs from the streets to the prison. While President Richard Nixon declared a "war on crime," Mayor Richard J. Daley declared his own "war" on gangs in Chicago. Daley acted after the Blackstone Rangers organized a successful boycott of the 1968 presidential elections, costing Democratic candidate Hubert H. Humphrey Illinois' crucial votes and throwing the national election to Richard Nixon.

Incarcerating gangs and revolutionaries together occurred in many countries and often had the effect of destroying the political organizations while providing the gangs with useful organizational advice. In Brazil the policy of putting all bank robbers, criminals, and revolutionaries together, had the unintended effect of organizing Rio de Janeiro's armed drug factions. In the United States, revolutionary nationalism among Black, Puerto Rican, and Mexican inmates gave shape to a more business-oriented style of gang organization and parallel ethnic prison gangs.

Throughout the world, the decisive defeat of most left-wing political movements shattered hopes of progress in the ghettos, barrios, and favelas and gave priority to an ideology of "survival." The defeat of the revolutionary movements in the 1960s and 1970s led to more cynical, alienated, and depoliticized gangs. This demoralization, the emergence of the drug cartels, the fall of the Soviet Union, and the overwhelming power of global corporations would shape the political involvement of gangs at the end of the millennium.

Gangs, as organizations of the street and participants in the drug economy, play an important political role in the global era. Nation-states throughout the world have been weakened as multinational corporations move vast sums of money at the click of a mouse, destabilizing entire countries and regions. The demise of the USSR meant that countries could no longer play one superpower off against another. Aid from Western countries and the World Bank often is predicated on cutting domestic social spending in countries with desperately poor populations. At the same time the enormous profits of the drug economy made the powerful Colombian and Mexican cartels major political players. Working for the traffickers is often the only well-paid employment for young men in barrios, ghettos, and favelas.

All these factors led to a strengthening of nonstate actors, among them gangs, which often exercise effective social control over urban and rural territories of weakened states. And the uncertainties of globalization also sparked a crisis in identity. Secular and revolutionary identities were replaced by more traditional notions of religion and race. "Gangsta rap" music, based on gang life in American ghettos, became an influential force among youth globally.

Political activity by gangs took three forms at the end of the twentieth century. First, in countries like Jamaica, the political parties recruited gangs to help them gain or hold on to power. Very much like the U.S. voting gangs of a century before, these gangs engaged in violence at the behest of politicians. This also meant de facto protection of their criminal activity, especially the drug trade. Throughout South America, gangs were recruited by the traffickers for protection of their interests and often to support one political faction against another. There are now thousands of children in organized armed violence, some child soldiers, in South America, Africa, and Asia. Death squads, drug cartels, revolutionary groups, and the military all recruit from the same pool of poor, angry young men who are attracted to gangs.

In Mumbai (Bombay), India, the Shiv Sena, a militant, fundamentalist Hindu party, came to power through a shrewd mixture of *hinduvata*, or appeals to Hindu dominance, and use of *dada*, or gangs, to provide electoral and anti-Muslim violence. In Nigeria gangs were organized by some states with Muslim majorities enforcing *Sharia*, or Muslim law. At the same time, in gangland tradition, they supported themselves through the drug economy.

A second form of political activity was the devolution of some nationalist or revolutionary groups into gangs. In Northern Ireland, Protestant militias, once violent killers of Catholics, began to lose heart as the peace process and Catholic birthrate accelerated. Violence in Belfast today is not mainly between Protestants and Catholics but overwhelmingly between former Protestant militias fighting over local drug markets.

In South Africa, the Spear of the Nation armed warriors returning home after liberation were faced with stark alternatives. Having little education and few skills other than armed struggle, a handful of these ex-revolutionaries got jobs as policemen.

The others had to choose between starvation and working for the drug gangs. In South America, guerrilla groups such as FARC in Colombia and the Shining Path in Peru tax and cooperate with the traffickers to fund their armed struggle.

In Eastern Europe, the demise of the Soviet Union brought the underground economy out into the open. As socialism's safety net unraveled, young men were recruited into drug organizations and mafias. In Albania, the World Bank reports, one-quarter of all the young men are now employed in the drug economy. In Yugoslavia, Serbian leaders used gangs to precede their army into Bosnia on the grisly road to "ethnic cleansing."

Finally, a few gangs were drawn into grassroots movements, mainly based on racial or religious identity. In New York City, the Puerto Rican and Dominican Almighty Latin King and Queen Nation attempted to transform itself from a street gang into a community organization. The short-lived attempt was met by fierce repression and the jailing of the political leadership. In Chicago, gangs participated in electoral politics both openly and behind the scenes. In Los Angeles, Crips and Bloods put forth a sweeping program for economic reform after the Rodney King riots. Muslim gangs in Africa and South Asia worked to advance the influence of Muslim law over their populations, while maintaining ties to the underground economy. Gangs in South America have been recruited by all political factions in armed and nonviolent roles.

Gangs today are drawn into political activity under many different circumstances. The power of globalization and weakness of the nation-state guarantees a continuing role of gangs in political activity. As organizations of the most marginalized populations, they mobilize in support of their perceived interests. Often this includes defense of the underground economy, but it can take on many political hues.

Contemporary gangs have strong ethnic and/or religious identities. Their political agendas often coincide with those of their ethnic-religious group. When their group is in power, gangs can be used as shock troops in repression. When street organizations are drawn from oppressed or marginalized national or religious groups, they can engage in a politics of opposition. Lack of hope in the future, however, often means gangs cynically manipulate politicians in the interests of "survival," a euphemism for the underground economy. These different orientations are often represented in hip-hop music and culture, which has spread from the United States to urban settings worldwide.

It is this aspect of gangs that makes them so important for political activism of the twenty-first century. Where social movements provide hope for those on the streets, gang organizations can be won over to political activism, as the ALKQN in New York City. Where movements advance the interests of the professionals, business, or unions and neglect the streets, gangs will stay attached to the underground economy and their politics, when present, will be for sale to the highest bidder.

See also Child Soldiers; Gangs; Hip-Hop Generation; Juvenile Justice; State and Youth, The; Urban Communities, Youth Programming in.

Recommended Reading

Dowdney, Luke (2003). *Children of the Drug Trade: A Case Study of Children in Organised Armed Violence in Rio de Janeiro*. Rio de Janeiro: 7Letras.
Gangresearch.net. See http://gangresearch.net.
Glaser, Clive (2000). *Bo-Tsotsi: The Youth Gangs of Soweto, 1935–1976*. Westport, CT: Heinemann.
Vigil, Diego (2002). *A Rainbow of Gangs: Street Cultures in the Mega-City*. Austin: University of Texas.

John M. Hagedorn

Gay Activism. *See* Gay-Straight Alliances in Schools (GSAs); Queer, Sexuality, and Gender Activism.

Gay-Straight Alliances in Schools (GSAs). Gay-Straight Alliances (GSAs) are school-based clubs that are based on partnerships between sexual minority and heterosexual students for the purposes of supporting lesbian, gay, bisexual, and transgender (LGBT) students and their allies and for promoting positive change in the school climate for these students. These clubs have received significant public attention in recent years. The historical roots of GSAs are based in the first community programs that were created in the 1980s and 1990s to meet the unique needs of LGBT young people. These community agencies emerged in response to the significant basic needs of urban LGBT youth, many of whom had been drawn to cities after leaving or being kicked out of their homes because of their sexual identities. Their needs included housing, mental-health and substance-abuse services, and safety.

These first agencies grew to become outlets for social support, and over time they became venues for LGBT youth-community activism. Thus, community-based programs were the precursors to the first school-based organization for LGBT youth, the Los Angeles counseling and support group founded in 1984 by Virginia Uribe called Project 10 (Uribe 1994). Following the founding of Project 10, counseling and support groups specifically created to meet the needs of LGBT students began to emerge across the country. Like the historical progression of the community-based LGBT youth organizations, these school-based groups began initially as counseling and support groups but eventually evolved into social and recreational clubs or clubs whose purpose was to educate about LGBT issues and improve the school climate. By the mid-1990s the name "Gay-Straight Alliance" emerged as a common name for these school-based clubs.

The role of adults was central in the origins of these precursor organizations to contemporary GSAs, which were grounded in providing support and counseling to LGBT youth. Caring teachers and school counselors who were either gay themselves or who were straight allies became impassioned advocates for the well-being of gay students, often as a result of their experiences with the HIV/AIDS crisis, their relationships with LGBT family members or friends, or their own exposure to the hostile school climate either during their own adolescence or as adult teachers. These first brave teachers and counselors fought educational systems that were fundamentally resistant to challenging heteronormativity.

Over the course of the last ten years the GSA movement has transformed from adult-initiated school clubs into youth-led organizations aimed at activism for social change in schools. Parallel to the rise in youth leadership for the GSA movement has been the growth of regional and national infrastructures that link and support local youth leaders and their GSAs. Several sentinel events prompted an explosion in the number of GSAs during the past decade, including the banning of the Salt Lake City, Utah, high-school GSA and the resulting legislative and court battles in 1995; the death of University of Wyoming student Matthew Shepard in October 1998; and the controversy surrounding the GSA at El Modino High School in Orange County, California, in the fall of 1999. Each of these events received significant media attention and was followed by a groundswell of response in local communities and schools across the nation. Many communities became concerned for the first time about the unique needs of LGBT youth and turned attention to the schools both as a source of pervasive harassment and discrimination of youth and as an important site for support and strategic change.

During the same period, two other important social changes were taking place. First, the Internet was emerging as a powerful tool for connecting isolated and marginalized communities; it was becoming a resource for sharing stories and strategies for youth activism. For the first time, many hitherto isolated LGBT young people found communities of peers online. The result was that the Internet became a site for discourse and for LGBT issues in schools. The Internet literally connected young people

who had previously been isolated and linked them to each other's stories of local transformation in their schools. The second change has been the emergence of national, regional, and local organizations that focused their attention on LGBT youth and schools. These organizations were prompted in part by the sentinel events that propelled the GSA movement, as well as by the growing LGBT movement. Organizations such as the Gay, Lesbian, and Straight Education Network (GLSEN) and the GSA Network, a California-based organization, began as small activist organizations but took off during the 1990s and grew exponentially. Not surprisingly, these organizations use the Internet as a strategic means to reach out to young people, both to link them to one another through virtual communities and to equip them with the tools to create and sustain social change in their school climates. Young people have played prominent roles in the histories of these organizations. For example, GSA Network is a youth-led organization governed by regional youth councils made up of leaders of their local high-school GSAs. Its work to support local GSAs is based on youth-led and youth-created training guides and resources, available to young people online (GSA-Network 2004).

Linked to one another and supported by each other and by state and national advocacy organizations, GSAs are now more likely to be organized and sustained by students than by adult school personnel. As a result of these social changes and the changing role of youth activists in the GSA movement, the purposes and functions of GSAs have changed. While the first GSAs were established to provide support for LGBT students, contemporary GSAs may continue to play that role, but two GSA forms have become prominent: the social organization and the activist club. Some GSAs exist as an alternative social environment in the school, a place to "hang out" that is safe and supportive for a wide range of "alternative" students who don't fit in with the dominant culture of the high school. In contrast, activist GSAs focus their attention on changing the school's gender and sexual-orientation climate. GSA club activities have included displaying posters that challenge heterosexism, hosting a queer prom, organizing a day to recognize the silence that has characterized attention to sexual minorities called "Day of Silence," holding training for teachers on LGBT issues and homophobia in the school, and surveying fellow students and school personnel administrators to report on the school's LGBT climate. Through these efforts, GSAs work to increase visibility of LGBT people and issues in the school.

Not since the 1960s have we witnessed youth activism at the level and intensity that we see among contemporary GSAs. While the student activism of the 1960s is best characterized as emerging from political concerns, the motivations for the activism of the 1960s arguably was partly based in or was a response to cultural changes with regard to sexuality. That activism emerged from older students, mostly on college and university campuses across the country. GSAs are notable in that they have been based at high-school and even middle-school campuses. Contemporary schools are one of the most important social contexts or institutions that guide young people in their development. GSAs present a unique example of youth activism not only because they push the boundaries of heteronormativity but because they do so within the context of high schools (and in some cases middle schools), which are institutions that are fundamentally normative-creating in the lives of young people. GSAs are remarkable not only because young people are leading the social change; they are remarkable because it is young people who are challenging and even transforming an institution that has historically been the site of adolescent social control.

See also Diversity Education; Feminism; Gender Differences in the Political Attitudes of Youth; Queer, Sexuality, and Gender Activism.

Recommended Reading

Griffin, P., Lee, C., Waugh, J., and Beyer, C. (2004). "Describing Roles That Gay-Straight Alliances Play in Schools: From Individual Support to Social Change." *Journal of Gay and Lesbian Issues in Education*, 1 (3): 7–22.

GSA-Network (2004). *About GSA Network*. See http://www.gasnetwork.org.

Heineman, J. (1994). "Building a GLOBE in Nebraska." In *One Teacher in 10*, edited by K. Jennings. Los Angeles: Alyson Books, pp. 208–211.

Herdt, G., and Boxer, A. (1993). *Children of Horizons*. Boston: Beacon Press.

McGarry, M., and Wasserman, F. (1998). *Becoming Visible: An Illustrated History of Lesbian and Gay Life in Twentieth-Century America*. New York: Penguin Studio.

McKenna, K. Y. A., and Bargh, J. A. (1998). "Coming Out in the Age of the Internet: Identity 'Demarginalization' Through Virtual Group Participation." *Journal of Personality and Social Psychology*, 75 (3): 681–694.

Sweat, J., Russell, S. T., and Ryan, C. (2004). "Media Framing of a Youth Social Movement: The Case of Gay-Straight Alliances." Unpublished manuscript, University of California, Davis.

Uribe, V. (1994). "Project 10: A School-Based Outreach to Gay and Lesbian Youth." *High School Journal*, 77 (Special issue): 108–112.

Stephen T. Russell

GCE. *See* Global Citizenship Education (GCE) in the United States.

Gender Activism. *See* Queer, Sexuality, and Gender Activism.

Gender Differences in the Political Attitudes of Youth. Citizenship is an important area of adult functioning, yet until now research has not examined in depth its development well enough to understand how to promote its positive development. Adolescence and young adulthood are crucial times for examining the development of civic engagement because individuals are on the verge of exercising their citizenship for the first time in terms of behaviors such as voting. The study of attitudes and interests allows an examination into civic engagement even in youth who are not active in terms of actual participation. Interestingly, considerable research shows that considerable and important gender differences exist in political views and these differences are present by adolescence.

At one time it was thought that girls were less interested and involved in politics than boys. We now know that boys and girls are just different politically, but one sex is not more involved than the other. Research throughout the world has found that adolescent girls tend to be more prosocial in their political orientation. They are interested in and concerned about issues such as poverty that reflect a concern for other people. They are also more likely to do community service. Recent research in the United States shows also that boys are not just less prosocial but are in fact more politically conservative than girls, being concerned about political issues such as taxes and defense. Interestingly, these gender differences are independent of adolescent age and are expressed across domains, applying to political issues deemed important, political policies supported, and political topics discussed outside class. These results demonstrate that by adolescence, teens have developed a political orientation that is consistent and can be reliably measured across domains, and there are meaningful gender differences in these views.

Developmental research suggests that adolescence, a period of intense change, is likely to be an important time for the emergence of gender differences in politics. During adolescence, such developmental tasks as personal identity and cognitive abilities such as formal operations are reaching adult capacities. Although teens experience an array of other changes, such as puberty, these developmental achievements are the ones most relevant to the emergence of gender differences in politics. Perhaps most relevant to this topic is that the socialization pressures for gender-typical behavior increase during adolescence; this gender intensive socialization may also influence the development of gender differences in political views.

The fact that youth's attitudes and the gender differences in such attitudes are present by adolescence indicates that we need to examine childhood or even early development for the origins of such differences. Certainly research has shown continuity in individuals' prosocial orientation, independent of gender, from preschool to young adulthood. The question is when and how do these differences map onto politics. Other core gender differences such as interests in math seem to relate to socialization as well as to biology; one interesting question for future research is whether biology as well as socialization might affect gender differences in politics.

Age and gender also interact in that the developmental trajectories of the two sexes vary. For example younger males and older females endorse more prosocial policies. That is, male youth seem to become less prosocial with age, whereas females become more prosocial with age. That is, as cognitive and social development maturity is reached in adolescence, youth come to increasing match the gender differences in political views they show as adults. These results also support the notion that adolescence and young adulthood are critical periods for the final consolidation of gender differences in political orientation and behavior.

Yet, to explore the development of gender differences in civic engagement, we need to investigate the relationship between socialization factors and political views. A number of correlates, such as school activities, community services, and civic education, have been identified between childhood or youth experiences and later, adult civic engagement. Generally, research shows that certain school activities such as working on the newspaper and playing sports show gender differences and relate to political views. Other activities, such as doing community service and taking civics classes, do not show gender differences.

As might be expected, boys participate more in sports and girls in newspapers and yearbooks. And these gender differences in school activities relate to the gender differences in views, that is, newspaper and yearbook related to prosocial views and sports related to conservative views. Hence, participation in gender-related school activities is one means by which the gender differences in politics may emerge. Yet, participation in other activities with no gender differences, such as school government, also relate to political views, in this case, to decreased support for prosocial policies and increased discussion of conservative topics. Interestingly, community service, which has long been shown to relate to later civic engagement, does not relate to political views. Civic education in school seems to serve as a means to expose youth to politics, increasing attention to both sides of the issues. Having had a civics course relates to discussion of politics outside class, both conservative and prosocial topics. Hence, it does not seem that the socialization variables that previous research has shown relate to civic engagement do so in a general way; when looking at views, different activities relate to different views, and there are gender differences both in the activities pursued and in their relationship to views. More research is needed to relate specific socialization variables to specific forms of civic engagement.

See also Chat Rooms, Girls' Empowerment and; Feminism; Gay-Straight Alliances in Schools (GSAs); Riot Grrrl.

Recommended Reading

Eccles, J., Jacobs, J., and Harold, R. (1990). "Gender Role Stereotypes, Expectancy Effects, and Parents' Socialization of Gender Differences." *Journal of Social Issues*, 46: 183–201.

Sherrod, L. R. (April 2003). "Promoting the Development of Citizenship in Diverse Youth." *PS: Political Science and Politics*, 287–292.

Sherrod, L. R., and Baskir, L. R. (In Press). "Gender Differences in the Political Interests of U.S. High School Students." *Journal of Social Issues*.

Tilley, J. (March 2002). "Is Youth a Better Predictor of Sociopolitical Values Than Is Nationality?" *Annals of the American Academy of Political and Social Science*, 580: 226–256.

Torney-Purta, J. (2002). "The School's Role in Developing Civic Engagement: A Study of Adolescents in Twenty-eight Countries." *Applied Developmental Science*, 6 (4): 202–211.

Lauren Baskir

Generational Conflict. Generational conflict involves the competition and expression of differences, divisions, and discord between age-groups. Tension and clashes between age-groups have been observed throughout history. The biblical book of Job (30:12) contains the generational lament: "Upon my right hand rise up the youth; they push away at my feet, and they raise up against me the ways of their destruction." Ancient Greek dramas pitted youth against their elders, and Plato and Aristotle both viewed generational strife as a primary cause of social and political change. Town-and-gown riots punctuated medieval university life throughout Europe as students clashed with professors and townspeople. And from 1815 onward young people periodically organized youth movements to challenge adult authority and demand reform.

The question is how can generational conflict be explained? After outlining the various types of age-based disagreement and explanations for generational conflict, focus is given to understanding the opposition and dynamics involved in generational movements, using political generations as an example. Discussion then turns to the future of generational conflict, some cautions concerning the use of the terms "generation" and "generational conflict," and considerations in dealing with antagonistic age-groups and generational relations.

What is generational conflict, and why is it important? Occurring at both the individual and collective levels, generational conflict may range from routine misunderstandings and friction between youth and their elders to the vitriolic animosity and hostility reflected in organized rebellions. Scholars and journalists are on a perpetual quest for the proverbial "generation gap," which, if sufficiently wide, may signal the arrival of an extraordinary or decisive generation in history. What sets the generations apart? Sometimes the distinguishing feature is an especially large-size birth cohort, such as the baby-boom generation in the United States (an estimated 76 million adults born in the late 1940s and 1950s) or the more recent Generation Y or new millennium generation (approximately 70 million young people born from the late 1970s to the early 1990s). Other times the distinguishing characteristic is a cultural divide that differentiates the age-groups, such as the *Wandervögel* (Wandering Birds) youth movement in early twentieth-century Germany that rejected adults' bourgeois, middle-class values to trek through the countryside singing folk songs and celebrating youthful freedom. And frequently it is politics that splits apart the generations, such as the 1980s generational movements that fractured the Soviet Union and created turmoil in Western Europe, the Middle East, Africa, Asia, and Latin America.

Generational conflict is important not only because of the tension, instability, and disruption it may create but because it is a driving force for societal renovation and change. The change may be gradual and evolutionary as one generation replaces another in the rhythm of birth and death. Or the change may be radical and dramatic as reflected in age-based movements for reform and revolution in politics, science, literature, culture, and the arts.

Why does generational conflict occur? Essentially, generational antagonism and opposition are rooted in the relationship between age-groups. Age is one of the most fundamental human categories and sources of identification in all societies, with each age-group accorded distinct characteristics, roles, and expectations for behavior, as well as levels of status and power. On the one hand, the age-groups need each other, and generations are a major source of institutional stability—most fundamentally when the adult generation transmits its cultural heritage and socializes the

younger generation to the ways of society in order to prepare youngsters for future adulthood. The socialization process is never complete or total, however, due to a number of underlying biological, psychological, and social differences separating youth and adults. Moreover, since human development occurs within a specific set of sociohistorical conditions, societal trends and events may influence generational relations and help explain why generational conflict may become more pronounced during certain periods in history rather than others.

The tensions between age-groups are reflected in what is meant by generation. The different meanings of the term "generation" are discussed, and the formation and principal explanations for generational conflict are reviewed. See table titled "Formation and Explanations of Generational Conflict" for an overview.

One meaning of generation is *genealogical* and concerns lineage and kinship descent from a common ancestor, such as the parent generation and the offspring generation or the generations of a family. The age-based tensions in this case are derived from the parent generation's normative and psychological need to socialize, guide, and control their offspring. These parental duties are juxtaposed against the younger generation's developmental need to come into their own by struggling against, competing with, and attempting to replace or perhaps surpass the parent generation.

The conflict between fathers and sons is a frequent theme in literature, and the conscious and unconscious emotional conflicts and antagonistic relations between parents and offspring are a cornerstone of Freudian psychology. A popular explanation for youthful protests and activism is that young people are asserting their independence and working out their emotional conflicts with their parents through their rebellious actions in the social, cultural, or political arenas. However, the generational-rebellion hypothesis has been criticized on

Formation and Explanations of Generational Conflict

Formation	Age-group membership		
	Genealogical explanation	Life-cycle explanation	Cohort-generational explanation
Definitions	Generation based on family or kinshiplineage (e.g., parents versus offspring).	Generation based on age-group differences in life-cycle characteristics, needs, and orientations (e.g., young versus old).	Generation based on cohort membership and distinct growing-up experiences shared with contemporaries (e.g., 1940s cohort versus 2000s cohort).
Sources of generational tension	Parents need to socialize, guide, and control offspring versus offspring's need to become independent and come into their own by replacing or surpassing the parents' generation.	Psychosocial incompatibilities of the different stages of life; developmental advances during adolescence and youth that make young people critical of adults, egocentric, and concerned about their identity and place in society; expectation that the attitudes and behaviors formed during youth will change with age to become more conservative.	Cohorts grow up and come of age in modern societies under different sets of social conditions, which affect the formation of their attitudes and behaviors; youth have a fresh contact with society and are apt to be critical of adult society; a generation is an age-group "for itself"; youth may form a bond and generational consciousness based on shared cohort experiences to become an active generation.
Examples	Sigmund Freud and anecdotal accounts emphasize the conscious and unconscious emotional conflicts between parents and offspring, and working out conflicts through actions and movements for change.	Erik Erikson and developmental research emphasize the different orientations of youth and adults, age-based tensions, and the appeal of movements for change to youth.	Karl Mannheim and cohort-generational research indicate that events, cultural styles, and intellectual thought influence generational consciousness, bonding, conflict, and movements for change.
Limitations	Research only partially supports explanation; most teens feel close to their families; most activists learned parents' orientations in the home; many parents of activists support their offspring.	This predicts that generational conflict is constant when, in fact, it is more pronounced at certain times than others; most committed activists do not change orientations with age; it ignores impact of society and history on generational relations.	Problems determining when a generation has come into existence; deciding on criteria and boundaries defining a generation; misapplying concept of generations to cohorts; exploiting generational conflict.

several grounds. First, although national surveys of youth indicate that adolescents report frequent arguments with their parents, the overwhelming majority of teens claim that they love their parents and feel close to their families. And second, researchers generally find that rather than rebelling against their parents, most youthful activists are carrying out the values learned in the home, with many parents supporting their offspring's activity.

Another meaning of generation concerns *age-group membership*. In this case, the tensions between age-groups are grounded in the life-cycle incompatibilities of the various stages of life (e.g., young versus old) and in the cohort differences associated with growing up and coming of age with one's peers during dissimilar eras in history (e.g., the youth cohort coming of age today in the new millennium versus the cohort that grew up during World War II in the 1940s). A cohort is defined as a group exhibiting a common demographic characteristic—in this case, age or birth years. By being born around the same time in history, the members of a cohort experience a particular set of societal conditions together during the same stages of life and are likely to form similar attitudes and behaviors based on their shared experiences. Each of these forms of age-group membership is described in relation to generational conflict.

According to the *life-cycle explanation* of generational conflict, the adult generation has a different set of developmental needs and interests than a youth generation, and it is these biological and psychological incongruities that strain age-group relations. Nash (1978) notes that the ancient Greeks were keenly aware of the role that stage of life plays in generational conflict, observing that the youthful characteristics of high energy, idealism, impetuousness, and hubris put them at odds with adults, who like contemplation and caution, and that each age-group prefers the company of its contemporaries. The life-cycle explanation for generational conflict is reflected in Erik Erikson's life-stage theory (1968) and in contemporary research conducted by developmental psychologists and social scientists.

The life-cycle explanation addresses the question of why young people but not children are likely to challenge their elders. The answer revolves around the physiological, cognitive, and emotional develop-ments that transpire during adolescence. For example, as teenagers become able to think more abstractly, they are inclined to become critical of their parents and the adult world, as they begin searching for who they are, how they will fit into their communities, and what kind of a society it is they are about to enter. In addition, adolescents are apt to be egocentric, viewing themselves and society from their own perspectives and finding it difficult to understand the perspectives of others, especially adults. Striving for independence, moving away from family to peers, and lacking experience, the youth generation is likely to believe that the adult generation is overly traditional and old-fashioned.

At times, young people concur that the status quo is outmoded and that it is up to the younger generation to forge a better world—in which case they may take action by mobilizing for change. For example, political youth movements do not happen often but when they do, young people begin to see their personal lives linked to politics. This is one reason why movements for freedom, liberty, and equality are so appealing to youth, as evidenced by some of the slogans from the 1989 Beijing uprising in Tiananmen Square in China: "Down with Dictatorship!" "Down with Corruption!" and "Long Live Freedom!" In art, the expressionist movement in the early twentieth century shocked the conventional world, as young artists eschewed representational art in favor of portraying their emotions and inner feelings in their work. Yet, as one French adage says, "He who is not a revolutionary at age twenty has no heart; he who is still a revolutionary at age forty has no head." According to the life-cycle perspective, the radical inclinations of youth will ebb, and with adulthood will come greater caution and conservatism.

There are some limitations to the life-cycle explanation for generational conflict. First, the life-cycle interpretation implies that generational conflict is a constant feature of modern society, whereas historical evidence suggests that conflict between youth and their elders becomes heightened during certain periods but remains relatively quiescent during others. Second, studies of former activists, revolutionaries, and the members of prominent generations in history indicate that the most highly committed participants do not substantially change their attitudes as they age but adhere to the values and precepts formed in their youth. Essentially, the life-cycle explanation pays scant attention to society's role in fostering generational strife and age-based movements for reform or revolution.

The link between society and generational conflict is more fully addressed in the *cohort-generational explanation*—most prominently reflected in Karl Mannheim's essay "The Problem of Generations" (1952) and in recent studies conducted by sociologists and political scientists. In rapidly changing modern societies, the growing-up experiences of younger and older age-groups are likely to be quite disparate, and herein lay the seeds of generational conflict.

According to this explanation, the stage of youth is a critical time for formulating one's beliefs and patterns of behavior. As youngsters move from childhood to adolescence, they become more cognizant of the larger community and less accepting of adults' socialization efforts. It is young people's "fresh contact" with society, Mannheim says, that makes them more sensitive to what is going on in the world around them and also may make them more critical of adults and the kind of society adults have created for youth. Dramatic events such as unpopular wars, economic depressions, scientific revolutions, and technological and cultural innovations affect all age-groups but are considered to have an especially strong impact on young people as they crystallize their values and beliefs. It has also been noted that it is not so much the events per se that influence generational conflict as it is the intellectual thought and cultural styles that express and articulate the desires of youth to rid themselves of the "old" and create "new" forms and trends. Unlike the life-cycle interpretation, which predicts greater conservatism with advancing age, the cohort interpretation contends that the social attitudes and behavior formed during youth are not substantially altered with age and with life course, and survey research generally supports the cohort-generational explanation.

While age-based differences and animosities have erupted into collective youthful outbursts, riots, and insurrections throughout history, most forms of overt generational conflict are short-lived. Beginning in the early nineteenth century, however, generational conflict took a new, more organized and sustained form—generational movements that brought about significant social and political change. How do age-group differences become transformed into overt conflict and a full-fledged generation? The explanation is as follows. Naturally peer-oriented, young people share social and cultural growing-up experiences with their contemporaries and look to each other rather than adults to bond. Especially when a youth cohort comes of age under very different circumstances from the adult generation, adults will have a more difficult time transmitting their values, beliefs, and practices to the young, who may view adults' efforts as antiquated and irrelevant. At times, the disparities between youth and adults can become so pronounced that young people become conscious of themselves as a unique or special age-group in history, further promoting intergenerational misunderstanding, miscommunication, and conflict. Mannheim makes an important distinction between a cohort and a generation, noting that a cohort is an age-group "in itself," whereas a generation is a dynamic age-group "for itself." A full-blown, active youth generation may challenge adults in any number of arenas, including culture, science, and the arts, although most of the social-science research has focused on social and political generations.

While research has provided support for the cohort-generational explanation of generational conflict, there are some problems with this perspective as well. One problem is deciding when a generation gap has become so pronounced that a bona fide generation has come into existence. A second problem involves determining the criteria and cutoff points defining a generation. Should generations be defined by age and cohort birth year, by the distinct societal events that condition a generational mentality, or by new cultural forms and thought? More concretely, where does one generation or cohort end and another begin? Third, if generational consciousness is the key to defining a generation, how can such an abstract construct be operationalized and measured?

It is important to note that the term "generation," in a Mannheimian sense, was meant to designate an active generation struggling against other generations for power and control. In practice, however, the term "generation" often is used haphazardly to apply to age cohorts that are not really at odds with the adult generation, do not demonstrate an identifiable generational consciousness, nor do they view themselves as a special age-group bound together as an organized force for change. For example, *Generation X* is the title of a 1991 Douglas Coupland novel that describes the hopeless lives of young people who are well educated but frequently unemployed or underemployed as well as turned off and tuned out to the materialistic and status-obsessed adult world. The media then applied the Generation X label to the post–baby-boom generation (a relatively small cohort born roughly from 1965–1980), characterizing Xers as cynical slackers. Despite the attention and hype, Generation X is a cohort and not an age-conscious generation that is mobilized against adult society for innovation or change.

To make the distinction between an age cohort and a generation, the term *decisive generation* has been used to describe extraordinary generations in history that mobilize to reform or revolutionize social institutions, the political system, science-technology, or culture. See table titled "Formation and Dynamics of Decisive Generations" for a description of the formation and dynamics of decisive generations. When a decisive generation forms, routine eras are replaced by destabilization and disruption. For example, the Roaring Twenties in the United States represented a cultural revolution in values and lifestyles, to be followed by economic depression in the 1930s that resulted in more than a decade of organized youth movement activity in the arts and politics as part of the Great Depression generation. American society was ultimately transformed by the movements, government decisions, and changes that transpired during the 1930s, the divisions and impact of which continue today. In examining decisive generations in history, generational conflict is a central dynamic involved in the formation, mobilization, and maintenance of age-based efforts to bring about or resist change.

As an illustration, consider political generations as an example of decisive generations in history, and note the significance of generational conflict in forming and sustaining youth movements. A political generation occurs when politics divides along age-group lines and young people openly challenge the adult generation's handling of local, national, or international affairs. A political generation begins with youth movement activity coalescing around issues that young people believe need to be addressed and resolved. Inspired by the values of the Enlightenment and modern nationalism (*liberté, égalité, fraternité*), the first youth movement or political generation occurred in 1815 with the formation of the *Burschenschaften* (student associations) movement in Germany, when students disparaged their elders and called for a written constitution, individual rights, and the consolidation of the German states. Youth movement activity then spread rapidly to Italy, Austria, France, Ireland, and

Formation and Dynamics of Decisive Generations

Formation	Dynamics of Generational Conflict
Origins	Life-cycle needs of young people and extraordinary cohort experiences forge a bond and the generational consciousness among youth that they are a special generation with a mission to work together for change.
Intergenerational conflict	Youth "deauthorize" adult society (the "establishment") for its failings through young leaders and organizers, speeches, songs, intellectual thought, and social criticism, which appeal to young people's life-cycle needs to find identity, bond with peers, and link their lives to society. Young people then authorize themselves to mobilize and change society, especially when the youth population is large, educated, and forms a generational consciousness of being a special age-group in history participating in a common destiny.
Intragenerational conflict	Although a generation of youth may concur that society needs to be changed, different groups within the youth generation compete and conflict over the direction that change should take. Generation groupings or units form because the members of the youth generation come from different social backgrounds, and therefore perceive, interpret, and respond to society in different ways. Much of the momentum for a generation comes from intragenerational conflict.
Types of generational conflict and generational revolutionists	These include large-size generations (the baby boom, Generation Y); cultural generations (bohemians, the Jazz Age, hippies); political generations (Young Ireland, Young Communists, Young Fascists, Oxford Pledge, *Intifada*); artistic generations (expressionists, cubists, Dadaists); literary generations (romanticism, Bloomsbury Circle, Lost Generation, Beat Generation); scientific generations (Copernican, Darwinian, Olympia Academy); medical generations (Jenner, Pasteur, psychoanalysis).
Patterns of generational conflict	Routine eras of little generational conflict are followed by the eruption of generational opposition and movements for change. Decisive political generations occur in waves or clusters called historical generations (Young Europe, post-Victorian, Great Depression, 1960s, and 1980s). Thus far, it has been young people who have mobilized into decisive generations against adult society; older adults may mobilize in the future. Generational conflict is now global in scope.

later Russia, as young people banded together to reject absolutism and the *Ancien Régime* in their struggle for nationalism, independence, and freedom.

A survey of modern history indicates that youth movements erupt in waves or clusters. These clusters of political generations are called historical generations, and thus far, there have been five identifiable historical generations: Young Europe (1815–1848, 1860–1890), the post-Victorian generation (1890–1918), the Great Depression generation (1930–1940), the 1960s generation (1960–1970), and the 1980s generation (1980–1990). The issues galvanizing these recurring youth movements

largely revolved around the desire for greater citizenship, with particular commitments to individual and collective rights, personal freedom, equality, democracy, and self-determination.

When youthful political generations arise, they are especially threatening to adult authorities and create a dynamic of confrontation and turmoil that may last a decade or longer. Once mobilized, conflict between the generations predominates. Regime leaders and supporters of the status quo often fuel an escalating spiral of hostility and confrontation by depicting youthful activists as hooligans and cracking down on them as a way of deflecting attention from the issues of protest. Youthful political generations have toppled governments and reformed societies, though often not without injury, destruction, repression, and death. It should also be mentioned that while most youth movements have favored progressive change, some youth movements have endorsed right-wing or reactionary goals—most notably the 1930s fascist generations in Europe. For example, it was young Germans whose youth movement supported Hitler and the Nazi party—championing slogans such as "step down you old ones" and "National Socialism is the organized will of youth."

In examining political generations in history, generational conflict comes into play in several ways. First, *intergenerational conflict* has been a principal dynamic for rallying and sustaining youth movements and historical generations. A survey of more than one hundred political generations in history indicated a common pattern shared by most of the movements. Disgusted with the world created by adults, young people organize to discredit and challenge their elders. Adult society is "deauthorized" by a generation of youth, largely through the efforts of young charismatic leaders, a cadre of youthful organizers, and speeches, songs, political writings, intellectual thought, and social criticism. Young people in late adolescence and early adulthood are receptive to such appeals, partially because of their life-cycle needs and partially because of their shared cohort experiences during a period of disappointing trends and events. Historically, young people are particularly apt to be perturbed and organize against adult-run institutions over issues related to unpopular or corrupt leadership, labor and educational reform, colonial or military repression, economic discontinuities, and institutional breakdowns. Typically, the adult regime is disparaged as "old," repressive, and out of touch, and appeals are made to youth to band together to reform society for a bold "new" generation.

Once young people have expressed their dissatisfaction with adult society, a critical dimension of intergenerational conflict involves young people "authorizing" themselves to bring about the desired changes. Youthful dissatisfaction with adults, after all, is a relatively constant theme of modern times, whereas youth movements and political generations are not routine. To authorize a generation, youthful discontent must be mobilized and channeled, creating the belief that something can be done to alleviate the perceived problem. Several factors come into play in the authorization process. First, there are large numbers of young people receptive to change and located where they can be organized and take direct action. Political generations, in fact, are most likely to occur when the size of the youth population is unusually large and increasing numbers of young people are becoming educated on university campuses. Beyond sheer numbers and critical mass, of utmost importance is the formation of generational consciousness—forging a recognition and connection among like-minded youth that they are part of a significant force in history whose mission is to mobilize and to transform the status quo.

Intergenerational conflict is not sufficient to produce a generational movement. A second principal dynamic involves *intragenerational conflict* or the opposition and competition within a generation. While a generation of youth may agree that society needs to be changed, its members often disagree over the direction change should take. As Mannheim noted, various generation units arise within a youth generation to compete and struggle over the control of the larger movement. Essentially, generation units form because young people come from different social backgrounds (class, status, gender, religion, region) and, as a result, interpret their common generational experiences in different ways. For example, within the highly active 1960s generation in the United States, the left-wing Students for a Democratic Society (SDS), who were raised in middle- and upper-middle class Jewish or Protestant homes, openly competed with the right-wing Young

Americans for Freedom (YAF), who were drawn largely from middle- and working-class Protestant or Catholic homes. Although the members of both SDS and YAF agreed that American society needed to be restructured, SDS wanted social change in a more progressive liberal-left direction, whereas YAF favored highly conservative and reactionary changes. Much of the momentum for the 1960s generation was derived from the competition and antagonism between these two opposing generational units, which waged nearly a decade of uninterrupted intragenerational conflict. Other youthful generation units were evident as well during the 1960s, including the politically moderate Young Democrats and Young Republicans, the radical Black Panthers, a variety of youthful civil rights and feminist organizations as well as the countercultural hippies and Yippies. Each decisive political generation in history has been partially sustained by the competition and conflict within the youth generation (Braungart 1993).

What might be expected for generational conflict in the future? What began as a few political generations in early nineteenth-century Europe increased in number and scope in the twentieth century, with the 1960s generation and the 1980s generation occurring on a worldwide scale. Many of these generational movements were spontaneous and organized by young people themselves, but they also have been sponsored by adult organizations as part of a larger movement for change or to combat and counter a movement for change. Much of the dynamic and momentum for these youth movements was derived from the conflict between and within generations. Thus far, it has been mostly young people organizing against adult society, and often over issues related to citizenship rights, corporate and civic responsibility, university reform, and enfranchisement. Generational movements also may be organized by older age-groups, such as the Townsend movement for Social Security benefits in the 1930s and the Gray Panthers in the 1960s.

With increased modernization and globalization, generational conflict is universal today and will continue to erupt into youth movements and political generations. While the patterns of inter- and intra-generational conflict set in motion an age-based struggle to transform or maintain the status quo, changes in generational dynamics also may be expected. Some of the issues of generational conflict will shift, with predictions that clashing cultures, human and animal rights, mininationalisms (submerged nations), environmental pollution, corporate and state corruption, and destructive biological technology may provide the sources of age-group contention in the future. And, since these issues transcend national boundaries, generational movements are likely to be transnational and perhaps international in scope. Moreover, the strategies and tactics of generational movements have expanded beyond the standard protest model. The Internet has become a powerful tool for swift communication, organization, and mobilization, as evidenced by the worldwide dissemination of information and rapid formation of protests over America's 2003 war against Iraq. Another recent strategy is to utilize litigation and the court systems (local, national, and international, i.e., the United Nations) to articulate dissatisfaction and try to bring about the desired reform and change.

For the most part it has been young people challenging the adult generation and organizing for change. Given the improving health and life expectancy of older people in advanced nations, it may someday be the elder generation that takes the initiative and mobilizes for change—especially when the large baby-boom generation reaches older adulthood and perhaps becomes disgruntled over health care and public policy issues. After all, it is part of the baby-boomer's youthful cohort legacy to mobilize and demand political reform. It also has been suggested that as the population of older adults increases and resources become more scarce, generational resentment and animosity may erupt between the young and the old over the special benefits given to retired citizens yet denied to equally needy children and youth. Finding a common ground and ways to bridge the generational divide will be required as the elderly population doubles from the year 2000 to 2050.

A few caveats or cautions are in order. Although the concepts of "generation," "generation gap," and "generational conflict" have intuitive appeal, there is a risk of overemphasizing and misapplying these terms, thereby promoting stereotypes, myths, and mindless interpretations. For example, the haphazard use of the term "generation" fosters a false representation of reality, as illustrated by the media's fondness for references to Generation X, despite the lack of survey evidence to support Generation X's existence or alleged attributes and animosities.

In addition, terms like "generation" and "generational conflict" have been used to manipulate and exploit youth in several ways. For example, the marketing, media, and advertising sectors have seized upon the appeal of generations in order to sell products and entertainment. As an illustration, *Businessweek* (February 15, 1999, 80, 82–83) celebrated the arrival of Generation Y: "To malls across America, a new generation is voting with its feet.... These kids ... [are] part of a generation that rivals the baby boom in size—and will soon rival it in buying clout.... Marketers haven't been dealt an opportunity like this since the baby boom hit.... Soon a lot of ... companies are going to have to learn the nuances of Gen Y marketing." In addition, since the dynamics of generational conflict and the formation of active generations have been recognized, adult efforts have focused on co-opting and directing youthful energies toward activities adults consider acceptable. Political regimes, nongovernmental organizations (NGOs), religious organizations, and a plethora of interest groups explicitly target and recruit youth to carry out their goals. Sometimes the goals are healthy and foster young people's develop-

ment, but young people's idealism, energy, and dependence also have been exploited for war (children soldiers), terrorism (suicide bombings), and other nefarious adult agendas. Politicians, in particular, may manipulate generational conflict to their advantage, as, for example, during the 1989 Tiananmen Square democracy movement in China when the Politburo hardliners used the student protests to consolidate their power and to squelch both the political opposition and the student movement.

Generational conflict is a fundamental dynamic in human relationships at the individual and group levels. It is derived from life-course needs and orientations and is exacerbated by modernization and rapid technological development. A first step is to understand the range, depth, and nuances of generational conflict, recognizing that the conflict of generations may promote personal growth and creative new forms, or it may foster misconceptions, exploitation, hostility, and outright physical combat that destroys lives and communities. Most of the research attention thus far has been on generational conflict over social and political issues. However, in examining innovation, change, and resistance, the generational conflict model also can be applied to other fields, such as the arts, sciences, and medicine. In exploring age-based relations, the emphasis has been on generational differences, rifts, and discord. Focus also needs to be given to understanding generational caring, healing, and rapprochement, especially with the rapidly increasing older populations in modern nations and the escalating numbers of young people in developing countries. Part of the solution to age-based dissonance and strife may lie in author J. F. Clarke's statement: "The politician thinks of the next election; a statesman, of the next generation."

See also Anti-Nazi Youth Resistance; Digital Divide; Generational Replacement; Intergenerational Programs and Practices; Palestinian *Intifada*; Tiananmen Square Massacre (1989); United Nations, Youth Activism and the.

Recommended Reading

Braungart, R. G. (1993). "Historical Generations and Generation Units: A Global Perspective." In *Life Course and Generational Politics*, edited by R. G. Braungart and M. M. Braungart. Lanham, MD: University Press of America, pp. 113–135.

Braungart, R. G., and Braungart, M. M. (1993). "Historical Generations and Citizenship: Two Hundred Years of Youth Movements." *Research in Political Sociology*, 6: 139–174.

Erikson, E. (1968). *Youth: Identity and Crisis*. New York: Norton.

Feuer, L. S. (1969). *The Conflict of Generations*. New York: Basic Books.

Inglehart, R. (1986). "Intergenerational Changes in Politics and Culture: The Shift from Materialist to Postmaterialist Value Priorities." *Research in Political Sociology*, 2: 81–105.

Keniston, K. (1971). *Youth and Dissent*. New York: Harcourt Brace Jovanovich.

Mannheim, K. (1952). *Essays on the Sociology of Knowledge*. London: Routledge and Kegan Paul.

Nash, L. L. (1978). "Concepts of Existence: Greek Origins of Generational Thought." *Daedalus*, 107: 1–21.

Richard G. Braungart and Margaret M. Braungart

Generational Replacement. "Nothing is certain," the popular saying goes, "except death and taxes." While one can disagree with the certainty of taxes, there is no disputing the inevitability of death. This fact of life is the driving force behind the notion of *generational replacement*. In the broadest sense, generational replacement refers to the gradual dying off of older age cohorts and their substitution in the population with younger ones.

The relevance of this natural and indisputable process to the amount, type, goals, and impact of youth activism is far more complex, however. At the heart of this complexity is a number of factors—from formal efforts to socialize youth to certain beliefs and behaviors; to the political, economic, cultural, and technological environments in which particular cohorts come of age; to major public events that affect public life and citizens' relationships to it; to the competing effects of aging and the development of more stable generational identities. These factors can come together in unique and unpredictable combinations, resulting in patterns of activism that distinguish young people from not only their older siblings, parents, and grandparents but also from youth of earlier eras.

In theory, there is no more fundamental transfer of power, and therefore no more fundamental *potential* for change, than that which occurs as a result of generational replacement. This is so because unlike any other type of political and social change it is inevitable, all inclusive, and untested. As noted by Ferrari (1874), approximately every thirty years the reigns of control of a sociopolitical system are handed to a completely new set of citizens and leaders, the unavoidable result of our mortality. Despite the magnitude of this reality, however, generationally inspired sociopolitical changes are arguably more the exception than the rule. Members of a new generation do not develop their values, opinions, and behaviors independently of the generations that came before but instead learn them from these older cohorts. This process of socialization occurs formally and informally through institutions such as the family, schools, media, and the workplace, which serve both as the repositories of the cumulative beliefs of prior generations and as transmitters of these beliefs to future generation.

The socialization process, especially in modern, complex societies, is imperfect and interactive, however, seldom resulting in the exact replication of specific orientations from generation to generation. In addition, because the social, economic, political, technological, and cultural environments are constantly changing, new generations are often raised under unique circumstances that complicate the socialization process. Finally, the pluralistic nature of most modern societies means that different socializing agents often send different, competing messages. It is in this inability of society to control all the relevant aspects of the socializing environment and the resultant inability to guarantee its own replication that the potential impact of generational replacement resides. The distinction between the study of political socialization in general and the particular study of generational replacement is that the former emphasizes *continuity* in attitudes, opinions, and behaviors between age cohorts while the latter is more likely to focus on *discontinuity*. Indeed, the study of generational replacement becomes most important when the process of political socialization fails.

The short- and longer-term impact of generational replacement is affected by a number of other, related factors. Included among these are the rates of political, cultural, economic, and technological change, which can affect both the pace of generational change and the distinctiveness among different generations. Also important is the size of different age cohorts, which can influence both the likelihood that a particular cohort comes to see itself as unique (i.e., *as a generation*) and a generation's impact on the larger social and political environment. And, of course, the economic, social, and ethnic diversity *within* newly emerging cohorts is crucial to consider, since these circumstances (along with gender) influence both the socialization process and the development of a coherent generational identity.

Perhaps the thorniest issue in considering the impact of generational replacement is the confounding effects of the life cycle. Put simply, age can be important for two reasons: because of the different developmental and circumstantial stages associated with being young, middle-aged, or elderly and because of the interaction of environmental changes with political learning (especially during the crucial ages of late adolescence and early adulthood), which lead to more permanent generational worldviews that do not dissipate with age. While both life cycle and generational effects are important to understanding youth activism, the implications of each can be very different.

For example, if young people are more liberal in their political views, more likely to engage in nontraditional political activities such as protests, or less likely to engage

in more traditional participation such as voting *because* they are young, then one would expect this distinctiveness to dissipate as they age, resulting in relative stability overall as generational replacement occurs. If, however, these patterns are due to a more permanent difference in a generation's identity, then these cohort-specific changes might portend more fundamental, structural change as they take the reigns of power. Further complicating this picture are "period effects," or the impact of incremental (e.g., the growth of the Internet) or sudden (e.g., the terrorist attacks of September 11, 2001) changes that can interact with the life cycle and generational identity to produce unique patterns of response.

While these factors make disentangling the impact of generational replacement on youth activism difficult, it is clear that youth throughout history have often approached their civic and political roles differently from both older cohorts and past cohorts of young people. Young people, whether because they were young or because of more permanent differences, have played a key role in many periods of political and social upheaval.

Studies (focusing largely on the United States) of age-related patterns in civic and political engagement suggest intriguing though inconclusive differences among the cohorts that make up the current population. Taken as a whole these and other studies suggest the existence of four somewhat distinct generations—"matures" or "the fifties generation" (those born before 1946), "baby-boomers" or "the sixties generation" (those born between 1946 and 1964), "Generation X" (those born between 1965 and 1976) and "DotNets" or "millennials" (those born after 1976)—each with their own approach to civic and political life. The most direct and comprehensive comparison of these cohorts to date is provided by Keeter, Zukin, Andolina, and Jenkins (2002), whose study includes over two dozen indicators of electoral engagement (e.g., voting), civic engagement (e.g., volunteering), cognitive engagement (e.g., following politics and public affairs in the media), and public voice (e.g., protesting, contacting a public official, boycotting). Simplifying somewhat, they find that members of the DotNet and Generation X cohorts are more cognitively disengaged from public affairs and less likely to participate in electoral politics than contemporary older cohorts or young people from prior eras but that the generation gap is less pronounced (especially for DotNets, given their relative youth) in most indicators of civic engagement and public voice. They also find evidence of generational differences in public attitudes with younger cohorts more tolerant of diversity and more accepting of an activist role for government. Whether these differences result from life cycle or true generational effects remains uncertain, although research by Keeter, Zukin, Andolina, Jenkins, and others suggests that both processes are at play. Answering this question more definitively is crucial to knowing whether we are witnessing a more typical pattern of age-based participation or a more fundamental shift, driven by generational replacement, in the nature of civic and political activism.

See also Demographic Trends Affecting the World's Youth; Digital Divide; Generational Conflict; Intergenerational Programs and Practices; Youth Bulge.

Recommended Reading

Braungart, R. G., and Braungart, M. M., eds. (1993). *Life Course and Generational Politics.* Totowa, NJ: Rowman and Littlefield.
Craig, S. C., and Bennett, S. E., eds. (1997). *After the Boom: The Politics of Generation X.* Totowa, NJ: Rowman and Littlefield.
Delli Carpini, M. X. (1986). *Stability and Change in American Politics: The Coming of Age of the Generation of the 1960s.* New York: New York University Press.
Delli Carpini, M. X. (1989). "Age or History: Generations and Sociopolitical Change. In *Political Learning in Adulthood: A Sourcebook of Theory and Research*, edited by R. S. Sigel. Chicago: University of Chicago Press, pp. 11–55.
Howe, N., and Strauss, W. (2000). *Millennials Rising: The Next Great Generation.* New York: Vintage Books.
Jennings, M. K., and Niemi, R. G. (1981). *Generations and Politics.* Princeton, NJ: Princeton University Press.
Keeter, S., Zukin, C., Andolina, M., and Jenkins, K. (2002). *The Civic and Political Health of the Nation: A Generational Portrait.* College Park, MD: The Center for Information and Research on Civic Learning and Engagement, University of Maryland.
Putnam, R. D. (2000). *Bowling Alone: The Collapse and Revival of American Community.* New York: Simon and Schuster.

Michael X. Delli Carpini

Girls. *See* Chat Rooms, Girls' Empowerment and; Feminism; Riot Grrrl.

Global Citizenship Education (GCE) in the United States. Global citizenship expands upon the traditional definition of citizenship in a national context to include social responsibility, community involvement, and political literacy in the global community. Whereas programs promoting citizenship have historically encouraged engagement and participation within national boundaries, global citizenship education (GCE) strives to create a generation of individuals who understand the interdependence of the world's systems (economic, political, social, cultural, technological, and environmental), believe that solutions to global challenges are attainable, feel morally compelled to confront these challenges, and take responsible actions to promote a just, peaceful, and sustainable world. While the need to prepare young people for informed participation and responsible action in the global community has never been more pressing, GCE remains largely absent from the educational experience in the United States. In overcoming challenges and promoting effective, wide-scale GCE in the United States, a range of organizations involving young people are addressing issues of content, pedagogy, and scale. By updating traditional global studies curricula, applying appropriate pedagogy, and devising innovative approaches to overcome traditional distribution barriers, American youth may yet join the GCE movement already underway in other countries around the world.

Global citizenship education prepares young people to exercise their duties and responsibilities in the global community. Rooted in a human rights framework, GCE ultimately aims to engage the global citizenry in actions that support the alleviation of poverty and inequity and to ensure the protection of all people's basic rights and opportunities. To this end, GCE is designed to help participants develop the three following learning outcomes:

Knowledge: A deepened understanding of global dynamics, systems, and frameworks, as well as concepts such as poverty, development, and global citizenship.

Perspectives: A value for diversity, a sense of empathy for others around the world, a commitment to social justice and equity, and the belief that the elimination of poverty and protection of human rights is an attainable goal which individuals and governments have the responsibility to achieve.

Skills: The ability to engage as both a leader and collaborator in effectively communicating, advocating, networking, and mobilizing resources to safeguard human rights and alleviate poverty.

The content of GCE is different from traditional approaches to teaching about the world, which have often focused on the study of countries and cultures as discrete units. As the world becomes increasingly globalized and the fates of its diverse inhabitants increasingly intertwined, the focus on *international education* is giving way to an emphasis on *global education*. The latter emphasizes the values, transactions, actors, and issues that transcend national and regional bounds and affect all humanity. GCE takes this practice one step further by encouraging and supporting real-world engagement around these themes in order to complete the learning cycle.

Ultimately, GCE seeks not only to affect understanding but also to influence attitudes and behaviors. Thus, learning about global citizenship cannot be presented as a simple set of facts for rote memorization.

Instead, in order to potentially reframe the way people conceive of the world and their roles within it, GCE is delivered through a participatory and experiential pedagogy which transcends the limits of the traditional "knowledge-banking" approach to classroom instruction. To accomplish this, GCE engages students in investigative and individualized learning which helps them realize a sense of global interdependence and develop a personal understanding of what it means to be a global citizen.

An additional component of effective GCE is promoting dialog and exchange through international contact to promote understanding, coordination, and networking with others. Through a dialogic encounter with others from around the world, young people can break from the stereotypes about other places. This can lead to an openness to develop the perspectives and skills fundamental to global citizenship. Recent advances in transportation and telecommunications technology make international collaboration less expensive and more feasible, thus offering new ways to support the pedagogical demands of GCE. Through the growth of international exchange programs, an increasing number of students have the opportunity to experience a reality outside their own. However, even as opportunities for travel expand, historic and enduring barriers to access make these programs unlikely to ever involve significant or diverse proportions of the U.S. student population. Telecommunication, on the other hand, offers a far lower-cost opportunity for dialog and exchange between students from around the world through online collaboration, as we see with emerging networks such as Taking it Global and I*earn and videoconferencing through organizations like the Global Nomads Group.

To give a sense of the potentials for GCE among students in the United States, it is useful to look at examples of programs that have successfully reached broad national constituencies in other parts of the world. Most often, these initiatives succeed when governments take the lead by incorporating GCE into formal curricular standards and then collaborate with domestic and international nongovernmental organizations (NGOs) to develop and distribute engaging materials.

In the United Kingdom the national curriculum for citizenship includes standards for knowledge, skills, and understanding relating to human rights and provides opportunities for individuals and volunteer groups to bring about social change locally, nationally, and internationally. To support the distribution of GCE materials and activities throughout the United Kingdom (UK), the government has launched a Web site, the Global Gateway, which serves as a clearinghouse for such curricula and the platform for their ambitious "e-twinning" scheme. This initiative aims to pair all schools in the United Kingdom with schools in other countries via the Internet by 2009. Nongovernmental efforts, like Oxfam's Cool Planet Web site and catalog for schools, offer a wide array of materials which directly support UK standards and help teachers bring GCE to their students both online and in the classroom.

In Norway, 70 percent of youth aged fifteen to twenty-one engage in GCE through Operation Day's Work. This program allows students and teachers to select a development challenge faced by a specific world region and to structure classroom activities around this issue. This classroom-based learning is then applied in practice when participants engage in a day of service through which they donate a day's worth of wages—totaling over $3 million annually—to a NGO development project of their choice.

In Canada, the Canadian International Development Agency (CIDA) has instituted the Global Classrooms Initiative to encourage young Canadians to become active and engaged global citizens. The initiative funds Canadian NGOs to develop activities and materials to use in promoting GCE around the country.

While the United Kingdom, European Union member-states, and Canada have made notable strides promoting global citizenship education through the formal education system, comparable initiatives remain largely absent in the United States. The lack of government support, limited notions of global studies, as well as a decentralized school system and rather narrow standards, have left the United States far behind other developed countries in preparing youth for responsible engagement in a rapidly globalizing world.

At a national level, government-supported international programming in the United States tends to focus on developing knowledge of different regions and cultures as a means of supporting U.S. foreign policy and economic and security interests. The decentralized nature of the U.S. school system in which curricular standards vary from state to state makes it incredibly difficult to develop a single nationwide GCE program. Moreover, the lack of priority given to general social studies, under the pressures of "high-stakes testing" and the strict curricular standards to which teachers are held, make it ever more difficult to incorporate a nonmandated curriculum such as GCE in the U.S. classroom.

A variety of educational and humanitarian nongovernmental organizations have developed GCE curricula for teachers. However, due to the challenge of distribution through the formal school system, these resources remain largely untapped and underused. Distribution typically relies on posting materials online or mailing curriculum to a self-selecting group of interested teachers—thus limiting the dissemination of these valuable resources.

Supplementing any materials that make their way into U.S. classrooms are a handful of programs that can help students in the United States develop a more global perspective through extracurricular involvement (e.g., the World Affairs Challenge, Global Relief Conference). These programs, while highly effective in engaging self-selecting students in GCE, have to date remained limited in both scale and impact.

At the same time, for young students whose global social consciousness is awakened—through participation in these extracurricular programs or international exchange—there remain few, if any, outlets for those who ask, "What next?" While college students have myriad opportunities—from joining the Peace Corps or Oxfam's Change initiative to becoming involved in one of the many campus movements focused on global social justice—younger students with a burning desire to *do something* to help alleviate global inequities remain largely unsupported in transferring this energy into sustained action.

NetAid, a New York–based nonprofit organization is meeting the challenge of supporting these students and distributing comprehensive and pedagogically sound GCE in the U.S. context. In its work to inspire, educate, and empower young people to take action in the fight against global poverty, NetAid has developed the Global Citizen Corps (GCC), a peer-education model that draws directly on lessons learned from the international community while simultaneously addressing barriers to widespread distribution which are specific to the United States.

The NetAid Global Citizen Corps (GCC) is an innovative youth leadership and service-learning program designed to provide high-school students in the United States with the training and resources they need to raise awareness and mobilize a domestic youth movement in the fight against global poverty. Through the recruitment and training of a dynamic corps of young change agents who implement a series of Global Action Days at their schools, the GCC aims to significantly increase the number of students in the United States who internalize a sense of global interdependence and the value of civic responsibility in the global community.

The GCC is grounded in sociological, educational, and cognitive research about message framing and resonance to address the challenge of making global issues salient for today's youth. The pedagogical approach which informs the GCC draws on the research of the Global Interdependence Initiative, which suggests the most effective ways to engage people in the United States on global issues, as well as on the work of psychologists and educational theorists who have articulated the cognitive requirements for making a message stick. Choosing an effective messenger is as important as defining the message and its mode of delivery. Research shows that by age ten young people are far more likely to have their minds changed by their peers than by their parents or other adult figures in their lives. Given this, the promise of a peer-education model that empowers young people themselves to be the messengers of global citizenship—particularly in light of the constraints of school-based distribution—is a particularly promising approach to the distribution of GCE in the context of the United States.

NetAid recruits GCC leaders from a broad and diverse audience through collaboration with networks of educators (e.g., Teach for America, Global TeachNet, Peace Corps Teaching Fellows), associations of schools (e.g., International Studies Schools Association, International Baccalaureate Organization, regional departments of education), and other youth-serving organizations (Model United Nations, Global Youth Action Network, Voices of Youth, American Field Service, and other student exchange programs). The process is highly selective and identifies those who are likely to be the most effective as messengers of global citizenship in their schools. Successful candidates demonstrate leadership ability, entrepreneurial flair, significant interest in global issues, and a commitment to inspire others to action.

Once selected, GCC leaders compile baseline measurements for their year of service by completing an online self-assessment and administering a peer survey designed to gauge the "global temperature" at their schools. With these baseline measures in place, GCC leaders embark on a yearlong program designed to deepen their own understanding of global issues and strengthen their ability to raise their schools' "global temperature" by promoting GCE among their peers.

The GCC program begins with an intensive multiday training for GCC leaders. Through activities that draw on experiential and service-learning pedagogy, participants are challenged to think critically about the United States' role in the world while beginning to develop a more global perspective—one characterized by a sense of individual responsibility to the global community, a commitment to social justice, and a belief that individuals have the power and responsibility to make a difference. To complement this substantive learning, a series of skills-building workshops, emphasizing leadership, message framing, working with the media, networking, and resource mobilization, help GCC leaders develop effective peer education and campaigning skills. At the conclusion of the training GCC leaders receive a "global citizenship toolkit" which equips them with key resources (e.g., banners, videos, games and activities, and a CD-ROM with downloadable posters, fact sheets, and slide shows) to help promote global citizenship at their schools and in their communities.

Throughout the school year, GCC leaders receive ongoing support in planning and implementing their activities through a dynamic GCC Online Action Center. Employing new and promising tools that are increasingly second nature to today's tech-savvy youth, the GCC Online Action Center combines organizing and campaigning tools (which have made recent headlines through organizations like MoveOn. org) with innovative approaches to information sharing through community boards (as seen with the successes of Idealist.org and Craigslist.org) and Web logs or "blogs." Through this innovative forum, participants can post directly to a group home page to share learning resources and organizing tools, as well as to personal blogs which track their campaigns and showcase

their accomplishments. The Online Action Center helps GCC leaders to collaborate with one another in planning their Global Action Days; access key resources about current events, campaigns and new opportunities for involvement; and receive direct feedback and ongoing support from NetAid and a network of mentors throughout their planning process.

By allowing participants to interact closely with each other, the GCC Online Action Center promotes a sense of cooperation and community among participants from disparate parts of the country. Additionally, by connecting the GCC to other organizations and networks of youth from around the world, this online platform completes the global citizenship education learning cycle. As additional support, GCC leaders are also encouraged to collaborate with the GCC faculty advisors at their schools and a network of local mentors, individuals who are eager to help train the next generation of global citizens (e.g., returned Peace Corps volunteers, college activists, community leaders, international development professionals) and who can provide support both online and in person throughout the year.

The greatest impact of the GCC will come through a series of Global Action Days organized by each GCC leader and implemented with the support of his or her faculty advisor and/or group of peers. By mobilizing schools throughout the United States to join global campaigns, the Global Action Day concept leverages the attention and publicity that exist around a series of internationally recognized days, such as World AIDS Day on December 1 or the Global Campaign for Education's Access to Education Week in April of each year. During Global Action Days, GCC leaders are encouraged to devise creative ways to raise awareness about key development issues, awaken a sense of empathy for others around the world, and build momentum for campaigns to provide direct support to grassroots projects working to alleviate global poverty.

For each Global Action Day, NetAid provides GCC leaders with a variety of resources and suggested activities which can be adapted to work in a variety of settings—from hosting a classroom hunger banquet to convening a school-wide simulation to demonstrate the prevalence of HIV/AIDS around the world. Actions might include collecting signatures for a petition calling for increased U.S. humanitarian aid, conducting a virtual e-card campaign online, or organizing a fundraising event to collect resources to help support a specific grassroots development project. Thus, Global Action Days pair experiential activities with concrete opportunities for action.

NetAid's Global Citizen Corps is designed to complement existing global education programs in the United States and abroad by growing the network of youth in the United States who are active and engaged global citizens. In bringing these inspired young leaders together, the GCC helps create a momentum greater than the sum of its parts, a coordinated national youth movement with the aim of alleviating global poverty. Ultimately, by promoting connections between young global citizens in developed and developing countries, the GCC supports the emergence of a global partnership for international development among today's youth.

See also Character Education; Citizenship Education Policies in the States; Civic Virtue; Democratic Education; Digital Divide; Diversity Education; Environmental Education (EE); Global Justice Activism; IEA Civic Education Study; Just Community High Schools and Youth Activism; National Alliance for Civic Education (NACE); New Media; Prosocial Behaviors; School Engagement; School Influences and Civic Engagement; United Nations, Youth Activism and.

Recommended Reading

Arnove, Robert F. (1999). "Reframing Comparative Education: The Dialectic of the Global and the Local." In *Comparative Education: The Dialectic of the Global and the Local*, edited by R. F. Arnov and C. A. Torres. Boulder, CO: Rowman and Littlefield.

Boulding, Elise (1988). *Building a Global, Civic Culture: Education for an Interdependent World*. New York: Teacher's College Press.

Canadian International Development Agency (2004). *The Global Classrooms Initiative*. See http://www.acdicida.gc.ca/cida_ind.nsf/vall/F06E7C95140BF76985256B12005AD8F5?Open Document.

Department for Education and Employment Advisory Group on Citizenship (1988). *Education for Citizenship and the Teaching of Democracy in Schools: Final Report of the Advisory Group on Citizenship*. London: Qualifications and Curriculum Authority.

Department for Education and Skills (2004). *International Strategy for Education Putting the "World" into World Class Education*. Press Notice 2004/0193. See http://www.dfes.gov.uk/pns/DisplayPN.cgi?pn_id=2004_0193.

Gardner, Howard (2004). *Changing Minds: The Art and Science of Changing Our Own and Other People's Minds*. Boston: Harvard Business School Publishing.

NetAid (2003). *Learning for Change: Strategies to Build a Domestic Constituency for International Development*. See http://www.netaid.org/documents/learning_for_change.pdf.

Qualifications and Curriculum Authority (2004). *National Curriculum Online: Citizenship Key Stage Four*. See http://www.nc.uk.net/webdav/servlet/XRM?Page/@id=6001andSession/@id=D_8UXoJSAR81sTcv6TpiTDandPOS[@stateId_eq_main]/@id=4188andPOS[@stateId_eq_note]/@id=4188.

Reimers, Fernando (2003). *Rethinking Social Studies to Develop Global Literacy and Global Trust*. Boston Research Center for the Twenty-first Century Newsletter #21 2003: 1, 1.

United States Department of Education (2004). *Our Role in International Education*. See http://www.ed.gov/about/offices/list/ous/international/edlite-edrole.html.

The World Conservation Union Commission on Education and Communication (2003). *What is Education for Sustainable Development?* See http://www.iucn.org/themes/cec/education/whatis.htm.

Abigail Falik and Justin van Fleet

Global Justice Activism. The rise of mass-based transnational movements against corporate globalization during the past decade represents one of the most important expressions of radical grassroots dissent of the past generation. Beginning in November 1999, when 50,000 protesters converged on Seattle to shut down the

Young Brazilian anarchists march against war and neoliberalism at the World Social Forum in Porto Alegre in January 2002. *Courtesy of Jeffrey S. Juris.*

World Trade Organization (WTO) meetings, anticorporate globalization activists have organized highly visible direct-action protests against multilateral institutions and alternative forums in cities such as Prague, Barcelona, Genoa, Quito, Porto Alegre, and Cancun, uniting diverse movements and networks in opposition to growing corporate influence over people's lives, communities, and resources. At the same time, a new form of networking politics has emerged involving decentralized coordination, open participation, consensus decision-making, and the free and open circulation of information.

Although anticorporate globalization movements are intergenerational, youth activists have occupied their leading edge, infusing them with a confrontational spirit and emphasis on technological, political, and social innovation. Young people have assumed prominent roles within many important struggles since the 1960s, including student, peace, and environmental activism. Contemporary anticorporate globalization movements are characterized by three features, which make them particularly attractive to younger generations. First, they are organized around informal network-based forms facilitated by new information and communication technologies, such as the Internet. Second, they involve nontraditional and highly theatrical forms of direct-action protest. Finally, anticorporate globalization movements are global in their geographic reach and thematic scope, as activists increasingly link their locally rooted struggles to diverse movements elsewhere.

By significantly enhancing the speed, flexibility, and global reach of information flows, allowing for communication at a distance in real time, digital computer networks provide the technological infrastructure for the emergence of contemporary network-based social-movement

An anarchist group known as the Pink & Silver Bloc protests at a meeting of the G8 in Genoa, Italy, in July 2001. *Courtesy of Jeffrey S. Juris.*

forms. Anticorporate globalization movements thus belong to a new class of "computer-supported social movements," as activists use new digital technologies to communicate and coordinate on local, regional, and global scales, while moving back and forth between online and off-line political activity. Given that younger generations have grown up using computers, it should come as no surprise that they have been at the forefront of incorporating new technologies into their everyday organizing routines.

Specifically, anticorporate globalization activists have employed digital networks to organize direct actions and share information and resources, as well as plan and coordinate activities. Although activists primarily use e-mail and electronic Listservs, they also create temporary Web pages during mobilizations to provide information, resources, and contact lists; post documents and calls to action; and sometimes, to house discussion forums and IRC chat rooms. Moreover, particular movement networks, like People's Global Action (PGA) and the World Social Forum (WSF), and individual organizations have their own Web pages where activists post reflections, analyses, updates, calls to action, and links along with more logistical information. Interactive Web sites offering multiple tools for coordination are becoming increasingly popular, including open publishing projects like the Independent Media Center (IMC), or Indymedia, which allow users to freely post news and information without editorial selection and control.

Moreover, independent media activism increasingly forms part of an emerging radical media culture among young anticorporate globalization activists. For example, Indymedia, established during the anti–WTO protests in Seattle, has become a global network of local Web-based media projects, allowing activists to create and circulate alternative news and information. During mass actions and gatherings, hundreds of activists take to the streets to record video footage, snap photos, and conduct interviews, while IMCs become dynamic communication hubs, buzzing with activity as protesters upload files, swap reports and information, and edit videos. There are now more than 120 local IMC sites around the world, while the global network receives up to 2 million page views per day. Younger media activists have also practiced "tactical media," including the playful parodying of corporate advertisements, as in "culture jamming," or new kinds of electronic civil disobedience, such as the "virtual sit-in." Beyond specific objectives, activists also use new digital technologies within temporary media hubs to experiment with horizontal collaboration, while expressing directly democratic political ideals.

New technologies have greatly reinforced the most radically decentralized network-based organizational forms within anticorporate globalization movements, leading to highly flexible, diffuse, and often ephemeral formations, like the Direct Action Network (DAN) in the United States, the Movement for Global Resistance (MRG) in Catalonia, or People's Global Action (PGA) on a global scale. Grassroots movements and collectives can now directly connect up across space without the need for organizational hierarchy. In contrast to traditional parties and unions, network-based politics involve the creation of broad umbrella spaces where diverse organizations, collectives, and networks converge around a few common hallmarks while preserving their autonomy and specificity. Young people are typically attracted to such informal, grassroots forms of political participation, which are increasingly seen as concrete political alternatives in and of themselves, particularly given the widely perceived crisis of representative democracy.

Younger activists are also characteristically drawn to more unconventional forms of direct-action protest, involving creative, expressive, or violent repertoires. Despite emerging in different cultural contexts, the various tactics employed by young anticorporate globalization activists all produce theatrical images for mass-mediated consumption, including the following: giant puppets and street theater; mobile street carnivals; militant protesters advancing toward police lines with white outfits, protective shields, and padding; and black-clad, masked urban warriors smashing the symbols of corporate capitalism. Whether broadcast images depict samba dancers dressed in pink and silver, thousands of Michelin men advancing toward a "red zone," or skirmishes between robocops and hooded stone throwers, mass actions are powerful image events, while the overall summit blockade strategy where diverse formations "swarm" their target produces high-powered social drama.

In addition to their more utilitarian purpose of shutting down major summit meetings, mass actions are complex cultural performances that allow participants to communicate symbolic messages to an audience while also providing a forum for producing and experiencing shared meaning and solidarity. The theatrical performances staged by activists associated with diverse networks—including physical confrontation (black bloc), symbolic conflict (white overalls) or carnivalesque revelry (pink bloc)—capture mass-media attention but also embody and express alternative political identities.

Beyond putting their bodies on the line to communicate political messages, direct-action activists also express themselves stylistically through clothing and bodily adornment. During mass anticorporate globalization actions, youth activists consciously appropriate, recombine, and assemble diverse products and cultural symbols, including white overalls, industrial tubes and tires, black boots and masks, wigs, and pink dresses, to express the values and identities associated with alternative activist youth subcultures.

Among more radical anticapitalist networks, squatting and the use of aggressive tactics, styles, and icons associated with the "black bloc" comprise central elements of a militant youth counterculture organized around performative violence. The black bloc is not an organization or even a network but rather a specific set of direct-action tactics involving the destruction of private property, usually banks and transnational storefronts, ritualized confrontation with the police, and a series of defensive practices, including "de-arrests," marching in small, compact groups with elbows linked, and jail solidarity. These tactics are connected to a broader militant style, including the use of black pants and jumpers, combat boots, and black masks or bandanas to cover the face, and an aggressive, confrontational attitude. Masks are worn for instrumental purposes—to protect activist identity for individual security—but also serve symbolic functions, such as expressing collective solidarity through anonymity or portraying

archetypical images of youth rebellion. Militant styles and practices are the physical embodiment of a political vision based on anticapitalism, direct confrontation, and a total rejection of the market and the state.

Young people have grown up in a more globalized world then ever before, given that geographically dispersed actors can now communicate and coordinate through transnational networks in real time. Contemporary anticorporate globalization movements, which extend from largely middle-class, youth-based movements in Europe and North America to mass-based poor people's struggles throughout Latin America, Asia, and Latin America, are thus truly global in reach. Indeed, despite their uneven geographic distribution, transnational activist networks like PGA, the WSF process, or Indymedia provide the infrastructure for the emergence of global fields of meaning and political identification, which accord with the life experiences and political imaginations of many young activists in the global North and urban areas of the global South. As a young Barcelona-based activist once put it, "This is a global protest.... We are building networks in Barcelona but with a global consciousness. If there is a revolt around water in Bolivia or in Washington or Monterrey, wherever, even if far away, I feel part of what is happening."

In addition to a more general sense of global solidarity, youth activists have also used the Internet to plan and coordinate concrete actions, gatherings, and activities across transnational space, while periodically coming together in concrete locales. For example, young people from countries around Europe, including Spain, Italy, France, Germany, Holland, and England have used Listservs to organize European PGA conferences and No Border camps, while many have also helped coordinate the more radical fringe of the regional and global social forum process. A Barcelona-based Indymedia activist had this to say regarding the excitement generated through such long-distance collaboration:

I learned how a group of people, some in the U. S., others in London, and others, who knows where, coordinated through a global Listserv. Suddenly someone would send an e-mail saying, "I think this story is important, what do you think?" In less than a week, ten people had answered, one or two saying it wasn't clear, but most feeling it was important, so we distributed the tasks: "I'll reduce it to so many characters," "I'll translate it into German," and "I'll do Italian." The next day we started working, and the messages began arriving: "Spanish translation done," "Italian done," "French done." Then someone sent a photo, "What do you think about this picture?" The comments went around, and then someone sent another picture, and suddenly we had created an article!

Moreover, now that images and slogans travel instantaneously through alternative and mainstream global media networks, protest styles and practices circulate rapidly from one site to another. Despite local variation, black-bloc, pink-bloc, or white-overalls tactics are increasingly similar in places as diverse as Italy, Spain, the United States, Brazil, and Mexico. Indeed, today's anticorporate globalization movements have ushered in a truly global youth culture of protest.

Beyond geographic reach, contemporary anticorporate globalization movements are also global in their thematic scope, bringing together diverse struggles in opposition to growing corporate influence over politics, society, and the economy, as well as increasing commercial penetration into the most intimate aspects of everyday lives. Corporations have specifically targeted adolescents with their ever more aggressive "branding" campaigns, and consequently, young people have been at the forefront of forging a broad resistance to corporate domination and, increasingly, to global capitalism itself. An emphasis on corporate power and the symbols of corporate capitalism, including the WTO, World Bank, and International Monetary Fund (IMF), has thus allowed previously disconnected movements to unite against a common enemy. At the same time, young people are also more likely to be motivated by the "postmaterial" values associated with anticorporate activism, including respect for human rights and the environment, gender and class equality, egalitarianism, direct democracy, and global solidarity.

Building on previous youth involvement in antisweatshop campaigns, radical ecology, squatting, Zapatista activism, and other forms of global solidarity, anticorporate globalization movements have provided a forum for the emergence of globally linked radical youth countercultures. Although, as mentioned above, anticorporate globalization movements are intergenerational, young people have played key roles, particularly within the more grassroots, technologically innovative, and direct-action oriented sectors. Indeed, the importance of new technologies, flexible network-based forms, informal channels of political participation, nontraditional styles of symbolic protest, as well as their global reach and thematic scope make anticorporate globalization movements particularly conducive to youth engagement. Young anticorporate globalization activists are thus experimenting with new technological, cultural, and political practices and forms that may one day lead to broader social transformation.

See also Global Citizenship Education (GCE) in the United States; Global Youth Action Network (GYAN); United Students Against Sweatshops (USAS); Zapatista Rebellion (Mexico).

Recommended Reading

Arquilla, John, and Ronfeldt, David (2001). *Networks and Netwars.* Santa Monica, CA: Rand.

Castells, Manuel (1997). *The Power of Identity.* Oxford: Blackwell.

Inglehart, Ronald (1977). *The Silent Revolution.* Princeton: Princeton University Press.

Juris, Jeffrey S. (2004). *Networked Social Movements: The Network Society*, edited by Manuel Castells. London: Edward Elgar.

Klein, Naomi (1999). *No Logo.* New York: Picador.

Meikle, Graham (2002). *Future Active*. New York: Routledge.

Peterson, Abby (2001). *Contemporary Political Protest*. Aldershot: Ashgate.

Starhawk. *Webs of Power*. Gabriola Island, B.C.: New Society Publishers.

Starr, Amory (1999). *Naming the Enemy*. London and New York: Zed Books.

Yuen, Eddie, Burton-Rose, Daniel, and Katsiaficas, George, eds. (2004). *Confronting Capitalism*. Brooklyn, NY: Soft Skull Press.

Jeffrey S. Juris

Global Youth Action Network (GYAN). Why do many young people today demonstrate interest in activism but fail to get fully engaged? Why are new social movements inspired by globalization capable of mobilizing tens of thousands of protestors yet develop few links to lobbies that promote alternative economic policy? The Global Youth Action Network (GYAN) asserts that society and development are limited by "fragmentation" and that defragmentation—defined as the creation of new relationships between traditionally segregated groups combined with the new availability of quality information—can liberate many new opportunities. The WTO protester in Seattle and the overwhelmed finance minister of sub–Saharan Africa need each other. How can they be linked? GYAN facilitates the integration of global issues and local processes through a program that links personal relationships, collaborative projects, centralization of information on the Internet, and youth participation in democratic structures. This program was first implemented in June 2004 in São Paulo, Brazil, and is called the "local jam."

GYAN was founded in 1999 to support collaboration between youth organizations. In just five years it has launched several dozen global projects and incubated partnerships between youth organizations while supporting diverse activities ranging from campaigns and research to conferences and political lobbies. When designing a program, GYAN examines the actors in the field and proposes a structure for collaborative action, taking into account five levels of youth participation in social change: (1) awareness, (2) action and recognition, (3) networking, (4) collaboration of social groups, and (5) policy. GYAN recently used this five-level model to design youth campaigns that support the United Nations millennium development goals (MDGs). It consulted hundreds of youth experts, wrote a white paper on the contributions of youth to MDG implementation, and published a campaign framework for groups to take action. Two of GYAN's largest projects include Global Youth Service Day, the world's largest celebration of youth volunteerism, and www.TakingITGlobal.org, a Web site with the Internet's largest community of youth activism.

The local jam is dedicated to "defragmenting youth" and was developed by GYAN's South American regional office in São Paulo, Brazil. It created a youth network in the city in response to two observations of local researchers: a majority of young people in the city wanted to get more involved in some cause, and as of 2003, only 8 percent of youth participated in cause-related groups. As a network-driven organization focused on international youth mobilization and participation in global decision-making processes, GYAN developed a program to integrate the activism of local youth organizations while addressing international goals.

In the first stage the organization mapped international youth movements and sought their contacts in São Paulo. It then mapped local youth movements, joining the work of the mayor's office, and placed the results into a municipal Web site that is integrated within the TakingITGlobal Web platform. The mapping process, originally led by the mayor's office of São Paulo, identified more than 1,700 youth groups. The Web site became a virtual space for ongoing local networking and at the same time became a node within the wider global youth movement.

For the second stage GYAN launched an outreach and selection process to connect with groups and identify representative young leaders from diverse backgrounds in the city. They received applications from hundreds of activists and chose sixty to participate in thematic working groups, all focused on developing collaborative projects and facilitated by local partner organizations in the city. Two months of dialog culminated in a retreat or "local jam," a one-week informal gathering dedicated to building personal relationships, celebrating diversity, launching collaborative projects, and developing a strategy for youth political participation from the local to the global level. Thirty-seven people attended for seven days: twenty-five from São Paulo, five from other Brazilian states, five from other countries in the region, and two from other continents. Representatives of the mayor's office and other organizations attended for one day.

In the third and final stage GYAN evaluated the process and incubated some of the collaborative projects. A remarkable twenty new projects were created and set in motion (a handful adapted from preexisting activities). They ranged from the development of the São Paulo Center for Indigenous and Environmental Education to the launch of the Brazilian campaign for youth participation in municipal elections. The projects also helped network diverse groups and defragment the youth of São Paulo, creating opportunities to engage more youth in activism and to help more groups become politically active at local, national, and international levels.

In summary, a process of mapping and dialog between diverse groups culminated in a one-week jam. The process, with the exception of the mapping, lasted six months and has inspired similar efforts in other cities around Brazil and the rest of the world, most notably in Porto Alegre, Brazil, as a lead up to the World Social Forum 2005 and in the United States in New York City with a grant from the Rockefeller Brothers Fund. The concept of a "jam" was originally developed by Youth for Environmental Sanity in Santa Cruz, California, and focused on building rela-

tionships at the global level. GYAN adapted the concept to focus on three goals, especially at the local level: (1) developing new projects, (2) building networks, and (3) strengthening the political power of youth. This local emphasis inspired the name "local jam."

The network created by the local jam continues to function, hopefully in perpetuity, decentralized from GYAN. At the same time its members have an ongoing strategy for youth political participation set in place that never existed before, encouraging youth dialog with political structures ranging from the local level in the case of the São Paulo mayor's office to the global level with the United Nations. GYAN sees itself as a catalyst that helps groups celebrate diversity and in the process generates new projects that facilitate development and renews democracy with fresh participation from new, young actors with local roots and global vision, members of a global network.

Where did GYAN come from? In 1996 seventeen-year-old Benjamin Quinto participated in a small discussion and networking session of international NGOs at the United Nations secretariat in New York. He was inspired to meet people whose lives were dedicated to global problem solving. At the same time, however, he was shocked to learn that few young people were involved. He read the UN charter, observed its call for the participation of young people, and set out to create a youth assembly within the UN system. After three years of consultation with politicians, international organizations, and youth from all over the world, he concluded that a youth assembly could not function in the UN system without demand for such a body from member countries. Quinto also concluded that young people around the world needed to get better organized among themselves, celebrate their differences, collaborate on projects, and exercise greater political influence at local and national levels. With an initial grant from the singer Jewel and the Lifebridge

Foundation, Quinto, together with Jonah Wittkamper and Bremley Lyngdoh, set up the Global Youth Action Network in New York to support collaboration between youth organizations. Since its launch five years ago, GYAN has grown into one of the largest networks of youth organizations in the world.

Young people are attracted to the concept of GYAN as a network because they recognize the weakness of separation—or fragmentation—in the face of the overwhelming challenges and opportunities in the world today. The network and the Web site, TakingITGlobal.org, offer them connection to more than 50,000 other young activists in all countries of the world. Connecting to youth in other countries and contributing to the common cause of alliance building invites young organizers to step out of their local realities and consider the larger picture. Local organizers are attracted to the vision of "global community" while international organizers are attracted to a serious engagement with local realities. Together they integrate agendas, defragment, involve more and more "under-involved" youth, and create a new kind of movement.

The five-level model of youth participation that GYAN uses when designing its programs such as the local jam was inspired by integral theory, a concept of philosopher Ken Wilber that encourages planners to examine the internal and external dimensions of both individual organizers and their communities. Correspondingly, GYAN and its five-level model call for building an "integrated youth movement," a movement in which youth participate actively in the following:

1. *Awareness*: raising awareness of social issues and critical thinking about the future

2. *Action and recognition*: taking action to solve community problems and providing recognition

3. *Networking*: communicating to share information, relationships, resources, and knowledge

4. *Collaboration and trust*: facilitating collaboration and building trust between diverse social groups

5. *Political participation*: engaging with formal decision-making structures

The model suggests both a strategy for defragmentation and a framework for selecting and designing indicators to measure integral participation. Each level of the model builds upon the others. For example, political participation of young people (level five) will be mere tokenism if youth representatives do not have networks to support them—or if networks distrust each other and refuse to cooperate—thereby weakening the collective political power of youth.

The local jam process joins with existing groups working at the levels of *awareness* (level one) and *action and recognition* (level two), and then facilitates their partnership to strengthen the levels of *network* (level three), *collaboration and trust* (level four) and *political participation* (level five). To understand how the model works it is helpful to examine each level and consider how to measure progress.

Level one (*awareness*). The São Paulo youth network of the local jam involves many groups from diverse religions, social classes, races, and political parties. Among these are groups that raise awareness and run campaigns to educate youth about social and environmental issues. The prevalence of these campaigns and youth participation in them is a key measure of progress at this level.

Level two (*action and recognition*). In response to increasing awareness, more and more individuals take action to address issues. Within the São Paulo network there are groups that "take action" and clean litter from parks, organize cultural presentations, offer training courses to give young people skills, and much more. To support role models and encourage greater action it is important to recognize the contributions of young people to society, especially in the media. Frequent mobilizations of young people for volunteer activities and recognition of their work in the media are indicators of healthy activity at this level. Although not part of the local jam process, GYAN addresses this issue of "recognition" at the global level by organizing the International Youth in Action Award and donating $1,000 (U.S.) to the top ten youth-led community projects in the world every year.

Level three (*network*). To facilitate networking and information sharing GYAN encouraged the local jam participants to take part in several collaborative projects. Although these projects are components of the local jam process, GYAN encourages other youth organizations to replicate them around the world. The presence of youth-focused publications (off-line or online) and forums (such as conferences) for young people to build meaningful relationships across traditional barriers are important signs of progress at this level. Below are a few examples:

Informal monthly meetings—On the first Monday of every month young activists in São Paulo gather for an informal dinner to sustain their relationships, make new connections, and discuss their movement. Diverse groups from various backgrounds participate. Many uninvolved young people enter the movement for the first time by participating in such meetings. Organizing the event in a place not affiliated with any one organization (e.g., a restaurant) allows for decentralization of the process, thereby encouraging collective responsibility instead of singular leadership.

E-mail bulletins of local opportunities and events for youth activists—There are many communication networks of youth activists, too many to keep track of. To facilitate the flow of information within the movement, young volunteers gather information, package it into a calendar, and send it out to youth networks via e-mail. Such calendars help educators and other adults get students involved by providing a snapshot of what is happening in the city. As a goal for the future in São Paulo, organizers will try to convince community newspapers to publish the calendars as well.

Municipal Web site—The São Paulo Web site within the TakingITGlobal infrastructure contains profiles and blogs of young activists, lists of events, a database of organizations, articles written by young people about key issues, and much more. Started in 2000 for the global level, the site remains free for anyone on the Internet with more and more local-level sites opening up.

Level four (*collaboration and trust*). The local jam is GYAN's chief tool for building trust among diverse groups and facilitating collaboration. Building from the Web of trust created by the local jam, GYAN and the jam participants develop new projects ranging from exchange programs and campaigns to cultural exhibitions and conferences. An evaluation made three months after the retreat counted more than twenty activities and projects that resulted from the local jam process. In the future, GYAN plans to use the local jam methodology to build trust between entire social groups, hoping that it will change the political landscape for future generations and lower the barriers to entry in society and divisions by religion, race, social class, and so forth. Two important partner organizations already support GYAN's movement toward this goal. The Interfaith Youth Core convenes young people of diverse religions to educate each other about their faiths and organizes volunteer activities. The Indigenous and Non-Indigenous Youth Alliance organizes dialog between urban and aboriginal youth to build solidarity and foster partnership. GYAN believes that the celebration of diversity is the best mechanism for uniting young people and fostering greater activism. Many factors indicate progress at this level, primarily the size and frequency of collaborative projects and the diversity of youth involved.

Level five (*political participation*). GYAN believes that young people, united in their diversity, can form a powerful political force. To crosslink networks and build upon the collaboration and trust of diverse youth groups, GYAN promotes highly visible debates between political candidates and youth during election years. As a result of the relationships that formed at the local jam, GYAN was able to promote debates this year in Brazil for the first time. The organizers created a partnership with MTV to promote political awareness among youth and encourage young people to organize debates throughout the country. GYAN also publishes information, facilitates networking, and lobbies for greater youth participation in political processes of local, national, and international governmental structures. The prevalence of youth participation in political processes and government spending on youth-led programs are important indicators of progress at this level.

Suggested Indicators for a Youth Participation Index

Level one (*awareness*):	(1) Youth participation in issue-oriented awareness raising campaigns. (2) Successful responses of youth to questionnaires that measure awareness (3) Government spending to support youth-led campaigns
Level two (*action and recognition*):	(1) Percentages of youth who volunteer (2) Percentage of youth who participate in youth-led groups (3) Number of positive reports in the media about youth (4) Government spending to support youth-led action and recognition
Level three (*networking*):	(1) Numbers of young people who participate in networking focused gatherings (2) Numbers of youth-led publications (3) Quality of information available on youth opportunities (4) Cross pollination of youth networks identified by the number of young people who act in multiple networks (5) Government spending to support youth-led publications
Level four (*collaboration and trust*):	(1) Prevalence of groups dedicated to building trust between youth of different social groups (2) Diversity of young people participating in key organizations—such as government youth councils (3) Number and diversity of alliances and partnerships held by youth organizations (4) Number of collaborative projects run by diverse youth organizations (5) Government spending to support youth-led trust building projects
Level five (*political participation*):	(1) Percentage of young people who voluntarily vote (2) Percentage of youth who participate in political parties (3) Prevalence of youth participation within government structures (4) Government spending to support youth-led participation in government

GYAN uses the five-level model with the hope that it will integrate youth movements and support those working to "defragment" society. To guide this process, GYAN is calling for the development of a youth participation index for documenting and measuring progress toward these goals. By tracking and compiling diverse indicators, it may be possible to create a composite index that measures the integration of youth and their participation in shaping society. Local youth organizations could draw from available data about their cities and design their own indices, potentially forming a political tool to measure the performance of elected officials and hold them accountable. The following list of six sample indicators, drawn from data that is readily available in many countries, could provide a good "integrated" measure of youth participation in a given city or country:

1. Youth participation in issue-oriented awareness raising campaigns
2. Percentage of youth who participate in youth-led groups
3. Number of positive reports in the media about youth
4. Government and grant-maker spending to support youth-led publications
5. Diversity of young people participating in key organizations such as government youth councils
6. Percentage of young people who voluntarily vote

The preceding table provides a more comprehensive list of potential indicators, suggested by GYAN, for developing a youth participation index.

Finally, the diversity among youth and the obstacles for marginalized young people need to be taken into account. Organizers must recognize that many young people from impoverished communities with inadequate access to education, health care, and employment will not be able to participate fully in youth movements unless they are empowered to do so. As a result, the analysis of the indicators above must be considered carefully in tandem with other development indicators. Such measurements could enhance planning, improve distribution of resources, indicate factors such as violence and poverty that inhibit participation, and strengthen democracy. Perhaps most useful for the near future of youth movements and decision-makers would be a global survey of existing youth participation indicators. The result could be a conceptual framework that aids groups in the selection of indicators and the design of indices that are relevant for local, national, and international bodies where needed.

GYAN's pilot project in São Paulo, Brazil, has had much success defragmenting the youth movements of the city and supporting youth activism from a local to a global level. But it is only a start, and much remains to be learned as the jam process and similar experiments take place around the world.

See also Global Citizenship Education (GCE) in the United States; Global Justice Activism; Statute of the Child and Adolescent (Brazil); Transnational Youth Activism.

Recommended Reading

Wilber, Ken (2001). *A Theory of Everything.* Boston: Shambhala.

Jonah Wittkamper and Luis Davila

Grassroots Youth Movements. Free bus passes for young people in Portland, a voting-age reduction in Cambridge, ethnic-studies classes for students in Los Angeles, and a brownfield turned into a park and recreation center in the Bronx—all of these are examples of victories young people have won to improve their communities. All are part of a growing movement called "youth organizing."

Young people have a long history of leading social movements. In the early 1990s, however, a new kind of youth activism began, a youth-led youth movement, that is, a movement dedicated to issues that directly concern youth also led by youth. Groups of young people from around the country began forming organizations and joining together to create change in their schools and communities. What makes these new efforts different than past ones is that young people are not simply a part or the core of an organized constituency but instead are the subject or "issue" of the organizing efforts. In the past young people have participated in general movements around issues that affect the entire community. Now young people are often organizing around youth-specific issues such as aiming to improve the quality of public schools or opposing criminal-justice policies designed to incarcerate more young people. In addition, the vast majority of these organizations are led by poor young people and young people of color. Campaigns often address institutionalized racism and economic injustice as they relate directly to young people's lives. These youth organizing campaigns are overtly political and often involve addressing fundamental inequities through direct interaction with institutional power structures.

Many youth organizing groups place a strong emphasis on being youth-led, although different organizations define this in different ways. The spectrum ranges from organizations that are entirely youth run with little involvement from adults to organizations where young people make decisions with strong support and guidance from adults. Other groups utilize an intergenerational approach (see Intergenerational Programs and Practices).

Another unique feature of these new youth organizing shops is that they intentionally bring together the fields of community organizing and youth development. In the 1980s, a significant paradigm shift began in youth work. Traditional youth programs that viewed young people as problems needing help began rethinking their approach and philosophy using ideas of positive youth development. Positive youth development takes a more holistic view of young people, their needs, and what they can offer to address real community problems.

Like youth development, many youth organizing groups see helping young people become stable adults as a major part of their missions. Members of youth organizing groups also get access to social services because these groups recognize that it is difficult for young people to engage in organizing campaigns if their basic needs are unmet. Organizing groups also recognize that young people have a great deal to offer their communities. However, beyond equipping young people to help others through community service, organizing groups help young people develop knowledge, skills, and passion to prepare them for a lifetime of community activism and leadership. Young people in organizing groups learn how to analyze the problems affecting their communities and bring people together to create solutions. Organizing campaigns allow young people to develop important skills such as research, public speaking, and negotiation. Perhaps most importantly young people learn through firsthand experience that it is possible to create real change. This experience helps combat the hopelessness that often prevents people from organizing and prepares many young people to become committed lifelong leaders.

Another pillar of youth organizing is the belief that young people develop most effectively in the context of their communities. Simply put, young people and communities must change together. For this "mutuality" to emerge, young people must understand their communities, issues, and power structures so they can bring tangible value to the table and establish themselves as bona fide players in the public discourse.

These organizations have begun to receive some strong support from foundations. The Funders' Collaborative on Youth Organizing is a group of funders and representatives of organizing groups who have come together to support the growth of this new field.

The Philadelphia Student Union is an organization some friends and I founded in 1995, the year after I graduated from high school. We started very small with a group of twelve young people meeting in a socially progressive West Philadelphia restaurant whose owner had agreed to sponsor us. Since that time, the Student Union has become a major force in the struggle to improve Philadelphia's high schools.

The Student Union has two primary goals: to organize young people to transform public schools and to help a generation of young people become lifelong community leaders. Our guiding principle is that if we are to eliminate problems like racism and poverty in order to create a more just society, we need a public-school system that ensures that all young people, regardless of race or class, receive a high-quality education. We also need a school system that teaches people to be critical thinkers and skilled leaders who can bring people together to create solutions to pressing social problems.

For this magnitude of transformation to happen, however, young people must lead the change. The Student Union believes that public education will not truly work until students feel a sense of ownership of their schools, and this will not happen until students have a voice in decision-making. For too long young people have been treated as passive beneficiaries of their education rather than participants who can and must be actively engaged in shaping their education and holding their schools accountable.

To drive this important agenda, the Student Union has created chapters in seven public high schools in Philadelphia. Each chapter meets once a week after school. Chapter meetings are split between participating in leadership-development workshops and working on campaigns. The leadership-development program has three main goals: (1) to help young people analyze root causes of social problems and make connections between larger social issues and the problems facing them everyday; (2) to help young people

develop concrete leadership skills such as working with the media, public speaking, and community organizing strategies; and (3) to build supports around young people that will help them achieve their life goals.

The Student Union has continued to refine its methodology and organizing model over the past decade. The Student Union's organizing model emphasizes critical analysis, research, negotiation, and direct action. First, students in each chapter complete the initial training to set a foundation necessary to begin the process of choosing an issue around which to organize. This process begins with workshops on learning theory. Then students design their ideal school, complete an analysis of the current state of affairs in their own school, and then actively compare the two. Next, they survey and interview a cross section of students, teachers, parents, and administrators to find out their concerns and learn more about the root cause of the problems. Based upon this firsthand research and analysis, an issue is selected, and a campaign is designed to make the necessary changes.

The Student Union's theory of action is based in large part on supporting individual school campaigns. The advantage of school-centered campaigns is that students are empowered to address immediate needs, which they and their fellow students have identified. Furthermore, school campaigns are often winnable in relatively short time periods, sometimes during a single semester or school year. These early wins are directly felt by students, creating an important momentum and sense of efficacy.

When we first started doing individual school campaigns, we organized around relatively simple issues. Students at Simon Gratz High School organized to get textbooks for students with no books. The West Philadelphia High School chapter pressured the school administration to make some long overdue building repairs.

As time has passed, our capacity to take on more complex issues has grown. Students at Simon Gratz organized to ensure more interactive and engaging teaching. These students ran a professional development session for all teachers in their school and helped create a committee to improve teacher training. Students at Bartram High School convinced the school district to pay for a special three-day training session to bring together thirty-five students and thirty-five staff members to create a plan to improve the school climate and build a culture of respect and trust.

Another major campaign is now going on at West Philadelphia High School, one of the most troubled schools in Philadelphia. When students found out that their school was scheduled to receive a new building, they seized the opportunity not just to get a new physical environment but to completely change the way that instruction and decision-making would happen in their school. They did research about effective high-school transformation models and wrote a plan to break their school into four small schools that would be designed by the community. They have now brought a coalition of community groups, churches, teachers, students, and parents together to support their plan.

The second major component of the Student Union's theory of action is working on district-wide issues with students from across all chapters and other organizational allies. In the fall of 2000, we organized a student convention in which over 400 students from twenty-seven high schools came together to discuss and adopt the "student platform on school reform." This platform was designed by Student Union activists and was heavily informed by our work at the school level. The platform contains issues that students have identified as requiring policy change at the district level by the superintendent and school board. The student platform continues to provide the basis for selecting district-wide campaign issues.

One major plank of the student platform involves school climate and student rights. Many Student Union members feel that they are treated like criminals while in school, with more emphasis on preparing them for prison than for college or the workforce. Philadelphia's neighborhood high schools all have metal detectors, airport-style bag scanners, surveillance cameras, and metal bars on the windows. School buildings are secured by a school police force that is bigger than all but three other public forces in Pennsylvania. Students must wear their identification badges around their necks at all times. Many students feel that their school deals with violence by treating students like criminals rather than by supporting troubled students or looking to get at the root of the problem. Case in point is that following the Columbine shooting, students at that high school received counseling and support services. However, when a vice-principal was accidentally shot in the foot at Bartram High School in Philadelphia, every high school in the city was mandated to have metal detectors.

With the goal of moving toward a system of supporting students, the Student Union won two major victories in 2003. We convinced the district to double the number of guidance counselors in high schools so that each counselor would serve an average of 500 students. Previously, some schools had as many as 1,200 students per counselor. This victory represents a $9.5 million commitment from the district, which we believe is money well spent. We also convinced the district to open "student success centers" at ten neighborhood high schools. Student Union members and allies are playing a major role in designing these centers. The centers, being brought online this year, provide places where students can receive counseling, social-service referrals, and help with problems in school.

Perhaps the largest citywide campaign in which the Student Union has been engaged was the high-profile fight against school privatization. In the summer of 2001, the school district of Philadelphia was running out of money. In an attempt to force the commonwealth of Pennsylvania to provide additional funding, the district threatened to close in March when money would run out, rather than make huge program cuts. The commonwealth responded by passing legislation authorizing the commonwealth itself to take over the district. In a highly visible game of brinksmanship, then-governor Mark Schweiker threatened a state takeover under which the central administration of the district and as many as one hundred schools would be turned over to the Edison Schools Corporation, a for-profit enterprise headquartered in New York City. Upon hearing about this threat, Student Union members became angry. They were fully aware of the significant funding gap between the Philadelphia school district and suburban districts in Pennsylvania. Student Union activists felt strongly that this posturing was a diversion from the fact that the commonwealth was blatantly underfunding Philadelphia schools. Moreover, not only were students concerned about the corporatization of public schools, they also were outraged about Edison's well-established track record as a poor manager of schools and as a contributor to political campaigns.

Public-education advocates in Philadelphia, including the Student Union and Youth United for Change, another youth organizing shop, formed a broad-based coalition to fight against privatization. By many accounts, students led this fight. Students from the two youth organizations began educating their peers about the situation and then organized several major actions. On November 20, 2002, we took over 1,000 students for a rally and lobbying visit to the state capitol in Harrisburg. One month later students in almost half of Philadelphia's public high schools walked out, and 3,000 students met at city hall for a rally. Then on April 17, the day before the state-controlled School Reform Commission (which had replaced Philadelphia's Board of Education following the state takeover) was to vote on which schools to privatize, the Student Union organized an overnight vigil in the courtyard of the school district administration building. At six a.m., before district employees arrived for work, students stood tall and linked arms, blocking each of the doorways. We blockaded the building and refused to let anyone inside. One student was arrested. The meeting of the School Reform Commission could not proceed as scheduled and needed to be moved to another building.

In the end, we were able to fully stop the privatization of the central administration and of any high schools in Philadelphia. In addition, Edison Schools received a contract to manage only twenty schools, eighty less than the governor was threatening. Although twenty out of 264 were ultimately turned over to Edison, the limited number of schools was seen as a major blow to the school privatization industry.

The Student Union's efforts in Philadelphia are not unique. Similar youth organizing shops are springing up across the country to address a wide variety of issues including neighborhood revitalization, economic justice, environmental justice, and education. Young people are continuing their long and proud tradition of being on the front lines of social change. They are also getting ready for a lifetime of activism. The youth organizing movement is also sparking a change in how leading experts view effective youth-development work. Experts are realizing the positive impact that young people can have on their communities and in turn the value that youth derive from participating in social-change efforts. This burst of youth activism provides a ray of hope that a generation of young people is acquiring the knowledge, skills, and determination to create a just and equitable society.

See also Community Service; Earth Force; Empowerment; National and Community Service; Palestinian *Intifada*; Social Networks; Student Political Activism; Volunteerism.

Recommended Reading

Funders' Collaborative on Youth Organizing (2003). Occasional Papers Series on Youth Organizing. New York. See http://www.fcyo.org.

Kim, J., ed. (2002). *Future 500*. New York: Active Element Foundation.

Males, M. (1996). *The Scapegoat Generation: America's War on Adolescents*. Monroe, ME: Common Courage Press.

Tolman, J., and Pittman, K. (2001). *Youth Acts, Community Impacts*. Takoma Park, MD: The Forum for Youth Investment.

Eric Braxton

GSAs. *See* Gay-Straight Alliances in Schools (GSAs).

GYAN. *See* Global Youth Action Network (GYAN).

H

High-School Students' Rights Movement of the 1960s. Historians agree that one of the defining features of the 1960s was the "rights revolution," the expansion of democracy to include people formerly excluded from full citizenship. These groups included African Americans, American Indians, Latinos, women, gays, college students—and minor schoolchildren. Although the latter group has been overshadowed by the social movements and achievements of the others, they nonetheless constituted an identifiable interest group and managed to claim new rights for themselves. Moreover, for the first time in history American high-school students attempted, albeit without much success, to form a mass movement. While activist students succeeded in some cities in creating citywide student organizations and failed at forming national groups, they did manage to forge some tentative bonds with students across the country.

Just as historians root the more well-known movements of the 1960s in the previous decade or even earlier, the high-school student movement also grew out of soil seeded in earlier times. Following World War II, despite the significant participation of young people in the war, parents, educators, and legislators managed for the first time to ensure that the vast majority of children under eighteen were in school. This changed the class character of the public schools and the baby boom dramatically augmented the number of students in school. The cold-war emphasis on conformity meshed with school administrators' need to manage this larger, more diverse student body. Thus the high schools of the

1950s, in the eyes of critics, tended to be inflexible and controlling.

However, two social currents ran counter to the authoritarianism of the public schools. The first was what came to be called, pejoratively, "permissive parenting" among the white middle class. Permissive parenting meant taking babies off the rigid scheduling advocated by an earlier school of experts and making family life more open and democratic. Experts advised parents to reason with children rather than forcing them to submit to adult decrees. At the same time, the schools themselves taught students that the American way of life was grounded in freedom and that democracy was superior to any other form of government. Students were thus doubly primed to notice the gap between official veneration of democracy and the practice of autocracy in the schools.

The convergence of these forces help to explain the much-studied phenomenon of college activism, but it fed a burgeoning high-school movement as well. The high-school student movement is difficult to date, in part because there was more than one high-school movement. Arguably the first emerged among black high-school students, as an integral part of the civil rights movement. Many of these students quickly learned that however problematic their status as blacks in a white world, their youth status also worked against them. The first legal assault on the restrictiveness of high-school authorities came from African American students who challenged school rules prohibiting them from wearing buttons on campus for freedom or the SNCC

(Student Non-Violent Coordinating Committee), an interracial organization of college students working for civil rights (*Burnside v. Byars* 1966; *Blackwell v. Issaquena* 1966).

A second strand of the student-rights movement grew out of popular culture, not political protest. The ardent desire of many high-school students, boys in particular, to imitate their rock 'n' roll idols threw them up against school dress codes, which forbade long hair on boys. In the same year that black high-school students demanded the right to advertise their political passions through buttons, white high-school boys went to court demanding control over their own hair, the first in an avalanche of similar cases (*Ferrell v. Dallas* 1966).

Dress codes in fact became one of the primary hot-button issues galvanizing high-school students into activism and protest. According to a congressional study of high-school unrest for 1968 and 1969, nearly 70 percent of high-school protests involved either student discipline or dress codes. While some students demanded the right to make fashion or political statements through their physical appearance, others simply wanted a voice in forming the rules that governed them. In addition to lawsuits, students held sit-ins, circulated petitions, or simply ignored dress codes, forcing authorities either to suspend them, compromise with them, or quietly let the rules dissolve.

Dress and hair regulations affected the majority of high-school students, so activists frequently found it easy to mobilize large numbers of students around these issues. When activists attempted to recruit others in pursuit of a particular issue or reform, however, they felt the full weight of administrators' power. Administrators could and did censor student newspapers; when activists turned to underground publications, administrators confiscated the papers and suspended students caught distributing or even possessing them; administrators denied students access to school bulletin boards or copying machines; they

forbade the formation of certain student organizations; they refused to give students a voice in inviting outside speakers to campus. Some even punished students for taking part in demonstrations that occurred off campus and outside of school hours. Suspensions and expulsions formed the most formidable weapons in officials' arsenals, but they also banned students from graduation, expelled them from student government or other organizations, kept them off athletic teams, and prevented their pictures from being included in school yearbooks.

School officials had possessed and used all of these powers in earlier years; they did not suddenly become autocratic in the 1960s. However, by the mid-1960s the social context had altered dramatically. High-school students observed the reform efforts of other groups and profited by their example. Moreover, the heightened democratic expectations of the era convinced them that the law was on their side. By and large, they were correct. A series of lawsuits established the rights of high-school students to a free press, to free speech, to assemble, to pass out literature, to petition, to participate in political activities, and to demonstrate peacefully. Courts imposed new standards of due process for student discipline and limited school officials' freedom to search and seize student belongings. None of these freedoms were absolute, and the courts carefully maintained distinctions between the freedoms possessed by adults and those doled out to children; nevertheless, the relatively untrammeled power of school authorities over schoolchildren in 1960 had been considerably curtailed by 1975 (ACLU 1971).

The federal courts and the American Civil Liberties Union (ACLU) proved powerful friends to youthful activists, but students frequently reached out to other allies as well. Sometimes they turned to each other. High-school students concerned with press freedom created fragile bonds through underground newspapers. John Birmingham, a student and publisher of a high-school underground newspaper in Hackensack, New Jersey, established ties with other high-school underground writers and published a compilation of their works. Two short-lived high-school underground press services appeared, one in New York City and the other in Chicago. Of the thousand or more high-school underground newspapers estimated to exist in this era, however, the majority bloomed and faded locally, aware of but not in touch with the larger underground high-school movement.

Other student activists tried to form high-school organizations that would breach the walls of individual schools and unite students for larger causes. Student unions appeared in New Jersey, Minnesota, Maryland, Ohio, the District of Columbia, Delaware, California, Texas, and New York, at least. There may in fact have been many more such organizations, but since the activities of youth are rarely comprehensively documented, this cannot be proven. Black student unions (BSUs) appeared in many large, urban schools with substantial black populations; in New York City, the Black High School Coalition worked to unite all of the city's BSUs. Frequently, high-school students rallied around the demand for a high-school student bill of rights, as students did in Homestead, Pennsylvania; Detroit, Michigan; and New York City.

College students sometimes ventured to help high-school students organize. Some high-school students became involved with the college association Students for a Democratic Society (SDS), and a number of high schools formed SDS chapters. In the spring of 1968, disillusioned with mainstream politics, the national organization decided to recruit high-school students, among others, for the inevitable revolution it foresaw. A more moderate college antiwar group, the Student Mobilization Committee, invited high-school students to its spring antiwar conference in 1969 to hammer out a high-school bill of rights.

Many school officials and law enforcement workers recoiled from a threatened alliance between college radicals and volatile high-school students. Not fully crediting high-school students with brains and their own agenda, these adults often exaggerated the strength of ties between older and younger activists and missed the significant strains in their relationships, where those relationships even existed. While high-school activists were not averse to using college allies when it suited their purposes, many complained that the college students were attempting to manipulate them and had little knowledge of or concern about the issues that high-school students found most compelling. Overall, most high-school activists in this period acted independently of older activists and of each other.

Although their struggles do not form part of our collective memory of the 1960s, contemporaries took the high-school movement very seriously. Pundits and educational experts wrote articles attempting to explain the origins and goals of the movement. Teachers and principals traveled to other schools investigating the scope of the movement. For the first time, the White House Conference on Youth invited mostly young people to attend and listened seriously to their critiques of education, racism, the war in Vietnam, the environment, and the overall trends in American society. President Richard Nixon created an Office of Youth, headed by a twenty-five-year-old, under the Department of Education, and several cities elected high-school students to the school board or board of education.

Not surprisingly, not all adults embraced dialog with young activists. Many perceived the high-school students' rights movement as an attack on their authority or as a faddish imitation of the other social rebellions then in progress. These adults, sometimes working with nonactivist high-school students or local police forces, attempted to quell the movement without giving an inch. Again, because the documentation of the high-school movement is so sparse, we may never know how many local movements collapsed under adult pressure.

Nevertheless, a cursory glance through contemporary journals of education reveals an explosion of pedagogical experiments, many of which emerged at the prodding of activist high-school students. Some schools tried new styles of teaching, brought in new subjects, or even tried to redefine the teacher-student relationship. Others maintained a traditional curriculum but worked to enhance communication between students and school authorities. In some instances, intransigent administrators had their wings clipped by federal judicial rulings. While the student activists of the 1960s did not win all of their battles, this first high-school movement succeeded in altering the content and context of public education—at least briefly.

See also School Engagement; School Influences and Civic Engagement.

Recommended Reading

American Civil Liberties Union (1968). *Academic Freedom in the Secondary Schools.* Originally printed in September 1968; reprinted in December 1969 and May 1971.
Blackwell v. Issaquena County Board of Education (1966), 363 F. 2d 749.
Birmingham, John (1970). *Our Time Is Now: Notes from the High School Underground.* New York: Praeger.
Burnside v. Byars (1966), 363 F. 2d. 744, 749.
Ferrell v. Dallas Independent School District (1966, 1968), 261 F. Supp. 545 (1966), 392 F. 2d 697 (1968), 393 89 S. Ct. 98 (1968).
Gilbert, James (1986). *A Cycle of Outrage: America's Reaction to the Juvenile Delinquent in the 1950s.* New York: Oxford University Press.
Libarle, Marc, and Seligson, Tom (1970). *The High School Revolutionaries.* New York: Random House.
Palladino, Grace (1996). *Teenagers: An American History.* New York: Basic Books.
Peck, Abe (1985). *Uncovering the Sixties: The Life and Times of the Underground Press.* New York: Pantheon Books.

Gael Graham

Hip-Hop Generation. Youth organizing as a strategy for civic participation among urban youth of color presents both challenges and promise. Youth organizing is shaped by coercive public policies that present barriers to civic participation for youth of color. Proponents of civic engagement and youth development often fail to acknowledge and address the ways in which the lives of working-class youth of color are embedded within a terrain of changing political, economic, and social landscapes where youth and their families struggle for economic survival, physical safety, and decent educational opportunities. Organizing also is an important strategy for working-poor youth of color because it confronts quality-of-life issues in communities and transforms oppressive economic, educational, and social conditions. Organizing moves beyond service to the community by encouraging youth to explore systemic root causes of social issues and encourages young people to use their own power to change school policies, organizational practices, and community conditions. The convergence of hip-hop culture and youth organizing has been a vehicle to engage youth of color in meaningful social-change efforts.

Urban youth now more than ever experience tremendous social, economic, and political pressures. Fewer jobs and after-school opportunities, combined with a growing fear of crime, all have shaped a national consciousness about urban communities as well as the youth within them. Although policymakers express concern about the future of young people, few actually understand how economic, political, and social conditions shape young people's lives. This is particularly true for working-class communities of color where punitive public policies exacerbate rather than ameliorate community problems. Increasingly, however, youth are responding to local and state policies by organizing their peers and developing partnerships and allies to address issues ranging from environmental racism to police harassment.

Through organizing, young people confront unjust school policies, alter institutional power relationships between adults and youth and ultimately improve quality-of-life issues in their communities. Central to our understanding of activism among urban youth of color is precisely the relationship between institutionalized processes of social control and how young people negotiate, challenge, and respond to these forces. Youth organizing involves a political understanding of how systems and institutions promote or hinder progress toward social equality and a set of common practices about how to achieve equity in the context of social, political, and economic barriers to health and well-being.

Youth organizing among urban youth of color can be best understood against the backdrop of economic despair, social isolation, and political apathy. These challenges present substantial barriers to civic participation and are supported by policies that usually respond to youth problems either by blaming youth themselves or simply treating them as civic problems. As a result, there are three primary issues that shape opportunities for civic participation among youth of color.

The first is coercive public policy which views young people of color as threats to social order and public life. *Coercive policies* are characterized by harsh punitive measures and policies aimed at deterring young people from delinquent behavior. These strategies view youth as the source of civic problems and have resulted in a growing trend for more punitive rather than restorative youth policy. Over the past seven years, for example, forty-three states have instituted legislation that facilitated the transfer of children to adult court. The result of these laws was the dismantling of a longstanding belief on the part of juvenile courts that special protections and rehabilitation were necessary to protect children and youth from the effects of the adult justice system. Since 1980, however, the juvenile justice system's explicit purpose to "rehabilitate" youth has come under attack for being too lenient with

regard to its capacity to handle supposedly more violent, delinquent youth of the 1980s and 1990s. Critics of the juvenile justice system believed the allegedly unprecedented numbers of delinquent and violent youth during the 1980s was a direct result of the absence of harsh treatment on the part of the juvenile justice system. In response, states adopted harsher sentencing for youth, which disproportionately impacted youth of color from poor and working-class communities.

For example, while minority youth represent only 34 percent of the U.S. population, in 1997 they comprised 62 percent of incarcerated youth. Additionally, in 1997, African American youth were six times more likely to be incarcerated and receive longer sentences than their white counterparts. Between 1985 and 1990, the number of African American and Latino state prisoners under the age of eighteen increased by almost 10 percent, while the incarceration rate for white youth declined by 11 percent. Coercive policies are substantial barriers to productive civic engagement for youth and are serious threats to overall safety and well-being. To engage disconnected youth of color in meaningful social-change efforts, we need to look beyond superficial behavioral explanations for youth-related problems toward more fundamental issues related to economic conditions, social isolation, and political power.

The second primary issue that shapes opportunities for civic participation among youth of color is *generational tension* between adults and youth who hold divergent and sometimes opposing sociopolitical ideas. These tensions are evident among youth who are first-generation immigrants and are highly critical of American society, as well as black youth who express frustration for silence on the part of black leaders to confront issues relevant to black urban poverty. For example, many black youth of the hip-hop generation (youth who have grown up in the post–civil rights era) have lost faith in the ability of black adults to address issues related to urban poverty and economic decay. Kitwana (2002) noted that black youth have grown cynical of systems that tolerate corporate corruption and seem to protect the wealthy at the expense of their communities and increasingly skeptical of black adult leadership who are unresponsive to the economic, political, and cultural devastation that has occurred in black communities since the 1980s.

Some black adults simply do not understand, and others reject outright, the ways in which today's youth express their frustration with these issues through hip-hop culture. Kitwana (2002) noted that adults from the civil rights generation cannot fully understand the complex modes of oppression confronting today's black youth. Oppression for today's hip-hop generation "is not simply a line in the sand with white supremacists blocking access— us over here and them over there" (Kitwana 2002, 4). The older generation's views of poverty, unemployment, and limited job options "exacerbate tensions between black youth and black adults because older black adults view poverty as simply something many of them overcame. Why can't your generation do the same? Or why does your generation use poverty as an excuse?" (42). For youth from the hip-hop generation, oppression is just as pervasive but much more ambiguous. Black youth today experience abusive police practices from both whites and blacks, witnessed the destruction of black families from crack cocaine, and struggle to find viable job opportunities, all of which sometimes obscure the real source of oppression. Because older black adults and young blacks hold divergent views of oppression, many young black youth often see their own parents and other black adults as the enemy within the race.

Third, the prolonged effects of *racism* have fostered a sense of fatalism and despair among some black youth. Moving beyond the discussions about how racism limits opportunities, we also consider the psychological trauma racism has waged on the lives of youth of color in urban America. The prolonged effects of institutional racism in America have bred a profound sense of apathy and hopelessness among youth of color. Countless acts of police harassment and violence, daily racial indignities at schools, and the general public's perception of black youth as a menace to society amount to a sustained assault on the emotional, spiritual, and mental health of youth.

The cumulative impact of coercive policies, political impotence regarding urban economic decay, and ongoing racial discrimination has resulted in unresolved rage, aggression, depression, and fatalism. Dr. Alvin Poussaint, professor of psychiatry at the Harvard Medical School in Boston, showed that from 1980 to 1995 suicides among black youth increased 114 percent. He attributed the rise to increased racial discrimination and violence in low-income urban communities. "Post-traumatic slavery syndrome," a term he uses to describe the long-term impact of racism on the lives of blacks, reveals the ways in which black youth engage in ongoing life-threatening activities such as drug use and gun violence. He argued that the impact of racism has contributed to high rates of stress-related illnesses in the black community (Poussaint and Alexander 2000).

Taken together, coercive policies, generational tensions, and racism all are formidable barriers to civic participation among urban youth of color. Although researchers agree that urban youth of color are less likely to participate in civic activities, growing evidence suggests that traditional measures of civic competence such as civic knowledge and participation in volunteer activities may be simply inappropriate for understanding civic and political participation among urban youth of color. For example, Sanchez-Jankowski (2002) suggested that youth who have histories of racial discrimination and exclusion from mainstream civic activities such as volunteering or community service have different strategies for engagement that often are overlooked by social scientists. Civic engagement for minority youth is a function of their ethnic group's history, social class, and the social context in which they live. Often, civic participation among minority youth is reflected in contributing to efforts that impact their families, friends, and communities rather than contributing to society as a whole. For youth of color community and neighborhood issues shape how young people participate in civic activities.

This conceptual shift highlights important distinctions between traditional youth civic participation and how youth of color engage in youth organizing. First, rather than focusing on service to the poor, youth organizing focuses on changing systems that create the need for service in the first place. Youth organizing is shaped by a political understanding of race, economic inequality, and political power. From this perspective youth civic engagement is not simply a strategy to develop individual youth but rather a process where individuals and communities acquire the knowledge, analytical skills, and emotional faculties necessary for democratic participation and social change. Second, this conceptual shift underscores the ways that young people develop as a collective body rather than as individuals. By focusing on identity issues related to gender identity, body image, sexuality, self-image, and internalized racism, youth explore collective identities and build communities that confront and challenge pressing community issues. Third, youth organizing conceptualizes young people as agents who can transform the conditions in the neighborhoods in which they live rather than subjects who simply participate in their communities. This is particularly important in a democratic society in which consistent, informed, and active engagement in the civic process exemplifies the "good citizen."

Youth organizing is especially appealing for young people traditionally considered "at risk" by traditional youth developers.

For a variety of reasons, traditional youth development strategies often fail to capture the imaginations of young people whose lives are most marred by injustice and poverty. What is the point of joining a mentorship program, for example, or participating in after-school tutoring, if the mentorship won't land you a living-wage job and the school has no heat? In the face of these barriers and the social and political inequalities that engendered them, cynicism and despair are reasonable reactions. Overcoming this cynicism requires that youth be engaged in civic activities that are relevant to improving quality-of-life issues through active engagement with ameliorating the injustices and inequalities that circumscribe their lives.

Yet youth development practitioners as a whole are just beginning to understand youth organizing as a promising civic engagement strategy for youth of color. Young people in working-class communities of color confront formidable economic and social pressures, and despite the lack of effective public policy directed at improving the lives of urban youth, there are numerous examples of youth in low-income communities challenging, influencing, and creating public policy in ways that meet their needs.

Youth organizing, a strategy in which young people organize their peers to challenge or change issues related to their schools, communities, and their identities, has largely gone unnoticed both among researchers and public policymakers. Youth organizing has been described as a process through which young people identify issues and act collectively and strategically to change power relations, create meaningful institutional relations, and strengthen indigenous leadership within communities.

Youth organizing usually involves analysis, action, and reflection related to changing systemic causes of social and community problems. This process may also encompass issues related to personal identity, such as gender or sexual orientation, as well as broader community issues of poverty and racism. *Analysis* entails transforming a problem into an issue and identifying parties responsible for bringing about desired changes. *Action* involves a collective public activity that confronts decision-makers and pressures them to make a desired change. Action includes a range of activities: speaking at a city council meeting, informational picketing, writing letters to officials, circulating petitions, displaying banners, and holding walk-outs. *Reflection* is an important component of youth organizing because it fosters personal, intellectual, and spiritual growth. Reflection might include journaling, debriefing with peers about an issue or experience, or discussing the effectiveness of a particular event and yields insight and "lessons learned" about experiences that can be applied to other areas of young people's lives.

Youth organizing builds civic capacity for youth of color both by meeting the basic needs of young people and increasing the possibilities for community and social change. Through organizing, youth build positive racial, ethnic, sexual, gender, and class identities, while at the same time working with community members to confront relevant social problems related to inequalities within their own communities. Young people develop strong political identities when they collectively work on community issues, develop alliances with institutions, organizations, and individuals, and shape policies that improve the quality of life for members of a given community. Often these practices foster awareness of common community problems and broader political and social issues. Through political education young people become familiar with the various historical forms of oppression as well as the larger processes and systems that have caused the suffering of numerous people around the globe.

For many youth of color, hip-hop has been the vehicle for youth organizing. Rap, poetry, and graffiti art have been utilized as politicizing tools to inform youth about

significant social problems. Since the mid-1980s, groups such as Public Enemy seized the attention of many urban youth of color because of their ability to boldly criticize and reveal serious contradictions in American democracy. Rap artists such as Chuck D, KRS1, and Arrested Development called for youth to raise their consciousness about American society and become more critical about the conditions of poverty. Hip-hop groups such as Dead Prez, the Coup, and the Roots now provide them with an analysis of racism, poverty, sexism, and other forms of oppression.

In many ways, progressive hip-hop encourages young people to change their thinking about themselves and community problems and act to create a more equitable world. While progressive hip-hop culture functions as the voice of resistance for America's youth, it also provides a blueprint of the possibilities for social change. Similar to other forms of aesthetic modes of expression such as jazz, art, and poetry, young people use hip-hop culture as a vehicle to express pain, anger, and the frustration of oppression. In fact, hip-hop icon Ice-T was quoted saying that rap music was like CNN for black youth, referring to the idea that rap music provided a voice for black youth in the absence of political interests in black urban America.

Hip-hop culture can also be used as a strategy to organize, to inform, and to politicize young people who would otherwise not be involved in youth organizing. For example, while youth organized to defeat Proposition 21 in California, youth organizations, community activists, and local hip-hop artists joined forces and organized hip-hop concerts to conduct mass political education and distributed flyers with youthful graffiti art that encouraged disenfranchised youth to vote and participate in the political process. A well-known Bay Area hip-hop artist and participant in the organizing effort commented as follows: "Culturally, a lot of young people do not read newspapers, or even if you pass them a flyer, they might read it, but it's not as real to them because it's an old way of organizing. So hip-hop can bring us new tools to organize people with."

Although we acknowledge that aspects of hip-hop culture can be politically inspiring, it also can promote homophobic, misogynistic, and fatalistic messages that are counterproductive to a social-change agenda. (For a good example of fatalistic hip-hop listen to Tupac Shakor's "Machievelli." For political inspiration, listen to Lauren Hill or Dead Prez.) What is important, however, is that hip-hop culture has defined youth identity in America and throughout the world. In fact, while hip-hop emerges from the experiences of black and Latin urban struggles, it has also shaped the political identities of suburban whites. Recognizing hip-hop as a potential political vehicle for disconnected urban youth, hip-hop media entrepreneur Russell Simmons has formed the Hip Hop Summit Action Network aimed at channeling the hip-hop movement toward political issues. In fact, in June 2004 America witnessed the first National Hip-Hop Political Convention in Newark, New Jersey.

The convergence of youth organizing and hip-hop reflects a burgeoning political identity and new forms of civic participation among young people in urban communities. Similar to the 1960s rebellions in urban America, urban youth are using new and innovative organizing strategies to bring about social change. For example, Kids First—a multiracial organization that creates opportunities for youth in Oakland, California, to transform their schools and communities through advocacy, leadership training, and alliance building—uses rap as an organizing strategy by inviting local youth into their makeshift recording studio so that youth who otherwise couldn't record their music could have access to quality recording equipment. Once they get involved in the production of their music, they are also exposed to a host of programs that support their personal and political development. They have used this strategy to engage youth in political activities and have been successful at winning campaigns that provide free public transportation to school for youth in Oakland and have opposed high-stakes standardized testing for students in poorly funded public schools. The organization also realized that successful youth organizing requires a break from traditional organizing, which relied heavily on stable adult constituents. Similarly, the Huey P. Newton Foundation in Oakland, California, launched its own recording label to harness the energy of local hip-hop artists and channel their efforts toward political goals.

While some programs use hip-hop as an organizing strategy, others focus on collective identities such as race, class, or gender. For example, Sisters in Action for Power is an intergenerational, multiracial, community-based organization that focuses on strengthening the leadership skills of low-income women and girls of color in Portland, Oregon. By teaching girls about the historical and contemporary impact of colonialism, the organization provides youth with a broad conceptual framework to understand gender inequity. Through political education and historical and political analysis of contemporary issues, youth develop political explanations for challenges and barriers in their lives. For example, girls use political explanations to describe how images of women in the media shape the way they feel about their own bodies. Amara Perez, executive director of Sisters in Action for Power, says that colonialism, the domination of one group's beliefs over another, shapes how girls feel about themselves because "what the dominant culture says what a girl or woman should be isn't healthy and does not contribute toward collective power." This analytical tool gives youth a powerful lens to understand relationships between individual or personal challenges as well as larger social and historical issues.

As girls develop a more critical understanding of issues related to gender roles and power, they are better able to articulate, challenge, and develop solutions for policies that subjugate women's issues. For example, young women in the program led a 1996 campaign which prompted the school district to track and report sexual harassment cases and encouraged Multnoman County to pass a resolution to incorporate gender violence in all violence prevention and intervention language. U.S. policymakers and government officials, as well as youth-serving institutions could stand to learn from this type of commitment to young people. The most crucial lesson would be to comprehend how young people's personal development must be concomitant with the amelioration of their communities' living conditions.

Contrary to Putnam (2000) who believes that America is experiencing dangerously low levels of civic, community, and political participation, young people of color are engaged in efforts to transform their schools and communities. Youth organizing opens new and exciting possibilities for our understanding of civic engagement among youth of color in urban communities. The social and economic conditions youth face on a daily basis need much greater attention on the part of youth-development proponents, educational reformers, and policymakers. Young people in urban communities strive to create safe communities, supportive learning environments, and meaningful activities for themselves as well as others. If scholars, educators, and policymakers would simply listen to what they have to say, we would learn that they have analytical capacity, creative energy, and the desire to make good things happen in their schools and communities. Hip-hop culture has the capacity to inform, politicize, and speak more directly to issues facing urban youth; our challenge is to acknowledge this creative energy and make real investments in their efforts for social change.

See also Digital Divide; MTV's Choose or Lose Campaign (1992–); New Media; Punk Rock Youth Subculture; Religiosity and Civic Engagement in African American Youth; Riot Grrrl.

Recommended Reading

Ayman-Nolley, S., and Taira, L. L. (2000). "Obsession with the Dark Side of Adolescence: A Decade of Psychological Studies." *Journal of Youth Studies*, 3 (1): 35–48.

California Tomorrow and Californians for Justice (2002). *The Need for Change Is Now … Students Demand Justice in Their Schools.* Oakland: California Tomorrow in partnership with Californians for Justice.

Cervone, B. (2002). *Taking Democracy in Hand: Youth Action for Educational Change in the San Francisco Bay Area.* Providence, RI; Takoma Park, MD: What Kids Can Do, Inc.; the Forum for Youth Investment.

Ginwright, S. (2003). *Youth Organizing: Expanding Possibilities for Youth Development.* New York: Funders' Collaborative on Youth Organizing: Occasional Papers Series.

Hosang, D. (2003). *Youth and Community Organizing Today.* New York: Funders' Collaborative on Youth Organizing: Occasional Papers Series.

Kelley, R. (1996). "Kickn' Reality, Kickn' Ballistics: Gangsta Rap and Postindustrial Los Angeles." In *Droppin' Science: Critical Essays on Rap Music and Hip-Hop Culture*, edited by W. E. Perkins. Philadelphia: Temple University Press.

Kitwana, B. (2002). *The Hip-Hop Generation: Young Black and the Crisis in African American Culture.* New York: Basis Civitas Books.

Males, M., and Macallair, D. (2000). *The Color of Justice.* Washington, D.C.: Building Blocks for Youth.

Martinez, E. (1998). "High School Students in the Lead: Massive Walkouts in California Have Important Lessons for All Organizers." *Z Magazine*, 11 (6): 41–45.

Poussaint, Alvin, and Alexander, Amy (2000). *Lay My Burden Down: Unraveling Suicide and the Mental Health Crisis among African-Americans.* Boston: Beacon Press.

Putnam, R. D. (2000). *Bowling Alone: The Collapse and Revival of American Community.* New York: Simon and Schuster.

Sanchez-Jankowski, M. (2002). "Minority Youth and Civic Engagement: The Impact of Group Relations." *Applied Developmental Science*, 6 (4): 237–245.

Sydell, L. (Writer) (2000). "Morning Edition: Hip Hop and Youth Organizing" [Radio Broadcast Transcript]. Burrelle's Information Services, Box 7, Livingston, NJ 07039.

Watts, R. J., Williams, N. C., and Jagers, R. J. (2002). "Sociopolitical Development." *American Journal of Community Psychology* 27 (2), 255–272.

Shawn Ginwright

Homies Unidos. On November 2, 1996, twenty-two members of El Salvador's opposing gangs joined together to discuss shared problems and common solutions in San Salvador. These visionary youth decided to create an organization that could help curb gang violence and attend to the needs of gang members and at-risk communities.

They called the group Homies Unidos and enlisted the help of Magdaleno Rose-Ávila to help them get started. As a Mexican American living in El Salvador, Magdaleno was an unlikely mentor for the fledgling group, but his experience as a former gang member, a farm worker organizer in California, and a human-rights activist made him particularly well equipped for the task. He understood that gangs fulfill certain needs for their members, who often lack stable families, jobs, and support networks.

Today, Homies Unidos is a full-fledged community-based organization committed to violence prevention and intervention in at-risk communities through creative alternatives to violence and drug use. The bulk of their work combines alternative education, leadership development, self-esteem building, and health-education programs. Commonly referred to as "Homies," the organization formally began operating in Los Angeles, California, two years after its founding in Central America.

In 1992 El Salvador's brutal twelve-year civil war between the U.S.-backed, right-wing Salvadoran government and a leftist guerrilla movement ended with the signing of the peace accords. During the conflict droves of Salvadorans fled their war-torn country for the United States. Many settled in the inner city of Los Angeles, where young Salvadorans banded together in gangs when they found themselves clashing with already established black and Latino gangs at school.

U.S. immigration policy toward Salvadorans shifted with the signing of the peace accords, and many Salvadorans lost their refugee status. "The INS launched its Violent Gang Task Force in 1992," writes Donna DeCesare, who has written widely on Salvadoran gangs and was instrumental in helping Homies Unidos in its early days, "ushering in a new era of immigration and criminal justice policy by targeting large numbers of immigrants with criminal records for deportation to their countries of origin—even if they had lived most of their lives in the United States."

Since then, the deportation of noncitizens with criminal records has continued. The flood of deported gang members from Los Angeles and other U.S. inner cities to El Salvador and the rest of Central America fueled a gang problem of epidemic proportions. Although gangs existed in the region before the deportations, the importation of U.S. gang structures and practices, which were further solidified in U.S. prisons, ensured their proliferation and entrenchment abroad.

Transnational problems require equally transnational solutions, and Homies Unidos exemplifies this strategy with their projects in San Salvador and Los Angeles. The L.A. office has become the headquarters of the group's activities and is staffed by an executive director, program directors and program assistants. A core of about twenty-five volunteers supports the five-person staff in L.A., and the Salvador office has three staff members. Since many are former gang members, the staff and volunteers at Homies Unidos are acutely aware of the causes of, and the potential solutions to, youth violence and gang membership.

Homies does not have official membership. Repressive antigang measures in the United States and Central America make belonging to a gang illegal, so "membership" in the organization would put participants—even those not involved in gangs—at risk of "illicit association." Moreover, those who are no longer in gangs, or "inactive gang members" as they prefer to call themselves, become the targets of active members. For many—if not most—of the original twenty-two *homies*, their organizing efforts had fatal consequences.

The implementation of the *mano dura* (heavy hand) legislation—an aggressive, zero-tolerance, antigang measure—throughout Central America has severely aggravated violence against youth and their criminalization. In San Salvador the authorities barely allow the Homies branch to operate; one tactic employed by the government is to deny the group nonprofit status, making it harder for the organization to get grants. Indeed, one of the few places the group has managed to carry out successful programs is in El Salvador's prison system. Most alarmingly, recent human-rights reports warn of right-wing death squads that have begun to target suspected gang members in an obscene form of social cleansing.

Rehabilitated gang members are often arrested because their visible tattoos make them indistinguishable from active members in the eyes of police. In response, Homies has initiated a weekly tattoo removal program in partnership with local health clinics. To be admitted into the program, participants are required to attend a ten-week alternative education program called the Epiphany Project, which has a curriculum that includes anger management, drug and alcohol education, and life-skills development sessions.

Practically all of the organization's programs, including the Epiphany Project, are open to all at-risk teenagers, not just gang members that have renounced violence. Homies holds weekly community workshops that combine featured speakers, group discussions, and other activities and runs classes for "anyone, young or old," interested in taking their high-school diploma equivalency exam. All of these services are free of charge.

The art program is one of their most successful projects. Participants are exposed to forms of alternative expression through workshops, lectures, and field trips. They also learn the power of art as an educational tool.

The leadership of the organization has sought strong ties with a range of progressive organizations with more experience and resources working for social justice. During relief efforts for the Hurricane Mitch disaster in Central America, for example, Homies reinforced their relationship with the leaders of the Central American immigrant community in California.

More recently, Homies partnered with Remy Sol Coffee, a gourmet coffee company that supports small-scale coffee farmers in Costa Rica. Part of the proceeds from coffee purchases made through the Homies Unidos Web site helps fund its programs. The group also seeks funding from private foundations and donations but has deliberately decided to not accept any government money, which they consider to have too many strings attached.

Since many of the deportees to El Salvador are almost wholly unfamiliar with their native country, Homies tries to ease their transition. The organization facilitates communication between deportees in El Salvador and their families in the United States. In fact, strengthening families is a central tenet of their organizational philosophy, particularly because many participants in the programs have children themselves.

In response to gross human-rights violations stemming from the antigang laws in El Salvador and Honduras, where the group is currently expanding its activities, Homies Unidos launched *Libertad con Dignidad* (Liberty with Dignity), an international human-rights campaign calling for the end of these repressive and unconstitutional policies. The campaign seeks coalitions with international human-rights groups and promotes education and public-awareness initiatives in the United States and Central America.

"We recognize that within gang structures there exists delinquency, organized crime, drugs, and other negative factors," reads a Homies press release on the *mano dura* policy, "but we at Homies Unidos also recognize the untapped potential of youth that become involved with gangs. We understand that gangs exist not because youth are delinquent, but rather because civil society and communities lack in resources."

See also Gangs; Gangs and Politics; Immigrant Youth in the United States; Juvenile Justice; Student Action with Farmworkers (SAF); Transnational Identity; Transnational Youth Activism.

Recommended Reading

DeCesare, Donna (July–August 1998). "The Children of War: Street Gangs in El Salvador." *NACLA Report on the Americas: Latin American Youth: Anger and Disenchantment on the Margins*. Vol. 32, No. 1.

Homies Unidos. See the group's Web site at http://www.homiesunidos.org.

Teo Ballvé

ICP. *See* Innovations in Civic Participation (ICP).

Identity and Activism. While identity negotiation occurs in many sites, it is of particular relevance to activists in social movements, especially the ways in which participation in movements impacts the lives of young activists. Many young people participate to varying degrees in social movements and these movements provide an important alternative means for voicing opinions and affecting the political process. While activists participate in social movements, not all individuals who participate in these movements are activists. Participation in such movements can vary with regard to the extent of commitment, expenditure of resources and time, and level of identification with the group. In general, activists show high levels of commitment, expend significant portions of their time and energy, and strongly identify with the social movements in which they participate. Rebecca Klatch notes that "commitment to a social movement involves not only conviction about what is wrong with the world, but also the decision to act on these beliefs, to strive for social change. Commitment also means a conception of oneself as someone who takes action in defense of deeply held values, someone who cares."

Identities are the names that humans impute to others or avow themselves in the course of social interaction. They are not static; rather, individuals work constantly to negotiate and maintain their identities. Identity negotiation is a particularly salient issue for young adults as adolescence is a time of flux and is often characterized by a search for identity. In fact, some observers posit that youth experience a normative "identity crisis," which makes issues of identity paramount at this life stage. Social movements are critically important phenomena to explore issues of youth identity. However, while considerable research exists on the external aspects of social movements, there is limited understanding of how activism affects participants. It is worth considering that some of the major effects of social movements have less to do with the public claims their leaders make than with the effects that these movements have on the individuals who participate in them, such as the effects that these movements have on the identity of activists.

Participating in social movements can have many significant consequences for activists. Individuals who have been involved in social movements, even at a low level of commitment, often carry the consequences of that participation throughout their lives. While the social-psychological consequences of activism are many, four major effects can be highlighted. First, activism can lead to the development of a collective identity. Second, partly because of the development of a collective identity, activists are often required to recreate congruence, or "fit," between the ways that they had previously seen themselves and this new collective identity. Third, activism can lead individuals to have higher levels of self-esteem. Finally, activism is associated with higher levels of self and collective efficacy.

Identity is a multidimensional concept, and in order to understand the ways in which activism can affect a young person's identity, this concept must be understood in a broader framework. Social scientists have distinguished three main types of identity: *social*, *personal*, and *collective*. A social identity is an identification in terms of membership in a social category. For example, a person can have a social identity based on a broad social category, such as being a member of a particular gender, ethnicity, age, or class. Individuals can also have social identities based on social roles, such as an occupational or family role. In both of these cases, social identities, which are often rooted in categorical ascriptions or memberships, are based on social interaction and through this process are given to an actor by other actors.

A personal identity, on the other hand, is a self-definition. It includes aspects of one's biography and life experiences that congeal into a relatively distinct personal or idiosyncratic whole. Social and personal identities may overlap in that how an individual sees herself can be consistent with how others see her. This, however, is not always the case as others may attribute an identity to an individual that he does not find accurate or favorable. In this situation the individual can refuse to accept this identity and may consequently experience inconsistency between his personal and social identity.

A third type of identity, collective identity, is a sense of "we-ness" or "oneness" that derives from perceived shared attributes or experiences among those who comprise a group, often in contrast to one or more perceived sets of others. These identities can be based on an individual's social or personal identity, such as identifying as a member of an ethnicity or gender. This is not necessary, however, as an individual's personal or social identity may not give rise to a collective identity. A collective identity is more likely to occur when there is contestation between two or more groups or when there are threats to the integrity or viability of a group.

The experience of being an activist can have many significant consequences for the individual. Four primary social-psychological consequences are especially relevant: the growth of a new collective identity; the convergence of personal and collective identities; increased self-esteem; and increased self and collective efficacy.

When individuals come together and interact within a social movement, they often construct a collective identity which can serve as the basis for both collective action and members' definition of self. This collective identity is a shared definition of a group that derives from members' common interests, experiences, and solidarity and articulates the group's goals, beliefs, and vision of social change. As mentioned, a collective identity is more likely to occur when there is contestation between two or more groups or when there are threats to the integrity or viability of a group. Consequently, social movements are a site ripe for the formation of collective identities. These collective identities are often very positive for individuals as they can be the basis of feelings of collective solidarity, efficacy, and agency, which individuals are not as likely to experience through their personal or social identities.

Whenever individuals develop new identities or transform existing ones, they are faced with the task of aligning these identities with other identities that they already had. So, for example, a new collective identity as an activist has to be made to "fit" with all the other personal and social identities that an individual already has. This alignment can occur through the enlargement of the personal identity of an individual to include the relevant collective identity as part of their definition of self. In order for an individual to enlarge his or her personal identity he or she must engage in identity construction, the process through which personal and collective identities are aligned. This process occurs so that the individual can come to regard their engagement in the movement as being consistent with their interests and how they see themselves in general.

This alignment can happen through four main processes: *identity amplification*, *identity consolidation*, *identity extension*, and *identity transformation*. First, identity amplification entails the establishment and strengthening of an existing identity that is congruent with a movement's collective identity. Through this process an identity that was previously not felt to be particularly important now takes on more meaning. Second, identity consolidation is the adoption of an identity that combines two prior identities that appear to be incompatible because they are typically associated with strikingly different subcultures or traditions. Third, identity extension is the process whereby an individual's personal identity expands so that its reach is congruent with that of the movement. Finally, identity transformation entails the development of a new identity through biographical reconstruction in which one changes how one sees oneself and consequently develops a new identity. All four of these processes of alignment of personal and collective identities can occur when an activist attempts to align his or her new activist collective identity with one's personal identities.

Partially because of the identity changes that often ensue from social-movement participation, activists may experience changes in their levels of self-esteem and self-efficacy. Self-esteem is an individual's positive and negative self-evaluations. Individuals are motivated to see themselves favorably and to try to maintain or enhance favorable views of the self. Participating in a group in which other activists provide positive evaluations of the individual and in which feelings of solidarity are fostered can lead an individual to have more positive self-evaluations.

Also, individuals may experience changes in their level of self-efficacy, their belief that they, as individuals, are capable of the specific behaviors required to produce a desired outcome in a given situation. A high level of self-efficacy in an individual indicates that he or she feels self-confident and sees himself or herself as a causal agent in one's environment and, consequently, able to produce desired changes in the world. Experiences of collective efficacy, the feeling that it is possible to create change through working with others, which is often fostered through activism, can lead individual group members to experience higher levels of self-efficacy.

It is clear that activism can lead to fundamental changes in the ways in which individuals see themselves, their levels of self-esteem, and their beliefs that they can affect the world around them. This occurs through two main processes: *framing* and *social interaction*. Individuals use frames to organize their experiences and guide action. According to Erving Goffman, frames allow individuals to "locate, perceive, identify, and label" occurrences and events in their lives (Goffman 1974, 21). Through the framing that occurs in social movements, identities are announced or renounced, avowed or disavowed, embraced or rejected. Social-movement frames delineate what the group is and who the opponents of the group are. It also focuses attention on what it means to be in the group, what type of person is in the group, and so forth. Social-movement participation may also lead to changes in a young person's identity or view of himself or herself because of the interaction that occurs between like-minded individuals in the process of activism. For example, a young person's identity may be altered through interaction with other activist youth as individual identities are created, negotiated, and sustained through social relations. Peers are important in solidifying commitment to a movement and in helping articulate and develop a broader analysis of social issues. Therefore, through interaction with other activist youth, young people in social movements recreate biographies highlighting certain aspects of their lives and personalities, reaffirm their common values, and align their personal and collective identities.

Social movements have the ability to radically alter the world in which we live. They can change laws, social values, and can further the goals of social justice. In addition, these movements often have significant consequences for the activists who form them. Participating in social movements can lead individuals to develop new collective identities, lead to a convergence of their new collective identity with their other social and personal identities, increase their self-esteem, and increase their feelings of self and collective efficacy. These social-psychological effects occur through the processes of framing and social interaction. Participation in social movements, for these reasons, can be an important part of the identity formation and negotiation, which is of fundamental importance to young people.

See also Civic Identity; Ethnic Identity; Identity and Organizing in Older Youth; National Identity and Youth; Social Movements; Transnational Identity.

Recommended Reading

Erikson, Erik H. (1968). *Identity, Youth, and Crisis*. New York: W. W. Norton.

Gamson, William (1992). "The Social Psychology of Collective Action." In *Frontiers in Social Movement Theory*, edited by A. D. Morris and Carol Mueller. New Haven, CT: Yale University Press.

Goffman, Erving (1974). *Frame Analysis: An Essay on the Organization of Experience*. Cambridge, MA: Cambridge University Press.

Klatch, Rebecca (1999). *A Generation Divided: The New Left, The New Right, and the 1960s*. Berkeley, CA: University of California Press.

McAdam, Doug (1989). "The Biographical Consequences of Activism." *American Sociological Review*, 54: 744–760.

McCall, George J., and Simmons, J. L. (1978). *Identities and Interactions: An Examination of Human Associations in Everyday Life*. New York: Free Press.

Melucci, Alberto, Keane, John, and Mier, Paul (1989). *Nomads of the Present: Social Movements and Individual Needs in Contemporary Society*. Philadelphia: Temple University Press.

Poletta, Francesca, and Jasper, James M. (2001). "Collective Identity and Social Movements." *Annual Review of Sociology*, 283.

Reger, Jo (2002). "More than One Feminism: Organizational Structure and the Construction of Collective Identity." In *Social Movements: Identity, Culture, and the State*, edited by D. S. Meyer, Nancy Whittier, and Belinda Robnett. New York: Oxford University Press.

Snow, David A., Oselin, Sharon S., and Corrigall-Brown, Catherine (Forthcoming). "Identity." *The Encyclopedia of Social Theory*. Thousand Oaks, CA: Sage.

Stryker, Sheldon, Owens, Timothy J., and White, Robert W., eds. (2000). *Self, Identity, and Social Movements*. Minneapolis: University of Minnesota Press.

Catherine Corrigall-Brown

Identity and Organizing in Older Youth. As civic participation among youth continues to trail behind that of older Americans in the area of electoral politics, researchers are paying considerable attention to how to better engage youth, especially older youth between the ages of fifteen and twenty-three. Research shows that poor youth and youth of color face numerous barriers to traditional forms of political and community engagement, including the lack of resources, knowledge, skills, and social networks to participate actively in civic life. These barriers similarly inhibit the ability of youth and young adults to recognize collective interests and to engage in forms of activism on behalf of themselves and their communities. To better understand factors that inhibit or promote youth civic participation and activism, some researchers have examined the role of identity in fostering youth's commitment to civic groups and collective action. Researchers have also begun to look closely at youth organizing as one successful model for actively engaging older youth in community issues. Activism herein is defined broadly as strategies to enhance individual- and community-level change. These strategies may include a focus on youth's internal capacities (as a citizen and family member) as well as a focus on supporting youth's civic skills and behaviors.

Research shows that early- and mid-adolescence are distinguished by the start of the search process for identity, which entails the need for social affirmation and peer and social group identification. Most adolescents do not become aware, however, of "ideological forces" (i.e., injustice, racism) that shape their worlds until late in their teenage years. Hence, young people in their early- to mid-adolescence (ages eleven to fourteen) are often drawn to youth and civic organizations by the desire to meet and interact with diverse peers and learn new skills. Older youth or young adults (ages fifteen to twenty-three), on the other hand, are often more interested in conceptual or critical discussions of civic or social issues (e.g., social justice). Older youth are also more likely to be interested in applying their civic knowledge and leadership skills in real-life settings rather than in safe, controlled settings.

Although there is consensus that increased civic participation among older and disenfranchised youth is needed, there is no consensus as to the most developmentally appropriate and effective strategies for engendering such engagement. Some youth organizations have responded by engaging young people in two related approaches: (1) *identity support* and (2) *youth organizing.*

Identity support is the creation of safe spaces where youth can develop a sense of affirmation and belonging rooted in their ethnic, racial, sexual, and/or other identities (both their own and that of others). It is the creation of spaces where youth can learn about their identities and share experiences of oppression without the fear of being stereotyped, harassed, or rejected. Identity-support organizations recruit youth from specific marginalized ethnic, racial, or cultural groups and stress the importance of hiring culturally and socially appropriate role models. Strategies used by these organizations include a focus on history and its relevance for current social conditions, celebration of cultural symbols and values, support groups, critique of the dominant culture (particularly values and practices that discredit or discriminate against their identity group), and community outreach, education, and advocacy.

Identity-support organizations focus on raising awareness and strengthening individuals' ability to navigate and negotiate the challenges they face. In doing so, they seek to "make the personal political" among youth from marginalized social groups in the United States. This type of activism prioritizes building an awareness of collective interests to address shared oppressions rather than discrete civic knowledge, skills, behaviors, or attitudes.

By contrast, the strength of *youth organizing* is that it provides youth with opportunities to build civic skills by engaging them actively on social issues. Youth organizing is the union of grassroots community organizing and positive youth development with an explicit commitment to social change and political action. Youth organizing is based on the premise that young people are capable of taking leadership to transform their communities. Youth-organizing approaches include membership development, political education, issue identification (through community surveys and mapping of community services), public protest, letter-writing campaigns, and public-awareness campaigns. In most cases, community-change goals are the ultimate driving force behind the work of the organizations, while youth development is seen as essential to building the capacity and sustaining the commitment of youth organizers. Youth-organizing groups often have youth on staff as paid organizers and an unpaid "membership" base of individuals who participate in meetings and events. Issues addressed by youth organizing groups often arise from the context of their local communities. For instance, youth organizers have organized against toxic-waste facilities in their low-income communities and sought to create new forms of community policing. Often in parallel to local campaigns, however, organizing groups will team with other local and national organizations to weigh in on matters of state or national policy. For instance, youth organizers across California have lobbied against punitive California legislation that would lead to increased youth incarceration.

Although youth organizing and identity support are potentially powerful strategies for engaging older, marginalized youth populations, research is just beginning to demonstrate how effective they are for achieving desired community engagement outcomes and supporting the holistic development of youth. One initial study suggests that identity-support and youth-organizing approaches are significantly better at supporting developmental outcomes such as civic activism and identity than are traditional youth-development approaches. This study also suggests that identity-support and youth-organizing agencies are relatively successful at building supportive adult-youth relationships, youth leadership, decision-making, and community involvement. This research concludes that deliberate approaches to staffing and youth-led decision-making structures positively influence the quality of participation and level of outcomes from youth experiences.

In sum, youth organizing and identity support address issues of poverty and discrimination by providing models for extending and deepening the youth-development approach so that they are more inclusive of older marginalized youth and are more successful at engaging youth as activists in their communities.

See also Civic Identity; Ethnic Identity; Identity and Activism; National Identity and Youth; Transnational Identity.

Recommended Reading

Erikson, E. H. (1965). "Youth: Fidelity and Diversity." In *The Challenge of Youth*, edited by E. Erikson. Garden City, NY: Anchor, pp. 1–28.

Gambone, M.A., Yu, H. Cao, Lewis-Charp, H., Sipe, C. L., and Lacoe, J. (2004). *A Comparative Analysis of Community Youth Development Strategies*. CIRCLE Working Paper 23. See http://www.civicyouth.org/research/areas/race_gender.htm.

Ginwright, S., and James, T. (2002). "From Assets to Agents of Change: Social Justice, Organizing, and Youth Development." *New Directions in Youth Development*, 96 (winter), 27–46.

Larson, R., and Richards, M. (1991). "Boredom in the Middle School Years: Blaming Schools Versus Blaming Students." *American Journal of Education*, 91: 418–443.

Lewis-Charp, H., Yu, H. C., Soukamneuth, S. (2004). *Examining Youth Organizing and Identity-Support Two Civic Activist Approaches for Engaging Youth in Social Justice*. Social Policy Research Associates.

Lewis-Charp, H., Yu, H. C., Soukamneuth, S., and Lacoe, J. (2003). *Extending the Reach of Youth Development through Civic Activism: Outcomes of the Youth Leadership Development Initiative*. Social Policy Research Associates.

Michelsen, E., Zaff, J. F., and Hair, E. C. (2002). *Civic Engagement Programs and Youth Development: A Synthesis*. Washington, D.C.: Child Trends.

Sherrod, L. (2000). "The Development of Citizenship in Today's Youth." *Journal of Applied Developmental Science*, (special issue).

Hanh Cao Yu, Sengsouvanh Soukamneuth, and Heather Lewis-Charp

IEA Civic Education Study. John F. Kennedy said, "Liberty without learning is always in peril; learning without liberty is always in vain." This quotation aptly describes the democratic atmosphere within which dispositions supporting youth activism are formed. Although Kennedy was speaking as an American leader, the same spirit has animated concerns about ways of increasing (or at least stemming decreases) in young people's political engagement in many democratic countries of the world. Sentiments such as this provided the animating spirit behind the IEA Civic Education Study. It was a research project collaboratively constructed by researchers in nearly thirty countries (including the United States, four other Pacific Rim nations, and twenty-three European countries). A central focus of the study was on student engagement, participation, and activism. Ideas about solidarity as well as more conventional civic engagement were part of the study's conceptualization.

The first phase of this massive study consisted of a consensus-building process about the empirical measures and a collection of twenty-four national case studies in which researchers from different countries delineated expectations about what the average fourteen- or fifteen-year-old should know about topics such as elections, rights to protest, political parties, and civil society (see for example, Torney-Purta, Schwille, and Amadeo 1999; Steiner-Khamsi 2002). In the second phase, beginning in 1999, nationally representative school-based samples of fourteen-year-olds in twenty-eight countries (totaling 90,000 students) spent two class periods answering a test and questionnaire (see Torney-Purta, Lehmann, Oswald, and Schulz 2001; http://www.wam.umd.edu/~iea). Samples of upper-secondary students (aged seventeen to eighteen) in sixteen countries (not including the United States) also responded to the instrument. To give some perspective, the age cohort of fourteen-year-olds sampled in the United States in 1999 became eligible to vote in national elections for the first time in 2004.

Respondents in all the countries took a test of conceptual knowledge of democracy and skills in interpreting political materials such as cartoons or mock party leaflets (carefully developed to be common across countries) and also a survey of concepts of democracy and of good citizenship, political attitudes, and behaviors (including several measures used in previous studies of adults' political activities). In fact, the study's assessment of activism and precursors to action related to previous studies in most areas in which research relating to political socialization has taken place—political science, developmental and educational psychology, community studies, and social-studies education. To take one example, perceptions of the efficacy of one's actions (including political action) is familiar to political scientists but also has roots in psychology in Bandura's social cognitive theory (1997) as well as in Erikson's developmental theory (1968), in Hahn's research on social studies (1998), and Watt's sociopolitical development theory from community psychology (2003). Three aspects of the IEA study are of special interest to understanding youth political activism: first, similarities and differences in the political cultures

surrounding activism that were visible in the responses of students; second, the extent to which a broad range of student characteristics as well as school and out-of-school factors have an impact on potential activism; and third, the role of different types of motivation in participation and activism.

There were some *similarities across countries* in the norms about political engagement and activism to which fourteen-year-olds subscribed. There was consensus across countries in the belief that it was important for adult citizens to obey the law and to vote. Moving beyond voting, however, one can contrast conventional political activities (joining a political party or engaging in political discussion) with more activist citizenship behaviors outside the conventional realm (taking part in activities to promote human rights or protect the environment and joining a volunteer organization). In the large majority of the countries the latter, less conventional but nonprotest types of activities, were more positively viewed than conventional activities. When young people think of becoming engaged in a cause, it is very unlikely that they will actively protest (block traffic or occupy a building) and quite unlikely that they will join a political party's efforts. Rather, it is likely that they will become mobilized in relation to a nongovernmental or community-based organization. The relative youth of fourteen-year-olds is not the explanation for these preferences. Among upper-secondary students (aged seventeen and eighteen), when many students are already eligible to vote and are welcome to join partisan organizations, the same consensus about the importance of community participation and action in support of human rights and the environment was observed.

There were also *differences across countries*, however. Four country-level patterns of activism were observed among fourteen-year-olds. First, youth in countries such as Greece and Cyprus, showed high levels of potential activism of several types. Large proportions of respondents in these two countries believed that it was good for democracy when citizens demanded their rights and engaged in peaceful protests against unjust laws, and they also strongly subscribed to norms that it was part of the good citizen's role to protest and to join organizations promoting human rights (and believed that they themselves would engage in such activities when they became adults). These were the only two countries out of the twenty-eight in which more than one-quarter of the students expected to occupy buildings or block traffic as part of protest activities.

Second, Sweden had a somewhat contrasting pattern (which was partially replicated in some other Northern and Western European countries). Swedish students were likely to believe that it was good for democracy when citizens participated in activities demanding their rights or protesting injustice in the legal system, but they did not see this kind of activity as especially important for adult citizens. Furthermore, these students were confident of the value of activism in their schools, but their own levels of expected participation outside of school (at the national or local level) were modest. In other words, they believed that activism contributed to a strong national democracy, but it was not up to them to do it.

Third, the average student in countries such as the Czech Republic and Estonia did not see the value of activism for democracy, did not believe that citizens had much responsibility for political engagement, and did not plan to be active themselves. The respondents in some other postcommunist countries had a much more participant orientation, however.

Finally, the United States was in an intermediate position. Students were less convinced than the Cypriot, Greek, or Swedish students that protest was good for democracy, but they were more convinced of its importance than the students in many of the other countries. Students in the United States stood out in valuing volun-

teer service in the community more than either conventional political activity or protest participation. They believed voluntary action was good for democracy, that it was a responsibility of citizens, and that they personally should participate in this way. In fact 50 percent of fourteen-year-olds in the United States said they had already participated in activities to help the community. In general, the activities they favored were of a nonconflictual and nonpolitical character.

Voting and political protest are well-known forms of action among young people. However, the precursors of young people's activism (and the activism itself) are multidimensional and extend beyond structured classes in civics and participation in conventional political activities such as voting. There is evidence that schools, postsecondary institutions, and other organizations are fostering civic engagement and activism when they help students to do the following:

- Gain meaningful historical and contemporary civic knowledge
- Link knowledge gained in an abstract form to more concrete situations and to skills in interpreting political communication
- Acquire skills in reading newspapers (and interest in doing so)
- Learn how to participate in respectful discussion of issues
- Acquire respect for the rule of law and civil liberties, and the history of groups' struggles to realize these liberties
- Develop a sense of identity that incorporates civic and political dimensions
- Understand different types of activism, ranging from becoming informed and informing others to conventional activities such as campaigning to peaceful protest activities
- Demonstrate the willingness to spend time in bettering their communities and also learn about the root causes of problems they see there
- Experiment with new media and cultural forms for expressing political messages

The IEA data show that although all of these are potentially valuable, some are more closely linked to certain types of participation than are others.

Young people need meaningful *civic knowledge*, both historical and contemporary, in order to overcome commonly held misconceptions. For example, the role of representation in democracy is often not well understood. An analysis of patterns of response on individual test items from the IEA study shows that many young people believe that direct democracy (in which every citizen can vote on laws, for example) is the only real democratic form of government. Students also have difficulty recognizing that most political decisions require trade-offs and compromises.

Even if there were no widespread misconceptions among young people, the IEA study shows that knowledge of civic and political processes and concepts by itself would not be sufficient to ensure participation. In the IEA study, civic knowledge was strongly related to the expectation of voting but not to the expectation of other forms of adult engagement such as conventional political activities going beyond voting, volunteer activities, or protest actions.

Schools do have an important role to play in civic education, however. Studying in class about political topics such as elections or voting is related to the expectation of several types of participation and activism. The explicit emphasis on this topic by teachers appears to convey the importance of voting to students that goes beyond the factual knowledge they acquire.

To look at the role of schools from another point of view, in Central and Eastern Europe in the early 1990s the education system changed drastically in response to demands for increased preparation for democracy. In some countries there was a strong academic curriculum in place. Many teachers in those countries effectively integrated concepts of democracy into this curriculum. Less than ten years later in the IEA Civic Education Study several Central and Eastern European countries had stu-dents who excelled when they were asked about abstract democratic concepts, such as what role political parties or constitutions play in democracy. Students in the United States ranked tenth out of twenty-eight countries in this conceptual knowledge. However, U.S. students had the highest score of any of the twenty-eight countries on skills in interpreting political communication, such as newspaper articles or cartoons. Students in the postcommunist countries, where hands-on teaching and the use of political media were not emphasized, performed much less well on the part of the test dealing with skills.

A common practice in schools in the United States is to strongly encourage community service. The IEA study's data allowed an examination of the extent and effectiveness of this experience. As noted earlier 50 percent of students in the United States said they belonged to an organization conducting activities to benefit the community, a larger proportion than in any other country. Students who had both experiences of volunteering in the community and had also studied in their classes about the community and its problems were more likely to expect to volunteer or be active in charitable giving as adults (and slightly more likely to expect to vote and engage in other types of conventional participation). The effects of service learning were most powerful in the United States (and quite substantial in England as well). In many of the other countries there were either very small numbers of students participating in volunteer activities (less than 10 percent in several postcommunist countries), or these activities showed only a weak relationship to political participation. In the large majority of countries surveyed by IEA (including the United States) volunteer or service-learning experience was not correlated with the likelihood of political protest. Although service learning may be valuable in itself (or as a vehicle encouraging academic achievement or future volunteering), for most students it does not seem to be a precursor of activism in standing up against injustice or for an unpopular political position.

The IEA study included measures of several different types of efficacy, but one of the most important was students' sense of confidence in the collective efficacy of participation in their own schools. That measure was among the most powerful predictors across socioeconomic groups and countries of the expectation of participating in conventional participation such as voting and joining a political party, community volunteering, and protest participation. School culture is important in fostering engagement and activism. There is also considerable evidence that a classroom culture or climate in which issues are discussed in an atmosphere of respect also plays a positive role.

Finally, the discussion of political issues with parents is important in many countries in fostering future activism such as participation in peaceful political protests and more conventional types of political participation, according to the IEA analysis (see Flanagan, Bowes, Csapo, and Sheblanova 1998 for a similar finding in another cross-national study).

The IEA study shows substantial differences in civic knowledge and in the expectation of voting (and some other types of activity) between students from home backgrounds with more resources and those with fewer, between those who plan to go on to higher education and those who expect to drop out before secondary-school graduation and between those attending schools with many students on the free or reduced lunch program and those with few students on this program. If schools are to assist in ensuring equal opportunities in preparation for citizenship, the factors in schools that make substantial contributions to civic preparation need to be especially strengthened where there are few family-home literacy resources. These school factors include explicit curricula for civic education starting in late elementary school, moving beyond a focus on knowledge to activities likely to motivate students to participate (as well as learning in order to pass a test), and a school and classroom climate that gives students a sense that they can make a difference.

A sense of the efficacy of political and social action is part of a broader pattern of motivation to be engaged. There are several types of relevant motivation. First, acquiring knowledge and practicing citizenship in the community is sometimes a byproduct of the pursuit of another goal. Students may learn facts about the Constitution because passing a test on these facts is required for promotion, or they may volunteer in the community because of a college application. This type of learning does not necessarily promote a long-lasting disposition that will sustain engagement.

A second more positive view is that young people become motivated when they are surrounded by practices, symbols, and groups which communicate that people whom they care about value their nation or their neighborhood and the democracy practiced there. Community service undertaken in a partnership with respected adults and open classroom discussion are both important sources of this kind of motivation.

Third, motivation may result when students get upset or angry about something, often about injustice that they feel personally or see in the lives of others in the community. Channeling this motivation into constructive action is sometimes important but also likely to be challenging.

Finally, the knowledge and cognitive skills acquired in and out of school serve as motivators and promote realistic efficacy when they help young people develop understanding of what happens in their communities or nation and a reason for believing that their action matters. This has several aspects: knowledge, accepting norms that participation is worthwhile, having the skills to assess a situation from different points of view, and having the dispositions and skills to actually participate. Enhancing young people's skills encourages them to believe in their own self-efficacy and in the efficacy of getting together with others to take action. This depends on experience in settings in which students can feel empowered (or understand their lack of power) and on feedback from respected adults (including parents and teachers). Unfortunately this combination of experience and motivation is rare for the majority of students, not only in the United States but also in other democratic countries.

See also Character Education; Citizenship Education Policies in the States; Civic Engagement in Diverse Youth; Civic Virtue; Democratic Education; Diversity Education; Environmental Education (EE); Just Community High Schools and Youth Activism; National Alliance for Civic Education (NACE); Prosocial Behaviors; School Engagement; School Influences and Civic Engagement.

Recommended Reading

Amadeo, J., Torney-Purta, J., Lehmann, R., Husfeldt, V., and Nikolova, R. (2002). *Civic Knowledge And Engagement: An IEA Study of Upper Secondary Students in Sixteen Countries.* Amsterdam, The Netherlands: International Association for the Evaluation of Educational Achievement.

Baldi, S., Perie, M., Skidmore, D., Greenberg, E., and Hahn, C. (2001). *What Democracy Means to Ninth Graders: U.S. Results from the IEA Civic Education Study.* Washington, D.C.: National Center for Education Statistics.

Hahn, C. L. (1998). *Becoming Political: Citizenship Education in a Comparative Perspective.* Albany, NY: SUNY Press.

Hahn, C. L. (2001). "Student Views of Democracy." *Social Education,* 65: 456–469.

Steiner-Khamsi, G., Torney-Purta, J., and Schwille, J., eds. (2002). *New Paradigms and Recurring Paradoxes in Education for Citizenship.* Oxford: Elsevier Service.

Torney-Purta, J., and Amadeo, J. (2004). *Strengthening Democracy in Latin America Through Civic Education: An Empirical Analysis of the Views of Students and Teachers.* Washington, D.C.: Organization of American States (USDE).

Torney-Purta, J., Lehmann, R., Oswald, H., and Schulz, W. (2001). *Citizenship and Education in Twenty-eight Countries.* Amsterdam: International Association for the Evaluation of Education Achievement.

Judith Torney-Purta

Immigrant Youth in Europe—Turks in Germany. Migration to Europe is not a new phenomenon and has a long history. However, the postwar migratory movements, particularly those beginning in the 1960s, underline what is understood as immigration—and more often than not as the "immigration problem"—in Europe today. Accordingly, the story of Turkish migration to Europe begins in the 1960s—in 1963, to be exact. Throughout the 1960s, the Turkish government signed bilateral agreements with various European states, leading to "guest-worker" programs.

Under the provisions of these agreements Turkish laborers journeyed to the industrialized center of Europe (i.e., Austria, Belgium, Germany, France, the Netherlands, Sweden, and Switzerland). The guest-worker programs, however, were not exclusive to the Turks. In this massive labor movement, workers from the countries at Europe's southern periphery and nearby North Africa—Italy, Spain, Portugal, Greece, the former Yugoslavia, Algeria, and Morocco—sought jobs and fortunes in the core of Europe, as well. Also in movement toward Europe (Britain, France, and the Netherlands) in this period were migrants from the colonies and former colonies—India, Pakistan, the Caribbean, Algeria, Surinam, and Indonesia.

The formal policies of labor recruitment in Europe ended in the mid-1970s (in Germany in 1973). By this time the presence of foreign populations in Europe had risen substantially. In 1976 there were about 12 million foreigners in the above-mentioned European countries, whereas in 1960 this number had been only 5 million. Germany's share in the number of foreigners in 1976 was close to 4 million, about 6.4 percent of the total population of what was then the Federal Republic.

This migration is commonly perceived and told as a story of poor villagers leaving their homes and traditions and settling in a foreign place—urban and modern Germany. They are taken to be the "first generation," dislocated and yearning for lost cultures in their new "home away from home."

Starting in 1980s the migration picture in Europe begins to include immigrant youth, the so-called "second generation." The attention of the media, academia, and policymakers turned to this growing section of the immigrant population, increasingly visible in schools, work, and public places. Seen through the lens of the generational model, the "second generation" youth are considered to be disoriented on the streets and disconnected from the larger society and its institutions, resources, and discourses. They are said to be neither here nor there, neither Turkish nor German, neither traditional nor modern. With the "third generation," the migrant youth are expected to become indistinguishable from the native youth.

Although intuitive, the generational model locates migrant youth in shadows of a precarious "Nowhere," standing at an incommensurable distance from the modernity and present tense of the West. This tends to overlook Europe's migrant youth as active participants in the societal projects of their place and time who cultivate youthful imaginations. From the public spaces of "Now-and-Here" in Europe, migrant youth speak of their conditions, expectations, and solutions. They speak to the world at large, articulating utopias in response to the uncertainties encompassing their lives. Since the 1980s, as they increasingly get incorporated into the European imagination, their activism testifies to their resilience, inventiveness, and engagement.

Chronologically, immigrant youth activism in Germany, and in Europe in general, can be broken down into two periods, each roughly covering a decade and with the turning point approximately around mid-1990s. The first period is marked by more visible instances of street activism, gangs, and fights with neo-Nazi groups.

Starting in the mid-1980s, and following in the footsteps of black youth movements in the United States, graffiti and hip-hop made headway into Europe. As elsewhere, youth "gangs" became the rage in Germany. Gang graffiti covered the walls and subway cars, and youth groups with "cool" names (36 Boys, Red Cobs, Black Panthers, Fighters, and *die Barbaren*) proliferated in Berlin and then spread to other cities amid enthusiastic media attention and serious debates on youth violence. According to police accounts, there were about 500 youth gangs in and around the Frankfurt metropolitan area, mostly prone to violence and comprising migrant youths. These gangs had names fashioned either after ethnic identities such as Kroatia Boys, Italy Boys, and Russ Boys, or after neighborhoods, as in Ring Boys, Gingheimer Posse, and Ahorn Boys.

The "gangs" were comprised mostly of boys and affirmed a masculine language of violence—although there were a small number of girls' gangs. Some of these groupings engaged in skirmishes with other gangs and patrolled the city streets, looking for skinheads and picking fights with them. Some were involved in petty crimes. In Berlin some gang members took part in the annual May Day clashes between the police and the autonomous antifascist groupings, following the "alternative" May Day parade in Kreuzberg (a section of Berlin where many migrants have settled).

Mostly, though, they spectacularly posed for the cameras, in proper gang wear, with baseball bats and caps, black hoods, and expensive bomber jackets. The Turkish daily *Hürriyet*'s Berlin supplement and Berlin's high-circulation tabloid *Berliner Zeitung* consumed their pictures to the limit—one with pride, the other with alarm. Every other news show on television devoted at least one show to expert discussion on gangs after a lead story exhibiting Turkish youth gangs in their hoods and complaining about Berlin becoming a new Los Angeles. Then, toward the end of the summer of 1991, the gang story lost its media appeal, and youth gangs disappeared from the urban agenda, almost as suddenly as they had appeared.

Perhaps it was a coincidence that one of the last gang pictures published in *Hürriyet* was of a Turkish girls' gang, the symbolic last act in the procession of the gang story. Typically, the stories of girls follow the abundant attention given to the boys, almost as small, last-minute amendments to the prolific legends of the boys.

Fights with neo-Nazi groupings were a prominent feature of youth activism in the late 1980s and early 1990s. Turkish, German, and other immigrant youth groups, organized in gangs or in political clusters with leftist and anarchist orientations, frequently came to blows with neo-Nazis. Notable graffiti then covered the walls in Berlin that read in English: "Ayhan did the right thing!"—an obvious reference to Spike Lee's film *Do the Right Thing*. Ayhan was a Turkish boy who went to prison for reportedly picking fights with neo-Nazis and injuring one. The writers of the graffiti were members of a radical multiethnic youth group that called itself Revolutionary Communists. Their other wall writing declared that "*Graffiti ist Kein Verbrechen*" (graffiti is not a crime). To the searching eye, both writings are still legible on walls in Kreuzberg and its vicinity.

In the early 1990s, antiforeigner attacks in Germany escalated to a more violent level. Starting with the attacks on asylum seekers in Rostock in the fall of 1992 and continuing with the firebombings of Turkish homes in Moelln in 1992 and Solingen in 1993, violence was no longer a matter of street fights between youth gangs. In Moelln, the attack resulted in the deaths of a Turkish woman and two girls. In Solingen, the victims of the firebomb attacks were two Turkish young women and three girls from the same family. In each instance of violence, the perpetrators were the neo-Nazi *Kameraden* (comrades).

Once it had become apparent that antiforeigner violence was a political act perpetrated by organized neo-Nazi groupings, the response to the violence shifted to the terrain of mass political protests and state action. The attack in Solingen especially generated public outrage and triggered mass demonstrations in Solingen and in other parts of Germany. In a parallel development to mass protests, various state authorities in Germany gave themselves the task of promoting hip-hop as a solution to the "problem" of youth violence and allocated ample resources to this end. Berlin's Foreigners' Office took the lead in establishing the Mete Eksi Prize, given in memory of a Turkish youth killed in a street fight in Kreuzberg in November of 1991. The prize is still awarded to youth projects that promote diversity and tolerance and endorse dialogs against violence.

The availability of extensive organizational resources complemented the expanding popularity of hip-hop among the migrant youth of Berlin and other metropolitan centers of Germany and eventually led to the post-1990 period in youth activism. Rappers and break-dancers took the place of "gangs" at center stage and attracted media attention as the new marvels of the immigrant ghettos. The hip-hop styles they cultivated had contributed to the incorporation of Berlin and Germany into the global hip-hop scene.

In terms of youth activism, the pre-1990 phase was also marked by overt political involvement, first around labor issues then around rights. In the 1970s and well into 1980s, Turkish youth took part in leftist revolutionary political organizations, which were closely connected to their parent organizations in Turkey and advanced demands related to the rights of workers and improvement of working and living conditions of immigrants. By their nature, these organizations were anticapitalist and were allied with now defunct German revolutionary parties and organizations. Their radicalism was in line with the radicalism sweeping the world and Europe at the time, and they were highly successful in mobilizing Turkish youth. In opposition to this left-radical organizing stood two major political movements, one nationalist and one religious, Gray Wolves and National Vision. These two movements were also offshoots of respective political movements in Turkey, the National Action Party and the National Salvation Party. The politics and rivalry of all three strands had much to do with the political landscape of Turkey than Germany. Nonetheless, Turkish immigrant associations of the time had been slowly but surely moving in the direction of mobilizing around migration-specific issues such as language and cultural and political rights.

When one looks at other centers of migration in Europe, one observes similar developments. On the one hand we encounter political street protests, at times taking violent forms. On the other hand we witness a movement with claims concerning workers' rights and migrant rights—primarily in the domains of language, culture, and political participation. Throughout the 1980s, Britain had been a stage for countless major "race riots," the most notable ones being the Southall, Brixton, Tottenham, and Handsworth riots. A combination of conservative socioeconomic policies of the Thatcher times, the rise of racist parties and movements, and growing immigrant activism around "race relations" were key components of the contexts in which the riots took place. In Hanif Kureishi's films *Sammy and Rosie Get Laid* (1987) and *My Beautiful Launderette* (1985), for example, young white, black, and Pakistani immigrant protagonists walk through London and conduct their lives against a backdrop of racial clashes, fights with racist skinheads, and streets ablaze. France in the 1980s had been the scene of immigrant collective action and large street protests. In 1983, for instance, 100,000 people walked from Marseille to Paris in the March for Equality. Subsequent mass marches became stages for immigrant demands. *Memoire Fertile*, an umbrella movement of about twenty immigrant organizations, and *France Plus*, mainly an organization of Maghrebi immigrants (*beurs*), advanced demands for a *nouvelle citoyenneté* (new citizenship) and protested against racism and exclusion.

In the post-1990 phase, migrant youth activism steadily has moved away from overt political action to the sphere of cultural politics and production. In a sense youth action has been more subdued and constricted—although there has been occasional street activism such as the anti–Le Pen rallies in France following the 2002 presidential elections, race riots in the north of England in cities like Bradford, Oldham, Leeds, and Burnley, and ritualized May 1st riots in Berlin. The new emphasis in youth activism has been on rights that are defined in cultural terms and celebrated in spectacles, festivals, and various other performance venues.

Given this shift in content and form, migrant youth activism at the start of the twenty-first century can be viewed as following the two overlapping paths of political engagement and cultural production. The "political" engagement involves demands for recognition of cultural difference and identity work (identity-related claims and displays of identity), on the one hand, and institutionalized political activism (work within political entities, home and host parties and associations), on the other.

In the 1990s, Germany, the Netherlands, Britain, and France moved toward establishing and implementing "multicultural" policies. Within this framework cultural demands such as *halal* food (food prepared according to Islamic customs), language instruction in mother tongue (Turkish in Germany), and after-school religious instruction have been met with resistance from state officials at times but mostly with positive outcomes. In Berlin's high schools, Turkish has been offered as the second foreign language to pupils of Turkish origin. After a long court battle, the Islamic Federation in Germany has attained the right to give after-school religion courses to Muslim students. Alevites, members of a Sufi branch of Islam from Turkey, can teach their religious and cultural precepts as after-school courses to pupils of Alevite descent. Unlike in France, wearing of headscarves in school has not been a contentious issue for a long time in Germany.

Migrant youth have been at the forefront of these struggles for recognition. Not only are they the "natural" subjects in these debates over cultural differences, but also as youth they have been actively involved in politics. Most Turkish associations, as well as ethnic and religiously oriented ones such as Kurdish, Alevite, and Sunni organizations, depend on the youth in carrying out their activities and thus vigorously seek to mobilize the youth in their political campaigns. The German political parties have made a special effort to recruit young Turkish immigrants. Since the end of the 1990s, every political party from the environmentalist Greens to conservative Christian Democrats has had prominent immigrant politicians in their ranks, mostly of Turkish origin, serving as local leaders and members of state, federal, and European parliaments. Although small in number, immigrant youth are also involved in alternative, anarchist-leaning "antifa" (short for antifascist) groups, antiglobalist associations such as Attac, and various Islamic and nationalist (Turkish, as well as Kurdish) radical organizations.

When it comes to "cultural" work, immigrant youth are becoming increasingly visible in the art and culture landscape of Germany, both as audiences and producers. From informal cultural scenes to the institutional art and culture industries—in other words from street festivals, youth centers, immigrant associations, mosques' auxiliaries, and wedding halls to television, theaters, concert halls, fashion houses, exhibitions, and movie studios—it is not unusual to encounter Turkish youth as writers, actors, singers, designers, directors, and producers. Their names are too many to list and are recurrently cited for award-winning films, best-selling novels and books, celebrated TV shows, and outstanding art shows and exhibitions. They are no longer marginally related to cultural production in an alien place but central to the production of culture in metropolitan cities like Berlin, Frankfurt, and Hamburg, as well as in Germany at large.

The diversity of migrant youth's cultural production notwithstanding, hip-hop (rap, graffiti, and break dancing) is the most visible of the art forms, one which associates migrant youth with global cultural flows and spaces. Hip-hop is also the most conspicuous art form associated with migrant youth. Among the more obvious reasons for this visibility is the indisputable visual, vocal, and commercial presence of hip-hop worldwide. Another factor behind this fascination with migrant hip-hop and its exoticness is the notion (and perhaps the stereotype) of "the ghetto." Irrespective of whether they are truly ghettos, Kreuzberg in Berlin and Altona in Hamburg are designated as such and Turkish and other migrant youth emerge and rise to prominence as natural "homeboys."

By 1993, for instance, the hip-hop scene in Kreuzberg had its prominent names, MC Gio, writer Neco, and DJ Derezon (Sony), the dancer Storm, and the rapper Boe B. Their pictures and words were eminently featured in the stylish pages of cosmopolitan Berlin biweeklies *Zitty* and *Tip*. Their stories and art were interpreted and promoted as necessary for the social harmony and the multicultural unity of Berlin.

In March of 1994, a youth festival called Street '94 was the rage in Kreuzberg with the mottos "TO STAY IS MY RIGHT" and "WE ALL ARE ONE" proudly displayed. Street '94 included two months of intense activity, revolving around an art exhibition, workshops and panel discussions on graffiti writing, street dancing, rap music, dance parties, and open-air screenings of films such as *Juice*, *New Jack City*, *Menace II Society*, and *Boyz 'N the Hood*. The festival was organized under the auspices of NaunynRitze, a prominent youth center in Kreuzberg, and co-sponsored by Kreuzberg's municipal government and Berlin's Ministry of Youth and Family. Street '94 was closely associated with another Berlin-wide youth project, an upscale "Youth Art+Culture" project called X–'94 with the subtitle "FIFTY DAYS TO BLOW YOUR MIND," organized by Berlin's *Akademie der Kuenste* (Academy of the Arts). In the grand design of X–'94, Street '94 represented the cool art of the street, subcultural undercurrents of the metropolis, and the raw skill of ghetto boys and girls.

Street '94 was also connected to the global hip-hop scene in tangible ways. Prominent graffiti writers from other metropolitan centers, such as T-KID from New York and JAY-ONE from Paris, came to Berlin as invited artists. They participated in workshops and conversed with Berliner writers in panel discussions. They lectured on writing, exchanged views on aesthetics and style, told tales of their fortunes, and reflected on the ethics of hip-hop. Their names attracted renowned street artists and numerous rappers and writers-to-be to the various festival events.

Street '94 was not the only mega-project undertaken by NaunynRitze in the 1990s. Over the next few years they organized the *Multinationales Anti-rassistiches Performance Project* (MAPP) in 1995 and the *Personen Ohne Wohnung* (POW, People Without Homes). Like Street '94, both MAPP and POW were designed to activate the productive potential of the youth. MAPP was a joint production with three other youth organizations from Sheffield, Rotterdam, and Luxembourg. The project was part of the European Council Initiative's Campaign on Combating Racism, Xenophobia, Anti-Semitism, and Intolerance, and was sponsored through the European Union's Youth for Europe program. The show was a multigenre performance, a mix of dance, theater, graffiti, acrobatics, and music. POW was also a European co-production, this time between Sheffield and Berlin. It was conceived as a performance piece and a multimedia installation, performed by youth from Berlin and Sheffield, both native and immigrant, with four of the participants actually being homeless youth.

In 1995 for the first time in Germany an immigrant rap group named Cartel made a sensational entry into the world of hip-hop. In the words of its young Turkish music impresarios, Cartel rocked the market like a "bomb." Their CD, comprising twelve songs delivered in four languages (Turkish, English, German, and Spanish), sold widely. The Turkish, German, and Spanish rappers of Cartel—Karakan from Nürnberg, Erci E. from Berlin, and Da Crime Posse from Kiel—soon made it to the cover of *Spex*, the main music journal in Germany. In the same year they were on tour in Germany and Turkey, performing to sold-out crowds.

Cartel's CD was migrant hip-hop at its best: playful samples of Turkish music, bullet-fast rhymes, and melodic couplets skillfully blended with bass and drums. It connected familiar Turkish tunes with rhymes verbalized in the foreignness of Spanish and German and mischievous allusions covering the vast terrain of popular culture. However, Cartel's claim to fame was not so much a result of its musical accomplishments but its defiant lyrics couched in the vernacular of hip-hop. Their song "You Are a Turk" became their defining message, mostly interpreted as a sign of resistance to integration, ardent nationalism, and gang violence. Despite the alarmist debate around Cartel's lyrics, their songs were hip-hop manifestos, diligently following the script of rap—the usual array of ghetto problems (drugs and violence) and adolescent masculinity (riding cars and chasing girls), woven in narratives of migrancy (longing for homes far away, displacement, broken families).

Another important hip-hop group was Islamic Force, the creation of Boe B. (after his high-school nickname, Bobby of Dallas fame) and his DJ and producer Derezon (short for "there is only one") with the addition of Killa Hakan (a nickname from his gang days with 36 Boys), and Nellie (an aspiring soul singer migrated from Kosovo). From the beginning, Boe B. sought his claim to fame by making *harbi* (true, original) rap his trademark and staying faithful to the authentic sounds and language of rap. Accordingly, in their rap Islamic Force plainly spoke of a typical ghetto, tormented by drugs, violence, and exclusion, and called for respect, diversity, and tolerance.

In a sense Turkish rap has been Germany's response to Rai and rap in France and post–Bhangra rap in Britain. The music of Cartel and Islamic Force resonates with sounds and verses written elsewhere in the world—for instance, by NTM and MC Solaar in Paris and Fun'da'mental and Asian Dub Foundation in London. They all speak in the *vernacular of rap*, a variety of angry street talk, preaching against discrimination, celebrating brotherly solidarity, and calling for diversity, tolerance, and human rights.

The institutional resources available to immigrant youth have been instrumental in shaping the parameters of resistance and creativity, as well as creating global cultural affinities and bonds. Without question, in Berlin's youth centers hip-hop emerged as the most popular art form, as well as the pedagogical tool of choice among social workers and governmental officials for channeling youth away from violence and into productive artistic endeavors.

The calls for diversity and tolerance booming from Berlin's hip-hop stages have been in line with the multiculturalist policies in vogue in Germany's major metropolitan centers. Over the course of 1990s, Berlin's Foreigners' Office has waged a diversity campaign under the motto *Miteinander Leben* (Living Together), promoting a city of tolerance and pluralism. In 1992 a poster published by the office covered the billboards of the city, pronouncing "*Wir sind Berlin*" (We are Berlin). The Berlin in the poster showed portrait photos of persons of diverse professions, ages, colors, and genders, all different but all Berliners. Since then the office has been involved in other campaigns, some successful, some utterly misguided (e.g., posters of love between a migrant black girl and a neo-Nazi youth, for instance), all in the service of achieving a cosmopolitan Berlin.

In addition to German authorities, the European Union is also actively involved in shaping the prospects of the cultural and artistic production of immigrant youth. In this respect, the EU progressively funds and sponsors youth projects that promote intercultural understanding and "European" principles of antiracism and diversity. Through the Youth for Europe program the EU had allocated about $113.6 million during the five years between 1995 and 1999.

As we move into the twenty-first century, migrant youth activism is moving from the "marginal" to the "mainstream." The prominent presence of immigrant youth in the fields of sports, music, literature, and politics is astonishing. Cartel and Islamic Force are distant memories from the 1990s, but Erci E., Derezon, and Killa Hakan continue their careers as rappers. Aziza A., who entered the hip-hop scene as the first female rapper with the pointedly titled CD *Es ist Zeit* (*It Is the Time*), takes stages as the elder stateswoman of rap.

With every passing day, commercially viable new rap stars such as Kool Savas enter the hip-hop scene. Fatih Akin's film *Gegen die Wand* (*Against the Wall*) won the Golden Bear award in the Berlin Film Festival as the German entry. Neco, the graffiti writer of the 1990s, made *Alltag* (*Everyday*), a stylized depiction of ghetto life in Kreuzberg, and was dubbed "the Spike Lee of Germany." To speak of elected officials of Turkish origin in Germany's state and federal parliaments and in the European parliament is now ordinary. It is even difficult to talk about "immigrant youth" since most have citizenship in their countries of residence.

However, in the post–9/11 world "Islam" still colors public opinion in Europe. Immigrant youth, irrespective of their politics, bear the burden of being characterized as fundamentalists and at times as potential terrorists and become subjects of superfluous headscarf debates. The accent put on Islam has led to suggestions that Europe is essentially racist and anti-Muslim and has animated reaction among immigrant youth.

This notwithstanding, migrant youth identity—Muslim, Turkish, or otherwise—is in the process of becoming an aestheticized art project, losing its marginal and subversive disposition. Instead of speaking in rebellious ghetto languages immigrant youth, in their words and images, rebel against the constraints and stereotypes of "the ghetto." They speak to the world in the contemporary discourses of tolerance, equality, and diversity. As the inhabitants of cosmopolitan metropolises of the new Europe, their cultural productions display a diversity of experiences and their experiences are displays of diversity.

See also Australia, Youth Activism in; Demographic Trends Affecting the World's Youth; Eastern Europe, Youth and Citizenship in; Europe, Comparing Youth Activism in; European Identity and Citizenship; Hip-Hop Generation; Immigrant Youth in the United States; India, Youth Activism in; Indonesia, Youth Activism in; Nigeria, Youth Activism in; Palestinian *Intifada*; Russia, Youth Activism in; Serbia, Youth Activism in (1990–2000); Soweto Youth Activism (South Africa); State and Youth, The; Statute of the Child and Adolescent (Brazil); Tiananmen Square Massacre (1989); Transnational Identity; Transnational Youth Activism; Turkey, Youth Activism in; United Nations, Youth Activism and; Xenophobia; Zapatista Rebellion (Mexico); Zionist Youth Organizations.

Recommended Reading

Anwar, M. (1998). *Between Cultures: Continuity and Change in the Lives of Young Asians*. London: Routledge.

Bauman, G. (1996). *Contesting Culture: Discourse of Identity in Multi-ethnic London*. Cambridge: Cambridge University Press.

Hall, K. D. (2002). *Lives in Transition: Sikh Youths as British Citizens*. Philadelphia: University of Pennsylvania Press.

Keppel, G. (1997). *Allah in the West: Islamic Movements in America and Europe*. Stanford, CA: Stanford University Press.

Loh, H., and Güngör, M. (2002). *Fear of a Kanak Planet: Hiphop zwischen Weltkultur and Nazi-Rap*. Höfen, Austria: Hannibal.

Mitchell, T., ed. (2001). *Global Noise: Rap and Hip-Hop outside the USA*. Middletown, CT: Wesleyan University Press.

Modood, T., Berthoud, R., Lakey, J., Nazroo, J., Smith, P., Virdee, S., and Beishon, S. (1997). *Ethnic Minorities in Britain: Diversity and Disadvantage*. London: Public Policy Institute.

Sharma, S., Hutnyk, J., and Sharma, A., eds. (1996). *Dis-Orienting Rhythms: The Politics of the New Asian Dance Music*. London: Zed Books.

Soysal, L. (1999). "Projects of Culture: An Ethnographic Episode in the Life of Migrant Youth in Berlin." PhD diss., Harvard University.

Levent Soysal

Immigrant Youth in the United States. The fastest-growing youth population in the United States, those in immigrant families, is at the leading edge of the race-ethnic transformation of America. Public activism among youth in immigrant families is limited, but their rapidly growing numbers and unprecedented racial, ethnic, and cultural diversity ensure that their influence will reverberate through American society during the coming decades. The precise nature of this influence cannot be known in advance, but it is clear that the ways this influence plays out will depend on two sets of factors. The first relates to the resources and circumstances of these youth and their families as they arrive in their newly adopted homeland, while the second reflects the reception they receive and the ways in which they are incorporated into local communities and the broader American society. Attention focuses first on the demographic transformation that is being wrought by these youth, followed by discussion of each of these two broad sets of factors.

Historically, fewer than half of Americans were Hispanic, Black, Asian, or American Indian, but rapid growth of these groups is creating a new American majority. This transformation does not, however, reflect the emergence of a singular, numerically dominant group. Instead, it is characterized by a mosaic of diverse racial, ethnic, and cultural groups from around the world. This demographic transformation is occurring rapidly and will become a reality first among children and youth. U.S Census Bureau projections indicate that soon after 2030 these race-ethnic minority children and youth will outnumber non-Hispanic whites. Driven by world population growth and economic opportunities in the United States, immigration and births to immigrants and their descendents is fueling this transformation because most immigrants are Hispanic or Asian. In fact, by 2000 one-in-five children and youth under age eighteen were immigrants or lived in immigrant families, and of these 52 percent were Hispanic, 14 percent were Asian, and 7 percent were black. Thus, as America entered the twenty-first century, 73 percent of all children and youth who were immigrants or had immigrant parents belonged to race-ethnic minorities.

Even our most senior citizens will feel the consequences of this transformation of America's youth. By 2030, when the baby-boom generation will be of retirement age, Census Bureau projections indicate that 72 percent of the elderly sixty-five years will be non-Hispanic white, compared to only 56 percent of working-age adults, and 50 percent of children. As a result, as the growing elderly population of the predominantly white baby-boom generation reaches the retirement age, it will increasingly depend for its economic support during retirement on the productive activities and civic participation (e.g., voting) of working-age adults who are members of racial and ethnic minorities. Many of these workers will have grown up in immigrant families. Thus, resources for and the mode of incorporation of these youth in American society deserve increasing attention from government officials and the American public.

The experiences of youth in immigrant families differ profoundly depending on the timing of migration. First-generation immigrant youth who arrive as adolescents or young adults were immersed for many formative years in the culture of their homeland before entering American society, while younger immigrants spend their childhoods living simultaneously in two cultures, that of the foreign-born parents who provide for their care and upbringing and that of the wider American society. The many youth born in the United States to immigrant parents, "second-generation immigrants," have much more in common with the bicultural foreign-born youth who arrived as young children than with youth whose grandparents or earlier generations were immigrants. In fact, second-generation immigrant youth often are the younger siblings of first-generation immigrants.

Children and youth in immigrant families are spread widely across the United States. For example, they account for about half of all children and youth in California and between one-fourth and one-third of those in eight states, including the next three largest states of Texas, New York, and Florida. In most of the remaining states, the number in immigrant families more than doubled between 1990 and 2000, including many where immigration was historically quite limited, among them North and South Carolina, Georgia, Tennessee, and Arkansas in the South, and Minnesota, Iowa, Nebraska, Utah, and Idaho in the Midwest and West.

Because of enormous changes in the living situations and activities of youth as they transition to adulthood, it is important to distinguish adolescents under age eighteen who mainly are living at home and attending middle or high school from older youth who may be attending college or supporting themselves through work and who may be living on their own or married, sometimes with their own young children.

The future prospects of adolescents in immigrant families, like other adolescents, are influenced by the circumstances of their parents. Insofar as race-ethnic minorities often have experiences quite different from non-Hispanic whites, it is important to distinguish immigrants by their race and ethnicity, as well as by country of origin. Among adolescents in immigrant families, five groups stand apart with regard to key family circumstances. These groups are adolescents with origins in Mexico, Central America, Indochina (Cambodia, Laos, Thailand, Vietnam), the Caribbean (other than Cuba), and blacks from Africa. These countries or regions of origin account for about half of all adolescents aged thirteen to seventeen in immigrant families. For ease of presentation, youth in immigrant families with these origins will be referred to here as minority youth (or adolescents) from selected third-world countries. Youth in immigrant families from other third world countries (e.g. China, Cuba) are not included in this group.

Most adolescents in immigrant families, regardless of their origins, benefit from living in two-parent families with a strong work ethic. More than three-fourths of adolescents in white native-born families and in immigrant families live with two parents, and more than 90 percent living with fathers have a father who is employed. There are large differences in parental education, however. For example, about one-tenth of minority adolescents from selected third-world countries have a father who graduated from college, similar to the level for Hispanics in native-born families, but the proportion is half again higher for blacks in native-born families, three times greater for whites in native-born families, and nearly four times higher for youth with other immigrant origins. At the opposite extreme, only one-tenth of whites in native-born families have a father who has not graduated high school, compared to about 60 percent for minority adolescents from selected third-world countries.

Even more striking, only one-in-fifty white adolescents in native-born families has a father with less than nine years of school, but this jumps to four-in-ten for the minorities from selected third-world countries. In addition, two-thirds of these adolescents have a father who is not English proficient. As a consequence, about three-in-ten minority adolescents from selected third-world countries have fathers who are not able to find full-time, year-round work,

a level double that of white adolescents in native-born families. Similarly, while about two-thirds of these immigrant groups have employed mothers, this rises to eight-in-ten for the white native group.

Not surprisingly then, about one-third of minority adolescents from third-world countries live in poverty, a level only slightly higher than for minority adolescents in native-born families but twice the level for other adolescents in immigrant families and four times the level experienced by whites in native-born families. The pattern of differences across these groups is broadly similar with regard to health-insurance coverage and with regard to the chances of not being in excellent or very good health. Recent immigrants are comparatively healthy overall, but health tends to deteriorate through time, the longer that immigrants live in the United States and from one generation to the next.

Despite the strong family structure and work ethic experienced by minority adolescents from selected third-world countries and despite the high educational aspirations that their parents hold for them, the limited parental educational attainments and economic resources in their families contribute to a substantial high-school dropout rate. Combining high dropout rates with the limited educational attainments of new immigrants who are aged eighteen or older when they arrive in the United States, about four-in-ten minority youth from selected third-world countries have not graduated from high school by age twenty, a level more than three times greater than for other youth in immigrant families or whites in native-born families.

Not surprisingly, only about one-fourth of minority youth from selected third-world countries are enrolled in school (mainly college) by age twenty-one, compared to one-third of minorities in native-born families and about half overall for those in white native-born and other immigrant groups. Of course, many immigrant youth arrive during their early twenties. Among those aged twenty-five, only one-in-ten minority youth from selected third-world countries are college graduates, slightly below the level of youth in minority native-born families, but only one-third the level of whites in native-born families and less then one-fourth the level of other immigrants.

Despite differences in school enrollment and educational attainments, about two-thirds of youth are employed at age twenty-one, with the noteworthy exception of blacks in native-born families, only half of whom are employed. Although employment rates are similar for most groups, roughly one-fourth of minority youth aged eighteen to twenty-two from selected third-world countries are officially poor, slightly below the level of minorities in native-born families but nearly twice as high as the level for whites in native-born families. Thus comparable levels of work among these youth in immigrant families does not translate into similar levels of economic resources.

Youth in immigrant and native-born families are about equally likely to live with a parent at age twenty-one, with one-half of them doing so. But by age twenty-two one-fourth of minority youth from selected third-world countries are married, compared to one-fifth of Hispanics in native-born families, a sixth of whites in native-born families, and about one-in-ten for other immigrant groups. Also, as of age twenty-two, one-fourth of minority youth from selected third-world countries have a child of their own in the home, about midway between the one-in-five among whites in native-born families and the one-in-three among minorities in native-born families. Youth in immigrant families from other regions of the world are least likely to be married or to have children of their own.

Cleary, there are sometimes large differences between minority youth from selected third-world countries and other youth in immigrant families both in their parental family circumstances during adolescence and in their own educational attainments, economic resources, and family-building activity during their early twenties. There also often are substantial differences between minority youth from these selected immigrant regions and whites in native-born families. These differences are often to the disadvantage of the long-term prospects of minority youth from selected third-world countries.

Despite the substantial family strengths experienced by minority youth from selected third-world countries, by their early twenties their education and poverty levels are most similar to black, Hispanic, and American Indian minorities in native-born families. This raises a critical question for these youth and for America's future about the reception that they and their families experience in their adoptive communities and the broader American society. Is the promise of the American dream that draws these youth and their families a reality or a false hope?

Historically, immigrant groups arriving with substantial economic, educational, and other social resources have achieved considerable success in their adoptive homeland, while others have been met with discrimination or exclusion from access to economic, political, and educational institutions. At the end of the nineteenth and beginning of the twentieth century, many Southern and Eastern European groups suffered from discrimination, but blacks, Native Americans, Mexican Americans, and Puerto Ricans confronted a color line that excluded them from the benefits of full participation in American society.

Today, at the dawn of the twenty-first century, a similar pattern is unfolding. Youth who are highly educated in immigrant families from Canada and Europe and Asian countries are afforded easy access to a rich array of opportunities and often achieve considerable success. But Hispanics from Mexico and Central America, blacks from the Caribbean and Africa, as well as the much smaller group of Asian refugees from Indochina, often find that limited economic resources and residential segregation confine them to neighborhoods where schools are poorly funded and inadequate and where other public resources are quite sparse compared to more affluent suburban neighborhoods.

While an occasional individual from these groups manages to overcome these severe constraints, most find the challenges to achieving the American dream quite daunting. Rather than assisting the efforts of immigrants to contribute productively and successfully to the American economy and culture, public policies often create unnecessary hurdles for those who are not already well-educated and English fluent and effectively exclude immigrants from access to a quality education, basic health services, and other resources.

America has been a land of opportunity for many generations of immigrants who have shown initiative and worked hard over the past two centuries, but blacks and Hispanics have often been excluded by public policy or social convention from having access to these opportunities. We face momentous decisions today as immigration is transforming the race-ethnic composition of America, creating a new American majority. Will youth in immigrant families, not only those in highly educated and resource-rich families but also those who arrive with fewer resources but no less desire to succeed, be afforded the opportunity to realize for themselves and their children the promise of the American dream? We are at a critical juncture in our national history, and the path we follow will have repercussions not only for immigrant youth but for all Americans during the years and decades ahead.

See also Australia, Youth Activism in; Demographic Trends Affecting the World's Youth; Eastern Europe, Youth and Citizenship in; Europe, Comparing Youth Activism in; European Identity and Citizenship; Immigrant Youth in Europe—Turks in Germany; India, Youth Activism in; Indonesia, Youth Activism in; Nigeria, Youth Activism in; Palestinian *Intifada*; Russia, Youth Activism in; Serbia, Youth Activism in (1990–2000); Soweto Youth Activism (South Africa); the State and Youth; Statute of the Child and Adolescent (Brazil); Tiananmen Square Massacre (1989); Transnational Identity; Transnational Youth Activism; Turkey, Youth Activism in; United Nations, Youth Activism and; Xenophobia; Zapatista Rebellion (Mexico); Zionist Youth Organizations.

Recommended Reading

"Children of Immigrant Families." *The Future of Children*, (Summer 2004) 14 (2): 1–160.

Hernandez, D. J. (1993). *America's Children: Resources from Family, Government, and the Economy*. New York: Russell Sage Foundation.

Hernandez, D. J. (1999). *Children of Immigrants: Health, Adjustment, and Public Assistance*. Washington, D.C.: National Academy Press.

Hernandez, D. J., and Charney, E. (1998). *From Generation to Generation: The Health and Well-Being of Children in Immigrant Families*. Washington, D.C.: National Academy Press.

Pedraza, S., and Rumbaut, R. (1996). *Origins and Destinies: Immigration, Race, and Ethnicity in America*. Belmont, CA: Wadsworth Publishing Company.

Portes, A., and Rumbaut, R. (2001). *Legacies: The Story of the Immigrant Second Generation*. New York: Russell Sage Foundation.

Rumbaut, R., and Portes, A. (2001). *Ethnicities: Children of Immigrants in America*. Berkeley, CA: University of California Press.

Donald J. Hernandez

India, Youth Activism in. In India today, "youth" is the social category most immediately paired with consumerism. Indeed, one of India's dominant features is an ideology of consumerism and a practice of ostentatious consumption. Development itself is often equated with ostentatious consumption. However, the relation between consumption and young people in developing countries like India is complex. While some Indian youth are prominent consumers and consider consumption as a key element to their own identities, other young people are minimal or nonconsumers, whether by force, circumstance, or choice. Indian youth are growing up with high rates of economic growth yet, for most, very low levels of inclusiveness. The failure of the government of India (hereafter the GoI) to equitably deliver the fruits of development not only affects youth identities but also the way in which these young people formulate their *rights* and *duties as citizens* of India.

The increase in consumerism in India has taken place in a context of the transformation of India's economy. Since the beginning of the 1990s, economic policy has moved in the direction of liberalization and the nurturing of free markets. The newly introduced market-friendly policies aimed at developing outward-looking, internationally competitive economies have resulted in an ever-increasing influx of new goods, ideas, technologies, and lifestyles.

India is one of the *youngest nations* on the globe, that is, in 2004 it was estimated that around 54 percent of India's population is under twenty-five years of age. These young people live in huge metropolitan cities, in urbanized areas, and in towns as well as in remote villages and other rural settings. They live on the plains and vast agricultural tracts, in forests and mountain areas, or near seas, rivers, and oceans. They live in prosperous and posh bungalows and apartments or in slums, crammed hostel rooms, or just on the pavement. Yet, wherever they live and under whatever circumstances, they have all been influenced by the recent economic liberalization and are often called "*liberalization's children.*" However, these newly introduced policies have, far from uniting young people in India, created even greater divisions among them. In addition, while globalizing market forces have empowered some young people, others have become victims. Subjected to increasing impoverishment, these victims may well experience globally mediated images of consumption, but they are more frustrated than ever in fulfilling the proffered goal of actual consumption. In short, the most conspicuous difference among young people in India is the level of consumption.

In 1998, the GoI defined "youth" as all young people between the ages of fifteen and thirty-five. The United Nations estimated that in 2002 the youth population in India, defined as young people between the ages of fifteen and twenty-four, numbered 189,356,000, which formed around 18.6 percent of India's total population. Whereas a small percentage of these young people feel they have enough, and some even feel they have too much, most of them feel they want more. Yet, what they want more of varies. While economic growth has not brought social well-being to all, it is at times difficult to decide who is at the bottom. Poverty affects both young people's ability to organize and the form and content of protest. As a result, although both groups (i.e., the economically well-off and the poor) face problems and organize themselves to fight for their perceived *rights*, their demands and values are different and so are their ways of fulfilling them. At times, however, there is strategic convergence between the two groups.

Broadly speaking, poverty thus divides young people in India into two categories— "*the haves*" and "*the have-nots.*" Indeed, the unprecedented flow of capital, goods, and labor has made a small fraction of India's youth more prosperous. With more disposable income these young people are not only able to buy the new products that national and transnational companies are hoping to sell, they are also better equipped to make the most of the new prospects. They like wearing jeans, drinking fizzy sodas, and watching MTV. They also start their own businesses. They mostly belong to the urban middle and upper classes, and their educational level and computer literacy is comparatively high. Although much smaller in number than the "have-nots," it is often these "haves," known by a variety of labels such as *indies*, or financially independent young persons, *Generation Z* (succeeding *Generation X* and *Generation Y* but without carrying the social, political, economic, cultural, or ideological baggage of either), and *zippies*, or young city or suburban residents, who are presented as *the* youth of India. Besides, their numbers are increasing, as one now can even "buy" youth. In India, one can witness the global trend toward "down aging," that is, the tendency for older people to act and feel younger than they are. So forty is the new thirty; thirty is the new twenty. Conversely, ten is the new fifteen. The "youth image" as represented in films and advertisements is reshaping the collective consciousness of India.

Although rich enough to buy what they want to buy, these "haves" are not without life problems. In addition, although they appear to constitute a homogenous subgroup among the fifteen- to thirty-five-year-olds in India (i.e., through the way in which they experience and produce globalization accompanied by particular consumption patterns), diversity reigns among them as well. Profound and pervasive issues arise out of the social changes that accompany the economic transformation and the widespread diffusion of science and technology. The way in which individual young people grasp and interpret these issues is a complex process during which identities and demands are constructed and reconstructed. This can give rise to a series of conflicts on the basis of generation, class, ethnicity, religion, or gender.

In some sense, these "haves" feel deprived, too. They might now have more buying power, yet the new mind-sets, habits, and working styles are not only beneficial. Indeed, they can buy cell phones, visit Cafe Coffee Day outlets, discos, bowling alleys, pool parlors, frequent cyber-cafés, or even have a computer for themselves at home. Nevertheless, competition has increased enormously and apart from rising expectations among these young people of themselves, the state, teachers, parents, and peers also demand much more of them. Unfortunately, there are not many alternative roads open for those whose goals are not fulfilled or for those who have missed their targets. Like other groups in society, depression, suicide, drug addiction, other health-related problems (in their case due to lack of exercise and wrong

or excessive diets), and violence (both as victims and as perpetrators) are not absent among them.

Even with all the money in the world, girls cannot buy domestic and public security, and they thus continue their fight for more gender equality. Likewise, ostentatious consumption might set apart a few members of ethnic and religious minorities in India, such as tribals or *adivasis* and Muslims, yet during times of ethnic cleansing and communal riots, their property is destroyed, too, and they lack the same safety as the poorer members of the communities to which they belong. Therefore, these young people, though rich, continue their fight for religious, caste, ethnic, and regional equality.

It is this consuming class, targeted by multinationals and other companies, that is often identified as *the* youth of India. Yet, although they are the target of most youth lifestyle brands and the "hope of the nation," these "haves" number approximately only 16 million. The rest of the approximately 173 million young people in India are not able to practice ostentatious or conspicuous consumption, though they are youth nevertheless. In their case, the dominance of multinational corporations (MNCs) and international capital over markets, resources, and labor has not affected their economic status much, or rather frequently it has weakened them. But the *revolution of expectations* has not bypassed them. Locked in a struggle with poverty while picking up useful items and food from trash heaps in slums, working fifteen hours a day for low wages, which they often cannot keep themselves, or only for some food, these young people stare daily at boards advertising "youth" of both genders on new brands of bikes with "style and performance" called Zippy Spirit, Bravo, or Legend.

At night, or if possible also during the day, to escape boredom, hunger, (domestic) violence, or just for some fun, many (typically) boys and young men, try to see one of the latest Bollywood movies. In overcrowded and therefore overheated cinemas, these "have nots" are supposed to be the first to see the new releases. Yet often diaspora youth in other nations and other young people in India have already seen the same "new" movies on their (illegal) video players at home, weeks before these movies are shown in cinemas. In other respects, too, these young people go without. They cannot, for instance, afford the popcorn, burgers, softies, cold drinks, and fashions that are spotted in the hands of youth and shown in advertisements during movie intermissions.

Lower-class girls and young women can observe how the latest skin creams, shampoos, and fashions make a "Miss India." Generally, however, they do not see these advertisements shown in between soaps portraying middle-class dramas on their own televisions, as many live in dwellings without electricity. Instead, they watch them on sets belonging to the middle-class families where they sweep, cook, and look after the owner's children. In rural areas boys play soccer but without Nikes, Reeboks, or the Indian variety called Liberty sneakers. In fact, they play without wearing shoes at all. Young women carry stones on their heads, work in the fields, and drink self-made beer or water from the Pepsi bottles discarded by other youth who just had a picnic in the same fields.

These "have-nots" feel excluded from the rich dividends that economic reforms in the early 1990s have paid. Undoubtedly, these youth, too, have their way of consuming. Beyond or instead of their daily bare necessities, they might sniff petrol or glue, buy huge quantities of relative cheap tranquilizers that are available everywhere without a prescription, and might use cannabis. Girls sport gold jewelry at weddings and new saris, too, yet their parents are now also expected to provide a Bajaj scooter, a Philips TV, or Titan watches as part of the dowry to be given to the prospective husband's family. Marriages are canceled and girls harassed or even worse, if parents cannot come up with these luxury articles. Some boys and young men would rather spend hard-earned money on a pair of fancy-looking sunglasses than on books or a school uniform—that is, if they are enrolled in schools in the first place. Most of them never attend schools either because they do not exist, there is no incentive, they are too far away, or because no teachers are available. In any case, many drop out before they have finished their basic education, as they or their guardians do not feel this education is of any use to them. Those who desire to study further cannot afford the fees for private tutors or the bribes needed to get admission to schools and colleges. Instead, they start working at ages when other young people are called mere children.

As among the "haves," crime, health-related problems, substance addiction, depression, low self-esteem, suicide, and violent conflicts are part of their daily lives, too. Yet, in the case of most of these less economically well-off youths, it is the lack of consumption, whether or not accompanied by the craving for it, which often inflames violence and crime and leads to destructive and self-destructive behaviors.

Ostentatious consumption has not only divided young people in India into two groups of "haves" and "have-nots" it also antagonizes them. Indeed, although some of these "haves" strive for more equality or denounce ostentatious consumption, others among these young, affluent cosmopolitans along with a few other rich youngsters residing in rural areas, perceive themselves to be miles apart from the "local nuisance" of "third-world India." At the same time, the "have-nots" either aspire to become part of Indian youth culture by listening to Madonna, wearing fake designer jeans, and by eating hamburgers, if they can afford them at all, or they vehemently condemn the forces that preserve inequality. Yet, it is not only poverty that separates consumers from nonconsumers. It is much more and often combined with dimensions of social class. Gender differences divide youth into girls and boys, young women and young men who have to live with separate consumption rules. Some observers have found that the New Economic Policy (NEP) has marginalized women more than men and deprived girls and young women of adequate nourishment, medical care, clothing, and education. Thus, these latest economic reforms adversely affect these girls as consumers. Patriarchal notions that depict them as the preservers of the nation might, for example, prescribe a dress style that rules out Western fashion. Although the rules are different for boys and young men, they must also comply with prescriptions regarding their lifestyle, ideas, and activities.

Apart from gender and class, such things as ethnic, linguistic, and religious differences among young people place them in various hierarchically ordered subcategories and often exclude them from the very category of youth. Rather, they are identified as indigenous people (or *adivasis*), as Muslim minorities, or as lower (or scheduled) castes with different, although formally equal, rights and duties than those pertaining to upper-caste Hindu) youth. Besides, those speaking English or Hindi figure much more in debates on Indian youth than those who are (only) versed in one of the many other Indian languages. There are regional differences as well, as in India the distribution of natural resources and wealth is not equal and consequently youth in various regions face different problems.

Yet, although young people in India are certainly divided by poverty, such things as regional, gender, or ethnic similarities among them can sometimes bridge the gap caused by class hierarchies. They are also uniquely united in their views on adults, in particular those ruling the country. The level of official political involvement among young people in India is considered to be lower than that of previous generations. This is not, however, due to young people being more satisfied with those adults who rule. To the contrary, many young people seem to have lost interest in

politics. They particularly mention the corruption among politicians and the mismanagement of state officials as reasons for dissatisfaction. Clearly, the Indian nation-state and its young people have expectations of each other, and both are often disappointed by the behavior of the other.

The GoI knows that globalization, in the sense of economic restructuring and the increased reliance on market mechanisms or the general increased inflow of new and different goods, ideas, and technologies, has not only created new openings for young people in India but has also caused stagnation and regression. In order to be able to depend on its youth as "the future of the nation," the nation-state therefore has to protect the interests of not only economically privileged young people but of all privileged and disadvantaged young people between the ages of fifteen and thirty-five. The GoI thus purports to bridge the gap between "the haves" and "the have-nots," by making the former category less exclusive. In practice this has meant special policies for unemployed youth, youth of scheduled castes in rural settings, youth in urban settings, Muslim youth, mentally and physically challenged youth, girls, youth in backward areas, and youth with drug addictions. Of the fifteen major international legal instruments adopted by intergovernmental bodies of the UN system relating to the human rights of youth, the GoI has ratified or acceded to the following six: medical examination of young persons; night work of young persons (in industries); suppression of the traffic in persons and of the exploitation of the prostitution of others; abolition of slavery, the slave trade, and institutions and practices similar to slavery; civil and political rights and economic, social, and cultural rights.

The GoI has also set up the Committee on National Youth Programmes (CONYP) to develop guidelines for the national youth policy, chaired by the prime minister of India. The committee, an advisory body, has members who are ministers in charge of various youth-related depart-ments, provincial ministers, members of parliament, representatives of political parties and of several nongovernmental youth organizations, and young people of various socioeconomic backgrounds. This body advises the government on measures for implementing the plan of action of the national youth policy, reviews coordina-tion between departments of the central and state governments and voluntary orga-nizations involved, and provides feedback on the implementation of the national youth programs. The government has also established youth centers aimed at the employment capabilities of rural youth by organizing leadership training programs and social services. National services schemes are aimed at involving university and high-school students in rural recon-struction activities to assist the weaker sec-tions of society.

The ultimate goal of the GoI seems to be to unite all young people as one Indian youth. Through its national youth policy, the Department of Youth Affairs and Sports in the Ministry of Human Resources Devel-opment, in cooperation with other youth-serving ministries, youth organizations, and a network of youth research centers, tries to do the following: (1) instill in youth a deep awareness of and respect for the principles and values enshrined in the Indian constitution; (2) promote among youth an awareness of Indian historical and cultural heritage and imbue them with a sense of pride and national identity; (3) help develop in youth the qualities of dis-cipline, self-reliance, justice and fair play; (4) provide youth with maximal access to education, which apart from developing their all-around personality would equip them with professional and vocational training for employment and self-employ-ment opportunities; and (5) make youth aware of international issues and involve them in promoting world peace.

Yet, confronted with young people's pro-tests organized in student and ethnic move-ments, youth wings of political parties, feminist organizations, peace movements, or movements for environmental protec-tion and protest in less organized ways, the GoI does not always see young people as preservers of the nation-state, at least as it would define it. These movements have also shown that youth cannot be defined on the basis of age alone, and the GoI is also aware that its young citizens do not constitute a homogeneous category but are divided by class, gender, ethnicity, and religion. Responding to these various and dissimilar movements in which young people take part and which the GoI at times considers threatening, the GoI has set up two youth coordinating bodies in India.

First, there is the Indian Committee of Youth Organizations (IYCO), founded in 1981. In 1996 there were about 360 mem-bers of the IYCO. It is directed by a national conference, which elects officers who administer the daily work of the organiza-tion. Its main aim is to provide a common platform for Indian youth organizations, thus to establish communication channels between them and to coordinate their activities. It is engaged in training mem-bers of their organizations and disseminat-ing information about the activities of their members, relevant policies and programs of youth-serving ministries, and the activ-ities of transnational youth and youth-serving organizations. The IYCO cooperates with all governmental youth-serving agen-cies and is affiliated with the World Assem-bly of Youth (WAY) on the international level.

Second, there is another youth-coordi-nating body called the Indian Assembly of Youth (IAY). This organization was estab-lished in 1955 with the objective of promot-ing the interests and social and economic conditions of Indian youth. To reach that aim, the IAY focuses on problems related to youth and analyzes them on national and international levels. The organization describes itself as a national voluntary youth organization, but the number of affili-ated youth groups is not stated. Its activi-ties are mainly the holding of conferences, seminars, workshops, camps, and campaigns and the sponsoring of an international youth center. Those activities concentrate especially on the environment and sustainable development but also on education and literacy, rural development, the advancement of girls and young women, and the fight against hunger and poverty. On the international level the IAY is affiliated with the Asian Youth Council and the Caretakers of Environment International (CEI).

The GoI has not succeeded in its goal of creating unity out of diversity. Judging from the various voices of young people in India, the overall picture demonstrates diversity. These young people not only have different values and orientations but also exhibit dissimilar behaviors. Young people all over India are involved in massive movements related to issues of cultural identity and economic backwardness. An overview of the numerous and extremely diverse activities undertaken by young people in India indeed shows young people want more and to transform India. Yet, whereas some fight for more student power, others unite for the rights of *dalits* or lower castes, child laborers, female children, mentally and physically challenged children, or more regional and cultural autonomy. At times, "the have" and "the have-not" youth fight together to save a forest, ban nuclear experimentation, stop the construction of big dams, or in support of or against a war; yet at other times and for different reasons they oppose each other, be it on the basis of caste, class, or religion. There is indeed growing unrest and protest among these young people, warning and demonstrating that wealth alongside abject poverty can, in turn, lead to violence and anarchy-like conditions. They express concern that globalization and consumerist capitalism lead to overconsumption of resources and aberrations such as global warming. Some young people warn that globalization can cause greater divisions among young people—nationally as well as globally. Other Indian youth feel that (Western) consumerism, that is, production for unending con-

sumption, will never put them on equal footing with other young people on the globe as there is simply not enough for all. They fear that with the rapid depletion of nonrenewable resources, consumerism involves an unstoppable march toward ecological suicide. Others feel that the culture of consumerism leads not only to the (economic) marginalization of some but also to cultural impoverishment of all.

Thus, values and political positions differ widely. Whereas some fight against decisions made by the International Monetary Fund (IMF), the World Trade Organization (WTO) and support the Nuclear Non-Proliferation Treaty and abolishment of the capital punishment in India, others fight against job reservations, reject the Comprehensive Test Ban Treaty (CTBT), support antiterrorism laws and *Hindutva* or the supremacy of Hinduism in India. There are young people whose main concern is the alleged lower birthrate among Hindus compared to that of Muslims, the increased unemployment among upper-caste Hindus, and the erosion of "Indian" values. Others put all effort in literacy missions, agitation against displacement, or fight for the rehabilitation of rape victims and girls involved in the "flesh trade."

All Indian youth, at least at the level of national law, have equal civil, political, economic, social, and cultural rights, and all citizens aged eighteen and over are eligible to vote. Moreover, one of the central themes of the national youth policy is *youth empowerment*. Yet, it is difficult for certain groups to avail themselves of some or even any of these rights. Consequently, a huge difference exists not only between female and male youth, but also between those who are literate and illiterate, employed and unemployed, poor and rich, and members of so-called minority communities and young people who belong to so-called forward communities, or the "creamy layer" of society. Some ask for drinking water, electricity, food, or a dwelling place other than the pavement on which they live, whereas others demand jobs, tax cuts, and lower fuel prices and plane fares. Their battles are unequal as globalization is not an even phenomenon and influences social groups among these young people in different ways and equips them with more or less social, economic, and cultural power.

Yet, diversity of demands and values does not mean utter confusion among young people. Indeed, young people (rich or poor) live in an India where, amid extreme poverty, a few enjoy ostentatious consumption. But this is the world they know, one in which they are growing up and finding their ways. In this India some young people prefer to educate street children in their free time rather than shopping at malls; some work in the malls while living in *chawls* and prefer to buy fake designer jeans and T-shirts instead of fruit with the little money they have earned by selling real jeans to young university students. Globalization has thus indeed divided young people into "the haves" and "the have-nots," as well as into those who want more and those who want less.

However, this fact seems to cause much more confusion among older people than among youth themselves. For the older generations this is a new India, which has resulted in a new battleground among themselves: between the traditional and the modern, the old and the new, often understood as a battleground between Western versus Indian values and lifestyles, between consumerism and adequate consumption. Although the GoI seems to have difficulty in defining the kind of national identity it wants to instill in the younger generations, the latter have never lived in another India and clearly have their own, albeit diverse, coping mechanisms. They do not show much interest in organized politics and, only a very small percentage believes that the government is able to solve their problems. Nevertheless, many among these fifteen- to thirty-five-year-olds feel they have their own solutions. Although the solutions designed by these youth might not produce a unified Indian youth culture or will mean the victory for "Indian culture" as defined by adults, the GoI should not be seeing these demands of its "liberalization's children" as a threat. After all, *they* constitute new India, and they might teach adults how to develop in it.

See also Australia, Youth Activism in; Demographic Trends Affecting the World's Youth; Eastern Europe, Youth and Citizenship in; Europe, Comparing Youth Activism in; European Identity and Citizenship; Immigrant Youth in Europe—Turks in Germany; Immigrant Youth in the United States; Indonesia, Youth Activism in; Nigeria, Youth Activism in; Palestinian *Intifada*; Russia, Youth Activism in; Serbia, Youth Activism in (1990–2000); Soweto Youth Activism (South Africa); State and Youth, The; Statute of the Child and Adolescent (Brazil); Tiananmen Square Massacre (1989); Transnational Identity; Transnational Youth Activism; Turkey, Youth Activism in; United Nations, Youth Activism and; Xenophobia; Zapatista Rebellion (Mexico); Zionist Youth Organizations.

Recommended Reading

Baruah, A. K., ed. (2002). *Student Power in North East India: Understanding Student Movements*. New Delhi: Regency Publications.

Devasia, L., and Devasia, V. V., eds. (1991). *Girl Child in India*. New Delhi: Ashish Publishing House.

Jayaswal, R. (1992). *Modernization and Youth in India*. Jaipur and New Delhi: Rawat Publications.

Kripalani, M. (October 11, 1999). "India's Youth: They Are Capitalist-Minded and They Are Changing the Nation Forever." *Business Week*.

Liechty, M. (1995). "Media, Markets and Modernization: Youth Identities and the Experience of Modernity in Kathmandu, Nepal." In *Youth Cultures: A Cross-Cultural Perspective*, edited by V. Amit-Talai and H. Wulff. London and New York: Routledge, pp. 166–202.

Mishra, V. D. (1993). *Youth Culture: A Comparative Study in the Indian Context*. New Delhi: Inter-India Publications.

Mohammed, N., and Matin, A., eds. (1995). *Indian Youth: Problems and Prospects*. New Delhi: Ashish Publishing House.

Ruhela, S. P., ed. (2001). *Sociology of the Youth Culture in India*. New Delhi: Indian Publisher Distributors.

Sethi, R. M., ed. (1999). *Globalization, Culture and Women's Development*. New Delhi and Jaipur: Rawat Publications.

Sinha-Kerkhoff, K. (1999). "The Experience of Globalization: Indian Youth and Non-Consumption." In *Modernity on a Shoestring. Dimensions of Globalization, Consumption and Development in Africa and Beyond*, edited by R. Fardon, W. van Binsbergen, and R. van Dijk. Leiden. London: EIDOS, pp 117–141.

United Nations (2002). Country Profiles on the Situation of Youth: India. See http://esa.un.org/socdev/unyin/countrya.asp? countrycode=in.

Kathinka Sinha-Kerkhoff

Indonesia, Youth Activism in. Youth activism in Indonesia takes many forms, violent and nonviolent, and occurs for a variety of political and social reasons. Youth activism has a long and rather heroic history in the archipelago, signaling not only civic engagement but also political and religious struggles. There have been a number of unified mass protests and actions by youth that have led to the removal of colonial powers and the overthrow of governments. The logic and practices of contemporary youth activism have been greatly influenced by the rapid growth of easily accessible information technology and by urban expansion. In Indonesia the term "youth" in relation to "activism," connotes protest actions and agitation by people under the age of thirty (*pemuda*), rather than by adolescent youth (*remaja*). For example, the nationalist revolution is sometimes referred to as the *revolusi pemuda*. *Pemuda Rakyat* was the Communist youth organization under President Sukarno, while *Pemuda Pancasila* was the anticommunist youth organization under President Suharto.

Significant motivations for youth activism in Indonesia have included indigenous rights and national unity (1945–1949), pro-communism (1950s), anticommunism (1965–1966), pro-democracy (1998), and militant Islam (ongoing). In short, young people, especially students, have been the motor for political change during the last four decades. In the new century, however, youth activism seems fragmented around a number of causes and dissatisfactions with little observable unity between groups. Moreover, it is often difficult to distinguish between genuine political and religious youth activism and vigilante groups of young men (*preman*)—a shadowy "civil militia" of mercenary thugs—available for hire to anybody who will pay them to agitate and cause unrest. Many commentators argue that contemporary violent "political" activism in Indonesia has its origins in the repressive strategies of the Suharto state since 1965 and 1966, starting with the original bloodbath in which over 1 million alleged Communists were killed.

Youth activism can be found in all regions of Indonesia, not just major cities. Demonstrations are almost daily events. The attitude of older people seems to be that nonviolent protest by youth, especially students, is really just part of normal everyday life. During political campaigns, a common form of youth activism is *massa*—an impressive cavalcade of motorbikes, trucks, banners held aloft, music, and loudspeakers, followed by young people on foot. *Massa* cavalcades are male dominated, hold up traffic, and usually end with a rally and address by political leaders or clerics, often followed by a rock concert. Large-scale protests against price increases and unemployment in the relentless economic crisis, by contrast, tend to be more static and include both sexes. Hundreds of young people sit or stand for hours outside government buildings, chanting with placards. This is also common practice for anti-Western protests by large Muslim youth organizations like KAMMI. Other forms of nonviolent public protest include street theater enactments, *berpoesi* (reading revolutionary poetry aloud), performing revolutionary songs, and burning flags and effigies.

Violent public youth activism, when distinguished from the activities of civil militia groups, is driven by strong political or religious convictions. Furthermore, it is not uncommon for youthful supporters of rival political groups, or even rival Muslim groups, to fight pitched battles in the streets. Tactics include throwing stones or missiles at opponents and police, blockading streets with uprooted trees, vandalism, spraying graffiti, and looting businesses and shops (usually Chinese owned). More violent forms include overturning and torching cars; bombing and burning homes, shops, churches, and government buildings; mugging, robbing, and raping householders; occupying target offices and throwing workers bodily into the street; and even torture and murder. Identification of perpetrators of these actions does not happen often because they wear cloths over their faces or conduct activities at night. Members of the public fear retaliation if they come forward with evidence. The police and the military often retreat altogether from street events of political or religious violence, sometimes because they are outnumbered, sometimes to avoid provocation, and sometimes because they are behind the violence in the first place for profit motives.

Youth activism in Indonesia also has a less public face. During the Suharto years, leftist groups—indeed any groups that questioned the political status quo—were outlawed with only three political parties permitted and no free and open elections. In such conditions, groups of young people desiring political change or those in favor of an Islamic state, for example, had to meet in secret and find covert ways of disseminating information to members and followers. As faxes, Web-connected computers, and mobile phones started to become available, it became easier and easier to communicate inside and between such groups through e-mail, SMS, and faxed updates. Technologically facilitated communication and dissemination of information made these activist groups much more effective in the final years of the Suharto regime. Leaders and organizers could contact supporters and sympathizers very quickly to organize protests and actions. Many of those who took leading roles were university students with skills and ready access to information technology. Around the same time, Indonesians were able to watch satellite television through *parabola* dishes. Young activists could therefore see with their own eyes the nonviolent mass protests that brought down the Marcos government in the neighboring Philippines, even if Indonesian television stations downplayed or ignored the event. Connecting to the World Wide Web meant that Indonesian activist groups could learn about ideas, strategies, and examples from similar groups worldwide.

Some of the significant characteristics of youth activism in Indonesia can be understood through two important examples: the expansion of Islamic youth activism since the 1980s and the massive youth-led protests which brought down the Suharto government in 1998. Turning first to Islamic extremism, the resurgence of religious fundamentalism can be understood as an apparent coping mechanism for the recent rapid changes experienced by many young people around the world as an outcome of globalization. Liberal Islam was actually the dominant trend among committed Muslims in the student movement throughout the 1970s, but by the 1980s more radical trends had appeared. Van Bruinessen argues that it was the depoliticization imposed on local (Indonesian) Islam under Suharto that caused a turn to "global" Islamic thought, particularly by young intellectuals. After the crucial involvement of youth activists in the demise of Sukarno in 1966, student activism on both sides of the political spectrum continued into the reign of President Suharto, prompting him to introduce the 1978 campus normalization law, which squelched all political activity at universities. The ideas of the Saudi Arabia–based Muslim Brotherhood then became a major focus of orientation, as young Islamic activists turned their attention to the Middle East, claiming this as an intellectual, rather than political, exercise.

A loosely affiliated movement called *tarbiyah* (education) came to replace overt Islamic political activism on campuses after 1978. In particular, groups met for discussion of radical Islamic texts at the Salman mosque in Bandung at the Institute of Technology. During this time of marked repression, their actions and teachings were quietly disseminated, inspiring young Muslims elsewhere, particularly in universities and Islamic boarding schools. The Bandung group itself was inspired by two Iranian authors, Ali Shari'ati and Murtaza Mutahhari, associated with the revolution in Iran. The daring interpretations and revolutionary message of these two writers fostered a widespread interest in Shi'ism among politically disaffected students. At the same time, young Indonesian scholars were traveling overseas and becoming exposed to sometimes radically opposed Islamic ideas, for example mystical Sufism on the one hand, and ascetic Wahhabi'ism on the other.

Support for Shi'a Islam brought its youthful, campus-based followers into conflict with older Muslim radicals from the DDII, the proselytizing *dakwah* council established in 1967 and fiercely opposed to Shi'a teachings. At the same time, remnant sympathizers of the *Darul Islam* group which had fought against Communism in the mid-1960s were encouraging the emergence of a violently political group of young men—the *Komando Jihad.* The sentiments of this group, supported by the DDII and influenced by the teachings of clerics such as Abu Bakar Ba'asyir (later associated with terrorist group *Jema'ah Islamiyah*), were virulently anti-Western and anti-Christian, committed to creating an Islamic state in Indonesia, in the region, and eventually in the world. Arson and bombing of churches, night clubs, and cinemas occurred in the 1970s and 1980s. The mid-1980s saw the heavy-handed enforcement of *Pancasila* (the secular constitutional doctrine of unity in diversity) by the state on all groups and associations. Anyone who publicly expressed other ideolog-ical positions was arrested. The year 1984 saw the violent repression of a public protest in Tanjung Priok Harbour, Jakarta. The outrage of key underground Islamic activist groups precipitated a wave of violent incidents including the bombing of the Buddhist Borobudur Temple, symbol of Indonesia's pre-Islamic past. Furthermore, traveling via Malaysia, numbers of young Indonesian Muslims traveled to Pakistan and Afghanistan to receive guerrilla training in the cause of *jihad.*

By the mid-1990s, some Islamic activist groups had come together for the purposes of nonviolent political activism to bring about *reformasi* in Indonesia, while others had diverged further into violent (but usually covert) *jihad,* the latter favoring the union of the whole Muslim world as a superpower governed by a caliphate like those in ancient times. Two Muslim activist groups attractive to young people which serve as examples of ideological divergence are KAMMI on the one hand, and Laskar Jihad on the other. A nonviolent student protest organization, KAMMI was founded by *dakwah* groups from some sixty campus mosques and had links with the earlier *tarbiyah* movement which proposes that, in theory, Islam and democracy are compatible. Many young women wearing the white *jilbab* (veil) were enthusiastic members. Some mass protests against the Suharto government in 1997 were made solely by girls and women, sitting silently in rows and blocking the street. By contrast, Laskar Jihad, which first came to public attention in early 2000, was opposed to democracy and in favor of revolutionary armed struggle in the face of alleged "war" by the United States and Israel on Islam. Until 2000, Laskar Jihad was a puritanical intellectual movement, influenced by Saudi-based Wahhabi Salafism. Spurred on by zeal for *jihad* against Christian enemies of Islam and supported by Middle East mentors, Laskar Jihad opened secret camps to train young men as "holy warriors" ready to die in battle against infidels (Christians) in the eastern islands of the

Moluccas, which many of them did. It is reported that after the tragedy of September 11, support funds were suddenly severed, leaving many of these young men penniless, stranded far from Java in a hostile environment.

The second example of contemporary youth activism concerns the forced resignation of President Suharto in 1998. Suharto's Indonesia, usually referred to as the New Order period, attempted an expansionist model of modern industrialization and development, while keeping authority firmly centralized and a tight lid on political dissent and activism. At the same time, an entire generation of young people was growing up better educated than their parents, earning more, and far more open to the world through new technologies. In short, the nascent political knowledge possessed by the age cohort of young people in Indonesia in the 1980s and 1990s was different than that of preceding generations. During Suharto's New Order regime, families across the archipelago who had survived the turmoil and bloody purges of the beginning of the New Order (1965–1968) tended to avoid even talking about politics, and their children were similarly discouraged. There were sham "elections" and the Golkar party was always reelected with Suharto as president. Political repression was a way of life. By the end of the 1980s though, international pressure led to some deregulation and the society seemed more open. Certainly, the following decade saw the emergence of many radical Islamic and political youth groups. However, these groups were only the tip of an iceberg of discontent. In Indonesia by 1997 there was a whole generation of young people who were not willing to shut up, who wanted to talk about politics and did so loudly. The president, his family, his cronies, his political party (Golkar), and the military were involved in ever-increasing amounts of corruption, graft, cover-up, and violent actions against civilians. By the time the Asian economic crash hit Indonesia in 1997 most people had had enough. Young

people, particularly students, took to the streets.

By then, sophisticated communications and information technology meant that significant news updates about government corruption and the economic crisis (although censored in the official press) were widely available to student activists, labor activists, and nongovernmental organizations (NGOs). Many of the young activists who came to prominence during this decade grew up in the rapidly expanding middle class, in which confidence and entrepreneurship had become valued personal qualities. There was sufficient anger and shared desire for change among young people by 1997, as well as organizational capacities and skills, to bring about a loose coalition of youth activist groups committed to bringing down the Suharto government, even if they had different ideas about what they wanted afterward. Significantly, it was youth activism—student groups, including KAMMI and a number of other Muslim youth activist groups, as well as thousands of ordinary university and high-school students in major cities, that constituted the major force of this movement. Senior public figures and older activists only joined later.

At first the military and police cracked down heavily on the young protesters, detaining over 300 as political prisoners in March 1998. In early May, six students from Trisakti University in Jakarta were shot and killed during demonstrations. Countless other activists disappeared. Meanwhile at an international level, Suharto had lost the confidence of the international community and the rupiah (Indonesia's currency) was in free fall. The print media started telling the truth about the corruption, nepotism, and the political crisis, even as newspapers and journals were progressively banned for doing this. We may perhaps draw some parallels with the student uprising of 1968 in Paris, France. In both cases what began as a primarily student-led mass demonstration grew into a situation of mass civil unrest involving workers as well as public intellectuals, so that whole cities shut down as street violence raged. In 1998 there were riots almost everywhere lasting over five days. Most of the actual violence was likely carried out not by activists and demonstrators but by *preman*, militia-style gangs acting for vested state interests, including the military, to bring about instability and the chance to snatch political power. Around May 20, 1998, in significant public spaces across the country, but particularly outside the parliament in Jakarta, youth-led demonstrations assembled in largely nonviolent protests to call for the resignation of President Suharto. Thousands and thousands chanted "*reformasi*" (reform) and "*turunkan Suharto*" (bring down Suharto) for many hours. The military did not intervene. Senior figures in government and business had turned against the president. Suharto made a public speech of resignation on May 21.

This example, as well as the evolution of contemporary Islamic activist groups, demonstrates three important aspects of youth activism in Indonesia. First, there is a long history of youth activism in the country. At certain significant historical points in time, the majority of the population has supported the radical stand taken by a loose coalition of youth groups (*pemuda*) to force constitutional change. Second, at such times there can be mass rioting and violence one day and silent mass protest the next. This is because there are youth activist groups—political, religious, and NGOs—committed to intellectual expansion, public involvement, and nonviolent action for change. However, around the same set of causes, there are also extremist groups committed to indoctrination of followers, covert operations, and violent action in pursuit of their revolutionary goals. Third, contemporary Indonesian youth activism, while emphatically local in its location and practices, looks outside the country more and more for inspiration and examples, using modern information technology.

A final point is that the history of youth activism in Indonesia is cyclical. Groups of activists are drawn together in common cause on specific, often spectacular, occasions, then split apart to follow sectarian goals. For example, after the resignation of Suharto, while many Muslim activists supported the swearing in of Habibie, the deputy president, to lead the country, the secular wing of the *reformasi* movement considered Habibie a relic of the New Order and demanded total reform. In the aftermath of Habibie's appointment, extreme polarization of previously cooperating groups occurred. Certain new militant Muslim groups came to dominate street politics and strove to intimidate leftist and liberal groups, often with the assistance of *preman* civilian militias. Meanwhile, other young Islamic activists were searching for a relevant non-Western liberalism via intellectually open Islamic discourse, initiating a dialog with the heirs of the Marxist left. On January 22, 2003, a secular and leftist National Coalition to bring about *reformasi total* (total reform of the nation) was created. Of forty-five affiliated organizations, twenty-eight were NGOs, trade unions, and political parties; twelve were student groups, the largest source of membership; five were youth activist groups. However, since then the National Coalition has not found a unified political voice.

The early years of the twenty-first century thus find Indonesian youth activism rather fragmented. Certainly there is no single unifying cause at present. Yet demonstrations by ordinary citizens and students over food prices, civic decay, and unemployment still occur almost daily in Indonesian cities, as significant economic problems have not been solved. And rarely a day goes by without public protest from one of the radical Islamic groups. We may note that recent events of global and local terrorism have changed the way the world regards Islamic youth activism in Indonesia. Moreover, the tragedy of September 11, 2001, the Bali bombing in October 2002 in which over 200 were killed (mostly Australians), the arrest of Abu Bakar Ba'asyir, and the subsequent U.S. military actions in Afghanistan and Iraq have only served to strengthen the divide between different kinds of Islamic activist groups inside Indonesia. The September 2004 bombing of the Australian embassy in Jakarta further illustrates this point with many moderate Islamic youth groups condemning the action. Certainly many of these same groups still argue stridently for the installation of *Syari'ah* (Koranic) law in the firm belief that this is the only answer to endemic practices of corruption and graft in their nation. Yet most contemporary Muslim student and youth activism involves public debate. It should not be automatically assumed that young Islamic activists are members of extreme fundamentalist groups involved in terrorist conspiracies. Real Islamic terrorist groups such as Jema'ah Islamiyah certainly do exist, just as violent Christian militia groups do, but the very nature of their revolutionary projects means they operate underground rather than in the public domain.

See also Australia, Youth Activism in; Demographic Trends Affecting the World's Youth; Eastern Europe, Youth and Citizenship in; Europe, Comparing Youth Activism in; European Identity and Citizenship; Immigrant Youth in Europe—Turks in Germany; Immigrant Youth in the United States; India, Youth Activism in; Nigeria, Youth Activism in; Palestinian *Intifada*; Russia, Youth Activism in; Serbia, Youth Activism in (1990–2000); Soweto Youth Activism (South Africa); State and Youth, The; Statute of the Child and Adolescent (Brazil); Tiananmen Square Massacre (1989); Transnational Identity; Transnational Youth Activism; Turkey, Youth Activism in; United Nations, Youth Activism and; Xenophobia; Zapatista Rebellion (Mexico); Zionist Youth Organizations.

Recommended Reading

Aditjondro, G. (2002). "Suharto Has Gone—But the Regime Has Not Changed." In *Stealing from the People: Sixteen Studies of Corruption in Indonesia*, edited by R. Holloway. Jakarta: Aksara Foundation.

Aspinall, E. (1999). "The Indonesian Student Uprising of 1998." In *Reformasi: Crisis and Change in Indonesia*, edited by A. Budiman, B. Hatley, and D. Kingsbury. Clayton: Monash Asia Institute.

Lane, M. (July 17, 2002). "Indonesia: No Change without Youth." *Green Left Weekly*. See http://www.greenleft.org.au/back/2002/500/500p22.htm.

Lindsey, T. (2001). "The Criminal State: *Premanisme* and the New Indonesia." In *Indonesia Today: Challenges of History*, edited by G. Lloyd and S. Smith. Singapore: Institute of Southeast Asian Studies.

Nilan, P. (Winter 2003). "Young People, Politics and Religion in Indonesia." *The International Scope Review*, 4, 8.

Robison, R., and Goodman, D. (1996). "The New Rich in Asia: Economic Development, Social Status and Political Consciousness." In *The New Rich in Asia*, edited by R. Robison and D. Goodman. London: Routledge.

Salim, A., and Azyumardi, A., eds. (2003). *Shari'a and Politics in Modern Indonesia*. Singapore: Institute of Southeast Asian Studies.

Schwarz, A. (1994). *A Nation in Waiting: Indonesia in the 1990s*. Sydney: Allen and Unwin.

Van Bruinessen, M. (2002). "Genealogies of Islamic Radicalism in Post-Suharto Indonesia." *South East Asia Research*, 10 (2): 117–154.

Winter, J. (April 2002). "The Political Impact of New Information Sources and Technologies in Indonesia." *Gazette*, 64 (2): 109–119.

Pam Nilan

Innovation Center for Community and Youth Development. *See* Youth Leadership for Development Initiative (YLDI).

Innovations in Civic Participation (ICP). Service is an important form of youth activism and the field is growing worldwide. On six continents millions of ordinary young people of both privileged and disadvantaged backgrounds are using their heads, hearts, and hands to tackle local and global problems through national and community service. Innovations in Civic Participation (ICP) is at the forefront of these efforts, and its experiences working to provide young people around the world with opportunities to play an active role in their communities through service is instructive.

The word service means different things to different people around the world. Some people associate service with the military. Others equate it with sporadic volunteering. Still others think that an activity can only be considered service if the participants are not paid. The Global Service Institute (GSI) defines service as "an organized period of substantial engagement and contribution to the local, national, or world community, recognized and valued by society, with minimal or no monetary contribution to the participant." This working definition of service most closely describes the type of activity that ICP supports through program and policy development.

Service is an important and effective strategy for addressing contemporary social, political, and economic challenges and it is essential for engaging young people. At 1.7 billion, today's youth (ages fifteen to twenty-four as defined by the United Nations) comprise the largest generation ever to enter the transition to adulthood. In many developing countries three-quarters of the population is under the age of thirty. The values, attitudes, and skills acquired by youth—and especially the choices made by the current generation of young people—will influence the course of current events and shape the future in fundamental ways.

At the same time, there is increasing concern about the status of young people, particularly in countries transitioning from war where many demilitarized youth possess limited education and life skills. For many youth limited access to employment or further education and training opportunities translates into disempowerment and often results in an increased sense of fatalism and weakened initiative. In the absence of opportunities risky behaviors such as drug use, unsafe sex, and gang violence all too often fill the void and perpetuate the cycle of poverty, unemployment, illegal activity, lost production, and lost opportunity.

The causes for the problems that youth face worldwide are complex and the solutions will not be simple. Nevertheless, it is imperative to engage youth in the process. Although the concept of "youth as resources" is increasingly acknowledged, the practice of actively engaging youth in activities as full partners is still not fully accepted. International experience has shown that service organizations that engage young people build citizenship skills and can help society to appreciate young people—and help young people to view themselves as a resource for change, rather than as a troubled, at-risk group.

By serving their communities in meaningful, structured ways, young people are gaining invaluable life skills that are as important as mathematics and writing. They are learning to work with others who are different from themselves, learning to be entrepreneurs, but also to be team players. They are learning about complex issues firsthand by talking to people affected by them and becoming part of the solution. Both in the United States and around the world there are efforts to encourage, strengthen, and expand this new approach to activism.

Founded in 2001, ICP envisions a world in which people of all ages and in every nation are actively engaged in improving their lives through national and community service. To achieve this goal, ICP provides expertise, ideas, information, research, and advocacy support in the United States and around the world to develop and strengthen policies and programs that promote civic engagement through service. ICP's recent work includes conducting research to assess the youth-service policy environment worldwide, awarding small grants to support innovative youth-service policy development around the world, building the field of service through regional centers in Latin America and southern Africa, and hosting and participating in national and international forums. ICP has worked with numerous universities, national and local governments, nongovernmental organizations, and multilateral organizations in over twenty countries on five continents.

ICP grew out of an international Ford Foundation workshop in Costa Rica in

2000, Youth Involvement as a Strategy for Social, Economic, and Democratic Development. Organized by Susan Stroud, now executive director of ICP, the workshop looked at what society is doing to prepare young people to address problems in their communities and around the world. The consensus was that while education and job training are essential, another strategy is emerging as a new and necessary way for youth to prepare for life's challenges: service.

Stroud and professor Michael Sherraden of the Center for Social Development (CSD) at Washington University then created the idea of the Global Service Institute (GSI). GSI would increase the understanding of service by supporting and disseminating research and information, assisting governments and nonprofit organizations around the world to design and implement innovative service programs and policies based on best practices, and building a global information network. In 2001 they received funding to realize their dream and developed a partnership to move the project forward—CSD would head up GSI's research and global information network while ICP would focus on program and policy development.

Three years later ICP remains dedicated to helping build the international field of youth service through program and policy development. To do this, ICP does the following: (1) provides technical assistance to organizations and governments for service policy and program development, (2) supports research and policy development targeting civic participation and youth service in different countries, (3) stimulates new thinking in the field of national and community service in the United States and around the world, (4) shares a wealth of knowledge about what works in national and community service, and (5) encourages dialog between disciplines in order to illustrate the potential of service in addressing critical social issues. The following examples demonstrate some of the different ways that ICP is working to support the field.

Before founding ICP, Stroud worked on various service initiatives in Russia, Mexico, and Italy and was one of the White House architects of the National and Community Trust Act of 1993, the legislation that led to the creation of a national service program in the United States called AmeriCorps. As ICP's executive director, she is now helping the British government develop a national service program, as an expert advisor to a commission launched in May 2004. This commission is investigating the feasibility of implementing a national youth-volunteering program in England. The commission will look to other national youth-volunteering strategies, such as AmeriCorps, as possible models. The creation of the commission has been accompanied by an increase of over 1.3 million volunteers in England between 2001 and 2003, a number that exceeds expectations and further highlights the growth of the service movement.

ICP is supporting the development of youth-service policy through its global youth-service policy scan, an ongoing exploratory study assessing the status and configuration of policies that involve young people in community service and volunteerism in every country around the world. The study is seeking to develop the knowledge base by providing descriptive information and to explore the context within which national youth-service policies can emerge and thrive.

ICP is also supporting the development of youth-service policy through its small grants program. Out of 170 applicants, eleven grants were given to organizations in different countries around the world to support the creation, implementation, and sustainability of youth-service policy. In Bosnia and Herzegovina (BiH), OSMIJEH, the Association for Psychosocial Help and Development of Voluntary Work, is the national volunteer center. OSMIJEH has mobilized over 6,000 youth, including people from all groups of society. Muslims, Serbs, and Croats work side by side; local people interact with refugees and displaced people. Young volunteers help reconstruct rural villages, tutor in elementary schools, and care for disabled children and the isolated elderly. Youth run radio programs, help with translation, and organize public events, elections, seminars and conferences. These programs help to combat feelings of hopelessness by providing young people with opportunities to become actively involved in the rebuilding of their country. OSMIJEH is now working to create a national network of NGOs and government agencies that will work to further youth service and advocate for a national youth-service policy.

Another critical activity is stimulating new thinking in the field of national and community service. ICP and the National Association of Service and Conservation Corps (NASCC) are working to encourage AmeriCorps programs to offer more transitional support to their corps members. By facilitating an extensive network of national and site-based partnerships, leveraging additional resources for transition services, and offering technical assistance, NASCC and ICP are focusing on opportunities that allow at-risk corps members to use the skills they have acquired as a result of their experience in a service or conservation corps and the AmeriCorps education award. The goal is to build toward future educational opportunities and careers with long-term potential.

New thinking is also needed about different ways in which service might help alleviate the teacher shortage and teacher-retention issues in the United States. Most AmeriCorps programs involve service in an educational setting, and many AmeriCorps members are interested in staying in the field. Over 50 percent of the members in the Washington Reading Corps (an AmeriCorps program in Washington state) said they were interested in a career in teaching. Most were committed to staying in the high-need areas where they served as AmeriCorps members. Working with the Washington Commission on National and Community Service (WCNCS)

and office of the superintendent of public instruction (OSPI) in Washington state, ICP is finding ways to encourage more AmeriCorps members to remain in the field of education. Some of the ideas on the table include an outreach strategy and partnership development between the Washington Reading Corps and universities and colleges that provide teacher certification in Washington.

In Latin America and the Caribbean, ICP has organized a series of working meetings with the Inter-American Development Bank Youth Unit (IDB Youth), Centro Latinoamericano de Aprendizaje y Servicio Solidario (CLAYSS), and numerous other leaders in Latin America and the Caribbean (LAC) to discuss ways to strategically build the field of youth service and civic participation in the region. Some of the activities discussed include organizing regional workshops; developing networks of practitioners, policymakers, scholars, youth organizations, and funders; developing information clearinghouses; publishing newsletters and other periodicals; collecting research on service; pursuing regional resource development; and offering training opportunities. Similarly, working with the Volunteer and Service Enquiry Southern Africa in Johannesburg (VOSESA), ICP is encouraging dialog in southern Africa with the ultimate goal of strengthening good practice in the region.

An integral component of ICP's work is information dissemination, especially with regard to what works in national and community service. Much of this information is shared through *Service News Worldwide*, a monthly newsletter intended to highlight information pertaining to the rapidly evolving field of service. Each issue includes updates on new service programs and initiatives, articles on work in progress regarding service policy development, information on upcoming events, awards, and opportunities, and a virtual discussion forum.

Another publication, *Service Enquiry*, analyzes the experience of service and volunteerism in different parts of the world.

It targets practitioners, nongovernmental organizations, academics in higher education, policymakers, and researchers and analysts in different parts of the world. The first edition was published in the fall of 2003 and focused on the latest developments in service policy, service programs, and the impact of service on democratic values, citizenship, and socioeconomic development.

These examples highlight some of the work that ICP is doing to ensure that more people around the world can play active roles in improving their lives through national and community service. However, it is the energy and commitment of young people that are driving this movement on the ground.

See also AmeriCorps; Civic Engagement in Diverse Youth; Community Service; National and Community Service; Positive Youth Development, Programs Promoting; Social Movements; Social Responsibility; Student Political Activism.

Recommended Reading

Global Service Institute (GSI). See http://gwbweb.wustl.edu/csd/gsi/.
Innovations in Civic Partnerships. See www.icicp.org.
UK Home Office. See http://www.homeoffice.gov.uk/n_story.asp?item_id=949.

Adam Desrosiers, Brett Alessi, Grace Hollister,
and Susan Stroud

Intergenerational Programs and Practices.
The International Consortium for Intergenerational Programs defines intergenerational programs as "social vehicles that create purposeful and ongoing exchange of resources and learning among older and younger generations." As the phrase is used by human-service professionals, it generally refers to the wide range of ways in which young people, generally twenty-one years of age and younger, and older adults, sixty years of age and older, can be brought together to interact, support, and provide care for one another. Although the focus is generally on bringing together children/youth and older adults, intergenerational programs do not necessarily exclude participation from generations in the middle.

The intergenerational (re-)connection theme is far-reaching. It includes programs of intervention developed in a wide variety of settings, including schools, community organizations, hospitals, and places of worship. Yet, it goes beyond programs. There are instances in which the generations are brought together as part of local or cultural traditions with the process not quite fitting into a formal program-development framework. We can also speak of an intergenerational perspective which has implications for how we construct social policy and develop our basic institutions. Intergenerational policies, for example, include investment in the education of the young, financial security for older adults, and support for families as they care for their members. The phrase "intergenerational programs and practices" encompasses this broad range of intergenerational phenomena.

Intergenerational programs and practices provide an important venue for mobilizing the talents, skills, energy, and resources of older adults in service to young people and vice versa. For example, some initiatives enlist older adults as tutors, mentors, school volunteers, and childcare workers. In other initiatives youth serve as friendly visitors to isolated elders in the community, oral historians, volunteers to help elders with chores, and as tutors for those older adults interested in learning more about computers and the Internet. More recently, programs have been evolving in which youth and older adults together serve their communities. All of these initiatives provide opportunities for youth and older adults to participate in meaningful activities, share involvement with others, and increase their responsibility in their communities.

The intergenerational "movement" calls for the recognition that all generations are interdependent and that optimal community functioning would harness the oldest and youngest members' strengths to meet pressing social problems. A goal of many intergenerational programs is to develop a concern for the common good of older and younger generations as well as a sense of connectedness between them.

Intergenerational programs have been characterized as an effective countermeasure to negative consequences associated with the residential and social segregation of age-groups. Geographical segregation from grandparents and extended kin, limited roles for older adults in society, age segregation in institutions (e.g., day care, school, congregate living, and so forth) and in popular culture (e.g., TV shows, magazines, movies, music), as well as our society's emphasis on youthfulness have resulted in a lack of opportunities for old people and young people to interact with one another in meaningful ways. Among the undesirable outcomes associated with the trend toward increased intergenerational segregation are a decline in senior adults' life satisfaction, an increase in negative stereotypes toward the aged and aging among younger people, and a reduction in the extent and quality of the social networks of children and senior adults.

Over the past twenty-five years we have witnessed tremendous growth in the number and diversity of intergenerational programs. The call for increased intergenerational engagement is coming from many directions. We see it in newspaper editorials providing commentary on the increased sense of social isolation experienced by many young people and older adults. The theme is also finding its way into the publications and meetings conducted by professional societies in a broad range of fields, including education, volunteerism, child development, service learning, and gerontology. In 2003 Haworth Press launched the first journal in the field, *Journal of Intergenerational Relationships: Programs, Policy, and Research.*

The design of intergenerational programs is influenced to a large extent by the objectives of the participating organizations and the goals inherent in the settings in which the initiatives are implemented. In schools, for example, intergenerational programs are typically designed to enhance and reinforce the educational curriculum and contribute to student learning and personal growth. Programs have been developed to support virtually any curriculum subject and academic skill. There are numerous examples of programs in which senior adults are enlisted to contribute to math, English language arts, fine arts, science, physical education, health, and social studies curricula. One of the most common premises for bringing senior adults into classrooms is in the context of contributions they might make in the teaching of history. Senior adults enhance classroom history lessons by sharing their personal experiences and opinions. In the process, students gain an understanding of history as a living, ongoing process. They also learn how to develop, conduct, and document results from structured interviews.

Intergenerational mentoring programs establish relationships of mutual caring, commitment, and trust between young people and people with more experience. Mentoring programs often target youth who are considered at risk for truancy, criminal activity, drug abuse, and premature sexual experimentation, which can lead to pregnancy and sexually-transmitted diseases. Some mentoring programs target immigrant children and youth and have an emphasis on literacy as well as social support. Several studies of intergenerational mentoring programs focus on the impact of senior mentors' styles of interaction on their relationships with youth. The best mentors tend to be patient listeners who are relationship-oriented in their dealings with youth. The least effective tend to be those who have ready-made prescriptions in their mind about how they are going to influence their young mentees.

Children and youth in service-learning or community-service programs engage senior adults in a variety of services and in a variety of contexts. They contribute to senior adults' health, expand their social-support networks, and help them stay longer in their homes. For seniors living in assisted-care/long-term-care institutions, such initiatives provide needed options for recreation and socialization. At the same time, the students fulfill the service requirements of their schools.

Intergenerational programs are now being called upon to assist in the creation of intentional, caring communities and to offset the civic dissolution resulting from societal changes. Accordingly, some programs are beginning to market themselves as "community building" efforts and as strategies for promoting civic education and community participation. These programs aim to involve young people and older adults in positively changing their communities together, whether through joint service to other populations, activism around an issue of common concern, or providing input into community planning and development. In addition to benefiting the community, such initiatives benefit participants by teaching youth and seniors—both frequently disempowered groups—that they have something to give to society. Participants feel valued, empowered, and socially engaged. An important component of these programs is that time and opportunity are provided for planned reflection.

Examples of intergenerational community-service programs include the following:

- Adjudicated youth and Retired Senior Volunteer Program (RSVP) older adult volunteers in Allentown, PA, work together to maintain a community garden. The fresh vegetables harvested from the garden are donated to the Second Harvest Food Bank.
- Senior Corps volunteers and at-risk youth deliver in-home chore, homemaker, and respite services for frail older adults in Florida.
- Academically, emotionally, and physically challenged middle- and high-school students and isolated older adults join together to make soup and sandwiches for the homeless, Valentine's Day cards

for hospitalized children, and decorations for institutionalized elders through a Maryland program entitled Self-Esteem Through Service.

Slightly different from intergenerational community service is intergenerational community advocacy or action. Examples include the following:

- The Intergenerational Citizens Action Forum in Miami, Florida, allows older adults to help students organize and conduct a town meeting to address issues critical to senior citizens such as Social Security reform, crime, and environmental protection. Then, students and their elder mentors form caucuses, write bills, and contact legislators to urge action.
- An annual intergenerational advocacy conference, sponsored by the Agency on Aging in Phoenix, Arizona, in collaboration with other administrations and foundations, gathers fifty high-school students and fifty older adults from across the state for a day and a half of advocacy training and strategizing for change. A recent theme of a conference was protecting oneself from fraud.

What these programs have in common is that they highlight a view of citizenship that involves people of all ages as active participants in local issues. Participants learn that they share concerns with members of other generations and that together they have the potential to make a difference in their communities.

Whether intergenerational programs are designed to contribute to change at the individual or community level, to be successful attention needs to be paid to how programs are designed. Here are some program development themes and considerations noted in the intergenerational literature:

Involve existing and potential participants in the program planning process. The general principal is that the more participation included before the program begins, the greater participants' motivation and "buy-in" throughout the program.

Prepare participants before the program begins: orient them to how people in the other groups think and experience the world. Even before youth and older adult participants of an intergenerational program meet each other, orientation sessions can be developed to promote understanding about generational differences regarding views about education, money, recreation, and so forth.

Design developmentally appropriate activities. This includes taking into account competencies (e.g., readiness to create and explore) as well as limitations (such as in terms of mobility and cognitive functioning).

Design activities in a culturally appropriate manner. It is important to pay attention to cultural differences regarding expected patterns of intergenerational communication. Activities need to be planned in a manner that is consistent with cultural norms in terms of things like touch, humor, and dealing with illness and loss (including death).

Design activities that relate to participants' real-world concerns. When activities are designed to address participants' personal and community needs, they are more likely to pursue further opportunities for intergenerational exchange.

Start light. Intergenerational communication is a sequential process that most naturally begins with the type of superficial contact that is generated by "icebreakers" (or "warm-ups"). Warm-up activities can give way to additional activities designed to yield more intensive, in-depth communication. As in any relationship, it takes time.

It is also important to consider what happens to intergenerational programs after they are planned and implemented. Sustainability, the current catchword in intergenerational programming circles, tends to be a problem even when there is great excitement at the onset of a new program. There are many barriers to the systematic growth and development of intergenera-

tional programs, including age-segregated public and private funding streams, lack of systematic collaboration among funding sources at the local, state, and national levels, lack of integration of programs into existing service systems or large-scale initiatives, and limited mechanisms for identifying and sharing best practices.

One strategy for addressing many of these barriers is to make sure that policymakers and the public understand how intergenerational programs contribute to individual and community development. The intergenerational literature provides a growing body of evidence attesting to how program participants benefit from their involvement. Evidence is accumulating which suggests that young people gain valuable knowledge and skills from their intergenerational experiences. This includes gaining social skills and learning things as varied as handicrafts, performing-arts skills, horticultural skills, traditional games, and cultural history.

Various studies have been conducted which demonstrate the efficacy of intergenerational program experiences to promote more positive attitudes toward older persons and the aging process. Several of these studies incorporate pre- and posttesting of the participants, include control group comparisons, and demonstrate a statistically significant impact on student attitudes toward older adults. In some cases, young participants learn to see past negative stereotypes that attribute mental limitations to people with physical limitations. Through direct contact with senior adults, the young volunteers learn that despite physical limitations, many senior adults have extensive knowledge, motivation, abilities, and engaging personalities.

There are also several studies, however, which indicate mixed results in terms of program impact on young participants' attitudes toward the elderly. In these studies, although the student participants were uniformly positive in their assessments about their interactions with the senior adults, they did not consistently show a change in understanding of issues relating to aging. Some of the factors contributing to such mixed results include variation in the frequency and quality of intergenerational contact, inconsistencies in how participants were recruited and oriented to their program experiences, and variation in the types of participants involved in the programs that were studied (e.g., healthy elders versus frail elders).

Older adults benefit, too, from their participation in intergenerational programs. Within modern gerontology, the health (physical and mental) of older adults is viewed in relational terms; social connectedness and active community engagement are of paramount importance. And this is consistent with how most adults define successful aging, that is, mostly in terms of relationships, specifically caring about and getting along with others. Intergenerational programs provide opportunities for seniors to remain active, contributing members of society, and this has important psychological benefits such as improved self-esteem, a heightened sense of social connectedness, and a more optimistic view toward life.

There is undoubtedly a need for further research. Intergenerational scholars and practitioners readily admit that as an emerging field, there remains much work to be done in terms of documenting the impact of various intergenerational program approaches and charting the factors that determine their success or failure. More research is needed to answer questions such as the following:

Do the experiences of program participants carry over into their relationships with family members?

Do intergenerational programs influence the career and recreational direction decisions made by project participants?

What are the community-level outcomes of intergenerational programs?

In what ways is intergenerational programming useful for different racial, cultural, ethnic, or religious groups?

What barriers exist to intergenerational programming in diverse communities?

What role does socioeconomic status play in different outcomes of intergenerational programs?

With more research and careful planning some of the many benefits of intergenerational initiatives noted by those who plan and participate in them can be more effectively substantiated, and this is likely to contribute to efforts to support and extend intergenerational work.

See also Adult Roles in Youth Activism; Adultism; Community Collaboration; Generational Conflict; Generational Replacement; Social Responsibility; Social Trust; Volunteerism; Voice; Youth Commissions.

Recommended Reading

Brabazon, K., and Disch, R. (1997). *Intergenerational Approaches in Aging: Implications for Education, Policy, and Practice.* New York: Haworth Press.

Bressler, J. (In Press). *Connecting Generations, Strengthening Communities: A Handbook for Intergenerational Programs.* Philadelphia: Center for Intergenerational Learning at Temple University.

Generations United (2002). *Young and Old Serving Together: Meeting Community Needs through Intergenerational Partnerships.* Washington, D.C.: Generations United.

Kaplan, M. (1994). *Side-by-Side: Exploring Your Neighborhood through Intergenerational Activities.* San Francisco: MIG Communications.

Kaplan, M., Henkin, N., and Kusano, A., eds. (2002). *Linking Lifetimes: A Global View of Intergenerational Exchange.* Lanham, MD: University Press of America.

Kingston, E., Hirshorn, B., and Cornman, J. (1986). *Ties That Bind: The Interdependence of Generations.* Cabin John, MD: Seven Locks Press.

Kuehne, V. S. (1999). *Intergenerational Programs: Understanding What We Have Created.* Binghamton: The Haworth Press.

Newman, S., Ward, C. R., Smith, T. B., and Wilson, J. (1997). *Intergenerational Programs: Past, Present and Future.* Bristol, PA: Taylor and Francis.

Winston, L. (2001). *Grandpartners: Intergenerational Learning and Civic Renewal, K–6.* Portsmouth, NH: Heinemann.

Matthew Kaplan and Abigail Lawrence-Jacobson

International Association for the Evaluation of Educational Achievement. *See* IEA Civic Education Study.

J

Jesuit Volunteer Corps (JVC). The Jesuit Volunteer Corps (JVC) is a faith-based organizational program that enlists young people in full-time service for social justice and peace. Similar to other service programs like the Peace Corps, Teach for America, and Vista, JVC offers recent college graduates an attractive alternative to regular employment by providing opportunities to contribute to the betterment of society while growing professionally, personally, and spiritually. JVC is the largest Catholic lay-volunteer program in the country and each year provides service placements for about 360 individuals domestically and about eighty internationally. All told, since its inception in 1956, more than 11,000 people in their early twenties have served as Jesuit volunteers (JVC and the Society of Jesus 2000).

What makes the Jesuit Volunteer Corps unique among full-time service opportunities is its program model, which integrates service with the four values of *community*, *simplicity*, *social justice*, and *spirituality*. In this framework, Jesuit volunteers (JVs) live in low-income neighborhoods, advocate for social justice by working with the poor and marginalized, and reflect on the service in light of the gospel and Catholic social teachings. JVs contribute to local schools, social-service agencies, and other beneficiaries with their skills and commitment. JVs themselves stand to benefit by serving in unfamiliar and difficult circumstances and by gaining new awareness and insights about the society in which they live. In many ways, the Jesuit Volunteer Corps epitomizes the term "youth activism." This entry describes the Jesuit Volunteer Corps as a program that promotes the development of activism among recent college graduates.

Jesuits and JVC: Known formally as the Society of Jesus, the Jesuits were founded by Saint Ignatius Loyola in 1540 as a religious order in the Roman Catholic Church. The Jesuits' mission is based on Loyola's social teachings and spiritual exercises and seeks to integrate prayer with active work for others. Today, more than 20,000 Jesuit priests serve in 122 countries. In the United States more than one hundred high schools and twenty-eight colleges and universities are considered Jesuit. It is a hallmark of Jesuit educational institutions to have a well-rounded liberal arts curriculum and to frame the teachings of the church from a social justice perspective (see http://www.jesuits.org for more information).

The Jesuit Volunteer Corps was launched in 1956 when Jesuit priests from the Oregon province invited a handful of college graduates to serve the poor in Nome, Alaska. Soon after, JVC communities began to emerge in the Pacific Northwest along with a more structured program model. A main priority of the JVC is to form leaders committed to faith and justice in the emerging role of lay people in the Catholic Church (JVC and the Society of Jesus 2000).

In the past half century, the Jesuit Volunteer Corps has grown to eighty-six communities in six regions in the United States, as well as on the intentional level. JVC West has eighteen communities in sixteen cities. JVC East has sixteen communities in fifteen cities. JVC Midwest has six communities in six cities. JVC Southwest has fifteen communities in eight cities. JVC South has eight communities in eight cities. JVC International has twenty-three communities in eleven countries.

Overview and Figures: Although JVC was founded by a religious order and is privately run, young people of any faith are eligible to join. Figures show that about 85 percent of volunteers are Catholic, about 75 percent are female, about 95 percent are recent college graduates, about 55 percent graduated from Jesuit colleges and universities, about 15 percent graduated from non-Jesuit Catholic institutions, and about 30 percent graduated from secular institutions (Gaunt 2000). Jesuit priests and laypersons continue to provide guidance, training, and professional development to the directors and staff and lead the retreats for the volunteers. Jesuits also provide local support and spiritual guidance within the towns and locales in which Jesuit volunteers serve (JVC and the Society of Jesus 2000).

Despite variability across personal characteristics and placement locations, the JVC program model is designed to ensure that all JVs share as common an experience as possible. The program model is based on the young persons' openness to the four values and being matched with an agency that suits a particular volunteer's interests and needs. The model also provides support and opportunities for embedded reflection to help ensure that the JVs' experience is a success. The following is a brief description of the most central components of the JVC program model.

Each young person who applies to the Jesuit Volunteer Corps is expected to be open and accepting of each of the four values of *community, social justice, spirituality*, and *community*. These values represent the cornerstone of the Jesuit vocation, and the JVC program model purposefully and concretely integrates these values within the whole of the JVs experience.

Community: JVs live in a low-income area *in community* with three to nine fellow JVs. Community life centers around daily routines, such as household chores, cooking, eating, and "hanging out." Community members often form deep relationships based on their common working experiences through reflections on the challenges, failures, and successes of their efforts. Many JVs become close friends, and research shows that relationships formed in community endure over time long after leaving JVC (Gaunt 2000). As well as JVs immediate in-house community, community is experienced on broader levels through relationships with neighbors, co-workers, and members of the local parish (http://www.jesuitvolunteers.org).

Social Justice: The term "social justice" from a Catholic social-teaching perspective emphasizes the least of our brothers and sisters and holds such values as solidarity and the common good. JVs are assigned to live and work in low-income and poverty-stricken neighborhoods despite being in some of the nicest cities. JVs work in conditions that expose them to the realities and complexities of systemic injustice faced by the marginalized and disenfranchised. Through their jobs, retreats, and community living, JVs are encouraged to understand the term "social justice" by examining the causes of injustice and searching for faith-filled responses and long-term solutions (http://www.jesuitvolunteers.org).

Simplicity: JVs are instructed to care less about money, material objects, and consumption, in order to understand and focus on the basic necessities of life, such as conversation and relationships. Living simply helps JVs to understand the plight of the poor and marginalized and allows JVs to disentangle themselves from a culture of wealth and power (http://www.jesuitvolunteers.org). Each community decides on the specifics of how to *live simply*, such as decisions on purchasing food and material objects, recycling, appliance usage, and so on.

Spirituality: While there is no explicit guideline that JVs have to be Catholic or even religious, JVC was created as a faith-based program. Thus, JVC is structured to enhance JVs communal and individual prayer life. The purpose of the spirituality value is so that JVs can further understand and seek God's presence in their work and in their relationships. JV communities are encouraged to have a "spirituality night" at least once a week and are free to search for their own style of spirituality (http://www.jesuitvolunteers.org). Research shows that spirituality is very important to many Jesuit volunteers and to former volunteers during and after their JVC experience (Hendry 1999). The emphasis on Jesuit and Ignatian spirituality is one fundamental difference between JVC and other full-time secular service programs.

The JVC program model is designed to match an applicant with a nonprofit community-based agency that assists the needy. Applicants first choose a region to apply to and a specific employment type. JVC staff facilitates the process by putting the applicant in touch with the potential agency for an interview to determine if a placement would be a good match. The agencies in which JVs serve cover a spectrum of interests, from assisting the poor or disenfranchised directly, to working in schools, coordinating programs, or advocating for social justice. Some examples of JV job placements include:

- Advocating for domestic-violence prevention in a local shelter
- Assisting poor pregnant women who have no health insurance at a neighborhood health office
- Coordinating an after-school program for children whose parents cannot afford day care
- Answering calls on a crisis hotline at a local mental-health agency
- Assisting the elderly at a St. Vincent de Paul community center
- Offering counsel to illegal immigrants at a community law office

Most positions in JVC can be filled by young people who have a general educational background and a willingness to learn new skills (http://www.jesuitvolun-teers.org). All JVs have job descriptions, training, and ongoing supervision. The agencies pay JVs a stipend of around $80 a month and also cover living expenses and health insurance.

The commitment to work for justice and peace requires support and the program model ensures that JVs are supported before, during, and after their year of service (http://www.jesuitvolunteers.org). Support mainly comes in the forms of retreats and through a network of fellow volunteers.

Retreats: All JVs attend a week-long orientation to discuss the four values, become acquainted with their community mates, and to prepare for the year ahead. During the year JV communities attend several retreats and workshops to reflect on and discuss the four values and to recharge. At the end of the year a retreat is dedicated to closure and to preparing JVs for the challenges of returning to normal life.

Network of Support: Support comes from all angles during and after JVC. Community living is the main source of support for JVs on a daily basis. The Jesuit Volunteer Corps has an office in each region with a director and staff. JVC staff is familiar with local situations and provides personal and programmatic support to each JV and each community (http://www.jesuitvolunteers.org). JV communities have local support, including former Jesuit volunteers (FJVs) and families that "adopt" JVs for a year by hosting potluck dinners and through general involvement in the JVs lives. When their JVC service ends, FJVs continue the spirit of JVC through gatherings in many cities and by attending retreats specifically for FJVs.

The JVC program model purposefully embeds reflection throughout the JVs experience—from the application process to retreats, daily life in community, and years after JVC. Reflection prompts JVs to step back and evaluate their lives in relation to others who are less fortunate. The reflection element helps JVs focus on program goals and values, reaffirms and renews the efforts of the community on a whole, and helps JVs make sense of complicated situations and experiences.

In the Jesuit Volunteer Corps young people actively and directly respond to society's ills, reflect on causes, question and sometimes object to laws, and come up with solutions to systemic problems. The JVC program model is structured so that JVs are continually challenged to reevaluate their experiences in relation to their own personal, communal, and spiritual development as individuals. Clearly, the program model of the Jesuit Volunteer Corps supports and promotes the development of youth activism for social change. Anecdotal accounts and descriptive research speak to the JVC experience as a transforming and an enduring experience over time (see Gaunt 2000; Hendry 1999). To date, no longitudinal or empirical research has assessed the nature and form of youth activism in JVC. Two points seem worthy of speculation in regard to the Jesuit Volunteer Corps and youth activism and raise many interesting questions that future research will be sure to address.

First, JVC enlists many young people who are already activists. In an age of consumerism and competition to get the highest paying and best jobs, JVs work for social justice and are willing to dirty their hands and minds for causes in which they believe. Research could help explain the factors that lead young people to join the Jesuit Volunteer Corps. For example, are most JVs active volunteers through high school and college? Do most JVs have friends or parents who volunteer? How does a young person's spirituality and political beliefs tie into the decision to join the Jesuit Volunteer Corps?

Second, it seems fair to speculate that a year of service as a Jesuit volunteer enhances young people's activism. Future research is needed to examine *how* and *in what conditions* this process may occur. For example, what kinds of activism does JVC enhance? Are young people more likely to become politically active and more likely to volunteer after a year of service as a JV? Are young people more likely to become spiritually active and to link their spiritual development to civic and moral causes? What are the longer-term developmental effects of programs such as JVC on adults who served in JVC as youth? Are Jesuit volunteers' career choices in part determined by their experiences as JVs? What kinds of experiences during JVC are most likely to enhance youth activism? Each of these important questions has ramifications for program models that give young people an opportunity to develop skills to be active and effective democratic citizens.

As stated on the Jesuit Volunteer Corps Web site, "JVC is more than just a job. Social justice, simple lifestyle, community, and spirituality: these values provide the cornerstone for living out a commitment to faith and social justice." Given the strong program model and the energy with which young people perform service, it is not surprising that the motto of the Jesuit Volunteer Corps reflects the transforming experience through which young people are "ruined for life."

The following is the mission statement of the Jesuit Volunteer Corps:

The Jesuit Volunteer Corps offers women and men an opportunity to work full-time for justice and peace. Jesuit Volunteers are called to the mission of serving the poor directly, working for structural change in the United States, and accompanying people in developing countries. The challenge to Jesuit volunteers is to integrate Christian faith by working and living among the poor and marginalized, by living simply in the community with other Jesuit volunteers, and by examining the causes of social injustice. Since 1956, the Jesuit Volunteer Corps has worked in collaboration with Jesuits, whose spirituality the volunteers incorporate in their work, community, and prayer life. The Jesuit Volunteer Corps offers volunteers a year or more experience that will open their minds and hearts to live always conscious of the poor, committed to the church's mission of promoting justice in the service of faith (http://www.jesuitvolunteers.org).

Note: In 1995–1996 the author volunteered with JVC Northwest in Yakima,

Washington, as a crisis-line counselor and sexual-assault victims' advocate at a neighborhood mental-health clinic.

See also Campus Crusade for Christ International (CCC); Catholic Education and the Ethic of Social Justice; Religiosity and American Youth; Religiosity and Civic Engagement in African American Youth; Spirituality.

Recommended Reading

Gaunt, T. (2000). "Ruined for Life: The Enduring Influence of a Volunteer Service Program." See http://comm-dev.org/conf2002/session.php?session=III.

Hendry, S. (1999). "Ruined for Life: The Spirituality of the Jesuit Volunteer Corps Christian Spirituality." JVC and the Society of Jesus. See http://www.jesuitvolunteers.org.

The Jesuit Volunteer Corps (2004). See http://www.jesuitvolunteers.org.

JVC and the Society of Jesus (2000). "Affirming Our Relationships and Exploring New Directions." See http://www.jesuitvolunteers.org/files/jvc_sj.pdf.

Society of Jesus (2004). See http://www.jesuit.org.

Edward Metz

Just Community High Schools and Youth Activism. The school is considered an important socialization agent during the adolescent years. Adolescents spend most of their time in school and school-related activities interacting with peers and teachers on both academic and personal levels. During adolescence there is generally a lack of participation in the work force, a transition in family roles, and a lack of effective roles in most societal contexts. This is also true for the school environment. Adolescents often feel that schools are controlled solely by adults and that students are not given an opportunity to create rules and create their own environment. Research has found that increased involvement in the school environment can stimulate more positive attitudes toward school and decrease negative behaviors. Schools like the Just Community are set up specifically to foster a positive school culture as well as students' academic learning, responsibility, and moral behavior by actively engaging students in the school's culture. A Just Community such as the Scarsdale Alternative High School is one that creates structures designed to meet these conditions by making democracy as moral and civic education a major focus.

There are three broad ideologies in Western education. The romantic ideology contends that what comes from within the child is the most important aspect of development. Therefore, the teaching of ideas and attitudes through rote or drill would result in meaningless learning and the suppression of inner spontaneous tendencies. The romantic notion recognizes the natural development of the child as part of a larger romantic philosophy of discovering the inner self.

Cultural-transmission ideology asserts that education's primary task is the transmission to the present generation of information, rules, and moral values collected in the past. Such educators believe that it is their duty to convey such knowledge to children and that such knowledge is driven by the changing or static nature of the society. While the romantic notion emphasizes the child's freedom, the cultural-transmission ideology emphasizes the child's need to learn the discipline of social order and views the educational ends as the internalization of the moral values and knowledge of the culture.

In contrast, progressivism holds that education should support the child's natural interaction with a developing society or environment. Philosopher John Dewey stated that "education is the work of supplying the conditions which will enable the psychological functions, as they successively arise, to mature and pass into higher functions in the freest and fullest manner." This aim requires an educational environment that actively stimulates development through the presentation of resolvable but genuine problems, and such experiences make the child think—think in ways that organize both cognition and emotion.

Progressive educators see the development of morality as an active change in patterns of response to problematic social situations rather than learning culturally accepted rules. Dewey believed that a moral education is most potent when lessons are taught to children and adolescents in the course of real events, not just as abstract lessons. Progressivism believes that it is the educators' duty to facilitate the child's advancement to the next stage of development, which involves exposure to conflict requiring the effective application of the current level of thought and being exposed to a higher level of thought. Foundations of character education include self-discipline and self-control as well as being able to motivate and guide oneself. Being able to put aside one's self-centered focus and impulses has social benefits: it opens the way to empathy, to real listening, and to taking another person's perspective. Schools have a central role in cultivating character by including self-discipline and empathy, which in turn enable true commitment to civic and moral values. In so doing, it is not enough to lecture children about values; they need to practice them, which will occur as children build the essential emotional and social skills.

The Scarsdale Alternative School was founded in 1972 as a free school that broke away from the cultural-transmission ideology of the traditional high school to embrace the romantic notion of education with the belief that public schools impeded education because students were denied the basic right of directing their own education. Like many other alternative schools, the Scarsdale Alternative School was founded on the premise of freedom. However, the ambiguity of this freedom (freedom from, freedom toward, freedom for, and so forth) led to a great deal of trouble in the alternative-school movement and the eventual demise of most of them. In 1977 the Scarsdale Alternative School consciously made the choice to become a Just Community School and to embrace the progressive ideology of education. It was designed upon the concepts of Lawrence

Kohlberg. Kohlberg's research stipulates certain conditions for moral growth: exposure to cognitive moral conflict, role taking, consideration of fairness and morality, exposure to the next higher stage of moral reasoning, and active participation in group decision-making.

When the Scarsdale Alternative School became affiliated with Lawrence Kohlberg, the school based its practices on a theory of cognitive moral development that has guided the school in the creation of various structures through which students deliberate issues of justice, fairness, and caring. Having to resolve these issues causes students, over time, to develop more mature reasoning. The goal is to learn to take various perspectives into consideration, to become less egocentric and bound by peer norms, and to become more able to take an institutional perspective that represents the common good. The theory helps educators understand that good teaching does involve carefully planned intervention and direction and that students grow and learn in important ways from challenge and conflict despite the claims of the romantic educators.

The Scarsdale Alternative School evolved by developing and implementing structures designed to affect the manner in which students and teachers interacted and to allow for more meaningful participation of students in the decision-making process of the school. The result of this effort has been the institutionalization of the major structural components of the Just Community: community meeting, agenda meeting, core group, and fairness committee.

Throughout the academic year community meetings are held one afternoon a week for one-and-a-half hours. The agenda is the outgrowth of the deliberations of an agenda meeting that has clarified the issues at hand and has ranked them in the order of importance to the community. At the community meeting the discussions sometimes result in the establishment of new rules, expectations, or procedures. Although community meeting is the legislative branch of government at the school, some of the most important dialog is not legislative in its intent. Rather, there is often open sharing of concerns, disagreements, sources of conflict, and areas of agreement that have no goal beyond greater understanding among members of the community.

Once a week each student also participates in a smaller meeting called core group, with fifteen students and a teacher/advisor. In addition to forging close relationships among students and teachers, core group also serves important administrative functions. As an organizational structure, core group can significantly personalize and improve the entire monitoring process of a student's life in school. Agenda, core group, and community meeting are closely linked structures designed to help the school define its pressing concerns and address them.

In a community in which students are encouraged to make public their expectations of others, to debate proper behavioral norms, and to formalize these expectations and norms through rules, it is important to provide a structure that will enable the community to determine fair consequences for those who do not abide by those rules. The fairness committee consists of a representative group of students, one of whom, trained in the fairness committee leadership course, leads the case, and one teacher. The task of the fairness committee is to hear and decide cases of alleged rule violations and to determine appropriate action, as well as to try to settle any type of grievance brought before it.

While not a part of the school governance system, one other structure supports the character-education initiative at the Scarsdale Alternative School: the internship. In 1973 the Just Community began its career internship program (CIP) in order to make the structure of the overall curriculum reflect the philosophy that students learn in different ways and that experimental learning can be a powerful experience for students. For the month of January classes are suspended, and all students are responsible for finding an internship with some agency, institution, or individual. The CIP is a direct response to one of the original educational challenges set for the school, to make the school less isolated from and more responsive to the larger community. Also, students and faculty vote democratically each year to commit themselves to mandatory community service separate from their internship responsibilities. The internship and community-service structures were created in the hopes of promoting perspective taking when students have real responsibility in the adult world.

Institutions for youth, like high schools, tend to develop a characteristic moral atmosphere which may stimulate moral growth or retard it. The Just Community approach involves an effort to develop more responsible moral action as well as improving moral reasoning. The central theme of the Just Community is the actual experience of participatory democratic decision-making in an environment stressing norms of justice and community in the relations of students and teachers and to one another. Traditional high schools maintain hierarchical relationships between students and teachers and among teachers themselves. They are large formal bureaucratic institutions in which problems are settled by the administration and teachers. In contrast, the Just Community encourages more equal relationships between teachers and students and among students themselves. At the core of this practice is the idea of participatory government—one person, one vote—whether student or teacher, in dealing with issues of fairness and community issues. Students along with teachers are expected to create the rules and govern the school. Discussions in weekly community meetings regarding issues of justice, fairness, and morality are encouraged in hopes of promoting moral reasoning and enhancing community and social responsibility. A more basic part, however, is to help the adolescent construct a moral community that can stimulate and support altruism and a sense of conscientious obligation.

Over the years, the Scarsdale Alternative High School has benefited from evaluation research from affiliates of the Harvard University Center for Moral Education and, more recently, Fordham University. Research shows that alternative high-school students' moral-reasoning development was significant while comparison group students' moral reasoning showed almost no growth over three years. The alternative-school environment appears to be successful in promoting civic involvement and academic achievement, as well as the moral and prosocial development of students and teachers. Alternative school students reported feeling responsible for helping their peers and upholding the rules they had made as a group, whereas comparison students did not feel responsible for their peers, nor for maintaining school rules. Students in the alternative school demonstrated a strong sense of school belongingness and believed that their school culture was more positive than students in traditional high schools. Teachers and students alike depict student-student and teacher-student relationships more positively than their high-school counterparts. Also, students in traditional high schools did not value their schools as communities whereas alternative school students do. Furthermore, when faced with ethical dilemmas, two-thirds of alternative school students believed that their peers would act prosocially, while only one-third of traditional high-school students believed this of their peers. The democratic nature of the alternative school also has a profound impact on students' activism, especially concerning local involvement. Alternative school students are satisfied with their input in school decisions and the quality of these decisions. The alternative school atmosphere exerts a strong effect on the development of positive feelings of personal political effectiveness.

See also High School Students' Rights Movement of the 1960s.

Recommended Reading

Kohlberg, L. (1981). *The Philosophy of Moral Development: Moral Stages and the Idea of Justice.* San Francisco, CA: Harper and Row.

Kohlberg, L., and Higgins, A. (1987). "School Democracy and Social Interaction." In *Moral Development Through Social Interaction*, edited by W. M. Kurtines, and J. L. Gewirtz. Oxford, England: John Wiley and Sons, pp. 102–128.

Kohlberg, L., and Mayer, R. (1972). "Development as the Aim of Education." *Harvard Educational Review*, 42: 449–496.

Powers, F. C., Higgins, A., and Kohlberg, L. (1989). *Lawrence Kohlberg's Approach to Moral Education.* New York: Columbia University Press.

Jason J. Barr, Howard Rodstein,
Ann Higgins-D'Alessandro

Juvenile Justice. Few issues challenge a society's ideas about both the nature of human development and the nature of justice as much as serious juvenile crime. Because we neither expect children to be criminals nor expect crimes to be committed by children, the unexpected intersection between childhood and criminality creates a dilemma that most people find difficult to resolve. Indeed, the only ways out of this problem are either to redefine the offense as something less serious than a crime or to redefine the offender as someone who is not really a child.

For much of the past century American society has chosen to treat most juvenile infractions as matters to be adjudicated as delinquent acts within a separate juvenile justice system designed to recognize the special needs and immature status of young people and emphasize rehabilitation over punishment. The presumption behind the juvenile justice system is that, while teenagers are certainly more mature than children, the same factors that make them ineligible to vote or to serve on a jury require us to treat them differently than adults when they misbehave.

During the 1990s there was a shift in the way juvenile crime was viewed by policymakers and the general public, in large part in response to the dramatic increase in violent juvenile crime that took place during the 1980s. This shift was reflected in an increase in the number of juveniles whose cases were adjudicated in adult criminal court, either by statute (i.e., where a state's law calls for the automatic filing of certain charges in criminal court, even when the offender is a juvenile, or where the state's boundary between juvenile and criminal court is drawn at an age below eighteen), prosecutorial discretion (i.e., where a state permits a prosecutor to charge a juvenile in adult court if circumstances are believed to warrant it), or judicial waiver (i.e., where a judge determines that the appropriate venue for a juvenile's adjudication is criminal, not juvenile, court). Approximately 200,000 individuals under the age of eighteen are tried in criminal court annually in the United States.

Transferring a juvenile to criminal court has three sets of implications that lend themselves to a developmental analysis. First, transfer to adult court alters the legal process by which a minor is tried. Criminal court is based on an adversarial model, while juvenile court has been based, at least in theory, on a more cooperative model. Second, the legal standards applied in adult and juvenile courts, especially those pertaining to competence to stand trial and the determination of criminal responsibility, are different in a number of ways. Finally, the choice of trying a young offender in adult versus juvenile court often determines the possible outcomes of the adjudication. In adult court the outcome of being found guilty of a serious crime is nearly always some sort of punishment. In juvenile court the outcome of being found delinquent also may be some sort of punishment, but juvenile courts typically retain the option of a rehabilitative disposition, alone or in combination with some punishment.

The transition from adolescence to adulthood does not occur at a single, fixed, well-defined age. Not only do different individuals mature at different rates and

times, but different abilities may develop along different timetables. Accordingly, instead of asking where to draw the line between adolescence and adulthood for the purposes of deciding when to try juveniles as adults, it is more sensible to ask at what ages individuals can be presumed to possess (or to not possess) the various attributes that are potentially relevant to this issue.

To do this, one must identify the aspects of development that are relevant and ask whether, how, and on what timetable these aspects of development change during the transition from adolescence to adulthood. The following three questions are especially important:

When do individuals become competent to be adjudicated in an adversarial court context? This question concerns the proper venue for an adolescent's adjudication. Given the adversarial nature of criminal court proceedings, at what age are adolescents likely to possess the skills necessary to protect their own interests in the courtroom and participate effectively in their own defense?

When do individuals meet the criteria for adult blameworthiness? This question concerns the appropriate amount of punishment for a juvenile offender who has been judged to have committed the offense in question. Is there an age before which individuals, by virtue of "normal" psychological immaturity, should be considered to be of "diminished responsibility" and therefore held less accountable, and proportionately less punishable, for their actions?

Is there a point in development at which individuals cease to be good candidates for rehabilitation by virtue of the diminished likelihood of change in the psychological and behavioral characteristics thought to affect criminal behavior or because of diminished amenability to treatment? This concerns the type of sanction imposed on an adolescent who is deemed responsible and, more specifically, the relative emphasis placed on rehabilitation versus punishment. A fundamental tenet of the juvenile justice system is that juveniles can be rehabilitated because their characters are not yet fully formed. In general, children are presumed to be more malleable than adults. But is there a predictable timetable along which individuals change from relatively changeable to relatively unchangeable?

Two specific types of competencies are needed to be tried in criminal court. First, the individual must be able to consult with his or her lawyer with a reasonable degree of rational understanding and an understanding of the proceedings. Second, the individual must also demonstrate the ability to make decisions about waiving rights, entering pleas, proceeding without an attorney, and so on.

Numerous cognitive and social-cognitive competencies that change during the adolescent years likely underlie the development of competence to stand trial, among them, the ability to engage in hypothetical and logical decision-making (in order to weigh the costs and benefits of different pleas), demonstrate reliable episodic memory (in order to provide accurate information about the offense in question), extend thinking into the future (in order to envision the consequences of different pleas), engage in advanced social perspective-taking (in order to understand the roles and motives of different participants in the adversarial process), and understand and articulate one's own motives and psychological state (in order to assist counsel in mounting a defense). Developmental research indicates that these abilities emerge at somewhat different ages, but that it would be highly unlikely that an individual would satisfy all of these criteria much before the age of twelve. At the other extreme, research suggests that the majority of individuals probably have these abilities by age sixteen.

Although direct research regarding adolescents' understanding of court proceedings is limited, there is evidence to raise concerns regarding the competence of adolescents under age fifteen to participate in

criminal trials. One comprehensive study of age differences in competence to stand trial found that about one-in-five fourteen- and fifteen-year-olds and one-in-three eleven- to thirteen-year-olds is as impaired as defendants as are mentally-ill adults who have been found not competent to stand trial. In that study there were no differences between adults and adolescents sixteen and older in the abilities relevant to competence to stand trial. Other studies have found similar patterns of age differences when individuals are asked to explain their Miranda rights.

It is important to understand the implications of the fact that adolescents may not fully comprehend the meaning of their right to remain silent or of a decision to accept a plea bargain or take the stand as a defendant. The juvenile court acknowledges diminished competence by attempting to function in a way that protects the interests of the youngster who may not be able to participate fully in his or her own defense and by limiting the punitiveness of the punishments to which a less-than-competent defendant might be exposed. The adversarial system of adult criminal courts, in contrast, relies in large part on the competence of the defendant to ensure that his or her attorney has the information necessary to prepare an effective defense and that the defense is pursued in a manner consistent with the defendant's interests. In the criminal system it is the defendant who must ultimately make plea decisions and other critical choices throughout the course of a trial. If an adolescent does not have the understanding necessary to make such decisions, the perspective to comprehend the long-term consequences of such decisions, or the ability to articulate his or her priorities to counsel criminal court is an inappropriate venue for adjudicating the offense or determining a sentence.

The adult justice system presumes that defendants who are found guilty are responsible for their own actions and should be held accountable and punished accordingly. Historically, those who are guilty but less responsible for their actions (e.g., because of one or more mitigating factors, such as one's mental state at the time of the crime) receive proportionately less punishment. It is therefore worth considering whether, because of the relative immaturity of minors, it may be justified to view them as being less blameworthy than adults for the very same infractions—that is, whether developmental immaturity should be viewed as a relevant mitigating factor in the way that we view mental illness or self-defense. If, for example, adolescents below a certain age cannot foresee the consequences of their actions, or cannot control their impulses, one should not hold them as blameworthy for their actions as one would hold an adult. And if adolescents below a certain age are less blameworthy than adults, perhaps they should receive less, or different, punishment as well.

Are there age differences in blameworthiness that are substantial enough to affect legal judgments about culpability? Specifically, is there an age below which we can presume sufficiently diminished responsibility to argue that immaturity is a mitigating factor that should prevent an individual from being tried as an adult? Is there an age beyond which we can presume sufficient maturity of judgment to hold an individual accountable enough to proceed with a trial in an adult venue and expose the person to the possibility of adult punishment?

Many of the cognitive and social-cognitive capabilities that are potentially relevant to the assessment of blameworthiness are the same as those that are relevant to the assessment of adjudicative competence. To be fully accountable for an act, for example, a person must commit the act voluntarily, knowingly, and with some ability to form reasonable expectations of the likely or potential consequences of the act. In this respect, logical decision-making and ability to foresee the future ramifications of one's decisions are important to determinations of blameworthiness, just as they are to determinations of adjudicative competence.

Judging an individual as blameworthy presumes certain capacities that are emotional and interpersonal and not simply cognitive in nature, however. Among these psychosocial capabilities, for example, are the ability to control one's impulses, to manage one's behavior in the face of pressure from others to violate the law, or to extricate oneself from a potentially problematic situation. Many of these capabilities have been examined in research on what we broadly refer to as "judgment," because deficiencies in these realms would likely interfere with individuals' abilities to act in ways that demonstrate mature enough decision-making to qualify for adult-like accountability. Importantly, studies show that there are significant age differences in traits such as resistance to peer pressure, future orientation, and impulse control, with adults consistently demonstrating more responsibility, greater time perspective, and more temperance. Moreover, individuals who score higher on these measures of psychosocial maturity are more likely to make socially responsible decisions in the hypothetical situations than those who were less psychosocially mature. Viewing a criminal act as the result of *immature* judgment, rather than as the outcome of *bad* judgment, has important implications for debates over whether we should try juveniles as adults and hold them to adult standards of criminal blameworthiness.

In legal practice, amenability refers to the likelihood of an individual desisting from crime and/or being rehabilitated when treated with some sort of intervention that is available within the community at the time of adjudication. Amenability is probably the most practical basis on which to make decisions about how a serious juvenile offender should be treated. It makes little sense to invest the rehabilitative resources of the juvenile justice system in individuals who are unlikely to change and a great deal of sense to target such resources at those individuals most likely to respond to intervention or treatment. For this reason amenability is frequently a factor in decisions regarding the transfer of juveniles to criminal court. The U.S. Supreme Court has defined the due process requirements for transfer hearings, listing eight criteria to be considered in making transfer decisions. Foremost among these are the seriousness of the offense and the need to protect the community, the maturity of the juvenile, and the juvenile's likely amenability to treatment and rehabilitation.

In practice, judgments about amenability are made not on the basis of age but on an individualized basis, with decision-makers taking into account a juvenile's current circumstances, psychological history, and responses to prior interventions, if any. From a developmental perspective, however, the amenability question can be reframed as a question about general tendencies toward malleability at given ages, rather than statements about particular individuals. In other words, developmental scientists might ask whether there is an age below which one can presume that most individuals have the capacity to change and an age above which most people's amenability has diminished enough that they are unlikely to respond effectively to rehabilitation. If these questions could be answered definitively, at least some of the decision-making about an individual's amenability to treatment could be done on the basis of age.

Unfortunately, developmental research does not provide a satisfactory answer to these questions. The bulk of the data on the stability of personality traits suggests that individuals do indeed become less likely to change over the course of adolescence and adulthood, suggesting a possible decline in malleability over the course of development. But data on the over-time increase in the stability of personality characteristics do not speak to the question of whether change is *possible*, because estimates of personality stability do not inform questions about malleability. Observing boulders for long periods of time might suggest that they tend to remain where they are put but provide no indication of whether these boulders might move if pushed. Similarly, even if it were shown that antisocial tendencies were stable over time, this does not tell us that such tendencies cannot be changed by altering the individual's environment—it only tells us that these tendencies do *not* change if the environment is *not* altered.

A developmental perspective can inform, but cannot settle, debates over whether and under what circumstances juveniles should be tried as adults. Even setting aside the weighty political, practical, and moral questions that impinge on the discussion, the developmental analysis we have presented here does not point to any one age that politicians and practitioners should use in formulating transfer policies or practices.

In general, however, it is appropriate to raise serious concerns based on developmental evidence about the transfer of individuals under thirteen to adult court owing to their limited adjudicative competence as well as the very real possibility that most individuals this young will not prove to be sufficiently blameworthy to warrant exposure to the harsh consequences of a criminal court adjudication. At the other end of the continuum it appears, from a developmental perspective, appropriate to conclude that the vast majority of individuals seventeen and older are not appreciably different from adults in ways that would prohibit their fair adjudication within the criminal justice system. Variability among individuals between the ages of thirteen and sixteen requires that some sort of individualized assessment of an offender's competence to stand trial, blameworthiness, and likely amenability to treatment be made before reaching a transfer decision.

The irony of employing a developmental perspective in the analysis of transfer policy is that the exercise reveals the inherent inadequacy of policies that draw bright-line distinctions between adolescence and adulthood. Indeed, an analysis of the developmental literature indicates that variability among adolescents of a given chronological age is the rule, not the exception. In order to be true to what we know about development, a fair transfer policy must be able to accommodate this variability. The most effective way to do this is to widen the "bright-line" distinction between juveniles and adults into a formally acknowledged "gray area" that includes youth for whom age alone is an unreliable indicator of their development and, hence, of the appropriateness of their waiver to criminal court.

See also Community Justice; Global Justice Activism; Rights of Participation of Children and Youth; Rights, Youth Perceptions of; Social Justice; State and Youth, The.

Recommended Reading

Cauffman, E., and Steinberg, L. (2000). "(Im)maturity of Judgment in Adolescence: Why Adolescents May Be Less Culpable Than Adults." *Behavioral Sciences and the Law*, 18: 1–21.

Grisso, T. (1997). "The Competence of Adolescents as Trial Defendants." *Psychology, Public Policy, and Law*, 3: 3–32.

Grisso, T., Steinberg, L., Woolard, J., Cauffman, E., Scott, E., Graham, S., Lexcen, F., Reppucci, N., and Schwartz, R. (2003). "Juveniles' Competence to Stand Trial: A Comparison of Adolescents' and Adults' Capacities as Trial Defendants." *Law and Human Behavior*, 27: 333–363.

Scott, E., and Grisso, T. (1997). "The Evolution of Adolescence: A Developmental Perspective on Juvenile Justice Reform." *Journal of Criminal Law and Criminology*, 88: 137–189.

Scott, E., Reppucci, N., and Woolard, J. (1995). "Evaluating Adolescent Decision Making in Legal Contexts." *Law and Human Behavior*, 19: 221–244.

Steinberg, L., and Cauffman, E. (1996). "Maturity of Judgment in Adolescence: Psychosocial Factors in Adolescent Decision-Making." *Law and Human Behavior*, 20: 249–272.

Steinberg, L., and Scott, E. (2003). "Less Guilty by Reason of Adolescence: Developmental Immaturity, Diminished Responsibility, and the Juvenile Death Penalty." *American Psychologist*, 58: 1009–1018.

Laurence Steinberg and Elizabeth Cauffman

JVC. *See* Jesuit Volunteer Corps (JVC).